SHAZAM

THE ECONOMETRICS COMPUTER PROGRAM

VERSION 8.0

USERS'S REFERENCE MANUAL

SHAZAM
#997-1873 East Mall
Vancouver, B.C. V6T 1Z1
CANADA

World Wide Web site
http://shazam.econ.ubc.ca/

Order Information
1-604-822-5062   -Voice-
1-604-822-5915   -Fax-
info@shazam.econ.ubc.ca   -Email-

Technical Help
1-604-822-9436
1-604-822-5915
help@shazam.econ.ubc.ca

McGraw-Hill
A Division of The McGraw·Hill Companies

ISBN 0-07-069870-8

http://www.mhcollege.com

Acknowledgment

Most programming for SHAZAM is done by Kenneth J. White and Diana Whistler with some portions based on programs by John Cragg, Robert Davies, Bill Farebrother, Amos Golan, Gordon Hughes, Tony Hall, Roger Koenker, Doug Miller, Charles Nelson, David Ryan, and Leigh Tesfatsion. In addition S. Donna Wong, Jeremy Boyd, Shirley Haun, Nancy Horsman, Cherie Metcalf, Robert Picard, Heather Waples, Maureen Chin, and Marsha Courchane have contributed substantial portions of this manual. Many other individuals have aided in improving the program and documentation. In particular, SHAZAM would not have been possible without the assistance of Justin Wyatt, Mary Beth Walker, Terry Wales, Keith Wales, Steve Theobald, Eleanor Tao, John Small, Meridith Scantlen, Gene Savin, Esther Ruberl, Hedley Rees, Angela Redish, Michel Poitevin, Joris Pinkse, Jeff Perloff, Branko Peric, Doug Pearce, Harry Paarsch, James Nason, Junji Nakano, Robert McRae, Mark McBride, Michael McAleer, Stuart Logie, David Levy, Bert Kritzer, Stan Kita, George Judge, Fred Joutz, David Jaeger, Al Horsman, Malcolm Greig, Bill Griffiths, Mark Greene, Quentin Grafton, David Gow, Gene Golub, Dorothy Golosinski, Debra Glassman, David Giles, Judy Giles, John Geweke, Frank Flynn, Robert Engle, Stephen Donald, Erwin Diewert, John Deegan, Melanie Courchene, James Chalfant, Oral Capps, Trudy Cameron, Ray Byron, Linda Bui, Alex Bui, Andrew Brownsword, Peter Berck, David Bates, Fellini's Espresso Bar, and Duke's Gourmet Cookies.

An appropriate reference for SHAZAM is:

SHAZAM User's Reference Manual Version 8.0, McGraw-Hill, 1997. ISBN 0-07-069870-8.

Additional references for SHAZAM keyed to popular econometrics textbooks are:

White, K.J. and Bui, L.T.M., *Basic Econometrics: A Computer Handbook Using SHAZAM*, McGraw-Hill, 1988. ISBN 0-07-834463-8, *Gujarati (2nd Edition) Handbook*.

White, K.J. and Bui, L.T.M., *The Practice of Econometrics: A Computer Handbook Using SHAZAM*, Addison-Wesley, 1991. ISBN 0-201-50048-5, *Berndt Handbook*.

White, K.J., Haun, S.A., and Gow, D.J., *Introduction to the Theory and Practice of Econometrics: A Computer Handbook Using SHAZAM and SAS*, Wiley, 1988. ISBN 0-471-85946-X, *Judge Handbook*.

White, K.J. and Theobald, S.A., *Basic Econometrics: A Computer Handbook Using SHAZAM*, McGraw-Hill, 1995. ISBN 0-07-069864-3, *Gujarati (3rd Edition) Handbook*.

White, K.J., Wong, S.D., Whistler, D., Grafton, R.Q., and Scantlen, M., *Econometric Models & Economic Forecasts: A Computer Handbook Using SHAZAM*, McGraw-Hill, 1991. ISBN 0-07-050101-7, *Pindyck-Rubinfeld Handbook*.

Chotikapanich, D. and Griffiths, W.E., *Learning SHAZAM™: A Computer Handbook for Econometrics*, Wiley, 1993. ISBN 0-471-58592-0, *Griffiths-Hill-Judge Handbook*.

Coelli, T.J. and Griffiths, W.E., *Computer and Exercise Solutions Manual*, Wiley, 1989. ISBN 0-471-63821-8, *Judge 85 Handbook*.

Student guides to SHAZAM are:

White, K.J., Boyd, J.A.J., Wong, S.D. and Whistler, D., *SHAZY: The SHAZAM Student Version*, McGraw-Hill, 1993. ISBN 0-07-833562-0.

Nguyen, T.T., *Statistics with SHAZAM*, Narada Press, 1993. ISBN 1-895938-00-7.

Whistler, D., "An Introductory Guide To SHAZAM", http://shazam.econ.ubc.ca/intro/.

"...sound research cannot be produced merely by feeding data to a computer and saying SHAZAM."

Peter Kennedy
A Guide to Econometrics

"A casual reader may wonder whether the names of some of these programs, particularly ORACLE and SHAZAM, reflect in any way the Delphic nature of econometric predictions."

Ivor Francis
Statistical Software: A Comparative Review

"...detailed implementation in concrete computer programs or systems. Hence, names familiar to many such as...GREMLIN, TROLL, AUTOREG, SHAZAM..."

Richard E. Quandt
Handbook of Econometrics

"The easiest solution to an inconclusive bounds test is to use a program such as SHAZAM..."

Judge, Hill, Griffiths, Lütkepohl and Lee
Introduction to the Theory and Practice of Econometrics, 2nd Edition

"In instances where d falls within the inconclusive region the exact critical value d* can be found numerically, providing appropriate computer software [e.g., SHAZAM, White(1978)] is available."

Judge, Griffiths, Hill, Lütkepohl and Lee
The Theory and Practice of Econometrics, 2nd Edition

"Beach and MacKinnon devised an iterative procedure for maximizing Equation (8-77), which has now been incorporated in White's SHAZAM program..."

Jack Johnston
Econometric Methods, 3rd ed.

"Some Computer Programs (e.g. SHAZAM, White (1978)) allow for the estimation of ρ and provide an unconditional covariance matrix."

Fomby, Hill and Johnson
Advanced Econometric Methods

Senator:	"Do you realize that I got a bill passed today that's going to put a million people to work? You know how I did it? I said one word."
Wife:	"SHAZAM?"
Senator:	"No. Subcommittee."

From the movie:
The Seduction of Joe Tynan

Econometrics Laboratory
Department of Economics
Evans Hall #3890
Berkeley, CA 94720-3890

TABLE OF CONTENTS

1. INTRODUCTION

"I think there is a world market for about five computers."
Thomas J. Watson
Chairman of the Board-IBM, 1943

SHAZAM is a comprehensive computer program for econometricians, statisticians, biometricians, engineers, sociometricians, psychometricians, politicometricians and others who use statistical techniques. The primary strength of SHAZAM is for the estimation and testing of many types of regression models. The SHAZAM command language has great flexibility and provides capabilities for programming procedures. SHAZAM has an interface to the GNUPLOT package for high quality graphics.

SHAZAM includes features for:

- data transformations, handling missing observations, matrix manipulation, evaluation of derivatives and integrals, data sorting, calculation of price indexes, computation of cumulative distribution functions for a variety of probability distributions;

- descriptive statistics, nonparametric density estimation, Dickey-Fuller and Phillips-Perron unit root tests, tests for cointegration;

- OLS estimation, restricted least squares, weighted least squares, ridge regression, distributed lag models, generalized least squares, estimation with autoregressive or moving average errors, estimation with heteroskedastic errors, ARCH and GARCH models, ARIMA (Box-Jenkins) time series models, Box-Cox regressions, probit models, logit models, tobit models, estimation using regression quantiles (including MAD estimation), regression with non-normal errors (including exponential regression and beta regression), regression with time varying coefficients, nonparametric methods, generalized entropy methods;

- linear and nonlinear hypothesis testing, calculation of confidence intervals and ellipse plots, computation of the Newey-West autocorrelation consistent covariance matrix, regression diagnostic tests (including tests for heteroskedasticity, CUSUM tests, RESET specification error tests), computation of p-values for many test statistics (including the p-value for the Durbin-Watson test), forecasting;

- nonlinear least squares, estimation of systems of linear and nonlinear equations by SURE, 2SLS and 3SLS, generalized method of moments (GMM) estimation, pooled time-series cross-section methods;

- principal components and factor analysis, principal components regression, linear programming, minimizing and maximizing nonlinear functions, solving nonlinear simultaneous equations.

Users should always be aware of the version of SHAZAM being used. This manual describes Version 8.0 of SHAZAM. Some options and commands described in this manual were not available in earlier versions so users should be certain an old version of SHAZAM is not used with this manual.

SHAZAM has thousands of users in more than 70 countries and is one of the most popular econometric computer programs in the world. It can be found at the Northernmost (University of Tromso, Norway) and Southernmost (University of Otago, New Zealand) Universities in the world and also in Antarctica.

WARNING: SHAZAM COMMANDS FROM VERSIONS 1.0-4.6 WILL NOT WORK IN LATER VERSIONS. See the chapter *NEW FEATURES IN SHAZAM* for further details.

HOW TO RUN SHAZAM

To effectively use SHAZAM users should be familiar with how to maintain files on their computer including how to use an editor. The SHAZAM system makes use of data files (that contain a data set to analyze), command files (that contain a list of SHAZAM commands), output files (that contain the results of a SHAZAM analysis) and procedure files (that contain a set of SHAZAM commands that perform a specific task). The chapter *HOW TO RUN SHAZAM* gives detailed information on the appropriate system control commands.

There are two modes of operation in SHAZAM: BATCH and TALK. BATCH mode is active when the commands are in a separate file. TALK mode is active when SHAZAM commands are typed interactively and output is received after each command. In TALK mode the user is prompted to type in new commands with the prompt:

```
TYPE COMMAND
```

Most computer systems will automatically recognize TALK mode but if you do not get the `TYPE COMMAND` prompt, simply type the command: **SET TALK** to force SHAZAM into TALK mode.

THE **DEMO** *COMMAND*

A good way for new users to learn SHAZAM is to run the SHAZAM on-line tutorial. On many systems to run SHAZAM interactively (TALK mode) you either type:

shazam (or shazame or shazamw)

or click on the SHAZAM icon with a mouse. When SHAZAM begins execution it will start with a greeting like:

```
Hello/Bonjour/Aloha/Howdy/G Day/Kia Ora/Konnichiwa/Buenos Dias/Nee Hau
Welcome to SHAZAM - Version 8.0  -  DEC 1996 SYSTEM=MSDOSEXT  PAR=  500

TYPE COMMAND
:_
```

When you see the prompt: TYPE COMMAND it means SHAZAM is waiting for you to type a SHAZAM command. To begin the SHAZAM tutorial type **DEMO**. The **DEMO** command automatically loads the Theil textile data set that is used for demonstration purposes for many of the examples in this user manual. You can then do any of the following:

- Follow the instructions as they appear.

- Experiment with the textile data set by typing any SHAZAM command (the **READ** command is not allowed).

- Continue with the tutorial by typing **DEMO**.

- Restart the tutorial at any time by typing the command **DEMO START**.

- Exit SHAZAM completely by typing **STOP**.

It typically takes about 30 minutes to complete the entire tutorial.

SHAZAM ON THE INTERNET

The SHAZAM World Wide Web page can be viewed at:

```
http://shazam.econ.ubc.ca/
```

The WWW page has useful information for all SHAZAM users. Some of the topics are:

General Information

- Description of the features and options available in SHAZAM.
- A list of the computer hardware requirements for each platform version of SHAZAM.
- Information on ordering a copy of SHAZAM from the WWW page.

Documentation

- An "Introductory Guide To SHAZAM" describes the basics of using SHAZAM and illustrates the use of SHAZAM with examples that include data files, command files and output files.
- Sample chapters from the *SHAZAM User's Reference Manual* .
- A list of published SHAZAM computer handbooks that accompany econometrics textbooks. The computer handbooks illustrate how to use SHAZAM to replicate the numerical examples within each chapter of the corresponding textbooks.

Applications

- Running a short SHAZAM program from the WWW page. For further details see the chapter *HOW TO RUN SHAZAM FROM THE INTERNET*.
- Examples of SHAZAM command and procedure files from the *SHAZAM User's Reference Manual*, and as well, other examples that are not in the manual.

  If you have written an interesting procedure and you would like to share it with other SHAZAM users send it to us and we will put it on the WWW site.

Other Useful Links

- Information about the GNUPLOT program.

Newsgroups and Email

SHAZAM information and advisory services available on the internet are:

- The Usenet News group `comp.soft-sys.shazam` offers general discussion about the features of SHAZAM. This includes discussion on the problems with the use of SHAZAM and how to solve them.

- For technical questions on SHAZAM send an E-mail message to:

   `help@shazam.econ.ubc.ca`

- For ordering information send an E-mail message to:

   `info@shazam.econ.ubc.ca`

If none of the above is successful then questions on SHAZAM can be referred to your local SHAZAM consultant or:

SHAZAM
#997-1873 East Mall
Vancouver, B.C., V6T 1Z1
CANADA

1-604-822-9436 (Technical Help)

1-604-822-5062 (Ordering Information)

1-604-822-5915 (Fax)

In addition, services can be contracted from *Northwest Econometrics*, a professional consulting company which has authorized SHAZAM consultants in several cities.

SHAZAM *AWARDS AND BENEFITS*

SHAZAM *Research Incentive Plan (SRIP)*

The SHAZAM Research Incentive Plan offers free personal SHAZAM upgrades to any user who has published an article in which SHAZAM is cited. To apply, simply send a reprint of the article, along with your original diskette(s) or tape, to the SHAZAM address given above.

All articles in a refereed printed journal are eligible and free upgrades must be claimed in the year of publication. In the case of co-authored articles, only one author may get the upgrade.

A list of articles that cite SHAZAM is available at the SHAZAM World Wide Web site.

SHAZAM *Hall Of Fame*

SHAZAM users who have cited SHAZAM in at least 5 refereed printed articles during their careers will be granted membership into the SHAZAM Hall of Fame. There are 3 categories:

> **Regressor**   - Cite SHAZAM in 5 articles
>
> **Executive Regressor**   - Cite SHAZAM in 10 articles
>
> **Lifetime Achievement Award**   - Cite SHAZAM in 15 or more articles

Hall of Famers are eligible for many free SHAZAM benefits. Current members of the SHAZAM Hall of Fame are:

> James A. Chalfant, William A. Donnelly, Susan Feigenbaum, Ira N. Gang, David E.A. Giles, David M. Levy, Albert A. Okunade, and Joachim Wagner.

Frequent Regressors Club

To become a member of the Frequent Regressors Club refer to the application form at the back of this manual.

2. A CHILD'S GUIDE TO RUNNING REGRESSIONS

"Difficult? A child could do it."
> Arthur S. Goldberger
> Professor of Economics, 1971

This chapter should be read by all users as it provides step-by-step basic information on how to run Ordinary Least Squares (OLS) regressions.

A Data File

A simple data set to analyze is the textile demand data set from Theil [1971, p. 102]. There are 17 years of observations on the variables *YEAR, CONSUME, INCOME,* and *PRICE*. The data can be entered in a file, say **MYDATA**, and a listing of the file is:

```
1923  99.2  96.7 101.0
1924  99.0  98.1 100.1
1925 100.0 100.0 100.0
1926 111.6 104.9  90.6
1927 122.2 104.9  86.5
1928 117.6 109.5  89.7
1929 121.1 110.8  90.6
1930 136.0 112.3  82.8
1931 154.2 109.3  70.1
1932 153.6 105.3  65.4
1933 158.5 101.7  61.3
1934 140.6  95.4  62.5
1935 136.2  96.4  63.6
1936 168.0  97.6  52.6
1937 154.3 102.4  59.7
1938 149.0 101.6  59.5
1939 165.5 103.8  61.3
```

Setting the Sample Size

The first required SHAZAM command is usually **SAMPLE** to specify the sample size. The sample size is the number of observations in the data. The general format of the **SAMPLE** command is:

SAMPLE *beg end*

where *beg* is the first observation to be used (usually 1), and *end* is the last observation. If your data has 17 observations your **SAMPLE** command will look like:

```
SAMPLE 1 17
```

This **SAMPLE** command sets the sample size to 17 observations and the data will be placed in observations 1 through 17 (because *beg* is specified as 1).

Data Input

Having set the sample size, you are ready to enter your data with the **READ** command. In general, the **READ** command will look like:

READ(*datafilename*) *vars* / *options*

where *datafilename* is the name of the data file (this is optional), *vars* is a list of variable names for the data and *options* is a list of desired options. Variable names may be up to 8 characters long and must consist only of letters or numbers and start with a letter. If the data on *YEAR, CONSUME, INCOME* and *PRICE* is stored in the file named **MYDATA** the **READ** command would be:

```
READ(MYDATA) YEAR CONSUME INCOME PRICE
```

Alternatively, it may be convenient to enter the data directly in a SHAZAM command file following the **READ** command so no data filename is used. The command file is then available for a BATCH session. The SHAZAM command file would contain the lines:

```
READ YEAR CONSUME INCOME PRICE
   1923   99.2   96.7 101.0
   1924   99.0   98.1 100.1
   1925  100.0  100.0 100.0
   1926  111.6  104.9  90.6
   1927  122.2  104.9  86.5
   1928  117.6  109.5  89.7
   1929  121.1  110.8  90.6
   1930  136.0  112.3  82.8
   1931  154.2  109.3  70.1
   1932  153.6  105.3  65.4
   1933  158.5  101.7  61.3
   1934  140.6   95.4  62.5
   1935  136.2   96.4  63.6
   1936  168.0   97.6  52.6
   1937  154.3  102.4  59.7
   1938  149.0  101.6  59.5
   1939  165.5  103.8  61.3
```

Normally, data is typed observation by observation where the observations for all variables begin on a new line. You may use more than one line per observation. If your data is set up variable by variable instead of observation by observation you will have to use the **BYVAR** option on your **READ** command. For details on the **BYVAR** option see the chapter *DATA INPUT AND OUTPUT*. All variables entered on a **READ** command must have an equal number of observations. In the above example, the first column read will be stored in variable *YEAR*, the next in *CONSUME*, and so on.

NOTE: Be sure that the number of variables you give on the **READ** command matches the number of variables in your data.

The STAT Command

The **STAT** command will print some useful descriptive statistics including the means, standard deviations, variances, minimums and maximums for the variables listed. The format of the **STAT** command is:

STAT *vars*

where *vars* is a list of variables. There are many options available on the **STAT** command which are described in the chapter *DESCRIPTIVE STATISTICS*.

The OLS Command

The **OLS** command will run an ordinary least squares regression. The format of the **OLS** command is:

OLS *depvar indeps / options*

where *depvar* is the name of the dependent variable, *indeps* are the names of the independent variables and *options* is a list of options desired. A very simple **OLS** command might look like this:

```
OLS CONSUME INCOME PRICE
```

This will run a regression of the variable *CONSUME* on variables *INCOME* and *PRICE*. A *CONSTANT* is automatically included in the regression. No options were requested. There are many available options which are described in the chapter *ORDINARY LEAST SQUARES*. Some common ones are:

ANOVA	Prints the **AN**alysis **O**f **VA**riance tables
GF	Prints **G**oodness-of-**F**it statistics testing for normality of residuals
LIST	**LIST**s residuals plus residual summary statistics
NOCONSTANT	Suppresses the intercept
PCOV	Prints a **COV**ariance matrix of coefficients
RSTAT	Prints **R**esidual summary **STAT**istics (Durbin-Watson etc.)

Users should note that the **LIST** option will substantially increase the amount of output, particularly if the sample size is large. An example of an **OLS** command with options is:

```
OLS CONSUME INCOME PRICE / RSTAT PCOV
```

This example runs an **OLS** regression of *CONSUME* on *INCOME*, *PRICE* and a *CONSTANT* and prints residual summary statistics and a covariance matrix of coefficients along with the standard output. Do not forget to separate the options from the list of variables by a slash (/). The options may be listed in any order.

The **SHAZAM** *Command File*

The command file for a complete SHAZAM run might look like the following :

```
*  I HOPE THIS WORKS!
SAMPLE 1 17
READ YEAR CONSUME INCOME PRICE
    1923   99.2   96.7 101.0
    1924   99.0   98.1 100.1
    1925  100.0  100.0 100.0
    1926  111.6  104.9  90.6
    1927  122.2  104.9  86.5
    1928  117.6  109.5  89.7
    1929  121.1  110.8  90.6
    1930  136.0  112.3  82.8
    1931  154.2  109.3  70.1
    1932  153.6  105.3  65.4
    1933  158.5  101.7  61.3
    1934  140.6   95.4  62.5
    1935  136.2   96.4  63.6
    1936  168.0   97.6  52.6
    1937  154.3  102.4  59.7
    1938  149.0  101.6  59.5
    1939  165.5  103.8  61.3
STAT CONSUME INCOME PRICE
OLS CONSUME INCOME PRICE / RSTAT PCOV
OLS CONSUME INCOME
STOP
```

NOTE: The line in the example beginning with an asterisk (*) is a SHAZAM *comment*. You can insert these at various places in the run, except within the data. Comment lines are printed on the output and sometimes help document the output. Comment lines must begin with an asterisk (*) in column 1. The rest of the line may contain anything.

In this simple example there are 4 input variables *YEAR, CONSUME, INCOME* and *PRICE* and 17 observations. The **SAMPLE** command sets the sample size to 17 observations. The **STAT** command is used to get descriptive statistics of the variables.

Two **OLS** regressions are run. Both regressions use *CONSUME* as the dependent variable.

The **STOP** command is a signal to SHAZAM that it has reached the end of the commands.

SHAZAM *output from the* **STAT** *Command*

The output for the **STAT** command is shown below. Note that SHAZAM commands typed by the user appear in SHAZAM output following the symbol |_.

```
|_STAT CONSUME INCOME PRICE
NAME      N     MEAN      ST. DEV     VARIANCE     MINIMUM     MAXIMUM
CONSUME  17    134.51     23.577      555.89        99.000     168.00
INCOME   17    102.98     5.3010      28.100        95.400     112.30
PRICE    17    76.312     16.866      284.47        52.600     101.00
```

For a variable X with N observations denoted by X_t, t=1,...,N the statistics listed by the **STAT** command are calculated as follows.

MEAN
$$\overline{X} = \frac{1}{N}\sum_{t=1}^{N} X_t$$

VARIANCE
$$\hat{\sigma}_X^2 = \frac{1}{N-1}\sum_{t=1}^{N}(X_t - \overline{X})^2 = \frac{1}{N-1}\left[\sum_{t=1}^{N}X_t^2 - N\overline{X}^2\right]$$

ST. DEV
$$\sqrt{\hat{\sigma}_X^2} \quad \text{(Standard Deviation)}$$

MINIMUM   the smallest value of X_t

MAXIMUM   the largest value of X_t

SHAZAM *output from the* **OLS** *Command*

The output for the first **OLS** command is:

```
|_OLS CONSUME INCOME PRICE / RSTAT PCOV
 OLS ESTIMATION
       17 OBSERVATIONS      DEPENDENT VARIABLE = CONSUME
...NOTE..SAMPLE RANGE SET TO:    1,    17

 R-SQUARE =     .9513    R-SQUARE ADJUSTED =     .9443
 VARIANCE OF THE ESTIMATE-SIGMA**2 =    30.951
 STANDARD ERROR OF THE ESTIMATE-SIGMA =    5.5634
 SUM OF SQUARED ERRORS-SSE=    433.31
 MEAN OF DEPENDENT VARIABLE =    134.51
```

```
LOG OF THE LIKELIHOOD FUNCTION = -51.6471

VARIABLE     ESTIMATED  STANDARD   T-RATIO          PARTIAL STANDARDIZED ELASTICITY
  NAME       COEFFICIENT  ERROR     14 DF   P-VALUE CORR. COEFFICIENT  AT MEANS
INCOME       1.0617     .2667      3.981     .001   .729     .2387      .8129
PRICE        -1.3830    .8381E-01  -16.50    .000  -.975    -.9893     -.7846
CONSTANT     130.71     27.09      4.824     .000   .790     .0000      .9718

VARIANCE-COVARIANCE MATRIX OF COEFFICIENTS
INCOME       .71115E-01
PRICE        -.39974E-02   .70248E-02
CONSTANT     -7.0185      -.12441       734.10
             INCOME        PRICE        CONSTANT

DURBIN-WATSON = 2.0185    VON NEUMANN RATIO = 2.1447    RHO =  -.18239
RESIDUAL SUM =  -.12434E-12   RESIDUAL VARIANCE =   30.951
SUM OF ABSOLUTE ERRORS=   72.787
R-SQUARE BETWEEN OBSERVED AND PREDICTED =  .9513
RUNS TEST:      7 RUNS,     9 POSITIVE,     8 NEGATIVE, NORMAL STATISTIC = -1.2423
```

The calculations for the OLS output are now described. The linear regression model can be written as:

$$Y_t = \beta_1 X_{1t} + \beta_2 X_{2t} + \beta_3 X_{3t} + \ldots + \beta_K X_{Kt} + \varepsilon_t \quad \text{for } t=1,\ldots,N$$

where there are N observations and Y_t is observation t on the dependent variable, X_{kt} is observation t on the kth explanatory variable for k=1,. . .,K, β_k are parameters to estimate and ε_t is a random error that is assumed to have zero mean and variance σ^2.

In matrix notation this can be stated as:

$$Y = X\beta + \varepsilon$$

where β is a K x 1 vector of parameters, $Y = [Y_1\ Y_2 \ldots Y_N]'$ and X is the N x K matrix:

$$X = \begin{bmatrix} X_{11} & X_{21} & \cdot & X_{K1} \\ X_{12} & X_{22} & \cdot & X_{K2} \\ \cdot & \cdot & \cdot & \cdot \\ X_{1N} & X_{2N} & \cdot & X_{KN} \end{bmatrix}$$

If a constant term is included in the model then one of the columns of the X matrix will be a column where every element is a 1. SHAZAM automatically makes the last column of the X matrix the one that corresponds to the constant term.

The OLS estimated coefficients are calculated as:

$$\hat{\beta} = (X'X)^{-1}X'Y$$

The N x 1 vector of OLS estimated residuals denoted by e are obtained as:

$$e = Y - X\hat{\beta}$$

and the predicted values are $\hat{Y} = X\hat{\beta}$.

With $\overline{Y}$ the mean of the dependent variable the deviations from the sample mean are denoted by $y_t = Y_t - \overline{Y}$ and $\hat{y}_t = \hat{Y}_t - \overline{Y}$ for t=1, ... ,N.

The output from the **OLS** command includes:

R-SQUARE

$$R^2 = 1 - \frac{\sum_{t=1}^{N} e_t^2}{\sum_{t=1}^{N}(Y_t - \overline{Y})^2} = 1 - \frac{e'e}{y'y}$$

R-SQUARE ADJUSTED

$$\overline{R}^2 = 1 - \left(1 - R^2\right)\frac{N-1}{N-K}$$

VARIANCE OF THE ESTIMATE-SIGMA**2

$$\hat{\sigma}^2 = \frac{1}{N-K}\sum_{t=1}^{N} e_t^2 = \frac{e'e}{N-K}$$

STANDARD ERROR OF THE ESTIMATE-SIGMA

$$\hat{\sigma} = \sqrt{\hat{\sigma}^2}$$

SUM OF SQUARED ERRORS-SSE

$$\sum_{t=1}^{N} e_t^2 = e'e$$

MEAN OF DEPENDENT VARIABLE

$$\overline{Y} = \frac{1}{N}\sum_{t=1}^{N} Y_t$$

With the assumption that the residuals are normally distributed the log-likelihood function for the linear regression model can be expressed as:

$$-\frac{N}{2}\ln(2\pi) - \frac{N}{2}\ln(\sigma^2) - \frac{1}{2\sigma^2}(Y - X\beta)'(Y - X\beta)$$

On the SHAZAM output the LOG OF THE LIKELIHOOD FUNCTION is evaluated as:

$$-\frac{N}{2}\ln(2\pi) - \frac{N}{2}\ln(\tilde{\sigma}^2) - \frac{N}{2} \quad \text{where } \tilde{\sigma}^2 = \frac{e'e}{N}$$

The above uses the result: $(Y - X\hat{\beta})'(Y - X\hat{\beta}) / \tilde{\sigma}^2 = e'e / \tilde{\sigma}^2 = N$.

When the **NOCONSTANT** option is used on the **OLS** command the SHAZAM output reports the RAW MOMENT R-SQUARE that is calculated as:

$$1 - \frac{e'e}{Y'Y}$$

The variance-covariance matrix of the OLS parameter estimates (printed with the **PCOV** option) is estimated as:

$$V(\hat{\beta}) = \hat{\sigma}^2 (X'X)^{-1}$$

Denote $V(\hat{\beta}_k)$ as the kth diagonal element of the $V(\hat{\beta})$ matrix. For the OLS estimated coefficients the SHAZAM output reports the following.

STANDARD ERROR $\left(\text{of } \hat{\beta}_k\right)$ $\qquad SE_k = \sqrt{V(\hat{\beta}_k)} \qquad$ for k=1, ... , K

T-RATIO $\qquad\qquad\qquad t_k = \dfrac{\hat{\beta}_k}{SE_k}$

PARTIAL CORRELATION $\qquad \dfrac{t_k}{\sqrt{t_k^2 + N - K}}$

STANDARDIZED COEFFICIENT $\qquad \hat{\beta}_k\left(\dfrac{\hat{\sigma}_{X_k}}{\hat{\sigma}_Y}\right)$

ELASTICITY AT MEANS $\qquad E_k = \hat{\beta}_k\left(\dfrac{\overline{X}_k}{\overline{Y}}\right)$

The p-values reported on the OLS output are the tail probabilities for a two-tail test of $H_0: \beta_k = 0$. The p-value is the exact level of significance of a test statistic. If the p-value is less than a selected level of significance (say 0.05) then there is evidence to reject H_0. For a discussion of p-values see, for example, Griffiths, Hill and Judge [1993, p. 138] or Gujarati [1995, p. 132, p.788].

Residual Statistics

If the **RSTAT, LIST,** or **MAX** options are used the SHAZAM output also includes a number of residual statistics calculated as follows.

DURBIN WATSON	$DW = \dfrac{\sum_{t=2}^{N}(e_t - e_{t-1})^2}{\sum_{t=1}^{N} e_t^2}$	VON NEUMANN RATIO	$DW\left(\dfrac{N}{N-1}\right)$
RHO	$\hat{\rho} = \dfrac{\sum_{t=2}^{N} e_t e_{t-1}}{\sum_{t=2}^{N} e_{t-1}^2}$	RESIDUAL SUM	$\sum_{t=1}^{N} e_t$
RESIDUAL VARIANCE	$\hat{\sigma}^2 = \dfrac{1}{N-K}\sum_{t=1}^{N} e_t^2$	SUM OF ABSOLUTE ERRORS	$\sum_{t=1}^{N} |e_t|$

The statistic R-SQUARE BETWEEN OBSERVED AND PREDICTED is calculated as:

$$R^2 = \frac{\left(\sum \hat{y}_t y_t\right)^2}{\sum \hat{y}_t^2 \sum y_t^2}$$

For discussion on goodness-of-fit measures see, for example, Judge, Griffiths, Hill, Lütkepohl and Lee [1985, pp. 29-31] and Kvalseth [1985].

The runs test (discussed in, for example, Gujarati [1995, p. 419]) gives a test for independent residuals. A run is defined as an uninterrupted sequence of either positive or negative residuals. Let N_1 be the total number of positive residuals and N_2 be the total number of negative residuals (so that $N_1+N_2=N$). Let n be the total number of runs. The RUNS TEST reported on the SHAZAM output is computed as:

$$\frac{n - E(n)}{\sigma_n} \qquad \text{where}$$

$$E(n) = \frac{2N_1N_2}{N_1 + N_2} + 1 \quad \text{and} \quad \sigma_n^2 = \frac{2N_1N_2(2N_1N_2 - N_1 - N_2)}{(N_1 + N_2)^2(N_1 + N_2 - 1)}$$

Under the null hypothesis of independence and assuming $N_1>10$ and $N_2>10$ the runs test statistic has an asymptotic standard normal distribution. If N_1 or N_2 are less than 10 then tables of critical values available in Gujarati [1995] can be consulted.

Model Selection Test Statistics and Analysis of Variance

When the **ANOVA** option is specified the SHAZAM output will also include a series of model selection test statistics as well as two analysis of variance tables. The output from the model selection tests will appear as:

```
MODEL SELECTION TESTS - SEE JUDGE ET AL. (1985,P.242)
 AKAIKE (1969) FINAL PREDICTION ERROR - FPE =        36.413
    (FPE IS ALSO KNOWN AS AMEMIYA PREDICTION CRITERION - PC)
 AKAIKE (1973) INFORMATION CRITERION - LOG AIC =   3.5912
 SCHWARZ (1978) CRITERION - LOG SC =               3.7382
MODEL SELECTION TESTS - SEE RAMANATHAN (1992,P.167)
 CRAVEN-WAHBA (1979)
    GENERALIZED CROSS VALIDATION - GCV =           37.583
 HANNAN AND QUINN (1979) CRITERION =               36.811
 RICE (1984) CRITERION =                           39.392
 SHIBATA (1981) CRITERION =                        34.485
 SCHWARZ (1978) CRITERION - SC =                   42.023
 AKAIKE (1974) INFORMATION CRITERION - AIC =       36.277
```

With $\tilde{\sigma}^2 = \dfrac{e'e}{N}$ the calculations for the above statistics are:

AKAIKE (1969) FINAL PREDICTION ERROR - FPE $\qquad \tilde{\sigma}^2\left(\dfrac{N+K}{N-K}\right)$

AKAIKE (1973) INFORMATION CRITERION - LOG AIC $\qquad \ln\tilde{\sigma}^2 + \dfrac{2K}{N}$

SCHWARZ (1978) CRITERION - LOG SC $\qquad \ln\tilde{\sigma}^2 + \dfrac{K\ln N}{N}$

CRAVEN-WAHBA (1979) GENERALIZED CROSS VALIDATION $\qquad \tilde{\sigma}^2\left(1-\dfrac{K}{N}\right)^{-2}$

HANNAN AND QUINN (1979) CRITERION $\qquad \tilde{\sigma}^2\,(\ln N)^{2K/N}$

RICE (1984) CRITERION $\qquad \tilde{\sigma}^2\left(1-\dfrac{2K}{N}\right)^{-1}$

SHIBATA (1981) CRITERION $\qquad \tilde{\sigma}^2\left(\dfrac{N+2K}{N}\right)$

SCHWARZ (1978) CRITERION - SC $\qquad \tilde{\sigma}^2\,N^{K/N}$

AKAIKE (1974) INFORMATION CRITERION - AIC $\qquad \tilde{\sigma}^2\exp\left(\dfrac{2K}{N}\right)$

The output for the analysis of variance tables is:

```
              ANALYSIS OF VARIANCE - FROM MEAN
               SS           DF           MS              F
REGRESSION    8460.9        2.          4230.5        136.683
ERROR         433.31        14.         30.951        P-VALUE
TOTAL         8894.3        16.         555.89          .000

              ANALYSIS OF VARIANCE - FROM ZERO
               SS           DF           MS              F
REGRESSION    .31602E+06    3.          .10534E+06    3403.474
ERROR         433.31        14.         30.951        P-VALUE
TOTAL         .31646E+06    17.         18615.          .000
```

The calculations for this output are:

ANALYSIS OF VARIANCE - FROM MEAN

	SS	DF	MS	F
REGRESSION	$y'y - e'e$	$K-1$	$\dfrac{y'y - e'e}{K-1}$	$\dfrac{N-K}{K-1}\left(\dfrac{y'y - e'e}{e'e}\right)$
ERROR	$e'e$	$N-K$	$\dfrac{e'e}{N-K}$	
TOTAL	$y'y$	$N-1$	$\dfrac{y'y}{N-1}$	

ANALYSIS OF VARIANCE - FROM ZERO

	SS	DF	MS	F
REGRESSION	$Y'Y - e'e$	K	$\dfrac{Y'Y - e'e}{K}$	$\dfrac{N-K}{K}\left(\dfrac{Y'Y - e'e}{e'e}\right)$
ERROR	$e'e$	$N-K$	$\dfrac{e'e}{N-K}$	
TOTAL	$Y'Y$	N	$\dfrac{Y'Y}{N}$	

Tests for Normality of the Residuals

If the **GF** and **LM** options are specified the SHAZAM output includes some tests for normality of the residuals as follows.

```
COEFFICIENT OF SKEWNESS =   -0.0343 WITH STANDARD DEVIATION OF 0.5497
COEFFICIENT OF EXCESS KURTOSIS =  -0.8701 WITH STANDARD DEVIATION OF 1.0632

     GOODNESS OF FIT TEST FOR NORMALITY OF RESIDUALS -  6 GROUPS
OBSERVED   0.0   2.0   6.0   7.0   2.0   0.0
EXPECTED   0.4   2.3   5.8   5.8   2.3   0.4
CHI-SQUARE =     1.1126 WITH  1 DEGREES OF FREEDOM

JARQUE-BERA ASYMPTOTIC LM NORMALITY TEST
  CHI-SQUARE =              .6662 WITH  2 DEGREES OF FREEDOM
```

For the estimated residuals the sample k^{th} central moments are:

$$m_k = \frac{1}{N}\sum_{t=1}^{N}(e_t - \bar{e})^k$$

Define:

$$S_k = \frac{1}{N}\sum_{t=1}^{N}e_t^k \; , \; k = 1,2,3,4$$

then the sample central moments can be computed as:

$$m_2 = S_2 - S_1^2 \; , \qquad m_3 = S_3 - 3S_1S_2 + 2S_1^3 \qquad \text{and}$$

$$m_4 = S_4 - 4S_1S_3 + 6S_1^2S_2 - 3S_1^4$$

A measure of skewness is: $\qquad\qquad\qquad \gamma_1 = \frac{m_3}{m_2^{3/2}}$

and a measure of excess kurtosis is: $\qquad \gamma_2 = \frac{m_4}{m_2^2} - 3$

The above statistics are biased estimators of skewness and kurtosis that can be used for large N. Unbiased estimators of skewness and kurtosis are described in, for example,

Smillie [1966]. The SHAZAM calculations incorporate these small sample adjustments as follows. The COEFFICIENT OF SKEWNESS is calculated as:

$$g_1 = \frac{k_3}{k_2^{3/2}}$$

and the COEFFICIENT OF EXCESS KURTOSIS is calculated as:

$$g_2 = \frac{k_4}{k_2^2}$$

where the k-statistics are:

$$k_2 = \frac{N}{N-1} m_2 \quad , \qquad k_3 = \frac{N^2}{(N-1)(N-2)} m_3 \qquad \text{and}$$

$$k_4 = \frac{N^2}{(N-1)(N-2)(N-3)} \left[(N+1)m_4 - 3(N-1)m_2^2 \right]$$

If the residuals are normally distributed then g_1 and g_2 have zero means and standard deviations:

$$\sigma_{g_1} = \sqrt{\frac{6N(N-1)}{(N-2)(N+1)(N+3)}} \qquad \text{and}$$

$$\sigma_{g_2} = \sqrt{\frac{24N(N-1)^2}{(N-3)(N-2)(N+3)(N+5)}}$$

The chi-square GOODNESS OF FIT TEST FOR NORMALITY OF RESIDUALS is computed by dividing the estimated residuals into m groups. The number of groups is automatically set by SHAZAM based on the sample size. The observed frequency of residuals in group i is denoted by o_i. The number of values theoretically expected in group i if the residuals are normally distributed is denoted by d_i. The test statistic is:

$$\chi^2 = \sum_{i=1}^{m} \frac{(d_i - o_i)^2}{d_i}$$

Under the hypothesis of normality this test statistic has a χ^2 distribution with m–K–2 degrees of freedom. Further discussion of the goodness of fit test is in, for example, Klein [1974, p.372].

The JARQUE-BERA ASYMPTOTIC LM NORMALITY TEST is developed in Jarque and Bera [1987] and is computed as:

$$N\left[\frac{\gamma_1^2}{6} + \frac{\gamma_2^2}{24}\right]$$

In large samples, under the null hypothesis of normally distributed residuals, the test statistic has a chi-square distribution with 2 degrees of freedom.

More Information

Detailed command descriptions are in the chapters that follow. Users may also find it helpful to review the *MISCELLANEOUS COMMANDS AND INFORMATION* chapter. It gives some of the "rules and regulations" you should follow when running SHAZAM.

3. DATA INPUT AND OUTPUT

"All the waste in a year from a nuclear power plant can be stored under a desk."

Ronald Reagan
Former Movie Star and U.S. President, 1980

This chapter provides complete information on how to assign a **FILE**, set a **SAMPLE** period, and **READ**, **PRINT**, and **WRITE** data.

THE FILE COMMAND

In most situations SHAZAM users will have a command file and one or more data files. In addition a number of other files may be used including output files, procedure files, etc. It will become necessary to tell SHAZAM the name of the files and you may also have to assign a particular file to a SHAZAM *input-output unit* before it can be used. The **FILE** command is used whenever some action is required on a particular file. Different operating systems have different rules for assigning names of files and you should become aware of the rules for your particular operating system. While the **FILE** command can also be used to assign the command (INPUT) file and the OUTPUT file these file assignments can often be more easily done at the time you begin execution of SHAZAM. Instructions for assigning INPUT and OUTPUT files at execution time are available in the *HOW TO RUN SHAZAM* chapters.

The format of the **FILE** command is:

FILE *option filename*

where *option* is either one of the keywords (**CLOSE, DELETE, HELPDEMO, INPUT, KEYBOARD, LIST, OUTPUT, PATH, PRINT, PROC, PROCPATH, SCREEN** or **TEMP**) or an input-output unit number (range is 11-49).

FILE CLOSE *filename*	Closes the specified *filename*. This is usually only needed if you wish to re-assign a file for another purpose.
FILE DELETE *filename*	Delete the specified *filename*.
FILE HELPDEMO *pathname*	Specifies a directory path to use to search for the SHAZAM HELP and DEMO files. This is usually only used at installation time.

FILE INPUT *filename*	Reads SHAZAM commands from *filename*.
FILE KEYBOARD *filename*	Makes a copy of all commands typed on a keyboard and writes them into *filename*.
FILE LIST *filename*	Lists the specified *filename* on the screen.
FILE OUTPUT *filename*	Puts the output in the assigned *filename*. If used, this is often the first **FILE** command. No output will appear at the screen.
FILE PATH *pathname*	Specifies a directory path to append to all filenames used in subsequent **FILE, READ** or **WRITE** commands.
FILE PLOTPATH *pathname*	Specifies a directory path for the GNUPLOT program.
FILE PRINT *filename*	Prints the specified *filename* on a printer (not available on some operating systems).
FILE PROC *filename*	Loads a SHAZAM PROCEDURE from the specified *filename*.
FILE PROCPATH *pathname*	Specifies a directory path to use to search for SHAZAM PROCEDURES.
FILE SCREEN *filename*	Puts the output in the assigned filename and simultaneously displays the output on the computer screen. Alternative to **FILE OUTPUT** command.
FILE TEMP *pathname*	Specifies a directory path to use for creating and writing to temporary scratch files.

There are occasions (described in this manual) when a file must be assigned to an input-output unit number. Any unit number from 11-49 is available. Unit numbers are sometimes required as some SHAZAM commands do not allow you to write the full filename and are expecting a unit number instead. In this case you must first use the **FILE** command to assign a unit number to the file then use the unit number instead of the filename in any further SHAZAM commands. For example:

```
FILE 11 MYDATA
```

If the file is Binary (as is the case for the **OUT=** option in **SYSTEM** and **NL** problems or the **BINARY** option on a **WRITE** command) a decimal point (.) should be placed next to the unit number. For example:

FILE 12. DUMP.DAT

THE SAMPLE COMMAND

The **SAMPLE** command has the following format:

SAMPLE *beg end*

where *beg* and *end* are numbers specifying the beginning and ending observations. For example, to input the first 10 observations of the data with the **READ** command the following **SAMPLE** command should be used:

SAMPLE 1 10

The **SAMPLE** command should not set a sample size larger than the number of observations available in the data.

An expanded form of the **SAMPLE** command can be used after all the data has been read to control which observations are used for estimation. Note, however that the expanded form is not available for use with the **READ** command described below. In the expanded form you can select certain groups of observations. For example:

SAMPLE 1 8 11 15

would skip observations 9 and 10. Another example is:

SAMPLE 1 1 5 5 12 12 15 15 20 20

which would only use observations 1, 5, 12, 15, and 20.

With time series data the **SAMPLE** command can specify dates. This form of the **SAMPLE** command is described in the chapter *MISCELLANEOUS COMMANDS AND INFORMATION*.

THE READ COMMAND

The **READ** command inputs the data and assigns variable names. When data is not in a separate file the data directly follows the **READ** command. However, if the data is in a separate file the **READ** command must specify the file containing the data with either a filename or unit number. If a unit number is used there must be a previous **FILE** command which assigns the file to the unit number. The three possible formats for the **READ** command are:

READ *vars / options*

READ(*unit*) *vars / options*

READ(*datafilename*) *vars / options*

where *vars* is a list of variable names and *options* is a list of desired options (see details below). In the first case, no unit number or filename is specified so the data must immediately following the **READ** command. The second case specifies a unit number which was assigned on a previous **FILE** command. The third case specifies a filename so no previous **FILE** command is required. An example of a **READ** command where the data file **MYDATA** is assigned to unit 11, and contains 4 variables is the following:

```
FILE 11 MYDATA
SAMPLE 1 17
READ(11) YEAR CONSUME INCOME PRICE
```

If the *datafilename* method is used, the commands are:

```
SAMPLE 1 17
READ(MYDATA) YEAR CONSUME INCOME PRICE
```

This method may NOT work on binary files on some operating systems and instead the **FILE** command with the decimal point following the unit number must be used. IBM mainframe operating systems must use unit numbers as assigned by the system control language.

Some computer programs (but not SHAZAM!) will interpret a "." as a missing data character. If your data file has missing data you will be required to use an editor to change the "." to an arbitrary numerical value. For example, you may want to set all the missing data to the value of −99999 which is the SHAZAM default missing data code as explained in the chapter *SET AND DISPLAY*.

The following options are available on the **READ** command:

BINARY	Used when the data is in Double Precision **BINARY** (unformatted). If the **FILE** command is used to assign the **BINARY** file, follow the instructions above to include a "." after the unit number on the **FILE** command. For example, the binary file **DUMP.DAT** can be assigned with:

```
FILE 11. DUMP.DAT
```

BYVAR	Used when the data is to be read variable **BY VAR**iable rather than observation by observation. When this option is used, the data for each new variable must begin on a new line. If this option is not used, the data for each new observation must begin on a new line. Observations deleted by the **SKIPIF** command or the expanded form of the **SAMPLE** command are included when this option is used.
CLOSE	**CLOSE**s a file that was opened for the **READ** or **WRITE** command. Most operating systems do not require that files be closed, but sometimes it is desirable to do so to free up memory or a unit number. If this option is used, the file will no longer be assigned to the unit number as specified with the **FILE** command.
DIF	Used when data is to be read from a DIF file. DIF files can be produced by *Lotus 1-2-3 TRANSLATE* and other spreadsheet or statistics programs. Refer to the section on *USING DIF FILES* in this chapter.
EOF	Forces SHAZAM to read to the End Of the data File regardless of the **SAMPLE** command in effect. This is the default if no **SAMPLE** command has been previously specified.
FORMAT	Data will be read in according to the **FORMAT** previously specified on the **FORMAT** command. The format will be stored in a SHAZAM variable called **FORMAT**. Details on the **FORMAT** command are given later in this chapter.
LIST	**LIST**s all data read. This option is equivalent to a **READ** command together with a **PRINT** command. Details on **PRINT** are given below.
REWIND	Used to **REWIND** the input data file BEFORE reading any data. The default is NOT to **REWIND** the data file. The **REWIND** option makes it possible to reread a data file. It is also used to read a file created with SHAZAM **WRITE** commands.
TSP	Used when data is to be read from a file with data in **TSP .DB** format. Some programs produce this type of file. Refer to the section on *USING TSP DATA FILES* in this chapter.

BEG=, END=   Sets a sample range which overrides the sample size set on the latest
                  SAMPLE command. The sample size set by these options will only be
                  used for the current **READ** command. Subsequent problems will be
                  performed according to the sample range set by the latest **SAMPLE**
                  command.

ROWS=, COLS=   Specifies the number of **ROWS** and **COLumnS** when a matrix is
                  being read in. Only one matrix can be read in on a given **READ**
                  command and if a matrix is being read in, no other variables may be
                  read in on that **READ** command. **SKIPIF** commands are not in effect
                  when a matrix is read. The beginning observation on the **SAMPLE**
                  command is used as the first row number for the matrix. Use the
                  option **BEG=1** to ensure that the matrix begins at row 1.

SKIPLINES=   **SKIP**s the number of **LINES** specified before reading in any data. It is
                  used if a data file contains a certain number of lines such as labels or
                  comments which need to be skipped before reading in the data.

Reading from Several Data Files

If you use **READ** commands to read from several files, the command file might look
like:

```
SAMPLE beg1 end1
READ(data1) vars1
SAMPLE beg2 end2
READ(data2) vars2
SAMPLE beg3 end3
READ(data3) vars3
```

When the second **READ** command is encountered the first data file is closed. When a
filename is specified on the **READ** or **WRITE** command the file is closed when another
READ or **WRITE** command specifies a filename. If a unit number is specified then the
files will stay assigned to each unit as shown in the next list of SHAZAM commands.

```
FILE 11 data1
FILE 12 data2
FILE 13 data3
SAMPLE beg1 end1
READ(11) vars1
SAMPLE beg2 end2
READ(12) vars2
SAMPLE beg3 end3
READ(13) vars3
```

This method uses up three input-output units. On some computer systems there may
be a limit on the number of open data files.

THE PRINT COMMAND

The **PRINT** command is used to list variables on the screen or the SHAZAM output file. Note that this command does not direct output to the printer. The **PRINT** command has the following format:

PRINT *vars / options*

where *vars* is a list of variable names and *options* is a list of desired options. The available options on the **PRINT** command are:

BYVAR   Specified variables will be printed variable **BY VAR**iable rather than observation by observation. If only one variable is printed this option is automatically in effect. It can be turned off with **NOBYVAR**. If **BYVAR** is specified, observations that have been omitted either with **SKIPIF** command or the expanded form (defined later in this chapter) of the **SAMPLE** command will also be printed.

FORMAT   The data will be written according to the format previously specified on the **FORMAT** command. The format will be stored in a variable called **FORMAT**. Details on the **FORMAT** command are given later in this chapter.

NEWLINE   These options will start a new line, page or sheet before printing. The
NEWPAGE   **NEWSHEET** option will only work on page printers which use a
NEWSHEET   colon (:) as the new sheet carriage control character.

NONAMES   Omits printing the heading of variable **NAMES**.

WIDE/   **WIDE** uses 120 columns and **NOWIDE** uses 80 columns. The default
NOWIDE   setting is described in the chapter *SET AND DISPLAY*.

BEG=, END=   Only the observations within the range specified by **BEG=** and **END=** will be printed. If these are not specified, the range from the **SAMPLE** command is used.

THE WRITE COMMAND

It is possible to write selected data from a SHAZAM run into a file by using the **WRITE** command. The **WRITE** command has the following format:

FILE *unit filename*
WRITE(*unit*) *vars / options*

or

WRITE*(filename) vars / options*

where *unit* is a unit number (assigned to a file with an operating system command or the SHAZAM **FILE** command), *filename* is the name of the data file, *vars* is a list of variable names and *options* is a list of desired options. The available units for writing data are 11-49. The available options on the **WRITE** command are similar to those available for the **PRINT** and **READ** commands, that is, **BYVAR, CLOSE, DIF, FORMAT, NAMES, WIDE, BEG=, END=** and the following additions:

BINARY   Specified variables will be written into the specified file in Double Precision **BINARY**. If the **FILE** command is used to assign the **BINARY** file, follow the instructions for the **FILE** command in this chapter and be sure to include a decimal point (.) after the unit number.

REWIND   Used to rewind the output data file before any data is written. If the **WRITE***(filename)* form is used then the file will be overwritten if there is a subsequent **WRITE** command with the same filename. That is, the **REWIND** option is not required. However, if the file is first assigned to a unit number with a **FILE** command then the data file will not be rewound as the default on the **WRITE** command. The **REWIND** option makes it possible to reuse a data file.

NOTE: The default on the **WRITE** command is **NONAMES**. Therefore, if a heading of variable names is desired the **NAMES** option should be used.

An example of the use of the **WRITE** command to write data to an output file is:

```
READ(MYDATA) YEAR CONSUME INCOME PRICE
GENR LNCON=LOG(CONSUME)
GENR LNINC=LOG(INCOME)
GENR LNPR=LOG(PRICE)
WRITE(THEIL.DAT) YEAR LNCON LNINC LNPR
STOP
```

THE **FORMAT** *COMMAND*

The **FORMAT** command can precede a **READ, WRITE** or **PRINT** command that specifies the **FORMAT** option. It gives the column positions of the data. The general format is:

FORMAT(*list*)

where *list* contains edit descriptors of the form:

nX   advances the column position by n spaces.

nFw.d   the field is w characters wide and contains a number such that d digits
                occur after the decimal point. The field is repeated n times.

                On a **READ** command fields that are all blanks are interpreted as zero
                values. Also, an explicit decimal point in the input field will override
                any specification of the decimal-point position given in the **FORMAT**
                command.

Aw   the field is w characters wide and contains a SHAZAM character
                variable. Character data is described later in this chapter.

/   skip to the next line.

The above descriptors follow FORTRAN rules. FORTRAN I format is not allowed. The
command line of a **FORMAT** statement must not exceed 248 characters. (Do not
confuse this with the data file record length). The use of the **FORMAT** command is
shown in the next example.

EXAMPLES

The following examples will illustrate the proper use of options on **READ** and **PRINT**
commands, as well as present the output that can be expected from the use of these
commands. The following is a listing of the Theil textile data set typed observation by
observation. The variables are, from left to right, *YEAR, CONSUME INCOME* and
PRICE.

```
1923   99.2   96.7 101.0
1924   99.0   98.1 100.1
1925  100.0  100.0 100.0
1926  111.6  104.9  90.6
1927  122.2  104.9  86.5
1928  117.6  109.5  89.7
1929  121.1  110.8  90.6
1930  136.0  112.3  82.8
1931  154.2  109.3  70.1
1932  153.6  105.3  65.4
1933  158.5  101.7  61.3
1934  140.6   95.4  62.5
1935  136.2   96.4  63.6
1936  168.0   97.6  52.6
1937  154.3  102.4  59.7
1938  149.0  101.6  59.5
1939  165.5  103.8  61.3
```

Suppose that the file **MYDATA** contains the data set. To input this data, all that is needed is a **SAMPLE** command and a very simple **READ** command:

```
SAMPLE 1 17
READ(MYDATA) YEAR CONSUME INCOME PRICE
```

Alternatively, this same data could be read using a **FORMAT** command. The appropriate commands are a **SAMPLE** command, a **FORMAT** command and a **READ** command with the **FORMAT** option:

```
SAMPLE 1 17
FORMAT(F4.0,3F6.0)
READ(MYDATA) YEAR CONSUME INCOME PRICE / FORMAT
```

The above **FORMAT** means to read the first variable in the first 4 columns, then read 3 variables of 6 columns each.

To print all or some of the variables the **PRINT** command is used. The sample size can be reset as many times as desired within a run. The sample size in effect will be the last one specified. This allows extensive manipulation of data. For example, in the following SHAZAM output the sample size is set twice, first to read the entire data file with the **READ** command, and then to print a subset of observations with the **PRINT** command.

```
|_SAMPLE 1 17
|_READ(MYDATA) YEAR CONSUME INCOME PRICE
|_PRINT YEAR CONSUME INCOME PRICE
     YEAR            CONSUME          INCOME             PRICE
    1923.000        99.20000         96.70000          101.0000
    1924.000        99.00000         98.10000          100.1000
    1925.000        100.0000         100.0000          100.0000
    1926.000        111.6000         104.9000          90.60000
    1927.000        122.2000         104.9000          86.50000
    1928.000        117.6000         109.5000          89.70000
    1929.000        121.1000         110.8000          90.60000
    1930.000        136.0000         112.3000          82.80000
    1931.000        154.2000         109.3000          70.10000
    1932.000        153.6000         105.3000          65.40000
    1933.000        158.5000         101.7000          61.30000
    1934.000        140.6000         95.40000          62.50000
    1935.000        136.2000         96.40000          63.60000
    1936.000        168.0000         97.60000          52.60000
    1937.000        154.3000         102.4000          59.70000
    1938.000        149.0000         101.6000          59.50000
    1939.000        165.5000         103.8000          61.30000
|_SAMPLE 10 17
|_PRINT YEAR CONSUME INCOME PRICE
     YEAR            CONSUME           INCOME            PRICE
    1932.000        153.6000         105.3000          65.40000
    1933.000        158.5000         101.7000          61.30000
    1934.000        140.6000         95.40000          62.50000
```

```
    1935.000         136.2000         96.40000         63.60000
    1936.000         168.0000         97.60000         52.60000
    1937.000         154.3000         102.4000         59.70000
    1938.000         149.0000         101.6000         59.50000
    1939.000         165.5000         103.8000         61.30000
|_PRINT YEAR INCOME / BEG=1 END=4
    YEAR             INCOME
    1923.000         96.70000
    1924.000         98.10000
    1925.000         100.0000
    1926.000         104.9000
```

An expanded form of the **SAMPLE** command can also be used to select portions from the larger sample. For example, to select observations 1 through 4 and 12 through 15, the following **SAMPLE** command would be used:

```
|_SAMPLE 1 4 12 15
|_PRINT YEAR CONSUME INCOME PRICE
    YEAR             CONSUME          INCOME           PRICE
    1923.000         99.20000         96.70000         101.0000
    1924.000         99.00000         98.10000         100.1000
    1925.000         100.0000         100.0000         100.0000
    1926.000         111.6000         104.9000         90.60000
    1934.000         140.6000         95.40000         62.50000
    1935.000         136.2000         96.40000         63.60000
    1936.000         168.0000         97.60000         52.60000
    1937.000         154.3000         102.4000         59.70000
```

It is possible to read in data from more than one file in a single SHAZAM run. If, for example, the Textile data were divided into two portions, 1923-1930 and 1931-1939, and each portion were in a different file, SHAZAM could not only read in both data files, but could also combine the two files so the variables were complete. Since the maximum number of observations of a variable is set by the first **READ** command in the absence of a **SAMPLE** command, it is necessary to first create the variable with the **DIM** command. The **DIM** command will reserve enough space for all the observations from both data files. In this example **MYDATA1** is used for observations 1 to 8 and **MYDATA2** is used for observations 9 to 17:

```
|_DIM YEAR 17 CONSUME 17 INCOME 17 PRICE 17
|_READ(MYDATA1) YEAR CONSUME INCOME PRICE / BEG=1 END=8 LIST
    4 VARIABLES AND       8 OBSERVATIONS STARTING AT OBS       1
...SAMPLE RANGE IS NOW SET TO:           1           8
    1923.000         99.20000         96.70000         101.0000
    1924.000         99.00000         98.10000         100.1000
    1925.000         100.0000         100.0000         100.0000
    1926.000         111.6000         104.9000         90.60000
    1927.000         122.2000         104.9000         86.50000
    1928.000         117.6000         109.5000         89.70000
    1929.000         121.1000         110.8000         90.60000
    1930.000         136.0000         112.3000         82.80000
|_READ(MYDATA2) YEAR CONSUME INCOME PRICE / BEG=9 END=17 LIST
    4 VARIABLES AND       9 OBSERVATIONS STARTING AT OBS       9
```

```
    1931.000          154.2000          109.3000          70.10000
    1932.000          153.6000          105.3000          65.40000
    1933.000          158.5000          101.7000          61.30000
    1934.000          140.6000          95.40000          62.50000
    1935.000          136.2000          96.40000          63.60000
    1936.000          168.0000          97.60000          52.60000
    1937.000          154.3000          102.4000          59.70000
    1938.000          149.0000          101.6000          59.50000
    1939.000          165.5000          103.8000          61.30000
|_SAMPLE 1 17
|_PRINT YEAR CONSUME INCOME PRICE
      YEAR               CONSUME             INCOME              PRICE
    1923.000          99.20000          96.70000          101.0000
    1924.000          99.00000          98.10000          100.1000
    1925.000          100.0000          100.0000          100.0000
    1926.000          111.6000          104.9000          90.60000
    1927.000          122.2000          104.9000          86.50000
    1928.000          117.6000          109.5000          89.70000
    1929.000          121.1000          110.8000          90.60000
    1930.000          136.0000          112.3000          82.80000
    1931.000          154.2000          109.3000          70.10000
    1932.000          153.6000          105.3000          65.40000
    1933.000          158.5000          101.7000          61.30000
    1934.000          140.6000          95.40000          62.50000
    1935.000          136.2000          96.40000          63.60000
    1936.000          168.0000          97.60000          52.60000
    1937.000          154.3000          102.4000          59.70000
    1938.000          149.0000          101.6000          59.50000
    1939.000          165.5000          103.8000          61.30000
```

In the above example, the **DIM** command set the length of all four variables to 17. (For further details on the **DIM** command see the chapter *MISCELLANEOUS COMMANDS AND INFORMATION.*) Then, using the **BEG=** and **END=** options, the variables *YEAR, CONSUME, INCOME* and *PRICE* were read in from two data files, observations 1 to 8 are read in from **MYDATA1** and observations 9 to 17 are read in from **MYDATA2**.

READ *command with* BYVAR *option*

When the data is typed variable by variable the **BYVAR** option is needed on the **READ** command. The following is a listing of a file which contains the same data as that used above, but it is typed variable by variable rather than observation by observation:

```
    1923  1924  1925  1926  1927  1928  1929  1930
    1931  1932  1933  1934  1935  1936  1937  1938  1939
     99.2  99.0 100.0 111.6 122.2 117.6 121.1 136.0
    154.2 153.6 158.5 140.6 136.2 168.0 154.3 149.0 165.5
     96.7  98.1 100.0 104.9 104.9 109.5 110.8 112.3
    109.3 105.3 101.7  95.4  96.4  97.6 102.4 101.6 103.8
    101.0 100.1 100.0  90.6  86.5  89.7  90.6  82.8
     70.1  65.4  61.3  62.5  63.6  52.6  59.7  59.5  61.3
```

Each variable may extend over more than one line. However, *new variables must start on a new line*. With the **BYVAR** option the **SAMPLE** command is especially important.

SHAZAM needs the sample size in order to know when to stop reading observations into the first variable listed on the **READ** command and start reading them into the second, etc.

To input the above data a **SAMPLE** command and a **READ** command with the **BYVAR** option are needed:

```
SAMPLE 1 17
READ(MYDATA) YEAR CONSUME INCOME PRICE / BYVAR
```

Alternatively, this same data could be read by using a **FORMAT** and **READ** command. The appropriate commands are a **FORMAT** command and a **READ** command with the **FORMAT** and **BYVAR** options:

```
SAMPLE 1 17
FORMAT(8F6.0/9F6.0)
READ(MYDATA) YEAR CONSUME INCOME PRICE / FORMAT BYVAR
```

The above **FORMAT** needs 8 variables of 6 columns each on the first followed by 9 variables of 6 columns each. The "/" in the **FORMAT** is an indicator to skip to the next line. It is also possible to use the **BYVAR** option on the **PRINT** command. The variables will be printed horizontally by variable rather than in columns:

```
|_PRINT YEAR CONSUME / BYVAR
 YEAR
    1923.0    1924.0    1925.0    1926.0    1927.0    1928.0    1929.0    1930.0
    1931.0    1932.0    1933.0    1934.0    1935.0    1936.0    1937.0    1938.0
    1939.0
 CONSUME
     99.20     99.00    100.00    111.60    122.20    117.60    121.10    136.00
    154.20    153.60    158.50    140.60    136.20    168.00    154.30    149.00
    165.50
```

READ *command with* **ROWS=** *and* **COLS=** *option*

It is often useful to read data as a matrix. To read in a matrix, the **ROWS=** and **COLS=** options are needed on the **READ** command. If the original Theil textile data were all to be placed in a single matrix named *W*, the appropriate **READ** command would be:

```
READ(MYDATA) W / ROWS=17 COLS=4 BEG=1
```

To print *W* the **PRINT** command is used:

```
|_PRINT W
 W
    17 BY     4 MATRIX
    1923.000       99.20000      96.70000      101.0000
    1924.000       99.00000      98.10000      100.1000
```

```
 1925.000        100.0000        100.0000        100.0000
 1926.000        111.6000        104.9000        90.60000
 1927.000        122.2000        104.9000        86.50000
 1928.000        117.6000        109.5000        89.70000
 1929.000        121.1000        110.8000        90.60000
 1930.000        136.0000        112.3000        82.80000
 1931.000        154.2000        109.3000        70.10000
 1932.000        153.6000        105.3000        65.40000
 1933.000        158.5000        101.7000        61.30000
 1934.000        140.6000        95.40000        62.50000
 1935.000        136.2000        96.40000        63.60000
 1936.000        168.0000        97.60000        52.60000
 1937.000        154.3000        102.4000        59.70000
 1938.000        149.0000        101.6000        59.50000
 1939.000        165.5000        103.8000        61.30000
```

It is also possible to print only one column of the matrix using the **PRINT** command with the column number of the matrix specified after a colon (:) as follows:

```
|_PRINT W:4
    101.0000   100.1000   100.0000   90.60000   86.50000
    89.70000   90.60000   82.80000   70.10000   65.40000
    61.30000   62.50000   63.60000   52.60000   59.70000
    59.50000   61.30000
```

The above **PRINT** command prints the data occupying the fourth column of the matrix *W*.

Reading Character Data

It is possible to read character data in SHAZAM, using the **FORMAT** command and option. The following example illustrates how to read the names of nine of the provinces of Canada into a variable called *PROVINCE* and shows that it is possible to read non-character data on the same **READ** command when the appropriate **FORMAT** is specified (i.e. using A format to read characters). The data is the unemployment and vacancy rates of each province for January 1976 as provided by Statistics Canada. Data on the 10th province, Prince Edward Island, was not available.   The first **FORMAT** below says to read a variable that is 8 characters followed by two data variables of 5 columns each.   The second **FORMAT** uses "1X" to skip one column then prints 8 characters for the variable *PROVINCE*.

```
|_SAMPLE 1 9
|_FORMAT(A8,2F5.1)
|_READ PROVINCE UR VR / FORMAT
NEWFOUND 14.9   4.0
NOVA SCO  9.1   5.0
NEW BRUN 12.2   7.0
QUEBEC    9.1   6.0
ONTARIO   7.1   5.0
MANITOBA  6.7   8.0
SASKATCH  4.8   8.0
```

```
ALBERTA    5.3 11.0
BRITISH   10.0  4.0
|_PRINT UR VR
        UR                  VR
   14.90000          4.000000
    9.100000          5.000000
   12.20000          7.000000
    9.100000          6.000000
    7.100000          5.000000
    6.700000          8.000000
    4.800000          8.000000
    5.300000          11.00000
   10.00000          4.000000
|_FORMAT(1X,A8)
|_PRINT PROVINCE / FORMAT
 PROVINCE
 NEWFOUND
 NOVA SCO
 NEW BRUN
 QUEBEC
 ONTARIO
 MANITOBA
 SASKATCH
 ALBERTA
 BRITISH
```

Note, in the above example, that some systems do not permit printing in column 1, so two different **FORMAT** commands are needed, one for the **READ** command and one for the **PRINT** command. Note also that all of the variables *PROVINCE, UR* and *UV* could have been printed on the same **PRINT** command if a **FORMAT** command of the form **FORMAT(1X,A8,2F5.1)** had been specified.

Each observation of character data may be only 8 characters long, but if the user wishes to have longer character variables, more than one variable should be specified on the **READ** command and a **FORMAT** command specifying the appropriate A format should also appear. For example, if each observation were to be at most 16 characters long, the appropriate **FORMAT** command would be **FORMAT(2A8)** and 2 variables would be read in on the **READ** command and printed out on the **PRINT** command. The following example illustrates this procedure for the case where 16 characters are permitted:

```
|_SAMPLE 1 9
|_FORMAT(2A8,2F5.1)
|_READ PROV1 PROV2 UR UV / FORMAT
NEWFOUNDLAND      14.9  4.0
NOVA SCOTIA        9.1  5.0
NEW BRUNSWICK     12.2  7.0
QUEBEC             9.1  6.0
ONTARIO            7.1  5.0
MANITOBA           6.7  8.0
```

```
SASKATCHEWAN       4.8   8.0
ALBERTA            5.3  11.0
BRITISH COLUMBIA  10.0   4.0
|_FORMAT(1X,2A8,2F5.1)
|_PRINT PROV1 PROV2 UR VR / FORMAT NONAMES
NEWFOUNDLAND      14.9   4.0
NOVA SCOTIA        9.1   5.0
NEW BRUNSWICK     12.2   7.0
QUEBEC             9.1   6.0
ONTARIO            7.1   5.0
MANITOBA           6.7   8.0
SASKATCHEWAN       4.8   8.0
ALBERTA            5.3  11.0
BRITISH COLUMBIA  10.0   4.0
```

USING THE CITIBASE DATABANK

The **RESTORE** command is used to restore data from a Databank. At present only the CITIBASE Databank is supported. To use it, the CITIBASE Databank must be available at your installation in its original form as distributed by Citibank. Since this is often on a tape, you may need to mount the tape and assign it to a unit number with the **FILE** command. You must specify the option **CITIBASE** and the **UNIT=** number on the **RESTORE** command. If using a Citibase Databank in the new format (available since 1986) use the **CITINEW** option instead of **CITIBASE**. In addition you must use the **TIME** command to set the date since the date form of the **SAMPLE** command will be used, (see the chapter *MISCELLANEOUS COMMANDS AND INFORMATION*). In general, the format of the **RESTORE** command is:

RESTORE *vars* / **CITINEW UNIT=***unit*

The names on the **RESTORE** command must be CITIBASE names. In the following example it is assumed that the CITIBASE file has been assigned to unit 11 and the user wishes to read the annual variables *VAR1, VAR2* and *VAR3* from the CITIBASE file for the years 1960 to 1980.

```
FILE 11 CITIFILENAME
SAMPLE 121
TIME 1960 1
SAMPLE 1960.0 1980.0
RESTORE VAR1 VAR2 VAR3 / CITINEW UNIT=11
PRINT VAR1 VAR2 VAR3
```

Since it is time consuming to restore data from the CITIBASE databank you should check your commands carefully. In particular, you should make sure you have typed the variable names correctly or a search of the entire databank will be made looking for a variable that probably does not exist. Once the data has been restored you may want to use the SHAZAM **WRITE** command to put the data in a separate file for later use.

USING DIF FILES

Many spreadsheet and statistical programs (for example: *Lotus 1-2-3*) have adopted a standard for transferring files between programs. The standard is widely used and is called a DIF (DATA-INTERCHANGE-FORMAT) file. A DIF file often contains information about the variable names, number of variables and number of observations. DIF files are a very convenient way to read data into SHAZAM that have been previously used in another program like *Lotus 1-2-3*. The *TRANSLATE* program supplied with *Lotus 1-2-3* can change a regular *Lotus* file into a DIF file which can be read by SHAZAM and other programs.

When data is prepared in a spreadsheet program to read into SHAZAM it is best to set up the data as a rectangular matrix where each column of the matrix corresponds to a SHAZAM variable and each row of the matrix corresponds to an observation in SHAZAM. Hence, if your data contained 11 variables and 37 observations your spreadsheet program would show 11 columns and 37 rows. If the first row of the spreadsheet contains the names of the variables then the spreadsheet would have 11 columns and 38 rows. When variable names are included you should be careful that they correspond to SHAZAM variable name rules or SHAZAM may not be able to access the data properly.

Assume you have created a DIF file from another program (or from SHAZAM using the **WRITE** command with the **DIF** option). Suppose the file is called **MYDATA.DIF** and no names have been included in the first row of the spreadsheet but you wish to assign the variable names *YEAR, CONSUME* and *INCOME* and there are 17 rows and 3 columns. Your SHAZAM commands would appear as:

```
READ(MYDATA.DIF) YEAR CONSUME INCOME / DIF
```

Be sure to include the **DIF** option on the **READ** command. If variable names are included in the DIF file, then you MUST NOT include them on the **READ** command, hence you would use:

```
READ(MYDATA.DIF) / DIF
```

The above two examples assume that the data file **MYDATA.DIF** is located in the same directory as your SHAZAM command files. If your data file is located in a separate directory/folder called *LOTUS* then, for the MSDOS version of SHAZAM, the above **READ** commands would be:

```
READ(C:\LOTUS\MYDATA.DIF) YEAR CONSUME INCOME / DIF        or
READ(C:\LOTUS\MYDATA.DIF) / DIF
```

It is assumed that the hard disk on the personal computer is called "C". If the hard disk is called something other than "C" then replace it with the appropriate name.

For the Macintosh version of SHAZAM, the **READ** commands would be:

```
READ(DISK:LOTUS:MYDATA.DIF) YEAR CONSUME INCOME / DIF          or
READ(DISK:LOTUS:MYDATA.DIF) / DIF
```

It is assumed that the hard disk on the Macintosh is called "DISK". If the hard disk is called something other than "DISK" then replace it with the appropriate name.

It is extremely important to remember that you must specify exactly where the data file is located in your **READ** command. Otherwise, SHAZAM will not know where to look for the file and there will be an error.

The number of observations for each variable must be identical in the DIF file. This means that you cannot have any missing observations for any of the variables. If missing observations exist in the data file then you must enter a value of zero or some other value like the SHAZAM default missing data code of −99999.

In some cases you may find that your data file has to be cleaned up a bit in the spreadsheet program before a proper DIF file can be produced. For example, you may find that your spreadsheet program has produced a large number of blank rows and columns. It may be necessary to delete these blank rows and columns first. It is required that an equal number of rows are present for each column in the spreadsheet. Some spreadsheet programs actually transpose the data matrix when writing a DIF file. If this happens it may be necessary to perform some data manipulations using SHAZAM **MATRIX** commands to transpose the data into the proper form.

SHAZAM can also create a DIF file for use in another program. For example, if your SHAZAM run currently has the variables *YEAR*, *PRICE* and *INCOME* and you wish to create a DIF file with these three variables you would need the following commands:

```
WRITE(NEWFILE.DIF) YEAR PRICE INCOME / DIF NAMES
```

If you did not wish to include the variable names in the DIF file then the **NAMES** option would not be used. In order to learn how to use DIF files, it is often easier to first **WRITE** a DIF file in SHAZAM and then examine it and **READ** it back into SHAZAM. If you are successful in this exercise you will understand the DIF file process.

USING TSP FILES

Occasionally SHAZAM users may find it necessary to read data files that have been produced in the **.DB** format used by the TSP microcomputer program. TSP files usually contain five header lines before the data which describe the sample, provide information about the frequency (Quarterly, Monthy, Annual, etc.) and the beginning and ending year of the sample. SHAZAM can read TSP files directly if the **TSP** option is specified on the **READ** command. It is also necessary to first use the SHAZAM **TIME** command described in the chapter *MISCELLANEOUS COMMANDS AND INFORMATION* to ensure that the data is read properly.

For example, assume you have data on the variables *CONSUME* and *INCOME* and they are contained in the separate TSP files called **CONSUME.DB** and **INCOME.DB**. Now you wish to assign the variable names as *C* and *Y* instead of *CONSUME* and *INCOME* when you read the data in. The data is quarterly for the years 1974 first quarter to 1988 fourth quarter. In this case the SHAZAM commands are:

```
TIME 1974 4
SAMPLE 1974.1 1988.4
READ(CONSUME.DB) C / TSP
READ(INCOME.DB) Y / TSP
```

4. DESCRIPTIVE STATISTICS

"Jupiter's moons are invisible to the naked eye and therefore can have no influence on the earth, and therefore would be useless, and therefore do not exist."

Francisco Sizzi
Professor of Astronomy, 1610

The **STAT** command computes descriptive statistics.

Mean, Variance and Other Statistics

For a variable X with N observations denoted by X_t, t=1,...,N the statistics listed by the **STAT** command are calculated as follows.

Mean
$$\overline{X} = \frac{1}{N}\sum_{t=1}^{N} X_t$$

Variance
$$\hat{\sigma}_X^2 = \frac{1}{N-1}\sum_{t=1}^{N}(X_t - \overline{X})^2 = \frac{1}{N-1}\left[\sum_{t=1}^{N} X_t^2 - N\overline{X}^2\right]$$

Standard deviation
$$\hat{\sigma}_X = \sqrt{\hat{\sigma}_X^2}$$

Minimum   Min = the smallest value of X_t

Maximum   Max = the largest value of X_t

When the **WIDE** option is specified the output also reports:

Coefficient of variation $\hat{\sigma}_X/\overline{X}$

Constant digits statistic
$$= \begin{cases} -\log_{10}(R/|Min|) & \text{if } R < |Min| \text{ and } Min \neq Max \\ 0 & \text{otherwise} \end{cases}$$

where R=(Max−Min) is the sample range. The fraction R/|Min| gives the relative change from the smallest to the largest value. For discussion see Simon and Lesage [1989].

When the **PMEDIAN** option is specified the output reports the median, the mode and quartiles. Let $X_{(1)}, X_{(2)}, \ldots, X_{(N)}$ be the observations that are ordered from smallest to largest. The median is:

$$\begin{cases} \text{when } N \text{ is odd:} & X_{((N+1)/2)} \\ \text{when } N \text{ is even:} & \text{the average of } X_{(N/2)} \text{ and } X_{((N+2)/2)} \end{cases}$$

The mode is the most frequently occurring value in the set of observations. The quartiles are obtained as:

first quartile (lower 25%)	$X_{((N+1)/4)}$
second quartile	the median
third quartile (upper 25%)	$X_{(3(N+1)/4)}$
interquartile range	difference between the third and first quartiles (a measure of dispersion).

Interpolation is used to compute the quartiles when $(N+1)/4$ is not an integer. Discussion and examples are given in Newbold [1995, Chapter 2].

The **PFREQ** option reports frequencies, relative frequencies and cumulative relative frequencies. For the ordered data the frequency f_t is the number of occurrences of $X_{(t)}$. The relative frequency is f_t/N and the cumulative relative frequency is $(f_1 + \ldots + f_t)/N$. Note that the frequency distribution for grouped data is obtained with a histogram display that is available with the **HISTO** option on the **PLOT** command (see the chapter *PLOTS*).

Covariance and Correlation

Statistics involving relationships between variables are also produced with the **STAT** command. Consider K variables such that the k-th variable has observations X_{kt} for $t=1,\ldots,N$ and mean $\overline{X}_k$ and standard deviation $\hat{\sigma}_{X_k}$ for $k=1,\ldots,K$. The cross-products (printed with the **PCP** option) are:

$$\sum_{t=1}^{N} X_{it} X_{jt} \qquad\qquad \text{for } i,j=1,\ldots,K$$

The cross-products of deviations about the mean (printed with the **PCPDEV** option) are:

$$\sum_{t=1}^{N}(X_{it}-\overline{X}_i)(X_{jt}-\overline{X}_j) \qquad \text{for } i,j=1,\ldots,K$$

The covariances (printed with the **PCOV** option and saved with the **COV=** option) are:

$$Cov(X_i,X_j) = \frac{1}{N-1}\sum_{t=1}^{N}(X_{it}-\overline{X}_i)(X_{jt}-\overline{X}_j) = \frac{1}{N-1}\left[\sum_{t=1}^{N}X_{it}X_{jt}-N\overline{X}_i\overline{X}_j\right]$$

The correlations (printed with the **PCOR** option and saved with the **COR=** option) are:

$$Cor(X_i,X_j) = Cov(X_i,X_j) / \hat{\sigma}_{x_i}\hat{\sigma}_{x_j}$$

The correlation coefficients may be seriously affected by extreme outliers. An alternative measure of correlation that is not as sensitive to extreme values is based on ranks. Let S_{it} be the rank of X_{it} where the ranking is in ascending order of values. Spearman's rank correlation coefficients are calculated as:

$$r_s(X_i,X_j) = 1 - \frac{6}{N(N^2-1)}\sum_{t=1}^{N}(S_{it}-S_{jt})^2$$

The **PRANKCOR** option computes the Spearman rank correlation coefficients. For further details see Gujarati [1995, p. 88 and p. 372], Newbold [1995, p. 436] or Yule and Kendall [1953, p. 455].

Testing for Equality of Mean and Variance

The **ANOVA** option constructs an analysis of variance table that gives a framework for testing for equality of population means (see, for example, Newbold [1995, pp. 598-605]). Consider K variables such that the k-th variable has observations X_{kt} for $t=1,\ldots,n_k$. That is, the design allows for unequal sample sizes. Define:

$$N = \sum_{k=1}^{K}n_k\,, \qquad \overline{X}_k = \frac{1}{n_k}\sum_{t=1}^{n_k}X_{kt} \qquad \text{and} \qquad \overline{X} = \frac{1}{K}\sum_{k=1}^{K}\overline{X}_k$$

The analysis of variance (ANOVA) table is constructed as follows.

	SS	DF	MS	F
BETWEEN	$SSB = \sum_{k=1}^{K} n_k (\overline{X}_k - \overline{X})^2$	$K-1$	$\dfrac{SSB}{K-1}$	$\dfrac{SSB/K-1}{SSW/N-K}$
WITHIN	$SSW = \sum_{k=1}^{K} \sum_{t=1}^{n_k} (X_{kt} - \overline{X}_k)^2$	$N-K$	$\dfrac{SSW}{N-K}$	
TOTAL	$SST = \sum_{k=1}^{K} \sum_{t=1}^{n_k} (X_{kt} - \overline{X})^2$	$N-1$	$\dfrac{SST}{N-1}$	

Under the null hypothesis of equal means the F-test statistic has an F distribution with (K–1, N–K) degrees of freedom.

The **BARTLETT** option computes Bartlett's statistic for testing for equality of population variance (see, for example, Judge, Griffiths, Hill, Lütkepohl and Lee [1985, p. 448]). The sample variances are:

$$\hat{\sigma}_k^2 = \frac{1}{(n_k-1)} \sum_{t=1}^{n_k} (X_{kt} - \overline{X}_k)^2 \qquad \text{and} \qquad \hat{\sigma}^2 = \frac{1}{(N-K)} \sum_{k=1}^{K} (n_k - 1) \hat{\sigma}_k^2$$

A statistic for testing for equality of variance is:

$$u = \sum_{k=1}^{K} \left(\hat{\sigma}_k^2 / \hat{\sigma}^2 \right)^{n_k/2}$$

Bartlett's test statistic is based on a modification of $-2\ln(u)$ and is constructed as:

$$M = \frac{(N-K)\ln\hat{\sigma}^2 - \sum_{k=1}^{K}(n_k-1)\ln\hat{\sigma}_k^2}{1 + [1/\{3(K-1)\}]\left[\sum_{k=1}^{K} \dfrac{1}{(n_k-1)} - \dfrac{1}{(N-K)} \right]}$$

The test statistic M has an approximate χ^2 distribution with (K–1) degrees of freedom under the null hypothesis of equal variances. The derivation of exact critical values for the case of equal sample sizes is given in Dyer and Keating [1980].

STAT *COMMAND OPTIONS*

In general, the format of the **STAT** command is:

STAT *vars / options*

where *vars* is a list of variable names and *options* is a list of desired options. The available options on the **STAT** command are:

ALL   Statistics are computed for **ALL** the variables in the data. Therefore, no variable names need be specified.

ANOVA   Prints an **AN**alysis **O**f **VA**riance table and an F-value that tests the null hypothesis that the means of all the variables listed on the given **STAT** command are the same. An **ANOVA** example appears later in this chapter.

BARTLETT   Computes **BARTLETT**'s homogeneity of variance test statistic to test the hypothesis that the variances of all the variables listed are equal. An example of this option is given later in this chapter.

DN   Uses N (number of observations) as a divisor rather than N–1 when computing variances and covariances.

MATRIX   Any **MATRIX** or matrices contained in the list *vars* will be treated as a single variable if this option is used. If this option is not specified SHAZAM will treat each column of the matrix as a separate variable.

MAX   Prints all the output of the **PCOR, PCOV, PCP, PCPDEV** and **PRANKCOR** options.

PCOR   Prints a **COR**relation matrix of the variables listed.

PCOV   Prints a **CO**Variance matrix of the variables listed.

PCP   Prints a **C**ross**P**roduct matrix of the variables listed.

PCPDEV   Prints a **C**ross**P**roduct matrix of the variables listed in **DEV**iations from the means.

PFREQ   Prints a table of **FREQ**uencies of occurrence for each observed value in the data. Also prints the median, the mode and quartiles. This option is *not* recommended for large sample sizes with many different possible values since pages and pages of output would result.

PMEDIAN	Prints the **MEDIAN**, mode and quartiles for each variable. This option could be time-consuming when the sample size is large.
PRANKCOR	Prints a matrix of Spearman's **RANK COR**relation coefficients.
REPLICATE	Used with **WEIGHT=** when the weights indicate a sample replication factor.
WIDE	Requires 120 columns of output. When this option is used the coefficient of variation and the constant digits statistic will be printed in addition to the regular descriptive statistics.
BEG=, END=	Specifies the **BEG**inning and **END** observations to be used in the **STAT** command.
COR=	Stores the **COR**relation matrix in the variable specified.
COV=	Stores the **CO**Variance matrix in the variable specified.
CP=	Stores the **CrossProduct** matrix in the variable specified.
CPDEV=	Stores the **CrossProduct** matrix in **DEV**iations from the mean in the variable specified.
MAXIM=	Stores the **MAXIM**ums as a vector in the variable specified.
MEAN=	Stores the **MEAN**s as a vector in the variable specified.
MEDIANS=	Stores the **MEDIANS** as a vector in the variable specified.
MINIM=	Stores the **MINIM**ums as a vector in the variable specified.
MODES=	Stores the **MODES** as a vector in the variable specified.
RANKCOR=	Stores the Spearman's **RANK COR**relation matrix in the variable specified (see the **PRANKCOR** option above).
STDEV=	Stores the **ST**andard **DEV**iations as a vector in the variable specified.
SUMS=	Stores the sum of each variable as a vector in the variable specified.
VAR=	Stores the **VAR**iances as a vector in the variable specified. Note that when the **DN** option is used the divisor is N instead of N–1.

WEIGHT=   Specifies a variable to be used as a **WEIGHT** if weighted descriptive statistics are desired. Consider K variables such that the k-th variable has observations X_{kt} for t=1,...,N and k=1,...,K. Let W_t be the weights. The weighted statistics are:

Mean
$$\overline{X}_k^w = \frac{1}{S} \sum_{t=1}^{N} W_t X_{kt} \quad \text{where} \quad S = \sum_{t=1}^{N} W_t$$

Variance
$$\hat{\sigma}_{x_k w}^2 = \frac{c}{S} \cdot \left[\sum_{t=1}^{N} W_t X_{kt}^2 - S \cdot (\overline{X}_k^w)^2 \right]$$

where c=N/(N–1). When the **DN** option is used then c = 1. When the **REPLICATE** option is used then c=S/(S–1). The **REPLICATE** option is not effective when **DN** is specified.

The weighted covariances and correlations are computed as:

$$\text{Cov}\left(X_i, X_j\right)_w = \frac{c}{S} \cdot \left[\sum_{t=1}^{N} W_t X_{it} X_{jt} - S \cdot \overline{X}_i^w \overline{X}_j^w \right]$$

$$\text{Cor}\left(X_i, X_j\right)_w = \text{Cov}\left(X_i, X_j\right)_w / \hat{\sigma}_{x_i w} \hat{\sigma}_{x_j w}$$

It is important to note that options beginning with **P** will merely print results on the output file. Options ending in an equal sign (=) are used to store the matrix or vector in the variable specified or to specify input requirements.

EXAMPLES

The examples below use Theil's textile data to illustrate some options on the **STAT** command. First, a **STAT** command with the **PCOR** , **PCOV** and **WIDE** options are specified and the output is:

|_STAT CONSUME INCOME PRICE / PCOR PCOV WIDE					
NAME	N	MEAN	ST. DEV	VARIANCE	MINIMUM	MAXIMUM
CONSUME	17	134.51	23.577	555.89	99.000	168.00
INCOME	17	102.98	5.3010	28.100	95.400	112.30
PRICE	17	76.312	16.866	284.47	52.600	101.00

COEF.OF.VARIATION	CONSTANT-DIGITS
.17529	.15679
.51475E-01	.75166
.22102	.36140E-01

```
CORRELATION MATRIX OF VARIABLES -        17 OBSERVATIONS

CONSUME    1.0000
INCOME     .61769E-01  1.0000
PRICE     -.94664       .17885      1.0000
           CONSUME     INCOME       PRICE



 COVARIANCE MATRIX OF VARIABLES -        17 OBSERVATIONS

CONSUME    555.89
INCOME     7.7201       28.100
PRICE     -376.44       15.990      284.47
           CONSUME     INCOME       PRICE
```

The next example shows the use of the **STDEV=** and **COR=** options. The standard deviations of the variables *CONSUME, INCOME* and *PRICE* are stored in a variable called *SD*. The correlation matrix is stored in a variable called *CMATRIX*. These variables are then available for future computations.

```
|_STAT CONSUME INCOME PRICE / STDEV=SD COR=CMATRIX
NAME        N    MEAN      ST. DEV     VARIANCE     MINIMUM      MAXIMUM
CONSUME    17   134.51     23.577       555.89      99.000       168.00
INCOME     17   102.98     5.3010       28.100      95.400       112.30
PRICE      17   76.312     16.866       284.47      52.600       101.00

|_PRINT SD CMATRIX
   SD
  23.57733         5.300972        16.86623


   CMATRIX
  1.000000
   .6176945E-01   1.000000
 -.9466377         .1788466        1.000000
```

The next examples use the housing data from Pindyck and Rubinfeld [1991, p. 131]. Each variable contains data for housing expenditure for five families with identical incomes. The income levels are 5, 10, 15 and 20 thousand dollars and are identified here by the variable names *A, B, C* and *D*. The output below shows the use of the **ANOVA** and **BARTLETT** options on the **STAT** command. Note that the **LIST** option on the **READ** command is used to obtain a listing of the housing expenditure data.

```
|_SAMPLE 1 5
|_READ (HOUSE.DAT) A B C D / LIST

   4 VARIABLES AND        5 OBSERVATIONS STARTING AT OBS       1


       A              B              C              D
   1800.000       3000.000       4200.000       4800.000
   2000.000       3200.000       4200.000       5000.000
   2000.000       3500.000       4500.000       5700.000
   2000.000       3500.000       4800.000       6000.000
   2100.000       3600.000       5000.000       6200.000
```

```
|_STAT A B C D / ANOVA BARLETT
NAME       N    MEAN        ST. DEV      VARIANCE      MINIMUM       MAXIMUM
A          5    1980.0      109.54       12000.        1800.0        2100.0
B          5    3360.0      251.00       63000.        3000.0        3600.0
C          5    4540.0      357.77       .12800E+06    4200.0        5000.0
D          5    5540.0      614.82       .37800E+06    4800.0        6200.0

                        ANALYSIS OF VARIANCE
                    SS          DF            MS                    F
BETWEEN         .35346E+08      3.        .11782E+08         81.114
WITHIN          .23240E+07      16.       .14525E+06
TOTAL           .37670E+08      19.       .19826E+07

BARLETTS HOMOGENEITY OF VARIANCE TEST =        9.0525
   APPROXIMATELY CHI-SQUARE WITH      3 DEGREES OF FREEDOM
```

The above results show that Bartlett's test statistic is 9.0525. The 5% critical value from a chi-square distribution with 3 degrees of freedom is 7.81. The test statistic exceeds this critical value and so there is evidence for unequal variance between populations. The F-test statistic from the ANOVA table is designed to test for equality of means. However, the construction assumes that the populations have equal variance and so the F-test statistic may not be meaningful in this example.

In the next example the housing expenditure data is read in as a matrix, M. If the **MATRIX** option is used on the **STAT** command the matrix variable will be treated as a single variable as shown in the following output.

```
|_SAMPLE 1 5
|_READ (HOUSE.DAT) M / ROWS=5 COLS=4

     5 ROWS AND          4 COLUMNS, BEGINNING AT ROW          1

|_STAT M / MATRIX
NAME       N    MEAN        ST. DEV      VARIANCE      MINIMUM       MAXIMUM
M          20   3855.0      1408.1       .19826E+07    1800.0        6200.0
```

However, if the **MATRIX** option is not specified, each column of the matrix specified will be treated as a single variable as shown in the next output.

```
|_STAT M
NAME       N    MEAN        ST. DEV      VARIANCE      MINIMUM       MAXIMUM
...NOTE...TREATING COLUMNS OF M        AS VECTORS
M          5    1980.0      109.54       12000.        1800.0        2100.0
M          5    3360.0      251.00       63000.        3000.0        3600.0
M          5    4540.0      357.77       .12800E+06    4200.0        5000.0
M          5    5540.0      614.82       .37800E+06    4800.0        6200.0
```

5. PLOTS

"When the President does it, that means it is not illegal."
Richard Nixon
Former U.S. President, 1977

The **PLOT** command will plot variables. The **GNU** option provides an interface to the GNUPLOT program. An alternative method for obtaining high quality graphics is available with the **GRAPHICS** option.

PLOT *COMMAND OPTIONS*

In general, the format of the **PLOT** command is:

PLOT *depvars indep / options*

where *depvars* is one or more dependent variables to be plotted against a single independent variable, *indep*, and *options* is a list of desired options. The available options are:

ALTERNATE   Alternates the symbols "X" and "O" in plotting columns of the histogram when the **HISTO** option is used. It is especially useful with the **GROUPS=** option described below.

DASH   Used with the **GRAPHICS** and **LINE** options to obtain dashed lines when more than one variable is plotted.

GNU   Gives an interface to the **GNUPLOT** program. For more information on this option see the section *GNUPLOT* at the end of this chapter.

GOAWAY   Used with the **GRAPHICS** option if you wish the PLOT window to go away after the plot appears on the screen. Alternatively, you can click the GO AWAY box in the upper left corner. The option is in effect except in **TALK** mode. It can be turned off with **NOGOAWAY**.

GRAPHICS/   <u>MSDOS Operating System.</u>
VGA/EGA   Specifies the type of graphics monitor on your PC. If you do not have
HERCULES   an EGA, VGA, or HERCULES graphics monitor try using the **GRAPHICS** option which can be used for CGA monitors. The **HOLD, NOBLANK, HISTO, RANGE** and **SYMBOL** options are not supported, but the following options are supported: **LINE, LINEONLY** and **DASH**. See also the **PAUSE** and **PRINT** options.

GRAPHICS   Macintosh.
This option will display a separate PLOT window for the graphics
plot. After the plot is displayed the window can be removed by
clicking the GO-AWAY box in the upper left corner. See also the
GOAWAY and **PAUSE** options.

HISTO   Plots **HISTO**grams for the variables specified on the **PLOT** command.
The histogram could be centered around the mean with a scale of 3
standard deviations on either side of the mean, or, with the use of the
RANGE option described below, the entire range of the variable(s)
could be plotted. The first method is the default and is useful if there
are a few outliers which would complicate the scaling of the
histogram. However, if all the data must be plotted, the **RANGE**
option should be used to get the entire range. A separate histogram is
done for each variable in the list. Each histogram takes one page of
computer output. If **NOWIDE** is specified the histogram will be half
the regular size. See also the **ALTERNATE, RANGE** and **GROUPS=**
options.

HOLD   **HOLD**s the printing of the plot. The contents of this plot will be saved
for the next **PLOT** command. At that time the plot will be blanked out
unless the **NOBLANK** option is used. This option may not work on
GRAPHICS plots.

LINE   Used with the **GRAPHICS, GNU, EGA, VGA,** or **HERCULES** option
to draw a line connecting the data points and plot a symbol at each
point.

LINEONLY   Used with the **GRAPHICS, GNU, EGA, VGA,** or **HERCULES** option
to only draw a line connecting the data points. No symbols at the data
points will be plotted.

NOBLANK   Prevents the plot from being initialized with blanks, to allow the plot
to be imposed on the plot previously specified with the **HOLD** option.
The **HOLD** and **NOBLANK** options would be used if, for example, a
plot with different symbols for each part of the sample were desired.
This option may not work on **GRAPHICS** plots.

NOPRETTY   SHAZAM attempts to make pretty intervals on the axes by checking
the range of the data. This usually works, but sometimes the labels
are not acceptable. The **NOPRETTY** option will tell SHAZAM not to
attempt to make the axes pretty and just use the range of the data
directly.

PAUSE Used with one of the **GRAPHICS** options on DOS or Macintosh computers to temporarily stop the screen after a graphics plot appears so it can be examined. To resume the run, simply press the RETURN key. This option is automatically in effect in **TALK** mode.

PRINT Used with one of the **GRAPHICS** options on DOS computers to **PRINT** the plot on a printer. It may not work on some printers.

RANGE Utilizes the entire **RANGE** of the data for plotting the histogram when the **HISTO** option is used.

SAME/
NOSAME Plots *depvars* against the *indep* on the **SAME** plot. The two relationships are distinguishable by their differing point symbols. See the **SYMBOL=** option for further details. No more than 8 dependent variables should be plotted against the independent variable on the same plot. The default is **SAME**.

TIME Plots the listed *depvars* sequentially against **TIME**. In this case, *indep* is not specified.

WIDE/
NOWIDE **NOWIDE** reduces the size of the plot in the printed output. All of the reduced plot can be seen on a terminal screen as it takes up less than 80 columns. The default value is explained in the chapter *SET AND DISPLAY*.

BEG= , END= Sets a sample range for the particular **PLOT** command. This sample size is in effect only for the **PLOT** command with this option. If these options are not specified, the sample range for the current **SAMPLE** command is used.

CHARSIZE= Used with the **GRAPHICS** option on some MSDOS versions to specify the size of characters to be used as labels. The default is **CHARSIZE=0** which uses a predefined size. A smaller character size may be obtained with **CHARSIZE=.1**.

DEVICE= Used with the **GRAPHICS** option on some MSDOS versions to specify the type of device for the plot output. A complete list of settings is in the **README** installation instructions file. The use of this option with the **GNU** option is described in the *GNUPLOT* section.

GROUPS= When the **HISTO** option is used SHAZAM normally places data into 6 groups. This option can be used to specify up to 60 groups. The values allowed for **GROUPS=** are 2, 3, 4, 5, 6, 10, 12, 15, 30 or 60.

PORT=   Used with the **GRAPHICS** option on some DOS versions to specify the output destination. If a filename is specified then the output will be saved in the file. A complete list of settings is in the **README** installation instructions file. The use of this option with the **GNU** option is described in the *GNUPLOT* section.

SYMBOL=   Specifies the **SYMBOL**s to be used. The default symbols, in order, are * + 0 % $ # ! @.

XMIN=   Specifies the desired range for either the **X** or **Y** axis. The **NOPRETTY**
XMAX=   option must be used with these options otherwise SHAZAM attempts
YMIN=   to make pretty intervals on the axis by checking the range of the data.
YMAX=   If these are not specified the computed **MIN**imum and **MAX**imum for the variables will be used.

The following is an example of the **PLOT** command using Theil's textile data. Each of the variables *CONSUME, INCOME* and *PRICE* are plotted against time.

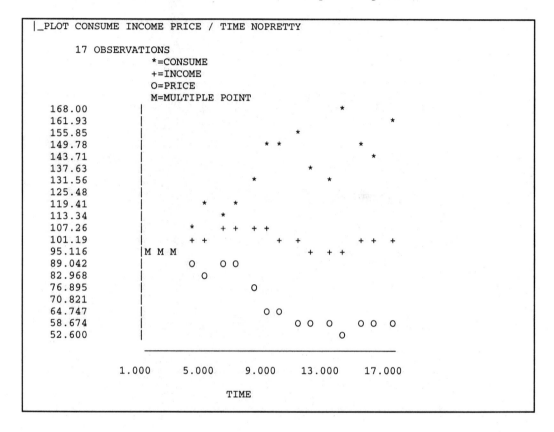

```
|_PLOT CONSUME INCOME PRICE / TIME NOPRETTY

        17 OBSERVATIONS
                        *=CONSUME
                        +=INCOME
                        O=PRICE
                        M=MULTIPLE POINT
     168.00         |                                    *
     161.93         |                                          *
     155.85         |                          *
     149.78         |                    * *             *
     143.71         |                                  *
     137.63         |                        *
     131.56         |                *              *
     125.48         |
     119.41         |        *     *
     113.34         |           *
     107.26         |      *    + +   + +
     101.19         |      + +          +   +       + +   +
     95.116         |M M M              +     + +
     89.042         |      O       O O
     82.968         |        O
     76.895         |             O
     70.821         |
     64.747         |           O O
     58.674         |                  O O   O     O O   O
     52.600         |                           O

                    _____

          1.000      5.000     9.000     13.000    17.000

                             TIME
```

The next example shows the use of the **HOLD** and **NOBLANK** options:

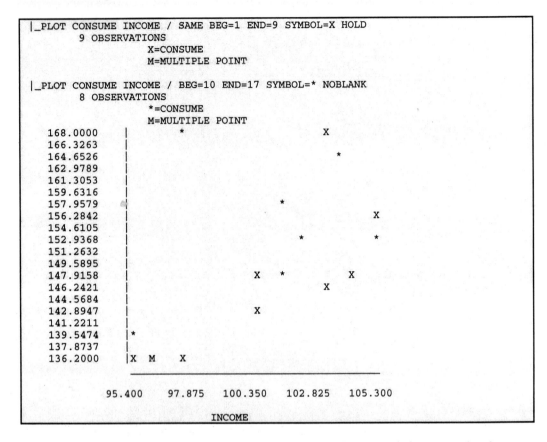

```
|_PLOT CONSUME INCOME / SAME BEG=1 END=9 SYMBOL=X HOLD
         9 OBSERVATIONS
                     X=CONSUME
                     M=MULTIPLE POINT

|_PLOT CONSUME INCOME / BEG=10 END=17 SYMBOL=* NOBLANK
         8 OBSERVATIONS
                     *=CONSUME
                     M=MULTIPLE POINT
      168.0000   |         *                        X
      166.3263   |
      164.6526   |                                      *
      162.9789   |
      161.3053   |
      159.6316   |
      157.9579   |                            *
      156.2842   |                                          X
      154.6105   |
      152.9368   |                        *           *
      151.2632   |
      149.5895   |
      147.9158   |                    X   *       X
      146.2421   |                            X
      144.5684   |
      142.8947   |                    X
      141.2211   |
      139.5474   |*
      137.8737   |
      136.2000   |X   M    X
                  _____
                  95.400     97.875   100.350   102.825   105.300
                                    INCOME
```

The **HOLD** and **NOBLANK** options may be used in this way if, for example, the user wished to see if the relationship between two variables changed during a given sample period. Of course, this would only be a visual test of the hypothesis that the relationship had changed and would in no way be conclusive.

GNUPLOT

GNUPLOT is a freely distributable command-driven plotting program developed by Thomas Williams, Colin Kelley and others. The gnuplot program is distributed with SHAZAM for the PC, VAX, UNIX (including SUN SPARCstations and NeXT) and Macintosh. The **GNU** option on the **PLOT** command can be used to generate gnuplot graphs and histograms. When the **GNU** option is used the following **PLOT** options are also available:

HISTO, LINE, LINEONLY, TIME , BEG=, END= and **GROUPS=**

Additional options are:

APPEND   Specifies that the gnuplot command file is to be appended to a command file that was created with the use of a previous **GNU** option in the SHAZAM program.

AXIS   By default, an x-axis and y-axis is drawn at x=0 and y=0. Use **NOAXIS**
NOAXIS   to omit the axes.

KEY   By default, a key is displayed in the upper right-hand corner. Use
NOKEY   **NOKEY** to suppress the key.

COMMFILE=   Gives the filename for the gnuplot command file (8 characters maximum).

DATAFILE=   Gives the filename for the gnuplot data file (8 characters maximum).

DEVICE=   Specifies the type of device for gnuplot output. The default is the terminal screen. The option **DEVICE=POSTSCRIPT** sends output to a PostScript file. The gnuplot command **set term** gives the complete list of valid options.

OUTPUT=   Gives the filename for the gnuplot output file (8 characters maximum) when the **DEVICE=** option is used. When **DEVICE=POSTSCRIPT** is used the default output filename is **GNU.ps**. On DOS computers use **OUTPUT=PRN** to send the output directly to the printer.

PORT=   Use **PORT=NONE** to obtain gnuplot command and data files but no gnuplot output.

An example of the use of the **GNU** option for plotting the Theil textile data is:

```
PLOT CONSUME INCOME PRICE YEAR / GNU LINEONLY
```

This will initiate the creation of gnuplot command and data files with the extension **.GNU**. The gnuplot command file is **COMM.GNU**. When the SHAZAM run has finished the plot can be displayed. At the system command prompt type:

```
gnuplot   COMM.GNU
```

The plot can be printed on paper. If a PostScript printer is available the plot can be saved to a PostScript file for subsequent printing. For example, the plot can be saved to the PostScript file **MYPLOT.PS** with the SHAZAM command:

```
PLOT CONSUME INCOME PRICE YEAR / GNU LINEONLY DEVICE=POSTSCRIPT OUTPUT=MYPLOT.PS
```

Customizing the Plot

SHAZAM prepares a basic gnuplot command file. This command file is then available for the user to customize with additional labels, arrows, titles, scaling of axes etc. to obtain report quality graphics. The gnuplot command file **COMM.GNU** may look like:

```
load "C000.GNU"
```

The file **C000.GNU** has the gnuplot commands and, for the Theil textile data example, a listing of this file is:

```
set samples            17
set title
set key
set xlabel "YEAR      "
set ylabel
plot   "D000.GNU" using  1: 2   title "CONSUME "  w lines      ,\
       "D000.GNU" using  1: 3   title "INCOME  "  w lines      ,\
       "D000.GNU" using  1: 4   title "PRICE   "  w lines
```

This file gives a simple example of gnuplot commands for plotting time series data. The **plot** command plots the time series from the data file **D000.GNU**. If the gnuplot files are to be saved for future use then the **.GNU** files should be renamed so they will not be overwritten by future SHAZAM runs. If gnuplot files from a SHAZAM run are not needed for future work then the **.GNU** files can be deleted.

GNUPLOT is case sensitive and commands are typically lower case only. To obtain on-line documentation about gnuplot features at the system command prompt type: **gnuplot**. Then at the gnuplot command prompt type: **help**. To exit the gnuplot program type: **exit**.

The gnuplot command file can be customized by using the various options available with the **set** command. This is illustrated below. The **C000.GNU** file is modified to include titles and labelling of the time series. Note that the # symbol is used for a gnuplot comment. The first two commands are required to send the output to the PostScript file **MYPLOT.PS**. The **set nokey** command is used to omit the key that gives the data description. Then, as a replacement to the key, the **set label** commands are used to place identifiers on the time series.

```
set term postscript
set output "MYPLOT.PS"
set samples         17
set title "Textile Demand in the Netherlands (Source: Theil [1971])"
set nokey
set xlabel "YEAR"
set ylabel "Index  (1925=100)"
# Put in labels for the time series
set arrow 1 from 1930.5,130 to 1930,136
set label "Textile consumption per capita" at 1930.7,130
set arrow 2 from 1932.5,107 to 1932,105.3
set label "Income per capita" at 1932.7,107
set arrow 3 from 1930.5,84 to 1930,82.8
set label "Relative price of textiles" at 1930.7,84
#
plot   "D000.GNU" using  1: 2     w lines     ,\
       "D000.GNU" using  1: 3     w lines     ,\
       "D000.GNU" using  1: 4     w lines
```

The gnuplot graph follows on the next page.

Creating Images for Publishing on the World Wide Web

The PBMPLUS program (developed by Jef Poskanzer and modified by others) can be used for converting gnuplot graphs to **.GIF** files. Instructions are available at the SHAZAM Web site. The URL is: http://shazam.econ.ubc.ca/

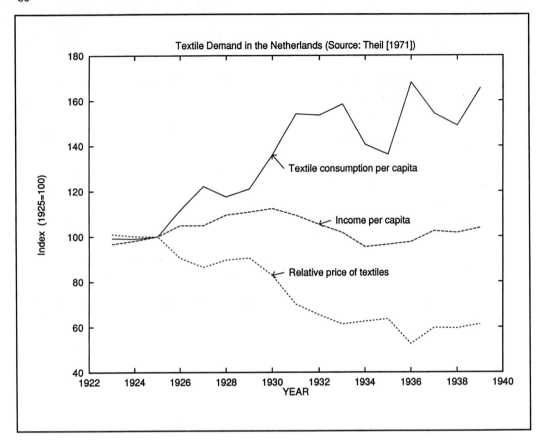

6. GENERATING VARIABLES

"The government are very keen on amassing statistics. They collect them, add them, raise them to the nth power, take the cube root and prepare wonderful diagrams. But you must never forget that everyone of these figures comes in the first instance from the village watchman, who just puts down what he damn well pleases."

Anonymous, Quoted in Sir Josiah Stamp,
Some Economic Factors in Modern Life

This chapter describes commands for generating variables, selecting sub-sets of observations and performing numeric differentiation and integration.

THE GENR COMMAND

The **GENR** command will create new variables from old ones and do a variety of data transformations. The **SAMPLE** command defines the observation range used in **GENR** commands.

In general, the format of the **GENR** command is:

GENR *var = equation*

where *var* is the name of the variable to be generated and *equation* is any arithmetic equation which involves variables, constants and mathematical functions.

The following mathematical operators may be used:

Priority-level	*Operator*
1	unary $-$ (for example, $X^{**}-A$ is treated as $X^{**}(-A)$)
1	unary functions (see list below)
2	$**$ (exponentiation)
3	$*$, $/$ (multiplication, division)
4	$+$, $-$ (addition, subtraction)
5	.EQ., .NE. , .GE. , .GT. , .LE. , .LT. (relational operators)
6	.NOT. (logical operator)
7	.AND. (logical operator)
8	.OR. (logical operator)

The available unary functions are:

ABS(x)	absolute value
DUM(x)	dummy variable generator
EXP(x)	e^x
INT(x)	integer truncation
LAG(x)	lag a variable one time period
LAG(x,n)	lag a variable n time periods
LGAM(x)	log gamma function, $\log(\Gamma(x))$
LOG(x)	natural logs
MAX(x,y)	maximum of two variables
MIN(x,y)	minimum of two variables
MOD(x,y)	modulo arithmetic, remainder of x/y
NCDF(x)	standard normal cumulative distribution function
NOR(x)	normal random number with standard deviation x
SAMP(x)	draw a sample with replacement from the variable x
SEAS(x)	seasonal dummy variable with periodicity x
SIN(x)	sine (x measured in radians)
SQRT(x)	square roots
SUM(x)	cumulative sum of variable x
SUM(x,n)	sum of n observations on variable x starting at observation 1
TIME(x)	time index plus x
UNI(x)	uniform random number with range (0,x)

The order of operations of mathematical expressions in SHAZAM conforms to the priority levels given above. Among operations of the same priority, expressions are executed from left to right. To avoid confusion use as many levels of parentheses as desired. Multiplication is assumed with ") (" and is treated as ") * (".

A variable with a common scalar element everywhere can be created by using the command format:

GENR *newvar=var(element)*

where *element* is a number or the name of a scalar variable. For example, to generate a variable that takes on the value of the third observation of the variable *A*, the following command is appropriate:

```
GENR ATHREE=A(3)
```

The following example illustrates the use of **GENR** commands for a case where Theil's [1971, p. 102] textile data has been read in and a series of new variables needs to be created.

```
SAMPLE 1 17
READ(11) YEAR CONSUME INCOME PRICE
GENR PRICE=PRICE/100
GENR PCCONS=(CONSUME-LAG(CONSUME))/LAG(CONSUME)
GENR T=TIME(0)
```

The first **GENR** command is used to change the units of the variable *PRICE*. The second **GENR** command is used to generate a variable for the percentage change of consumption from the preceding year. Note that observation 1 of *PCCONS* will not be defined properly since *LAG(CONSUME)* does not exist for the first observation. A warning message will be printed. The third **GENR** command is used to generate a variable *T* with observation values 1, 2, 3, . . . , 17.

DUM *function*

The DUM(x) function will create a dummy variable equal to one when x is positive and equal to zero for observations when x is not positive. For example:

```
GENR D1=DUM(3)
GENR D2=DUM(TIME(0)-6)
GENR D3=DUM(CONSUME-INCOME-1)
```

The first example of the DUM(x) function creates a dummy variable that is always equal to one. The second creates a dummy variable that is equal to zero for the first 6 observations and equal to one otherwise. The last example uses the variables *CONSUME* and *INCOME* from Theil's textile data and creates a dummy variable equal to one when the relation inside parentheses is positive or zero and equal to zero otherwise. It is also possible to create a matrix of seasonal dummy variables. For information on this procedure, see the chapter *MATRIX MANIPULATION*.

LAG *function*

The LAG(x,n) function will lag the variable x, n times. When only one lag is desired the n can be left off the function (i.e. LAG(x)). The first n observations are undefined when the LAG(x,n) function is used. SHAZAM replaces these observations with zeros. It is not necessary to change the sample size to use the LAG(x,n) function, but warning messages will appear whenever this function is used without proper sample commands. In fact, changing the sample size before generating new variables can cause further sample size problems. However, the sample size should be changed to start at n+1 before estimation. The LAG(x,n) function must be used only on predefined variables and not on functions of variables. So, for example:

```
GENR X=LAG(SQRT(Y),3)
```

will result in an error message. To avoid this error two **GENR** commands can be used:

```
GENR Z=LAG(Y,3)
GENR X=SQRT(Z)
```

or one:

```
GENR X=SQRT(LAG(Y,3))
```

It is possible to lead future variables by using a negative value for n on the LAG(x,n) function. For example:

```
GENR XT=LAG(X,-1)
```

Note that in this case the final observation of *XT* may not be defined.

The next example shows the computation of a 3-period centered moving average for the variable *P*. The result is stored in the variable *SMA3*.

```
GENR SMA3=(LAG(P)+P+LAG(P,-1))/3
```

The **GENR** command implements recursive calculations when the right hand side variables are LAG functions of the left hand side variable. For example, the series:

$$X_t = .8X_{t-1} + Z_{t-1}$$

can be generated with the command:

```
GENR X=.8*LAG(X)+LAG(Z)
```

Note that the command:

```
GENR X=LAG(X)
```

does not give the same result as the command:

```
GENR Y=LAG(X)
```

That is, when using the LAG function, if a recursive calculation is not required then the left side variable must not be one of the variables in the LAG function.

LGAM *function*

The LGAM(x) function is used to compute the log of the mathematical gamma function $\Gamma(x)$ which is used in a number of probability distributions, including the gamma, beta, chi-square and F distributions.

LOG *function*

The LOG(x) function is used to take natural logarithms. The relationship between natural log and logarithm to the base 10 is:

$$\ln_e(x) = 2.3026 \cdot \log_{10}(x)$$

Therefore, a command that will obtain the logarithm to the base 10 of each element in the variable A is:

```
GENR L10A=LOG(A)/2.3026
```

MOD *function*

The MOD(x,y) function is used to compute the remainder of a division. For example: MOD(15,4)=3.

NCDF *function*

The NCDF(x) function returns the probability associated with the standard normal cumulative distribution function at the value x. The probability will be in the [0,1] range. The use of the NCDF(x) function is illustrated below. In the example Z is generated to take on the values 0 to 2.0.

```
|_SAMPLE 1 21
|_GENR Z=(TIME(0)-1)/10
|_GENR P=NCDF(Z)
|_PRINT Z P
          Z                    P
    0.0                  0.5000000
    0.1000000            0.5398278
    0.2000000            0.5792597
    0.3000000            0.6179114
    0.4000000            0.6554217
    0.5000000            0.6914625
    0.6000000            0.7257469
    0.7000000            0.7580363
```

0.8000000	0.7881446
0.9000000	0.8159399
1.000000	0.8413447
1.100000	0.8643339
1.200000	0.8849303
1.300000	0.9031995
1.400000	0.9192433
1.500000	0.9331928
1.600000	0.9452007
1.700000	0.9554345
1.800000	0.9640697
1.900000	0.9712834
2.000000	0.9772499

To obtain the inverse NCDF and save the result in the variable Z use the commands:

```
GENR PA=1-P
DISTRIB PA / INVERSE TYPE=NORMAL CRIT=Z
```

Further information on the **DISTRIB** command is in the chapter *PROBABILITY DISTRIBUTIONS*.

NOR *function and* **UNI** *function*

If **GENR** commands are used to generate random variables, the random number generators are usually initialized by the system clock. Users can generate all their data if they have none to be read in. In this case, the user specifies the number of observations to be generated on the **SAMPLE** command. For example, the **GENR** command can be used to calculate probability distributions:

```
SAMPLE 1 30
GENR X1=UNI(2)
GENR X2=5+NOR(1)
GENR CHI3=NOR(1)**2+NOR(1)**2+NOR(1)**2
GENR CHI5=NOR(1)**2+NOR(1)**2+NOR(1)**2+NOR(1)**2+NOR(1)**2
GENR F35=(CHI3/3)/(CHI5/5)
```

The first **GENR** command generates a new variable called *X1* from a uniform distribution with a range of 0 to 2. The second **GENR** command generates a new variable called *X2* from a normal distribution with a mean equal to 5 and a standard deviation equal to 1.

The final three **GENR** commands show how to generate a variable from a F distribution. Consider $Z_1, Z_2,...$ as independent standard normal random variables then

$$Z_1^2 + Z_2^2 + ... + Z_{n_1}^2 \sim \chi_{n_1}^2$$

is a chi-square random variable with n_1 degrees of freedom. With $\chi^2_{n_1}$ and $\chi^2_{n_2}$ as independent chi-square random variables then a variable with the F-distribution with n_1 and n_2 degrees of freedom is constructed as:

$$F_{n_1,n_2} = \frac{n_2}{n_1}\chi^2_{n_1} \Big/ \chi^2_{n_2}$$

The **GENR** commands generate the variables *CHI3* and *CHI5* as chi-square variables with 3 and 5 degrees of freedom respectively. The variable *F35* is then from an F distribution with 3 and 5 degrees of freedom.

The command **SET RANFIX** (described in the chapter *SET AND DISPLAY*) typed before the **GENR** statement will prevent the random number generator from being set by the system clock. Therefore, the same set of random numbers will be generated when specified. Otherwise, the random number generator will generate a different set of random numbers when requested. The normal random number algorithm is described in Brent [1974]. In this example all of the data is generated internally. Note also that when the data is generated internally a sample size must be specified with the **SAMPLE** command, otherwise SHAZAM will not know how many observations to generate.

SAMP *function*

The SAMP(x) function can be used to draw a sample (with replacement) from another variable. In the example below the variable *BIGX* has 100 observations. A new variable with 20 observations is generated by sampling with replacement.

```
SAMPLE 1 100
READ(X.DAT) BIGX
SAMPLE 1 20
GENR NEWX=SAMP(BIGX)
```

The SAMP function is useful for bootstrapping experiments (see the example in the chapter *PROGRAMMING IN SHAZAM*).

SIN *function*

For any number x sine and cosine are related by the rule $\cos(x)=\sin(x+\pi/2)$. Therefore the cosine function for a variable X can be generated with the command:

```
GENR COSX=SIN(X+$PI/2)
```

Note that *$PI* is a SHAZAM temporary variable that contains the value of π.

The tangent function is defined as $\tan(x)=\sin(x)/\cos(x)$. Therefore the tangent function for a variable X can be generated with the command:

```
GENR TANX=SIN(X)/SIN(X+$PI/2)
```

SUM *function*

The SUM(x) function creates a cumulative sum of the variable x. For example,

```
GENR X=SUM(2)
```

creates a variable that takes on the values 2,4,6, . . . The SUM function can be used to create a capital stock series from a net investment series. For example, if the initial capital stock is 25.3 then the **GENR** command is:

```
GENR KAPITAL=25.3+SUM(INVEST)
```

The SUM(x,n) function will sum up n successive observations on the variable x starting at observation 1. This can be used to convert monthly data to quarterly or yearly data, as in the following example:

```
SAMPLE 1 120
READ(CPI.DAT) MCPI
* Convert to annual data using 12-month averages
SAMPLE 1 10
GENR YCPI=(SUM(MCPI,12))/12
```

SHAZAM calculates the sum of the first 12 observations of the variable *MCPI* and then divides the sum of *MCPI* by 12 and makes this number the first observation in the new variable *YCPI*. It continues this for subsequent observations in *MCPI*, until it has created 10 observations for *YCPI*. The **SAMPLE** command which precedes the **GENR** statement tells SHAZAM the size of the new variable. This is only necessary if the new variable is to have a different length than that specified by the current **SAMPLE** command.

It is often useful to compute a variable total. The recommended way of doing this is with the **SUMS=** option on the **STAT** command (see the chapter *DESCRIPTIVE STATISTICS*). For example, to compute the sum of all elements of *X* and save the result in *TOTX* the following command can be used:

```
STAT X / SUMS=TOTX
```

TIME *function*

The TIME(x) function creates a time index. For example, the command:

```
GENR T=TIME(0)
```

creates a time index so that the first observation is equal to 1 and the rest are consecutively numbered. The command:

```
GENR T=TIME(1929)
```

will create a time index so that the first observation is equal to 1930. See the **TIME** command in the chapter *MISCELLANEOUS COMMANDS AND INFORMATION* for an alternate way to create a time index.

Relational and logical operators

The operators that are available for use in **GENR** commands are as follows.

Operator	Meaning
.EQ.	Equal (=)
.NE.	Not equal ($\neq$)
.GE.	Greater than or equal ($\geq$)
.GT.	Greater than (>)
.LE.	Less than or equal ($\leq$)
.LT.	Less than (<)
.AND.	Logical conjunction
.OR.	Logical disjunction
.NOT.	Logical negation

A value of 1 is generated if an expression is true, and a value of 0 if it is false. Parentheses should be used to ensure the correct order of processing. For example:

```
GENR X5=(X1.EQ.X2)
GENR X6=(X1.LE.X2).OR.(X3.GT.0.5)
GENR X7=(TIME(0).EQ.18)
GENR X8=(UNI(1).LE.0.6)
GENR X1=(X1.GE.0)*X1
```

The first two examples create dummy variables equal to 1 if the condition is met, and 0 otherwise. The third example creates a dummy variable equal to 1 for observation 18 only. The fourth example creates a binomial random variable from the uniform random number generator. The variable will take on a value of 1 for approximately 60% of the observations and a value of 0 for the rest. Of course, the probabilities are true only for the population and may differ for any sample. The last example will set all negative values of *X1* to 0. Note that the old *X1* is replaced by the new *X1*.

THE GEN1 COMMAND

The **GEN1** command is used to generate a scalar variable or constant. The **GEN1** command is equivalent to using both a **SAMPLE 1 1** command and a **GENR** command to generate a variable with only one observation. It is faster because it removes the need for the **SAMPLE 1 1** command. **SKIPIF** commands do not affect the **GEN1** command.

The format of the **GEN1** command is:

GEN1 *constant = equation*

For example:

```
GEN1 NOB=$N
```

saves the value of the number of observations in the variable *NOB*. See the chapter *ORDINARY LEAST SQUARES* for a description of the temporary variable *$N*.

An element of a vector can be saved as a scalar with the following command format:

GEN1 *constant=var(element)*

The next example saves the coefficient estimates from OLS estimation in the variable *BETA*. Then element *K* of the variable *BETA* is saved in the scalar *B0*.

```
OLS CONSUME INCOME PRICE / COEF=BETA
GEN1 K=$K
GEN1 B0=BETA(K)
```

A useful feature of the **GEN1** and **GENR** commands is to use it as a desk calculator. If the = sign is left out of the equation, SHAZAM will simply print the result. For example, the command:

```
GEN1 LOG(2*3.14159)
```

will give the output:

```
|_GEN1 LOG(2*3.14159)
    1.8378762
```

THE IF COMMAND

The **IF** command is a conditional **GENR** command. The format of the **IF** command is:

IF(*expression*)

where *expression* is an expression in parentheses to be evaluated. If the expression is true or positive, the remainder of the **IF** command is executed. For example:

```
IF (X1.GE.0)X4=SQRT(X1)
IF(2+X2/6)X2=X2+12
IF (X2)X3=X2
```

The first **IF** condition states that if *X1* is greater than or equal to zero then *X4* is equal to the square root of *X1*. The second **IF** condition states that if *X2* divided by 6 plus 2 is positive then *X2* is equal to *X2* plus 12. The third **IF** condition states that if *X2* is positive then *X3* is equal to *X2*.

Note that some observations for a variable may not be defined if the **IF** condition is not true. In this case, the variable will be set to zero when the variable is initially created. For example, for the first **IF** command shown above, the variable *X4* is undefined when *X1* is less than zero and is thus equal to zero for these observations.

The **IF** command can also be used to conditionally execute any SHAZAM command on the line following the **IF** command. For example, if you only wanted to run an **AUTO** command when the Durbin-Watson statistic for the **OLS** regression is less than 1.0, you would use:

```
OLS Y X / RSTAT
IF($DW .LT. 1.0)
AUTO Y X
```

If the **IF** command is used on a vector of observations (rather than a scalar as in the example above) the command following the **IF** command will be executed if the **IF** condition is true for any observation in the sample.

A set of SHAZAM commands can be placed in a SHAZAM procedure as described in the chapter *SHAZAM PROCEDURES*. The **IF** command can then be used to conditionally execute the set of commands in the procedure. The format is:

IF(*expression*)
EXEC *proc_name*

THE IF1 COMMAND

The **IF1** command is equivalent to using both a **SAMPLE 1 1** command and a **IF** command to perform an operation only on the first observation. It is faster because it removes the need for the **SAMPLE 1 1** command. It is used primarily when checking either temporary variables or variables that have been generated with the **GEN1** command.

The format of the **IF1** command is:

IF1(*expression*)

For example:

```
GEN1 SIGG=$SIG2
IF1(SIGG.GT.0) SIG=SQRT(SIGG)
```

THE SKIPIF COMMAND

The **SKIPIF** command is used to specify conditions under which observations are to be skipped for most commands. (The observations will still be held in memory and in data files.) The format of the **SKIPIF** command is:

SKIPIF (*expression*)

where the *expression* may use arithmetic or logical operators such as those described for **GENR** and **IF** commands. The observation will be skipped if the value of the expression is positive; otherwise, the observation is retained.

Some examples of **SKIPIF** commands are:

```
SKIPIF (X3+X4.EQ.X5)
SKIPIF (X3.GT.X12)
SKIPIF ((X4.EQ.0).OR.(X5.EQ.0))
SKIPIF (TIME(0).EQ.6)
SKIPIF (X1)
SKIPIF (LAG(X2+3)/12-X4)
SKIPIF (PROVINCE.EQ."MANITOBA")
SKIPIF (ABS(X3+X4-X5).LE.0.0001)
```

The first **SKIPIF** example skips the observations when the sum of *X3* and *X4* is equal to *X5*. The second **SKIPIF** example skips the observations when *X3* is greater than *X12*. The third **SKIPIF** example skips the observations where *X4* is equal to zero or *X5* is equal to zero. The fourth **SKIPIF** example skips the observations where the *TIME* variable is equal to 6. The fifth **SKIPIF** example will skip the observations where *X1* is positive. The sixth **SKIPIF** example will skip the observations where the result of the lagged value of *X2* plus 3 divided by 12 minus *X4* is positive. The seventh **SKIPIF** example skips the observations where the variable *PROVINCE* is equal to MANITOBA. Note that if characters are used in the command they must be enclosed in double quotes (") and only upper case comparisons are valid. The final **SKIPIF** example skips the observations where the absolute value of *X3* plus *X4* minus *X5* is less than or equal to 0.0001.

Users should be aware that the test for equality between two numbers may sometimes fail due to rounding error in the computer. The first example above is a typical case where the problem might occur. The last example gives a possible remedy.

Users should take care to express **SKIPIF** commands accurately. A common error is to skip all the observations so that no data is left, for example:

```
SKIPIF (A.GE.0)
SKIPIF (A.LT.0)
```

If a large number of consecutive observations are to be skipped at the beginning or end of the data, it is more efficient to omit them with the **SAMPLE** command than with **SKIPIF** commands.

The **SKIPIF** command automatically creates a special variable called *SKIP$* and initializes it to be zero for each observation. Then, for any observation to be skipped, *SKIP$* is set equal to one.

Note that the *SKIP$* variable is set at the time the **SKIPIF** command is executed. For example:

```
GENR A=0
SKIPIF(A.EQ.1)
GENR A=1
PRINT A
```

would not skip any observations since all observations in *A* were zero at the time the **SKIPIF** condition was evaluated.

Sometimes the entire data set is required including those observations skipped on **SKIPIF** commands. It is possible to temporarily turn off the **SKIPIF** commands that are in effect. This requires the **SET** command:

```
SET NOSKIP
```

To put the **SKIPIF**'s back in effect the **SET** command is again used:

```
SET SKIP
```

To permanently eliminate all **SKIPIF** commands in effect, the **DELETE** command is used:

```
DELETE SKIP$
```

If the **DELETE** command has been used to eliminate all **SKIPIF** commands it is not necessary to use the **SET SKIP** command to use the **SKIPIF** command again.

SKIPIF commands are in effect for **READ, WRITE** and **PRINT** commands except when a matrix is used or the **BYVAR** option is used. The **BYVAR** option is the default for **WRITE** and **PRINT** commands when only one variable is specified.

The **SKIPIF** command will print out messages that tell you which observations have been skipped. If you have many skipped observations you could get many lines of messages. These warnings can be suppressed if you use the **SET   NOWARNSKIP** command.

For the automatic skipping of missing observations the **SET SKIPMISS** command can be used as described in the chapter *SET AND DISPLAY*. Then, if no longer required, a **SET NOSKIPMISS** command must be used.

THE ENDIF COMMAND

The **ENDIF** command works like the **IF** command except that when the condition is true for any observation, execution is stopped. If the **ENDIF** command is used inside a **DO**-loop, the **DO**-loop is terminated and execution will continue at the statement after **ENDO**. See the chapter *PROGRAMMING IN SHAZAM* for information on **DO**-loops.

The format of the **ENDIF** command is:

ENDIF(*expression***)**

For example:

```
ENDIF(A.LT.0)
```

The above execution will terminate when the variable *A* is less than zero.

THE DERIV COMMAND

The **DERIV** command can differentiate an equation with respect to any variable and return the derivatives as another variable. The format of the **DERIV** command is:

DERIV *variable resultvar=equation*

where *variable* is the variable in the *equation* for which the derivative should be taken with respect to and the result of the derivation will be placed in the variable *resultvar*. The current **SAMPLE** command will control the observations to be used. The method used is numeric differentiation. For example, if you wish to find the derivative of the equation:

```
2*(CONSUME/INCOME) + 3*PRICE
```

with respect to *INCOME*, use:

```
DERIV INCOME RESULT=2*(CONSUME/INCOME) + 3 * PRICE
```

Then, the variable *RESULT* will contain all the derivatives as in the following output:

```
|_DERIV INCOME RESULT=2*(CONSUME/INCOME) + 3*PRICE
|_PRINT RESULT
    RESULT
 -0.02121723 -0.02057439 -0.02000002 -0.02028352 -0.02221009
 -0.01961595 -0.01972853 -0.02156798 -0.02581511 -0.02770540
 -0.03064908 -0.03089716 -0.02931251 -0.03527277 -0.02943039
 -0.02886880 -0.03072085
```

THE INTEG COMMAND

The **INTEG** command can perform numeric univariate integration on any equation. The format of the **INTEG** command is:

INTEG *variable lower upper resultvar=equation*

where the integral of *equation* with respect to *variable* will be taken using the range specifed in *lower* and *upper*. The result of the integration will be placed in the variable *resultvar*. The current **SAMPLE** command will control the range of observations to be used in the integration. The variables *lower* and *upper* can either be existing variables or simple number values can be supplied.

For example, if you wish to find the cumulative probability for the standard normal distribution which has a density function of:

$$f(x) = \frac{1}{\sqrt{2\pi}} \exp(-\frac{x^2}{2})$$

you would use:

```
SAMPLE 1 1
GEN1 LOWER=0
GEN1 UPPER=1
INTEG X LOWER UPPER ANSWER=EXP(-.5*X**2)/SQRT(2*$PI)
PRINT ANSWER
```

The following output would be obtained:

```
|_SAMPLE 1 1
|_GEN1 LOWER=0
|_GEN1 UPPER=1
|_INTEG X LOWER UPPER ANSWER=EXP(-.5*X**2)/SQRT(2*$PI)
..NOTE..CURRENT VALUE OF $PI  =    3.1416
OBSERVATION  LOWERBOUND     UPPERBOUND       INTEGRAL
         1   .00000000      1.0000000        .34134475
|_PRINT ANSWER
    ANSWER
   .3413447
```

If the usual output from the **INTEG** command is not required, it can be suppressed with a "?" prefix, for example:

```
?INTEG X LOWER UPPER ANSWER=EXP(-.5*X**2)/SQRT(2*$PI)
```

EXAMPLES

Sampling Without Replacement

The SAMP function can be used for sampling with replacement. The SHAZAM commands in this example illustrate sampling without replacement. A variable called X is generated that has 300 observations of random integers between 1 and 2000 with no duplicate numbers in the data set.

```
SET RANFIX
SAMPLE 1 2000
GENR X=TIME(0)
GENR RAN=UNI(1)
SORT RAN X
SAMPLE 1 300
PRINT X / NOBYVAR
STAT X
STOP
```

The **SET RANFIX** command will prevent the random number generator from being set by the system clock so that the same set of random numbers will be generated each time this same command file is executed. The **SAMPLE** command sets the sample size. The **TIME(0)** function on the **GENR** command first generates a set of integers with a range of 1 to 2000. The next **GENR** command generates a uniform random number. The **SORT** command then sorts the variables *RAN* and *X* in ascending order according to *RAN*. The second **SAMPLE** command then selects 300 observations of the original 2000 observations. The **PRINT** command prints the variable *X* in vector format rather than **BYVAR**iable format.

Systematic Sampling

Suppose you wanted to take a sub-set of data from a larger data set that consisted of 100 observations. In this example, you want every 5th observation of variables *X* and *Y* to be in the new sub-set of data. The SHAZAM commands to achieve this result are:

```
SAMPLE 1 100
READ(DATA) X Y
SKIPIF(MOD((TIME(0),5)).NE.0)
STAT X Y
```

The **SAMPLE** command first sets the sample size to 100 observations. The **READ** command locates the data file called **DATA** and reads in the observations for variables *X* and *Y*. The **SKIPIF** command first evaluates the expression **TIME(0)** and generates a time index that begins at 1. Then the expression **MOD((TIME(0),5)** divides the time index by 5 and remainder is determined. If the remainder from the **MOD** function is not equal to 0 then the observation is skipped. If the **MOD** function is true then the observation is retained for the sub-set of data. The **STAT** command on *X* and *Y* will then print out the descriptive statistics on these two variables. The descriptive statistics should confirm that there are exactly 20 observations for each variable.

Replacing of Missing Values with the Mean

Suppose your data set has a missing observation in row 3 column 1 for the dependent variable, *Y*. There are two possible ways to deal with the missing data issue. The first method would be to omit the missing observation in the regression. For example, if your regression model is $Y = \beta_1 + \beta_2 X + \varepsilon$ and the dependent variable, *Y*, had a missing observation in row 3 then to estimate the model you would omit observation 3 for the dependent variable, *Y*, and the independent variable *X*. The number of observations in the regression must be the same for all variables. An example of the SHAZAM commands illustrating how to omit observation 3 assuming there are 7 observations in total is:

```
SAMPLE 1 7
READ(DATA.DAT) X Y
SAMPLE 1 2   4 7
OLS Y X
STOP
```

The second **SAMPLE** command tells SHAZAM to use observations 1 to 2 omit observation 3 and use observations 4 to 7 for the OLS regression.

The second method would be to take the average and use it for the missing observation. For example, the data set consists of variables X and Y and the following data:

```
X     Y
1     100
2     200
      300
4     400
5     500
6     600
7     700
```

As you will notice observation 3 is missing for variable X. To properly read these variables into SHAZAM you will be required to place a number such as the SHAZAM default missing data code of −99999 in row 3 column 1. SHAZAM will get confused reading in the data file if the number is not in the place of the missing value. For example, if the missing value in row 3 column 1 is left as a blank then the data would be read by SHAZAM as:

```
1          100
2          200
300        4
400        5
500        6
600        7
```

As you can see this is definitely not correct. The correct data file should look like:

```
1          100
2          200
-99999     300
4          400
5          500
6          600
7          700
```

To calculate the average for the missing observation in row 3 column 1 the SHAZAM commands would be:

```
 SAMPLE 1 7
 READ(DATA.DAT) X Y
 * SKIP OBSERVATION 3 USING THE SAMPLE COMMAND
 SAMPLE 1 2 4 7
 * CALCULATE THE MEAN OF X
 STAT X  / MEAN=XBAR
 * PLACE THE MEAN OF X IN ROW 3 COLUMN 1
 SAMPLE 3 3
 GENR X=XBAR
 SAMPLE 1 7
 PRINT X Y
```

The first **SAMPLE** command tells SHAZAM that there are 7 observations for variables X and Y. The **READ** command reads in the data for the variables. This includes the −99999 that is placed for the missing value. The second **SAMPLE** command tells SHAZAM to use observations 1 to 2 and 4 to 7 for the next command. The **STAT** command calculates the mean value of X and places it into the vector called *XBAR*. The third **SAMPLE** command then sets the sample range to observation 3. The following **GENR** command places the previous stored vector value of *XBAR* into the variable X at observation 3. Then the fourth **SAMPLE** command changes the sample range to the complete 7 observations and the **PRINT** command prints the results for X and Y. The SHAZAM output is:

```
|_SAMPLE 1 7
|_READ(DATA.DAT) X Y
    2 VARIABLES AND       7 OBSERVATIONS STARTING AT OBS       1
|_* SKIP OBSERVATION 3 USING THE SAMPLE COMMAND
|_SAMPLE 1 2 4 7
|_* CALCULATE THE MEAN OF X
|_STAT X / MEAN=XBAR
NAME         N    MEAN        ST. DEV      VARIANCE     MINIMUM      MAXIMUM
X            6   4.1667        2.3166        5.3667       1.0000       7.0000
|_* PLACE THE MEAN OF X IN ROW 3 COLUMN 1
|_SAMPLE 3 3
|_GENR X=XBAR
|_SAMPLE 1 7
|_PRINT X Y
   1.000000         100.0000
   2.000000         200.0000
   4.166667         300.0000
   4.000000         400.0000
   5.000000         500.0000
   6.000000         600.0000
   7.000000         700.0000
```

Also see the **MISSVALU=** and **SKIPMISS** options available on the **SET** command.

7. ORDINARY LEAST SQUARES

"Less is More."
Miës van der Rohe
Architect

The **OLS** command will perform **O**rdinary **L**east **S**quares regressions and produce standard regression diagnostics. This was introduced in the chapter *A CHILD'S GUIDE TO RUNNING REGRESSIONS*. In addition, the **OLS** command has an extensive list of options that provides many features for estimation and testing of the linear regression model. For example, tests on the residuals are available with the **DLAG**, **DWPVALUE**, **GF**, **LM**, and **RSTAT** options. Model selection tests (including the Akaike information criterion and the Schwarz criterion) are available with the **ANOVA** option. Standard errors adjusted for heteroskedasticity or autocorrelation are computed with the **HETCOV** or **AUTCOV=** options. Linear restrictions on the coefficients can be incorporated with the **RESTRICT** option. Ridge regression is available with the **RIDGE=** option and weighted least squares can be implemented with the **WEIGHT=** option.

The SHAZAM output from the **OLS** command includes elasticities evaluated at the sample means. However, the printed elasticities may not be correct if data has been transformed, for example the data is in logarithms. In this case, the **LINLOG**, **LOGLIN** or **LOGLOG** options can be specified to obtain meaningful elasticities.

The results from the **OLS** command can be accepted as input by other SHAZAM commands to obtain further analysis of the results. For example, the **DIAGNOS** command is described in the chapter *DIAGNOSTIC TESTS*, the **TEST** and **CONFID** commands are described in the chapter *HYPOTHESIS TESTING AND CONFIDENCE INTERVALS* and the **FC** command is described in the chapter *FORECASTING*.

OLS COMMAND OPTIONS

In general, the format of the **OLS** command is:

OLS *depvar indeps / options*

where *depvar* is the dependent variable, *indeps* is a list of independent variables and *options* is a list of desired options. If any variable in the list of independent variables is a matrix, SHAZAM will treat each column as a separate explanatory variable. To impose a lag structure on the independent variables see the chapter *DISTRIBUTED-LAG MODELS*. The available options on the **OLS** command are:

ANOVA

Prints the **AN**alysis **O**f **VA**riance tables and the F-statistic for the test that all coefficients are zero. In some restricted models, the F-test from an **ANOVA** table is invalid. In these cases the F-statistic will not be printed, but may be obtained with the **TEST** command. Model Selection Tests are also printed. This option is in effect automatically when running in BATCH mode. In TALK mode, the **ANOVA** option must be specified if the table is desired. In BATCH mode these statistics can be suppressed with the **NOANOVA** option.

AUXRSQR

Prints the R^2 statistics for the auxiliary regressions of each independent variable on all other independent variables. These R^2 statistics are useful in determining multicollinearity (see, for example, the discussion in Griffiths, Hill and Judge [1993, Chapter 13.5]).

DFBETAS

Computes the **DFBETAS** statistic. Also see the **INFLUENCE** option. Further details and an example are given later in this chapter.

DLAG

Computes Durbin's [1970] h statistic as a test for autocorrelation when there is a **LAG**ged **D**ependent variable in the regression. The lagged dependent variable *must* be the first listed independent variable when this option is used. The h statistic is useful since the Durbin-Watson statistic may not be valid in such situations. Durbin's h statistic cannot always be computed since the square root of a negative number may be required. In such cases, the h statistic will neither be computed nor printed. It is essential to remember that when lagged variables have been generated a **SAMPLE** command must be included to delete the beginning observations. The statistic is calculated as:

$$h = \hat{\rho}\sqrt{\frac{N}{1 - N\hat{\sigma}_\alpha^2}} \quad \text{where} \quad \hat{\rho} = \sum_{t=2}^{N} e_t e_{t-1} \bigg/ \sum_{t=2}^{N} e_{t-1}^2$$

and e_t are the estimated residuals and $\hat{\sigma}_\alpha^2$ is the estimated variance of the coefficient on the lagged-dependent variable. The Durbin h statistic is asymptotically normally distributed under the null hypothesis of no autocorrelation.

DN

Estimates the error variance $\hat{\sigma}^2$ by **D**ividing the residual sum of squares by **N** instead of N–K.

DUMP

DUMPs large amounts of output mainly useful to SHAZAM consultants.

DWPVALUE   Computes the Durbin Watson Probability-**VALUE**. The p-value is for a test of the null hypothesis of no autocorrelation in the residuals against positive autocorrelation. For example, if the Durbin Watson probability is .0437, the null hypothesis is rejected at less than the 5% significance level. This option automatically uses **METHOD=HH**. Also see the **ORDER=** option. The probability is saved in the temporary variable *$CDF*. Details on the computational method are given in the section *An Exact p-value for the Durbin-Watson Test* in the chapter *PROGRAMMING IN SHAZAM*.

GF   Prints **G**oodness of **F**it tests for normality of residuals. Coefficients of skewness and excess kurtosis are also computed as described in the chapter *A CHILD'S GUIDE TO RUNNING REGRESSIONS*. This option is automatically in effect when running in BATCH mode. In TALK mode, the **GF** option must be specified if this output is desired. In BATCH mode, this output can be eliminated by specifying **NOGF**.

GNU   Prepares **GNUPLOT** plots of the residuals and the fitted values. For more information on this option see the *GNUPLOT* section in the *PLOTS* chapter. With the **GNU** option the **APPEND, OUTPUT=, DEVICE=, PORT=** and **COMMFILE=** options are also available as described for the **PLOT** command.

HETCOV   Uses White's [1980] **HET**eroskedastic-Consistent **COV**ariance matrix estimation to correct the estimates for an unknown form of heteroskedasticity. This option is not available with **METHOD=HH**. If this option is used, the forecast standard errors computed by the **FC** command will not be correct. The formula is:

$$V\left(\hat{\beta}\right) = N(X'X)^{-1}S_0(X'X)^{-1} \quad \text{where} \quad S_0 = \frac{1}{N}\sum_{t=1}^{N} e_t^2 X_t X_t'$$

INFLUENCE   Computes the Belsley-Kuh-Welsch [1980, Chapter 2] diagnostics for detecting influential observations. See also the **DFBETAS** and **HATDIAG=** options. The **INFLUENCE** option is not valid with the **RIDGE=, HETCOV, AUTCOV=, RESTRICT** or Stepwise Regression options. Further details and an example are given later in this chapter.

LINLOG   Used when the dependent variable is **LIN**ear, but the independent variables are in **LOG** form. In this model the elasticities are estimated as $E_k = \hat{\beta}_k / \overline{Y}$. NOTE: This option does not transform the data. The data must be transformed by the user with the appropriate **GENR** commands.

LIST   LISTs and plots the residuals and predicted values of the dependent variable and residual statistics. When **LIST** is specified **RSTAT** is automatically turned on.

LM   Gives the Jarque-Bera [1980] Lagrange Multiplier test for normality of the OLS residuals. The test statistic is described in the chapter *A CHILD'S GUIDE TO RUNNING REGRESSIONS*.

LOGLIN   Used when the dependent variable is in **LOG** form, but the independent variables are **LIN**ear. In this model the elasticities are estimated as $E_k = \hat{\beta}_k \bar{X}$. The log-likelihood function is evaluated as:

$$-\frac{N}{2}\ln\left(2\pi\tilde{\sigma}^2\right) - \frac{N}{2} - \sum_{t=1}^{N}\ln Y_t \quad \text{where} \quad \tilde{\sigma}^2 = \frac{1}{N}\sum_{t=1}^{N}e_t^2$$

The R^2 calculation does not take anti-logs of the dependent variable. However, if the **RSTAT** option is also used the output will report:
R-SQUARE BETWEEN OBSERVED AND PREDICTED =
R-SQUARE BETWEEN ANTILOGS OBSERVED AND PREDICTED =
NOTE: This option does not transform the data. The data must be transformed by the user with the appropriate **GENR** commands.

LOGLOG   Used when the dependent variable and all the independent variables are in **LOG** form. In this model the elasticities are estimated as $E_k = \hat{\beta}_k$. The log-likelihood function and R^2 measure are evaluated as in the **LOGLIN** option above. NOTE: This option does not transform the data. The data must be transformed by the user with the appropriate **GENR** commands.

MAX   Prints Analysis of Variance Tables, Variance-covariance matrix, Correlation matrix, Residuals, Residual Statistics and Goodness of Fit Test for Normality. This option is equivalent to using the **ANOVA, LIST, PCOV, PCOR** and **GF** options. Users should be sure the **MAX** output is necessary, otherwise unnecessary calculations are required.

NOCONSTANT There will be **NO CONSTANT** (intercept) in the estimated equation. This option is used when the intercept is to be suppressed in the regression or when the user is supplying the intercept. This option should be used with caution as some of the usual output may be invalid. In particular, the usual R^2 is not well defined and could be negative. However, when this option is used, the raw moment R^2 may be of interest. The ANALYSIS OF VARIANCE - FROM MEAN table will not be computed if this option is used.

NOMULSIGSQ With this option, for classical OLS estimation, the $(X'X)^{-1}$ matrix is used as the complete covariance matrix of the estimated coefficients and is **NO**t **MUL**tiplied by $\hat{\sigma}^2$.

NONORM Used with **WEIGHT=** if you do not want normalized weights. Interpretation of output is sometimes difficult when weights are not normalized. Sometimes, the weights can be viewed as a sampling replication factor. Users are expected to know exactly what their weights represent.

PCOR Prints the **COR**relation matrix of the estimated coefficients. This should not be confused with a correlation matrix of variables which can be obtained with a **STAT** command. The elements of the correlation matrix are obtained as:

$$\mathrm{Cor}\left(\hat{\beta}_i,\hat{\beta}_j\right) = \mathrm{Cov}\left(\hat{\beta}_i,\hat{\beta}_j\right) / \sqrt{V\left(\hat{\beta}_i\right)V\left(\hat{\beta}_j\right)} \qquad i,j = 1,...,K$$

PCOV Prints the **COV**ariance matrix of the estimated coefficients (described in the chapter *A CHILD'S GUIDE TO RUNNING REGRESSIONS*). This should not be confused with the covariance matrix of variables which can be obtained with the **STAT** command.

PLUSH Prints the **LUSH** (**L**inear **U**nbiased with **S**calar covariance matrix using **H**ouseholder transformation) residuals. The Householder transformation method first finds the N x N orthogonal matrix P such that:

$$P'X = \begin{bmatrix} P_1'X \\ P_2'X \end{bmatrix} = \begin{bmatrix} R \\ 0 \end{bmatrix} \qquad \text{and} \quad X'X = R'R$$

where P_1 is NxK, P_2 is Nx(N–K) and R is a KxK upper triangular matrix. Note that R'R is a Cholesky factorization of X'X. The OLS coefficient vector is formed by solving $R\hat{\beta} = P_1'Y$. The N–K vector of LUSH residuals is computed as $P_2'Y$. For further details see Golub and Styan [1973].

REPLICATE Used with **WEIGHT=** when the weights indicate a sample replication factor. When this option is specified the **NONORM** option is often desirable. The effective sample size will then be adjusted upward to be equal to the sum of the weights. The **UT** option is automatically in effect.

RESTRICT Forces linear **RESTRICT**ions into the regression. It tells SHAZAM that **RESTRICT** commands follow. An example of this option is shown later in this chapter. Restrictions must be linear. This option may not be used with **DWPVALUE** or **METHOD=HH**.

RSTAT   Prints **R**esidual Summary **STAT**istics without printing each observation. The output includes the Durbin-Watson statistic and related residual test statistics. It also includes the Runs Test described in the chapter *A CHILD'S GUIDE TO RUNNING REGRESSIONS*. When the **LIST** option is specified **RSTAT** is automatically turned on.

UT   This option is used with **WEIGHT=** if you want the residuals and predicted values to be **U**n**T**ransformed so that the estimated coefficients are used with unweighted data in order to obtain predicted values. The regression estimates are not affected by this option. This option is not available with **METHOD=HH**.

AUTCOV=   Specifies the lag length L to use in the Newey and West [1987] variance estimator for models with autocorrelated disturbances. This option is the autocorrelation equivalent to the **HETCOV** option. An explanation of the method is in Greene [1993, p. 422]. Use **AUTCOV=1** until you really understand the method. The variance-covariance matrix of the estimated coefficients is estimated as:

$$V\left(\hat{\beta}\right) = N(X'X)^{-1}S_*(X'X)^{-1} \qquad \text{where}$$

$$S_* = S_0 + \frac{1}{N}\sum_{j=1}^{L}\sum_{t=j+1}^{N} w_j e_t e_{t-j}\left(X_t X'_{t-j} + X_{t-j}X'_t\right) \qquad \text{and} \qquad w_j = 1 - \frac{j}{L+1}$$

and S_0 is the White estimator described for the **HETCOV** option.

BEG=, END=   Specifies the **BEG**inning and **END**ing observations to be used in estimation. This option overrides the **SAMPLE** command and defaults to the sample range in effect.

COEF=   Saves the **COEF**ficients in the variable specified. If there is an intercept it will be stored as the last coefficient.

COV=   Saves the **COV**ariance matrix of coefficients in the variable specified.

FE=, FX=   Specifies the entering and exiting criteria in terms of **F**-values rather than probability levels when running Stepwise regressions. SHAZAM will use the user-supplied values of **FE=** and **FX=** only when no values are supplied for **PE=** or **PX=**. If either **FE=** or **FX=** is not specified, it will be defaulted to the other value. If **FX>FE** then SHAZAM will set **FX** to **FE**. If **FE=0** then all of the step variables will be allowed to enter. If the value specified for **FX=** is a large number then all of the step variables may be removed. See the section on *STEPWISE REGRESSION* in this chapter for further details.

HATDIAG=   Saves the diagonal elements of the Hat matrix $X(X'X)^{-1}X'$ in the variable specified.

IDVAR=   Specifies a character variable to be printed beside its corresponding observation when **LIST** or **MAX** options are used. For example, the data could consist of one observation for each of the Canadian provinces, in which case the user may identify the residual with the province. For information on reading and printing character variables, see the chapter *DATA INPUT AND OUTPUT*. An example of the **IDVAR=** option in use can be found later in this chapter.

INCOEF=   Specifies a vector of **COEF**ficients to **IN**put if you know what the coefficients are and do not want to estimate the equation. An example of this option is shown in the chapter *PROGRAMMING IN SHAZAM* for computing the Power of a Test. Also see the **INSIG2=** option described below.

INCOVAR=   Specifies a **COVAR**iance matrix to be used with the **INCOEF=** option. The covariance matrix must be a symmetric matrix stored in lower-triangular form such as that produced by the **COV=** option or the **SYM** function on the **MATRIX** command. When this option is used the **NOMULSIGSQ** option is automatically in effect.

INDW=   Specifies a value for the Durbin-Watson test statistic. This option may be used with the **DWPVALUE** option to get a p-value for the Durbin-Watson statistic.

INSIG2=   Specifies a value of σ^2 to be used. Also see the **INCOEF=** option described above.

METHOD=   Specifies the computational **METHOD** to be used on the **OLS** command. The default is **GS** (Gram Schmidt) as described in Farebrother [1974] and the alternatives are **HH** (Householder transformations), and **NORMAL** (Choleski solution of Normal equations). All methods should yield nearly identical results with most data, however **GS** is probably the most accurate.

ORDER=   Specifies the order of autocorrelation to test if the **DWPVALUE** option is used. The default is **ORDER=1**.

PCINFO=   This option is only used on **OLS** commands in conjunction with the **PC** command. For more information on this option see the chapter *PRINCIPAL COMPONENTS AND FACTOR ANALYSIS.*

PCOMP=   This option is only used on **OLS** commands in conjunction with the **PC** command. For more information on this option see the chapter *PRINCIPAL COMPONENTS AND FACTOR ANALYSIS.*

PE=, PX=   These options are similar to the **FE=** and **FX=** options described above, and are used to specify the Probability levels for Entering (**PE=**) and eXiting (**PX=**) variables that may be stepped into the equation when a Stepwise regression is being run. If a variable is more significant than the **PE** level, it will be included. If at any step a variable becomes less significant than **PX** it will be deleted from the equation. The default values are **PE=.05** and **PX=.05**. If either value is not specified it will be defaulted to the other value. If **PX< PE** then **PX** will be set to equal **PE**. If **PE=1** then all of the step variables will be allowed to enter. If **PX=0** then all of the step variables will be removed. See the section on *STEPWISE REGRESSION* in this chapter for further details.

PREDICT=   Saves the **PREDICT**ed values of the dependent variable in the variable specified.

RESID=   Saves the values of the **RESID**uals from the regression in the variable specified.

RIDGE=   Specifies a value of k to be used to convert the **OLS** regression to a **RIDGE** regression. This option only permits ordinary **RIDGE** regression where the diagonal elements of the X′X matrix are augmented by k. In order to do a **RIDGE** regression, a value for k must be specified. It may be necessary to run several regressions using different values of k in order to examine the stability of the coefficients. The value of k should be between zero and one. A value of k equal to zero will be an **OLS** regression. The user should be familiar with **RIDGE** regression before using this option. Watson and White [1976] provide good examples of Ridge regression. This option automatically uses **METHOD=NORMAL**. See the *PROGRAMMING IN SHAZAM* chapter for a Ridge Regression example. The ridge coefficients and covariance matrix are estimated as:

$$\hat{\beta}_R = [X'X + kI]^{-1}X'Y \quad \text{and} \quad V(\hat{\beta}_R) = \hat{\sigma}^2[X'X + kI]^{-1}(X'X)[X'X + kI]^{-1}$$

The **INSIG2=** option can be used to specify a value of σ^2 to be used in the estimate of the covariance matrix for the ridge regression estimates (see the discussion in Greene [1993, Chapter 9]).

STDERR=   Saves the values of the **STanDard ERR**ors of the coefficients in the variable specified.

TRATIO=   Saves the values of the **T-RATIO**s in the variable specified.

WEIGHT=   Specifies a variable to be used as the weight for a **WEIGHT**ed Least Squares regression. **OLS** with the **WEIGHT=** option is similar to a **GLS** regression with a diagonal Omega matrix. Users should also examine the **NONORM, UT** and **REPLICATE** options described above which can be used with the **WEIGHT=** option. More details and an example are given later in this chapter.

OLS TEMPORARY VARIABLES

There are many temporary variables available on the **OLS** command. These variables contain useful statistics from the most recent regression command in the SHAZAM run. (For a list of the temporary variables available on each regression command see the chapter *MISCELLANEOUS COMMANDS AND INFORMATION*.)

The temporary variables available after the **OLS** command are:

$ADR2	R-Square Adjusted
$DF	Degrees of Freedom
$ERR	Error Code
$K	Number of Coefficients
$LLF	Log of the Likelihood Function
$N	Number of observations used in the estimation
$R2	R-Square
$RAW	Raw-Moment R-Square
$SIG2	Variance of the Estimate - SIGMA**2
$SSE	Sum of Squared Errors - SSE

From the ANALYSIS OF VARIANCE - FROM MEAN table in the **OLS** output:

$ANF	ANOVA F Statistic
$SSR	Regression - SS
$SST	Total - SS

From the ANALYSIS OF VARIANCE - FROM ZERO table in the **OLS** output:

$ZANF	ANOVA F Statistic
$ZSSR	Regression - SS
$ZSST	Total - SS

If the **ANOVA** option is used the model selection test statistics are available in the temporary variables:

$FPE	Akaike (1969) final prediction error
$LAIC	Akaike (1973) information criterion - log AIC
$LSC	Schwarz (1978) criterion - log SC
$GCV	Craven-Wahba (1979) generalized cross validation
$HQ	Hannan and Quinn (1979) criterion
$RICE	Rice (1984) criterion
$SHIB	Shibata (1981) criterion
$SC	Schwarz (1978) criterion - SC
$AIC	Akaike (1974) information criterion - AIC

If the **DLAG** option is used the following temporary variable is available:

$DURH	Durbin's h statistic

If the **LM** option is used the following temporary variable is available:

$JB	Jarque-Bera normality test statistic

If the **RSTAT, LIST** or **MAX** option is used the statistics available in temporary variables are:

$DW	Durbin-Watson statistic
$R2OP	R-Square between observed and predicted
$RHO	Residual autocorrelation coefficient

If the **DWPVALUE** option is used then the following temporary variable is available:

$CDF	p-value for the Durbin-Watson statistic.

An example of the use of temporary variables follows in the next section.

Calculating a Chow Test

This example shows how temporary variables can be useful. Consider computing the Chow test statistic to test the hypothesis that the coefficients are the same in two regimes (this test is described in the chapter *DIAGNOSTIC TESTS*). The SHAZAM commands that compute the Chow test statistic are:

```
?OLS CONSUME INCOME PRICE
GEN1 CSSE=$SSE
GEN1 DF1=$K
GEN1 DF2=$N-2*$K
SAMPLE 1 9
?OLS CONSUME INCOME PRICE
GEN1 SSE1=$SSE
SAMPLE 10 17
?OLS CONSUME INCOME PRICE
GEN1 SSE2=$SSE
GEN1 F=((CSSE-(SSE1+SSE2))/DF1)/((SSE1+SSE2)/DF2)
SAMPLE 1 1
PRINT F
DISTRIB F / TYPE=F DF1=DF1 DF2=DF2
```

In the above example three **OLS** regressions are run. The first is run using all the observations in the sample. This is the combined regression. The second and third are run with the first 9 and last 8 observations in the sample, respectively. The purpose of the Chow test is to test the hypothesis that the coefficients are the same in each of the separate samples. The question mark (?) that appears before the **OLS** commands serves to suppress the output, since only the SSE variables are of interest in this problem. (For details on the ? output suppressor and temporary variables, see the chapter *MISCELLANEOUS COMMANDS AND INFORMATION*.) The contents of the SSE temporary variable are saved in a permanent variable before another regression is run because only the most recent values of temporary variables are saved. When saving a scalar variable, like SSE, the **GEN1** rather than **GENR** command should be used. The variable F contains the Chow test statistic computed as:

$$F=((CSSE-(SSE1+SSE2))/K)/((SSE1+SSE2)/(N1+N2-2K))$$

where SSE1 is the sum of squared errors for the OLS regression using the first 9 observations, SSE2 is the sum of squared errors for the OLS regression using the last 8 observations, CSSE is the sum of squared errors for the combined OLS regression, K is the number of parameters, N1 is the number of observations in the first separate OLS regression, and N2 is the number of observations in the last separate OLS regression.

The SHAZAM output from the above commands follows.

```
|_?OLS CONSUME INCOME PRICE
|_GEN1 CSSE=$SSE
..NOTE..CURRENT VALUE OF $SSE =    433.31
|_GEN1 DF1=$K
..NOTE..CURRENT VALUE OF $K   =    3.0000
|_GEN1 DF2=$N-2*$K
..NOTE..CURRENT VALUE OF $N   =    17.000
..NOTE..CURRENT VALUE OF $K   =    3.0000
|_SAMPLE 1 9
|_?OLS CONSUME INCOME PRICE
|_GEN1 SSE1=$SSE
..NOTE..CURRENT VALUE OF $SSE =    61.671
|_SAMPLE 10 17
|_?OLS CONSUME INCOME PRICE
|_GEN1 SSE2=$SSE
..NOTE..CURRENT VALUE OF $SSE =    189.35
|_GEN1 F=((CSSE-(SSE1+SSE2))/DF1)/((SSE1+SSE2)/DF2)
|_SAMPLE 1 1
|_PRINT F
   2.662815
|_DISTRIB F / TYPE=F DF1=DF1 DF2=DF2
F DISTRIBUTION- DF1=   3.0000      DF2=   11.000
MEAN=   1.2222     VARIANCE=   1.7072     MODE=    .28205


              DATA        PDF         CDF        1-CDF
   F
   ROW    1    2.6628    0.78980E-01   .90020    0.99796E-01
```

The final step is to calculate the p-value. That is, for an F-distribution with (K,N1+N2–2K) degrees of freedom find the area to the right of the calculated F-test statistic of 2.662815. This is done with the **DISTRIB** command which is described in the chapter *PROBABILITY DISTRIBUTIONS*. On the SHAZAM output this area is listed in the column marked 1-CDF. The p-value is .099796 so we can reject the null hypothesis at the 10% level although not at the 5% level.

Note that the **DIAGNOS** command (see the chapter *DIAGNOSTIC TESTS*) automatically computes Chow tests. That is, the same result can be obtained with the commands:

```
OLS CONSUME INCOME PRICE
DIAGNOS / CHOWONE=9
```

The **CHOWONE=** option on the **DIAGNOS** command specifies the number of observations in the first group.

Labelling Residual Output with the IDVAR= option

The next SHAZAM output shows the use of the **IDVAR=** option on **OLS** using the data that was read and printed in the chapter *DATA INPUT AND OUTPUT*. The variables are the unemployment and vacancy rates for some provinces of Canada for January, 1976 as provided by Statistics Canada.

```
|_SAMPLE 1 9
|_FORMAT(A8,2F5.1)
|_READ PROVINCE UR VR / FORMAT
|_OLS UR VR / IDVAR=PROVINCE LIST
 OLS ESTIMATION
        9 OBSERVATIONS      DEPENDENT VARIABLE = UR
...NOTE..SAMPLE RANGE SET TO:    1,    9

 R-SQUARE =     .4300     R-SQUARE ADJUSTED =     .3486
 VARIANCE OF THE ESTIMATE-SIGMA**2 =    6.9981
 STANDARD ERROR OF THE ESTIMATE-SIGMA =    2.6454
 SUM OF SQUARED ERRORS-SSE=    48.987
 MEAN OF DEPENDENT VARIABLE =    8.8000
 LOG OF THE LIKELIHOOD FUNCTION = -20.3949

VARIABLE     ESTIMATED  STANDARD   T-RATIO          PARTIAL STANDARDIZED ELASTICITY
  NAME       COEFFICIENT  ERROR      7 DF    P-VALUE CORR. COEFFICIENT  AT MEANS
VR           -.93553     .4071     -2.298     .055  -.656     -.6557     -.6851
CONSTANT     14.829      2.768      5.358     .001   .897      .0000     1.6851

   OBSERVATION            OBSERVED         PREDICTED        CALCULATED
      NO.                  VALUE            VALUE            RESIDUAL
        1 NEWFOUND        14.900           11.087            3.8132
        2 NOVA SCO         9.1000          10.151           -1.0513
        3 NEW BRUN        12.200            8.2803           3.9197
        4 QUEBEC           9.1000           9.2158           -.11579
        5 ONTARIO          7.1000          10.151           -3.0513
        6 MANITOBA         6.7000           7.3447           -.64474
        7 SASKATCH         4.8000           7.3447           -2.5447
        8 ALBERTA          5.3000           4.5382            .76184
        9 BRITISH         10.000           11.087           -1.0868

 DURBIN-WATSON = 1.9807    VON NEUMANN RATIO = 2.2283    RHO =  -.15456
 RESIDUAL SUM =  0.17764E-14  RESIDUAL VARIANCE =    6.9981
 SUM OF ABSOLUTE ERRORS=   16.989
 R-SQUARE BETWEEN OBSERVED AND PREDICTED =  .4300
 RUNS TEST:  6 RUNS,  3 POSITIVE,  6 NEGATIVE, NORMAL STATISTIC =    .8165
```

RESTRICTED LEAST SQUARES

The general command format for restricted least squares is:

OLS *depvar indeps* / **RESTRICT** *options*
RESTRICT *equation1*
RESTRICT *equation2*

. . .
END

The **RESTRICT** option informs SHAZAM that **RESTRICT** commands are to follow. More than one is allowed provided each is typed on a separate line. The *equation* is a linear function of the variables (that represent coefficients) involved in the estimation. NOTE: The restrictions *must* be a linear function of the coefficients. The **END** command marks the end of the list of **RESTRICT** commands and is required. Each restriction will add one degree of freedom.

Consider estimating the model $Y = X\beta + \varepsilon$ subject to the restrictions $R\beta = r$ where R is a known matrix and r is a known vector. The restricted least squares estimator is:

$$\hat{\beta}_r = \hat{\beta} + (X'X)^{-1}R'\left[R(X'X)^{-1}R'\right]^{-1}\left(r - R\hat{\beta}\right) \qquad \text{where} \qquad \hat{\beta} = (X'X)^{-1}X'Y$$

The covariance matrix of the restricted estimator is estimated as:

$$V\left(\hat{\beta}_r\right) = \hat{\sigma}^2(X'X)^{-1} - \hat{\sigma}^2(X'X)^{-1}R'\left[R(X'X)^{-1}R'\right]^{-1}R(X'X)^{-1}$$

The R^2 measure is calculated as: $\qquad 1 - \dfrac{e'e}{Y'Y - N\overline{Y}^2}$

where e is the estimated residuals from the restricted estimation. Note that this formula is not bounded at zero.

The following is an example of the use of the **RESTRICT** option and **RESTRICT** commands with **OLS** using Theil's textile data. The SHAZAM commands are:

```
OLS CONSUME INCOME PRICE / RESTRICT
RESTRICT INCOME+PRICE=0
END
```

The SHAZAM output follows.

```
|_OLS CONSUME INCOME PRICE / RESTRICT
 OLS ESTIMATION
      17 OBSERVATIONS      DEPENDENT VARIABLE = CONSUME
...NOTE..SAMPLE RANGE SET TO:    1,   17
|_RESTRICT INCOME+PRICE=0
|_END
F TEST ON RESTRICTIONS=   1.4715      WITH    1 AND   14 DF

 R-SQUARE =      .9462      R-SQUARE ADJUSTED =     .9426
VARIANCE OF THE ESTIMATE-SIGMA**2 =    31.924
STANDARD ERROR OF THE ESTIMATE-SIGMA =    5.6501
SUM OF SQUARED ERRORS-SSE=   478.86
MEAN OF DEPENDENT VARIABLE =    134.51
LOG OF THE LIKELIHOOD FUNCTION = -52.4966
```

VARIABLE NAME	ESTIMATED COEFFICIENT	STANDARD ERROR	T-RATIO 15 DF	P-VALUE	PARTIAL CORR.	STANDARDIZED COEFFICIENT	ELASTICITY AT MEANS
INCOME	1.3691	.8433E-01	16.24	.000	.973	.3078	1.0482
PRICE	-1.3691	.8433E-01	-16.24	.000	-.973	-.9794	-.7768
CONSTANT	97.991	2.634	37.21	.000	.995	.0000	.7285

An example of estimating equations with restrictions in a system of equations is shown in the chapter *TWO-STAGE LEAST SQUARES AND SYSTEMS OF EQUATIONS*.

WEIGHTED REGRESSION

Weighted regression has a number of applications and can be implemented in SHAZAM with the **WEIGHT=** option on the **OLS** command. One application is as a correction for heteroskedasticity. A second application is for replicated data that may be produced from a sample survey. First consider the regression model with heteroskedastic disturbances stated as:

$$Y_t = X_t'\beta + \varepsilon_t \qquad \text{where} \qquad E(\varepsilon_t^2) = \sigma^2 / W_t \qquad \text{for } t=1,\ldots,N$$

and Y_t, X_t and W_t are observed and the unknown parameters are β and σ^2. The values for W_t are specified in the **WEIGHT=** variable. SHAZAM normalizes the weights to sum to the number of observations. Each observation of the dependent and explanatory variables is multiplied by the square root of the normalized weight variable and the weighted least squares estimator $\hat{\beta}_w$ is then obtained by applying OLS to the transformed model:

$$\sqrt{W_t / \overline{W}}\, Y_t = \sqrt{W_t / \overline{W}}\, X_t'\beta + v_t \qquad \text{where} \qquad \overline{W} = \frac{1}{N}\sum_{t=1}^{N} W_t$$

The weighted residuals (that may be saved with the **RESID=** option) are calculated as:

$$\hat{v}_t = \sqrt{W_t / \overline{W}}\, (Y_t - X_t'\hat{\beta}_w)$$

The residual variance (reported as SIGMA**2 on the SHAZAM output) is estimated as:

$$\frac{1}{N-K}\sum_{t=1}^{N}(\hat{v}_t)^2$$

If the **DN** option is used the divisor is N instead of N–K. The log-likelihood function is evaluated as:

$$-\frac{N}{2}\ln\left(2\pi\tilde{\sigma}^2\right)-\frac{N}{2}+\frac{1}{2}\sum_{t=1}^{N}\log\left(\left|W_t / \overline{W}\right|\right) \quad \text{where} \quad \tilde{\sigma}^2 = \frac{1}{N}\sum_{t=1}^{N}(\hat{v}_t)^2$$

An example of applying weighted least squares to the heteroskedastic error model follows. With the Theil textile data set it is assumed that the error variance is directly related to the *PRICE* variable. The SHAZAM output is:

```
|_GENR PW=1/PRICE
|_OLS CONSUME INCOME PRICE / WEIGHT=PW
 OLS ESTIMATION
       17 OBSERVATIONS       DEPENDENT VARIABLE = CONSUME
...NOTE..SAMPLE RANGE SET TO:    1,   17
 SUM OF LOG(SQRT(ABS(WEIGHT)))  =  -.19396

  R-SQUARE =      .9426     R-SQUARE ADJUSTED =     .9344
 VARIANCE OF THE ESTIMATE-SIGMA**2 =    33.810
 STANDARD ERROR OF THE ESTIMATE-SIGMA =    5.8146
 SUM OF SQUARED ERRORS-SSE=    473.34
 MEAN OF DEPENDENT VARIABLE =    138.98
 LOG OF THE LIKELIHOOD FUNCTION = -52.5920

VARIABLE    ESTIMATED   STANDARD    T-RATIO          PARTIAL STANDARDIZED ELASTICITY
  NAME      COEFFICIENT   ERROR       14 DF    P-VALUE CORR.  COEFFICIENT  AT MEANS
INCOME        1.1543      .2922        3.950     .001   .726      .2626      .8529
PRICE        -1.4060    .9272E-01    -15.16      .000  -.971    -1.0080     -.7374
CONSTANT     122.92     28.96         4.244      .001   .750      .0000      .8845
```

Now consider an application to replicated data. In this case, consider that each observation Y_t, X_t is replicated N_t times. The values for N_t are specified in the **WEIGHT=** variable. The weighted least squares estimator $\hat{\beta}_w$ is obtained as before by applying OLS to the transformed model:

$$\sqrt{N_t}Y_t = \sqrt{N_t}X_t'\beta + v_t$$

When the **REPLICATE** option is used the estimated residuals are calculated as the untransformed residuals as:

$$e_t = Y_t - X_t'\hat{\beta}_w$$

When the **NONORM** option is used the residual variance (reported as SIGMA**2 on the SHAZAM output) is estimated as:

$$\frac{1}{\sum_{t=1}^{N}N_t - K}\sum_{t=1}^{N}N_t e_t^2$$

DETECTING INFLUENTIAL OBSERVATIONS

SHAZAM output from the **OLS** command with the **INFLUENCE** option follows.

```
|_OLS CONSUME INCOME PRICE / INFLUENCE
 OLS ESTIMATION
     17 OBSERVATIONS      DEPENDENT VARIABLE = CONSUME
...NOTE..SAMPLE RANGE SET TO:    1,   17

 R-SQUARE =    .9513     R-SQUARE ADJUSTED =     .9443
 VARIANCE OF THE ESTIMATE-SIGMA**2 =   30.951
 STANDARD ERROR OF THE ESTIMATE-SIGMA =   5.5634
 SUM OF SQUARED ERRORS-SSE=   433.31
 MEAN OF DEPENDENT VARIABLE =   134.51
 LOG OF THE LIKELIHOOD FUNCTION = -51.6471
```

VARIABLE NAME	ESTIMATED COEFFICIENT	STANDARD ERROR	T-RATIO 14 DF	P-VALUE	PARTIAL CORR.	STANDARDIZED COEFFICIENT	ELASTICITY AT MEANS
INCOME	1.0617	.2667	3.981	.001	.729	.2387	.8129
PRICE	-1.3830	.8381E-01	-16.50	.000	-.975	-.9893	-.7846
CONSTANT	130.71	27.09	4.824	.000	.790	.0000	.9718

	RESIDUAL	RSTUDENT	HT	COVRAT	DFFITS	DFFIT
1	5.5076	1.2294	.3279	1.3360	.8588	2.6871
2	2.5765	.5287	.2720	1.6096	.3232	.96281
3	1.4210	.2804	.2249	1.5824	.1510	.41223
4	-5.1814	-.9842	.1065	1.1268	-.3399	-.61780
5	-.25169	-.0456	.0858	1.3655	-.0140	-0.23617E-01
6	-5.3100	-1.0548	.1746	1.1827	-.4851	-1.1230
7	-1.9455	-.3829	.2167	1.5418	-.2014	-.53833
8	.57462	.1152	.2522	1.6652	.0669	.19384
9	4.3958	.8588	.1694	1.2743	.3879	.89668
10	1.5426	.2833	.1047	1.3696	.0969	.18045
11	4.5946	.8670	.1088	1.1839	.3029	.56078
12	-4.9571	-1.0007	.2072	1.2609	-.5116	-1.2953
13	-8.8975	-1.9206	.1734	.7142	-.8798	-1.8670
14	6.4156	1.3427	.2200	1.0846	.7131	1.8099
15	-2.5614	-.4770	.1197	1.3469	-.1759	-.34841
16	-7.2886	-1.4519	.1214	.9056	-.5396	-1.0067
17	9.3650	1.9629	.1147	.6475	.7064	1.2131

The HT values are defined as the diagonal values of the Hat matrix as described in Belsley, Kuh, and Welsch [1980, Equations 2.2 and 2.15] as follows:

$$h = \mathrm{DIAG}\left(X(X'X)^{-1}X'\right)$$

where DIAG() takes the diagonal of the matrix (the **HATDIAG=** option can be used to save the diagonal). The DFFIT values measure the effect of the coefficient change and measure the change in fit due to a deletion of one observation. Denote X(t) as the observation matrix with row t deleted and b(t) as the estimator obtained with this matrix. Then:

$$\text{DFFIT}_t = \hat{Y}_t - \hat{Y}_t(t) = X'_t[\hat{\beta} - b(t)] = \frac{h_t e_t}{1 - h_t} \qquad \text{where} \quad \hat{Y}(t) = X(t)b(t) \quad \text{and}$$

$$\text{DFFITS}_t = \left[\frac{h_t}{1 - h_t}\right]^{\frac{1}{2}} \frac{e_t}{\hat{\sigma}(t)\sqrt{1 - h_t}} \quad \text{where} \quad \hat{\sigma}^2(t) = \frac{1}{N - K - 1}\sum_{k \neq t}\left[Y_k - X'_k b(t)\right]^2$$

For further reference on these statistics see Belsley, Kuh, and Welsch [1980, Equations 2.10 and 2.11].

The RSTUDENT values are the Studentized Residuals as described in Belsley, Kuh, and Welsch [1980, Equation 2.26]:

$$e_t^* = \frac{e_t}{\hat{\sigma}(t)\sqrt{1 - h_t}}$$

The COVRAT statistic is defined as:

$$\text{COVRAT}_t = \frac{\hat{\sigma}(t)^{2K}}{\hat{\sigma}^{2K}}\left\{\frac{\det[X'(t)X(t)]^{-1}}{\det(X'X)^{-1}}\right\}$$

and compares the covariance matrices $\hat{\sigma}^2(X'X)^{-1}$ and $\hat{\sigma}^2(t)[X'(t)X(t)]^{-1}$ as described in Belsley et al. [1980, Equation 2.36].

If the **DFBETAS** option is specified on the **OLS** regression the following output is printed:

```
|_OLS CONSUME INCOME PRICE / DFBETAS
 OLS ESTIMATION
       17 OBSERVATIONS     DEPENDENT VARIABLE = CONSUME
...NOTE..SAMPLE RANGE SET TO:     1,    17

 R-SQUARE =    .9513     R-SQUARE ADJUSTED =     .9443
 VARIANCE OF THE ESTIMATE-SIGMA**2 =    30.951
 STANDARD ERROR OF THE ESTIMATE-SIGMA =    5.5634
 SUM OF SQUARED ERRORS-SSE=    433.31
 MEAN OF DEPENDENT VARIABLE =     134.51
 LOG OF THE LIKELIHOOD FUNCTION = -51.6471

VARIABLE    ESTIMATED   STANDARD    T-RATIO            PARTIAL STANDARDIZED ELASTICITY
  NAME      COEFFICIENT   ERROR      14 DF    P-VALUE CORR. COEFFICIENT  AT MEANS
INCOME       1.0617      .2667       3.981     .001   .729    .2387       .8129
PRICE       -1.3830     .8381E-01   -16.50     .000  -.975   -.9893      -.7846
CONSTANT    130.71      27.09        4.824     .000   .790    .0000       .9718
```

DFBETAS:	INCOME	PRICE	CONSTANT
	-.5514	.6385	.4262
	-.1847	.2480	.1362
	-.0659	.1218	.0418
	-.0556	-.2070	.0927
	-.0031	-.0065	.0041
	-.3208	-.1693	.3511
	-.1455	-.0641	.1574
	.0572	.0024	-.0569
	.3011	-.1392	-.2610
	.0421	-.0552	-.0260
	-.0193	-.1976	.0773
	.3667	.1608	-.4232
	.5942	.2854	-.6951
	-.2951	-.4729	.4291
	-.0086	.1247	-.0269
	.0325	.3740	-.1399
	.1661	-.4864	-.0284

The DFBETAS statistic yields a scaled measure of the change on the estimated regression coefficients when row t is deleted (see Belsley et al. [1980, Equation 2.7]).

$$\text{DFBETAS}_{tj} = \frac{\hat{\beta}_j - b_j(t)}{\hat{\sigma}(t)\sqrt{(X'X)^{-1}_{jj}}} \qquad \text{for } j=1,\ldots,K$$

Another statistic not listed on the SHAZAM output is:

$$\text{DFBETA}_t = \hat{\beta} - b(t) = \frac{(X'X)^{-1}X_t e_t}{1 - h_t}$$

This statistic measures the effect of deleting row t on the estimated regression coefficients (see Belsley et al. [1980, Equation 2.1]).

STEPWISE REGRESSION

Stepwise regression is not widely used in econometrics because most economists use economic theory to determine which variables belong in the model. However it is available for those who think a computer algorithm is smart enough to replace economic theory. For stepwise regression, a slight modification of the **OLS** command is required. The format of the **OLS** command is:

OLS *depvar indeps (stepvars) / options*

where *depvar* is the name of the dependent variable, *indeps* (if present) are the names of the independent variables that are always forced into the equation, *stepvars* are the names of the the variables that may be stepped into the equation, and *options* are the desired options. (See the **FE=, FX=, PE=, PX=** options described above.) The **DWPVALUE, HETCOV, RESTRICT** and **RIDGE=** options may not be used when stepwise regressions are being run. Stepwise regression automatically uses **METHOD=NORMAL**.

```
|_OLS CONSUME (INCOME PRICE YEAR)
 OLS ESTIMATION
        17 OBSERVATIONS      DEPENDENT VARIABLE = CONSUME
...NOTE..SAMPLE RANGE SET TO:    1,   17

**** STEPWISE REGRESSION ****
***PARAMETERS FOR STEPWISE REGRESSION:   PE= .050000 AND  PX= .050000.


-----------------------------------------------------------------------
|**** STEPPING SEQUENCE ****|              |     |     |              |
|        |           |       |              |     |     |              |
| STEP   |VARIABLE   |       |              |D.F. | D.F.|              |
|NUMBER  | LABEL     | STATUS |    F-VALUE  |NUM. | DEN.|F-PROBABILITY |
|---------------------------------------------------------------------|
|     1  |PRICE      |STEPPED IN| 129.4014  | 1   |  15 |   0.000000   |
|     2  |INCOME     |STEPPED IN|  15.8508  | 1   |  14 |    .001365   |
|*SUMMARY FOR POTENTIAL VARIABLES NOT ENTERED INTO THE REG. EQUATION* |
|        |YEAR       |IF ENTERED|    .3869  | 1   |  13 |    .544702   |
|**** END OF STEPPING SEQUENCE ****         |     |     |              |
-----------------------------------------------------------------------

 R-SQUARE =      .9513     R-SQUARE ADJUSTED =      .9443
 VARIANCE OF THE ESTIMATE-SIGMA**2 =    30.951
 STANDARD ERROR OF THE ESTIMATE-SIGMA =    5.5634
 SUM OF SQUARED ERRORS-SSE=    433.31
 MEAN OF DEPENDENT VARIABLE =    134.51
 LOG OF THE LIKELIHOOD FUNCTION = -51.6471

VARIABLE     ESTIMATED  STANDARD   T-RATIO           PARTIAL STANDARDIZED ELASTICITY
  NAME       COEFFICIENT  ERROR     14 DF    P-VALUE CORR. COEFFICIENT  AT MEANS
INCOME        1.0617      .2667     3.981     .001   .729    .2387       .8129
PRICE        -1.3830     .8381E-01 -16.50     .000  -.975   -.9893      -.7846
CONSTANT      130.71     27.09      4.824     .000   .790    .0000       .9718
```

8. HYPOTHESIS TESTING AND CONFIDENCE INTERVALS

"God Himself could not sink this ship."
Titanic deckhand
April 10, 1912

The **TEST** command in SHAZAM can be used for linear or nonlinear hypothesis testing on regression coefficients after model estimation. The **CONFID** command can be used to compute confidence intervals and a confidence ellipse for two coefficients. Several **TEST** or **CONFID** commands can follow an estimation command. A discussion of hypothesis testing can be found in Judge, Hill, Griffiths, Lütkepohl and Lee [1988, Chapter 6.3-6.4] and Judge, Griffiths, Hill, Lütkepohl and Lee [1985, Chapter 6.6].

HYPOTHESIS TESTING

The **TEST** command follows an estimation command and the general format is:

estimation command
TEST *equation*

where *equation* is an equation made up of combinations of the variables involved in the estimation and represents the hypothesis to be tested. The equation must **not** contain logical relations such as .EQ., .NE., .LT., etc. (Note that to estimate models with inequality restrictions see the features in the chapter *INEQUALITY RESTRICTIONS*.) The equation may only include a variable in the estimated equation or one that has been previously generated with a **GEN1** or **GENR** command. Each single hypothesis must be placed on a separate **TEST** command.

If a *joint test* is required that involves several hypotheses, these should be grouped together with a blank **TEST** command to introduce them and an **END** command to mark the end of the group. The general command format for a joint hypothesis test is:

TEST
TEST *equation* 1
TEST *equation* 2
. . .

END

The **TEST** command calculates t, F, and chi-square test statistics. The appropriate test statistic to use depends on the form of the hypothesis. For example, when the hypothesis specified on the **TEST** command involves non-linear functions of the coefficients then the Wald chi-square statistic is generally used.

An example of hypothesis testing after OLS estimation is given in the next list of SHAZAM commands.

```
STAT CONSUME / MEAN=CBAR
STAT INCOME  / MEAN=IBAR
OLS CONSUME INCOME PRICE
TEST INCOME=1
TEST INCOME*(IBAR/CBAR)
TEST
  TEST INCOME=1
  TEST PRICE=-1
END
TEST INCOME*PRICE=-1
```

The Theil textile demand data set is analyzed. The first **TEST** command tests the hypothesis that the coefficient on *INCOME* is equal to one. The second **TEST** command computes a standard error for the income elasticity. Note that the equation does not have an = sign. This **TEST** command calculates a value for the function of the coefficients on the variables and then computes a standard error. The third **TEST** command initiates a joint hypothesis test. The final **TEST** command is an example of a non-linear hypothesis and the test statistics computed give a test for the hypothesis that the coefficient on *INCOME* multiplied by the coefficient on *PRICE* is equal to –1. SHAZAM output from the above **TEST** commands is included in the discussion that follows in this chapter.

If the **TEST** command follows non-linear estimation with the **NL** command then *equation* is an equation made up of combinations of the coefficients involved in the estimation. The next list of SHAZAM commands shows how to test hypotheses following nonlinear estimation with the **NL** command (see the chapter *NONLINEAR REGRESSION*). The commands estimate a CES production function with the variables *LOGQ*, *L* and *K*. The coefficients to estimate are B1, B2, B3, and B4. The **TEST** command then gives a test for $H_0: B3 = -1$.

```
NL 1 / NCOEF=4
EQ LOGQ=B1 + B4 * LOG ( B2*L**B3 + (1-B2)*K**B3)
COEF B1 .5 B2 .5 B3 -3 B4 -1
END
TEST B3=-1
```

For instructions on doing hypothesis testing on systems of equations, see the chapter *TWO STAGE LEAST SQUARES AND SYSTEMS OF EQUATIONS*.

Temporary variables available following a **TEST** command are:

$CHI	Wald chi-square statistic
$DF1, $DF2	Numerator and denominator degrees of freedom for the F distribution
$ERR	Error code
$F	F statistic

When a single hypothesis test is specified the temporary variables available are:

$DF	Degrees of freedom for the t distribution
$STES	Standard error of test value
$T	t statistic
$VAL	test value

When a joint test with exactly two **TEST** commands is used the temporary variables $VAL1, $VAL2, $CT11, $CT22, $CT12 are defined to give the two test values along with the elements of the covariance matrix of the two tests. For more information on temporary variables see the chapter *MISCELLANEOUS COMMANDS AND INFORMATION*.

Testing a Single Linear Combination of Coefficients

Consider testing $H_0: R_1\beta = r$ where R_1 is a known (1 x K) row vector and r is a known scalar. The simplest case is a hypothesis involving a single coefficient of the form $H_0: \beta_k = r$ (that is, R_1 has a 1 in element k and 0's for all other elements). The test statistic is:

$$t = \frac{R_1\hat{\beta} - r}{\sqrt{\hat{\sigma}^2 R_1(X'X)^{-1}R_1'}}$$

On the SHAZAM output the numerator is reported as the TEST VALUE and the denominator is reported as the STD. ERROR OF TEST VALUE. Under the assumption that $H_0: R_1\beta = r$ is true and with normally distributed errors the test statistic has a t-distribution with (N–K) degrees of freedom.

SHAZAM output from a **TEST** command is given below. The null hypothesis is that the coefficient on the variable *INCOME* is equal to 1.

```
|_TEST INCOME=1
TEST VALUE =    .61709E-01 STD. ERROR OF TEST VALUE   .26667
T STATISTIC =   .23140356      WITH   14 D.F.     P-VALUE=  .82035
F STATISTIC =   .53547606E-01 WITH    1 AND    14 D.F.   P-VALUE=  .82035
WALD CHI-SQUARE STATISTIC =  .53547606E-01 WITH    1 D.F.  P-VALUE=  .81700
UPPER BOUND ON P-VALUE BY CHEBYCHEV INEQUALITY = 1.00000
```

The p-value is the tail probability for a two-tailed test of $H_0: R_1\beta = r$ against the alternative that $H_1: R_1\beta \neq r$. The null hypothesis is rejected if the p-value is less than a selected level of significance (say 0.05). In this example, the p-value = $Pr[t_{(14)} < -0.2314$ and $t_{(14)} > 0.2314] = 2(1 - Pr[t_{(14)} < 0.2314]) = 0.82035$. Therefore, there is no evidence to reject the hypothesis that the coefficient on *INCOME* is equal to 1.

In the case of a single linear hypothesis the test statistic values satisfy: $t^2 = F$ statistic = Wald chi-square statistic.

Now consider calculating a standard error for an elasticity. With a linear regression equation an elasticity of the dependent variable with respect to the kth explanatory variable can be estimated as:

$$E_k = \hat{\beta}_k \frac{\overline{X}_k}{\overline{Y}}$$

where $\hat{\beta}_k$ is the estimated coefficient and $\overline{X}_k$ is the sample mean of variable k, and $\overline{Y}$ is the mean of the dependent variable. The SHAZAM estimation output reports this value in the column labelled ELASTICITY AT MEANS. However, it may also be of interest to compute a standard error for this statistic. The standard error can be estimated as:

$$\sqrt{V(\hat{\beta}_k)\left(\frac{\overline{X}_k}{\overline{Y}}\right)^2}$$

An example of the use of the **TEST** command to do this calculation is given below. With the Theil textile demand equation the standard error of the elasticity of consumption with respect to income is reported as the TEST VALUE. The T STATISTIC gives a test for the null hypothesis that the income elasticity is equal to 0.

```
|_TEST INCOME*(IBAR/CBAR)
TEST VALUE =    .81288        STD. ERROR OF TEST VALUE   .20417
T STATISTIC =   3.9813016      WITH   14 D.F.     P-VALUE=  .00137
F STATISTIC =   15.850762      WITH    1 AND    14 D.F.   P-VALUE=  .00137
WALD CHI-SQUARE STATISTIC =   15.850762      WITH    1 D.F.  P-VALUE=  .00007
UPPER BOUND ON P-VALUE BY CHEBYCHEV INEQUALITY = .06309
```

Testing More Than One Linear Combination of Coefficients

A general linear hypothesis can be expressed as $H_0: R\beta = r$ where R is a known (q x K) matrix and r is a (q x 1) column vector. The test statistic is:

$$F = \frac{1}{q}(R\hat{\beta} - r)'[RV(\hat{\beta})R']^{-1}(R\hat{\beta} - r)$$

where $V(\hat{\beta})$ is the (K x K) estimated variance-covariance matrix of $\hat{\beta}$. When the null hypothesis is true the F-statistic has an F-distribution with (q,N–K) degrees of freedom.

With the Theil textile demand equation consider testing the joint hypothesis that the coefficients on *INCOME* (β_1) and *PRICE* (β_2) are 1 and –1 respectively. The intercept parameter is β_3. In matrix notation this can be written as:

$$H_0: \begin{bmatrix} 1 & 0 & 0 \\ 0 & 1 & 0 \end{bmatrix} \begin{bmatrix} \beta_1 \\ \beta_2 \\ \beta_3 \end{bmatrix} = \begin{bmatrix} 1 \\ -1 \end{bmatrix}$$

The next SHAZAM output shows the results from the **TEST** command.

```
|_TEST
|_   TEST INCOME=1
|_   TEST PRICE=-1
|_END
F STATISTIC =    10.617226      WITH    2 AND    14 D.F.  P-VALUE=  .00156
WALD CHI-SQUARE STATISTIC =    21.234451      WITH    2 D.F.  P-VALUE=  .00002
UPPER BOUND ON P-VALUE BY CHEBYCHEV INEQUALITY =    .09419
```

The F test statistic is 10.617226. By consulting statistical tables it is found that the 5% critical value for F(2,14) is 3.74. The test statistic exceeds the critical value and so the conclusion is that the hypothesis is not supported by the data. The reported p-value of 0.00156 suggests that the null hypothesis is rejected even at a 1% significance level.

Note that in general the Wald chi-square statistic is equivalent to the F statistic multiplied by the number of hypotheses q and is distributed χ^2 with q degrees of freedom.

Testing Non-Linear Functions of Coefficients

Non-linear hypotheses can be stated in the general form H_0: $h(\beta) = 0$ where $h(\beta)$ is a set of q non-linear functions of the model parameters. The (qxK) matrix of partial derivatives is:

$$G = \frac{\partial h(\beta)}{\partial \beta}$$

The jth row of G is a vector of partial derivatives of the jth function with respect to β. The Wald test statistic is:

$$\text{Wald} = h(\hat{\beta})' \left[\hat{G} \, V(\hat{\beta}) \, \hat{G}' \right]^{-1} h(\hat{\beta})$$

where $\hat{G}$ is the matrix G evaluated at $\beta = \hat{\beta}$. When the null hypothesis is true the Wald statistic has an asymptotic chi-square distribution with q degrees of freedom. When q=1 then t=$\sqrt{\text{Wald}}$ has an asymptotic standard normal distribution under the null hypothesis.

Users should be aware that the value of the test statistic for a non-linear hypothesis is sensitive to the form of the equation (see Gregory and Veall [1985] and Lafontaine and White [1986]). Since the small sample distributions of non-linear test statistics are not known, the statistics reported as t, F, and Wald chi-square should be interpreted with caution.

SHAZAM uses analytical derivatives for the computation of the Wald test statistic. The nonlinear hypothesis specified on the **TEST** command can contain the functions LOG( ) and EXP( ). Other functions are not allowed. If a hypothesis with a square root function of coefficients is required then write the function in the form *(expression)***.5 and not SQRT(*expression*).

The next SHAZAM output shows the results of a test of the non-linear hypothesis that the product of two coefficients is equal to –1.

```
|_TEST INCOME*PRICE=-1
 TEST VALUE =   -.46833      STD. ERROR OF TEST VALUE    .39456
 T STATISTIC =   -1.1869717      WITH    14 D.F.     P-VALUE=  .25499
 F STATISTIC =    1.4089019      WITH     1 AND    14 D.F.  P-VALUE=  .25499
 WALD CHI-SQUARE STATISTIC =     1.4089019      WITH     1 D.F.  P-VALUE=  .23524
 UPPER BOUND ON P-VALUE BY CHEBYCHEV INEQUALITY =   .70977
```

The Chebychev Inequality

The table that follows summarizes the distributions of test statistics.

	Linear Model $Y=X\beta+\varepsilon$	Non-linear Model $Y=f(X,\beta)+\varepsilon$
Linear Hypothesis H_0: $R\beta=r$	$t_{(N-K)}$ for q=1, $F_{(q,N-K)}$ for q>1	asymptotic N(0,1) for q=1, asymptotic $\chi^2_{(q)}$ for q>1
Non-linear Hypothesis H_0: $h(\beta)=0$	asymptotic N(0,1) for q=1, asymptotic $\chi^2_{(q)}$ for q>1	asymptotic N(0,1) for q=1, asymptotic $\chi^2_{(q)}$ for q>1

In cases other than testing linear hypotheses of coefficients from the linear regression model the small sample distributions of the test statistics are unknown. We need to depend on the asymptotic distributions which are valid only in large samples. When applied to small samples the only probability known with certainty is the upper bound obtained from the Chebychev inequality.

For a random variable Z with zero mean and unit variance the univariate Chebychev inequality may be written:

$$\Pr[|Z|>D] \le \frac{1}{D^2}$$

where D is a positive constant. This gives an upper bound on the probability of $1/D^2$. For a t test statistic, in a circumstance in which we are uncertain if a t distribution is appropriate, an upper bound for the p-value is:

$$\frac{1}{t^2} \qquad \text{(the maximum is 1.0)}$$

For a sequence $\{Z_n\}$ for n=1, . . . , q the multivariate Chebychev inequality states:

$$\Pr[g(Z_n)>D] \le \frac{q}{D}$$

where g() is any non-negative continuous function. For a discussion, see Dhrymes [1978, pp. 382-384]. This result allows the computation of an upper bound for the p-value of a chi-square test statistic obtained from a joint hypothesis test.

The SHAZAM output below shows the results of a joint hypothesis test involving a non-linear function of the coefficients.

```
|_TEST
|_  TEST PRICE=-1
|_  TEST INCOME*PRICE=-1
|_END
F STATISTIC =    10.658128     WITH    2 AND   14 D.F.  P-VALUE=  .00154
WALD CHI-SQUARE STATISTIC =    21.316256     WITH    2 D.F.  P-VALUE=  .00002
UPPER BOUND ON P-VALUE BY CHEBYCHEV INEQUALITY =  .09383
```

The calculated chi-square statistic is 21.316256 and the reported p-value is 0.00002. This suggests rejection of the null hypothesis. But, with a small sample, we may be reluctant to rely on the asymptotic chi-square distribution. The Chebychev inequality yields an upper bound on the p-value as 2 / 21.316256 = 0.09383. Therefore, we do not reject the null hypothesis at a 5% level, but there is evidence to reject the null hypothesis at a 10% level.

CONFIDENCE INTERVALS

The **CONFID** command computes confidence intervals for coefficients from a previous estimation. The **CONFID** command can be used anywhere the **TEST** command can be used. In general, the format of the **CONFID** command is:

estimation   command
CONFID *coef1 coef2 ... / options*

where *coef1* and *coef2* are the names of coefficients and *options* is a list of available options. When only 2 coefficients are listed, the **CONFID** command will also compute a plot of the confidence ellipse. The available **PLOT** options (see the chapter *PLOTS*) are:

HOLD, NOBLANK, NOWIDE, SYMBOL, WIDE, XMAX=, XMIN=, YMAX= and **YMIN=**.

Other options available on the **CONFID** command are:

GNU   Prepares a **GNU**PLOT of the joint confidence region when 2
                    coefficients are specified. For more information on this option see the
                    GNUPLOT section in the *PLOTS* chapter. With the **GNU** option the
                    APPEND, AXIS, NOAXIS, OUTPUT=, DEVICE=, PORT= and
                    COMMFILE= options are also available as described for the **PLOT**
                    command.

GRAPHICS/ EGA/VGA/ HERCULES	Prepares a high quality plot of the joint confidence region when 2 coefficients are specified. The available **PLOT** options (see the chapter *PLOTS*) are: **GOAWAY, PAUSE, PRINT, XMAX=, XMIN=, YMAX=** and **YMIN=**.
NOFPLOT	Omits the joint confidence region plot when two coefficients are specified. This option would be used if you only wanted the individual confidence intervals for the coefficients.
NOMID	Omits the display of a symbol at the center of the confidence ellipse.
NORMAL	Specifies that the normal distribution rather than the t distribution should be used in computing confidence regions. Often, we only know that the coefficients are asymptotically normally distributed and the use of the t or F distribution would be inappropriate.
NOTPLOT	Omits the computation of the confidence intervals for individual coefficients. This might be used if only two coefficients were specified and you only want the joint confidence region plot (**FPLOT**). Normally, the individual confidence intervals are shown on the joint plot with a plus symbol (+) to show the outline of the confidence rectangle. The **NOTPLOT** option will suppress the drawing of the (+) symbol.
DF=	Specifies the degrees of freedom to use for obtaining 5% and 10% critical values from the t-distribution. With 2 coefficients this will be the denominator degrees of freedom for obtaining a 5% critical value from the F-distribution. The default setting is the degrees of freedom from the previous regression.
FCRIT=	Specifies the critical value from an F-distribution to be used for the joint confidence region plot. This option is similar to the **TCRIT=** option described below and is usually used to complement it. If the **FCRIT=** option is not specified a 5% critical value will be used.
POINTS=	SHAZAM usually constructs the confidence ellipse by evaluating the ellipse at approximately 200-205 points. The number used can be changed with this option if more or fewer points are desired to obtain a better looking plot.
TCRIT=	Specifies the t-distribution critical value for calculating confidence intervals. This value can be obtained from tables of the t-distribution or from output associated with use of the **DISTRIB** command. If this option is not specified then SHAZAM computes the critical values

for 90% and 95% confidence intervals. An example of the use of the **TCRIT=** option is given later in this chapter.

In some cases, users would like to compute the confidence region for coefficients that have been estimated in an earlier run and do not wish to re-estimate a model. This is possible for any set of two coefficients where you tell SHAZAM the estimated values of the coefficients, their estimated variances, and the covariance between the coefficients. In this case, the **CONFID** command does not need to follow an estimation command, but the following options *must* be included:

COEF1=   Specifies the coefficient estimate for the first coefficient you wish to plot. This coefficient will appear on the Y-axis of the plot.

COEF2=   Specifies the coefficient estimate for the second coefficient you wish to plot. This coefficient will appear on the X-axis of the plot.

COVAR12=   Specifies the estimated covariance between the two coefficients.

DF=   Specifies the number of degrees of freedom. This is typically (N–K). This option is also described above.

VAR1=   Specifies the estimated variance of the first coefficient.

VAR2=   Specifies the estimated variance of the second coefficient.

Interval Estimation for a Single Coefficient

The $100 \cdot (1-\alpha)\%$ confidence interval estimator for a coefficient β_k is:

$$\hat{\beta}_k \pm t_c \sqrt{V(\hat{\beta}_k)}$$

where t_c is the $\alpha/2$ critical value from a t-distribution with (N–K) degrees of freedom. SHAZAM sets values of t_c to give 95% and 90% confidence interval estimates. However, other values for t_c can be specified with the **TCRIT=** option on the **CONFID** command.

The next output shows the use of the **CONFID** command to compute interval estimates for the coefficients of the Theil textile demand equation.

```
|_OLS CONSUME INCOME PRICE
 OLS ESTIMATION
     17 OBSERVATIONS      DEPENDENT VARIABLE = CONSUME
...NOTE..SAMPLE RANGE SET TO:    1,   17
```

```
  R-SQUARE =      .9513      R-SQUARE ADJUSTED =     .9443
 VARIANCE OF THE ESTIMATE-SIGMA**2 =    30.951
 STANDARD ERROR OF THE ESTIMATE-SIGMA =    5.5634
 SUM OF SQUARED ERRORS-SSE=    433.31
 MEAN OF DEPENDENT VARIABLE =    134.51
 LOG OF THE LIKELIHOOD FUNCTION = -51.6471


 VARIABLE    ESTIMATED   STANDARD   T-RATIO              PARTIAL STANDARDIZED ELASTICITY
   NAME      COEFFICIENT   ERROR     14 DF    P-VALUE CORR. COEFFICIENT  AT MEANS
 INCOME       1.0617       .2667     3.981     .001   .729     .2387      .8129
 PRICE       -1.3830      .8381E-01 -16.50     .000  -.975    -.9893     -.7846
 CONSTANT    130.71       27.09      4.824     .000   .790     .0000      .9718

 |_CONFID INCOME PRICE CONSTANT
 USING 95% AND 90% CONFIDENCE INTERVALS

 CONFIDENCE INTERVALS BASED ON T-DISTRIBUTION WITH  14 D.F.
     - T CRITICAL VALUES =   2.145 AND   1.761
 NAME    LOWER 2.5%   LOWER 5%    COEFFICENT   UPPER 5%   UPPER 2.5% STD. ERROR
 INCOME     .4897       .5921      1.0617      1.531      1.634      .267
 PRICE    -1.563      -1.531      -1.3830     -1.235     -1.203      .084
 CONSTANT  72.59       82.99      130.71      178.4      188.8      27.094
```

The 95% interval estimate for the coefficient on *INCOME* is:

$$1.0617 \pm 2.145 \cdot 0.267 = [0.4897, 1.634]$$

Estimation of a Joint Confidence Region for Two Coefficients

Suppose β^* contains 2 coefficients from the β parameter vector and $V(\hat{\beta}^*)$ is a (2 x 2) sub-matrix of the full covariance matrix. A $100 \cdot (1-\alpha)\%$ confidence ellipse for β^* is the set of values that satisfies:

$$\frac{1}{2}(\hat{\beta}^* - \beta^*)'[V(\hat{\beta}^*)]^{-1}(\hat{\beta}^* - \beta^*) \leq F_c$$

where F_c is the α critical value from a F-distribution with (2,N–K) degrees of freedom. The rectangle that is formed by the two individual confidence intervals each with probability $1 - \alpha$ gives a confidence region with probability $\geq 1 - 2\alpha$ (see Theil [1971, p. 132]). SHAZAM sets F_c to give a 95% confidence ellipse. Other values for F_c can be set with the **FCRIT=** option.

The next example shows the use of the **CONFID** command to obtain a joint confidence region for the coefficients on the *INCOME* and *PRICE* variables from the Theil textile demand equation. Note that critical values are specified with the **TCRIT=** and **FCRIT=** options to give 99% interval estimates and a 99% confidence ellipse.

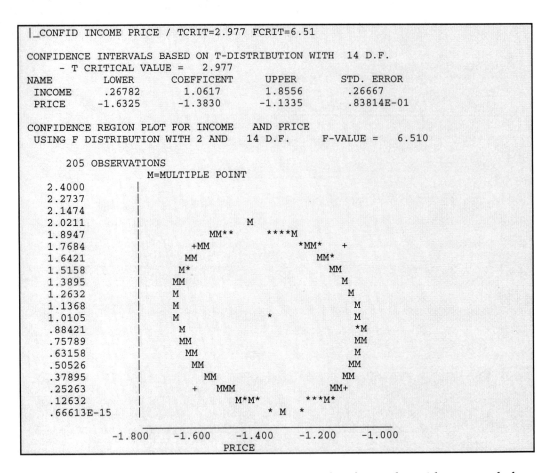

```
|_CONFID INCOME PRICE / TCRIT=2.977 FCRIT=6.51

CONFIDENCE INTERVALS BASED ON T-DISTRIBUTION WITH  14 D.F.
   - T CRITICAL VALUE =    2.977
NAME       LOWER       COEFFICENT       UPPER       STD. ERROR
 INCOME    .26782        1.0617         1.8556        .26667
 PRICE    -1.6325       -1.3830        -1.1335        .83814E-01

CONFIDENCE REGION PLOT FOR INCOME   AND PRICE
 USING F DISTRIBUTION WITH 2 AND   14 D.F.      F-VALUE =    6.510


     205 OBSERVATIONS
                    M=MULTIPLE POINT
    2.4000      |
    2.2737      |
    2.1474      |
    2.0211      |                          M
    1.8947      |          MM**        ****M
    1.7684      |         +MM            *MM*    +
    1.6421      |         MM              MM*
    1.5158      |        M*               MM
    1.3895      |        MM                M
    1.2632      |        M                 M
    1.1368      |        M                 M
    1.0105      |        M         *       M
    .88421      |         M                *M
    .75789      |        MM                MM
    .63158      |        MM                M
    .50526      |         MM               MM
    .37895      |          MM              MM
    .25263      |     +   MMM           MM+
    .12632      |            M*M*      ***M*
    .66613E-15  |              *  M   *
                _____
            -1.800    -1.600    -1.400    -1.200    -1.000
                                PRICE
```

The individual confidence intervals are shown on the above plot with a + symbol to show the outline of the confidence rectangle. The point estimate is displayed at the center of the confidence ellipse with the * symbol.

A GNUPLOT plot of the confidence ellipse can be obtained by specifying the **GNU** option on the **CONFID** command. This is illustrated in the next example. The example shows the use of the **CONFID** command after the **2SLS** command. The estimation is for the first equation of the Klein model (see the chapter *TWO STAGE LEAST SQUARES AND SYSTEMS OF EQUATIONS*). Since the 2SLS estimated coefficients are assumed to be asymptotically normally distributed and the small sample properties are unknown, the **NORMAL** option is specified. The **NOAXIS** option specifies to omit the vertical and horizontal lines drawn at 0. The SHAZAM commands are as follows:

```
SAMPLE 1 21
2SLS C PLAG P WGWP (WG T G TIME PLAG KLAG XLAG) / DN
CONFID PLAG P / NORMAL GNU NOAXIS
```

The SHAZAM output from the **CONFID** command is below.

```
|_CONFID PLAG P / NORMAL GNU NOAXIS
USING 95% AND 90% CONFIDENCE INTERVALS

CONFIDENCE INTERVALS BASED ON NORMAL DISTRIBUTION WITH
CRITICAL VALUES=   1.960 AND    1.645
NAME    LOWER 2.5%   LOWER 5%    COEFFICENT   UPPER 5%    UPPER 2.5%  STD. ERROR
PLAG       .5989E-02   .3978E-01   .21623       .3927       .4265       .107
P         -.2141      -.1769       .17302E-01   .2115       .2487       .118
CONFIDENCE REGION PLOT FOR PLAG      AND P
USING CHI-SQUARE DISTRIBUTION WITH CRITICAL VALUE=    5.990
```

The plot of the joint confidence region follows. The point estimate in the center of the confidence ellipse is marked at "x".

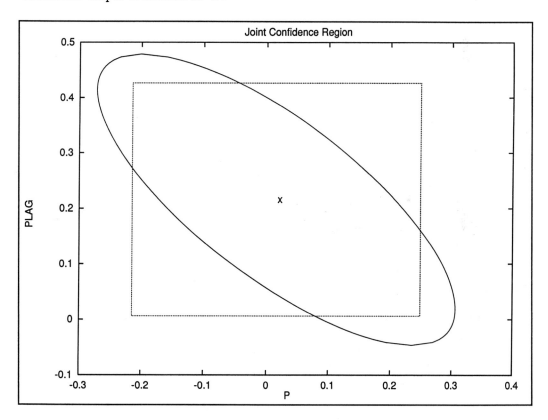

9. INEQUALITY RESTRICTIONS

"However, inequality constrained linear regression is not an option of any of the more popular econometrics software packages. Many practitioners may lack the gall (if not the resources) to determine the solution using ordinary least squares regression packages."

John Geweke, 1986

The **BAYES** command provides a procedure for estimation with inequality restrictions. The methodology is described in Geweke [1986]; Judge, Hill, Griffiths, Lütkepohl and Lee [1988, Chapter 20]; and Chalfant, Gray and White [1991]. The idea is to compute Bayes estimates as the mean of the truncated multivariate t posterior. Suppose that unrestricted estimation gives parameter estimates $\hat{\beta}$ with a variance-covariance estimate $V(\hat{\beta})$. The method uses a Monte Carlo numerical integration procedure that is implemented by generating replications from a multivariate t distribution. At replication i draw the vector w_i from a $N(0, V(\hat{\beta}))$ distribution and draw z_i from a χ^2 distribution with v degrees freedom (for the linear regression model, v=N–K). Then compute the replication:

$$\beta_i^A = \hat{\beta} + w_i / \sqrt{z_i^2 / v}$$

The antithetic replication is computed as:

$$\beta_i^B = \hat{\beta} - w_i / \sqrt{z_i^2 / v}$$

The antithetic replication simply changes the sign to essentially give an additional replication at low cost and ensuring a symmetric distribution (see Geweke [1988] for further details). The inequality constrained estimates and standard errors are reported as the mean and standard deviation of the values that satisfy the inequality restrictions.

Suppose that R is the number of replications and s is the number that satisfy the restrictions. On the SHAZAM output the PROPORTION is computed as $\hat{p} = s / R$ and this gives the probability that the restrictions are true. The NUMERICAL STANDARD ERROR OF PROPORTION (a standard error for numerical accuracy) is computed as $\sqrt{\hat{p}(1-\hat{p}) / R}$. The column with the label NUMERICAL SE is the standard deviation of the mean computed as the standard deviation divided by $\sqrt{s}$.

The method is computer intensive and initial experimentation with relatively few replications is recommended. Different machines will yield different results due to the machine differences in random number generation. The **SET RANFIX** command can be used to ensure the same set of random numbers in repeated runs.

BAYES *COMMAND OPTIONS*

In general, the format for estimation with inequality restrictions is:

estimation   command
BAYES / *options* **NSAMP=**
RESTRICT *inequality   restriction*

. . .

END

where *options* is a list of options and **NSAMP=** is the number of replications. The **NSAMP=** option is required. The **BAYES** command must follow an estimation command such as **OLS**. The **BAYES** command is followed by **RESTRICT** commands that specify the inequality restrictions, and an **END** command. The inequality restrictions must use one of the operators .LT., .LE., .GT. or .GE.. The inequality restrictions can be linear or non-linear.

The available options on the **BAYES** command are:

NOANTITHET   Omits the **ANTITHETIC** replications.

NORMAL   Assumes the coefficients are normally distributed rather than t distributed.

PSIGMA   Prints the ORIGINAL COVARIANCE MATRIX ESTIMATE and the NUMERICAL COVARIANCE MATRIX. The latter is computed as:

$$\frac{1}{R}\sum_{i=1}^{R} w_i w_i'$$

DF=   Specifies the degrees of freedom for the t distribution. The default setting is N–K.

NSAMP=   Specifies the number of replications. The **NSAMP=** option is required. This should be a small number (for example 100), while the user is experimenting. Readers of the Geweke article will realize that **NSAMP=** is often very high.

OUTUNIT=   Specifies an output unit number to write all the replicated coefficients that satisfy the inequality restrictions. The output unit should be assigned with the SHAZAM **FILE** command or an operating systems command. If **NSAMP=** is a large number the resulting file could be quite large.

EXAMPLES

Linear Regression with Inequality Restrictions

This example of the **BAYES** command uses the rental data set of Pindyck and Rubinfeld [1991, Table 2.1, p. 43] that is also analyzed in the Geweke [1986] article.

```
|_SAMPLE 1 32
|_READ RENT NO RM S DUM
   5 VARIABLES AND        32 OBSERVATIONS STARTING AT OBS        1
|_GENR Y=RENT/NO
|_GENR R=RM/NO
|_GENR SR=S*R
|_GENR OSR=(1-S)*R
|_GENR SD=S*DUM
|_GENR OSD=(1-S)*DUM
|_GENR ONE=1
|_* Run OLS. This gives results from column 1 of Geweke's Table II.
|_DISPLAY CPUTIME
CPUTIME     1.9990
|_OLS Y SR OSR SD OSD
OLS ESTIMATION
      32 OBSERVATIONS      DEPENDENT VARIABLE = Y


  R-SQUARE =    .4525    R-SQUARE ADJUSTED =    .3713
VARIANCE OF THE ESTIMATE-SIGMA**2 =   1395.5
STANDARD ERROR OF THE ESTIMATE-SIGMA =   37.356
SUM OF SQUARED ERRORS-SSE=   37678.
MEAN OF DEPENDENT VARIABLE =   138.17
LOG OF THE LIKELIHOOD FUNCTION = -158.544


VARIABLE   ESTIMATED   STANDARD   T-RATIO           PARTIAL STANDARDIZED ELASTICITY
  NAME     COEFFICIENT   ERROR     27 DF    P-VALUE CORR. COEFFICIENT  AT MEANS
SR         103.55       38.47      2.692    .012   .460   1.0083        .2264
OSR        122.04       37.36      3.267    .003   .532   1.1597        .5290
SD         3.3151       1.961      1.690    .102   .309    .3463        .0555
OSD        -1.1535      .5714      -2.019   .054  -.362   -.3480       -.0900
CONSTANT   38.562       32.22      1.197    .242   .224    .0000        .2791

|_DISPLAY CPUTIME
CPUTIME      2.6660
|_* Now use Geweke's method to impose inequality restrictions, and then
|_* run 1000 trials including antithetic replications.
|_* This will give results similar to column 3 of Geweke's Table II.
|_BAYES / NSAMP=1000
BAYESIAN (GEWEKE) INEQUALITY CONSTRAINED ESTIMATION
|_RESTRICT SR.GT.0
|_RESTRICT OSR.GT.0
|_RESTRICT SD.LT.0
|_RESTRICT OSD.LT.0
|_END
NUMBER OF INEQUALITY RESTRICTIONS =    4
NUMBER OF COEFFICIENTS=  5
NUMBER OF REPLICATIONS=      1000
ANTITHETIC REPLICATIONS ALSO INCLUDED
```

```
DEGREES OF FREEDOM FOR T DISTRIBUTION =        27
ORIGINAL COEFFICIENT ESTIMATES
   103.55288488897    122.03844729025   3.3151457566017  -1.1535408341482
   38.562062754257
      2000 REPLICATIONS        103 SATISFIED
PROPORTION= 0.05150 NUMERICAL STANDARD ERROR OF PROPORTION= 0.00494
VARIABLE  AVERAGE        STDEV        VARIANCE       NUMERICAL SE
SR         144.35        37.927       1438.5         3.7371
OSR        127.76        40.956       1677.4         4.0355
SD        -0.85167       0.83910      0.70410        0.82679E-01
OSD       -1.1220        0.58368      0.34069        0.57512E-01
CONSTANT   32.519        36.115       1304.3         3.5585
|_DISPLAY CPUTIME
CPUTIME      17.766
|_* Now attempt to impose the restrictions directly using the trick
|_* of squaring a coefficient to force it to be positive. This requires
|_* nonlinear estimation.
|_* This gives results similar to column 2 of Geweke's Table II.
|_NL 1 / NC=5
|_EQ Y=A + (B**2)*SR + (C**2)*OSR - (D**2)*SD - (E**2)*OSD
|_END
   5 VARIABLES IN  1 EQUATIONS WITH  5 COEFFICIENTS
      32 OBSERVATIONS


COEFFICIENT STARTING VALUES
A        1.0000      B       1.0000     C        1.0000
D        1.0000      E       1.0000
    100 MAXIMUM ITERATIONS, CONVERGENCE = 0.000010
INITIAL STATISTICS :
TIME =    0.733 SEC.   ITER. NO.    0    FUNCT. EVALUATIONS     1
LOG-LIKELIHOOD FUNCTION=  -207.0281
COEFFICIENTS
   1.000000      1.000000      1.000000      1.000000      1.000000
GRADIENT
 -0.1960723   -0.1349835   -0.2307822   1.165898   4.093769


FINAL STATISTICS :

TIME =    8.583 SEC.   ITER. NO.   33   FUNCT. EVALUATIONS   45
LOG-LIKELIHOOD FUNCTION=  -160.1530
COEFFICIENTS
   37.63371     11.40220     11.09239     0.8808439E-08  -1.073957
GRADIENT
 -0.6039829E-09 -0.4895324E-08 -0.1394745E-07  0.1627280E-07 -0.6853604E-07

MAXIMUM LIKELIHOOD ESTIMATE OF SIGMA-SQUARED =    1302.0

       COEFFICIENT    ST. ERROR   T-RATIO
A       37.634        30.255      1.2439
B       11.402        1.4500      7.8637
C       11.092        1.5915      6.9697
D       0.88084E-08   0.72146     0.12209E-07
E      -1.0740        0.25274     -4.2492
|_END
|_* The estimated coefficients are found by squaring each
|_* of the parameters. The TEST command can do this.
|_* The only interesting parts of the TEST output are the
|_* parts labeled 'TEST VALUE' and 'STD. ERROR OF TEST VALUE'
```

```
|_* which are the estimated coefficients we want.
|_* Be careful when using these standard errors.  For details
|_* see Lafontaine and White, "Obtaining Any Wald Statistic
|_* You Want", Economics Letters, 1986.
|_TEST B**2
TEST VALUE =    130.01     STD. ERROR OF TEST VALUE   33.066
T STATISTIC =    3.9318297    WITH    32 D.F.
F STATISTIC =   15.459285     WITH    1 AND   32 D.F.
WALD CHI-SQUARE STATISTIC =   15.459285     WITH    1 D.F.
|_TEST C**2
TEST VALUE =    123.04     STD. ERROR OF TEST VALUE   35.308
T STATISTIC =    3.4848358    WITH    32 D.F.
F STATISTIC =   12.144080     WITH    1 AND   32 D.F.
WALD CHI-SQUARE STATISTIC =   12.144080     WITH    1 D.F.
|_TEST -(D**2)
TEST VALUE = -0.77589E-16 STD. ERROR OF TEST VALUE  0.12710E-07
T STATISTIC = -0.61046306E-08 WITH    32 D.F.
F STATISTIC =  0.37266515E-16 WITH    1 AND   32 D.F.
WALD CHI-SQUARE STATISTIC =  0.37266515E-16 WITH    1 D.F.
|_TEST -(E**2)
TEST VALUE =   -1.1534     STD. ERROR OF TEST VALUE  0.54287
T STATISTIC =   -2.1245979    WITH    32 D.F.
F STATISTIC =   4.5139163     WITH    1 AND   32 D.F.
WALD CHI-SQUARE STATISTIC =   4.5139163     WITH    1 D.F.
|_DISPLAY CPUTIME
 CPUTIME     27.650
```

The resulting coefficient estimates satisfy the inequality constraints specified. However, in this example, the probability that the restrictions are true is only .0515. Users should be familiar with the Geweke paper before spending a large amount of computer time with the **BAYES** command. Note, that even with only 1000 replications the time required for the **BAYES** command is high. For example, on a VAX 750 computer unconstrained OLS took only 0.67 seconds of CPUTIME, while the BAYES procedure took 15.1 seconds and the constrained nonlinear procedure took 9.9 seconds. Note, however that only 1000 replications were done on the BAYES procedure here, and Geweke used from 10,000 to 250,000 in his examples. Bayesian inequality regression comes at a relatively high price, but SHAZAM makes it as painless as possible.

Seemingly Unrelated Regression with Inequality Restrictions

This example considers the estimation of firm investment relations using the data set in Judge, Hill, Griffiths, Lütkepohl and Lee [1988, Table 11.1, p. 453] (from an article by Boot and Dewitt and discussed by Theil). Data is available for General Electric and Westinghouse on investment (*IGE, IWH*), market value (*VGE, VWH*) and capital stock (*KGE, KWH*). Consider estimation of the system:

$$IGE = \beta_{11} + \beta_{12}VGE + \beta_{13}KGE + \varepsilon_1$$
$$IWH = \beta_{21} + \beta_{22}VWH + \beta_{23}KWH + \varepsilon_2$$

subject to the inequality restrictions $\beta_{12} > 0$, $\beta_{13} > 0$, $\beta_{22} > 0$,   and $\beta_{23} > 0$.

The commands that follow show how to set-up the estimation in SHAZAM. The **SET RANFIX** command is used to ensure the same random numbers in repeated runs. The **SYSTEM** command is used to obtain seemingly unrelated regression estimates. Note that when this is combined with the **BAYES** command the variable names should be different across equations. If the same variable is used across equations then the **GENR** command can be used to create a duplicate variable with a different name. With the **SYSTEM** command, SHAZAM saves the coefficients and variance-covariance matrix in a form that does not include the intercept terms. Therefore, if inequality restrictions on the intercept terms are required then a constant term must be generated and included as a variable and the **NOCONSTANT** option must then be specified on the **SYSTEM** command.

The **BAYES** command in this example specifies the **NORMAL** option. This may be appropriate when the estimation procedure is not OLS. If the **NORMAL** option is not used then the **DF=** option can be used to set the degrees of freedom for the t distribution. The **NSAMP=** option requests 5000 replications. SHAZAM will then generate 5000 antithetic pairs to effectively give 10,000 replications.

```
SET RANFIX
SAMPLE 1 20
READ (TABLE11.1) IGE VGE KGE IWH VWH KWH
SYSTEM 2 / DN
OLS IGE   VGE KGE
OLS IWH   VWH KWH
BAYES / NORMAL NSAMP=5000
RESTRICT VGE.GT.0
RESTRICT KGE.GT.0
RESTRICT VWH.GT.0
RESTRICT KWH.GT.0
END
STOP
```

10. ARIMA MODELS

"The end of the decline of the Stock Market will ... probably not be long, only a few more days at most."

Irving Fisher, Economist
November 14, 1929

The **ARIMA** command provides features for the Box-Jenkins approach (see Box and Jenkins [1976]) to the analysis of AutoRegressive Integrated Moving Average models of univariate time series. SHAZAM uses a modified version of programs written by Charles Nelson and described in Nelson [1973]. Other references are Harvey [1981]; Judge, Griffiths, Hill, Lütkepohl and Lee [1985, Chapter 7] and Griffiths, Hill and Judge [1993, Chapter 20]. The **ARIMA** command has three stages. The identification stage reports the sample autocorrelation function and the sample partial autocorrelation function that can be inspected to determine a specification for an ARIMA model. The estimation stage estimates the parameters of an ARIMA model and gives diagnostic tests for checking the model adequacy. The Box-Jenkins method is to repeat the identification and estimation stage until a suitable model is found. The forecasting stage provides point forecasts and confidence intervals.

In general, the format of the **ARIMA** command is:

ARIMA *var / options*

where *var* is a time series variable and *options* is a list of desired options. The options specified determine the stage as identification, estimation or forecasting.

IDENTIFICATION

For a time series z_t, $t=1, \ldots, N$ with sample mean $\bar{z}$ the sample autocovariances are:

$$c_j = \frac{1}{N} \sum_{t=j+1}^{N} \left[(z_t - \bar{z})(z_{t-j} - \bar{z}) \right] \quad j=0, 1, 2, \ldots$$

The sample autocorrelations are:

$$r_j = c_j / c_0 \qquad j = 1, 2, \ldots$$

A plot of the r_j gives the sample correlogram. If the order of the moving average process is q then the distribution of r_j for $j>q$ is approximately normal with zero mean and variance (Bartlett's formula):

$$\left(1 + 2\sum_{j=1}^{q} r_j^2\right) / N$$

The partial autocorrelations give information about the order of an autoregressive process. The jth partial autocorrelation coefficient is the estimated coefficient of z_{t-p} from a pth order autoregressive model with p=j. SHAZAM computes these by Durbin's recursive method (further discussion of this method is given at the end of this section). If the autoregressive order is p the higher order partial autocorrelations are approximately normally distributed with zero mean and standard deviation $1/\sqrt{N}$.

A test for a white noise process is given by the Ljung-Box-Pierce (see Box and Pierce [1970] and Ljung and Box [1978]) portmanteau test statistic. This test is constructed from the first J squared autocorrelations as:

$$Q = N(N+2) \sum_{j=1}^{J} \frac{1}{N-j} r_j^2$$

The choice of J is arbitrary (see, for example, the discussion in Harvey [1981, p. 148]). For a white noise process Q has an asymptotic χ_J^2 distribution.

For a stationary time series the correlogram function will decline at higher lags. If the correlogram shows slow decay this gives evidence for nonstationarity. Differencing is a technique to transform a nonstationary time series to a stationary process. The backward operator B is defined by:

$$B^d z_t = z_{t-d}$$

The first difference of z_t is given by $(1-B)z_t$ and the second difference is:

$$(1-B)^2 z_t = (z_t - z_{t-1}) - (z_{t-1} - z_{t-2})$$

When s is the number of periods in the seasonal cycle the first seasonal difference is:

$$(1-B^s)z_t = z_t - z_{t-s}$$

The general differencing transformation to consider is:

$$(1-B)^d (1-B^s)^D z_t$$

where d is the order of differencing and D is the order of seasonal differencing.

ARIMA *Identification Stage Command Options*

The following options are available in the identification stage of the **ARIMA** command:

ALL	Computes the time series properties for **ALL** orders of differencing up to the values specified with **NDIFF=** and **NSDIFF=**.
IAC	Computes inverse autocorrelations as described in Cleveland [1972]. The number of lags is as specified with the **NLAG=** option (the maximum is 20).
GNU	Prepares **GNUPLOT** plots for the **PLOTAC, PLOTDATA**, and **PLOTPAC** options. For more information on this option see the *GNUPLOT* section in the *PLOTS* chapter. With the **GNU** option the **APPEND, OUTPUT=, DEVICE=, PORT=** and **COMMFILE=** options are also available as described for the **PLOT** command.
LOG	Takes logs of the data.
PLOTAC	Plots the sample autocorrelation function. The number of lags is specified with the **NLAG=** option. The + symbols mark ± 2 standard errors to give an approximate 95% confidence interval for the autocorrelations.
PLOTDATA	Plots the data. If the **LOG, NDIFF=** or **NSDIFF=** options are used then the plot is of the transformed data.
PLOTPAC	Plots the sample partial autocorrelation function. The number of lags is specified with the **NLAGP=** option. The + symbols mark ± 2 standard errors to give an approximate 95% confidence interval for the partial autocorrelations.
WIDE **NOWIDE**	Sets the output width. **NOWIDE** uses 80 columns and **WIDE** uses 120 columns.
ACF=	Saves the sample AutoCorrelation Function in the variable specified.
BEG= **END=**	Sets the sample period. This option overrides the **SAMPLE** command. The values may be given as an observation number or as a date.
NDIFF=	Specifies the order of differencing to transform the data.

NLAG=　　　　Specifies the number of lags to consider in the calculation of the autocorrelations. The default is 24.

NLAGP=　　　Specifies the number of lags to consider in the calculation of the partial autocorrelations. The default is 12. (The value for **NLAGP=** must not exceed that for **NLAG=**).

NSDIFF=　　　Specifies the order of seasonal differencing. If this is specified then **NSPAN=** must be set.

NSPAN=　　　Specifies the number of periods in the seasonal cycle. For example, set **NSPAN=4** for quarterly data and **NSPAN=12** for monthly data.

PACF=　　　　Saves the sample Partial AutoCorrelation Function in the variable specified.

TESTSTAT=　Saves the Ljung-Box-Pierce statistics in the variable specified.

After the **ARIMA** identification command the temporary variables available are $ERR (error code) and $N (number of observations used in the identification phase). For more information on temporary variables see the chapter *MISCELLANEOUS COMMANDS AND INFORMATION* and the chapter *ORDINARY LEAST SQUARES*.

Example

The **ARIMA** command can be illustrated with the Theil textile data set (although a larger sample size is desirable). The output below gives the results from the ARIMA identification stage for the variable *CONSUME*.

```
|_ARIMA CONSUME / NLAG=8 NLAGP=8 PLOTAC PLOTPAC
      IDENTIFICATION SECTION - VARIABLE=CONSUME
NUMBER OF AUTOCORRELATIONS =    8
NUMBER OF PARTIAL AUTOCORRELATIONS =    8


             0      0 0
SERIES  (1-B) (1-B  )  CONSUME

  NET NUMBER OF OBSERVATIONS =    17
MEAN=    134.51       VARIANCE=    555.89     STANDARD DEV.=    23.577

  LAGS                      AUTOCORRELATIONS                    STD ERR
  1  -8      .72  .53  .42  .21  .16  .04 -.18 -.29                 .24

MODIFIED BOX-PIERCE (LJUNG-BOX-PIERCE) STATISTICS  (CHI-SQUARE)
    LAG     Q    DF  P-VALUE       LAG    Q    DF  P-VALUE
      1   10.59   1   .001          5   22.43   5   .000
      2   16.64   2   .000          6   22.48   6   .001
      3   20.64   3   .000          7   23.53   7   .001
      4   21.74   4   .000          8   26.51   8   .001
```

```
   LAGS                    PARTIAL AUTOCORRELATIONS                  STD ERR
   1   -8      .72   .01   .06 -.24   .17 -.22 -.26 -.12                .24

                                               0      0 0
AUTOCORRELATION FUNCTION OF THE SERIES     (1-B) (1-B  )  CONSUME

   1   .72 .                    +           RRRRRRRRRRRRRRRRRRRRRRRRRRRR
   2   .53 .           +                    RRRRRRRRRRRRRRRRRRRRR       +
   3   .42 .      +                         RRRRRRRRRRRRRRRR                +
   4   .21 .   +                            RRRRRRRR                          +
   5   .16 . +                              RRRRR                            +
   6   .04 . +                              RR                               +
   7  -.18 . +                          RRRRRRR                              +
   8  -.29 . +                      RRRRRRRRRR                               +

                                               0      0 0
PARTIAL AUTOCORRELATION FUNCTION OF THE SERIES   (1-B) (1-B  )  CONSUME

   1   .72 .                    +           RRRRRRRRRRRRRRRRRRRRRRRRRRRR
   2   .01 .                    +           R                   +
   3   .06 .                    +           RRR                 +
   4  -.24 .                    +       RRRRRRRR                 +
   5   .17 .                    +           RRRRRR               +
   6  -.22 .                    +       RRRRRRRR                 +
   7  -.26 .                    +       RRRRRRRRR                +
   8  -.12 .                    +           RRRR                 +      .
```

The correlogram shows that the sample autocorrelation function declines at higher lags to indicate a stationary process. Some judgement is required to determine a model specification that may describe this data. For example, to consider the suitability of an ARMA(1,1) process, the above results can be compared with theoretical patterns of autocorrelations and partial correlations of ARMA(1,1) processes that are given in Judge, Hill, Griffiths, Lütkepohl and Lee [1988, pp.698-699]. (More formal tests of stationarity are available in the chapter *COINTEGRATION AND UNIT ROOT TESTS*).

A Note on Calculating the Partial Autocorrelation Function

The partial autocorrelation function is approximated by a computationally fast recursive method of calculation described in Box and Jenkins [1976, Appendix A3.2, pp.82-84]. Box-Jenkins comment that "these estimates of the partial autocorrelations differ somewhat from the maximum likelihood values obtained by fitting autoregressive processes of successively higher order. They are very sensitive to rounding errors particularly when the process approaches nonstationarity." The potential for rounding error can be illustrated with monthly data on the 3-month treasury bill rate used in Pindyck and Rubinfeld [1991, Chapter 15]. The evidence is that the series is non-stationary but first differencing yields a stationary time series. The following SHAZAM commands first save the partial autocorrelation function generated by the **ARIMA** command in the variable *PACREC*. Then a set of SHAZAM commands computes the partial autocorrelation function by an exact method and saves the result in the variable *PACOLS*. This is then repeated for the first differences. The commands show SHAZAM features described in the chapter *PROGRAMMING IN SHAZAM*.

```
SAMPLE 1 462
ARIMA TBILL / NLAGP=6 PACF=PACREC
DIM PACOLS 6 BETA 6   PACDOLS 6
DO #=1,6
* Use ? to request no listing of OLS results
?OLS TBILL TBILL(1.#) / COEF=BETA
GEN1 PACOLS:#=BETA:#
ENDO
*
* Now analyze the first differences
ARIMA TBILL / NLAGP=6 PACF=PACDREC NDIFF=1
SAMPLE 2 462
GENR TBILLD=TBILL-LAG(TBILL)
DO #=1,6
?OLS TBILLD TBILLD(1.#) / COEF=BETA
GEN1 PACDOLS:#=BETA:#
ENDO
* Compare the results
SAMPLE 1 6
PRINT PACOLS PACREC PACDOLS PACDREC
```

The following output shows the numerical differences between the two computational methods. The variables *PACDOLS* and *PACDREC* are similar to show that the recursive approximation of the partial autocorrelation function is accurate for the first differences of the *TBILL* time series.

```
|_PRINT PACOLS PACREC PACDOLS PACDREC
      PACOLS            PACREC            PACDOLS           PACDREC
    .9853103          .9849570          .3211617          .3210678
   -.3292023         -.2853001         -.2370160         -.2369215
    .2268389          .1769929      -.1309987E-02     -.1195264E-02
  -.6588303E-02       .1690129E-01     -.2410939E-01    -.2402593E-01
    .1629670E-01      .5984347E-02      .2512562E-01     .2511988E-01
   -.3295990E-01     -.2934607E-01     -.2968467        -.2964889
```

ESTIMATION

A simple example of a time series model is the ARMA(1,1) process given by:

$$z_t - \phi_1 z_{t-1} = u_t - \theta_1 u_{t-1} + \delta$$

where u_t is a random error and the unknown parameters are ϕ_1, θ_1 and δ. To generalize this define polynomials in the backward operator as follows:

$$\phi(B) = 1 - \phi_1 B - ... - \phi_p B^p$$

and $\theta(B) = 1 - \theta_1 B - ... - \theta_q B^q$

where p is the order of the autoregressive process and q is the order of the moving average process.   The ARIMA(p, d, q) model has the form:

$$\phi(B)(1-B)^d z_t = \theta(B) u_t + \delta$$

Note that some authors define lag polynomials with opposite signs from that used here. Therefore, the computer output must be interpreted carefully.

A feature of economic time series is serial correlation at the seasonal lag. Seasonality can be modelled by defining the polynomials:

$$\Gamma(B^s) = 1 - \Gamma_1 B^s - ... - \Gamma_P B^{sP}$$

and $\Delta(B^s) = 1 - \Delta_1 B^s - ... - \Delta_Q B^{sQ}$

where P is the order of the seasonal AR process and Q is the order of the seasonal MA process. The multiplicative seasonal ARIMA model has the general form:

$$\Gamma(B^s)\,\phi(B)(1-B)^d(1-B^s)^D z_t = \Delta(B^s)\,\theta(B) u_t + \delta$$

Let $\beta' = [\phi'\ \theta'\ \Gamma'\ \Delta'\ \delta]$ be a   Kx1   vector of the model parameters where K=p+q+P+Q+1. Parameter estimates are obtained as the values that minimize the sum of squares function:

$$S(\beta) = \sum_{t=1}^{N} u_t(\beta)^2$$

A pure autoregressive model can be estimated by OLS (see the chapter *DISTRIBUTED LAG MODELS*). The inclusion of seasonal and moving average components means that nonlinear estimation methods are required.   The ARIMA estimation uses a version of Marquardt's algorithm [1963]. Each iteration uses a gradient estimate that is calculated by numerical approximation. Let $\hat{\beta}^{(i)}$ be the parameter estimates at iteration i. The following approximation is used:

$$\frac{\partial u_t}{\partial \beta_k}\left(\hat{\beta}^{(i)}\right) \approx \left[u_t\left(\hat{\beta}^{(i)} + h_k\,e_k\right) - u_t\left(\hat{\beta}^{(i)}\right)\right] / h_k \qquad \text{for } k = 1, ..., K$$

where e_k is a Kx1 zero vector with 1 in the kth element and $h_k = h\hat{\beta}_k^{(i)}$ where the scalar h is referred to as the step length. In SHAZAM h can be specified with the **STEPSIZE=** option and the default value is h=.01.

At each iteration the residuals are computed recursively. Presample values are required to start the recursion. The ARIMA estimation computes the presample values by a back-forecasting method. The treatment of presample values means that the parameter estimates from the **ARIMA** command will be different from estimates obtained with the **OLS** or **AUTO** SHAZAM commands (where applicable).

The ARIMA nonlinear estimation converges when one of two convergence criteria is met. The first criteria is based on the relative change in each parameter and requires:

$$\left|\hat{\beta}_k^{(i)} - \hat{\beta}_k^{(i-1)}\right| \,/\, \left|\hat{\beta}_k^{(i)}\right| < .0001 \qquad \text{for all k}$$

The second convergence criteria is based on the relative change in the sum of squares and requires:

$$\left|S\left(\hat{\beta}^{(i)}\right) - S\left(\hat{\beta}^{(i-1)}\right)\right| \,/\, S\left(\hat{\beta}^{(i-1)}\right) < .000001$$

As in any non-linear optimization, convergence to a global minimum is not guaranteed and the choice of good starting values is important. If the parameter estimates move into unacceptable regions then SHAZAM may terminate with overflow errors. If this occurs then the estimation can be restarted with different starting values or a different model specification. Users should carefully check their output for evidence of model convergence.

The variance of the estimated residuals (reported as SIGMA**2 on the SHAZAM output) is calculated as:

$$\hat{\sigma}_u^2 = \frac{1}{N-K} \sum_{t=1}^{N} u_t(\hat{\beta})^2$$

If the **DN** option on the **ARIMA** command is used then the divisor is N instead of (N-K). The variance-covariance matrix of the parameter estimates is estimated as:

$$\hat{\sigma}_u^2 \left(X_{\hat{\beta}}' X_{\hat{\beta}}\right)^{-1}$$

where the individual elements of the X matrix are:

$$x_{kt} = -\frac{\partial u_t}{\partial \beta_k}(\hat{\beta})$$

The calculation of the X matrix uses numerical derivatives as described above.

Following model estimation the SHAZAM output reports a number of statistics that are useful for evaluating the model adequacy. The Ljung-Box-Pierce statistic (see the identification stage) is constructed from the squared autocorrelations of the estimated residuals. This gives a test for white noise errors. With J lagged residual autocorrelations the test statistic can be compared with a χ^2_{J-K+1} distribution. If there is no constant term in the model (when the **NOCONSTANT** option is used) then the test statistic has an approximate χ^2_{J-K} distribution under the null hypothesis of white noise errors.

For model selection purposes the Akaike information criterion (AIC) and the Schwarz criterion (SC) are computed as follows:

$$AIC(K) = \log\left(\hat{\sigma}^2_u\right) + 2 \cdot K / N$$

$$SC(K) = \log\left(\hat{\sigma}^2_u\right) + K\log(N)/N$$

For the differenced series $y_t = (1-B)^d(1-B^s)^D z_t$ the cross-covariances between y_t and the estimated residuals $\hat{u}_{t-j}$ are:

$$c_{(y\hat{u})j} = \frac{1}{N}\sum_{t=j+1}^{N}(y_t - \bar{y})(\hat{u}_{t-j} - \bar{u}) \qquad j = 0, \pm 1, \pm 2, \ldots$$

where $\qquad \bar{y} = \frac{1}{N}\sum_{t=1}^{N} y_t \qquad$ and $\qquad \bar{u} = \frac{1}{N}\sum_{t=1}^{N}\hat{u}_t$

The cross-correlations are computed as:

$$r_{(y\hat{u})j} = c_{(y\hat{u})j} / \sqrt{c_{(yy)0}c_{(\hat{u}\hat{u})0}} \qquad j = 0, \pm 1, \pm 2, \ldots$$

The theoretical u_t are correlated with current and future values of y_t but are not correlated with past values. The estimated cross-correlations reported on the SHAZAM output can be inspected to see if they exhibit such a pattern.

ARIMA *Estimation Stage Command Options*

In general, the format of the **ARIMA** command for the estimation stage is:

ARIMA *var* / **NAR**= **NMA**= *options*

where *var* is a time series variable and *options* is a list of desired options. The options as described for the identification stage are:

LOG, WIDE/NOWIDE, BEG=, END=, NDIFF=, and **NSDIFF=.**

Options described for the **OLS** command that may be used are:

ANOVA, PCOR, PCOV, COV=, STDERR=, and **TRATIO=.**

Other options are:

DN	Uses a divisor of N instead of (N–K) when estimating SIGMA**2.
GNU	Prepares a **GNUPLOT** plot of the residuals. For more information on this option see the *GNUPLOT* section in the *PLOTS* chapter. With the **GNU** option the **APPEND, OUTPUT=, DEVICE=, PORT=** and **COMMFILE=** options are also available as described for the **PLOT** command.
NOCONSTANT	Excludes the constant term.
PITER	Prints the parameter estimates and the value of the sum of squares function at every iteration. By default only the results at the final iteration are listed.
PLOTRES	Plots the residuals.
RESTRICT	Uses zero starting values as zero restrictions. Also see the **START** and **START=** options. For example, with a quarterly time series *IINV*, an AR(5) process with zero coefficients for the 2nd and 3rd autoregressive coefficients may be estimated with the commands:

```
ARIMA IINV / NAR=5 START RESTRICT BEG=1950.1 END=1985.4
.5   0   0   .1   .1   5
```

START	Indicates that parameter starting values are entered on the line immediately following the **ARIMA** command. This option will not

work when the **ARIMA** command is in a **DO**-loop. Also see the **START=** option below.

ACF=   Saves the AutoCorrelation Function of the estimated residuals in the variable specified.

COEF=   Saves the estimated Coefficients in the variable specified. These values can be used as input to the **ARIMA** forecasting stage. This option should not be confused with the **COEF=** option used in the forecasting stage. In the estimation stage **COEF=** saves the coefficients while, in the forecasting stage, the **COEF=** option uses the coefficients as input parameters.

ITER=   Sets the maximum number of iterations. The default is 50. If this iteration limit is exceeded it may be sensible to try different starting values or a different model specification.

NAR=   Specifies the order of the AR (autoregressive) process.

NMA=   Specifies the order of the MA (moving average) process.

NSAR=   Specifies the order of the Seasonal AR process. If this is specified then **NSPAN=** must be set.

NSMA=   Specifies the order of the Seasonal MA process. If this is specified then **NSPAN=** must be set.

NSPAN=   Specifies the number of periods in the seasonal cycle. For example, set **NSPAN=4** for quarterly data and **NSPAN=12** for monthly data.

PREDICT=   Saves the Predicted values in the variable specified. These are the implied one-step-ahead forecasts.

RESID=   Saves the estimated Residuals in the variable specified.

START=   Specifies a vector of starting values. The input sequence for the starting values must correspond to **NAR=**, **NMA=**, **NSAR=**, and **NSMA=** with the constant term given as the last value. The calculation of numeric derivatives means that zero starting values can cause problems in starting the iterations. Therefore, SHAZAM sets a zero value to 0.01 to get the iterations started. Also see the **RESTRICT** option above.

STEPSIZE=   Specifies the stepsize to use in calculating the numeric derivatives. The default value is 0.01. The estimated covariance matrix of the parameter estimates may be sensitive to this value.

TESTSTAT=   Saves the Ljung-Box-Pierce statistics in the variable specified.

Following model estimation the available temporary variables as described for the **OLS** command are:

$ERR, $K, $LAIC, $LSC, $N, $R2, $SIG2, $SSE, $SSR,$ and $SST.$

The choice of good starting values will facilitate model convergence. If the **START** or **START=** option are not specified then SHAZAM will set default starting values. If **NAR=** or **NMA=** do not exceed 1 then default starting values of 0.5 are used for the coefficients. Otherwise, default starting values of 0.1 are used for the coefficients. The default starting value for the constant term is 1.0.

Example

The ARIMA estimation stage can be demonstrated with the *CONSUME* variable that was inspected in the identification stage. The example below shows the estimation of an ARMA(1,1) model. When the **START** option is used the starting values for the coefficients are entered on the line after the **ARIMA** command as follows:

```
ARIMA CONSUME / NAR=1 NMA=1 START
0.5  -0.2   100
```

The first value is the AR parameter, the second value is the MA parameter and the final value is the starting value for the constant term. Alternatively, starting values for the model estimation can be entered in a variable, say *ALPHA*, as shown in the next listing of SHAZAM commands.

```
DIM ALPHA 3
GEN1 ALPHA:1= 0.5
GEN1 ALPHA:2= -.2
GEN1 ALPHA:3= 100
ARIMA CONSUME / NAR=1 NMA=1 START=ALPHA
```

The output below gives results from the estimation of an ARMA(1,1) model.

```
|_ARIMA CONSUME / NAR=1 NMA=1 START=ALPHA
ESTIMATION PROCEDURE
STARTING VALUES OF PARAMETERS ARE:
  .50000       -.20000        100.00

MEAN OF SERIES =    134.5
VARIANCE OF SERIES =    555.9
```

```
STANDARD DEVIATION OF SERIES =    23.58

INITIAL SUM OF SQUARES =        17958.972

ITERATION STOPS - RELATIVE CHANGE IN EACH PARAMETER LESS THAN .1E-03

NET NUMBER OF OBS IS   17
DIFFERENCING: 0 CONSECUTIVE, 0 SEASONAL WITH SPAN  0
CONVERGENCE AFTER 30 ITERATIONS
INITIAL SUM OF SQS=   17958.972        FINAL SUM OF SQS=    2527.1076

 R-SQUARE =   .7159     R-SQUARE ADJUSTED =   .6753
VARIANCE OF THE ESTIMATE-SIGMA**2 =   166.02
STANDARD ERROR OF THE ESTIMATE-SIGMA =   12.885
AKAIKE INFORMATION CRITERIA -AIC(K) =    5.4650
SCHWARZ CRITERIA- SC(K) =    5.6121

              PARAMETER ESTIMATES      STD ERROR    T-STAT
              AR( 1)    .59682          .2130        2.802
              MA( 1)   -.94992          .9190E-01   -10.34
           CONSTANT   55.041          28.77         1.913

                          RESIDUALS
   LAGS                AUTOCORRELATIONS                       STD ERR
1 -12  -.37  .04  .23 -.12  .12 -.04  .00 -.16  .16 -.06 -.06 -.06    .24
13-16  -.05  .00 -.08 -.03                                           .30

MODIFIED BOX-PIERCE (LJUNG-BOX-PIERCE) STATISTICS  (CHI-SQUARE)
     LAG    Q     DF  P-VALUE     LAG    Q     DF  P-VALUE
      3    3.96    1   .047        10   6.93    8   .545
      4    4.34    2   .114        11   7.12    9   .624
      5    4.73    3   .193        12   7.37   10   .690
      6    4.77    4   .311        13   7.60   11   .748
      7    4.77    5   .444        14   7.61   12   .815
      8    5.69    6   .458        15   8.72   13   .793
      9    6.75    7   .456        16   9.09   14   .825

CROSS-CORRELATIONS BETWEEN RESIDUALS AND (DIFFERENCED) SERIES
CROSS-CORRELATION AT ZERO LAG =   .41
   LAGS                 CROSS CORRELATIONS Y(T),E(T-K)
   1-12     .49  .06  .24  .12 -.06  .13 -.04 -.09 -.12 -.08 -.14 -.12
   13-16   -.11 -.13 -.08 -.07
   LEADS                CROSS CORRELATIONS Y(T),E(T+K)
   1-12     .04  .26  .10  .08  .06 -.07 -.11 -.04  .01 -.15 -.03 -.21
   13-16   -.11 -.04 -.15 -.05
```

The estimation converged in 30 iterations. The estimated equation (where z_t denotes the variable *CONSUME*) is:

$$z_t - .59682\, z_{t-1} = \hat{u}_t + .94992\, \hat{u}_{t-1} + 55.041$$

Note that with different starting values the estimation may converge to different parameter estimates. Therefore, re-estimation with different starting values may be useful. The above output shows that the Ljung-Box-Pierce test statistics are less than the critical values from a chi-square distribution at any reasonable significance level and so the hypothesis of white noise errors is not rejected.

The *CONSUME* variable is annual data and therefore modelling of seasonal effects need not be considered. In economic analysis there is interest in modelling seasonally unadjusted quarterly and monthly data. A multiplicative seasonal autoregressive process that may be considered is:

$$(1 - \Gamma_1 B^4)(1 - \phi_1 B) z_t = u_t + \delta$$

That is,

$$z_t - \Gamma_1 z_{t-4} - \phi_1 z_{t-1} + \Gamma_1 \phi_1 z_{t-5} = u_t + \delta$$

Suppose that quarterly seasonally unadjusted data is available in the variable *ZQ*. The SHAZAM command for estimation of the above model is:

```
ARIMA ZQ / NSPAN=4 NSA=1 NAR=1
```

FORECASTING

An ARIMA model can be used to forecast future values of a time series. The goal is to obtain estimates $\hat{z}_{T+l}$ as the forecast at origin date T ($p \le T \le N$) for lead time l ($l \ge 1$) of z_{T+l}. The forecasting exercise is facilitated by recognizing that the data generation process for z_{T+l} can be expressed in different forms. The first form to consider is the difference-equation form. For example, the ARMA(1,1) process can be expressed as:

$$z_{T+l} = \phi_1 z_{T+l-1} + u_{T+l} - \theta_1 u_{T+l-1} + \delta$$

The second form to analyze is the random shock form. Any ARIMA process can be expressed as a linear function of the current and past random shocks as:

$$z_{T+l} = \mu + u_{T+l} + \Psi_1 u_{T+l-1} + \Psi_2 u_{T+l-2} + \dots$$

where the constant μ and the weights $\Psi_1, \Psi_2, \dots$ are determined as functions of the model parameters. The forecast can be written in the form:

$$\hat{z}_{T+l} = \mu + \Psi_l u_T + \Psi_{l+1} u_{-1} + \dots$$

The *l*-step ahead forecast error is:

$$e_{T+l} = [z_{T+l} - \hat{z}_{T+l}] = u_{T+l} + \Psi_1 u_{T+l-1} + \dots + \Psi_{l-1} u_{T+1}$$

The error has zero expectation and variance:

$$V[e_{T+l}] = \sigma_u^2 \left(1 + \Psi_1^2 + \ldots + \Psi_{l-1}^2\right)$$

In SHAZAM the forecasting procedure is made operational as follows. Input requirements from the estimation stage are the model parameter estimates $\hat{\beta}$ and the estimate of the error variance $\hat{\sigma}_u^2$ (the SHAZAM output labels this as SIGMA**2). If a moving average component is present then estimated residuals enter the forecast. Therefore, a sequence of one-step-ahead prediction errors is computed to the end of the sample period (including back-forecasting of pre-sample residuals). Point forecasts are calculated recursively from the difference-equation form of the process.

For example, for the ARMA(1,1) model the $l=1$ period ahead forecast is:

$$\hat{z}_{T+1} = \hat{\phi}_1 z_T - \hat{\theta}_1 \hat{u}_T + \hat{\delta}$$

The $l=2$ periods ahead forecast is: $\hat{z}_{T+2} = \hat{\phi}_1 \hat{z}_{T+1} + \hat{\delta}$

The $l=3$ periods ahead forecast is: $\hat{z}_{T+3} = \hat{\phi}_1 \hat{z}_{T+2} + \hat{\delta}$

The Ψ_i weights are calculated (these are listed on the SHAZAM output in the column marked PSI WT) and are used to estimate the forecast variance as $\hat{V}[e_{T+l}]$. A 95% confidence interval is computed as:

$$\hat{z}_{T+l} \pm 1.96\, \hat{V}[e_{T+l}]^{1/2}$$

Users should be aware that the 95% confidence interval is approximate. If the sample period set for the forecasting stage extends beyond the sample period used in the estimation stage then Nelson [1973, p. 224] notes that "the computations of the variance of residuals is restricted to the sample period so that any postsample deterioration in the fit of the model will not be reflected in standard errors and confidence intervals."

ARIMA *Forecasting Stage Command Options*

In general, the format of the **ARIMA** command for the forecasting stage is:

ARIMA *var* / **NAR= NMA= COEF= SIGMA= FBEG= FEND=** *options*

where *var* is the variable to forecast and *options* is a list of desired options. The options for differencing the data as used in the identification stage are:

NDIFF=, NSDIFF=, and **NSPAN=.**

The options for model specification as used in the estimation stage are:

NOCONSTANT, BEG=, END=, NAR=, NMA=, NSAR=, and **NSMA=.**

Other options are:

DN   Uses a divisor of N instead of (N–K) when estimating SIGMA**2. Also see the **SIGMA=** option below.

GNU   Prepares **GNUPLOT** plots of the forecast. For more information on this option see the *GNUPLOT* section in the *PLOTS* chapter. With the **GNU** option the **APPEND, OUTPUT=, DEVICE=, PORT=** and **COMMFILE=** options are also available as described for the **PLOT** command.

LOG   Takes logs of data. The data z_t is transformed to $y_t = \log(z_t)$. If this option is specified then it must also have been used in the estimation stage. SHAZAM first generates forecasts in log form, $\hat{y}_{T+l}$ and then generates antilog forecasts, $\hat{z}_{T+l}$. Some statistical theory is needed to understand how the forecasts in antilog form are obtained. Consider a random variable Y distributed as $N(\mu, \sigma^2)$ and define the random variable Z=exp(Y). Then the random variable Z has mean $\exp(\mu + \sigma^2/2)$ (see, for example, Mood, Graybill and Boes [1974]). Therefore, the conditional expectation forecast of $z_{T+l} = \exp(y_{T+l})$ is:

$$\hat{z}_{T+l} = \exp\left(\hat{y}_{T+l} + \frac{1}{2}\hat{\sigma}_u^2\right)$$

For the derivation of the standard errors of the anti-log forecasts, see Nelson [1973, p. 163]. Note that the confidence interval for $\hat{z}_{T+l}$ is not symmetric.

PLOTFORC   Plots the forecast with 95% confidence intervals.

STOCHAST   Computes the Beveridge/Nelson [1981] stochastic trend for first differenced models. This option is only valid when **NDIFF=1.**

COEF=   Gives the model coefficients. If this is not specified then values must be entered on the line following the **ARIMA** command. The input sequence for the coefficients must correspond to **NAR=, NMA=, NSAR=,** and **NSMA=** with the constant term given as the last value.

FBEG= **FEND=**	Specifies the origin date (**FBEG=**) and the last observation (**FEND=**) of the forecast. The origin date may not be greater than the final observation of the **SAMPLE** command or the value set with **END=**. Furthermore, the origin date must exceed the first observation of the **SAMPLE** command (or the value set with **BEG=**) by an amount at least equal to the maximum AR lag. These values may be given as an observation number or as a date. This option is required.
FCSE=	Saves the forecast standard errors in the variable specified.
PREDICT=	Saves the predictions in the variable specified.
RESID=	Saves the forecast residuals in the variable specified.
SIGMA=	Gives the value of **SIGMA** to use in calculating the forecast standard errors. By default the data for the current sample period will be used to estimate **SIGMA**. A recommended approach is to follow estimation with the command: `GEN1 S=SQRT($SIG2)` Then use the option **SIGMA=S** for the ARIMA forecasting. When this option is used the **DN** option is not applicable.

Example

A listing of SHAZAM commands for estimation and forecasting of an ARMA(1,1) model for the *CONSUME* variable is:

```
ARIMA CONSUME / NAR=1 NMA=1 COEF=BETA START=ALPHA
GEN1 S=SQRT($SIG2)
ARIMA CONSUME / NAR=1 NMA=1 COEF=BETA FBEG=14 FEND=19 SIGMA=S GNU
```

In the above commands the parameter estimates from the model estimation are saved in the variable *BETA* and the value of sigma**2 is available in the temporary variable *$SIG2*. These become input for the forecasting. The origin date for the forecast is set at observation 14 and the final forecast period is set at observation 19. This gives a 3 period ex post (within sample) forecast and a 2 period ex ante (out of sample) forecast.

SHAZAM output from the **ARIMA** forecast follows.

```
|_ARIMA CONSUME / NAR=1 NMA=1 COEF=BETA FBEG=14 FEND=19 SIGMA=S GNU

   ARIMA FORECAST
        PARAMETER VALUES ARE:
            AR( 1)=     .59682
            MA( 1)=    -.94992
```

```
              CONSTANT =      55.041

FROM ORIGIN DATE   14, FORECASTS ARE CALCULATED UP TO    5 STEPS AHEAD

FUTURE DATE     LOWER         FORECAST          UPPER        ACTUAL           ERROR
     15        141.881        167.136          192.390       154.300        -12.8356
     16        108.277        154.791          201.306       149.000        -5.79115
     17        95.3940        147.424          199.453       165.500         18.0763
     18        89.1687        143.027          196.885
     19        85.9081        140.402          194.897

        STEPS AHEAD      STD ERROR     PSI WT
             1            12.88        1.0000
             2            23.73        1.5467
             3            26.55         .9231
             4            27.48         .5509
             5            27.80         .3288

VARIANCE OF ONE-STEP-AHEAD ERRORS-SIGMA**2 =     166.0
STD.DEV. OF ONE-STEP-AHEAD ERRORS-SIGMA    =     12.88
```

A GNUPLOT plot of the forecast results follows. The plot shows that the ex post point forecast failed to predict the up-turn that occurred at observation 17.

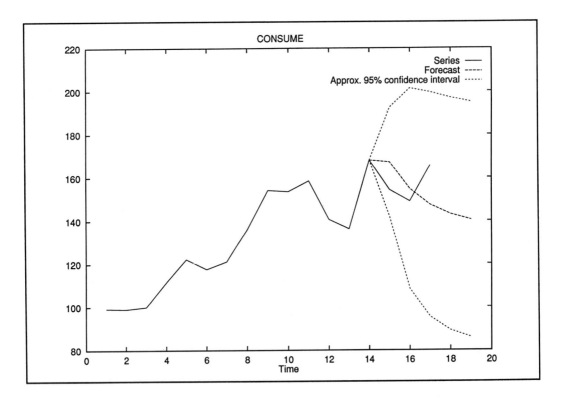

11. AUTOCORRELATION MODELS

> *"It can be predicted with all security that in fifty years light will cost one fiftieth of its present price, and in all the big cities there will be no such thing as night."*
>
> J.B.S. Haldane
> British Scientist, 1927

The **AUTO** command provides features for estimation of models with autocorrelated errors. Consider the linear model:

$$Y_t = X_t'\beta + \varepsilon_t \qquad \text{for } t=1,\ldots,N$$

where Y_t is an observation on the dependent variable, X_t is a vector of observations on K explanatory variables, and β is a vector of unknown parameters. Disturbances that follow an autoregressive process of order p (an AR(p) process) have the form:

$$\varepsilon_t = \sum_{j=1}^{p} \rho_j \varepsilon_{t-j} + v_t$$

Disturbances that follow a moving average process of order q (an MA(q) process) have the form:

$$\varepsilon_t = v_t + \sum_{j=1}^{q} \theta_j v_{t-j}$$

where the ρ_j and θ_j are unknown parameters and v_t is a random error. The order of the autoregressive process or the moving average process is specified with the **ORDER=** option on the **AUTO** command.

ESTIMATION WITH AR(1) ERRORS

The model with first-order autoregressive errors has the form:

$$Y_t = X_t'\beta + \varepsilon_t \qquad \text{and} \qquad \varepsilon_t = \rho\varepsilon_{t-1} + v_t \qquad \text{with} \qquad |\rho| < 1$$

where ρ is the autocorrelation parameter and v_t is a random disturbance. Using the assumptions $E[v_t] = 0$, $E[v_t^2] = \sigma_v^2$, $E[v_t v_s] = 0$ for $t \neq s$, the covariance matrix for ε can be expressed as:

$$E(\varepsilon\varepsilon') = \sigma_v^2\Omega = \frac{\sigma_v^2}{1-\rho^2}\begin{bmatrix} 1 & \rho & \rho^2 & . & \rho^{N-1} \\ \rho & 1 & \rho & . & \rho^{N-2} \\ \rho^2 & \rho & 1 & . & . \\ . & . & . & . & . \\ \rho^{N-1} & \rho^{N-2} & . & . & 1 \end{bmatrix}$$

SHAZAM provides a number of methods for estimating the parameters of the model with AR(1) errors.

Cochrane-Orcutt Iterative Estimation

The SHAZAM default estimation method for the model with AR(1) errors is Cochrane-Orcutt iterative estimation. The method proposed by Cochrane-Orcutt [1949] is extended to include the first observation with the Prais-Winsten [1954] transformation and the estimation is iterated until a convergence criteria is satisfied. The steps in the estimation procedure are as follows.

STEP 1: Estimate the regression equation by OLS and obtain estimated residuals e_t.

STEP 2: Run the regression:

$$e_t = \rho e_{t-1} + v_t^*$$

This gives the least squares estimate of ρ as:

$$\hat{\rho} = \frac{\sum_{t=2}^{N} e_t e_{t-1}}{\sum_{t=2}^{N} e_{t-1}^2}$$

STEP 3: Use the estimate $\hat{\rho}$ to obtain transformed observations Y^* and X^* as follows:

$$Y_1^* = \sqrt{1-\hat{\rho}^2}\ Y_1\,,\ X_1^* = \sqrt{1-\hat{\rho}^2}\ X_1 \quad \text{and}$$

$$Y_t^* = Y_t - \hat{\rho}Y_{t-1}\,,\ X_t^* = X_t - \hat{\rho}X_{t-1} \quad \text{for} \quad t = 2,3,\ldots,N$$

An estimate of β is obtained from an OLS regression of Y^* on X^*. A new set of estimated residuals is then calculated and steps 2 and 3 are repeated until successive estimates of ρ differ by less than .001 or the value set with the **CONV=** option on the **AUTO** command. The maximum number of iterations is 19 and this can be changed with the **ITER=** option. If the **DROP** option is used, the estimates are obtained by dropping the first observation.

The final estimate of ρ, say $\tilde{\rho}$, can be used to construct an estimate $\tilde{\Omega}$ of the matrix Ω. Then the final parameter estimates are given by:

$$\tilde{\beta} = \left(X'\,\tilde{\Omega}^{-1}\,X\right)^{-1} X'\,\tilde{\Omega}^{-1}Y$$

The transformed residuals are:

$$\left.\begin{array}{l} \tilde{v}_1 = \sqrt{1-\tilde{\rho}^2}\,\tilde{e}_1 \\[2mm] \tilde{v}_t = \tilde{e}_t - \tilde{\rho}\tilde{e}_{t-1} \quad t = 2,\ldots,N \end{array}\right\} \quad \text{where} \quad \tilde{e} = Y - X\tilde{\beta}$$

The estimate of the covariance matrix of $\tilde{\beta}$ is:

$$V\left(\tilde{\beta}\right) = \tilde{\sigma}_v^2 \left(X'\,\tilde{\Omega}^{-1}\,X\right)^{-1} \quad \text{where}$$

$$\tilde{\sigma}_v^2 = \frac{1}{N-K}(\tilde{v}'\tilde{v}) = \frac{1}{N-K}(Y-X\tilde{\beta})'\,\tilde{\Omega}^{-1}\,(Y-X\tilde{\beta})$$

The R^2 measure is: $\qquad 1 - \dfrac{\tilde{v}'\tilde{v}}{Y'Y - N\overline{Y}^2}$

The predicted values that are saved with the **PREDICT=** option are computed as:

$$\hat{Y}_1 = X_1'\tilde{\beta} \qquad \text{and}$$

$$\hat{Y}_t = X_t'\tilde{\beta} + \tilde{\rho}(\hat{Y}_{t-1} - X_{t-1}'\tilde{\beta}) \qquad \text{for} \quad t = 2,\ldots,N$$

The estimated residuals that are saved with the **RESID=** option are obtained as $Y - \hat{Y}$.

After estimation it may be useful to test for an AR(1) error term by testing the null hypothesis H_0: $\rho=0$ against the alternative H_1: $\rho\neq0$. Harvey [1990, pp. 200-201] discusses a Wald test that can be constructed as:

$$t = \frac{\tilde{\rho}}{\sqrt{V(\tilde{\rho})}} \qquad \text{where} \quad V(\tilde{\rho}) = (1-\tilde{\rho}^2)/N$$

This test statistic has an asymptotic standard normal distribution under the null hypothesis and is reported as the ASYMPTOTIC T-RATIO on the SHAZAM output.

Grid Search Estimation

The **GS** option on the **AUTO** command implements a Hildreth-Lu [1960] least squares grid search procedure. SHAZAM considers values of ρ ranging from –0.9 to 0.9 in increments of 0.1. For each of these values a regression of Y^* on X^* is estimated and the error sum of squares is computed. The value of ρ for which the sum of squared errors is smallest is chosen. Then, SHAZAM refines the value of ρ by searching in the neighbourhood of the chosen ρ in increments of 0.01. The refined value of ρ associated with the minimum sum of squared errors is selected as the optimal ρ. This method is illustrated later in this chapter.

Maximum Likelihood Estimation by the Beach-MacKinnon Method

Under the assumption of normality the log-likelihood function for the model with autocorrelated errors can be expressed as:

$$L\,(\beta,\Omega,\sigma_v^2) = -\frac{N}{2}\ln(2\pi) - \frac{N}{2}\ln\sigma_v^2 - \frac{1}{2}\ln|\Omega| - \frac{1}{2\sigma_v^2}(Y - X\beta)'\,\Omega^{-1}\,(Y - X\beta)$$

With the AR(1) error model $\left|\Omega^{-1}\right| = 1 - \rho^2$. The Beach and MacKinnon [1978] estimation procedure is to first maximize the log-likelihood function with respect to β holding ρ fixed (initially $\rho=0$) and then maximize L with respect to ρ considering β fixed. The solutions to these two maximization problems are developed in Beach and MacKinnon. The estimation is iterated until two successive estimates of ρ differ by less than .001 or the value set with the **CONV=** option.

Maximum Likelihood Estimation by Grid Search

The **GS** and **ML** options on the **AUTO** command give a variation on the previous grid search method. Dhrymes [1971, p. 70] shows that maximizing the likelihood function is equivalent to minimizing:

$$\frac{\sigma_v^2(\rho)}{(1-\rho^2)^{1/N}}$$

The minimum is located using the same grid search method described previously. Note that the previous method was concerned with minimizing $\sigma_v^2(\rho)$. Thus the two methods are based on different objective functions. Asymptotically the two grid search methods are equivalent since:

$$\lim_{N \to \infty} (1 - \rho^2)^{1/N} = 1 \quad \text{when} \quad |\rho| < 1$$

Nonlinear Least Squares

The **PAGAN** option on the **AUTO** command gives estimation by a nonlinear least squares method that is described in more detail later in this chapter.

TESTS FOR AUTOCORRELATION AFTER CORRECTING FOR AR(1) ERRORS

After correcting for first-order autocorrelation it is a good idea to check whether any autocorrelation remains in the v_t residuals. If so then it is possible that higher order autocorrelation exists. A simple procedure is to use a modification of the Durbin [1970] h test which is appropriate since a model corrected for autocorrelation could actually be rewritten as a lagged dependent variable model. Denote ϕ as the first order autoregressive parameter of the series v_t. An estimate is obtained as:

$$\hat{\phi} = \frac{\Sigma_{t=2}^{N} \; \tilde{v}_t \tilde{v}_{t-1}}{\Sigma_{t=2}^{N} \; \tilde{v}_{t-1}^2}$$

Consider testing the null hypothesis H_0: $\phi=0$ against the alternative H_1: $\phi \neq 0$. When the **RSTAT, LIST,** or **MAX** options is used with the AR(1) error model SHAZAM computes the test statistic:

$$h' = \hat{\phi} \sqrt{\frac{N}{1 - N\,V(\tilde{\rho})}}$$

This statistic is printed on the SHAZAM output as:

```
DURBIN H STATISTIC (ASYMPTOTIC NORMAL)
   MODIFIED FOR AUTO ORDER=1
```

If the original model has a lagged dependent variable then another modified Durbin h statistic can be derived. This model is:

$$Y_t = \gamma Y_{t-1} + X_t'\beta + \varepsilon_t \quad \text{with} \quad \varepsilon_t = \rho \varepsilon_{t-1} + v_t$$

Consider testing the null hypothesis H_0: $\phi=0$ in:

$$v_t = \phi v_{t-1} + w_t$$

The modified Durbin h test statistic is:

$$h' = \hat{\phi}\sqrt{\frac{N}{1-N[V(\tilde{\rho})+2Cov(\tilde{\rho},\tilde{\gamma})+V(\tilde{\gamma})]}}$$

In this case, if the **DLAG** option is used, the h statistic is labeled on the output as:

```
DURBIN H STATISTIC (ASYMPTOTIC NORMAL)
 MODFIED FOR AUTO ORDER=1 WITH LAGGED DEPVAR
```

In both cases the h statistics are asymptotically normally distributed if the null hypothesis is true.

ESTIMATION WITH AR(2) ERRORS

The model with AR(2) errors has the form:

$$Y_t = X_t'\beta + \varepsilon_t \qquad \text{and} \qquad \varepsilon_t = \rho_1\varepsilon_{t-1} + \rho_2\varepsilon_{t-2} + v_t$$

where $E[v_t]=0$, $E[v_t v_s]=0$ for $t \neq s$, and $E[v_t^2]=\sigma_v^2$. This process will be stationary if $\rho_1 + \rho_2 < 1$, $\rho_2-\rho_1 < 1$, and $\rho_1,\rho_2 \in (-1,1)$. The region in ρ_1 and ρ_2 space defined by these conditions is called the stability triangle. A discussion of the stability triangle is in Box and Jenkins [1976, pp. 58-65]. The covariance matrix of ε is $E[\varepsilon\varepsilon']=\sigma_v^2\Omega$. The form of Ω for the model with AR(2) errors is discussed in Judge, Griffiths, Hill, Lütkepohl and Lee [1985, Section 8.2.2]. As in the AR(1) error case SHAZAM offers a number of estimation methods.

Cochrane-Orcutt Iterative Estimation

The SHAZAM default estimation method for the model with AR(2) errors is a Cochrane-Orcutt iterative estimation procedure that is implemented as follows.

STEP 1: Estimate the regression equation by OLS and obtain estimated residuals e_t.

STEP 2: Get estimates $\hat{\rho}_1$ and $\hat{\rho}_2$ of ρ_1 and ρ_2 from the regression:

$$e_t = \rho_1 e_{t-1} + \rho_2 e_{t-2} + v_t^* \qquad \text{for} \quad t = 3,4,\ldots,N$$

STEP 3: Obtain transformed observations Y^* and X^* as:

$$Y_1^* = \sqrt{\hat{a}} Y_1 \ , \ X_1^* = \sqrt{\hat{a}} \ X_1 \qquad \text{where} \qquad \hat{a} = (1+\hat{\rho}_2)\left[(1-\hat{\rho}_2)^2 - \hat{\rho}_1^2\right]/(1-\hat{\rho}_2)$$

$$Y_2^* = \sqrt{1-\hat{\rho}_2^2}\left(Y_2 - \frac{\hat{\rho}_1}{1-\hat{\rho}_2}Y_1\right), \ X_2^* = \sqrt{1-\hat{\rho}_2^2}\left(X_2 - \frac{\hat{\rho}_1}{1-\hat{\rho}_2}X_1\right) \qquad \text{and}$$

$$Y_t^* = Y_t - \hat{\rho}_1 Y_{t-1} - \hat{\rho}_2 Y_{t-2} \ , \ X_t^* = X_t - \hat{\rho}_1 X_{t-1} - \hat{\rho}_2 X_{t-2} \qquad \text{for} \ \ t = 3, 4, \ldots, N$$

An estimate of β is obtained from an OLS regression of Y^* on X^*. A new set of estimated residuals is then calculated and steps 2 and 3 are repeated. The iterations stop when successive estimates of both ρ_1 and ρ_2 differ by less than .001 or the value set with the **CONV=** option.

Grid Search Estimation

When the **GS** and **ORDER=2** options are specified on the **AUTO** command the estimation method for ρ_1 and ρ_2 is by a grid search. The search is made within the stability triangle using initial spacing of .25 for the two values of ρ. The method is not guaranteed to yield a global maximum, particularly in small samples, but it usually works quite well. The **GS** option requires over 100 iterations for the search and so can be computationally expensive.

Maximum Likelihood Estimation by Grid Search

When the **ML** and **ORDER=2** options are specified on the **AUTO** command the model estimation considers maximizing the likelihood function under the assumption of normal disturbances. Schmidt [1971] discusses that the maximum likelihood estimators are those which minimize:

$$\frac{\sigma_v^2(\rho_1,\rho_2)}{\left|\Omega^{-1}\right|^{1/N}} \qquad \text{where} \qquad \left|\Omega^{-1}\right| = (1+\rho_2)^2\left[(1-\rho_2)^2 - \rho_1^2\right]$$

Estimation is by a grid search within the stability triangle as discussed above. An application can be found in Savin [1978].

Nonlinear Least Squares

The **PAGAN** and **ORDER=2** options on the **AUTO** command gives estimation by a nonlinear least squares method that is described in the next section.

ESTIMATION WITH HIGHER ORDER AR OR MA ERRORS

For the general estimation of models with autoregressive or moving average errors Pagan [1974] proposes the use of an iterative Gauss-Newton algorithm for the minimization of $S=v'v$. Using matrix notation the model with autoregressive errors can be expressed in the form:

$$v = M(\rho)(Y - X\beta) \qquad \text{where} \qquad \rho' = (\rho_1, \rho_2, \ldots, \rho_p)$$

and the model with moving average errors can be expressed in the form:

$$v = M(\theta)^{-1}(Y - X\beta) \qquad \text{where} \qquad \theta' = (\theta_1, \theta_2, \ldots, \theta_q)$$

M and M^{-1} are N x N lower triangular matrices. Specifically:

$$M(\rho) = \begin{bmatrix} 1 & 0 & . & . & . & 0 \\ \rho_1 & 1 & 0 & . & . & 0 \\ . & \rho_1 & 1 & . & & . \\ \rho_p & & . & . & . & . \\ & . & & . & . & 0 \\ 0 & & \rho_p & . & \rho_1 & 1 \end{bmatrix}$$

Note that the implementation sets the pre-sample values of ε equal to zero.

Matrix differentiation gives expressions for the computation of first derivatives and these are then used in the updating steps of the Gauss-Newton estimation algorithm.

The convergence criteria is based on the relative change in the error sum of squares. Let $S^{(i)}$ be the error sum of squares at iteration i. The estimation converges when:

$$\left| S^{(i)} - S^{(i-1)} \right| / S^{(i-1)} \leq \frac{\delta}{1000}$$

where δ can be specified with the **CONV=** option and the default is $\delta = .001$.

```
AUTO COMMAND OPTIONS
```

In general, the format of the **AUTO** command is:

AUTO *depvar indeps / options*

where *depvar* is the dependent variable, *indeps* is a list of independent variables, and *options* is a list of desired options. Options as defined for **OLS** that are available are:

ANOVA, DUMP, GF, LINLOG, LIST, LOGLIN, LOGLOG, MAX, NOCONSTANT, NOWIDE, PCOR, PCOV, RESTRICT, RSTAT, WIDE, BEG=, END=, COEF=, COV=, PREDICT=, RESID=, STDERR= and **TRATIO=**.

Additional options available with the **AUTO** command are:

DLAG   Used with first-order models to tell SHAZAM that the first independent variable is a **LAG**ged **D**ependent variable. With this option the estimated variances will be calculated using Dhrymes [1971, Theorem 7.1]. An example using this method can be found in Savin [1976].

DN   Computes the estimated variance of the regression line by **D**ividing the residual sum of squares by **N** instead of N–K. If the user believes that the model only has good large-sample properties and wants the maximum likelihood estimates of the variances, this option should be used.

DROP   **DROP**s the first observation in estimation. (In a second-order model, the first two observations will be dropped.) While this yields less efficient estimates, there are cases where this option might be chosen. If this option is not used, the beginning observations are saved with the usual transformation.   See any good econometrics text, and Poirier [1978] for discussions of this. If the **DROP** option is used, the **ML** option may not be used.

GS   Uses a **G**rid **S**earch to estimate ρ. For models with AR(1) errors 39 iterations will be required by a grid search. For models with AR(2) errors over 100 iterations will be required. The grid search will yield an accuracy of .01.

MISS   Adjusts the maximum likelihood estimates for any **MISS**ing observations that were deleted with **SKIPIF** commands. The method used is described in Savin and White [1978] and in Richardson and White [1979].

ML   Does Maximum Likelihood estimation for models with first or second order autoregressive errors. A reference is Dhrymes [1971, Theorem 4.4]. For the model with AR(1) errors the estimation method is a modified Cochrane-Orcutt procedure as developed by Beach and MacKinnon [1978]. With the **GS** option a grid search is used. A model with AR(2) errors is specified with the **ORDER=2** option and the estimation uses a grid search. Note that, with the **ML** option, the **DN** option will automatically be in effect and the **DROP** option may not be used.

NOPITER   Suppresses intermediate output from iterations.

PAGAN   May be used with **ORDER=1** or **ORDER=2** to estimate the model using Pagan's [1974] procedure.

CONV=   Used to set a **CONV**ergence criterion. The default is .001. This option is ineffective for a grid search.

GAP=   Provides an alternative way to indicate a single **GAP** in the data. It is used when the missing observations were not accounted for in the data. You should specify the observation number immediately before the gap. For example, **GAP=29** means that a gap exists in the data after observation 29. It will be assumed that only one observation is missing, unless the number of missing observations is specified with the **NMISS=** option.

ITER=   May be used when doing an **ITER**ative Cochrane-Orcutt procedure to control the number of iterations. If a value of **ITER=** is specified, this will be the maximum number of iterations allowed. **ITER=** should be a number between 2 and 99. The default is 19.

NMISS=   Used with the **GAP=** option to indicate the **N**umber of **MISS**ing observations from the data. For example, **GAP=29 NMISS=3** means that 3 observations were missing from the data after observation 29. This option is not to be confused with the **MISS** option described above.

NUMARMA=   Specifies the **NUM**ber of **AR** or **MA** coefficients to be estimated if some of the coefficients are to be restricted to be zero. For example, when **ORDER=4** is specified, but it is desired that the second autoregressive coefficient should be zero and not estimated then use **NUMARMA=3** and in the line following the **AUTO** command include the 3 coefficents to be estimated. For example:

```
AUTO CONSUME INCOME / ORDER=4 NUMARMA=3
1 3 4
```

If the **NUMARMA=** option is used with **ORDER=2** then the **PAGAN** option must also be specified.

ORDER=n   Used to estimate models with second or higher-**ORDER** autoregressive errors. If **ORDER=2** is specified, an iterative Cochrane-Orcutt procedure is done unless the **GS** or **ML** options are also specified. The missing data options are not valid for **ORDER=1** estimation.

If an **ORDER** larger than 2 is specified the model will be estimated using the least squares procedure described in Pagan [1974]. The **DLAG, DROP, GAP, GS, MISS, ML, NMISS, RESTRICT, RHO** and **SRHO** options are not permitted when **ORDER** is larger than 2. Also, the **FC** command will not work after an **AUTO** command that uses this option.

ORDER=–n   If a negative **ORDER** is specified the model will be estimated using a moving-average error model instead of an autoregressive error model. A least squares procedure is used as described in Pagan [1974]. For example, to estimate a model with first-order moving average errors use the option **ORDER=–1**. The **MISS, GAP, RHO, SRHO, DLAG, DROP, GS, ML** and **RESTRICT** options are not permitted. The **FC** command will not work after an **AUTO** command that uses this option.

RHO=   Allows the specification of any value of ρ desired for the regression. With the **RHO=** option neither a Cochrane-Orcutt nor a maximum likelihood estimation is done since SHAZAM already has the value of ρ. This is useful when ρ is already known as it eliminates expensive iterations.

SRHO=   Used with the **ORDER=2** and **RHO=** options when the Second-order ρ is to be specified for a model with AR(2) errors.

The available temporary variables on the **AUTO** command are:

$ADR2, $DF, $DW, $ERR, $K, $LLF, $N, $R2, $R2OP, $RAW, $RHO, $SIG2, $SSE, $SSR, $SST, $ZDF, $ZSSR and *$ZSST.*

For more information on temporary variables see the chapter *MISCELLANEOUS COMMANDS AND INFORMATION* and the chapter *ORDINARY LEAST SQUARES.*

EXAMPLES

The output below uses the Theil textile data set and shows the estimation results for a model with AR(1) errors. The estimation method is by an iterative Cochrane-Orcutt procedure with the modification that retains the first observation.

```
|_AUTO CONSUME INCOME PRICE

DEPENDENT VARIABLE =  CONSUME
..NOTE..R-SQUARE,ANOVA,RESIDUALS DONE ON ORIGINAL VARS

LEAST SQUARES ESTIMATION              17 OBSERVATIONS
BY COCHRANE-ORCUTT TYPE PROCEDURE WITH CONVERGENCE = 0.00100

    ITERATION              RHO               LOG L.F.                 SSE
        1              0.00000             -51.6470                 433.31
        2             -0.18239             -51.3987                 420.00
        3             -0.19480             -51.3972                 419.80
        4             -0.19535             -51.3972                 419.80


  LOG L.F. =   -51.3972        AT RHO =     -0.19535

                    ASYMPTOTIC  ASYMPTOTIC  ASYMPTOTIC
            ESTIMATE   VARIANCE    ST.ERROR    T-RATIO
RHO        -0.19535    0.05658     0.23786    -0.82129

  R-SQUARE =   0.9528     R-SQUARE ADJUSTED =   0.9461
VARIANCE OF THE ESTIMATE-SIGMA**2 =    29.986
STANDARD ERROR OF THE ESTIMATE-SIGMA =   5.4759
SUM OF SQUARED ERRORS-SSE=   419.80
MEAN OF DEPENDENT VARIABLE =    134.51
LOG OF THE LIKELIHOOD FUNCTION = -51.3972

VARIABLE     ESTIMATED    STANDARD    T-RATIO        PARTIAL STANDARDIZED ELASTICITY
  NAME       COEFFICIENT    ERROR     14 DF P-VALUE  CORR.   COEFFICIENT  AT MEANS
INCOME        1.0650       .2282      4.667    .000   .780     .2394       .8154
PRICE        -1.3751     .7105E-01  -19.35     .000  -.982    -.9837      -.7802
CONSTANT    129.62        23.05      5.624     .000   .833     .0000       .9637
```

The results of estimation by least squares grid search follows.

```
|_AUTO CONSUME INCOME PRICE / GS
DEPENDENT VARIABLE =  CONSUME
..NOTE..R-SQUARE,ANOVA,RESIDUALS DONE ON ORIGINAL VARS

LEAST SQUARES ESTIMATION              17 OBSERVATIONS
BY GRID SEARCH TO ACCURACY OF .01

    ITERATION              RHO               LOG L.F.                 SSE
        1             -0.90000             -54.6571                 559.98
        2             -0.80000             -53.7397                 521.94
        3             -0.70000             -53.0273                 489.91
        4             -0.60000             -52.4498                 463.89
        5             -0.50000             -51.9956                 443.87
```

6	-0.40000	-51.6661	429.85
7	-0.30000	-51.4657	421.82
8	-0.20000	-51.3971	419.75
9	-0.10000	-51.4594	423.60
10	0.00000	-51.6470	433.31
11	0.10000	-51.9500	448.77
12	0.20000	-52.3544	469.79
13	0.30000	-52.8436	496.06
14	0.40000	-53.3989	527.05
15	0.50000	-53.9999	561.91
16	0.60000	-54.6261	599.25
17	0.70000	-55.2597	637.07
18	0.80000	-55.9037	673.27
19	0.90000	-56.6566	708.48

ITERATION	RHO	LOG L.F.	SSE
20	-0.29000	-51.4529	421.35
21	-0.28000	-51.4414	420.93
22	-0.27000	-51.4313	420.57
23	-0.26000	-51.4224	420.28
24	-0.25000	-51.4149	420.04
25	-0.24000	-51.4087	419.86
26	-0.23000	-51.4038	419.75
27	-0.22000	-51.4003	419.69
28	-0.21000	-51.3981	419.69
29	-0.20000	-51.3971	419.75
30	-0.19000	-51.3975	419.87
31	-0.18000	-51.3992	420.05
32	-0.17000	-51.4022	420.29
33	-0.16000	-51.4065	420.58
34	-0.15000	-51.4122	420.94
35	-0.14000	-51.4190	421.35
36	-0.13000	-51.4272	421.83
37	-0.12000	-51.4367	422.36
38	-0.11000	-51.4474	422.95
39	-0.22000	-51.4003	419.69

```
LOG L.F. =   -51.4003      AT RHO =    -0.22000
```

	ESTIMATE	ASYMPTOTIC VARIANCE	ASYMPTOTIC ST.ERROR	ASYMPTOTIC T-RATIO
RHO	-0.22000	0.05598	0.23659	-0.92987

```
R-SQUARE =   0.9528    R-SQUARE ADJUSTED =   0.9461
VARIANCE OF THE ESTIMATE-SIGMA**2 =   29.978
STANDARD ERROR OF THE ESTIMATE-SIGMA =   5.4752
SUM OF SQUARED ERRORS-SSE=   419.69
MEAN OF DEPENDENT VARIABLE =   134.51
LOG OF THE LIKELIHOOD FUNCTION = -51.4003
```

VARIABLE NAME	ESTIMATED COEFFICIENT	STANDARD ERROR	T-RATIO 14 DF	P-VALUE	PARTIAL CORR.	STANDARDIZED COEFFICIENT	ELASTICITY AT MEANS
INCOME	1.0655	.2244	4.749	.000	.785	.2396	.8158
PRICE	-1.3744	.6981E-01	-19.69	.000	-.982	-.9832	-.7798
CONSTANT	129.51	22.65	5.719	.000	.837	.0000	.9628

When the **ML** option is chosen the method of estimation is a modified Cochrane-Orcutt procedure developed by Beach and MacKinnon [1978] and based on maximum likelihood estimation. Note that the **DN** option is automatically in effect when the **ML** option is chosen. The **DROP** option may not be used with the **ML** option. The output of the **ML** option with the **RSTAT** option is given below.

```
|_AUTO CONSUME INCOME PRICE / ML RSTAT
DEPENDENT VARIABLE = CONSUME
..NOTE..R-SQUARE,ANOVA,RESIDUALS DONE ON ORIGINAL VARS
DN OPTION IN EFFECT - DIVISOR IS N

MAXIMUM LIKELIHOOD ESTIMATION                    17 OBSERVATIONS
BY COCHRANE-ORCUTT TYPE PROCEDURE WITH CONVERGENCE = 0.00100

       ITERATION          RHO                LOG L.F.            SSE
           1            0.00000            -51.6470            433.31
           2           -0.18491            -51.3982            419.95
           3           -0.19741            -51.3971            419.77
           4           -0.19797            -51.3971            419.77

   LOG L.F. =   -51.3971      AT RHO =     -0.19797

                   ASYMPTOTIC  ASYMPTOTIC  ASYMPTOTIC
           ESTIMATE   VARIANCE   ST.ERROR    T-RATIO
RHO        -0.19797   0.05652    0.23774    -0.83275

  R-SQUARE =   0.9528     R-SQUARE ADJUSTED =    0.9461
VARIANCE OF THE ESTIMATE-SIGMA**2 =   24.692
STANDARD ERROR OF THE ESTIMATE-SIGMA =   4.9691
SUM OF SQUARED ERRORS-SSE=   419.77
MEAN OF DEPENDENT VARIABLE =    134.51
LOG OF THE LIKELIHOOD FUNCTION = -51.3971

                          ASYMPTOTIC
VARIABLE    ESTIMATED   STANDARD   T-RATIO        PARTIAL STANDARDIZED ELASTICITY
  NAME     COEFFICIENT    ERROR   ***** DF P-VALUE  CORR.  COEFFICIENT  AT MEANS
INCOME       1.0650      .2067     5.152    .000  .809      .2395       .8154
PRICE       -1.3750    .6436E-01  -21.37    .000 -.985     -.9836      -.7801
CONSTANT    129.61      20.88      6.209    .000  .856      .0000       .9636

DURBIN-WATSON = 1.8559    VON NEUMANN RATIO = 1.9719    RHO = -0.05282
RESIDUAL SUM =   1.0847     RESIDUAL VARIANCE =   24.761
SUM OF ABSOLUTE ERRORS=   73.221
R-SQUARE BETWEEN OBSERVED AND PREDICTED = 0.9527
RUNS TEST:    7 RUNS,    9 POSITIVE,    8 NEGATIVE, NORMAL STATISTIC = -1.2423
DURBIN H STATISTIC (ASYMPTOTIC NORMAL) =   -1.1000
  MODIFIED FOR AUTO ORDER=1
```

12. BOX-COX REGRESSIONS

"No model exists for him who seeks what he has never seen."
Paul Eluard
Artist

The **BOX** command provides features for estimation with Box-Cox transformations. References are Zarembka [1974, Chapter 3], Greene [1993, Chapter 11.4], Judge, Hill, Griffiths, Lütkepohl and Lee [1988, Chapter 12.5], Magee [1988], White [1972] and Savin and White [1978]. It is possible to restrict the exact power transformation on any of the variables by using the **LAMBDA** command. Any variable in the regression with non-positive values will automatically be restricted to be untransformed.

The Classical Box-Cox Model

For a variable $Y = (Y_1\ Y_2 \ldots Y_N)'$ consider the transformation:

$$
\begin{aligned}
Y_t^{(\lambda)} &= \frac{Y_t^\lambda - 1}{\lambda} & \lambda \neq 0 \\
&= \ln Y_t & \lambda = 0
\end{aligned}
$$

The Box-Cox model (from Box and Cox [1964]) is written:

$$
Y^{(\lambda)} = X\beta + \varepsilon
$$

where X is a $(N \times K)$ matrix of the observations on the independent variables and ε is a $(N \times 1)$ vector of random disturbances with $E(\varepsilon\varepsilon') = \sigma^2 I_N$.

The log-likelihood function is given by:

$$
L\left(\lambda, \beta, \sigma^2; Y, X\right) = -\frac{N}{2}\ln\left(2\pi\sigma^2\right) - \frac{1}{2\sigma^2}(Y^{(\lambda)} - X\beta)'(Y^{(\lambda)} - X\beta) + \ln J
$$

where
$$
J = \det\left[\frac{\partial Y^{(\lambda)'}}{\partial Y}\right] = \prod_{t=1}^{N} Y_t^{\lambda-1}
$$

is the Jacobian of the transformation on the dependent variable. Maximization of the above log-likelihood function with respect to σ^2 and β given λ gives the estimators:

$$\hat{\beta}(\lambda) = (X'X)^{-1} X'Y^{(\lambda)} \quad \text{and} \quad \hat{\sigma}^2(\lambda) = \frac{1}{N}(Y^{(\lambda)} - X\hat{\beta}(\lambda))'(Y^{(\lambda)} - X\hat{\beta}(\lambda)).$$

Substitution gives the concentrated log-likelihood function:

$$L^*(\lambda; Y, X) = -\frac{N}{2}\{\ln(2\pi) + 1\} - \frac{N}{2}\ln\hat{\sigma}^2(\lambda) + (\lambda - 1)\sum_{t=1}^{N}\ln Y_t$$

The first step of the estimation procedure is to find an estimate of λ to maximize L^*. SHAZAM does this by an iterative algorithm. Then the estimate $\tilde{\lambda}$ is used to obtain an estimate of β as:

$$\tilde{\beta} = (X'X)^{-1} X'Y^{(\tilde{\lambda})}$$

and the estimate of σ^2 is calculated as:

$$\tilde{\sigma}^2 = \frac{1}{N-K}(Y^{(\tilde{\lambda})} - X\tilde{\beta})'(Y^{(\tilde{\lambda})} - X\tilde{\beta})$$

When the **DN** option is used the divisor is N instead of N–K. An estimate of the covariance matrix of $\tilde{\beta}$ is:

$$\tilde{\sigma}^2 (X'X)^{-1}$$

Note that this covariance matrix gives conditional standard errors, conditional on $\lambda = \tilde{\lambda}$. For discussion on conditional vs. unconditional standard errors see Judge, Hill, Griffiths, Lütkepohl and Lee [1988, pp.558-9].

The elasticities evaluated at sample means for the Box-Cox model (see Savin and White [1978]) are found using:

$$E_k = \tilde{\beta}_k \frac{\overline{X}_k}{\overline{Y^{(\tilde{\lambda})}}}$$

Poirier and Melino [1978] discuss the derivation of the change in the expected value of Y with respect to a given regressor when a Box-Cox transformation is used.

The Extended Box-Cox Model

The Box-Cox model can be extended to applications in which both the dependent and the set of independent variables are transformed in the same way. This model is written:

$$Y^{(\lambda)} = X^{(\lambda)} \beta + \varepsilon$$

where the same value of λ is used to transform all the variables in the model. In this case, the log-likelihood function is as previously given except the regressors are transformed in addition to the dependent variable. As before the model estimation proceeds by implementing an iterative procedure to find a maximizing value $\tilde{\lambda}$. This is then used to find parameter estimates $\tilde{\beta}$. In this model, the elasticities evaluated at the variable means are computed as:

$$E_k = \tilde{\beta}_k \, \frac{\overline{X}_k^{(\tilde{\lambda})}}{\overline{Y}^{(\tilde{\lambda})}}$$

The Box-Tidwell Model

A variation of the Box-Cox model involves no transformation of the dependent variable but each of the independent variables is transformed by a different λ. This model is known as the Box-Tidwell model (see Box and Tidwell [1962]) and is given by:

$$Y = \beta_0 + \beta_1 X_1^{(\lambda_1)} + \beta_2 X_2^{(\lambda_2)} + \ldots + \beta_k X_k^{(\lambda_k)} + \varepsilon$$

Since there is no transformation on the dependent variable the log-likelihood function for the Box-Tidwell model has no Jacobian term. After model estimation the elasticities are computed as:

$$E_k = \tilde{\beta}_k \, \frac{\overline{X}_k^{(\tilde{\lambda}_k)}}{\overline{Y}}$$

The Combined Box-Cox and Box-Tidwell Model

The **FULL** option on the **BOX** command implements combined Box-Cox and Box-Tidwell estimation by allowing all variables, dependent and independent, to be transformed by a different value of λ.

The Box-Cox Autoregressive Model

The Box-Cox autoregressive model (described in Savin and White [1978]) is given by:

$$Y_t^{(\lambda)} = X_t'\beta + \varepsilon_t \quad \text{where} \quad \varepsilon_t = \rho\varepsilon_{t-1} + v_t \ , \quad |\rho| < 1 \ ,$$

and $\qquad E(v_t^2) = \sigma_v^2$

The log-likelihood function is:

$$L\left(\lambda, \rho, \beta, \sigma_v^2; Y, X\right) = -\frac{N}{2} \ln\left(2\pi\sigma_v^2\right) + \frac{1}{2} \ln\left(1-\rho^2\right)$$

$$-\frac{1}{2\sigma_v^2}\left(Y^{(\lambda)} - X\beta\right)' \Omega^{-1}\left(Y^{(\lambda)} - X\beta\right) + \ln J$$

where $\Omega^{-1} = E[\varepsilon\varepsilon']^{-1} = \begin{bmatrix} 1 & -\rho & 0 & \cdot & \cdot & \cdot & & & 0 \\ -\rho & 1+\rho^2 & -\rho & 0 & \cdot & \cdot & & \cdot & 0 \\ 0 & -\rho & 1+\rho^2 & -\rho & \cdot & \cdot & & \cdot & 0 \\ \cdot & 0 & -\rho & \cdot & & & & & \\ \cdot & & \cdot & & & & & & \\ \cdot & & & \cdot & & & & & \\ & & & & \cdot & & & & \\ & & & \cdot & & \cdot & & 1+\rho^2 & -\rho \\ 0 & 0 & 0 & & & & & -\rho & 1 \end{bmatrix}$

The Jacobian of the transformation on the dependent variable is:

$$J = \det\left[\frac{\partial Y^{(\lambda)'}}{\partial Y}\right] \qquad\qquad \text{where}$$

$$\left[\frac{\partial Y^{(\lambda)'}}{\partial Y}\right] = \begin{bmatrix} Y_1^{\lambda-1} & 0 & 0 & \cdot & \cdot & \cdot & 0 \\ \rho Y_2^{\lambda-1} & Y_2^{\lambda-1} & 0 & \cdot & \cdot & \cdot & 0 \\ \rho^2 Y_3^{\lambda-1} & \rho Y_3^{\lambda-1} & Y_3^{\lambda-1} & & & & \cdot \\ \cdot & & & \cdot & & & \cdot \\ \cdot & & & & \cdot & & \\ \cdot & & \cdot & & & \cdot & \\ \rho^{N-1}Y_N^{\lambda-1} & \rho^{N-2}Y_N^{\lambda-1} & & \cdot & \cdot & & Y_N^{\lambda-1} \end{bmatrix}$$

This is an N x N triangular matrix and the determinant of a triangular matrix is the product of the diagonal elements. Therefore:

$$J = \prod_{t=1}^{N} Y_t^{\lambda-1}$$

Maximizing the log-likelihood function with respect to β and σ_v^2 given both λ and ρ yields:

$$\hat{\beta}(\lambda,\rho) = \left(X' \Omega^{-1} X\right)^{-1} X' \Omega^{-1} Y^{(\lambda)} \qquad \text{and}$$

$$\hat{\sigma}_v^2(\lambda,\rho) = \tfrac{1}{N}[Y^{(\lambda)} - X\hat{\beta}(\lambda,\rho)]' \, \Omega^{-1} \, [Y^{(\lambda)} - X\hat{\beta}(\lambda,\rho)]$$

Substitution of these estimators into the log-likelihood function gives the concentrated log-likelihood function:

$$L^* (\lambda,\rho; Y, X) = -\tfrac{N}{2}\left\{\ln(2\pi)+1\right\} - \tfrac{N}{2} \ln \hat{\sigma}_v^2(\lambda,\rho) + \tfrac{1}{2} \ln\left(1-\rho^2\right) + (\lambda-1) \sum_{t=1}^{N} \ln Y_t$$

A grid search is used to find estimates $\tilde{\lambda}$ and $\tilde{\rho}$ that maximize L^*. Then an estimate for β is obtained as:

$$\tilde{\beta} = \left(X' \tilde{\Omega}^{-1} X\right)^{-1} X' \tilde{\Omega}^{-1} Y^{(\tilde{\lambda})}$$

and the estimated covariance matrix of coefficients conditional on λ is given by:

$$\tilde{\sigma}_v^2 \left(X' \tilde{\Omega}^{-1} X\right)^{-1}$$

where

$$\tilde{\sigma}_v^2 = \tfrac{1}{N-K} (Y^{(\tilde{\lambda})} - X\tilde{\beta})' \, \tilde{\Omega}^{-1} (Y^{(\tilde{\lambda})} - X\tilde{\beta})$$

When the **DN** option is used the divisor is N instead of N–K.

The Extended Box-Cox Autoregressive Model

The extended Box-Cox autoregressive model that transforms all variables by the same λ can be estimated in a similar fashion to the procedure described above. The extended Box-Cox autoregressive model requires the use of the **AUTO** and **ALL** options on the **BOX** command.

BOX *COMMAND OPTIONS*

In general, the format of the **BOX** command is:

BOX *depvar indeps / options*

where *depvar* is the dependent variable, *indeps* is a list of independent variables, and *options* is a list of desired options. Some of the available options on the **BOX** command are slightly different than those for the **OLS** command. In particular, the **NOCONSTANT** option produces a modified transformation (see details below), since the normal transformation requires an intercept in the regression. Options as defined for **OLS** that are available are:

ANOVA, GF, LIST, MAX, PCOR, PCOV, RSTAT, BEG=, END=, COV=, PREDICT= and **RESID=**

Additional options available for use with the **BOX** command are:

ACCUR   Normally, SHAZAM will estimate λ to an **ACCUR**acy of .01. However, if this option is used, SHAZAM will iterate to an **ACCUR**acy of 0.001 at some increase in computation time.

ALL   Used to extend the Box-Cox model so that **ALL** variables receive the same power transformation (unless restricted). Without this option only the dependent variable is transformed. The extended Box-Cox model is far more difficult to estimate than the classical model. For example, the classical model usually requires only four iterations. The **ALL** option often requires twenty iterations.

AUTO   Simultaneously estimate λ and the first-order **AUTO**correlation parameter ρ. The method is that of Savin and White [1978]. This option is very slow as over 100 iterations are required. An accuracy of 0.01 is obtained for λ and ρ (the **ACCUR** option is not available with this option). When using this option, the **DROP, NMISS=,** and **GAP=** options described in the chapter on *AUTOCORRELATION MODELS* may be used. The **RHO=** option described below can also be used. The λ range for the **AUTO** option is preset at (–2 , 3.5) and may not be altered. It is important to check for corner solutions.

DN   Uses a divisor of N instead of N–K when estimating σ^2.

DUMP   Used with the **AUTO** option to get some intermediate output on the iterations to be **DUMP**ed. This output is usually of little value, but sometimes contains useful information on the grid search.

FULL   Attempts a combined Box-Cox and Box-Tidwell estimation so that all variables in the equation have different λs. This option can be rather slow as many iterations are required. The warning on Box-Tidwell regressions also applies for the **FULL** option. In fact, overflows are quite common with this option so it should be used with care. **RESTRICT** commands are not permitted. The **ALL**, **AUTO**, **LAMBDA=**, **LAMS=**, **LAME=** and **LAMI=** options must not be used with the **TIDWELL** or **FULL** options.

NOCONSTANT Estimates a model with no intercept. The user should be aware that the Box-Cox model is not well defined for models without an intercept, and the model is generally not scale-invariant. The transformation that is used on this option is the one suggested by Zarembka [1974] so that $X_t^{(\lambda)} = X_t^{\lambda} / \lambda$ for $\lambda \neq 0$. A further result is that the likelihood function is not continuous at $\lambda=0$; SHAZAM will use a value of 0.01 instead of 0.0. A Golden Section search algorithm will be used.

RESTRICT   Forces linear parameter restrictions. The restrictions are specified with **LAMBDA** and/or **RESTRICT** commands as shown later in this chapter. The **RESTRICT** option is not available with the **FULL** or **TIDWELL** options.

TIDWELL   Does a Box-**TIDWELL** regression instead of a Box-Cox regression. Only the independent variables will be transformed and each variable will have a different λ. For details on the method see Box and Tidwell [1962]. All independent variables must be strictly positive for this technique. Users should be aware that, quite frequently, the Box-Tidwell method will not converge, thus causing the run to be terminated unsuccessfully. This happens most often in small samples where there is a high variance in one of the parameters. If this happens, the run might be successful if the data is scaled to a lower range (for example, divide all variables by 100). **RESTRICT** commands are not permitted. The **ALL**, **AUTO**, **LAMBDA=**, **LAMS=**, **LAME=** and **LAMI=** options must not be used with the **TIDWELL** or **FULL** options.

UT   UnTransforms the observed and predicted dependent variables for purposes of computing and plotting the residuals. All values will then be in their original form. This is a useful option since the transformed residuals and predicted values usually are difficult to interpret.   However, this option will raise computation time somewhat since an extra pass through the data is required. In addition, the untransformed residuals will no longer necessarily have a zero mean.   Note that this option does not affect the regression results. Only the residual listing will be affected.

COEF=   Saves the **COEF**ficients, the λs for each independent variable and the dependent variable, and ρ if the **AUTO** option is used.

LAMBDA=   Used to specify the value of **LAMBDA** desired by the user. Expensive iterations are eliminated with this option.

LAMS=   These options are used to do a manual grid test for λ. The **S**tarting
LAME=   value of **LAM**bda (**LAMS=**), the **E**nding value of **LAM**bda (**LAME=**)
LAMI=   and an **I**ncrement (**LAMI=**) should be specified. When the optimal λ has been determined it can be specified on the **LAMBDA=** option. The manual grid search is rarely needed. It may be necessary if the iterative procedure fails.   The manual grid search is not available when using the **AUTO** option.

RHO=   Specifies a fixed value for **RHO** to be used when the **AUTO** option is specified.

The available temporary variables on the **BOX** command are:

$ADR2, $ANF, $DF, $DW, $ERR, $K, $LLF, $N, $R2, $R2OP, $RAW, $RHO, $SIG2, $SSE, $SSR, $SST, $ZANF, $ZDF, $ZSSR and *$ZSST*.

For more information on temporary variables see the chapter *MISCELLANEOUS COMMANDS AND INFORMATION* and the chapter *ORDINARY LEAST SQUARES*.

As noted above, SHAZAM uses iterative methods to estimate Box-Cox regressions. In some cases the program will fail during the iterations with a floating-point overflow. If this happens, the data could be scaled by dividing all variables by a constant such as 100 or 1000. This is usually not a problem, however, unless the magnitude of the data is initially very large. Since many iterations are necessary for Box-Cox regressions, the costs will rise substantially for large sample sizes. The user should also be aware that the maximum likelihood methods used here are not for small samples, and the use of these techniques with small samples may yield nonsense results.

EXAMPLE

The output that follows shows the use of the **BOX** command with the Theil textile data set.

```
|_BOX CONSUME INCOME PRICE / DN ALL

DEPENDENT VARIABLE =CONSUME
DN OPTION IN EFFECT - DIVISOR IS N
BOX-COX REGRESSION          17 OBSERVATIONS

ITERATION LAMBDA   LOG-L.F.     GRADIENT   R-SQUARE      SSE        SSE/N
    1        .000  -46.5862    .466329E-01   .9744   .13613E-01   .80077E-03
    2       1.000  -51.6471   -5.06084       .9513   433.31       25.489
    3       -.618  -46.4049   -3.23983       .9762   .31739E-04   .18670E-05
    4      -1.000  -48.0606    4.33477       .9722   .92261E-06   .54271E-07
    5       -.382  -46.0401    3.26927       .9767   .30541E-03   .17965E-04
    6       -.236  -46.0919    -.354947      .9762   .12787E-02   .75217E-04
    7       -.472  -46.1138    .927319E-01   .9766   .12763E-03   .75075E-05
    8       -.326  -46.0353    .538015       .9766   .52622E-03   .30954E-04
    9       -.292  -46.0476    -.358561      .9765   .73786E-03   .43404E-04
   10       -.348  -46.0335    -.253926      .9766   .42730E-03   .25135E-04
   11       -.361  -46.0346    .861095E-01   .9766   .37579E-03   .22106E-04
   12       -.339  -46.0336    .457475E-01   .9766   .46264E-03   .27214E-04
   13       -.353  -46.0337    .536509E-02   .9766   .40683E-03   .23931E-04
   14       -.344  -46.0335    .302815E-01   .9766   .44046E-03   .25910E-04
   15       -.342  -46.0335    -.195690E-01  .9766   .44880E-03   .26400E-04
   16       -.346  -46.0335    -.136884E-01  .9766   .43538E-03   .25611E-04
   17       -.350  -46.0336    .235114E-01   .9766   .41708E-03   .24534E-04

BOX-COX REGRESSION FOR LAMBDA =     -.350000

 R-SQUARE =      .9766     R-SQUARE ADJUSTED =     .9733
VARIANCE OF THE ESTIMATE-SIGMA**2 =     .24534E-04
STANDARD ERROR OF THE ESTIMATE-SIGMA =    .49532E-02
SUM OF SQUARED ERRORS-SSE=    .41708E-03
MEAN OF DEPENDENT VARIABLE =     134.51
LOG OF THE LIKELIHOOD FUNCTION = -46.0336

                          ASYMPTOTIC
                          CONDITIONAL                                 BOX-COX
VARIABLE   ESTIMATED   STANDARD   T-RATIO        PARTIAL STANDARDIZED ELASTICITY
  NAME    COEFFICIENT   ERROR    **** DF   P-VALUE CORR. COEFFICIENT  AT MEANS
INCOME      1.1535     .1260       9.152      .000   .926     .3493     1.2665
PRICE       -.68995    .2606E-01  -26.48      .000  -.990   -1.0106     -.8413
CONSTANT    1.2292     .2810       4.375      .000   .760     .0000     6.8342
```

The **ALL** option is used and so SHAZAM transforms all the variables by the same λ. A value of $\lambda=1$ gives a linear model and a value of $\lambda=0$ gives a double log model.

Let $L^{(i)}$ be the value of the log-likelihood function and let $\tilde{\lambda}^{(i)}$ be the estimate of λ at iteration i. On the above estimation output the GRADIENT of the log-likelihood function with respect to λ is approximated as:

$$\left(L^{(i)} - L^{(i-1)} \right) \Big/ \left(\tilde{\lambda}^{(i)} - \tilde{\lambda}^{(i-1)} \right)$$

Likelihood ratio tests can be used to test hypotheses about the values of λ. For a test of the linear model the test statistic is:

$$2[L(\tilde{\lambda}) - L(\lambda = 1)]$$

This can be compared with a $\chi^2_{(1)}$ distribution. From the above output the test statistic is computed as:

$$2(-46.0336 + 51.647054) = 11.23$$

From statistical tables the 5% critical value is 3.84 and the 1% critical value is 6.64. The test statistic exceeds these critical values and, therefore, the linear model is rejected.

BOX-COX WITH RESTRICTIONS

The user may want to restrict some of the λs. When the **RESTRICT** option is used on the **BOX** command the **LAMBDA** command can be used to impose the restrictions. If the **ALL** option is not in effect, any of the right-hand side variables may be restricted to any λ. Those that are unrestricted will remain untransformed. If **RESTRICT** commands are used they must follow all **LAMBDA** commands (these are optional). For details on the **RESTRICT** command see the section *RESTRICTED LEAST SQUARES* in the chapter *ORDINARY LEAST SQUARES*. The **END** command should follow all the **LAMBDA** and **RESTRICT** commands. No λ may be restricted if the **TIDWELL** or **FULL** options are being used. The general format for restricted estimation is:

BOX *depvar indeps* / **RESTRICT** *options*
LAMBDA   *var1=value1   var2=value2* . . .
RESTRICT *equation*
END

The SHAZAM output that follows shows estimation results when the value of λ for *INCOME* is restricted to $\lambda=0$.

```
|_BOX CONSUME INCOME PRICE / DN ALL RESTRICT
|_LAMBDA INCOME=0
|_END

DEPENDENT VARIABLE =CONSUME
DN OPTION IN EFFECT - DIVISOR IS N

LAMBDA RESTRICTIONS --- VARIABLE     LAMBDA
                        INCOME        .0000
```

```
BOX-COX REGRESSION          17 OBSERVATIONS

ITERATION LAMBDA    LOG-L.F.     GRADIENT   R-SQUARE      SSE        SSE/N
    1      .000    -46.5862     .466329E-01   .9744     .13613E-01   .80077E-03
    2     1.000    -51.5842    -4.99795       .9516   430.12        25.301
    3     -.618    -46.3158    -3.25604       .9764     .31408E-04   .18475E-05
    4    -1.000    -47.8558     4.03182       .9728     .90064E-06   .52979E-07
    5     -.382    -46.0048     2.99505       .9768     .30414E-03   .17891E-04
    6     -.236    -46.0778    -.500439       .9763     .12766E-02   .75092E-04
    7     -.472    -46.0605    -.731765E-01   .9768     .12683E-03   .74606E-05
    8     -.326    -46.0092     .351498       .9766     .52461E-03   .30859E-04
    9     -.416    -46.0168     .842899E-01   .9768     .21753E-03   .12796E-04
   10     -.361    -46.0030     .248213       .9767     .37440E-03   .22023E-04
   11     -.348    -46.0040    -.803312E-01   .9767     .42582E-03   .25048E-04
   12     -.369    -46.0032    -.417153E-01   .9767     .34581E-03   .20342E-04
   13     -.356    -46.0032    -.311991E-02   .9767     .39325E-03   .23133E-04
   14     -.364    -46.0030    -.270137E-01   .9767     .36321E-03   .21365E-04
   15     -.366    -46.0030     .207597E-01   .9767     .35646E-03   .20968E-04
   16     -.363    -46.0030     .151163E-01   .9767     .36744E-03   .21614E-04
   17     -.360    -46.0030    -.120099E-01   .9767     .37689E-03   .22170E-04
```

BOX-COX REGRESSION FOR LAMBDA =   -.360000

R-SQUARE =   .9767   R-SQUARE ADJUSTED =   .9734
VARIANCE OF THE ESTIMATE-SIGMA**2 =   .22170E-04
STANDARD ERROR OF THE ESTIMATE-SIGMA =   .47085E-02
SUM OF SQUARED ERRORS-SSE=   .37689E-03
MEAN OF DEPENDENT VARIABLE =   134.51
LOG OF THE LIKELIHOOD FUNCTION = -46.0030

VARIABLE NAME	ESTIMATED COEFFICIENT	ASYMPTOTIC STANDARD ERROR	CONDITIONAL T-RATIO ***** DF	P-VALUE	PARTIAL CORR.	STANDARDIZED COEFFICIENT	BOX-COX ELASTICITY AT MEANS
INCOME	.21745	.2365E-01	9.196	.000	.926	.3504	1.2697
PRICE	-.68670	.2587E-01	-26.54	.000	-.990	-1.0113	-.8421
CONSTANT	2.7933	.1107	25.23	.000	.989	.0000	16.3104

13. COINTEGRATION AND UNIT ROOT TESTS

"It is interesting that Humans try to find Meaningful Patterns in things that are essentially random."

Mr. Data
Star Trek, 1992

The **COINT** command implements tests for unit roots and cointegration including Dickey-Fuller unit root tests, Phillips-Perron unit root tests and tests on the residuals of a cointegrating regression. References include Davidson and MacKinnon [1993, Chapter 20], Maddala [1992, Chapter 14] and special issues of the *Oxford Bulletin of Economics and Statistics* [1986], the *Journal of Economic Dynamics and Control* [1988] and the *Journal of Applied Econometrics* [1991].

UNIT ROOT TESTS

Dickey-Fuller Unit Root Tests

The finding of a unit root in a time series indicates nonstationarity which has implications for economic theory and modelling. Test statistics can be based on the OLS estimation results from a suitably specified regression equation. For a time series Y_t two forms of the "augmented Dickey-Fuller" regression equations are:

$$(1) \quad \Delta Y_t = \alpha_o + \alpha_1 Y_{t-1} + \sum_{j=1}^{p} \gamma_j \Delta Y_{t-j} + \varepsilon_t$$

$$(2) \quad \Delta Y_t = \alpha_o + \alpha_1 Y_{t-1} + \alpha_2 t + \sum_{j=1}^{p} \gamma_j \Delta Y_{t-j} + \varepsilon_t$$

where ε_t for $t = 1, \ldots, N$ is assumed to be Gaussian white noise. Equation (1) is with-constant, no-trend and (2) is with-constant, with-trend. The number of lagged terms p is chosen to ensure the errors are uncorrelated. The test statistics calculated are:

Null hypothesis	Test statistic	
$\alpha_1=0$ in (1)	(i) $N\hat{\alpha}_1$	z-test
$\alpha_1=0$ in (1)	(ii) t-ratio	τ-test
$\alpha_0= \alpha_1=0$ in (1)	F-test Φ_1	Unit root test (zero drift)
$\alpha_1=0$ in (2)	(i) $N\hat{\alpha}_1$	z-test
$\alpha_1=0$ in (2)	(ii) t-ratio	τ-test

$\alpha_0 = \alpha_1 = \alpha_2 = 0$ in (2)   F-test Φ_2 Unit root test (zero drift)

$\alpha_1 = \alpha_2 = 0$ in (2)   F-test Φ_3 Unit root test (non-zero drift)

When $\alpha_1 = 0$ the time series Y_t is nonstationary so that standard asymptotic analysis cannot be used to obtain the distributions of the test statistics. Various researchers have designed Monte Carlo experiments to generate critical values that can be used for testing purposes (see Fuller [1976], Dickey and Fuller [1981], Guilkey and Schmidt [1989], and Davidson and MacKinnon [1993]). The SHAZAM output reports asymptotic critical values.

The z-test depends on p (see the remarks in Davidson and MacKinnon [1993]) and, therefore, the SHAZAM output gives the z-test only when p=0. As a practical consideration, when p > 0, the treatment of initial values will affect the parameter estimates. In SHAZAM, the initial observations are deleted. Another method, that does not affect the asymptotic results, is to set the initial values of the ΔY_{t-j} to zero. Some researchers use the Akaike (AIC) and the Schwarz (SC) information criteria as a guide for selection of p and these statistics are reported on the SHAZAM output.

Phillips-Perron Unit Root Tests

As an alternative to the inclusion of lag terms to allow for serial correlation the Phillips-Perron method is to use a non-parametric correction for serial correlation. The approach is to first calculate the above unit root tests from regression equations with p=0. The statistics are then transformed to remove the effects of serial correlation on the asymptotic distribution of the test statistic. The critical values are the same as those used for the Dickey-Fuller tests. The formula for the transformed test statistics are listed in Perron [1988, Table 1, p.308-9]. The Newey and West [1987] method is used to construct an estimate of the error variance from the estimated residuals $\hat{\varepsilon}_t$ as:

$$\frac{1}{N} \sum_{t=1}^{N} \hat{\varepsilon}_t^2 + \frac{2}{N} \sum_{s=1}^{l} \omega(s,l) \sum_{t=s+1}^{N} \hat{\varepsilon}_t \hat{\varepsilon}_{t-s}$$

where l is a truncation lag parameter and $\omega(s,l)$ is a window. SHAZAM uses a window choice of:

$$\omega(s,l) = 1 - s/(l+1)$$

The selection of l is an important consideration and further discussion is available in Phillips [1987] and Perron [1988]. The **ARIMA** command (see the chapter *ARIMA MODELS*) can be used to inspect the time series properties of the variable to guide in the choice of the lag order. By default SHAZAM sets the order as the highest significant lag order from either the autocorrelation function or the partial autocorrelation function of the first differenced series.

TESTS FOR COINTEGRATION

An approach to testing for cointegration (or evidence of a long run relationship between non-stationary variables) is to construct test statistics from the residuals of a cointegrating regression. With M time series $Y_{t1}, \ldots, Y_{tM}$, each of which is I(1) (integrated of order 1), two forms of the cointegrating regression equations are:

(A) $Y_{t1} = \beta_0 + \sum_{j=2}^{M} \beta_j Y_{tj} + u_t$

(B) $Y_{t1} = \beta_0 + \beta_1 t + \sum_{j=2}^{M} \beta_j Y_{tj} + u_t$

Equation (A) is no-trend and equation (B) is with-trend. The choice of regressand is arbitrary and different choices can be considered. A test for no cointegration is given by a test for a unit root in the estimated residuals $\hat{u}_t$. The augmented Dickey-Fuller regression equation is:

$$\Delta \hat{u}_t = \alpha_* \hat{u}_{t-1} + \sum_{j=1}^{P} \phi_j \Delta \hat{u}_{t-j} + v_t$$

Test statistics are (i) $N\hat{\alpha}_*$ (the z-test) and (ii) a t-ratio test for $\alpha_*=0$ (the τ-test). Alternatively, Phillips unit root test statistics can be constructed that use a non-parametric correction for serial correlation. Sources of critical values include Phillips and Ouliaris [1990], MacKinnon [1991] and Davidson and MacKinnon [1993]. The SHAZAM output reports asymptotic critical values obtained from Davidson-MacKinnon. If a test statistic is smaller than the critical value then there is evidence for cointegration.

COINT COMMAND OPTIONS

In general, the format of the COINT command is:

COINT *vars / options*

where *vars* is a list of variable names and *options* is a list of desired options. The following options are available on the COINT command:

DN   Uses a divisor of N, rather than N-K (where K is the number of regressors), when estimating the variance used in calculating the t-statistics. The F-tests are computed with the standard finite sample adjustments.

DUMP   Gives output of interest to SHAZAM consultants.

LOG   Takes logs of the data.

MAX   Gives more detailed output including the correlogram of the first differenced series, the estimated lag coefficients of the augmented Dickey-Fuller regressions, and the parameter estimates of the cointegrating regressions.

BEG=, END=   Specifies the **BEG**inning and **END**ing observations to be used in the calculations. This option overrides the **SAMPLE** command and defaults to the sample range in effect.

NDIFF=   Specifies the order of differencing to transform the data.

NLAG=   Specifies the number of lag terms in the augmented Dickey-Fuller regressions or the truncation lag parameter for the Phillips tests. If this is not specified then the order is set as the highest significant lag order (using an approximate 95% confidence interval) from either the autocorrelation function or the partial autocorrelation function of the first differenced series (up to a maximum lag order of $\sqrt{N}$).

RESID=   Specifies a matrix to save the residuals from the regression equations used for the unit root tests. The first column is the residuals from the constant, no trend regression and the second column is the residuals from the constant, trend regression for the first series. The third and fourth column are the residuals for the second series (if requested). For example, to inspect the ACF of the residuals the following SHAZAM commands could be used.

```
SAMPLE 1 17
COINT CONSUME PRICE / NLAG=2 RESID=EMAT
* Adjust the sample period
SAMPLE 4 17
DO #=1,4
MATRIX E=EMAT(0,#)
ARIMA E
ENDO
```

SIGLEVEL=   Specifies the significance level for the critical values. The available choices are 1, 5 and 10. The default is **SIGLEVEL=10** for 10% critical values.

TESTSTAT=   Saves the test statistics in the variable specified.

TYPE=   Specifies the type of tests to calculate. The available options are:

DF for augmented Dickey-Fuller unit root tests. This is the default.

PP for Phillips-Perron unit root tests.

RESD for Dickey-Fuller tests on the residuals of cointegrating regressions.

RESP for Phillips tests on the residuals of cointegrating regressions.

For the cointegrating regressions the first variable given in the variable list for the **COINT** command is used as the regressand. Note that when the **TYPE=PP** or **TYPE=RESP** options are requested and the truncation lag order is set to 0 (**NLAG=0**) then the Dickey-Fuller unit root tests are calculated.

EXAMPLES

An example of Dickey-Fuller unit root tests for the Theil textile data follows.

```
|_COINT CONSUME PRICE

...NOTE..TEST LAG ORDER AUTOMATICALLY SET

 TOTAL NUMBER OF OBSERVATIONS =   17

 VARIABLE : CONSUME
 DICKEY-FULLER TESTS - NO.LAGS =  2   NO.OBS =   14

       NULL              TEST      ASY. CRITICAL
    HYPOTHESIS         STATISTIC     VALUE 10%
------------------------------------------------------------------
 CONSTANT, NO TREND
 A(1)=0   T-TEST        -1.4910      -2.57
 A(0)=A(1)=0             3.7439       3.78
                                             AIC =      5.143
                                             SC  =      5.326

------------------------------------------------------------------
 CONSTANT, TREND
 A(1)=0   T-TEST        -1.4131      -3.13
 A(0)=A(1)=A(2)=0        2.7911       4.03
 A(1)=A(2)=0             1.5715       5.34
                                             AIC =      5.187
                                             SC  =      5.416

------------------------------------------------------------------
```

```
VARIABLE : PRICE
DICKEY-FULLER TESTS - NO.LAGS =   0   NO.OBS =   16

      NULL            TEST        ASY. CRITICAL
   HYPOTHESIS       STATISTIC      VALUE 10%
--------------------------------------------------------------------
CONSTANT, NO TREND
A(1)=0   Z-TEST       -1.6049      -11.2
A(1)=0   T-TEST       -1.2120      -2.57
A(0)=A(1)=0            2.4019       3.78
                                              AIC =      3.502
                                              SC  =      3.599
--------------------------------------------------------------------
CONSTANT, TREND
A(1)=0   Z-TEST       -6.3269      -18.2
A(1)=0   T-TEST       -1.4458      -3.13
A(0)=A(1)=A(2)=0       2.0596       4.03
A(1)=A(2)=0            1.3886       5.34
                                              AIC =      3.533
                                              SC  =      3.678
```

In the above example the lag order p for the augmented Dickey-Fuller regression is set automatically (the method is described in the **NLAG=** option). For the *CONSUME* variable 2 lags were included and for the *PRICE* variable no lags were included. Note that the z-test is only reported when p=0. The unit root hypothesis can be rejected if the T-TEST statistic is smaller than the critical value. In all cases, the test statistic is not significant at the 10% level. For example, for the time series *CONSUME*, for the regression equation with constant and trend, the t-ratio test for $\alpha_1=0$ is -1.4131 which exceeds the critical value of -3.13. The listing shows that the tests for A(0)=A(1)=A(2)=0 and A(1)=A(2)=0 in the regression equation with constant and trend are not significant at the 10% level for any of the variables. Also, the Φ_1 test statistics for A(0)=A(1)=0 in the regression equation with constant and no trend do not exceed the critical values for the time series studied. The conclusion is that the null hypothesis of a unit root cannot be rejected for the *CONSUME* and *PRICE* time series.

The user should then verify that Dickey-Fuller tests on the first differences (not reported here) show stationarity so that the evidence is that the two time series are I(1). Unit root tests on first differences can be obtained by using the **NDIFF=1** option on the **COINT** command. Also, the sensitivity of the test results to different choices for the **NLAG=** option may be useful to examine. On the SHAZAM output the AIC test is the Akaike information criteria and the SC test is the Schwarz criteria. Another thing to consider is that, for macroeconomic time series, the **LOG** option may be sensible to use.

To evaluate whether a linear combination of the variables is stationary cointegrating regressions can be estimated as follows.

```
|_COINT CONSUME PRICE / TYPE=RESD

...NOTE..TEST LAG ORDER AUTOMATICALLY SET

COINTEGRATING REGRESSION - CONSTANT, NO TREND   NO.OBS =   17
REGRESSAND : CONSUME

  R-SQUARE =  .8961        DURBIN-WATSON =  1.191

  DICKEY-FULLER TESTS ON RESIDUALS - NO.LAGS =  0   M =  2

                        TEST      ASY. CRITICAL
                     STATISTIC     VALUE 10%
--------------------------------------------------------------------
NO CONSTANT, NO TREND
       Z-TEST       -9.8313       -17.1
       T-TEST       -2.3828       -3.04
                                          AIC =      4.035
                                          SC  =      4.083
--------------------------------------------------------------------

COINTEGRATING REGRESSION - CONSTANT, TREND      NO.OBS =   17
REGRESSAND : CONSUME

  R-SQUARE =  .8963        DURBIN-WATSON =  1.214

  DICKEY-FULLER TESTS ON RESIDUALS - NO.LAGS =  0   M =  2

                        TEST      ASY. CRITICAL
                     STATISTIC     VALUE 10%
--------------------------------------------------------------------
NO CONSTANT, NO TREND
       Z-TEST       -9.9990       -23.4
       T-TEST       -2.4364       -3.50
                                          AIC =      4.040
                                          SC  =      4.088
```

The output reports the R^2 and the Durbin-Watson test statistic from the cointegrating regressions. A high R^2 value and a low Durbin-Watson value is evidence of cointegration (for more discussion see Engle and Granger [1987]). The test statistics on the regression residuals can be compared with the critical values that are reported on the SHAZAM output. The results show that the null hypothesis of non-stationarity cannot be rejected. This suggests that the *CONSUME* and *PRICE* variables are not cointegrated.

TESTING USING SHAZAM PROCEDURES

For unit root testing other specifications of the regression equation can be used. For example, Ouliaris, Park and Phillips [1989] consider that a time series may be stationary around some polynomial trend. Perron [1989] proposes regressions that include dummy variables that recognize the possibility of exogenous changes in level or trend. Unfortunately, the asymptotic distribution of the unit root test statistic depends on the regressors included in the regression. Tests for seasonal unit roots are developed in Hylleberg, Engle, Granger and Yoo [1990] and applied examples of the methodology are given in Otto and Wirjanto [1990] and Lee and Siklos [1991]. Various testing methods can be implemented in SHAZAM by using the programming features illustrated in the chapter *PROGRAMMING IN SHAZAM*. A more general approach is to use SHAZAM procedures as described in the chapter *SHAZAM PROCEDURES*. This is demonstrated in the next example.

The Johansen Trace Test Procedure for Cointegration

The Johansen and Juselius [1990] procedure uses a maximum likelihood approach to construct test statistics for the number of cointegrating vectors. A SHAZAM procedure has been written to compute some test statistics for a model that includes quarterly seasonal dummy variables. The analysis uses logarithms of the data. To illustrate the use of this procedure the next list of SHAZAM commands reads 3 quarterly macroeconomic time series. It is assumed that previous investigation has established that the variables are I(1). The tests for cointegrating vectors, using log transformations of the data, are then run.

```
SAMPLE 1 164
READ(MACRO.DAT) Y C M
* Specify the filename of the SHAZAM procedure.
FILE PROC JOHANSEN
* Specify the maximum lag to use.
NLAG: 4
* Specify the variables.
VARS: Y C M
EXEC JOHANSEN
STOP
```

The SHAZAM output follows.

```
|_SAMPLE 1 164
|_READ(MACRO.DAT) Y C M
UNIT 88 IS NOW ASSIGNED TO: MACRO.DAT
   3 VARIABLES AND      164 OBSERVATIONS STARTING AT OBS       1

|_* Specify the filename of the SHAZAM procedure.
|_FILE PROC JOHANSEN

UNIT 82 IS NOW ASSIGNED TO: JOHANSEN
|_SET NOECHO
 _PROC JOHANSEN
   _         SET NODOECHO
    NLAG_
    4.000000
 Y C M
        R_              LTRACE_        LMAX_
        2.               2.295          2.295
        1.               8.596          6.301
        0.              26.763         18.167
```

```
  _        SET ECHO
           PROCEND
  _
|_STOP
```

On the SHAZAM output the column labelled LTRACE_ reports the trace test statistic and the column LMAX_ lists the maximal eigenvalue test statistic. The procedure illustrated here imposes no restrictions on the constant term so that the critical values tabulated in Johansen and Juselius [1990, Table A2] can be used. To test the hypothesis of no cointegrating relations (r=0) against the general alternative of r>0 the trace test statistic has a calculated value of 26.763. The 10% critical value is 28.4 and so the null is not rejected. To test the null that r=0 against the alternative that r=1 the maximal eigenvalue test statistic is reported as 18.167 and, again, this is less than the 10% critical value of 19.0. The general conclusion is that there is no significant evidence for any cointegrating relations in the data.

A complete listing of the SHAZAM procedure follows. The commands demonstrate many capabilities of the **MATRIX** command (see the chapter *MATRIX MANIPULATION*).

```
SET NOECHO
PROC JOHANSEN
* ==========================================================================
*              Johansen Tests for Cointegration
*
* Reference: S. Johansen and K. Juselius, "Maximum Likelihood Estimation
*     and Inference on Cointegration - with Applications to the Demand
*     for Money", OXFORD BULLETIN OF ECONOMICS AND STATISTICS, Vol 52,
*     1990, pp. 169-210.
*
* Equation numbers refer to the above paper.
*
* Notes:
* (1) The model includes a constant term and three seasonal dummies.
*     This is appropriate for quarterly time series.
* (2) No restrictions on the constant term are imposed. This allows
*     for linear trends in the data.
*
* Critical values for the test statistics are tabulated in
* Johansen and Juselius (1990), Table A2.
*
* TRACE TEST
* Null hypothesis: No. of cointegrating vectors is less than or equal to r.
*
*          10 % critical values           5 % critical values
*     r    p=2    p=3    p=4    p=5    r    p=2    p=3    p=4    p=5
*     ---------------------------------  ---------------------------------
*     4                          6.7     4                          8.1
*     3                   6.7   15.6     3                   8.1   17.8
*     2           6.7   15.6   28.4     2           8.1   17.8   31.3
*     1    6.7   15.6   28.4   45.2     1    8.1   17.8   31.3   48.4
*     0   15.6   28.4   45.2   66.0     0   17.8   31.3   48.4   70.0
*     r = number of cointegrating vectors
*     p = number of time series
```

```
*
* MAXIMUM EIGENVALUE TEST
* Null hypothesis: No. of cointegrating vectors is r.
* Alternative: r+1 cointegrating vectors
*
*           10 % critical values          5 % critical values
*      r    p=2    p=3    p=4    p=5    r    p=2    p=3    p=4    p=5
*      -----------------------------    -----------------------------
*      4                          6.7   4                          8.1
*      3                   6.7   12.8   3                   8.1   14.6
*      2            6.7   12.8   19.0   2            8.1   14.6   21.3
*      1     6.7   12.8   19.0   24.9   1     8.1   14.6   21.3   27.3
*      0    12.8   19.0   24.9   30.8   0    14.6   21.3   27.3   33.3
*
* ===> WARNINGS
* (1) The data is transformed to logarithms. If this is not desired then
* change the command MATRIX X_=LOG(X_) to MATRIX X_=X_
* (2) If quarterly seasonal dummies are not required then change the
* command MATRIX QD_=SEAS(T_,4) to GENR QD_=1
*
*   Use:
*     FILE PROC JOHANSEN
*     SAMPLE beg end
*     NLAG: lag k  (k > 1)
*     VARS: list of time series
*     EXEC JOHANSEN
*
* ========================================================================
SET NODOECHO
SET NOOUTPUT
COPY [VARS] X_ / TROW=1,$N
* Take logs of the data
MATRIX X_=LOG(X_)
GEN1 P_=$COLS
GEN1 T_=$ROWS
* Generate seasonal dummy variables
MATRIX QD_=SEAS(T_,4)
*GENR QD_=1
SAMPLE 2 T_
* Generate first differences
MATRIX DX_=X_-LAG(X_)
* Allocate arrays to store results
GEN1 NLAG_=[NLAG]
IF1(NLAG_.LT.2) NLAG_=2
PRINT NLAG_
GEN1 NLL_=NLAG_-1
GEN1 KK_=P_*NLL_
DIM  EA0_ T_ P_ EAK_ T_ P_  DXVEC_ T_ KK_
SET NOWARN
DO #=1,P_
* Generate NLAG-period lagged variables
GENR LY#_=LAG(X_:#,NLAG_)
ENDO
SET WARN
* Set up a matrix of lagged variables to use as regressors
GEN1 BEG_=NLAG_ + 1
SAMPLE BEG_ T_
GEN1 C1_=1
```

```
DO #=1,NLL_
GEN1 C2_=C1_+P_-1
MATRIX DXL_=LAG(DX_,#)
COPY DXL_ DXVEC_ / FROW=1;T_ TROW=1;T_ FCOL=1;P_ TCOL=C1_;C2_
GEN1 C1_=C2_+1
ENDO
* Obtain the residuals stated in Equation (3.6) and (3.7)
DO #=1,P_
* Regress first differences on the lagged differences
OLS DX_:# DXVEC_ QD_ / RESID=EA0_:# NOCONSTANT
* Regress NLAG-period lags on the lagged differences
OLS LY#_ DXVEC_ QD_ / RESID=EAK_:# NOCONSTANT
ENDO
GEN1 T1_=$N
COPY EA0_ E0_ / FROW=BEG_;T_ TROW=1;T1_ FCOL=1;P_ TCOL=1;P_
COPY EAK_ EK_ / FROW=BEG_;T_ TROW=1;T1_ FCOL=1;P_ TCOL=1;P_
* Note: the MATRIX command ignores the current SAMPLE command
* Do the calculations in Equation (3.9)
MATRIX S00_=E0_'E0_/T1_
MATRIX S0K_=E0_'EK_/T1_
MATRIX SKK_=EK_'EK_/T1_
* Cholesky decomposition - SKK=CC'
MATRIX C_=CHOL(SKK_)
MATRIX CINV_=INV(C_)
* Matrix B is a symmetric positive definite matrix
MATRIX B_=CINV_*S0K_'INV(S00_)*S0K_*CINV_'
* Get the eigenvalues of B (real and positive) in descending order
MATRIX LAMBDA_=EIGVAL(B_)
SAMPLE 1 P_
SORT LAMBDA_
GENR LMAX_=-T1_*LOG(1-LAMBDA_)
* Construct likelihood ratio test statistics from Equation (4.8)
GENR LTRACE_=-T1_*SUM(LOG(1-LAMBDA_))
GENR R_=P_-TIME(0)
** The variables analyzed are:
PRINT VARS / NONAMES
FORMAT(5X,F5.0,8X,F10.3,3X,F10.3)
PRINT R_ LTRACE_ LMAX_ / FORMAT
DELETE / ALL_
SET OUTPUT
SET DOECHO
SET ECHO
PROCEND
```

14. DIAGNOSTIC TESTS

"That is a question which has puzzled many an expert, and why? Because there was no reliable test. Now we have the Sherlock Holmes test, and there will no longer be any difficulty."
Holmes to Watson in "A Study in Scarlet" by A. Conan Doyle

SHAZAM can perform a number of diagnostic tests after estimating a single-equation regression model including tests on recursive residuals, Goldfeld-Quandt tests, Chow tests, RESET specification error tests, and tests for autocorrelation and heteroskedasticity. The **DIAGNOS** command is used for these tests and many other statistics. Some references are: Harvey [1990, Chapter 5]; Godfrey, McAleer, and McKenzie [1988]; Zarembka [1974, Chapter 1]; Breusch and Pagan [1979]; and Pagan and Hall [1983].

DIAGNOS *COMMAND OPTIONS*

The **DIAGNOS** command can be used following an **OLS** command. In general, the format of the **DIAGNOS** command is:

OLS *depvar indeps*
DIAGNOS / *options*

where *options* is a list of desired options. The options are summarized below and then are more fully described and demonstrated in the *EXAMPLES* section that follows.

The available options on the **DIAGNOS** command are:

ACF   Prints the AutoCorrelation Function of residuals and associated test statistics.

BACKWARD   Used with the **RECUR** option to compute **BACKWARD**s recursive residuals.

BOOTLIST   Used with the **BOOTSAMP=** option to print the entire list of Bootstrapped coefficients for every generated sample. This could generate a lot of output.

CHOWTEST   Produces a set of sequential **CHOW TEST** statistics and sequential Goldfeld-Quandt Test statistics which split the sample of dependent and independent variables in 2 pieces at every possible point. Some users may wish to sort the data first as suggested by Goldfeld and

Quandt [1972]. It also computes some recursive residuals test statistics. Also see the **CHOWONE=, GQOBS=** and **MHET=** options.

CTEST   Produces Pinkse's [1996] C-test for serial independence of error terms and stores the result in the temporary variable *$CTES*. The C-test tests for independence of the errors instead of lack of correlation. In the SHAZAM implementation the null hypothesis is independence and the alternative hypothesis is serial dependence of order one. The test is consistent against higher order dependence structures also, as long as under the alternative consecutive elements of the time series are not independent.

GNU   Prepares **GNUPLOT** plots of the recursive residuals when the **MAX** or **RECUR** options are specified. For more information on this option see the *GNUPLOT* section in the *PLOTS* chapter. With the **GNU** option the **APPEND, OUTPUT=, DEVICE=, PORT=** and **COMMFILE=** options are also available as described for the **PLOT** command.

HET   Runs a series of tests for **HET**eroskedasticity.

JACKKNIFE   Runs a series of regressions, successively omitting a different observation to get **JACKKNIFE** coefficient estimates. An example of jackknife estimation is in the Appendix to Chapter 9 in the *Judge Handbook*.

LIST   Prints a table of observed (Y) and predicted (Ŷ) values of the dependent variable, and regression residuals (e). This gives the same output as the **LIST** option on **OLS**.

MAX   Equivalent to specifying the **LIST, RECUR, ACF, BACKWARD, CHOWTEST, RESET**, and **HET** options. The computation of all these tests can be slow and can generate a lot of output.

RECEST   **NORECEST** suppresses the printing of the **REC**ursive **EST**imated
NORECEST   coefficients when the **RECUR** option is specified.

RECRESID   **NORECRESID** suppresses the printing of the **REC**ursive **RESID**uals
NORECRESID   when the **RECUR** option is specified.

RECUR   Performs **RECUR**sive Estimation by running a series of regressions by adding one observation per regression. It is often used for tests of structural change. Recursive residuals and CUSUM tests are printed along with a recursive t-test and Harvey's recursive residuals exact heteroskedasticity test. Also see the **MHET=** and **SIGLEVEL=** options.

RESET   Used to compute Ramsey [1969] **RESET** (regression specification error test) statistics.

WIDE   Reduces the width of output to 80 columns. The default value is
NOWIDE   explained in the chapter *SET AND DISPLAY*.

BOOTSAMP=   Specifies the number of samples desired for **BOOTSAMP** experiments on the previous OLS regression. This option is not appropriate with models that include lagged dependent variables as regressors. Examples of this option can be found in the Appendix to Chapter 9 of the *Judge Handbook*. Also see the example *Bootstrapping Regression Coefficients* in the chapter *PROGRAMMING IN SHAZAM*.

Initially, a regression is run and the K coefficients $\left(\hat{\beta}\right)$ and N residuals (e) are saved. Then, random samples of size N of residuals are drawn with replacement and the residuals are normalized using:
$$e_t^* = e_t / \sqrt{1 - K / N}$$
Next, a new dependent variable is generated as: $Y^* = X\hat{\beta} + e^*$

The bootstrap estimates are computed as: $\hat{\beta}^* = (X'X)^{-1} X'Y^*$

BOOTUNIT=   Writes out the generated coefficients for each sample in a **BOOT**strap experiment on the **UNIT** specified. It is used in conjunction with the **BOOTSAMP=** option. A file should be assigned to the unit with the SHAZAM **FILE** command or an operating system command. Units 11-49 may be used.

CHOWONE=   Specifies the number of observations in the first group for the Chow test and Goldfeld-Quandt test. (The **CHOWTEST** option reports test statistics at every breakpoint).

GQOBS=   Used with the **CHOWTEST** option to specify the number of central observations to be omitted for the Goldfeld-Quandt Test. The default is zero.

MHET=   Used with the **CHOWTEST** and **RECUR** options to specify M, the number of residuals to use in Harvey's recursive residuals exact heteroskedasticity test.

RECUNIT=   Used with the **RECUR** option if you want to write the **REC**ursive estimates and residuals on the **UNIT** specified. A file should be assigned to the unit with the SHAZAM **FILE** command or an operating system command. Units 11-49 may be used.

SIGLEVEL= Used with the **RECUR** option to specify the significance level desired for the CUSUM and CUSUMSQ tests. The available choices are 1, 5, and 10. The default is **SIGLEVEL=5**.

Warnings: After a regression with the **RESTRICT** option or a distributed lag model that incorporates restrictions the **DIAGNOS** command will not recognize these restrictions. That is, the **CHOWTEST** and **RECUR** options will work with the unrestricted model. After a weighted least squares regression with the **WEIGHT=** option the **DIAGNOS** command will compute test statistics with the untransformed residuals and so the **HET** option will not be appropriate for testing for heteroskedasticity in the transformed residuals.

EXAMPLES

For the regression equation $Y_t = X_t'\beta + \varepsilon_t$ with K coefficients β, denote the estimated residuals by e_t and the predicted values by $\hat{Y}_t$ for t=1,...,N .

Using Theil's textile data a complete listing of diagnostic tests is obtained with the SHAZAM commands:

```
OLS CONSUME INCOME PRICE
DIAGNOS / MAX
```

Users may want to be selective in the tests that they consider. The examples that follow show SHAZAM output for some of the **DIAGNOS** options that is obtained after the above OLS regression.

Tests for Autocorrelation

The output produced with the **ACF** option is:

```
RESIDUAL CORRELOGRAM
  LM-TEST FOR HJ:RHO(J)=0, STATISTIC IS STANDARD NORMAL
  LAG      RHO        STD ERR     T-STAT      LM-STAT     DW-TEST BOX-PIERCE-LJUNG
    1     -.1455       .2425      -.5998       .7014      2.0185       .4272
    2     -.2231       .2425      -.9200      1.2257      2.0359      1.4994
    3      .1871       .2425       .7716       .9975      1.1956      2.3074
    4     -.3002       .2425     -1.2377      1.7388      2.0133      4.5463
  CHI-SQUARE WITH   4  D.F. IS      3.333
```

The residual autocorrelations (RHO) are calculated as:

$$\hat{\rho}_j = \frac{\sum_{t=j+1}^{N} e_t e_{t-j}}{\sum_{t=1}^{N} e_t^2} \qquad \text{for } j=1,\ldots,p$$

Note that SHAZAM automatically sets the maximum lag order p based on the sample size of the data. In the above example p=4. If the autoregressive order is j the higher order autocorrelations are asymptotically normally distributed with zero mean and standard deviation $1/\sqrt{N}$ (given on the SHAZAM output in the column STD ERR). The t-statistics (T-STAT) are calculated as $\sqrt{N}\hat{\rho}_j$.

A Lagrange multiplier statistic for a test of H_0: $\rho_j=0$ is discussed in Breusch and Pagan [1980, Section 3.2]. Denote e_{-j} as the (N x 1) vector containing e_{t-j} (with zeroes for initial values). The test statistic is:

$$LM = N^2\hat{\rho}_j^2\tilde{\sigma}^2 \Big/ \left[e'_{-j}e_{-j} - e'_{-j}X(X'X)^{-1}X'e_{-j}\right] \qquad \text{where} \quad \tilde{\sigma}^2 = \frac{e'e}{N}$$

The value $\sqrt{LM}$ is reported as the LM-STAT statistic on the SHAZAM output. These test statistics have an asymptotic standard normal distribution. This test is appropriate when X contains lagged dependent variables.

A test for $H_0: \rho_1 = \rho_2 = \ldots = \rho_J = 0$ is given by the Box-Pierce-Ljung statistic (also see the chapter *ARIMA MODELS*) computed as:

$$Q = N(N+2)\sum_{j=1}^{J}\frac{1}{N-j}\hat{\rho}_j^2 \qquad \text{for } J=1,\ldots,p$$

This test is not appropriate when X includes lagged dependent variables. Under the null hypothesis Q has an asymptotic χ_J^2 distribution. The Q statistic incorporates a small sample adjustment to give a modified form of the Box-Pierce statistic. The chi-square statistic reported at the end of the ACF output is the Box-Pierce statistic for a test that the residual autocorrelations are jointly zero when there are no lagged dependent variables. The statistic is given by:

$$N\sum_{j=1}^{p}\hat{\rho}_j^2$$

This statistic can be compared with a χ_p^2 distribution.

Tests for Heteroskedasticity

The output produced with the **HET** option is:

```
HETEROSKEDASTICITY TESTS
  E**2 ON YHAT:          CHI-SQUARE =      2.495 WITH 1 D.F.
  E**2 ON YHAT**2:       CHI-SQUARE =      2.658 WITH 1 D.F.
  E**2 ON LOG(YHAT**2):  CHI-SQUARE =      2.303 WITH 1 D.F.
  E**2 ON X (B-P-G) TEST:      CHI-SQUARE =      4.900 WITH   2 D.F.
  E**2 ON LAG(E**2)  ARCH TEST: CHI-SQUARE =     1.490 WITH   1 D.F.
  LOG(E**2) ON X (HARVEY) TEST: CHI-SQUARE =     3.421 WITH   2 D.F.
  ABS(E) ON X (GLEJSER) TEST:   CHI-SQUARE =     4.202 WITH   2 D.F.
```

The test statistics are obtained from the results of auxiliary regressions of the form:

	Regressand	Regressors	Test Statistic	D.F.
	e_t^2	$\hat{Y}_t$, constant	NR^2	1
	e_t^2	$\hat{Y}_t^2$, constant	NR^2	1
	e_t^2	$\log(\hat{Y}_t^2)$, constant	NR^2	1
B-P-G	e_t^2	X_t	NR^2	$K-1$
ARCH	e_t^2	e_{t-1}^2, constant	NR^2	1
Harvey	$\log(e_t^2)$	X_t	$SSR/4.9348$	$K-1$
Glejser	$\lvert e_t \rvert$	X_t	$SSR/[(1-\frac{2}{\pi})\tilde{\sigma}_\varepsilon^2]$	$K-1$

where $\tilde{\sigma}_\varepsilon^2 = e'e/N$ and R^2 and SSR are the multiple coefficient of determination and the regression sum of squares respectively from the auxiliary regression. The tests can be compared with a χ^2 distribution with degrees of freedom as given in the D.F. column. (The null hypothesis is homoskedasticity). The B-P-G test is named from Breusch-Pagan-Godfrey (see Breusch and Pagan [1979] and Godfrey [1978]) and is discussed in Judge et al. [1985, Equation 11.3.4]. The ARCH test was introduced by Engle [1982]. The Harvey test is from Harvey [1976] and is discussed in Judge et al. [1985, Equation 11.2.60]. The Glejser test is due to Glejser [1969] and is in Judge et al. [1985, Equation 11.2.29].

It is useful to note that these tests can be calculated with SHAZAM commands. After most SHAZAM commands temporary variables are available that can be used in subsequent calculations. For example, N is the number of observations used in the regression, $R2$ is the R^2 and PI is the value of π. The SHAZAM commands that follow show how to replicate the statistics reported by **DIAGNOS / HET**. Note that the ? prefix instructs SHAZAM to suppress all output from the command.

```
?OLS CONSUME INCOME PRICE / DN RESID=E PREDICT=YHAT
?GEN1 SIG2=$SIG2
GENR E2=E*E
GENR YHAT2=YHAT*YHAT
GENR LYHAT2=LOG(YHAT2)
GENR LE2=LOG(E2)
GENR ABSE=ABS(E)
* E**2 ON YHAT
?OLS E2 YHAT
?GEN1 T1=$N*$R2
* E**2 ON YHAT**2
?OLS E2 YHAT2
?GEN1 T2=$N*$R2
* E**2 ON LOG(YHAT**2)
?OLS E2 LYHAT2
?GEN1 T3=$N*$R2
* B-P-G TEST
?OLS E2 INCOME PRICE
?GEN1 BPG=$N*$R2
* ARCH TEST
?OLS E2 E2(1.1)
?GEN1 ARCH=$N*$R2
* HARVEY TEST
?OLS LE2 INCOME PRICE
?GEN1 HARV=$SSR/4.9348
* GLEJSER TEST
?OLS ABSE INCOME PRICE
?GEN1 GLEJ=$SSR/( (1-2/$PI)*SIG2 )
PRINT T1 T2 T3 BPG ARCH HARV GLEJ
```

The SHAZAM output from the above commands is:

```
|_?OLS CONSUME INCOME PRICE / DN RESID=E PREDICT=YHAT
|_?GEN1 SIG2=$SIG2
|_GENR E2=E*E
|_GENR YHAT2=YHAT*YHAT
|_GENR LYHAT2=LOG(YHAT2)
|_GENR LE2=LOG(E2)
|_GENR ABSE=ABS(E)
|_* E**2 ON YHAT
|_?OLS E2 YHAT
|_?GEN1 T1=$N*$R2
|_* E**2 ON YHAT**2
|_?OLS E2 YHAT2
|_?GEN1 T2=$N*$R2
|_* E**2 ON LOG(YHAT**2)
|_?OLS E2 LYHAT2
|_?GEN1 T3=$N*$R2
|_* B-P-G TEST
|_?OLS E2 INCOME PRICE
```

```
|_?GEN1 BPG=$N*$R2
|_* ARCH TEST
|_?OLS E2 E2(1.1)
|_?GEN1 ARCH=$N*$R2
|_* HARVEY TEST
|_?OLS LE2 INCOME PRICE
|_?GEN1 HARV=$SSR/4.9348
|_* GLEJSER TEST
|_?OLS ABSE INCOME PRICE
|_?GEN1 GLEJ=$SSR/( (1-2/$PI)*SIG2 )
|_PRINT T1 T2 T3 BPG ARCH HARV GLEJ
    T1
   2.494585
    T2
   2.657886
    T3
   2.303134
    BPG
   4.899669
    ARCH
   1.490021
    HARV
   3.420607
    GLEJ
   4.202336
```

Recursive Residuals and the CUSUM and CUSUMSQ Tests

The output produced with the **RECUR** option is:

```
RECURSIVE COEFFICIENT ESTIMATES
     3    .58599        1.1338       -71.974
     4   -.54970E-01   -1.2802       233.31
     5   -.86357       -1.9976       384.60
     6    .92446E-01   -1.5186       242.54
     7    .60090       -1.2248       163.09
     8    .61319       -1.4191       180.66
     9    .36233       -1.6835       231.55
    10    .55817       -1.5320       197.07
    11    .59587       -1.5096       191.07
    12    .93135       -1.3893       145.05
    13   1.0961        -1.3266       122.08
    14   1.0210        -1.3876       135.31
    15   1.0177        -1.3746       134.45
    16   1.0213        -1.3458       131.41
    17   1.0617        -1.3830       130.71
```

OBS	REC-RES	CUSUM	BOUND	LOWER	CUSUMSQ	UPPER
RECURSIVE RESIDUALS - SIGNIFICANCE LEVEL = 5%						
4	.94469	.16379	4.0538	-.32902	.00206	.47188
5	2.2989	.56238	4.5605	-.25759	.01426	.54331
6	2.7913	1.04635	5.0673	-.18616	.03224	.61474
7	3.7605	1.69835	5.5740	-.11474	.06487	.68616
8	5.2155	2.60264	6.0807	-.04331	.12765	.75759
9	2.5217	3.03985	6.5875	.02812	.14232	.82902
10	-3.5083	2.43157	7.0942	.09955	.17073	.90045

11	-.95106	2.26667	7.6009	.17098	.17282	.97188
12	-9.1586	.67873	8.1076	.24241	.36639	1.04331
13	-8.5802	-.80893	8.6144	.31384	.53629	1.11474
14	7.2539	.44877	9.1211	.38526	.65773	1.18616
15	-2.4963	.01595	9.6278	.45669	.67211	1.25759
16	-6.5587	-1.12122	10.1345	.52812	.77138	1.32902
17	9.9530	.60447	10.6413	.59955	1.00000	1.40045

```
HARVEY-COLLIER  [1977] RECURSIVE T-TEST =           .1616  WITH    13 D.F.
HARVEY-PHILLIPS [1974] HETEROSKEDASTICITY TEST =   7.1480  WITH M =    4
```

A good discussion of recursive least squares is in Harvey [1990, Chapter 2.6]. The RECURSIVE COEFFICIENT ESTIMATES are OLS estimates based on the first t observations. Therefore, for t=N the recursive coefficients are identical to OLS. On the above output it can be verified that the coefficient estimates at 17 are the same as the coefficient estimates that are produced with the **OLS** command. Denote the recursive coefficients by b_t for t=K,...,N and define the t x K matrix $X_{(t)}$ as the matrix containing $X_1, X_2, \ldots, X_t$. The recursive residuals (in the column REC-RES on the SHAZAM output) are calculated as standardized prediction errors as:

$$v_t = (Y_t - X_t'b_{t-1})\Big/ \sqrt{1+X_t'\big(X_{(t-1)}'X_{(t-1)}\big)^{-1}X_t} \qquad \text{for } t=K+1,\ldots,N$$

The CUSUM (cumulative sum) of recursive residuals is:

$$W_t = \frac{1}{\hat{\sigma}} \sum_{j=K+1}^{t} v_j \qquad \text{for } t=K+1,\ldots,N, \quad \text{where} \quad \hat{\sigma}^2 = \frac{1}{N-K-1} \sum_{t=K+1}^{N} (v_t - \bar{v})^2$$

and $\bar{v}$ is the mean of the recursive residuals. The CUSUMSQ (cumulative sum of squares) is:

$$WW_t = \sum_{j=K+1}^{t} v_j^2 \Big/ \sum_{t=K+1}^{N} v_t^2 \qquad \text{for } t=K+1,\ldots,N$$

A test of misspecification can be based on the inspection of the CUSUM and CUSUMSQ of the recursive residuals. The construction of significance lines is developed in Brown, Durbin and Evans [1975]. The significance values for the CUSUMSQ test are tabulated in Durbin [1969] and reprinted in Harvey [1990, p. 366-7]. The SHAZAM output reports approximate 5% upper and lower bounds for the CUSUMSQ test. The **SIGLEVEL=** option can be used to request 1% or 10% bounds. Brown, Durbin and Evans [1975] recommend plots as a way of presenting these tests and they comment that "the significance tests suggested should be regarded as yardsticks for the interpretation of data rather than leading to hard and fast decisions". Plots are obtained with the **GNU** option. Note that these tests are not valid for models with lagged dependent variables.

Test statistics can be constructed to detect departures from randomness in the residuals. To test the hypothesis that the mean of the recursive residuals is zero the SHAZAM output reports the RECURSIVE T-TEST (from Harvey and Collier [1977] and given in Harvey [1990, Chapter 5, Equation 2.10]) calculated as:

$$\bar{v} \Big/ \sqrt{\hat{\sigma}^2/(N-K)}$$

The statistic can be compared with a t-distribution with (N–K–1) degrees of freedom. The second test statistic that the SHAZAM output reports is a HETEROSKEDASTICITY TEST proposed in Harvey and Phillips [1974] and given in Harvey [1990, Chapter 5, Equation 2.12]. This test statistic is based on the first set and last set of m recursive residuals and is calculated as:

$$\sum_{t=N-m+1}^{N} v_t^2 \Big/ \sum_{t=K+1}^{K+m} v_t^2$$

This has an $F_{(m,m)}$ distribution under the null hypothesis of homoskedasticity. SHAZAM sets m equal to (N–K)/3. Other choices of m can be set with the **MHET=** option.

The output produced with the **BACKWARD** and **RECUR** options is:

```
BACKWARDS
RECURSIVE COEFFICIENT ESTIMATES
    15    6.2400        1.5400       -576.61
    14    17.460       -12.984       -853.75
    13    2.1880        -2.4999        83.360
    12    1.8767        -2.3500       106.17
    11    2.0353        -2.2604        85.733
    10    2.0944        -2.2117        77.007
     9    2.1966        -2.1140        60.963
     8    2.1916        -2.0003        54.550
     7    2.0917        -1.8616        56.131
     6    2.1017        -1.8725        55.789
     5    1.8743        -1.7343        70.398
     4    1.8319        -1.7090        73.130
     3    1.3919        -1.5101       105.21
     2    1.2061        -1.4356       119.36
     1    1.0617        -1.3830       130.71

BACKWARDS
RECURSIVE RESIDUALS - SIGNIFICANCE LEVEL = 5%
  OBS    REC-RES       CUSUM    BOUND        LOWER    CUSUMSQ   UPPER
   14    5.6889      1.68608   4.0538       -.32902   .07469    .47188
   13   11.008       4.94850   4.5605       -.25759   .35432    .54331
   12    3.2906      5.92376   5.0673       -.18616   .37930    .61474
   11    4.9015      7.37648   5.5740       -.11474   .43475    .68616
   10    .98227      7.66761   6.0807       -.04331   .43698    .75759
```

9	2.1057	8.29170	6.5875	.02812	.44721	.82902
8	1.7982	8.82465	7.0942	.09955	.45467	.90045
7	3.0412	9.72602	7.6009	.17098	.47602	.97188
6	-.45786	9.59031	8.1076	.24241	.47650	1.04331
5	6.4177	11.49238	8.6144	.31384	.57155	1.11474
4	1.3958	11.90606	9.1211	.38526	.57605	1.18616
3	9.8188	14.81615	9.6278	.45669	.79854	1.25759
2	6.4933	16.74062	10.1345	.52812	.89584	1.32902
1	6.7182	18.73175	10.6413	.59955	1.00000	1.40045

```
BACKWARDS
HARVEY-COLLIER   [1977] RECURSIVE T-TEST =            5.0063 WITH   13 D.F.
HARVEY-PHILLIPS [1974] HETEROSKEDASTICITY TEST =       .9855 WITH M =      4
```

The backward recursive coefficients and recursive residuals estimates are calculated using the same formulas as given above, but the calculations are started at the end, instead of at the beginning, of the sample.

The CHOW Test and Goldfeld-Quandt Test

The output produced with the **CHOWTEST** option is:

```
HARVEY-COLLIER   [1977] RECURSIVE T-TEST =            .1616 WITH   13 D.F.
HARVEY-PHILLIPS [1974] HETEROSKEDASTICITY TEST =     7.1480 WITH M =      4

BACKWARDS
HARVEY-COLLIER   [1977] RECURSIVE T-TEST =            5.0063 WITH   13 D.F.
HARVEY-PHILLIPS [1974] HETEROSKEDASTICITY TEST =      .9855 WITH M =      4

SEQUENTIAL CHOW AND GOLDFELD-QUANDT TESTS
N1  N2   SSE1     SSE2      CHOW  PVALUE   G-Q       DF1  DF2 PVALUE
 4  13  .89245   247.66   2.7256   .095 .3604E-01    1   10  .147
 5  12  6.1774   206.47   3.8048   .043 .1346        2    9  .124
 6  11  13.969   206.26   3.5476   .051 .1806        3    8  .093
 7  10  28.110   197.02   3.3908   .058 .2497        4    7  .099
 8   9  55.312   193.78   2.7117   .096 .3425        5    6  .130
 9   8  61.671   189.35   2.6628   .100 .2714        6    5  .072
10   7  73.979   188.38   2.3892   .124 .2244        7    4  .042
11   6  74.883   164.36   2.9744   .078 .1709        8    3  .020
12   5  158.76   153.53   1.4209   .289 .2298        9    2  .048
13   4  232.38   32.364   2.3346   .130 .7180       10    1  .265

       CHOW TEST - F DISTRIBUTION WITH DF1=   3 AND DF2=  11
```

The Chow [1960] test gives a test for structural change. The SHAZAM output gives statistics that test for breaks at t=K+1,...,N–K–1. The Chow test statistic is calculated as:

$$\text{CHOW} = \frac{(\text{SSE} - \text{SSE1} - \text{SSE2})/K}{(\text{SSE1} + \text{SSE2})/(N_1 + N_2 - 2K)}$$

where SSE1 and SSE2 are the sum of squared errors from the first and second parts of the split sample, N is the number of observations in the entire sample, K is the number of estimated parameters, N_1 and N_2 are the observations in the first and second part of the split sample respectively, and SSE is the residual sum of squares from the regression over the entire sample. If the test statistic is less than the critical value from an $F_{(K, N_1+N_2-2K)}$ distribution then there is no evidence for a structural break.

The Goldfeld-Quandt [1965, 1972] (G-Q) statistic provides a test for different error variance between two subsets of observations. Denote the variance in the first subset by σ_1^2 and the variance in the second subset by σ_2^2. The null hypothesis is $H_0:\sigma_1^2 = \sigma_2^2$ and the alternative hypothesis is $H_1:\sigma_1^2 > \sigma_2^2$ (that is, the second subset of observations has smaller variance than the first subset). Note that many authors present the alternative as larger variance in the second subset of observations. Goldfeld and Quandt recommend ordering of the observations by the values of one of the regressors. This can be done with the **SORT** command. The **DESC** option on the **SORT** command should be used if it is assumed that the variance is positively related to the value of the sort variable. The test can be implemented by omitting r central observations. The value for r can be specified with the **GQOBS=** option and the default is r=0. The sample is split into two groups with N_1 and N_2 observations such that $N_1+N_2=N$ and the test statistic is calculated as:

$$G-Q = \frac{RSSE1 / DF1}{RSSE2 / DF2}$$

where RSSE1 and RSSE2 are the sum of squared errors from the first $N_1-r/2$ and the last $N_2-r/2$ observations respectively and DF1=$N_1-K-r/2$ and DF2=$N_2-K-r/2$. The statistic can be compared with an $F_{(DF1, DF2)}$ distribution.

If the G-Q test statistic is less than 1 then the p-value reported in the final column of the SHAZAM output is for a test of the null hypothesis of equal variance against the alternative hypothesis of $\sigma_1^2 < \sigma_2^2$ (larger variance in the second group). Therefore, there is evidence for *smaller* variance in the second group if G-Q>1 and the p-value is less than 0.05 (or some selected significance level). There is evidence for *larger* variance in the second group if G-Q<1 and the p-value is less than 0.05.

RESET Tests

The output produced with the **RESET** option is:

```
RAMSEY RESET SPECIFICATION TESTS USING POWERS OF YHAT
  RESET(2)=    11.787     - F WITH DF1=  1 AND DF2=  13
  RESET(3)=    5.4878     - F WITH DF1=  2 AND DF2=  12
  RESET(4)=    3.6049     - F WITH DF1=  3 AND DF2=  11
```

The Ramsey [1969] RESET tests (REgression Specification Error Test) are computed by running three additional regressions of the dependent variable on the independent variables, and on powers of $\hat{Y}$ (the predicted dependent variable - $\hat{Y}^2, \hat{Y}^3, \hat{Y}^4$) included in the same regression. The **RESET** Test is an F test that tests whether the coefficients on the new regressors are zero. That is, test statistics are constructed from auxiliary regressions as summarized in the table that follows. The multiple coefficient of determination from the initial regression is denoted by R_0^2 and the multiple coefficient of determination from the auxiliary regression is denoted by R^2.

	Regressand	Regressors	F-Test Statistic	D.F.
RESET(2)	Y_t	$X_t, \hat{Y}_t^2$	$\dfrac{(R^2 - R_0^2)}{(1 - R^2)/(N - K - 1)}$	(1, N–K–1)
RESET(3)	Y_t	$X_t, \hat{Y}_t^2, \hat{Y}_t^3$	$\dfrac{(R^2 - R_0^2)/2}{(1 - R^2)/(N - K - 2)}$	(2, N–K–2)
RESET(4)	Y_t	$X_t, \hat{Y}_t^2, \hat{Y}_t^3, \hat{Y}_t^4$	$\dfrac{(R^2 - R_0^2)/3}{(1 - R^2)/(N - K - 3)}$	(3, N–K–3)

The test statistics reported by the **RESET** option on the **DIAGNOS** command can be replicated with the following list of SHAZAM commands.

```
?OLS CONSUME INCOME PRICE / PREDICT=YHAT
?GEN1 R20=$R2
GENR YHAT2=YHAT**2
GENR YHAT3=YHAT**3
GENR YHAT4=YHAT**4
?OLS CONSUME INCOME PRICE YHAT2
?GEN1 RESET2=($N-$K)*($R2-R20)/(1-$R2)
?OLS CONSUME INCOME PRICE YHAT2 YHAT3
?GEN1 RESET3=($N-$K)*($R2-R20)/(2*(1-$R2))
?OLS CONSUME INCOME PRICE YHAT2 YHAT3 YHAT4
?GEN1 RESET4=($N-$K)*($R2-R20)/(3*(1-$R2))
PRINT RESET2 RESET3 RESET4
```

The SHAZAM output from the above commands is:

```
|_?OLS CONSUME INCOME PRICE / PREDICT=YHAT
|_?GEN1 R20=$R2
|_GENR YHAT2=YHAT**2
|_GENR YHAT3=YHAT**3
|_GENR YHAT4=YHAT**4
|_?OLS CONSUME INCOME PRICE YHAT2
|_?GEN1 RESET2=($N-$K)*($R2-R20)/(1-$R2)
|_?OLS CONSUME INCOME PRICE YHAT2 YHAT3
|_?GEN1 RESET3=($N-$K)*($R2-R20)/(2*(1-$R2))
```

```
|_?OLS CONSUME INCOME PRICE YHAT2 YHAT3 YHAT4
|_?GEN1 RESET4=($N-$K)*($R2-R20)/(3*(1-$R2))
|_PRINT RESET2 RESET3 RESET4
   RESET2
  11.78672
   RESET3
   5.487756
   RESET4
   3.604897
```

The Jackknife Estimator

The output produced with the **JACKKNIFE** option is:

```
JACKKNIFE COEFFICIENTS

COEFFICIENT    AVERAGE      ST.ERR
   INCOME       1.0259      .27080
   PRICE       -1.3694      .91245E-01
   CONSTANT    133.48      28.928
```

With this option SHAZAM runs a series of regressions, successively omitting a different observation to get jackknife coefficient estimates (see, for example, Judge et al. [1988, Section 9.A.2]). The jackknife coefficients are:

$$\hat{\beta}_{(t)} = \hat{\beta} - (X'X)^{-1} X_t e_t^+$$

where $e_t^+ = e_t / (1 - K_{tt})$ and K_{tt} is the tth diagonal element of the matrix $X(X'X)^{-1}X'$. A total of N (Kx1) coefficient vectors are generated each corresponding to a separate regression with the tth observation dropped. The average of the N (Kx1) coefficient vectors is calculated and reported on the SHAZAM output. The jackknife estimator of the covariance matrix of the parameter estimates is given in Judge et al. [1988, Section 9.A.2].

15. DISTRIBUTED-LAG MODELS

"Gentlemen, you have come sixty days too late. The depression is over."
Herbert Hoover
U.S. President, June 1930

Models that include lagged variables as explanatory variables can be specified with a special form of notation available only with the **OLS, AUTO, BOX, GLS,** and **POOL** commands. This is *not* available with the **SYSTEM, MLE, NL, PROBIT, LOGIT, TOBIT, ROBUST, ARIMA** or any other estimation command. An extension is available for the estimation of Almon polynomial distributed lags.

Discussion on the use of lagged variables in regression analysis is available in many econometrics textbooks. In particular, see Gujarati [1995, Chapter 17]; Griffiths, Hill and Judge [1993, Chapter 21]; Greene [1993, Chapter 18]; Maddala [1977, pp. 355-359]; Judge, Griffiths, Hill, Lütkepohl and Lee [1985, Chapter 9.3]; Judge, Hill, Griffiths, Lütkepohl and Lee [1988, Chapter 17]; Pindyck and Rubinfeld [1991, pp. 204-215]; and Johnston [1984]. The distributed lag model has the form:

$$Y_t = \alpha + \beta_0 X_t + \beta_1 X_{t-1} + \beta_2 X_{t-2} + ... + \beta_S X_{t-S} + \varepsilon_t$$

where S is the lag length.

A distributed lag for any explanatory variable on the estimation command (**OLS, AUTO, BOX, GLS,** or **POOL**) can be specified using the special form:

indep(first.last)

where *indep* is the name of an independent variable. The numbers in parentheses specify the *first* and *last* periods to use for lags. For example, (0.3) means to use the current period (0) and lags t–1, t–2, and t–3. Each explanatory variable may have a different lag structure.

An example, from Griffiths, Hill and Judge [1993, p. 683], is the response of quarterly capital expenditures (Y) to capital appropriations (X) in manufacturing. Assuming a lag length of 8 periods the SHAZAM commands to estimate the model are:

```
SAMPLE 1 88
READ (TABLE21.1) TIME Y X
OLS Y X(0.8)
```

SHAZAM will automatically delete the necessary number of observations corresponding to any undefined lagged variables at the beginning of the data, so this should not be done with the **SAMPLE** command. In the above example the estimation sample period will start at observation 9. However, if you wish to use the **SAMPLE** command and delete the observations yourself, you should use the **SET NODELETE** command. For example, the distributed lag model for manufacturing expenditure can be estimated with the following commands.

```
SAMPLE 1 88
READ (TABLE21.1) TIME Y X
SAMPLE 9 88
SET NODELETE
OLS Y X(0.8)
```

The SHAZAM output that corresponds to Table 21.2 of Griffiths et al. [1993, p. 685] is:

```
|_OLS Y X(0.8)
 LAG FOR X        RANGE =  0  8 ORDER= 0 ENDCON=0
 OLS ESTIMATION
        80 OBSERVATIONS      DEPENDENT VARIABLE = Y
...NOTE..SAMPLE RANGE SET TO:    9,    88

 R-SQUARE =    .9934    R-SQUARE ADJUSTED =    .9926
 VARIANCE OF THE ESTIMATE-SIGMA**2 =   35214.
 STANDARD ERROR OF THE ESTIMATE-SIGMA =    187.65
 SUM OF SQUARED ERRORS-SSE=   .24650E+07
 MEAN OF DEPENDENT VARIABLE =   4532.5
 LOG OF THE LIKELIHOOD FUNCTION = -526.942
```

VARIABLE	SUM OF LAG COEFS	STD ERROR	T-RATIO	MEAN LAG
X	.93923	.11736E-01	80.028	3.9170

VARIABLE NAME	ESTIMATED COEFFICIENT	STANDARD ERROR	T-RATIO 70 DF	P-VALUE	PARTIAL CORR.	STANDARDIZED COEFFICIENT	ELASTICITY AT MEANS
X	.38379E-01	.3467E-01	1.107	.272	.131	.0537	.0454
X	.67204E-01	.6851E-01	.9809	.330	.116	.0911	.0776
X	.18124	.8936E-01	2.028	.046	.236	.2243	.2019
X	.19443	.9254E-01	2.101	.039	.244	.2208	.2095
X	.16989	.9312E-01	1.824	.072	.213	.1814	.1779
X	.52360E-01	.9177E-01	.5706	.570	.068	.0526	.0534
X	.52461E-01	.9385E-01	.5590	.578	.067	.0494	.0521
X	.56178E-01	.9415E-01	.5967	.553	.071	.0499	.0544
X	.12708	.5983E-01	2.124	.037	.246	.1086	.1204
CONSTANT	33.415	53.71	.6221	.536	.074	.0000	.0074

The parameter estimates $\hat{\beta}_0, \hat{\beta}_1, \ldots, \hat{\beta}_8$ and $\hat{\alpha}$ are listed in the ESTIMATED COEFFICIENT column. The estimate $\hat{\beta}_0$ has an interpretation as an impact or short-run multiplier. The long-run or total distributed lag multiplier is estimated as the sum of the lag coefficients (SUM OF LAG COEFS):

$$\hat{\beta}^m = \sum_{i=0}^{S} \hat{\beta}_i$$

The standard error (STD ERROR) of the long run multiplier is calculated as:

$$\text{SE}(\hat{\beta}^m) = \left[\sum_{i=0}^{S} V(\hat{\beta}_i) + 2 \sum\sum_{i<j} \text{Cov}(\hat{\beta}_i, \hat{\beta}_j)\right]^{1/2}$$

A T-RATIO is computed as $\hat{\beta}^m / \text{SE}(\hat{\beta}^m)$.

The mean lag gives a measure of the speed of adjustment and is estimated as the weighted average:

$$\sum_{i=0}^{S} i \cdot \hat{\beta}_i \Big/ \sum_{i=0}^{S} \hat{\beta}_i$$

The mean lag may only have a useful interpretation if the lag coefficients are all positive.

In the above example the estimate of the long-run impact is 0.93923 and the t-statistic of 80.028 indicates that it is statistically significant. The estimate of the short-run impact is 0.038379 and this does not appear significantly different from zero. However, Griffiths et al. [1993, p. 683] discuss that multicollinearity may be a problem with unrestricted estimation of distributed lag models.

The special notation for lagged variables can be used to specify equations that include lagged dependent variables as regressors. For example, the next SHAZAM command implements OLS estimation of a model that includes a lagged dependent variable. The explanatory variables also include the current value of *INCOME* and the current and 2 lagged values of the variable *PRICE*.

```
OLS CONSUME CONSUME(1.1) INCOME PRICE(0.2)
```

Almon Polynomial Distributed Lag Models

The Almon [1965] method imposes restrictions on the coefficients of the distributed lag model. The coefficients are restricted to lie on a polynomial of degree r.

SHAZAM allows the user to specify a lag length, order of polynomial and endpoint constraints on any independent variable in the model. Each independent variable may have different order and endpoint constraints. An Almon polynomial distributed lag for any explanatory variable on the estimation command (**OLS, AUTO, BOX, GLS,** or **POOL**) can be specified using the special form:

indep(first.last,order,endcon)

where *indep* is the name of an independent variable. Each independent variable may have up to 3 parameters in parentheses which specify the form of the polynomial lag. The first parameter contains two numbers separated by a dot (.). These numbers specify the *first* and *last* periods to use for lags. The *order* parameter specifies the order of the Almon lag scheme. The *endcon* parameter specifies the endpoint restrictions as follows:

    0 = No Endpoint restrictions;
    1 = Endpoint restrictions on the left side of the polynomial;
    2 = Endpoint restrictions on the right side of the polynomial;
    3 = Endpoint restrictions on both left and right sides.

If *order* and *endcon* are not specified an unrestricted lag is used.

The Almon method imposes restrictions on the coefficients. In this case the **DWPVALUE, METHOD=HH,** and *STEPWISE REGRESSION* may not be used (see the chapter *ORDINARY LEAST SQUARES*). It should also be noted that some statistics on the **DIAGNOS** command like the Chow, Goldfeld-Quandt and recursive residuals tests will not incorporate the restrictions (see the chapter *DIAGNOSTIC TESTS*).

Note that other computer packages may use a different method to specify the degree of the polynomial. In particular the order may be equal to the SHAZAM definition plus 1.

The number of degrees of freedom is increased by the number of restrictions. Suppose J explanatory variables are specified and variable j has first and last lag period a_j, b_j with polynomial order r_j and number of endpoint restrictions m_j. When a constant term is included the number of variables in the regression is:

$$K = 1 + \sum_{j=1}^{J}(b_j - a_j + 1)$$

The number of restrictions is:

$$q = (K - 1) - \sum_{j=1}^{J}(r_j - m_j + 1)$$

The number of degrees of freedom is then N–K+q.

An estimation method is to construct variables as linear combinations of the X variables and apply unrestricted estimation using the constructed variables as regressors. The parameter estimates $\hat{\beta}_i$ are then recovered from linear combinations of the estimated coefficients. This method is described in Gujarati [1995] and other econometrics textbooks. The SHAZAM estimation method is to cast the problem in the framework of restricted estimation. That is, restrictions are imposed as with the **RESTRICT** option on the estimation command.

The restrictions on the parameter vector β due to the specification of the degree of the polynomial, and/or due to the specification of end-point constraints on the polynomial, may be found using Pascal's triangle (for discussion see Johnston [1984] or Greene [1993]). The restrictions have the form $R\beta = 0$ where the elements in the matrix R are obtained from Pascal's triangle given by:

$$
\begin{array}{ccccccc}
 & & & 1 & & & \\
 & & 1 & & -1 & & \\
 & 1 & & -2 & & 1 & \\
 1 & & -3 & & 3 & & -1 \quad \text{Polynomial of degree 2}\\
1 & -4 & & 6 & & -4 & \quad 1 \quad \text{Polynomial of degree 3}
\end{array}
$$

This can be illustrated with the manufacturing data set used previously. Assuming a lag length of 8 periods and a polynomial of degree 2 the parameter restrictions are:

$$\beta_0 - 3\beta_1 + 3\beta_2 - \beta_3 = 0$$
$$\beta_1 - 3\beta_2 + 3\beta_3 - \beta_4 = 0$$
$$\beta_2 - 3\beta_3 + 3\beta_4 - \beta_5 = 0$$
$$\beta_3 - 3\beta_4 + 3\beta_5 - \beta_6 = 0$$
$$\beta_4 - 3\beta_5 + 3\beta_6 - \beta_7 = 0$$
$$\beta_5 - 3\beta_6 + 3\beta_7 - \beta_8 = 0$$

The next output shows the estimation results that correspond to Table 21.5 of Griffiths, Hill and Judge [1993, p. 687].

```
|_OLS Y X(0.8,2)
 LAG FOR X        RANGE =   0  8 ORDER= 2 ENDCON=0
 OLS ESTIMATION
     80 OBSERVATIONS     DEPENDENT VARIABLE = Y
...NOTE..SAMPLE RANGE SET TO:    9,    88


F TEST ON RESTRICTIONS=    1.1500     WITH    6 AND    70 DF  P-VALUE=  .34309


 R-SQUARE =     .9928     R-SQUARE ADJUSTED =     .9925
 VARIANCE OF THE ESTIMATE-SIGMA**2 =    35631.
 STANDARD ERROR OF THE ESTIMATE-SIGMA =    188.76
 SUM OF SQUARED ERRORS-SSE=    .27079E+07
 MEAN OF DEPENDENT VARIABLE =    4532.5
 LOG OF THE LIKELIHOOD FUNCTION = -530.702


 VARIABLE    SUM OF LAG COEFS    STD ERROR       T-RATIO       MEAN LAG
 X              .93296            .11471E-01      81.335         3.8173
```

VARIABLE NAME	ESTIMATED COEFFICIENT	STANDARD ERROR	T-RATIO 76 DF	P-VALUE	PARTIAL CORR.	STANDARDIZED COEFFICIENT	ELASTICITY AT MEANS
X	.67168E-01	.1523E-01	4.411	.000	.451	.0941	.0794
X	.10022	.5114E-02	19.60	.000	.914	.1359	.1157
X	.12302	.5410E-02	22.74	.000	.934	.1522	.1370
X	.13556	.9413E-02	14.40	.000	.855	.1539	.1461
X	.13785	.1072E-01	12.86	.000	.828	.1472	.1444
X	.12988	.9079E-02	14.31	.000	.854	.1304	.1324
X	.11165	.5337E-02	20.92	.000	.923	.1051	.1109
X	.83175E-01	.7346E-02	11.32	.000	.792	.0739	.0806
X	.44442E-01	.1797E-01	2.473	.016	.273	.0380	.0421
CONSTANT	51.573	53.16	.9701	.335	.111	.0000	.0114

A test of the validity of the restrictions is given by testing the null hypothesis H_0: $R\beta = 0$. The F-statistic is calculated as:

$$ F = \frac{1}{q}\left[R\hat{\beta}\right]'\left[R\left(\hat{\sigma}^2(X'X)^{-1}\right)R'\right]^{-1}\left[R\hat{\beta}\right] $$

where q is the number of restrictions. Under the null hypothesis the F-statistic is distributed as $F_{(q,N-K)}$. N is the number of observations used in the estimation and K is the total number of coefficients estimated.

On the above output the F test on the restrictions has the value 1.1500. The p-value is reported as 0.34309 and so the null hypothesis of valid restrictions is not rejected. For the t-ratios the degrees of freedom is adjusted by the number of restrictions so that the degrees of freedom is N−K+q = 80−10+6 = 76.

Endpoint restrictions as described in Pindyck and Rubinfeld [1991, p. 213] may be specified for any polynomial. The use of endpoint restrictions increases the number of restrictions imposed in the model. For example, for the manufacturing data with a lag length of 8 periods and a second degree polynomial, an endpoint restriction on the left side can be incorporated with the command:

```
OLS Y X(0.8,2,1)
```

The additional restriction imposed is:

$$ -3\beta_0 + 3\beta_1 - \beta_2 = 0 $$

An endpoint restriction on the right side gives the added restriction:

$$ \beta_6 - 3\beta_7 + 3\beta_8 = 0 $$

16. FORECASTING

"The 1976 Olympics could no more lose money than I could have a baby."
Mr. Jean Drapeau
Mayor of Montreal, 1973

Forecasting can be implemented in SHAZAM with the **FC** command. Forecasts can be generated for models estimated with the **AUTO, BOX, LOGIT, OLS, POOL, PROBIT** and **TOBIT** commands. The **FC** command can use the estimated coefficients from the previous regression and then generate predicted values over any chosen set of observations. It is also possible to specify the coefficients with the **COEF=** option. The calculation of the forecast standard errors does not make any adjustments if lagged dependent variables are present. Useful references for forecasting are Salkever [1976], Pagan and Nichols [1984] and Harvey [1990].

The standard linear regression equation is written:

$$Y_t = X'_t\beta + \varepsilon_t \qquad\qquad t = 1, 2, \ldots, N$$

where Y_t is the dependent variable, X_t is a vector of explanatory variables, β is a Kx1 parameter vector and ε_t is a random error with zero mean and variance σ^2. Suppose that estimation with the **OLS** command yields the estimates $\hat{\beta}$ and $\hat{\sigma}^2$. For an origin date N_0, predictions of Y_{N_0+t} are obtained as:

$$\hat{Y}_{N_0+t} = X'_{N_0+t}\hat{\beta} \qquad\qquad t = 1, \ldots, M$$

The forecast error variance for period N_0+t is estimated as:

$$\hat{\sigma}^2\left[1 + X'_{N_0+t}(X'X)^{-1}X_{N_0+t}\right]$$

where X is the NxK matrix of regressors. The square root of the above gives the forecast standard error.

Forecast Evaluation

The mean squared error is computed as:

$$MSE = \frac{1}{M}\sum_{t=1}^{M}(Y_{N_0+t} - \hat{Y}_{N_0+t})^2$$

and the root mean squared error is $\sqrt{\text{MSE}}$. The mean absolute error is computed as:

$$\text{MAE} = \frac{1}{M} \sum_{t=1}^{M} \left| Y_{N_0+t} - \hat{Y}_{N_0+t} \right|$$

The mean squared percentage error is computed as:

$$\text{MSPE} = \frac{1}{M} \sum_{t=1}^{M} \left[100 \frac{Y_{N_0+t} - \hat{Y}_{N_0+t}}{Y_{N_0+t}} \right]^2$$

(when $Y_{N_0+t}=0$ the observation is excluded from the formula).

Consider $\overline{Y}$, $\overline{Y}^P$, s_a, and s_p as the means and standard deviations of the series Y_{N_0+t} and $\hat{Y}_{N_0+t}$ respectively for $t=1,\dots,M$. The calculation of the standard deviations uses a divisor of M. Denote r as the correlation between the observed and predicted values. SHAZAM reports two decompositions of the mean square error such that:

$$U^B + U^V + U^C = U^B + U^R + U^D = 1 \qquad \text{where}$$

$$U^B = \left(\overline{Y} - \overline{Y}^P\right)^2 / \text{MSE} \qquad \text{is the proportion due to Bias}$$

$$U^V = (s_a - s_p)^2 / \text{MSE} \qquad \text{is the proportion due to Variance}$$

$$U^C = 2(1-r) s_p s_a / \text{MSE} \qquad \text{is the proportion due to Covariance}$$

$$U^R = (s_p - r s_a)^2 / \text{MSE} \qquad \text{is the proportion due to the Regression}$$

$$U^D = \left(1 - r^2\right) s_a^2 / \text{MSE} \qquad \text{is the disturbance proportion}$$

Theil [1966, Chapter 2] and Maddala [1977, Section 15-6] give discussion on the interpretation of the results of the decomposition.

The Theil inequality coefficient (described in Theil [1966, p. 28]) is calculated as:

$$U = \left[\frac{\sum_{t=2}^{M}(Y_{N_0+t} - \hat{Y}_{N_0+t})^2}{\sum_{t=2}^{M}(Y_{N_0+t} - Y_{N_0+t-1})^2} \right]^{1/2}$$

For a perfect forecast $\hat{Y}_{N_0+t} = Y_{N_0+t}$ for all t and U=0. A value of U=1 results from a naive model where $\hat{Y}_{N_0+t} = Y_{N_0+t-1}$. A value of U > 1 results from a model that forecasts less precisely compared to a naive model.

Prediction for the Model with AR(1) Errors

The AR(1) error model has disturbances of the form:

$$\varepsilon_t = \rho\,\varepsilon_{t-1} + v_t$$

where ρ is the autoregressive parameter, v_t is a random error with zero mean and variance σ_v^2 and $E(\varepsilon\varepsilon') = \sigma_v^2\Omega$. Suppose that estimation with the **AUTO** command yields the estimates $\hat{\beta}$, $\hat{\rho}$, $\hat{\sigma}_v^2$ and $\hat{\Omega}$. For further details see the chapter *AUTOCORRELATION MODELS*. The BLUP (best linear unbiased predictor) is given by:

$$\hat{Y}_{N+t} = X'_{N+t}\,\hat{\beta} + \hat{\rho}^t\left(Y_N - X'_N\,\hat{\beta}\right) \qquad t = 1, 2, \ldots, M$$

where Y_N and X_N are the final observations of the estimation sample period. The IBLUP (predictor) uses information from the immediately preceding observation to obtain a series of one-step ahead predictions as:

$$\hat{Y}_{N+t} = X'_{N+t}\,\hat{\beta} + \hat{\rho}\left(Y_{N+t-1} - X'_{N+t-1}\,\hat{\beta}\right) \qquad t = 1, 2, \ldots, M$$

The mean-square-error of prediction (see Judge et al. [1985, Equation 8.3.13 p. 318] and Harvey [1990, Equation 7.10, p. 215]) is estimated as:

$$MSE\left(\hat{Y}_{N+t}\right) = \hat{\sigma}_v^2\left[\left(1-\hat{\rho}^{2t}\right)/\left(1-\hat{\rho}^2\right)\right]$$
$$+ \hat{\sigma}_v^2\left(X_{N+t} - \hat{\rho}^t X_N\right)'\left(X'\hat{\Omega}^{-1}X\right)^{-1}\left(X_{N+t} - \hat{\rho}^t X_N\right) \qquad t = 1, 2, \ldots, M$$

The asymptotic MSE of the predictor based on Baillie [1979] (see Judge et al. [1985, Equation 8.3.14, p. 318] and Harvey [1990, Equation 7.11, p. 215]) can be estimated as:

$$AMSE\left(\hat{Y}_{N+t}\right) \approx MSE\left(\hat{Y}_{N+t}\right) + \hat{\sigma}_v^2\,t^2\,\hat{\rho}^{2(t-1)}/N$$

where the last term is the MSE contribution due to estimation of ρ. If the **AFCSE** option is specified with the **BLUP** or **IBLUP** option on the **FC** command then the asymptotic forecast standard error is reported as the square root of the above.

FC COMMAND OPTIONS

In general, the format of the **FC** command, when the estimated coefficients from the immediately preceding regression are being used, is:

estimation command
FC / *options*

where *estimation command* can be **AUTO, BOX, LOGIT, OLS, POOL, PROBIT** or **TOBIT**. Note that the reported forecast standard errors are not valid when the **HETCOV** or **AUTCOV=** options are specified on the **OLS** command. The *estimation command* can also be **GLS, MLE,** or **2SLS**. For the latter cases the forecast standard errors are not available. The format when reading in all the coefficients is:

FC *depvar indeps* / *options* **COEF=**

where *depvar* is the variable name of the dependent variable, *indeps* is a list of variable names of the independent variables, **COEF=** is a required option used to specify the name of the variable in which the coefficients are stored, and *options* is a list of desired options.

When the coefficients from the previous regression are being used the variables must not be specified since SHAZAM has automatically saved them. However, when a new set of coefficients is being specified SHAZAM must be told which variables to use and the variable in which the coefficients have been saved must be specified on the **COEF=** option. The **FC** command is similar to the **OLS** command except no estimation is done. If the **PREDICT=** or **RESID=** options are used, the variable used for the results must have been previously defined with the **DIM** command. For a description of the **DIM** command see the chapter *MISCELLANEOUS COMMANDS AND INFORMATION*.

Options as described for **OLS** that are available are:

GF, LIST, BEG=, END=, PREDICT= and **RESID=**

Additional options are:

AFCSE   Used with the **BLUP** or **IBLUP** options to get Asymptotic Forecast
                        Standard Errors as described above.

BLUP, **IBLUP**	Used in autoregressive models when the user wishes the predicted values to be adjusted with the lagged residual, to give the **B**est **L**inear **U**nbiased **P**redictions. **BLUP** only uses information from the first observation specified while **IBLUP** uses information from the **I**mmediately preceding observation. Note, that correct forecast standard errors are only available for the first-order autoregressive model as described above.
DYNAMIC	Performs **DYNAMIC** forecasts for models with a lagged dependent variable. It is assumed that the lag variable is the first independent variable listed.
MAX	This option is equivalent to the **LIST** and **GF** options.
PERCENT	This option adds one line to every observation listing to display the **PERCENT**age change in the actual and predicted values (measured as the ratio of the current year to the previous year). In addition, it reports the ratio of the residual to the actual value. These ratios are printed in parentheses below the usual listing of actual, predicted, and residual values.
COEF=	Gives an input vector of model coefficients. If this is not specified then the estimated coefficients from the previous SHAZAM command are used.
CSNUM=	Specifies which cross-section to use on a Pooled Cross-Section Time-Series model for **POOL** models.
ESTEND=	Specifies the last observation of the estimation for **AUTO** and **POOL** models.
FCSE=	Saves the ForeCast Standard Errors in the variable specified. The option is only available when the coefficients from the previous regression are used for forecasting. The variable to be used for the forecast standard errors must be defined before the estimation with the **DIM** command. Note that if the **HETCOV** or **AUTCOV=** options were used on the previous **OLS** command, the forecast standard errors are incorrect.
NC=	Specifies the **N**umber of **C**ross-sections in a Pooled Cross-Section Time-Series model for **POOL** models.

When the **COEF=** option is specified the following options may also be included:

NOCONSTANT No intercept is included in the regression. In this case, a value for the intercept should not be included.

UPPER   Used with **MODEL=TOBIT** (see the chapter *TOBIT REGRESSION*).

LIMIT=   Used with **MODEL=TOBIT** (see the chapter *TOBIT REGRESSION*).

MODEL=   Specifies the type of **MODEL**. The available models are:

AUTO   When **MODEL=AUTO** is used the autoregressive order is specified with the **ORDER=** option and the default is AR(1). The **COEF=** vector must contain K values for β (the intercept coefficient is last) followed by the values for the autoregressive parameters.

BOX   When **MODEL=BOX** is used the **COEF=** vector must contain K values for β followed by K values for λ of each of the independent variables followed by the λ value on the dependent variable.

LOGIT   Use Coefficients from **LOGIT** command estimation.

OLS   The default is **MODEL=OLS.**

POOL   When **MODEL=POOL** is used the forecast must be done for only one Cross-Section. The relative position of the Cross-Section is specified with the **CSNUM=** and **NC=** options. The **COEF=** vector must contain K values for β, then a ρ value for each cross-section, and finally a standard error estimate for each cross-section. (See the chapter *POOLED CROSS-SECTION TIME-SERIES*).

PROBIT   Use coefficients from **PROBIT** command estimation.

TOBIT   When **MODEL=TOBIT** is used the *normalized* coefficients (including the one on the dependent variable) must be read in.

ORDER=   Specifies the **ORDER** of the model for **MODEL=AUTO**.

POOLSE=   Specifies the standard error of the cross-section in a Pooled Cross-Section Time-Series model when **MODEL=POOL**.

RHO=	Specifies a value of the first-order autoregressive parameter for the regression when **MODEL=AUTO** or **MODEL=BOX** or **MODEL=POOL** is specified.
SRHO=	Used with **MODEL=AUTO** and **ORDER=2** and the **RHO=** option to specify a value of the Second-order **RHO**.

EXAMPLES

An example of the use of the **FC** command after an **OLS** estimation is:

```
SAMPLE 1 17
OLS CONSUME INCOME PRICE / LIST
FC / LIST
```

Another example is:

```
SAMPLE 1 10
OLS CONSUME INCOME PRICE / COEF=BETA
TEST INCOME = -PRICE
FC CONSUME INCOME PRICE / BEG=1 END=17 COEF=BETA
```

In the above example, the **OLS** command saves the coefficient vector with the **COEF=** option. This is necessary since the **FC** command does not immediately follow the estimation command. On the **FC** command the dependent variable and the regressors are supplied along with the vector containing the estimated coefficients.

Another example of the use of the **FC** command is:

```
SAMPLE 1 10
OLS CONSUME INCOME PRICE
FC / LIST BEG=11 END=17
```

The output from the final example follows.

```
|_SAMPLE 1 10
|_OLS CONSUME INCOME PRICE
 OLS ESTIMATION
      10 OBSERVATIONS      DEPENDENT VARIABLE = CONSUME
...NOTE..SAMPLE RANGE SET TO:    1,    10


 R-SQUARE =    .9810    R-SQUARE ADJUSTED =    .9755
 VARIANCE OF THE ESTIMATE-SIGMA**2 =    10.568
 STANDARD ERROR OF THE ESTIMATE-SIGMA =    3.2509
 SUM OF SQUARED ERRORS-SSE=    73.979
 MEAN OF DEPENDENT VARIABLE =    121.45
 LOG OF THE LIKELIHOOD FUNCTION = -24.1954

 VARIABLE    ESTIMATED   STANDARD    T-RATIO        PARTIAL STANDARDIZED ELASTICITY
```

```
    NAME      COEFFICIENT    ERROR       7 DF     P-VALUE CORR. COEFFICIENT  AT MEANS
  INCOME        .55817       .2456       2.273     .057  .652      .1462      .4834
  PRICE       -1.5320        .1098     -13.95      .000 -.982     -.8976     -1.1060
  CONSTANT    197.07        32.44        6.075     .001  .917      .0000      1.6226


 |_FC / LIST BEG=11 END=17
 DEPENDENT VARIABLE = CONSUME            7 OBSERVATIONS
 REGRESSION COEFFICIENTS
     .558165798286      -1.53203247506       197.070728749

     OBS.     OBSERVED      PREDICTED    CALCULATED  STD. ERROR
     NO.       VALUE         VALUE        RESIDUAL
     11       158.50        159.92       -1.4226       4.863                   *I
     12       140.60        154.57      -13.968        5.729           *        I
     13       136.20        153.44      -17.241        5.472           *        I
     14       168.00        170.96       -2.9628       6.191                   *I
     15       154.30        162.76       -8.4646       4.898                *   I
     16       149.00        162.62      -13.624        5.016           *        I
     17       165.50        161.09        4.4053       4.613                    I *


 SUM OF ABSOLUTE ERRORS=    62.088
 R-SQUARE BETWEEN OBSERVED AND PREDICTED =  .6833
 RUNS TEST:    2 RUNS,    1 POS,     0 ZERO,    6 NEG  NORMAL STATISTIC = -1.5811
 MEAN ERROR =  -7.6111
 SUM-SQUARED ERRORS =    779.82
 MEAN SQUARE ERROR =   111.40
 MEAN ABSOLUTE ERROR=   8.8697
 ROOT MEAN SQUARE ERROR =   10.555
 MEAN SQUARED PERCENTAGE ERROR=   54.804
 THEIL INEQUALITY COEFFICIENT U =  .650
   DECOMPOSITION
     PROPORTION DUE TO BIAS =    .51999
     PROPORTION DUE TO VARIANCE =    .29305
     PROPORTION DUE TO COVARIANCE =   .18696
   DECOMPOSITION
     PROPORTION DUE TO BIAS =    .51999
     PROPORTION DUE TO REGRESSION =    .12868
     PROPORTION DUE TO DISTURBANCE =   .35133
```

The next example shows forecasting with a model with AR(1) errors. The **AUTO** command is used for estimation and the AR(1) parameter is estimated using the **ML** option. The first 13 observations are used for estimation. Forecasts are then made for observation 13 to 17 using the **BLUP** option on the **FC** command. In order to get correct estimates of the forecast standard error for the 14th through the 17th predictions, the forecast must begin at the 13th observation and end at the 17th using the **BEG=** and **END=** options in the **FC** command. This is necessary since each forecast must be adjusted by the lagged residual to get correct forecast standard errors. Note carefully the information contained in the output:

```
. . . FORECAST STD. ERRORS USE JUDGE (1985, EQ. 8.3.13)
IGNORE FORECASTS AND STD. ERRORS BEFORE OBSERVATION 14.
```

The forecasts and standard errors have been saved using the **PREDICT=** and **FCSE=** options on the **FC** command. Note that the **DIM** command is needed to allocate space for these variables. These variables could then be used as input for graphical display of the forecast. The **LIST** option on the **FC** command is used to obtain a listing of the predictions and prediction errors. The SHAZAM commands for the estimation and forecasting are as follows.

```
SAMPLE 1 13
DIM FC 17 SE 17
AUTO CONSUME INCOME PRICE / ML
FC / BLUP LIST BEG=13 END=17 MODEL=AUTO PREDICT=FC FCSE=SE
```

The SHAZAM output follows.

```
|_SAMPLE 1 13
|_DIM FC 17 SE 17
|_AUTO CONSUME INCOME PRICE / ML
DEPENDENT VARIABLE =  CONSUME
..NOTE..R-SQUARE,ANOVA,RESIDUALS DONE ON ORIGINAL VARS
DN OPTION IN EFFECT - DIVISOR IS N

MAXIMUM LIKELIHOOD ESTIMATION            13 OBSERVATIONS
BY COCHRANE-ORCUTT TYPE PROCEDURE WITH CONVERGENCE =  .00100

     ITERATION          RHO              LOG L.F.              SSE
         1             .00000           -37.1885            232.38
         2             .34495           -36.5653            209.09
         3             .34847           -36.5653            209.04
         4             .34853           -36.5653            209.04

 LOG L.F. =   -36.5653      AT RHO =       .34853

                  ASYMPTOTIC  ASYMPTOTIC  ASYMPTOTIC
            ESTIMATE  VARIANCE   ST.ERROR    T-RATIO
RHO         .34853    .06758     .25996     1.34070

 R-SQUARE =    .9617    R-SQUARE ADJUSTED =    .9541
VARIANCE OF THE ESTIMATE-SIGMA**2 =   16.080
STANDARD ERROR OF THE ESTIMATE-SIGMA =   4.0100
SUM OF SQUARED ERRORS-SSE=   209.04
MEAN OF DEPENDENT VARIABLE =   126.91
LOG OF THE LIKELIHOOD FUNCTION = -36.5653

                         ASYMPTOTIC
VARIABLE   ESTIMATED  STANDARD   T-RATIO          PARTIAL STANDARDIZED ELASTICITY
  NAME     COEFFICIENT  ERROR    --------   P-VALUE CORR. COEFFICIENT  AT MEANS
INCOME      1.0867     .2580      4.212      .000  .800     .2994       .8861
PRICE      -1.3087     .1044    -12.54       .000 -.970    -.9380      -.8442
CONSTANT  121.50      27.43       4.429      .000  .814     .0000       .9574
```

```
|_FC / BLUP LIST BEG=13 END=17 MODEL=AUTO PREDICT=FC FCSE=SE
..ASSUMING ESTIMATION ENDED AT OBSERVATION    13
DEPENDENT VARIABLE = CONSUME          5 OBSERVATIONS
REGRESSION COEFFICIENTS
   1.08666458513       -1.30867753239        121.501461408
AUTOCORRELATION RHO
   .3485269810734
USER SPECIFIED RHO=  .34853
USER SPECIFIED SRHO=  .00000
..FORECAST STD. ERRORS USE JUDGE(1985, EQ. 8.3.13)
IGNORE FORECASTS AND STD. ERRORS BEFORE OBS.   14

    OBS.    OBSERVED     PREDICTED    CALCULATED   STD. ERROR
    NO.      VALUE        VALUE        RESIDUAL
    13      136.20       143.02       -6.8240       4.879      *  I
    14      168.00       156.35       11.655        4.830         I       *
    15      154.30       153.82        .48106       4.947         *
    16      149.00       153.75       -4.7514       5.082      *  I
    17      165.50       153.97       11.525        5.053         I       *

BLUP IS ACTIVE - PREDICTED VALUES ADJUSTED WITH LAGGED RESIDUALS

SUM OF ABSOLUTE ERRORS=   35.237
R-SQUARE BETWEEN OBSERVED AND PREDICTED =  .7513
RUNS TEST:    4 RUNS,    3 POS,    0 ZERO,    2 NEG  NORMAL STATISTIC =    .6547
MEAN ERROR =   2.4172
SUM-SQUARED ERRORS =   338.04
MEAN SQUARE ERROR =   67.609
MEAN ABSOLUTE ERROR=   7.0473
ROOT MEAN SQUARE ERROR =   8.2225
MEAN SQUARED PERCENTAGE ERROR=   26.399
THEIL INEQUALITY COEFFICIENT U =  .441
  DECOMPOSITION
     PROPORTION DUE TO BIAS =   .86420E-01
     PROPORTION DUE TO VARIANCE =   .70030
     PROPORTION DUE TO COVARIANCE =   .21328
  DECOMPOSITION
     PROPORTION DUE TO BIAS =   .86420E-01
     PROPORTION DUE TO REGRESSION =   .42188
     PROPORTION DUE TO DISTURBANCE =   .49170
```

17. GENERALIZED ENTROPY

"Many economic-statistical models are ill-posed or under-determined. Consequently, it is important that we learn to reason in these logically indeterminate situations."

Ed Jaynes, 1985

Given a general linear model of the form:

$$Y = X\beta + \varepsilon$$

SHAZAM will recover estimates of β and ε according to the generalized maximum entropy (GME) and generalized cross-entropy (GCE) methods described in Golan, Judge and Miller [1996]. GME and GCE employ limited prior information, and the methods are robust alternatives to OLS and other estimation procedures. Users should be familiar with generalized entropy methods before attempting this procedure.

The unknowns are reparameterized as:

$$\beta = Zp = \begin{bmatrix} z_1' & 0 & . & 0 \\ 0 & z_2' & . & 0 \\ . & . & . & . \\ 0 & 0 & . & z_K' \end{bmatrix} \begin{bmatrix} p_1 \\ p_2 \\ . \\ p_K \end{bmatrix} \quad \text{and} \quad \varepsilon = Vw = \begin{bmatrix} v_1' & 0 & . & 0 \\ 0 & v_2' & . & 0 \\ . & . & . & . \\ 0 & 0 & . & v_N' \end{bmatrix} \begin{bmatrix} w_1 \\ w_2 \\ . \\ w_N \end{bmatrix}$$

where z_k is a vector of M ($2 \leq M$) support points for β_k and these are specified with the **ZENTROPY=** option on the **GME** command. Z is a K x KM matrix and p is a KM x 1 vector of weights. v_t is a vector of J ($2 \leq J$) support points for ε_t and these are specified with the **VENTROPY=** option.

The general linear model is rewritten as:

$$Y = X\beta + \varepsilon = XZp + Vw$$

The generalized maximum entropy (GME) problem is to choose p and w to maximize an entropy measure. If prior distributions are non-uniform the problem can be extended to employ a generalized cross-entropy (GCE) criterion. Let q be the KM x 1 vector of prior weights for β and let u be the NJ x 1 vector of prior weights on ε. Values for q and u can be specified with the **QPRIOR=** and **UPRIOR=** options respectively. The GCE problem is to select p and w to minimize:

$$I(p,q,w,u) = \sum_{k=1}^{K}\sum_{i=1}^{M} p_{ki}\ln(p_{ki}/q_{ki}) + \sum_{t=1}^{N}\sum_{j=1}^{J} w_{tj}\ln(w_{tj}/u_{tj})$$

subject to the set of data consistency constraints:

$$Y = XZp + Vw$$

and normalization constraints on p and w. This is a constrained minimization problem. A Lagrangian function can be stated with λ as the N x 1 vector of Lagrange multipliers on the data consistency constraints. The GCE solutions $\tilde{p}$ and $\tilde{w}$ are functions of $\tilde{\lambda}$. A solution method, that is implemented in SHAZAM, is to specify a dual version of the GCE problem. Numerical optimisation methods are then used to choose λ to maximize the objective function. Further discussion on the numerical solution procedure is in Golan, Judge and Miller [1996, Chapter 17].

Normalized entropy measures for the recovered coefficients are calculated as:

$$\sum_{i=1}^{M}\tilde{p}_{ki}\ln(\tilde{p}_{ki}) \bigg/ \sum_{i=1}^{M} q_{ki}\ln(q_{ki}) \qquad \text{for} \quad k=1,\ldots,K$$

The normalized entropy measure for p is:

$$\sum_{k=1}^{K}\sum_{i=1}^{M}\tilde{p}_{ki}\ln(\tilde{p}_{ki}) \bigg/ \sum_{k=1}^{K}\sum_{i=1}^{M} q_{ki}\ln(q_{ki})$$

GME COMMAND OPTIONS

In general, the format of the **GME** command is:

GME *depvar indeps / options*

where *depvar* is a vector of N observations. If the set of unknown model parameters, β, is a probability distribution, then the support of the distribution is specified in *indeps*. For a regression model, *indeps* should include the K vectors of explanatory variables, each containing N observations. Unlike the **OLS** command, **GME** does not require N>K.

Options as defined for the **OLS** command that are available are:

LINLOG, LIST, LOGLIN, LOGLOG, NOCONSTANT, PCOV, RSTAT, BEG=, END=, COEF=, COV=, PREDICT=, RESID=, STDERR= and **TRATIO=**

Options as defined for the **NL** command that are available are:

CONV=, ITER=, PITER= and **START=**

Additional options available on the **GME** command are:

DEVIATION	Specifies that the estimation is to use variables measured as deviations from their mean. This option automatically turns on the **NOCONSTANT** option.
LOGEPS=	Specifies a small constant to be included in each logarithmic term of the objective function in order to avoid numerical underflow. The default value is 1E–8.
QPRIOR=	Specifies a (K x M) matrix of prior probability distributions on the supports specified in **ZENTROPY=**. If this option is not used, the priors are assumed to be discrete uniform.
UPRIOR=	Specifies a (N x J) matrix of prior probability distributions on the supports specified in **VENTROPY=**. If this option is not used, the priors are assumed to be discrete uniform.
VENTROPY=	Specifies a (N x J) matrix containing the J support points for each of the N unknown disturbances. If this option is not used, the disturbance term, ε, is ignored.
ZENTROPY=	Specifies a (K x M) matrix containing the M support points for each of the K unknown parameters. If this option is not used, SHAZAM recovers a probability distribution for the K elements in *indeps*.

EXAMPLES

This example shows the estimation of a demand equation for beer using a data set from Griffiths, Hill and Judge [1993, Table 11.1, p. 372]. The variables are quantity demanded (*Q*), price of beer (*PB*), price of other liquor (*PL*), price of other goods (*PR*) and income (*Y*). The SHAZAM commands that follow first estimate a log-linear equation by OLS. The GME method is then applied.

```
SAMPLE 1 30
* Beer demand data set
READ (BEER.DAT) Q PB PL PR Y
* Consider a log-linear model
GENR LQ=LOG(Q)
GENR C=1
GENR LPB=LOG(PB)
GENR LPL=LOG(PL)
GENR LPR=LOG(PR)
GENR LY=LOG(Y)
* OLS estimation
OLS LQ C LPB LPL LPR LY / NOCONSTANT LOGLOG
* Specify the parameter and error support matrices Z and V
DIM Z 5 5 V 30 3
GENR Z:1=-5
GENR Z:2=-2.5
GENR Z:3=0
GENR Z:4=2.5
GENR Z:5=5
GENR V:1=-1
GENR V:2=0
GENR V:3=1
* Solve the dual problem and get the optimal Lagrange multipliers
GME LQ C LPB LPL LPR LY / NOCONSTANT ZENTROPY=Z VENTROPY=V LOGLOG
STOP
```

The OLS estimation results are below.

```
|_OLS LQ C LPB LPL LPR LY / NOCONSTANT LOGLOG

 OLS ESTIMATION
      30 OBSERVATIONS      DEPENDENT VARIABLE = LQ
...NOTE..SAMPLE RANGE SET TO:    1,    30
...WARNING...VARIABLE C        IS A CONSTANT


 R-SQUARE =    .8254     R-SQUARE ADJUSTED =    .7975
VARIANCE OF THE ESTIMATE-SIGMA**2 =    .35968E-02
STANDARD ERROR OF THE ESTIMATE-SIGMA =    .59973E-01
SUM OF SQUARED ERRORS-SSE=   .89920E-01
MEAN OF DEPENDENT VARIABLE =   4.0185
LOG OF THE LIKELIHOOD FUNCTION(IF DEPVAR LOG) = -75.9736
RAW MOMENT R-SQUARE =    .9998


VARIABLE   ESTIMATED   STANDARD   T-RATIO          PARTIAL STANDARDIZED ELASTICITY
  NAME    COEFFICIENT   ERROR     25 DF    P-VALUE CORR. COEFFICIENT  AT MEANS
C         -3.2432       3.743     -.8665    .394  -.171     .0000    -3.2432
LPB       -1.0204       .2390     -4.269    .000  -.649   -1.6871    -1.0204
LPL        -.58293      .5602     -1.041    .308  -.204    -.4095     -.5829
LPR        .20954       .7969E-01  2.629    .014   .465     .3971     .2095
LY         .92286       .4155      2.221    .036   .406     .9737     .9229
```

The GME solution follows.

```
|_GME LQ C LPB LPL LPR LY / NOCONSTANT ZENTROPY=Z VENTROPY=V LOGLOG
...NOTE..SAMPLE RANGE SET TO:     1,    30
       30 OBSERVATIONS

INITIAL STATISTICS :

TIME =    5.220 SEC.   ITER. NO.    1 FUNCTION EVALUATIONS     1
GENERALIZED MAXIMUM ENTROPY
FUNCTION VALUE=    -41.00556
COEFFICIENTS
   .0000000       .0000000       .0000000       .0000000       .0000000
   .0000000       .0000000       .0000000       .0000000       .0000000
   .0000000       .0000000       .0000000       .0000000       .0000000
   .0000000       .0000000       .0000000       .0000000       .0000000
   .0000000       .0000000       .0000000       .0000000       .0000000
   .0000000       .0000000       .0000000       .0000000       .0000000
GRADIENT
   4.403054       4.041295       4.160444       4.180522       4.160444
   4.062166       4.122284       4.178992       4.056989       4.151040
   4.188138       3.877432       4.018183       3.869116       4.043051
   3.943522       3.992681       3.945458       4.023564       3.953165
   3.960813       3.790985       4.055257       3.943522       3.985273
   3.912023       3.835142       3.845883       3.945458       3.910021

FINAL STATISTICS :

TIME =    7.810 SEC.   ITER. NO.    8 FUNCTION EVALUATIONS    16
GENERALIZED MAXIMUM ENTROPY
FUNCTION VALUE=    -40.88953
COEFFICIENTS
  -.7471853E-01   .7047584E-01  -.3980811E-01  -.2088085E-01   .1718525E-01
   .6260548E-01  -.4277361E-01  -.4776353E-01   .4011995E-02  -.9758509E-01
  -.1127975       .1687698      -.7855024E-01   .8392667E-01  -.1466195E-01
   .6197439E-01   .1182172E-01   .2583825E-01  -.3993996E-01  -.1753328E-02
  -.7051842E-01   .2650401      -.1504612      -.5927065E-01  -.7903290E-01
  -.3510743E-01   .1288732       .8452928E-01  -.3989216E-01   .1387945E-01
GRADIENT
   .1093738E-04   .1449848E-04   .1710085E-04   .1049372E-04   .1772534E-04
   .2659682E-04   .8632597E-05   .9548913E-05   .6241976E-05   .1157758E-04
   .4525873E-05   .1523205E-04   .9083578E-05   .2201034E-04   .2532559E-04
   .1897241E-04   .8911556E-05   .1447326E-04   .1181824E-04   .1539831E-04
   .1122714E-04  -.4600764E-05   .1419110E-04   .7498713E-05   .9664092E-05
   .9152785E-05   .2343221E-04   .2228759E-04   .1035147E-04   .1755680E-04

NORMALIZED ENTROPY FOR COEFFICIENT    1    .99983
NORMALIZED ENTROPY FOR COEFFICIENT    2    .98237
NORMALIZED ENTROPY FOR COEFFICIENT    3    .99906
NORMALIZED ENTROPY FOR COEFFICIENT    4    .99938
NORMALIZED ENTROPY FOR COEFFICIENT    5    .99365
NORMALIZED ENTROPY FOR P=   .99486
NORMALIZED ENTROPY FOR W=   .99774


 R-SQUARE =    .8072     R-SQUARE ADJUSTED =    .7764
VARIANCE OF THE ESTIMATE-SIGMA**2 =   .39710E-02
STANDARD ERROR OF THE ESTIMATE-SIGMA =   .63016E-01
SUM OF SQUARED ERRORS-SSE=   .99274E-01
MEAN OF DEPENDENT VARIABLE =   4.0185
LOG OF THE LIKELIHOOD FUNCTION(IF DEPVAR LOG) = -79.6664
```

RAW MOMENT R-SQUARE =   .9935

VARIABLE NAME	ESTIMATED COEFFICIENT	STANDARD ERROR	PSEUDO T-RATIO 25 DF	P-VALUE	PARTIAL CORR.	STANDARDIZED COEFFICIENT	ELASTICITY AT MEANS
C	.82291E-01	.5140E-03	160.1	.000	1.000	.0000	.0823
LPB	-.83969	.7717E-01	-10.88	.000	-.909	-1.3883	-.8397
LPL	-.19429	.9870E-01	-1.969	.060	-.366	-.1365	-.1943
LPR	.15767	.6495E-01	2.428	.023	.437	.2988	.1577
LY	.50497	.1945E-01	25.96	.000	.982	.2217	.5050

For the beer demand model, the parameter estimates may be interpreted as elasticities. Given that GME is a shrinkage estimator, the GME solution gives elasticities that are typically smaller in absolute value relative to the OLS estimates. That is, the parameter vector recovered by GME is a "shrunken" version of the OLS estimated parameter vector.

Note that the approximate standard errors and t-ratios are only valid in some settings. For further details see Golan, Judge and Miller [1996, Chapter 6].

18. GENERALIZED LEAST SQUARES

"50 years hence...we shall escape the absurdity of growing a whole chicken in order to eat the breast or wing, by growing these parts separately under a suitable medium."

Winston Churchill
Member of British Parliament, 1932

The **GLS** command performs Generalized Least Squares regressions. The method of generalized least squares is discussed in Judge, Hill, Griffiths, Lütkepohl and Lee [1988, Chapter 8], Greene [1993, Chapter 13] and other econometrics textbooks. Consider the linear model:

$$Y = X\beta + \varepsilon$$

where Y is an N x 1 vector of observations on the dependent variable, X is an N x K matrix of explanatory variables, β is a vector of unknown parameters and ε is a random error vector with zero mean and covariance matrix:

$$E(\varepsilon\varepsilon') = \sigma^2\Omega$$

The N x N matrix Ω is a known positive definite symmetric matrix that allows for a general error covariance structure and σ^2 is an unknown scalar. The GLS estimator is:

$$\hat{\beta} = \left(X'\Omega^{-1}X\right)^{-1}X'\Omega^{-1}Y$$

Another way of approaching the analysis is to express the Ω^{-1} matrix as $\Omega^{-1}=P'P$ where P is a non-singular N x N lower triangular matrix. The matrix P is used to transform the model to the form:

$$PY = PX\beta + P\varepsilon$$

Then OLS can be applied to the transformed model to get the GLS estimator. The transformed estimated residuals are calculated as:

$$\hat{v} = PY - PX\hat{\beta}$$

and the untransformed estimated residuals (available with the **UT** option) are:

$$e = Y - X\hat{\beta}$$

The estimate of σ^2 is: $\qquad \hat{\sigma}^2 = \frac{1}{N-K}(\hat{v}'\hat{v}) = \frac{1}{N-K}\left(e'\Omega^{-1}e\right)$

When the **DN** option is used the divisor for $\hat{\sigma}^2$ is N instead of N–K. An estimate of the covariance matrix of $\hat{\beta}$ is:

$$\hat{\sigma}^2\left(X'\Omega^{-1}X\right)^{-1}$$

With the assumption of normality the log-likelihood function can be written as:

$$-\frac{N}{2}\ln(2\pi) - \frac{N}{2}\ln\sigma^2 - \frac{1}{2}\ln|\Omega| - \frac{1}{2\sigma^2}(Y - X\beta)'\Omega^{-1}(Y - X\beta)$$

This is evaluated as:

$$-\frac{N}{2}\ln(2\pi) - \frac{N}{2}\ln\tilde{\sigma}^2 + \sum_{t=1}^{N}\ln(P_{tt}) - \frac{N}{2} \qquad \text{where} \qquad \tilde{\sigma}^2 = \frac{1}{N}(\hat{v}'\hat{v})$$

and P_{tt} is the tth diagonal element of P.

The Buse R^2 (see Buse [1973]) reported on the SHAZAM output gives a measure of goodness-of-fit and is calculated as:

$$R^2 = 1 - \frac{e'\Omega^{-1}e}{(Y - DY)'\Omega^{-1}(Y - DY)} \qquad \text{with} \quad D = \frac{jj'\Omega^{-1}}{j'\Omega^{-1}j}$$

where j is an N x 1 vector of ones. The expression Y–DY transforms the observations to deviations from a weighted mean. When the **NOCONSTANT** option is specified the raw moment R^2 (described in Theil [1961, p. 221]) is calculated by replacing Y–DY with Y. The raw moment R^2 is meaningful when the equation does not have an intercept.

The **GLS** command allows for general error covariance structures. It is useful to note that some special cases are implemented in other SHAZAM commands. For example, the **WEIGHT=** option on the **OLS** command (see the chapter *ORDINARY LEAST SQUARES*) provides weighted least squares estimation and models with autoregressive errors (see the chapter *AUTOCORRELATION MODELS*) can be estimated with the **AUTO** command. Another case of generalized least squares estimation is implemented with the **POOL** command (see the chapter *POOLED CROSS-SECTION AND TIME-SERIES*).

GLS *COMMAND OPTIONS*

In general, the format of the **GLS** command is:

GLS *depvar indeps / options*

where *depvar* is the dependent variable, *indeps* is a list of the independent variables, and *options* is a list of desired options. One of **OMEGA=, OMINV=** or **PMATRIX=** is required to tell SHAZAM which matrix to use for estimation. For example, to give SHAZAM the Ω matrix the **OMEGA=** option is used.

Options described for the **OLS** command that may be used are:

ANOVA, DLAG, DN, GF, LINLOG, LIST, LOGLIN, LOGLOG, MAX, NOCONSTANT, PCOR, PCOV, RESTRICT, RSTAT, BEG=, END=, COEF=, COV=, PREDICT=, STDERR= and **TRATIO=**

Other options are:

BLUP   The predicted values are adjusted using information obtained from previous period residuals according to the transformation specified by the P matrix. This option is not effective in forecasts using the **GLS** coefficients.

DUMP   Prints out the Ω, Ω^{-1} and P matrices. It is important to be aware that each of these matrices is of the order N x N and in large samples could require many pages of printout. The **DUMP** option is useful for checking to see if the input of the matrix has been done correctly.

FULLMAT   If the **FULLMAT** option is not specified, SHAZAM assumes that the specified matrix contains the diagonals of Ω (**OMEGA=**), Ω^{-1} (**OMINV=**) or the P matrix (**PMATRIX=**).

NOMULSIGSQ Uses $\left(X'\Omega^{-1}X\right)^{-1}$ as the estimate of the covariance matrix of the parameter estimates. It is **NO**t **MUL**tiplied by $\hat{\sigma}^2$.

UT   The estimated coefficients will be used with the original data to compute predicted values and residuals that are UnTransformed. Without this option, the residual output and predicted values given are transformed.

OMEGA=	Specifies the matrix to be used for estimation as Ω (**OMEGA=**), Ω^{-1}
OMINV=	(**OMINV=**) or the P matrix (**PMATRIX=**). One of these options *must*
PMATRIX=	be specified on each **GLS** command. The **FULLMAT** option must be used if the complete matrix, rather than just the diagonals of the matrix, is given. When just the diagonals are given the matrix must be set-up as follows. The main diagonal is entered in the first column in rows 1 to N. The first lower diagonal (if required) is entered in the second column in rows 1 to N–1 (the element in row N is ignored). The second lower diagonal (if required) is entered in the third column in rows 1 to N–2 (the elements in rows N–1 and N are ignored), etc.

RESID=	Saves the **RESID**uals in the variable specified. For details on which residuals are saved see the **UT** and **BLUP** options.

The available temporary variables on the **GLS** command are:

$ADR2, $ANF, $DF, $DW, $ERR, $K, $LLF, $N, $R2, $R2OP, $RAW, $RHO, $SIG2, $SSE, $SSR, $SST, $ZANF, $ZDF, $ZSSR$ and $ZSST$.

For more information on temporary variables see the chapter *MISCELLANEOUS COMMANDS AND INFORMATION* and the chapter *ORDINARY LEAST SQUARES*.

EXAMPLE

The **GLS** command can be demonstrated by estimating a model with first-order autoregressive errors for the Theil Textile data set. (Note that most SHAZAM users would use the **AUTO** command to estimate an AR(1) error model.) Consider an autoregressive parameter with a value of $\rho=0.8$. The form of the P matrix (see Judge, Hill, Griffiths, Lütkepohl and Lee [1988, Equation 9.5.29, p.390]) is:

$$
P = \begin{bmatrix}
\sqrt{1-\rho^2} & 0 & . & . & . & 0 \\
-\rho & 1 & 0 & . & . & 0 \\
0 & -\rho & 1 & 0 & & \\
. & & 0 & -\rho & . & . \\
. & & . & 0 & . & . & 0 \\
0 & & 0 & 0 & . & -\rho & 1
\end{bmatrix}
$$

The SHAZAM commands for the GLS estimation are:

```
* Set-up the P matrix
DIM P 17 2
SAMPLE 2 17
GENR P:1=1
GEN1 P:1=SQRT(1-.8*.8)
SAMPLE 1 17
GENR P:2=-.8
* Print the P matrix so that it can be checked.
PRINT P
* Get the GLS estimator
GLS CONSUME INCOME PRICE / PMATRIX=P
* Now verify the results with the AUTO command
AUTO CONSUME INCOME PRICE / RHO=.8
```

The **DIM** command is used to dimension the matrix P to be the size of the **PMATRIX** for the problem. (The **DIM** command is explained in the chapter *MISCELLANEOUS COMMANDS AND INFORMATION*.) Next, the **GENR** command is used to assign a value of 1 to observations 2 to 17 of the first column of the matrix P. Note that on the **GENR** command the first column of P is referred to as *P:1*. The first observation of this column is given a value of $\sqrt{(1-.8\cdot.8)}$. Finally, the second column is assigned a value of $-.8$.

The SHAZAM results from the GLS estimation follow.

```
|_* Set-up the P matrix
|_DIM P 17 2
|_SAMPLE 2 17
|_GENR P:1=1
|_GEN1 P:1=SQRT(1-.8*.8)
|_SAMPLE 1 17
|_GENR P:2=-.8
|_* Print the P matrix so that it can be checked.
|_PRINT P
    P
   17 BY      2 MATRIX
    .6000000       -.8000000
   1.000000       -.8000000
   1.000000       -.8000000
   1.000000       -.8000000
   1.000000       -.8000000
   1.000000       -.8000000
   1.000000       -.8000000
   1.000000       -.8000000
   1.000000       -.8000000
   1.000000       -.8000000
   1.000000       -.8000000
   1.000000       -.8000000
   1.000000       -.8000000
   1.000000       -.8000000
   1.000000       -.8000000
   1.000000       -.8000000
   1.000000       -.8000000
|_* Get the GLS estimator
|_GLS CONSUME INCOME PRICE / PMATRIX=P
```

```
...WARNING..ASSUMING P          CONTAINS DIAGONALS
GLS ESTIMATION
     17 OBSERVATIONS      DEPENDENT VARIABLE = CONSUME
...NOTE..SAMPLE RANGE SET TO    1,    17


 R-SQUARE DEFINITIONS BASED ON BUSE, AMSTAT(1973)
 R-SQUARE =    .7652     R-SQUARE ADJUSTED =     .7316
VARIANCE OF THE ESTIMATE-SIGMA**2 =   48.091
STANDARD ERROR OF THE ESTIMATE-SIGMA =   6.9348
SUM OF SQUARED ERRORS-SSE=   673.27
MEAN OF DEPENDENT VARIABLE =   134.51
LOG OF THE LIKELIHOOD FUNCTION = -55.9037
```

VARIABLE NAME	ESTIMATED COEFFICIENT	STANDARD ERROR	T-RATIO 14 DF	P-VALUE	PARTIAL CORR.	STANDARDIZED COEFFICIENT	ELASTICITY AT MEANS
INCOME	1.1240	.5595	2.009	.064	.473	.2527	.8606
PRICE	-1.6577	.2525	-6.565	.000	-.869	-1.1859	-.9405
CONSTANT	148.12	59.60	2.485	.026	.553	.0000	1.1012

19. HETEROSKEDASTIC MODELS

"The 'state of the world' is a serially correlated thing; hence, we find ARCH."

Francis Diebold and Marc Nerlove, 1989
Journal of Applied Econometrics

The **HET** command implements maximum likelihood estimation of models which require corrections for heteroskedastic errors. The model to consider is:

$$Y_t = X'_t\beta + \varepsilon_t$$

where Y_t is the dependent variable, X_t are the independent variables, β are unknown parameters and ε_t is a zero mean, serially uncorrelated process with variance given by the function h_t. A survey of approaches to the specification of h_t is available in Judge, Griffiths, Hill, Lütkepohl and Lee [1985, Chapter 11].

Forms of Heteroskedasticity

A form that has been applied to cross-section studies of household expenditure (for example, Prais and Houthakker [1955] and Theil [1971]) is "dependent variable heteroskedasticity" with

$$h_t = (X'_t\beta)^2\alpha^2$$

where α is a scalar parameter. Further flexibility is obtained with a variance specification that is a function of exogenous variables, say Z_t, as in

$$h_t = Z'_t\alpha \qquad \text{or} \qquad h_t = (Z'_t\alpha)^2$$

where α is a vector of unknown parameters. Another form is the "multiplicative heteroskedasticity" model described by Harvey [1976, 1990] with

$$h_t = \exp(Z'_t\alpha)$$

ARCH Models

When modelling heteroskedasticity in time series data the ARCH (autoregressive conditional heteroskedasticity) process developed by Engle [1982] is of interest. ARCH models recognize the presence of successive periods of relative volatility and stability and allow the conditional variance to evolve over time as a function of past errors. The variance conditional on the past is given by the equation:

$$h_t = \alpha_0 + \sum_{j=1}^{q} \alpha_j \varepsilon_{t-j}^2$$

where the α_j are unknown parameters and q is the order of the ARCH process.

Various extensions to the Engle ARCH model have been proposed in the literature. For example, ARMA models with ARCH errors are analyzed by Weiss [1984]. Bollerslev [1986] specifies a conditional variance equation, GARCH, that allows for a parsimonious parameterisation of the lag structure. Time varying risk premia can be considered by including some function of the conditional variance as an additional regressor in the mean equation. This gives the ARCH-M (ARCH-in-Mean) model discussed by Engle, Lilien and Robins [1987]. To incorporate these extensions consider the model:

$$Y_t = X_t'\beta + \gamma g(h_t) + \varepsilon_t + \sum_{j=1}^{r} \theta_j \varepsilon_{t-j}$$

where the ε_t is a GARCH(p,q) process with conditional variance function given by:

$$h_t = \alpha_0 + \sum_{j=1}^{q} \alpha_j \varepsilon_{t-j}^2 + \sum_{j=1}^{p} \phi_j h_{t-j}$$

and the unknown parameters are β, γ, θ, α, and ϕ. The function $g(h_t)$ in the ARCH-M model may be specified by the practitioner and possible choices are $\log(h_t)$ or $\sqrt{h_t}$. ARCH processes assume constant unconditional variance and the parameter restrictions for stationarity are:

$$\alpha_0 > 0, \alpha_j \geq 0 \text{ for all } j, \quad \phi_j \geq 0 \quad \text{for all } j, \quad \text{and} \quad \sum_{j=1}^{q} \alpha_j + \sum_{j=1}^{p} \phi_j < 1$$

Also, the ARCH variance equation can be extended to include exogenous variables.

Maximum Likelihood Estimation

Maximum likelihood estimates are obtained based on the assumption that the errors are conditionally Gaussian. With the assumption of normality the log-density for observation t is:

$$l_t = -\frac{1}{2}\log(2\pi) - \frac{1}{2}\log(h_t) - \frac{1}{2}\varepsilon_t^2 / h_t \quad \text{for } t = 1, \ldots, N$$

The log-likelihood function is:

$$L = \sum_{t=1}^{N} l_t$$

First derivatives of the log-likelihood function with respect to the mean equation parameters and the variance equation parameters can be derived and these are utilized by SHAZAM (with the exception of ARCH-in-Mean models where numerical derivatives are used). The nonlinear optimization method employed by SHAZAM is a quasi-Newton method and alternative algorithms can be selected with the **METHOD=** option as described for the **NL** command in the chapter *NONLINEAR REGRESSION*. For the **HET** command the optimization algorithm constructs an initial Hessian estimate from the outer-product of the gradient (with the exception of ARCH-in-Mean models where the model estimation uses numerical derivatives).

At model convergence there are a number of ways to compute an estimate of the variance-covariance matrix of the parameter estimates. The **HET** command computes the information matrix inverse (with the exception of ARCH-in-Mean models where the covariance matrix estimate is computed from a Hessian approximation). For ARCH models and the exogenous heteroskedasticity models the information matrix is block diagonal. For the dependent variable heteroskedasticity model the assumption of Gaussian errors leads to an information matrix that is not block diagonal. Analytic expressions for the information matrix are available in Harvey [1990, Chapter 3.4] (for the dependent variable heteroskedasticity and the multiplicative heteroskedasticity models), Engle [1982] (for ARCH models) and Bollerslev [1986] (for GARCH models). Alternative covariance matrix estimates are obtained by using the **NUMCOV**, **NUMERIC** or **OPGCOV** options as described for the **NL** command in the chapter *NONLINEAR REGRESSION*.

HET COMMAND OPTIONS

In general, the format of the **HET** command is:

HET *depvar indeps (exogs) / options*

where *depvar* is the dependent variable, *indeps* is a list of independent variables, *exogs* is an optional list of exogenous variables in the variance equation and *options* is a list of desired options. For models with exogenous heteroskedasticity an intercept term is always included in the variance equation and therefore should not be specified in the *exogs* variable list. For models with exogenous variables in the variance equation if the *exogs* option is not specified then SHAZAM will set the variance equation exogenous variables to be identical to the regression equation exogenous variables. However, users should be warned that this may not be the best choice. For example, it may be appropriate to consider some transformation of the regression variables in the variance equation.

The options as defined for **OLS** that are available are:

DUMP, LINLOG, LIST, LOGLIN, LOGLOG, MAX, NOCONSTANT, PCOR, PCOV, RSTAT, BEG=/END=, COEF=, COV=, PREDICT=, RESID=, STDERR= and TRATIO=.

The options as defined for the nonlinear regression command **NL** that are available are:

NUMCOV, NUMERIC, OPGCOV, CONV=, ITER=, METHOD=, PITER= and STEPSIZE=.

The following additional options are available on the **HET** command:

PRESAMP   The estimation of ARCH models requires pre-sample estimates of ε_t^2. The algorithm sets the pre-sample values as an additional parameter and then obtains an estimated value that maximizes the value of the likelihood function. Use the **PRESAMP** option to ensure that an initial value is fixed for the pre-sample data in all iterations. If this option is specified then the pre-sample values are set to the average of the squared errors evaluated at the starting parameter values or the square of the value specifed in the **START=** option.

ARCH=   Specifies the order q of the ARCH process.

ARCHM=   Specifies the functional form for the ARCH-in-Mean term. With **ARCHM=**x the term h_t^x is included as an additional regressor. Set **ARCHM=0** for $\log(h_t)$ in the ARCH-M model. Set **ARCHM=0.5** for

$\sqrt{h_t}$ in the ARCH-M model. When this option is used the model estimation uses numerical derivatives. The estimation algorithm provides a Hessian approximation that is used to compute the covariance matrix estimate. This may give unreliable standard errors. Therefore, the **NUMCOV** option (as described for the **N L** command) should also be considered with the **ARCHM=** option.

GARCH=   Specifies the order p of the lagged conditional variances in the GARCH process. If the **ARCH=** option is not set then the process estimated is GARCH(p,1). In applied work the GARCH process that is often considered practical is the GARCH(1,1) process. This is obtained by specifying **GARCH=1**.

GMATRIX=   Specifies an NxK matrix to use to store the derivatives of the log-likelihood function at each observation. This option is not available with the **NUMERIC** option. An example of the use of this option is given at the end of this chapter.

MACH=   Specifies the order of the moving average process in models with ARCH errors.

MODEL=   Specifies the form of heteroskedasticity. The available options are:
ARCH for ARCH models. When this option is requested the default for the ARCH order is **ARCH=1**.

DEPVAR for **DEP**endent **VAR**iable heteroskedasticity.

MULT for **MULT**iplicative heteroskedasticity.

STDLIN for $h_t = (Z'_t\alpha)^2$, (i.e. the **ST**andard **D**eviation is a **LIN**ear function of exogenous variables).

VARLIN for $h_t = Z'_t\alpha$, (i.e. the **VAR**iance is a **LIN**ear function of exogenous variables).

If the **ARCH=**, **ARCHM=**, **GARCH=** or **MACH=** options are requested then **MODEL=ARCH** is assumed. Otherwise, the default is **MODEL=DEPVAR**.

START=   Specifies a vector of starting values for the estimation. The values must be in the same order as on the SHAZAM output. In addition, for ARCH models, the final parameter may be the starting value for the standard deviation of the pre-sample innovations. If this option is not specified then the starting parameter values are chosen by default. The default starting estimate for β are obtained from an OLS regression. For ARCH models the default starting values for the α are obtained from a regression of the OLS squared residuals on a constant and q lags.

STDRESID=   Saves the standardized residuals in the variable specified. The standardized residuals are computed from the estimated parameters as $\hat{\varepsilon}_t / \sqrt{\hat{h}_t}$.

Following model estimation the available temporary variables as described for the **OLS** command are:

$ERR , $K, $LLF, $N,$ and $R2OP$.

A practical difficulty with **MODEL=VARLIN** is that the parameter values may wander into regions that give negative variance. If this is encountered the algorithm resets the negative variance to a small positive number. The ARCH models may also generate negative variance and overflows and the algorithm checks for this. Warning messages for negative variance corrections are given when the **DUMP** option is used. If the model does not converge then different starting values can be tried with the **START=** option.

For ARCH models, when the estimation results are displayed the variable name GAMMA_ gives the ARCH-in-Mean parameter, the variable names THETA_ give the moving average parameters, the variable names ALPHA_ give the ARCH parameters (the first is the constant term in the variance equation), and the PHI_ give the parameter estimates on the lagged variances in the GARCH conditional variance equation. Finally the variable name DELTA_ gives the estimate of the standard deviation of the pre-sample innovations.

EXAMPLES

Testing for Heteroskedasticity

To test for heteroskedasticity an approach is to first run an OLS regression and then apply Lagrange multiplier tests. The **DIAGNOS / HET** command reports a number of useful tests including a test for ARCH(1) errors. A test for ARCH(q) can be constructed by running a regression of the OLS squared residuals on a constant and q lags and comparing the $N \cdot R^2$ value with a χ^2 distribution with q degrees of freedom. The following SHAZAM commands generate tests for heteroskedasticity and ARCH(2) errors.

```
OLS CONSUME INCOME PRICE / RESID=E
DIAGNOS /HET
GENR E2=E**2
OLS E2 E2(1.2)
GEN1 LM=$N*$R2
PRINT LM
```

By examining the test statistics the user can verify that the null hypothesis of homoskedasticity is not rejected for this simple example. However, the examples that follow serve to illustrate the **HET** command.

Dependent Variable Heteroskedasticity

The estimation results for a model with "dependent variable heteroskedasticity" are given below:

```
|_HET CONSUME INCOME PRICE
...NOTE..SAMPLE RANGE SET TO:     1,    17
DEPVAR    HETEROSKEDASTICITY MODEL      17 OBSERVATIONS
          ANALYTIC DERIVATIVES


   QUASI-NEWTON METHOD USING BFGS UPDATE FORMULA

INITIAL STATISTICS :
TIME =    1.750 SEC.   ITER. NO.     1 FUNCTION EVALUATIONS     1
LOG-LIKELIHOOD FUNCTION=    -51.00134
COEFFICIENTS
   1.061709       -1.382986        130.7066       .3700365E-01
GRADIENT
   -13.82284      -21.68072       -.1674465       7.936759

FINAL STATISTICS :
TIME =    1.970 SEC.   ITER. NO.     6 FUNCTION EVALUATIONS     6
LOG-LIKELIHOOD FUNCTION=    -50.58788
COEFFICIENTS
    .9084240      -1.351451        144.0436       .3580546E-01
GRADIENT
   .6045146E-01  .6405245E-01   .5909730E-03    .5394427

SQUARED CORR. COEF. BETWEEN OBSERVED AND PREDICTED    .95040

ASY. COVARIANCE MATRIX OF PARAMETER ESTIMATES IS ESTIMATED USING
THE INFORMATION MATRIX

LOG OF THE LIKELIHOOD FUNCTION = -50.5879

                             ASYMPTOTIC
VARIABLE   ESTIMATED  STANDARD   T-RATIO         PARTIAL STANDARDIZED ELASTICITY
  NAME     COEFFICIENT  ERROR   ***** DF  P-VALUE CORR. COEFFICIENT  AT MEANS
           MEAN EQUATION:
INCOME      .90842      .2140     4.246    .000  .762     .2042       .6955
PRICE      -1.3515     .6706E-01 -20.15    .000 -.984    -.9668      -.7667
CONSTANT   144.04       22.78     6.324    .000  .869     .0000      1.0709
           VARIANCE EQUATION:
ALPHA_      .35805E-01 .6148E-02  5.823    .000  .85
```

The coefficient `ALPHA_` above can be interpreted as the estimate of the standard deviation of the ratio $\varepsilon_t / (X_t'\beta)$.

ARCH(1)

The following output shows the estimation of a first-order ARCH model.

```
|_HET CONSUME INCOME PRICE / ARCH=1
...NOTE..SAMPLE RANGE SET TO:      1,     17
ARCH      HETEROSKEDASTICITY MODEL       17 OBSERVATIONS
          ANALYTIC DERIVATIVES


   QUASI-NEWTON METHOD USING BFGS UPDATE FORMULA

INITIAL STATISTICS :
TIME =      .340 SEC.   ITER. NO.      1 FUNCTION EVALUATIONS     1
LOG-LIKELIHOOD FUNCTION=    -51.39268
COEFFICIENTS
    1.061709       -1.382986        130.7066        16.95086        .3812538
    5.048663
GRADIENT
   -2.568027        2.385548      -.4618551E-01   -.1685253E-01    .2616805
   -.9919629E-02

FINAL STATISTICS :
TIME =      .870 SEC.   ITER. NO.      8 FUNCTION EVALUATIONS     11
LOG-LIKELIHOOD FUNCTION=    -51.20214
COEFFICIENTS
     .9432237       -1.409199        145.0000        15.23096        .4810183
    5.203280
GRADIENT
   -.7149841E-01   -.7095763E-01   -.7350608E-03   -.4425543E-04   -.6301406E-03
   -.1273054E-03

SQUARED CORR. COEF. BETWEEN OBSERVED AND PREDICTED     .95035

ASY. COVARIANCE MATRIX OF PARAMETER ESTIMATES IS ESTIMATED USING
THE INFORMATION MATRIX

LOG OF THE LIKELIHOOD FUNCTION = -51.2021


                            ASYMPTOTIC
VARIABLE   ESTIMATED  STANDARD   T-RATIO          PARTIAL STANDARDIZED ELASTICITY
  NAME     COEFFICIENT  ERROR   **** DF   P-VALUE CORR. COEFFICIENT  AT MEANS
           MEAN EQUATION:
INCOME      .94322      .2019      4.672     .000  .815     .2121        .7222
PRICE     -1.4092      .6708E-01 -21.01      .000 -.988   -1.0081       -.7995
CONSTANT  145.00      20.63        7.029     .000  .904     .0000       1.0780
           VARIANCE EQUATION:
ALPHA_     15.231      9.221       1.652     .099  .44
ALPHA_      .48102      .5340       .9007    .368  .26
DELTA_     5.2033      8.321        .6253    .532  .18
```

The starting values listed in iteration 1 are obtained from OLS and the model converges in 8 iterations. Note that the estimated value for α_1 is 0.48102 which satisfies the stationarity constraints (although it is not statistically significant). The coefficient DELTA_ is the estimate of the standard deviation of the pre-sample innovations. If the

PRESAMP option is used then the pre-sample values are fixed. More model estimation output is obtained with the **DUMP** and **PITER=1** options.

Multiplicative Heteroskedasticity

A model with a variance equation that has a multiplicative parameterization can be estimated using the SHAZAM commands:

```
GENR LINC=LOG(INCOME)
GENR LPRICE=LOG(PRICE)
HET CONSUME INCOME PRICE (LINC LPRICE) / MODEL=MULT
```

Robust Standard Errors

Some applied workers report robust standard errors obtained from the covariance matrix calculation $A^{-1}BA^{-1}$ where A is the information matrix and B is the outer-product of the gradient (see White [1982], Weiss [1986] and Bollerslev [1986]). The standard errors are robust in the sense that conditional normality of the errors is not assumed. The next set of SHAZAM commands estimates a GARCH(1,1) model and computes robust standard errors. Starting values for the estimation are specified in the variable *INPUT*.

```
READ(filename) Y X1 X2
DIM INPUT 6
* Starting values for the mean equation
GEN1 INPUT:1=1
GEN1 INPUT:2=1
GEN1 INPUT:3=100
* Starting values for the GARCH(1,1) variance equation
GEN1 INPUT:4=.5
GEN1 INPUT:5=.2
GEN1 INPUT:6=.7
* Estimate a GARCH(1,1) model
HET Y X1 X2 / START=INPUT ARCH=1 GARCH=1 COEF=BETA COV=AINV &
             GMATRIX=G
* Compute robust standard errors
MATRIX V=AINV*(G'G)*AINV
MATRIX SE=SQRT(DIAG(V))
MATRIX T=BETA/SE
* Print parameter estimates with robust standard errors and t-ratios.
PRINT BETA SE T
```

20. MAXIMUM LIKELIHOOD ESTIMATION OF NON-NORMAL MODELS

"It's the work of a madman."
Ambroise Vollard
French art dealer, 1907
(viewing a Picasso painting)

In regression applications where the dependent variable is strictly positive the assumption of normally distributed errors may be inappropriate. The **MLE** command provides maximum likelihood estimation of linear regression models for a range of distributional assumptions. If regressions with multivariate-t errors are desired see the chapter in this manual titled *ROBUST ESTIMATION*. If the desired form of the model is not listed with the **TYPE=** option described below see the **LOGDEN** option in the chapter *NONLINEAR REGRESSION* where a user-specified density function may be estimated. This command should only be used if this type of regression model is fully understood. The derivations in this chapter were derived by Trudy Cameron. For a further description of these models see Cameron and White [1990].

Consider the class of linear regression models such that:

$$E(Y_t | X_t) = X'_t \beta$$

Assume Y_t are independent random variables from a distribution with probability density function $f(Y_t; X_t, \beta, \theta)$ where θ is a vector of parameters that describe the shape of the distribution. The log-likelihood function is obtained by summing the log densities over all observations:

$$L = \sum_{t=1}^{N} \log[f(Y_t; X_t, \beta, \theta)]$$

The maximum likelihood estimates of β and θ are found by a nonlinear algorithm as those that maximize the value of the log-likelihood function. The estimated covariance matrix of the coefficient estimates is found by computing the inverse of the matrix of second derivatives of the log-likelihood function and evaluating this matrix at the maximum likelihood estimates.

Exponential Regression

The exponential distribution is the default distribution for the **MLE** command and is used if the **TYPE=** option is not specified. The conditional density function for Y_t can be expressed as:

$$f(Y_t; X_t, \beta) = (1 / X_t'\beta) \exp(-Y_t / X_t'\beta)$$

Taking logs and summing over all N observations gives the log-likelihood function:

$$-\sum_{t=1}^{N} \log(X_t'\beta) - \sum_{t=1}^{N} \left(\frac{Y_t}{X_t'\beta} \right)$$

Generalized Gamma Regression

The generalized gamma distribution is a flexible distribution that contains the simple gamma, Weibull, exponential and lognormal distributions as special cases. The log-likelihood function for regression using the generalized gamma distribution is:

$$N \log(c) - N \log \Gamma(k) + N c k \log \left(\frac{\Gamma(k + (1/c))}{\Gamma(k)} \right)$$

$$- \sum_{t=1}^{N} \log(Y_t) + ck \sum_{t=1}^{N} \log \left(\frac{Y_t}{X_t'\beta} \right) - \sum_{t=1}^{N} \left(\left(\frac{\Gamma(k + (1/c))}{\Gamma(k)} \right) \frac{Y_t}{X_t'\beta} \right)^c$$

where c and k are shape parameters. When c=k=1 the exponential distribution is obtained. When k=1 the generalized gamma distribution reduces to the Weibull distribution and when c=1 the generalized gamma distribution reduces to the gamma distribution.

Model Discrimination

Since the exponential distribution is a special case of the gamma distribution and also of the Weibull distribution it is easy to compute Lagrange Multiplier (LM) statistics for testing the hypothesis of exponential versus the more general distributions. These test statistics are reported with the **LM** option on the **MLE** command. A LM statistic to test the exponential model against the gamma model is computed as:

$$LM = g'H^{-1}g$$

where g and H are the first (gradient) and second (Hessian) derivatives respectively of the gamma log-likelihood function evaluated at the point k=1. Under the null hypothesis that the exponential distribution is correct this statistic has an asymptotic chi-square distribution with 1 degree of freedom. A similar procedure is used to test the exponential model against the Weibull model.

An LM test of the Weibull or gamma model against the generalized gamma model can also be constructed. For nested models a likelihood ratio test statistic provides another basis for comparison (see the discussion in McDonald [1984] and Cameron and White [1990]). Wald test statistics (computed with the **TEST** command) can also be applied to aid in model selection.

Lognormal Regression

It can be shown (with difficulty) that the lognormal distribution becomes a special case of the generalized gamma distribution as the parameter k approaches infinity. For regression using the lognormal distribution the log-likelihood function is:

$$-N\log(\sqrt{2\pi}\sigma) - \sum_{t=1}^{N}\log(Y_t) - \frac{1}{2\sigma^2}\sum_{t=1}^{N}\left[\log\left(\frac{Y_t}{X_t'\beta}\right) + \frac{\sigma^2}{2}\right]^2$$

Beta Regression

It is also possible to derive a regression model for the beta distribution. The beta density function has two parameters: p and q and the mean of a beta distribution is equal to p/(p+q). One way to derive the model is to make one of the parameters a function of the independent variables. Therefore the beta regression model where the parameter q is conditional on X becomes:

$$E(Y_t|X_t) = X_t'\beta = \frac{p}{p + q(X_t)} \qquad \text{where} \qquad q(X_t) = \frac{p}{X_t'\beta} - p$$

Next, the conditional beta density function becomes:

$$f(Y_t; X_t, \beta, p) = Y_t^{(p-1)}(1 - Y_t)^{(q(X_t)-1)} \bigg/ \left\{ \frac{\Gamma(p)\Gamma(q(X_t))}{\Gamma(p + q(X_t))} \right\}$$

So the final beta regression log-likelihood function is:

$$-N\log\Gamma(p) + \sum_{t=1}^{N}\log\left[\frac{\Gamma(p + q(X_t))}{\Gamma(q(X_t))}\right] + (p-1)\sum_{t=1}^{N}\log(Y_t) + \sum_{t=1}^{N}\left(\frac{p}{X_t'\beta} - p - 1\right)\log(1 - Y_t)$$

Log-linear Models

An alternative model assumption is:

$$E\big(\log(Y_t)| X_t\big) = X_t'\beta$$

This form is obtained when **TYPE=EGAMMA, EGG, EWEIBULL** or **EXTREMEV** is specified on the **MLE** command. The dependent variable must first be transformed to log form. Define $Z_t = \log(Y_t)$. For the log-linear generalized gamma regression model (**TYPE=EGG**) the conditional density function for the logarithmically transformed variable Z_t is:

$$f(Z_t; X_t, \beta, \sigma, k) = \frac{1}{\sigma \Gamma(k)} \exp\left[k(Z_t - X_t'\beta)/\sigma - \exp((Z_t - X_t'\beta)/\sigma)\right]$$

where $\sigma = 1/c$. The log-likelihood function (see Cameron and White [1990, Equation 9]) can then be written as:

$$-N\log(\sigma) - N\log\Gamma(k) + k\sum_{t=1}^{N}(Z_t - X_t'\beta)/\sigma - \sum_{t=1}^{N}\exp\left[(Z_t - X_t'\beta)/\sigma\right]$$

The shape parameters reported on the SHAZAM output are σ and k. Note that for comparison purposes with the linear model the value of the log-likelihood function computed for the log-linear model must be adjusted to include the appropriate Jacobian transformation. This is implemented with the **LOGLIN** option as described for the **OLS** command. Also note that the log-linear lognormal model is simply OLS with $\log(Y_t)$ as the dependent variable.

MLE *COMMAND OPTIONS*

In general, the format of the **MLE** command is:

MLE *depvar indeps / options*

where *depvar* is the dependent variable, *indeps* is a list of independent variables, and *options* is a list of desired options. It is possible to specify the distribution of the errors when using the **MLE** command with the **TYPE=** option. Options as described for the **OLS** command that are available are:

ANOVA, DUMP, GF, LINLOG, LIST, LOGLIN, LOGLOG, MAX, NOCONSTANT, NONORM, PCOR, PCOV, RSTAT, BEG=, END=, COEF=, COV=, PREDICT=, RESID=, STDERR=, TRATIO= and **WEIGHT=**.

When the **WEIGHT=** option is specified the method explained under the **REPLICATE** option in **OLS** is used.

Options as described for the **NL** command (see the chapter *NONLINEAR REGRESSION*) that are available are:

CONV=, IN=, ITER=, OUT= and **PITER=**.

In addition, the following options are available:

LM   Performs a **L**agrange **M**ultiplier test of some models against a less restricted model. If **TYPE=EXP** is used, two **LM** Tests for the **GAMMA** or **WEIBULL** models will be done. If **TYPE=WEIBULL** or **TYPE=GAMMA** is used the **LM** test of a Generalized Gamma distribution is performed.

METHOD=   Specifies the nonlinear algorithm to use. The choices are **BFGS** (the default) or **DFP**. These **METHODS** are described in the chapter *NONLINEAR REGRESSION*.

TYPE=   Specifies the **TYPE** of distribution to be assumed for the errors. The available **TYPE**s are **WEIBULL, EWEIBULL, GAMMA, EGAMMA, GG** (Generalized Gamma), **EGG, LOGNORM** (Lognormal), **BETA, EXP** (Exponential) and **EXTREMEV** (Extreme Value Distribution). The default is **TYPE=EXP**. The types **EWEIBULL, EGAMMA, EGG** and **EXTREMEV** are used when the dependent variable is in log form. They correspond to the **WEIBULL, GAMMA, GG,** and **EXP** forms respectively.

The available temporary variables on the **MLE** command are:

$ADR2, $DF, $DW, $ERR, $K, $LLF, $N, $R2, $R2OP, $RAW, $RHO, $SIG2, $SSE, $SSR, $SST, $ZDF, $ZSSR and *$ZSST*.

For more information on temporary variables see the chapter *MISCELLANEOUS COMMANDS AND INFORMATION* and the chapter *ORDINARY LEAST SQUARES*.

EXAMPLES

The following is an example of **MLE** output using Theil's textile data and assuming an exponential distribution.

```
|_MLE CONSUME INCOME PRICE / LM
EXP       REGRESSION      17 OBSERVATIONS
SUM OF DEPVAR=   2286.6    SUM OF LOG DEPVAR=   83.069

   QUASI-NEWTON METHOD USING BFGS UPDATE FORMULA

INITIAL STATISTICS :
TIME =     .440 SEC.   ITER. NO.     1 FUNCTION EVALUATIONS      1
LOG-LIKELIHOOD FUNCTION=    -100.0802
COEFFICIENTS
```

```
     1.061709        -1.382986        130.7066
GRADIENT
  -.1963727E-01  -.3026843E-01  -.2327428E-03

FINAL STATISTICS :
TIME =    .470 SEC.   ITER. NO.     2 FUNCTION EVALUATIONS     2
LOG-LIKELIHOOD FUNCTION=    -100.0797
COEFFICIENTS
    .9188548       -1.348463        142.7181
GRADIENT
  -.1911043E-02  -.1817679E-02  -.1911542E-04

**** LM TEST OF EXP      AGAINST WEIBULL  ****
  LM GRADIENT
  -.1911043E-02  -.1817679E-02  -.1911542E-04  -16.97903
  LM SECOND DERIVATIVES
   10.898
   8.6995        7.2588
   .10593         .84822E-01   .10323E-02
   5.6534        4.3493        .54957E-01   20.051
  CHI-SQUARE =   16.931     WITH 1 D.F.

**** LM TEST OF EXP      AGAINST GAMMA     ****
  LM GRADIENT
  -.1911043E-02  -.1817679E-02  -.1911542E-04  -9.801741
  LM SECOND DERIVATIVES
   10.898
   8.6995        7.2588
   .10593         .84822E-01   .10323E-02
  -.19110E-02   -.18177E-02  -.19115E-04   10.964
  CHI-SQUARE =   8.7628     WITH 1 D.F.

SQUARED CORR. COEF. BETWEEN OBSERVED AND PREDICTED     .95056

 R-SQUARE =     .9499    R-SQUARE ADJUSTED =     .9428
VARIANCE OF THE ESTIMATE-SIGMA**2 =    26.204
STANDARD ERROR OF THE ESTIMATE-SIGMA =    5.1190
SUM OF SQUARED ERRORS-SSE=   445.46
MEAN OF DEPENDENT VARIABLE =    134.51
LOG OF THE LIKELIHOOD FUNCTION =  100.080
```

		ASYMPTOTIC					
VARIABLE	ESTIMATED	STANDARD	T-RATIO		PARTIAL	STANDARDIZED	ELASTICITY
NAME	COEFFICIENT	ERROR	**** DF	P-VALUE	CORR.	COEFFICIENT	AT MEANS
INCOME	.91885	5.996	.1532	.878	.041	.2066	.7035
PRICE	-1.3485	1.862	-.7241	.469	-.190	-.9646	-.7650
CONSTANT	142.72	642.6	.2221	.824	.059	.0000	1.0611

Note that if one simply wished to estimate the parameters of a univariate distribution rather than a full regression model it could be easily done by excluding all independent variables so that only the *CONSTANT* would be estimated as in:

```
MLE CONSUME / LM
```

21. NONLINEAR REGRESSION

"It may be safely asserted...that population, when unchecked, increases in geometrical progression of such a nature to double itself every twenty-five years."

Thomas Malthus
British Economist, 1830

The **NL** command provides general features for the estimation of nonlinear models. The model specification can be a single equation or a system of equations and estimation with autoregressive errors is available. A system of nonlinear simultaneous equations can also be estimated by Nonlinear Three Stage Least Squares (N3SLS) or by Generalized Method of Moments (GMM).

The **NL** command also has options for the estimation of a general nonlinear function. For example, the **LOGDEN** option can be used for estimation with non-normal errors (also see the chapter *MAXIMUM LIKELIHOOD ESTIMATION OF NON-NORMAL MODELS*). The **MINFUNC** and **MAXFUNC** options can be used to minimize or maximize simple functions and the **SOLVE** option can be used to solve a set of nonlinear simultaneous equations.

The estimation of nonlinear models requires the use of a numerical optimization algorithm. SHAZAM uses a quasi-Newton method also known as a variable metric method (see Judge et al. [1985, pp.958-960]). Each updating step of the algorithm requires a gradient (first derivative) estimate and SHAZAM provides for exact evaluation of the gradient. If exact derivatives cannot be computed then SHAZAM will use a numerical approximation to obtain the gradient and a message will indicate that numerical derivatives are used. Each updating step also requires an approximation of the Hessian (second derivatives). The quasi-Newton family of algorithms obtains a Hessian inverse approximation in each iteration by an updating scheme that involves adding a correction matrix. At model convergence this approximation is then used as the covariance matrix estimate of the estimated parameters.

NOTE: Users should be familiar with nonlinear estimation before attempting this procedure. The *Nonlinear Least Squares by the Rank One Correction Method* example in the *PROGRAMMING IN SHAZAM* chapter shows a simple updating algorithm. Some basic information can be found in Maddala [1977]. A more rigorous treatment of nonlinear estimation can be found in Judge, Griffiths, Hill, Lütkepohl and Lee [1985, Chapter 6, Appendix B]; Judge, Hill, Griffiths, Lütkepohl and Lee [1988, Chapter 12]; and in Amemiya [1983] and Gallant [1987]. A procedure for testing for autocorrelation in nonlinear models is described in White [1992].

Users experienced with nonlinear estimation will be aware that there is no guarantee that the model will converge. If it does, convergence to a local rather than a global maximum is likely. For this reason, the model should always be re-estimated with different starting values to verify that the global maximum has probably been achieved. Since the computational time required for nonlinear estimation can be extremely high it is often useful to attempt to get good starting values by first estimating a linear simplification of the model.

NONLINEAR MODEL SPECIFICATION

To set up a nonlinear model in SHAZAM, it is necessary to tell SHAZAM some basic information as well as give **EQ** commands indicating the form of each equation in the model. It is very important for users to give SHAZAM good starting values of the coefficients. The desired starting values should be specified on **COEF** commands or placed in a vector and specified with the **START=** option on the **NL** command.

In general, the format for nonlinear estimation is:

NL *neq* / **NCOEF=** *options*
EQ *equation*
. . .
EQ *equation*
COEF *coef1 value1 coef2 value2* . . .
END

where *neq* is the number of equations and *options* is a list of desired options.

For estimation by Nonlinear Two-Stage Least Squares (N2SLS) or Nonlinear Three-Stage Least Squares (N3SLS) the **NL** command has the general form:

NL *neq exogs* / **NCOEF=** *options*

where *exogs* is a list of instrumental variables. SHAZAM automatically includes a constant in the list of instrumental variables unless the **NOCONEXOG** option is used.

For generalized method of moments (GMM) estimation the **NL** command has the general form:

NL *neq exogs* / **NCOEF=** **GMM=** *options*

One **EQ** command is required for every equation in the model. The **EQ** command can be continued on additional lines if there is an ampersand (&) typed at the end of the line to be continued. An equation with continuation lines may contain a total of 4096 columns. **EQ** commands are similar to **GENR** commands. If functions like LOG( ) and EXP( ) are used then SHAZAM is able to compute exact derivatives. However, for some other functions SHAZAM will automatically impose the **NUMERIC** option. If the equation has square root terms then to enable analytic derivatives write the terms in the form (*expression*)**.5 and not SQRT(*expression*). SHAZAM will assume that anything in the equation that has not already been defined as a variable will be a coefficient to estimate. Coefficients that appear in one equation may also appear in other equations.

RESTRICT commands are not permitted. Parameter restrictions can be incorporated directly in the **EQ** command. No forecasting options are available. **TEST** commands may follow the **END** command. For a discussion about linear and non-linear hypothesis testing see the chapter *HYPOTHESIS TESTING*.

NL *Command Options*

Options as defined for the **OLS** command that are available are:

LIST, PCOV, RSTAT, BEG=, END=, COEF=, COV=, PREDICT=, RESID=, STDERR=, and **TRATIO=**

Additional options are:

ACROSS	Estimates the seemingly unrelated regressions model with vector autoregressive errors. This admits autocorrelation **ACROSS** equations as well as within a single equation. This option can be computationally slow. More details are in the section *ESTIMATION WITH AUTOREGRESSIVE ERRORS* later in this chapter.
AUTO	Estimates the model with **AUTO**regressive errors. The order is specified with the **ORDER=** option and the default is first order autoregressive (AR(1)) errors. More details are in the section *ESTIMATION WITH AUTOREGRESSIVE ERRORS* later in this chapter.
DRHO	Normally, when the **AUTO** option is specified SHAZAM gives the same value of ρ to each equation. With the **DRHO** option a **D**ifferent value of **RHO** is given to each equation. When the order of autocorrelation is specified as higher than one on the **ORDER=** option the **DRHO** option will also give more than one ρ for each equation.

DUMP   DUMPs the internal code that SHAZAM has generated for the **EQ** commands. This option is only useful for SHAZAM consultants. If **DUMP** is specified with **EVAL** there will be a large amount of output.

EVAL   EVALuates the likelihood function for the starting values and prints out the answer. If **ITER=0** is also specified no estimation will be done. This is useful for experimentation purposes. If **EVAL** and **DUMP** are specified all the data in the nonlinear system is dumped along with the computed residuals and derivatives of the function with respect to all parameters. First, the data for each observation will be printed. Then the residuals for each equation and the derivatives of each equation with respect to each parameter will be printed, and finally, the derivatives for the equations will be printed consecutively. This option may not be used with the **NUMERIC** option.

GENRVAR   Takes the vector of coefficients and generates a set of scalar variables using the same names as those used for the coefficients on the **EQ** command. These scalar variables can then be used for the rest of the SHAZAM run. This is an alternative to the **COEF=** method for saving the coefficients.
                NOTE: A large number of variables may need to be generated if the model is large. The coefficient names used may not be used on any **EQ** command later in the same run. Since the coefficients are now variables **TEST** commands will no longer work.

LOGDEN   Used to tell SHAZAM that the equation given on the **EQ** command is the **LOG-DEN**sity for a single observation rather than a regression equation. SHAZAM will then compute a complete likelihood function by summing the log-densities. This option allows maximum likelihood estimation of a large variety of functions. An example is in Chapter 12.3 of the *Judge Handbook*. Another example is in *Multinomial Logit Models* in the chapter *PROGRAMMING IN SHAZAM*.

MAXFUNC   Used to tell SHAZAM that the equation given on the **EQ** command is a function (such as a log-likelihood function) to be maximized rather than a regression equation. SHAZAM will find the values of the parameters that maximize the function. The **SAMPLE** command should be set to include only one observation. An example of the use of this option is given later in this chapter.

MINFUNC   Used to tell SHAZAM that the equation given on the **EQ** command is a function to be minimized rather than a regression equation. SHAZAM will then find the values of the parameters that minimize the function. The **SAMPLE** command should be set to include only one observation.

NOCONEXOG If a list of exogenous variables is included for either Nonlinear Two or Three Stage Least Squares SHAZAM will automatically add a *CONSTANT* to the list. If you do not want SHAZAM to automatically include a constant in the list of exogenous variables, specify the **NOCONEXOG** option.

NOPSIGMA Suppresses printing of the sigma matrix from systems estimation.

NUMCOV Uses numeric differences to compute the covariance matrix after estimation. If this option is NOT specified SHAZAM uses a method based on the Davidon-Fletcher-Powell algorithm which builds up the covariance matrix after many iterations. This method may not be accurate if the model only runs for a small number of iterations. The numeric method is more expensive and also may not necessarily be accurate. The differential to be used in numeric differences can be controlled with the **STEPSIZE=** option.

NUMERIC Uses the **NUMERIC** difference method to compute derivatives in the algorithm. SHAZAM normally computes analytic derivatives which are more accurate. However, in some models with many equations and parameters, considerable savings in required memory will result if the **NUMERIC** option is used to compute numeric derivatives. In some cases the **NUMERIC** option may even be faster. For large models SHAZAM may automatically switch to numeric derivatives. If this happens then analytic derivatives can be forced with the **NONUMERIC** option (this will not be effective if functions other than LOG() and EXP() are used in the model).

OPGCOV Uses the outer-product of the Gradient method to compute the covariance matrix. It is not valid with the **NUMERIC** option.

PCOV Prints an estimate of the **COV**ariance matrix of coefficients after convergence. This estimate is based on an estimate of the Hessian which SHAZAM computes internally. SHAZAM estimates the Hessian by building it up after repeated iterations. Therefore, if the model converges immediately, SHAZAM will have a very poor estimate of the Hessian or none at all. In this case, the covariance matrix will just be an identity matrix. If the **NUMCOV** or **OPGCOV** options are used the estimated covariance matrix is computed using alternate methods.

SAME   Runs the previous **NL** regression without repeating the **EQ** commands. This should only be used in TALK mode at a terminal.

SOLVE   Used to tell SHAZAM that the equations given on the **EQ** commands are to be solved as a set of nonlinear simultaneous equations. There should be one equation for each coefficient as specified by the **NCOEF=** option. An example is shown in *Solving Nonlinear Sets of Equations* in the chapter *PROGRAMMING IN SHAZAM*. The **SAMPLE** should be set to include only one observation.

AUTCOV=   Specifies the lag length to be used in computing the weighting matrix for the **GMM=** option. If this option is not specified automatic formulas are used.

CONV=   Specifies the **CONV**ergence criterion for the coefficients. This value will be multiplied by each coefficient starting value to compute the convergence condition for each coefficient. The default is **CONV=.00001**. Let $\tilde{\beta}^{(i)}$ be the parameter estimates at iteration i and let δ be the value set with **CONV=**. The iterations stop when:

$$\left|\tilde{\beta}_k^{(i)} - \tilde{\beta}_k^{(i-1)}\right| < \alpha_k \cdot \delta \quad \text{for all k;} \quad \text{where} \quad \alpha_k = \begin{cases} \left|\tilde{\beta}_k^{(0)}\right| & \text{for} \quad \tilde{\beta}_k^{(0)} \neq 0 \\ 0.1 & \text{for} \quad \tilde{\beta}_k^{(0)} = 0 \end{cases}$$

GMM=   Specifies the weighting matrix to use for Generalized Method of Moments Estimation. If a matrix is provided it should be a symmetric matrix conforming to the dimensions in the equations described in the section *GENERALIZED METHOD OF MOMENTS ESTIMATION* in this chapter. Alternatively, SHAZAM will automatically compute the matrix corresponding to the keywords **HETCOV, BARTLETT, TRUNC, QS, PARZEN** or **TUKEY**. See also the **AUTCOV=** option when using the **GMM=** option. If you don't know what you are doing and want to use GMM anyway, you should probably use either **HETCOV** or **BARTLETT**.

IN=unit   Reads back the values of the coefficients and log-likelihood function that were saved with the **OUT=** option. This option is only useful when there is something to **IN**put from a previous run. This option may be combined with the **OUT=** option to insure that the **IN=** file always contains the values of the coefficients from the most recent iteration. The **COEF** command should only be used with the **IN=** option if the starting values of some of the coefficients are to be modified. When both **OUT=** and **IN=** are used the same unit number is usually used. A binary file should be assigned to the unit with the SHAZAM **FILE** command or an operating system command.

ITER=   Specifies the maximum number of **ITER**ations. The default is 100.

METHOD=   Specifies the nonlinear algorithm to use for estimation. The default is a Davidon-Fletcher-Powell algorithm. An alternative **METHOD=BFGS**, Broyden-Fletcher-Goldfarb-Shanno (BFGS), is described in Belsley [1980]. Another alternative is a slightly different D-F-P algorithm which can be obtained with **METHOD=DFP**.

NCOEF=   Specifies the Number of different **COEF**ficients to be estimated. This option is required.

ORDER=   Specifies the **ORDER** of autocorrelation to be corrected when the **AUTO** option is used. The default is **ORDER=1**.

OUT=_unit_   Writes **OUT** on the unit specified the values of the coefficients and log-likelihood function after each iteration. This is quite useful for restarting the model in another run with the **IN=** option described above. When this option is used, a file must be assigned to the output unit as described in the chapter _DATA INPUT AND OUTPUT_. The values will be written in double precision (binary) all on one line. Units 11-49 are available for use.

PITER=   Specifies the frequency with which **ITER**ations will be Printed in the output. The default **PITER=15** indicates that one out of every 15 iterations will be printed.

SIGMA=   Saves the sigma matrix from systems estimation in the variable specified. For single equation estimation the estimate of σ^2 is saved.

START=   Uses the values in the specified variable as starting values for the estimation. The order of the parameters should be the same as normally printed by the SHAZAM **NL** command, namely, the order that they appear on the **EQ** commands (followed by autocorrelation coefficients when the **AUTO** option is used). In some cases this may be an easier way to input starting values than by using the **COEF** command. Be careful to make sure that the length of the **START=** vector is equal to the number of coefficients specified with the **NCOEF=** option (plus the number of autocorrelation coefficients if any).

STEPSIZE=   Specifies the stepsize to use with the **NUMCOV** and **NUMERIC** options to control the differential in numeric derivatives. The default is **STEPSIZE=1E-4**. The calculated covariance matrix may be very sensitive to this value.

ZMATRIX=   Specifies a matrix to create and use to store the derivatives of the nonlinear function with respect to each parameter. This option should be used only when there is only one equation that is estimated. The option is not valid if the **NUMERIC** option is also used. The Z matrix is described in Judge, Griffiths, Hill, Lütkepohl and Lee [1985, Equation 6.2.3].

After estimation the temporary variables as described for the **OLS** command are:

$ERR, $K, $LLF, and $N.

Note that the temporary variable LLF is used in all SHAZAM nonlinear estimation to hold the function value. This will be either the value of the log-likelihood function or the minimized function value.

NONLINEAR LEAST SQUARES

The nonlinear equation with additive errors has the general form:

$$Y_t = f(X_t, \beta) + \varepsilon_t \qquad \text{for } t=1, \ldots, N$$

The residual sum of squares is:

$$S(\beta) = \sum_{t=1}^{N} [Y_t - f(X_t, \beta)]^2$$

With $\varepsilon \sim N(0, \sigma^2 I_N)$ the maximum likelihood estimator for σ^2 is $\tilde{\sigma}^2 = S(\beta) / N$ and the maximum likelihood estimator is the value of β that maximizes the concentrated log-likelihood function (see Judge, Hill, Griffiths, Lütkepohl and Lee [1988, Equation 12.2.85]):

$$L(\beta) = -\frac{N}{2} \ln(2\pi) - \frac{N}{2} \ln\left(\frac{S(\beta)}{N}\right) - \frac{N}{2}$$

When the errors are normally distributed the maximum likelihood estimator is identical to the nonlinear least squares estimator which globally minimizes $S(\beta)$.

The estimates have an interpretation as estimates from a linearized model that is constructed from a Taylor series approximation. Define the matrix of first derivatives evaluated at the converged estimates $\tilde{\beta}$ as:

$$Z(\tilde{\beta}) = \left. \frac{\partial f(X,\beta)}{\partial \beta} \right|_{\tilde{\beta}}$$

(The Z matrix can be saved with the **ZMATRIX=** option on the **NL** command). The linear pseudomodel (see Judge et al. [1988, Equation 12.2.14]) is:

$$\overline{Y}(\tilde{\beta}) = Z(\tilde{\beta})\beta + \varepsilon \qquad \text{where} \qquad \overline{Y}(\tilde{\beta}) = Y - f(X,\tilde{\beta}) + Z(\tilde{\beta})\tilde{\beta}$$

An OLS regression of $\overline{Y}(\tilde{\beta})$ on $Z(\tilde{\beta})$ will reproduce the parameter estimate $\tilde{\beta}$.

The example below uses the **NL** command to estimate a demand equation with the Theil textile data. The model has one equation and three coefficients.

```
|_NL 1 / NCOEF=3
...NOTE..SAMPLE RANGE SET TO:      1,     17
|_EQ CONSUME=A+B*INCOME+C*PRICE
|_COEF  B  1  C  -1  A 50
   3 VARIABLES IN  1 EQUATIONS WITH   3 COEFFICIENTS
        17 OBSERVATIONS

COEFFICIENT STARTING VALUES
A         50.000      B          1.0000      C         -1.0000
     100 MAXIMUM ITERATIONS, CONVERGENCE =  .000010

INITIAL STATISTICS :
TIME =        .090 SEC.   ITER. NO.      0  FUNCT. EVALUATIONS    1
LOG-LIKELIHOOD FUNCTION=   -93.26261
COEFFICIENTS
   50.00000       1.000000      -1.000000
GRADIENT
   .2884071       29.68023       21.50215

INTERMEDIATE STATISTICS :
TIME =        .150 SEC.   ITER. NO.     15  FUNCT. EVALUATIONS   26
LOG-LIKELIHOOD FUNCTION=   -54.73018
COEFFICIENTS
   70.36305       1.643421      -1.360359
GRADIENT
  -.5982383      -68.90536      -52.52647

FINAL STATISTICS :
TIME =        .180 SEC.   ITER. NO.     26  FUNCT. EVALUATIONS   37
LOG-LIKELIHOOD FUNCTION=   -51.64706
COEFFICIENTS
   130.7066       1.061709      -1.382986
GRADIENT
   .6334375E-07   .6693914E-05   .5618457E-05

MAXIMUM LIKELIHOOD ESTIMATE OF SIGMA-SQUARED =   25.489
GTRANSPOSE*INVERSE(H)*G  STATISTIC  -  =   .10715E-13
```

```
          COEFFICIENT    ST. ERROR   T-RATIO
   A          130.71       24.827    5.2647
   B          1.0617       .24390    4.3531
   C         -1.3830     .76344E-01 -18.115
   END
```

Note that the **EQ** command supplies names for the coefficients to be estimated. In the above example, the coefficients are A, B and C, the variables are *CONSUME, INCOME* and *PRICE*. The **COEF** command immediately follows the **EQ** command and specifies starting values for the coefficients. An **END** command should follow the **COEF** command. Notice that the estimation results for this example are identical to that illustrated in the chapter *ORDINARY LEAST SQUARES*. In the case of a linear equation, the **NL** command gives the same estimated coefficients as the **OLS** command, but the computational time required to run **NL** regressions is much higher.

A sufficient number of starting values must be included for all coefficients or SHAZAM will not run the estimation. If the **COEF** command is omitted and no starting values are assigned then SHAZAM uses a starting value of 1.0 for all coefficients.

In the above example the starting values are specified with the command:

```
COEF   B 1   C  -1   A 50
```

If the coefficient names are not specified on the **COEF** command, SHAZAM assumes that the starting values appear in the same order as they appear on the **EQ** command. In the above example the coefficients on the **EQ** command appear in the order A, B and C. So an alternative way of entering starting values is with:

```
COEF
 50   1   -1
```

Testing for Autocorrelation

In a nonlinear model it is often desirable to use the Durbin-Watson statistic to test for autocorrelation. Following the method in White [1992] it is easy to approximate the exact distribution of the Durbin-Watson statistic using SHAZAM. In that article a reference was made to SHAZAM code to perform this test. Since the *Review of Economics and Statistics* does not like to print computer code, the method is shown here in the context of estimation of a CES (constant elasticity of substitution) production function. The form of the production function is:

$$Q = \alpha \, [\delta L^{-\rho} + (1-\delta)K^{-\rho}]^{-\eta/\rho} \qquad (\,\alpha > 0; \; 0 < \delta < 1; \; \rho > -1; \; \rho \neq 0, \text{ and } \eta > 0)$$

where Q is output, and L and K represent two factors of production. The statistical model can be expressed as:

$$\log(Q) = \gamma - \frac{\eta}{\rho} \log[\delta L^{-\rho} + (1-\delta)K^{-\rho}] + \varepsilon$$

where $\gamma = \log(\alpha)$ and ε is a random error term. The CES function is discussed and a data set is provided in Griffiths, Hill and Judge [1993, Chapter 22]. The next list of SHAZAM commands sets up the nonlinear estimation and then obtains a p-value for the Durbin-Watson test statistic.

```
SAMPLE 1 30
READ(TABLE22.4) L K Q
GENR LOGQ=LOG(Q)
* Estimate the CES production function
NL 1 / NCOEF=4 PCOV ZMATRIX=Z COEF=BETA PREDICT=YHAT
EQ LOGQ=GAMMA-(ETA/RHO)*LOG(DELTA*L**(-RHO)+(1-DELTA)*K**(-RHO))
COEF   RHO 1   DELTA .5   GAMMA 1   ETA 1
END
* Estimate the elasticity of substitution
TEST 1/(1+RHO)
* Generate the linear pseudomodel and compute the DURBIN-WATSON p-value
MATRIX YBAR=LOGQ-YHAT+Z*BETA
OLS YBAR Z / NOCONSTANT DWPVALUE
```

The option **NCOEF=4** on the **NL** command specifies that there are 4 coefficients to estimate. The coefficients are GAMMA, ETA, RHO and DELTA. The **COEF** command immediately follows the **EQ** command and gives the starting values for the iterative estimation. The Durbin-Watson p-value printed by the final **OLS** command above can be used with the Durbin-Watson statistic so it is not necessary to try to apply Durbin-Watson tables to a nonlinear problem.

MAXIMIZING A FUNCTION

This example is discussed in Greene [1993, Chapter 12, p. 352]. The problem is to maximize a function of a single variable: $f(\theta) = \ln\theta - \theta^2$

This problem can be solved by using the **MAXFUNC** option on the **NL** command. The SHAZAM commands that follow specify a starting value of $\theta=5$ for the iterative procedure.

```
SAMPLE 1 1
NL 1 / NCOEF=1 MAXFUNC
EQ LOG(THETA)-THETA**2
COEF THETA 5
END
```

NONLINEAR SEEMINGLY UNRELATED REGRESSION

A set of M nonlinear equations can be written as:

$$Y_i = f_i(X,\beta) + \varepsilon_i \qquad \text{for } i=1,\ldots,M$$

Note that the inclusion of the matrix X and the coefficient vector β in all equations allows for common explanatory variables and coefficients across equations. It is assumed that there is contemporaneous correlation between errors in different equations. Let S be the M x M matrix with (i,j)th element equal to:

$$\varepsilon_i'\varepsilon_j = [Y_i - f_i(X,\beta)]'[Y_j - f_j(X,\beta)]$$

With the assumption that the errors have a multivariate normal distribution the maximum likelihood estimator for β is obtained by maximizing the concentrated log-likelihood function (see Judge, Hill, Griffiths, Lütkepohl and Lee [1988, Section 12.4.2]):

$$L(\beta) = -\frac{NM}{2}\ln(2\pi) - \frac{N}{2}\ln(|S/N|) - \frac{NM}{2}$$

The maximum likelihood estimator is the value of β that minimizes $|S|$.

The next example shows how to set up a nonlinear estimation of the linear expenditure system as discussed in Judge et al. [1988, Section 12.4.3]. In this system it is assumed that consumer income Y is divided between 3 goods Q1, Q2 and Q3 whose prices are P1, P2 and P3 respectively. The coefficients to be estimated are the marginal budget shares (B1, B2, B3) along with the subsistence quantities (G1, G2, G3). Since this is a complete system of demand equations, it is well known that only 2 of the 3 equations need to be estimated (B3=1−B1−B2). Thus, there are 2 equations and 5 coefficients to estimate. The SHAZAM commands might look like:

```
SAMPLE 1 30
READ (TABLE11.3) P1 P2 P3 Y Q1 Q2 Q3
GENR PQ1=P1*Q1
GENR PQ2=P2*Q2
NL 2 / NCOEF=5 PCOV
EQ PQ1=P1*G1+B1*(Y-P1*G1-P2*G2-P3*G3)
EQ PQ2=P2*G2+B2*(Y-P1*G1-P2*G2-P3*G3)
COEF G1 2.903 G2 1.36 G3 13.251 B1 .20267 B2 .13429
END
* Compute B3
TEST 1-B1-B2
```

It is important to remember to eliminate 1 equation from the model when estimating systems of demand equations so that the system is not overdetermined.

ESTIMATION WITH AUTOREGRESSIVE ERRORS

The estimation of models with autoregressive errors is implemented with the **AUTO** option on the **NL** command. The estimation algorithm uses numeric derivatives and so the **NUMERIC** option is automatically set.

Single Equation Estimation

The nonlinear equation with errors that follow an autoregressive process of order p (AR(p) errors) has the form:

$$Y_t = f(X_t, \beta) + \varepsilon_t \qquad \text{with} \quad \varepsilon_t = \sum_{k=1}^{p} \rho_k \varepsilon_{t-k} + v_t$$

Parameter estimates are obtained by minimizing the objective function:

$$S(\beta, \rho) = \sum_{t=p+1}^{N} v_t^2 = \sum_{t=p+1}^{N} \left[(Y_t - f(X_t, \beta)) - \sum_{k=1}^{p} \rho_k (Y_{t-k} - f(X_{t-k}, \beta)) \right]^2$$

Note that initial observations are dropped. The method is a variation of the method described in Pagan [1974] and implemented for linear models with the **PAGAN** option on the **AUTO** command (see the chapter *AUTOCORRELATION MODELS*). Note that the Pagan method sets the pre-sample residuals to zero.

The number of coefficients to estimate is K+p where K must be specified with the **NCOEF=** option and p is specified with the **ORDER=** option. Starting values can be requested with the **START=** option and values must be specified for the K coefficients in β followed by the p autocorrelation coefficients.

Nonlinear Seemingly Unrelated Regression Estimation

For the SUR model with M equations let $\varepsilon_{(t)}$ denote the vector of M disturbances for observation t and assume an AR(p) process represented as:

$$\varepsilon_{(t)} = \sum_{k=1}^{p} R_k \varepsilon_{(t-k)} + v_{(t)}$$

where the R_k are M x M matrices of autocorrelation coefficients. Further discussion is in Judge, Griffiths, Hill, Lütkepohl, and Lee [1985, Section 12.3].

The default estimation method is to assume that $R_k = \rho_k I_M$. If the **DRHO** option is used then the assumption is that R_k is a diagonal matrix. The **ACROSS** option implements the general case of a vector autoregressive model with no restrictions on the R_k matrix. When the **ACROSS** option is specified the autocorrelation coefficients are printed in column order ($VEC(R_k)$).

Let S be the M x M matrix with (i,j)th element equal to:
$$\sum_{t=p+1}^{N} v_{it} v_{jt}$$

Parameter estimates are obtained by minimizing $|S|$.

NONLINEAR TWO-STAGE LEAST SQUARES (N2SLS)

Consider a model of the form:

$$Y = f(Z,\beta) + \varepsilon$$

where Y is an N x 1 vector of observations on the dependent variable, Z is the matrix of right-hand side variables in the equation, β is a p x 1 vector of unknown parameters and ε is a random error vector. With X as a matrix of instrumental variables (usually all the exogenous variables in the system) the parameter estimates are obtained by minimizing the objective function:

$$\varepsilon'X (X'X)^{-1}X'\varepsilon \qquad \text{where} \quad \varepsilon = Y - f(Z,\beta)$$

With estimated coefficients $\hat{\beta}$ the estimated N2SLS residuals are obtained as:

$$e = Y - f(Z,\hat{\beta})$$

The estimated covariance matrix of $\hat{\beta}$ is:

$$\hat{\sigma}^2 (g'X (X'X)^{-1}X'g)^{-1} \qquad \text{where} \qquad \hat{\sigma}^2 = e'e / N$$

and g is the N x p matrix of derivatives $\partial f(Z,\beta)/\partial\beta$ evaluated at $\hat{\beta}$.

An example of N2SLS using the first equation of the Klein Model described in the chapter *TWO STAGE LEAST SQUARES AND SYSTEMS OF EQUATIONS* follows. To implement N2SLS with the **NL** command the user must specify a set of instrumental variables to be used. In the example the list of instrumental variables is given as *W2, T,*

G, TIME1, PLAG, KLAG and *XLAG.* In addition, SHAZAM automatically includes a constant in the list of instrumental variables.

```
|_* NONLINEAR TWO STAGE LEAST SQUARES
|_NL 1 W2 T G TIME1 PLAG KLAG XLAG / NCOEF=4
...NOTE..SAMPLE RANGE SET TO:     1,     21
|_EQ C=A1*PLAG+A2*P+A3*W1W2+A0
|_END
  11 VARIABLES IN  1 EQUATIONS WITH   4 COEFFICIENTS
NONLINEAR TWO-STAGE LEAST SQUARES: USING   8 INSTRUMENTAL EXOGENOUS VARIABLES
        21 OBSERVATIONS


COEFFICIENT STARTING VALUES
A1        1.0000      A2        1.0000      A3        1.0000
A0        1.0000
        100 MAXIMUM ITERATIONS, CONVERGENCE =  .000010

INITIAL STATISTICS :
TIME =        .130 SEC.  ITER. NO.     0  FUNCT. EVALUATIONS     1
FUNCTION VALUE=   11111.95    FUNCTION VALUE/N =   529.1406
COEFFICIENTS
   1.000000       1.000000       1.000000       1.000000
GRADIENT
   16117.80       16557.11       39581.22       913.6000

FINAL STATISTICS :
TIME =        .250 SEC.  ITER. NO.     9  FUNCT. EVALUATIONS    13
FUNCTION VALUE=   9.157975    FUNCTION VALUE/N =   .4360940
COEFFICIENTS
   .2162340       .1730222E-01   .8101827       16.55476
GRADIENT
   .1799183E-04   .1988876E-04   .4711613E-04   .1456845E-05

MAXIMUM LIKELIHOOD ESTIMATE OF SIGMA-SQUARED =   1.0441
GTRANSPOSE*INVERSE(H)*G  STATISTIC  - =  .29445E-12


     COEFFICIENT    ST. ERROR   T-RATIO
A1      .21623        .10727     2.0158
A2      .17302E-01    .11805      .14657
A3      .81018        .40250E-01 20.129
A0     16.555        1.3208     12.534
|_END
```

N2SLS Estimation with Autoregressive Errors

If the **AUTO** option is used for estimation with autoregressive errors then an appropriate set of instrumental variables must be specified in the *exogs* list on the **NL** command (see, for example, the discussion in Greene [1993, p. 608]). For the model with AR(1) errors a choice of instrumental variables may be: Y_{t-1}, X_t and X_{t-1}.

NONLINEAR THREE STAGE LEAST SQUARES (N3SLS)

Now consider a system of M equations such that equation i has the general form:

$$f_i(Y,X,\beta) = \varepsilon_i \quad \text{for} \quad i=1,\ldots,M$$

The vector β has p parameters. The error covariances are given by $E(\varepsilon_i \varepsilon_j') = \sigma_{ij} I_N$. Denote Σ as the M x M matrix with individual elements σ_{ij} and stack the ε_i vectors to obtain an MN x 1 vector ε. The N3SLS estimator is obtained by minimizing the objective function:

$$\varepsilon' \left[\hat{\Sigma}^{-1} \otimes X(X'X)^{-1}X' \right] \varepsilon$$

where $\hat{\Sigma}$ is constructed from the N2SLS residuals. With the estimated N2SLS residuals for equation i in the N x 1 vector e_i the individual elements of $\hat{\Sigma}$ are obtained as $\hat{\sigma}_{ij} = e_i' e_j / N$. The covariance matrix of estimated coefficients is estimated as:

$$[G'(\hat{\Sigma}^{-1} \otimes X(X'X)^{-1}X')\,G]^{-1} \quad \text{where} \quad G = \begin{bmatrix} g_1 \\ . \\ g_M \end{bmatrix}$$

The g_i matrix is N x p and it contains the partial derivatives of $f_i(Y,X,\beta)$ with respect to β evaluated at the parameter estimates.

The example below gives SHAZAM output for N3SLS estimation of the Klein Model.

```
|_* NONLINEAR THREE STAGE LEAST SQUARES
|_NL 3 W2 T G TIME1 PLAG KLAG XLAG / NCOEF=12 PITER=50
...NOTE..SAMPLE RANGE SET TO:        1,     21
|_EQ C=A1*PLAG+A2*P+A3*W1W2+A0
|_EQ I=B1*PLAG+B2*KLAG+B3*P+B0
|_EQ W1=C1*TIME1+C2*XLAG+C3*X+C0
|_END
   14 VARIABLES IN  3 EQUATIONS WITH  12 COEFFICIENTS
NONLINEAR TWO-STAGE LEAST SQUARES: USING   8 INSTRUMENTAL EXOGENOUS VARIABLES
          21 OBSERVATIONS

COEFFICIENT STARTING VALUES
A1          1.0000       A2          1.0000       A3          1.0000
A0          1.0000       B1          1.0000       B2          1.0000
B3          1.0000       B0          1.0000       C1          1.0000
C2          1.0000       C3          1.0000       C0          1.0000
        100 MAXIMUM ITERATIONS, CONVERGENCE =   .000010

INITIAL STATISTICS :
TIME =          .090 SEC.  ITER. NO.      0   FUNCT. EVALUATIONS        1
FUNCTION VALUE=   1348508.     FUNCTION VALUE/N =    64214.68
```

```
COEFFICIENTS
     1.000000          1.000000          1.000000          1.000000          1.000000
     1.000000          1.000000          1.000000          1.000000          1.000000
     1.000000          1.000000
GRADIENT
    16117.80          16557.11          39581.22          913.6000          161577.1
    1970580.          165951.4          9806.800          46201.60          233550.0
    242535.3          3934.600

FINAL STATISTICS :
TIME =        2.130 SEC.   ITER. NO.      19    FUNCT. EVALUATIONS      31
FUNCTION VALUE=    17.62146       FUNCTION VALUE/N =    .8391173
COEFFICIENTS
     .2162340          .1730221E-01      .8101827          16.55476          .6159436
    -.1577876          .1502218          20.27821          .1303957          .1466738
     .4388591          .6594422E-01
GRADIENT
    -.9135559E-07     .1209752E-06     -.1557105E-07     -.2684200E-08     -.1069811E-06
    -.1600394E-05    -.1663395E-06     -.6411252E-08     -.1361892E-07     -.8107014E-07
     .1330693E-07    -.9246286E-07

SIGMA MATRIX
    1.0441
     .43785          1.3832
    -.38523           .19261            .47643

GTRANSPOSE*INVERSE(H)*G  STATISTIC  -  =    .99128E-14

          COEFFICIENT    ST. ERROR    T-RATIO
A1          .21623        .10727        2.0158
A2          .17302E-01    .11805        .14657
A3          .81018        .40250E-01    20.129
A0          16.555        1.3208        12.534
B1          .61594        .16279        3.7838
B2         -.15779        .36126E-01   -4.3677
B3          .15022        .17323        .86718
B0          20.278        7.5427        2.6885
C1          .13040        .29141E-01    4.4746
C2          .14667        .38836E-01    3.7767
C3          .43886        .35632E-01    12.316
C0          .65944E-01    1.0377        .63550E-01

*** NONLINEAR THREE STAGE LEAST SQUARES ***

INITIAL STATISTICS :
TIME =        2.340 SEC.   ITER. NO.       0    FUNCT. EVALUATIONS       1
FUNCTION VALUE=    28.61320       FUNCTION VALUE/N =    1.362534
COEFFICIENTS
     .2162340          .1730221E-01      .8101827          16.55476          .6159436
    -.1577876          .1502218          20.27821          .1303957          .1466738
     .4388591          .6594422E-01
GRADIENT
    -3.710973         -19.98431         -40.19389         -.1978416E-06     2.223335
    72.48382          11.97309          .1136923E-06     -79.17372         -57.11702
    -8.732483         -.4000084E-06
```

```
FINAL STATISTICS :
TIME =        6.560 SEC.   ITER. NO.     23   FUNCT. EVALUATIONS      29
FUNCTION VALUE=   24.29102      FUNCTION VALUE/N =    1.156715
COEFFICIENTS
    .1631441        .1248905        .7900809       16.44079      .7557240
   -.1948482      -.1307918E-01    28.17785        .1496741      .1812910
    .4004919        .1508024
GRADIENT
   -.1155376E-06  -.1648650E-06   -.4578952E-06  -.8789430E-07  -.1000770E-06
   -.4155699E-05  -.3814232E-06   -.2193214E-07  -.1618987E-05  -.2499567E-05
   -.1481715E-05  -.1650535E-06

SIGMA MATRIX
   .89176
   .41132          2.0930
  -.39361           .40305          .52003

GTRANSPOSE*INVERSE(H)*G  STATISTIC  -  =    .19942E-13

       COEFFICIENT    ST. ERROR    T-RATIO
A1        .16314       .10044       1.6243
A2        .12489       .10813       1.1550
A3        .79008       .37938E-01  20.826
A0      16.441        1.3045       12.603
B1        .75572       .15293       4.9415
B2       -.19485       .32531E-01  -5.9897
B3       -.13079E-01   .16190      -.80787E-01
B0      28.178        6.7938       4.1476
C1        .14967       .27935E-01   5.3579
C2        .18129       .34159E-01   5.3073
C3        .40049       .31813E-01  12.589
C0        .15080      1.0150        .14858
|_END
```

GENERALIZED METHOD OF MOMENTS ESTIMATION

Generalized method of moments (GMM) estimation is described in Andrews [1991], Davidson and MacKinnon [1993, Chapter 17], Gallant [1987], Greene [1993, Chapter 13], Hansen and Singleton [1982] and Newey and West [1987 and 1991].

Single Equation Estimation

In a single equation the model follows the notation of the Nonlinear Two-Stage Least Squares model which is a special case of GMM. The general form of the equation is:

$$Y = f(Z,\beta) + \varepsilon$$

where Y is an N x 1 vector of observations on the dependent variable, Z is the matrix of right-hand side variables in the equation, β is a P x 1 vector of unknown parameters and ε is a random error vector. The model assumptions are $E(\varepsilon)=0$ and $E(\varepsilon\varepsilon')=\Omega$ where Ω is unrestricted. With X as an NxK matrix of instrumental variables (usually all the predetermined variables in the system) the parameter estimates are obtained by minimizing the objective function:

$$\varepsilon'X \, (X'\Omega X)^{-1}X'\varepsilon \qquad \text{where} \quad \varepsilon = Y - f(Z,\beta)$$

The matrix $(X'\Omega X)$ is known as the weighting matrix and the user must specify this matrix with the **GMM=** option either as the name of a matrix variable which contains the desired values or as one of the pre-set SHAZAM options described below. The estimated covariance matrix of the GMM estimates $\tilde{\beta}$ is:

$$(g'X \, (X'\Omega X)^{-1}X'g)^{-1}$$

where g is the N x P matrix of derivatives $\partial f(Z,\beta)/\partial \beta$ evaluated at $\tilde{\beta}$.

There are a few preset options to allow SHAZAM to automatically compute the weighting matrix. If **GMM=HETCOV** is specified the White [1980] estimate of the matrix is used. The weighting matrix $(X'\Omega X)$ is estimated using the residuals e_t estimated from N2SLS as:

$$W_0 = \sum_{t=1}^{N} e_t^2 X_t X_t'$$

where X_t is a K x 1 vector of instrumental variables for observation t. If the disturbances are autocorrelated then the estimator proposed by Newey and West [1987] is:

$$W = W_0 + \sum_{j=1}^{L} \sum_{t=j+1}^{N} w_j e_t e_{t-j} \left(X_t X_{t-j}' + X_{t-j} X_t' \right)$$

The weights w_j and the maximum lag length L must be chosen in advance. A number of alternative schemes are implemented in SHAZAM with the **GMM=** option using the keywords **BARTLETT, TRUNC, PARZEN, QS** or **TUKEY**. The lag length L can be specified with the **AUTCOV=** option and if this option is not specified a default setting of L will be used. The weighting scheme and the default value of L for the alternative methods is as follows.

If **GMM=BARTLETT** is specified then:

$$w_j = 1 - \frac{j}{L+1}.$$

If the **AUTCOV=** option is not specified then the automatic bandwidth formula in Newey and West [1991] is used:

$$L = 4(N / 100)^{(2/9)}$$

If **GMM=TRUNC** is specified then:

$$w_j = 1 \quad \text{for all } j$$

$$L = 4(N / 100)^{(1/4)}$$

If **GMM=PARZEN** is specified then:

$$w_j = 1 - 6\left(\frac{j}{L+1}\right)^2 + 6\left(\frac{j}{L+1}\right)^3 \quad \text{for} \quad \left(\frac{j}{L+1}\right) \leq .5$$

$$w_j = 2\left(1 - \frac{j}{L+1}\right)^3 \quad \text{for} \quad \left(\frac{j}{L+1}\right) > .5$$

$$L = 4(N / 100)^{(4/25)}$$

If **GMM=QS** is specified then the **Q**uadratic **S**pectral estimator is used as suggested in Andrews [1991] with:

$$w_j = \left(\frac{25}{12\pi^2\left(\frac{j}{L+1}\right)^2}\right)\left(\frac{\sin(6\pi\left(\frac{j}{L+1}\right)/5)}{6\pi\left(\frac{j}{L+1}\right)/5} - \cos(6\pi\left(\frac{j}{L+1}\right)/5)\right)$$

$$L = 4(N / 100)^{(2/25)}$$

If **GMM=TUKEY** is specified then the Tukey-Hanning estimator is used with:

$$w_j = \left[1 + \cos(\pi\left(\frac{j}{L+1}\right))\right] / 2$$

$$L = 4(N / 100)^{(1/4)}$$

Estimation of a System of Equations

When there is more than one equation the notation follows that of the N3SLS model. Given a system of M equations such that equation i has the general form:

$$f_i(Y, X, \beta) = \varepsilon_i \qquad \text{for } i = 1, \ldots, M$$

Stack the ε_i vectors to obtain an MN x 1 vector ε. The GMM estimator minimizes:

$$\varepsilon'(X \otimes I) \, [(X \otimes I)' \Omega (X \otimes I)]^{-1} (X \otimes I)' \varepsilon$$

where I is an MxM identity matrix and Ω is now a (MNxMN) matrix. The matrix $(X \otimes I)$ is the block diagonal matrix:

$$\begin{bmatrix} X & 0 & . & 0 \\ 0 & X & . & 0 \\ . & . & . & . \\ 0 & 0 & . & X \end{bmatrix}$$

When **GMM=HETCOV** is used the weighting matrix $((X \otimes I)' \Omega (X \otimes I))$ is estimated as:

$$\sum_{t=1}^{N} (e_t \otimes X_t)(e_t \otimes X_t)'$$

where e_t is an Mx1 vector of estimated N3SLS residuals and X_t is a Kx1 vector of instrumental variables for observation t.

A similar multivariate procedure analagous to the single equation case is used for the other **GMM=** options. Note that the dimensions of the weighting matrix is now MKxMK. When the weighting matrix is shown on SHAZAM output it has been standardized by dividing by N. A TEST OF THE OVERIDENTIFYNG RESTRICTIONS is obtained by multiplying the minimized function value by N. This resulting test statistic (usually called J) is distributed χ^2 with MK–P degrees of freedom under the null hypothesis where P is the number of parameters in the system.

The minimized function value is available in the temporary variable *$LLF*. Note, however, that the function is not a log-likelihood function but the *$LLF* variable is used in all SHAZAM nonlinear estimation to hold the function value.

Users should be aware that the weighting matrix can easily be singular especially for small sample sizes. In this case it is not possible to compute the inverse of the matrix and estimation will not be successful. If alternative forms of the matrix are used with possibly different values for the **AUTCOV=** option then it may become possible to create a non-singular weighting matrix.

The following SHAZAM commands could be used to estimate the first two equations of the Klein Model:

```
* GENERALIZED METHOD OF MOMENTS ESTIMATION
NL 2 W2 T G TIME1 PLAG KLAG XLAG / NCOEF=8 GMM=HETCOV NOPSIGMA
EQ C=A1*PLAG+A2*P+A3*W1W2+A0
EQ I=B1*PLAG+B2*KLAG+B3*P+B0
END
```

22. NONPARAMETRIC METHODS

"What is sought is found."

Sophocles, *Oedipus Tyrannus*

The **NONPAR** command provides features for nonparametric density estimation and regression smoothing techniques.

DENSITY ESTIMATION

The Univariate Kernel Method

The kernel method is a nonparametric approach to density estimation and a good exposition of this method is in Silverman [1986]. For observations X_t t=1,...,N kernel estimates of the probability density function are obtained as:

$$\hat{f}_N(x) = \frac{1}{N \cdot h} \sum_{t=1}^{N} K\{(x - X_t)/h)\}$$

where h is a bandwidth or smoothing parameter and **K** is a kernel function with the property:

$$\int_{-\infty}^{\infty} K(u)du = 1$$

The **DENSITY** option on the **NONPAR** command is used to obtain kernel density estimates. The **METHOD=** option allows the use of the following kernel functions.

Kernel	**METHOD=** *option*	K(u)
Gauss	**NORMAL**	$\frac{1}{\sqrt{2\pi}}\exp(-u^2/2)$
Epanechnikov	**EPAN**	$I(|u| \le 1) \cdot \frac{3}{4}(1-u^2)$
Quartic	**QUARTIC**	$I(|u| \le 1) \cdot \frac{15}{16}(1-u^2)^2$
Triangular	**TRIANG**	$I(|u| \le 1) \cdot (1-|u|)$
Uniform	**UNIFORM**	$I(|u| \le 1) \cdot 0.5$

The indicator function I = 1 if $|u| \leq 1$ and 0 otherwise. The default setting for the bandwidth parameter is $h = \lambda \cdot \hat{\sigma}_x$ where

$$\lambda = \{4/(3\cdot N)\}^{1/5} \qquad \text{and} \qquad \hat{\sigma}_x^2 = \frac{1}{N}\sum_{t=1}^{N}(X_t - \overline{X})^2$$

This approximately optimal bandwidth for a normal kernel is described in Silverman [1986, p.45]. Alternative values for λ can be specified with the **SMOOTH=** option. The density estimates can be saved with the **PREDICT=** option.

The Multivariate Kernel Method

For the multivariate case where $X_t = (X_{1t}, \ldots, X_{Kt})$ a multivariate kernel function can be stated as a product of univariate kernel functions. A kernel function for K-dimensional u is:

$$\mathbf{K}(u) = \mathbf{K}(u_1, \ldots, u_K) = \prod_{j=1}^{K} \mathbf{K}(u_j)$$

The multivariate kernel density estimate can then be expressed as:

$$\hat{f}_N(x) = \frac{1}{N\cdot h}\sum_{t=1}^{N}\mathbf{K}_h(x - X_t) = \frac{1}{N\cdot h}\sum_{t=1}^{N}\prod_{j=1}^{K}\mathbf{K}\{(x_j - X_{jt})/h_j\} \qquad \text{where} \qquad h = \prod_{j=1}^{K}h_j$$

The bandwidth parameters are $h_j = \lambda \cdot \hat{\sigma}_{x_j}$ and default settings are:

$$\lambda = \{4/(N(2\cdot K + 1))\}^{1/(K+4)} \qquad \text{and} \qquad \hat{\sigma}_{x_j}^2 = \frac{1}{N}\sum_{t=1}^{N}(X_{jt} - \overline{X}_j)^2 \qquad \text{for } j=1,\ldots,K$$

Alternative values for λ can be specified with the **SMOOTH=** option and other estimates of the variance $\sigma_{x_j}^2$ can be requested with the **INCOVAR=** option.

To recognize covariance in the sample Rust [1988] uses a multivariate normal kernel function and this is implemented with the **METHOD=MULTI** option. Standardized variables are created as:

$$Z_t = A(X_t - \overline{X})/\lambda \qquad \text{where} \qquad A\hat{\Sigma}_x A' = I_K$$

The smoothing parameter λ can be set with the **SMOOTH=** option and the default setting is:

$$\lambda = \{4 / (N(2 \cdot K + 1))\}^{1/(K+4)}$$

The $\hat{\Sigma}_x$ matrix can be input with the **INCOVAR=** option and the default is to use the sample variance-covariance matrix with a divisor of N. The multivariate normal kernel is then obtained as a product of univariate standard normal kernel functions:

$$\hat{f}_N(x) = \frac{1}{N \cdot h} \sum_{t=1}^{N} K_h(x - X_t) = \frac{1}{N \cdot h} \sum_{t=1}^{N} \prod_{j=1}^{K} K(z_j - Z_{jt}) \qquad \text{where} \quad h = \lambda^K \cdot |\hat{\Sigma}_x|^{1/2}$$

NONPARAMETRIC REGRESSION

The **NONPAR** command provides nonparametric smoothing approaches to estimating the regression relationship:

$$Y_t = m(X_t) + \varepsilon_t \qquad \text{for} \quad t = 1, \ldots, N$$

where m=E(Y|X=x) is the unknown regression function. An informative presentation of the subject is contained in the monograph by Härdle [1990].

Kernel Estimators

The Nadaraya-Watson estimator is:

$$\hat{m}_N(x) = \frac{1}{N \cdot h} \sum_{t=1}^{N} W_{ht}(x) \cdot Y_t \qquad \text{where} \quad W_{ht}(x) = K_h(x - X_t) / \hat{f}_N(x)$$

The kernel function **K** can be specified with the **METHOD=** option. The **SMOOTH=** and **INCOVAR=** options can also be used as described above.

In matrix notation the predicted values can be stated as $\hat{Y} = S'Y$. The N x N smoother matrix S can be saved with the **SMATRIX=** option. A feature of S is that it does not depend on Y and so the nonparametric estimate is linear in Y. This property facilitates model evaluation that is described later in this chapter.

The selection of an optimal value for the smoothing parameter λ is the subject of much discussion in the literature. Smaller values of λ give rougher estimators (with more wiggles) and larger values of λ give smoother estimators. One selection approach is to choose λ to minimize the CV or GCV (described below).

The estimated residuals are $e_t = Y_t - \hat{Y}_t$. A variance estimate (see Härdle [1990, p.100]) conditional on X=x is:

$$\hat{\sigma}^2(x) = \frac{1}{N \cdot h} \sum_{t=1}^{N} W_{ht}(x) \cdot e_t^2$$

The conditional standard deviations evaluated at $X_1, \ldots, X_N$ can be saved with the **SIGMA=** option on the **NONPAR** command.

The asymptotic variance (from Algorithm 4.2.1 in Härdle [1990]) is:

$$V_N(x) = \frac{c_K \hat{\sigma}^2(x)}{N \cdot h \cdot \hat{f}_N(x)} \qquad \text{where} \qquad c_K = \int K^2(u) du$$

For the Gaussian kernel $c_K = 1/(2\sqrt{\pi})$, for the Epanechnikov kernel $c_K = 3/5$, for the quartic kernel $c_K = 5/7$, for the triangular kernel $c_K = 2/3$ and for the uniform kernel $c_K = .5$. An approximate 95 % confidence interval can then be constructed as:

$$\hat{m}_N(x) \pm 1.96 \sqrt{V_N(x)}$$

The prediction standard errors can be saved with the **FCSE=** option.

By taking derivatives of the regression function with respect to x_j slope estimates can be obtained at point x (see Härdle [1990, pp. 33-34]). The slope estimates are computed as:

$$b_j(x) = \frac{-1}{N \cdot h} \left[\sum_{t=1}^{N} G_{jt} \cdot K_h(x - X_t) \cdot Y_t - \hat{m}_N(x) \sum_{t=1}^{N} G_{jt} \cdot K_h(x - X_t) \right] \Big/ \hat{f}_N(x)$$

where, for the multivariate normal kernel,

$$G_{jt} = \frac{1}{\lambda^2} \sum_{k=1}^{K} \hat{\sigma}_x^{jk} (x_k - X_{kt}) \qquad \text{and} \qquad \hat{\sigma}_x^{jk} \text{ is the (j,k) element of } \hat{\Sigma}_x^{-1}$$

When the Gaussian kernel is selected, the slope estimates are evaluated at each point and printed with the **PCOEF** option.

Kernel smoothing methods are less accurate near the boundary of the observation interval. Boundary modifications have been proposed by Rice [1984] (also described in Härdle [1990, pp. 130-132]) and others (see Hall and Wehrly [1991]). A multivariate extension of the Rice method is available as a **NONPAR** command option. A Euclidean distance measure is used to select points near the boundary. The idea is that if x is more than the arbitrary rule of 2 1/2 bandwidths from the center then a boundary modified estimate is used. If

$$\sqrt{\frac{1}{K}\sum_{j=1}^{K}\{(x_j - \overline{X}_j)/h_j\}^2} > 2\tfrac{1}{2}$$

then the modified estimate is:

$$\tilde{m}_N(x) = \hat{m}_N(x;\lambda) + \gamma[\hat{m}_N(x;\lambda) - \hat{m}_N(x;\alpha\lambda)]$$

where $\gamma = R(\rho)/[\alpha R(\rho/\alpha) - R(\rho)]$, $R(v) = w_1(v)/w_0(v)$ and

$$w_0(v) = \int_{-1}^{v} K(u)du \qquad \text{and} \quad w_1(v) = \int_{-1}^{v} uK(u)du$$

The value for ρ (in the interval [0,1]) can be set with the **BRHO=** option. With $\rho \geq 1$, $\gamma=0$. A value for α must also be set and SHAZAM uses $\alpha=2-\rho$ as recommended in Rice [1984]. Note that this boundary modified estimate is still linear in Y.

SHAZAM makes direct use of the formula for the kernel regression estimator to compute estimates at each X_t t=1, . . ., N. The computation time increases rapidly with N and the use of efficient algorithms has been advocated. Algorithms that use fast Fourier transforms are available for calculating kernel estimators for bivariate data (see, for example, Härdle [1987]). The use of binning methods is described in Fan and Marron [1994]. These methods are not implemented here.

Locally Weighted Regression

The **METHOD=LOWESS** option on the **NONPAR** command implements the locally weighted regression method described in Cleveland [1979], Cleveland and Devlin [1988] and Cleveland, Devlin and Grosse [1988]. This method applies to the two-variable simple regression model. Suppose $X_{a(t)},...,X_{b(t)}$ are the ordered r nearest neighbors of X_t. For a value of f ($0 < f \leq 1$) let r be $f \cdot N$ rounded down to the nearest integer. The smoothing value f can be set with the **SMOOTH=** option.

For each t the locally weighted regression method finds estimates of β to minimize:

$$\sum_{\tau=a(t)}^{b(t)} w_{\tau}(X_t)\{Y_{\tau} - \beta(X_{\tau} - \overline{X}_t^w)\}^2$$

where $\overline{X}_t^w$ is the weighted average $\overline{X}_t^w = \sum_{\tau=a(t)}^{b(t)} w_{\tau}(X_t)X_{\tau}$.

The weights for the weighted least squares regression are computed as:

$$w_{\tau}(X_t) = W\big[(X_{\tau} - X_t)/h_t\big] \quad \text{where } h_t = \max(X_t - X_{a(t)}, X_{b(t)} - X_t)$$

and W is the "tricube" weight function $W(x) = I(|x| \leq 1) \cdot (1 - |x|^3)^3$.

The fitted values can be expressed as $\qquad \hat{Y}_t = \sum_{\tau=a(t)}^{b(t)} s_{\tau}(X_t)Y_{\tau}$

In matrix notation this can be stated as $\hat{Y} = S'Y$. The N x N matrix S is a linear smoother and can be saved with the **SMATRIX=** option. The estimated residuals are $e_t = Y_t - \hat{Y}_t$.

The prediction standard errors that can be saved with the **FCSE=** option are:

$$\hat{\sigma}_t = \sqrt{\hat{\sigma}^2 \sum_{\tau=a(t)}^{b(t)} s_{\tau}^2(X_t)}$$

The $\hat{\sigma}^2$ estimate is described in the section on model evaluation later in this chapter. An approximate $100 \cdot (1 - \alpha)\%$ confidence interval (see Cleveland and Devlin [1988, p. 599]) can then be obtained as:

$$\hat{Y}_t \pm t_{(\rho,\alpha/2)} \hat{\sigma}_t$$

where $t_{(\rho,\alpha/2)}$ is the critical value from a t-distribution with ρ degrees of freedom and

$$\rho = \text{tr}\{(I-S)(I-S)'\}^2 / \text{tr}\{[(I-S)(I-S)']^2\}$$

The value for ρ is reported on the SHAZAM output as the LOOKUP DEGREES OF FREEDOM and is saved in the temporary variable $DF1.

The weighted least squares procedure can be iterated with recalculated weights to get robust locally weighted regression estimates. Let m be the median of the $|e_t|$ and define robustness weights by:

$$\delta_t = K(e_t / 6m) \qquad \text{where } \mathbf{K} \text{ is the quartic kernel } K(u) = I(|u| \le 1) \cdot (1 - u^2)^2 .$$

The robustness weights δ_t can be saved with the **RWEIGHT=** option. The weighted least squares regression is repeated with the weights:

$$\delta_t \, w_\tau(X_t) \qquad \text{for} \quad \tau = a(t), \dots, b(t)$$

Robust locally-weighted regression is recommended for data sets with outliers or long-tailed error distributions (see Cleveland, Devlin and Grosse [1988, p.111]). However, the smoother matrix S now depends on the ε_t and so the model diagnostics described below are not valid.

Computations can be reduced by noting that if $X_{t+1} = X_t$ then $\hat{Y}_{t+1} = \hat{Y}_t$. Computations can be speeded by obtaining an interpolation for $\hat{Y}_{t+1}$ when $X_{t+1} \le X_t + \Delta$. A value for Δ can be specified with the **DELTA=** option.

A general implementation of the LOWESS method considers polynomial regressions and this is not available with the **NONPAR** command.

Model Evaluation

The R^2 measure that is reported on the SHAZAM output is calculated as:

$$R^2 = 1 - \frac{e'e}{Y'Y - N\overline{Y}^2}$$

The error variance reported as SIGMA**2 on the SHAZAM output is computed as:

$$\hat{\sigma}^2 = \frac{1}{n_1} \sum_{t=1}^{N} e_t^2 \qquad \text{where} \quad n_1 = \text{tr}\{(I - S)(I - S)'\}$$

The derivation of the degrees of freedom n_1 is discussed in Cleveland and Devlin [1988] and Hall and Marron [1990]. The "equivalent number of parameters" is obtained as $k_1 = N - n_1$. Note that k_1 is not necessarily an integer as is the case with OLS. Two other definitions for degrees of freedom are discussed in Buja, Hastie and Tibshirani [1989, pp. 469-470] and these compute the equivalent number of parameters as $k_2 = \text{tr}(SS')$ and alternatively $k_3 = \text{tr}(S)$. These measures are also reported on the SHAZAM output.

The value for n_1 is available in the temporary variable DF, the value for k_1 is stored in the temporary variable K and $\hat{\sigma}^2$ is saved in $SIG2$.

The adjusted R^2 and model selection statistics including the Akaike information criterion (AIC), the generalized cross-validation (GCV) statistic and others are calculated using the formula given in the chapter *A CHILD'S GUIDE TO RUNNING REGRESSIONS* where K is replaced with k_1.

The SHAZAM output also reports the cross-validation mean square error that is computed as:

$$CV = \frac{1}{N} \sum_{t=1}^{N} \{e_t / (1 - s_{tt})\}^2$$

where s_{tt} is the tth diagonal element of the smoother matrix S. The CV statistic is saved in the temporary variable CV. A discussion of the CV, GCV and other criterion is available in Eubank [1988, Chapter 2].

NONPAR *COMMAND OPTIONS*

In general, the format of the **NONPAR** command for regression estimation is:

NONPAR *depvar indeps / options*

where *depvar* is the dependent variable, *indeps* is a list of independent variables, and *options* is a list of options.

The format of the **NONPAR** command for kernel density estimation is:

NONPAR *vars /* **DENSITY** *options*

where *vars* is a list of variables.

Options as defined for the **OLS** command that are available are:

LIST, BEG=, and **END=**

The following additional options are available on the **NONPAR** command:

DENSITY   Calculates kernel density estimates. The kernel function is specified with the **METHOD=** option as **EPAN, MULTI, NORMAL, QUARTIC,**

TRIANG or **UNIFORM**. The default is **METHOD=NORMAL** for the univariate case and **METHOD=MULTI** for the multivariate case. An example of the use of this option is in the section on *Bootstrapping Regression Coefficients* in the chapter *PROGRAMMING IN SHAZAM*.

GNU   Prepares **GNUPLOT** plots of the residuals and the fitted values. With the **DENSITY** option a plot of the density function is given (available for univariate density estimation only). For more information on this option see the *GNUPLOT* section in the *PLOTS* chapter. With the **GNU** option the **APPEND, OUTPUT=, DEVICE=, PORT=** and **COMMFILE=** options are also available as described for the **PLOT** command.

PCOEF   For regression estimation with **METHOD=NORMAL, METHOD=MULTI** or **METHOD=LOWESS** this option prints the estimated slope coefficients evaluated at every point.

BRHO=   Used with kernel smoothing methods to specify a value of ρ $(0 \leq \rho < 1)$ to use in calculating the Rice [1984] boundary modified estimate. This is not available with the Epanechnikov kernel. With the Gaussian or triangular kernel the value for **BRHO=** is rounded down to the nearest tenth and numeric integration is used. Integrals are computed explicitly for other kernels. (When this option is used the **DENSITY** and **FCSE=** options are not available).

COEF=   For regression estimation with **METHOD=NORMAL, METHOD=MULTI** or **METHOD=LOWESS** this option saves the estimated slope coefficients in an N x K matrix.

DELTA=   Used with **METHOD=LOWESS** to group the observations as described above. The default is **DELTA=0**. When this option is used some model diagnostics are not provided and the **FCSE=** option is not available.

FCSE=   Saves the prediction standard errors in the variable specified. This option is not available with robust locally weighted regression.

HATDIAG=   Saves the diagonal elements of the smoother matrix S in the variable specified.

INCOVAR=   Used with kernel density estimation methods. For **METHOD=MULTI** the covariance matrix $\hat{\Sigma}_X$ must be a symmetric matrix stored in lower-triangular form such as that produced by the **COV=** option on the **STAT** command or the **SYM** function on the **MATRIX** command.

For the product kernel methods this must be a K x 1 vector of variance estimates $\hat{\sigma}^2_{x_i}$. If this option is not specified then default values will be set as described above.

ITER=   Used with **METHOD=LOWESS** to specify the number of iterations for robust locally weighted regression. The default is **ITER=0**. With **ITER=0** the estimation is by nonrobust locally weighted regression.

METHOD=   Specifies the kernel function or regression method. The available options are **EPAN, MULTI, NORMAL, QUARTIC, TRIANG, UNIFORM** and **LOWESS**. The default is **METHOD=NORMAL** for the univariate case and **METHOD=MULTI** for the multivariate case.

PREDICT=   Saves the predictions from the regression estimation in the variable specified. When the **DENSITY** option is used the **PREDICT=** option saves the density estimates in the variable specified.

RESID=   Saves the residuals from the regression estimation in the variable specified.

RWEIGHTS=   For **METHOD=LOWESS** saves the robustness weights in the variable specified. This is not used when **ITER=0**.

SIGMA=   For kernel smoothing methods saves the conditional standard errors $\hat{\sigma}_t$ in the variable specified.

SMATRIX=   Saves the N x N smoother matrix in the variable specified.

SMOOTH=   Specifies the value of the smoothing parameter. For kernel density estimation methods the default values are described above. For **METHOD=LOWESS** the default for the smoothing fraction f is **SMOOTH=.5**.

Temporary variables that are available following regression estimation are:

$ADR2, $CV, $DF, $DF1, ERR, $K, $N, $R2, $SIG2 and $SSE.

The model selection test statistics are available in the temporary variables:

$AIC, $FPE, $GCV, $HQ, $LAIC, $LSC, $RICE, $SC and $SHIB

EXAMPLES

This example is from Rust [1988] and is designed to show the limitations of OLS when the relationship is nonlinear. With N=50, values for X_t are generated from a uniform distribution on (0,1) and values for the errors ε_t are generated from a N(0, .1) distribution. The Y_t are generated as:

$$Y_t = 1 - 4(X_t - .5)^2 + \varepsilon_t$$

The SHAZAM command file is:

```
SAMPLE 1 50
SET RANFIX
GENR X=UNI(1)
GENR E=NOR(.1)
GENR Y = 1 - 4*(X-.5)**2 + E
OLS Y X / ANOVA
NONPAR Y X
STOP
```

The SHAZAM results comparing OLS regression and nonparametric regression with a normal kernel function follows.

```
|_SAMPLE 1 50
|_SET RANFIX
|_GENR X=UNI(1)
|_GENR E=NOR(.1)
|_GENR Y = 1 - 4*(X-.5)**2 + E
|_OLS Y X / ANOVA
 OLS ESTIMATION
      50 OBSERVATIONS    DEPENDENT VARIABLE = Y
...NOTE..SAMPLE RANGE SET TO:    1,    50


 R-SQUARE =     .0001    R-SQUARE ADJUSTED =    -.0208
VARIANCE OF THE ESTIMATE-SIGMA**2 =    .98797E-01
STANDARD ERROR OF THE ESTIMATE-SIGMA =    .31432
SUM OF SQUARED ERRORS-SSE=    4.7423
MEAN OF DEPENDENT VARIABLE =    .70496
LOG OF THE LIKELIHOOD FUNCTION = -12.0592


MODEL SELECTION TESTS - SEE JUDGE ET AL. (1985,P.242)
 AKAIKE (1969) FINAL PREDICTION ERROR - FPE =      .10275
    (FPE IS ALSO KNOWN AS AMEMIYA PREDICTION CRITERION - PC)
 AKAIKE (1973) INFORMATION CRITERION - LOG AIC =  -2.2755
 SCHWARZ (1978) CRITERION - LOG SC =              -2.1990
MODEL SELECTION TESTS - SEE RAMANATHAN (1992,P.167)
 CRAVEN-WAHBA (1979)
    GENERALIZED CROSS VALIDATION - GCV =           .10291
 HANNAN AND QUINN (1979) CRITERION =               .10578
 RICE (1984) CRITERION =                           .10309
 SHIBATA (1981) CRITERION =                        .10243
```

```
SCHWARZ (1978) CRITERION - SC =                    .11091
AKAIKE (1974) INFORMATION CRITERION - AIC =        .10274


VARIABLE    ESTIMATED  STANDARD   T-RATIO          PARTIAL STANDARDIZED ELASTICITY
  NAME     COEFFICIENT   ERROR    48 DF   P-VALUE CORR. COEFFICIENT  AT MEANS
X         -.82941E-02   .1595    -.5200E-01  .959 -.008    -.0075      -.0054
CONSTANT   .70876      .8555E-01  8.285      .000  .767    .0000      1.0054


|_NONPAR Y X
      50 OBSERVATIONS     DEPENDENT VARIABLE = Y
...NOTE..SAMPLE RANGE SET TO:   1,   50

THE BANDWIDTH/SMOOTHING PARAMETER IS SET BY DEFAULT
NONPARAMETRIC REGRESSION USING KERNEL=NORMAL
NUMBER OF VARIABLES=  1    NUMBER OF OBSERVATIONS=   50

        BANDWIDTH PARAMETER =    .48439

VARIABLE     MEAN        VARIANCE
X          .45826       .77671E-01


 R-SQUARE =    .7607    R-SQUARE ADJUSTED =    .7442
ERROR VARIANCE          SIGMA**2 =      .24756E-01
STANDARD ERROR          SIGMA =         .15734
SUM OF SQUARED ERRORS   SSE =           1.1347
EQUIVALENT NUMBER OF PARAMETERS - K1 =  4.1670
                                - K2 =  2.4716
                                - K3 =  3.3193


CROSS-VALIDATION MEAN SQUARE ERROR =    .27498E-01

MODEL SELECTION TESTS - SEE JUDGE ET AL. (1985,P.242)
 AKAIKE (1969) FINAL PREDICTION ERROR - FPE =     .26820E-01
    (FPE IS ALSO KNOWN AS AMEMIYA PREDICTION CRITERION - PC)
 AKAIKE (1973) INFORMATION CRITERION - LOG AIC = -3.6190
 SCHWARZ (1978) CRITERION - LOG SC =             -3.4597
MODEL SELECTION TESTS - SEE RAMANATHAN (1992,P.167)
 CRAVEN-WAHBA (1979)
    GENERALIZED CROSS VALIDATION - GCV =         .27007E-01
 HANNAN AND QUINN (1979) CRITERION =             .28486E-01
 RICE (1984) CRITERION =                         .27232E-01
 SHIBATA (1981) CRITERION =                      .26476E-01
 SCHWARZ (1978) CRITERION - SC =                 .31440E-01
 AKAIKE (1974) INFORMATION CRITERION - AIC =     .26809E-01
|_STOP
```

23. POOLED CROSS-SECTION TIME-SERIES

"Branch banking...will mean, I suggest in all humility, the beginning of the end of the capitalist system."
John T. Flynn
Business writer, 1933

Pooling methods can be used to combine cross-section and time series data. Suppose there are N cross-sectional units (a cross-sectional unit is, for example, a household, an industry or a region) observed over T time periods to give a total of N x T observations. The regression equation can be written as:

$$Y_{it} = X'_{it}\beta + \varepsilon_{it} \qquad \text{for } i = 1,...,N \quad t = 1,...,T$$

where β is a K x 1 vector of unknown parameters and ε_{it} is a random error. The parameters can be estimated by OLS. However, it may be interesting to incorporate assumptions that recognize cross-section specific effects.

The Parks [1967] method (described in Kmenta [1986, Section 12.2, pp.616-625] and Greene [1993, Section 16.3]) employs a set of assumptions on the disturbance covariance matrix that gives a cross-sectionally heteroskedastic and timewise autoregressive model. The **POOL** command in SHAZAM provides features for estimating this model and some variations of it. The assumptions of the model are:

$$E(\varepsilon_{it}^2) = \sigma_i^2 \qquad \text{heteroskedasticity}$$
$$E(\varepsilon_{it}\varepsilon_{jt}) = 0 \qquad \text{for } i \neq j, \quad \text{cross - section independence}$$
$$\varepsilon_{it} = \rho_i\varepsilon_{i,t-1} + v_{it} \qquad \text{autoregression}$$

and $E(v_{it})=0$, $E(v_{it}^2) = \phi_{ii}$, $E(v_{it}v_{jt}) = 0$ for $i \neq j$, $E(v_{it}v_{js})=0$ for $t \neq s$, and $E(\varepsilon_{i,t-1}v_{jt})=0$. The assumptions can be extended to allow for cross-section correlation so that $E(\varepsilon_{it}\varepsilon_{jt})=\sigma_{ij}$, $E(v_{it}v_{jt}) = \phi_{ij}$, and $E(v_{it}v_{js})=0$ for $t \neq s$.

An estimate for β is obtained by a generalized least squares (GLS) procedure. The estimation proceeds with the following steps.

STEP 1: Estimate β by OLS and obtain estimated residuals e_{it}.

STEP 2: Use the estimated residuals to compute $\hat{\rho}_i$ as estimates of the ρ_i. The **POOL** command allows for different estimation methods. The least squares estimation method (the default method) is:

$$\hat{\rho}_i = \sum_{t=2}^{T} e_{it}e_{i,t-1} \bigg/ \sum_{t=2}^{T} e_{i,t-1}^2 \qquad \text{for } i = 1,...,N$$

On the SHAZAM output the $\hat{\rho}_i$ are listed as RHO VECTOR. When the **SAME** option is specified the same autoregressive parameter is used for all cross-sections as follows:

$$\hat{\rho}_1 = ... = \hat{\rho}_N = \sum_{i=1}^{N}\sum_{t=2}^{T} e_{it}e_{i,t-1} \bigg/ \sum_{i=1}^{N}\sum_{t=2}^{T} e_{i,t-1}^2$$

The **CORCOEF** option ensures values in the interval $[-1,+1]$ by estimating the autoregressive parameter as the sample correlation coefficient between e_{it} and $e_{i,t-1}$.

STEP 3: Use the $\hat{\rho}_i$'s to transform the observations, including the first observation (see Kmenta [1986, Equation 12.27, p.619]) and apply OLS to the transformed model. The error variances and covariances ϕ_{ij} are estimated from the regression residuals of the transformed model. With transformed residuals $\hat{v}_{it}$ the estimated error covariances are:

$$\hat{\phi}_{ij} = \frac{1}{T-K}\sum_{t=1}^{T}\hat{v}_{it}\hat{v}_{jt}$$

In matrix notation, if V is the T x N matrix of residuals then:

$$\hat{\Phi} = \frac{1}{T-K}V'V$$

If the **DN** option is used the divisor is T instead of T−K. On the SHAZAM output the estimated error covariance matrix $\hat{\Phi}$ is reported as the PHI MATRIX.

STEP 4: Obtain the GLS estimator. The default estimation method of the **POOL** command is to use a diagonal PHI matrix. The **FULL** option ensures that the complete PHI matrix $\hat{\Phi}$ is employed to admit cross-section correlation. When T < N the matrix $\hat{\Phi}$ is singular and the **FULL** option cannot be used. The matrix V'V is N x N and the rank is the rank of V. When T < N the rank of V is T and so V'V is a singular matrix.

The procedure may be iterated to convergence with the **ITER=** option. However this may not lead to efficiency gains in small samples. Let $\tilde{\beta}^{(i)}$ be the parameter estimates at iteration i. The iterative estimation stops when the following convergence criteria is met:

$$\left|\tilde{\beta}_k^{(i)} - \tilde{\beta}_k^{(i-1)}\right| / \left|\tilde{\beta}_k^{(i)}\right| \;<\; \delta \qquad \text{for } k = 1,\ldots,K$$

where δ can be set with the **CONV=** option and the default is $\delta = .001$.

With final parameter estimates $\tilde{\beta}$ and $\hat{\rho}$ the transformed residuals are:

$$\left.\begin{array}{l} \tilde{v}_{it} = \tilde{e}_{it} - \hat{\rho}_i \tilde{e}_{i,t-1} \quad t = 2,\ldots,T \\[2mm] \tilde{v}_{i1} = \sqrt{1 - \hat{\rho}_i^2}\; \tilde{e}_{i1} \end{array}\right\} \quad \text{where} \quad \tilde{e}_{it} = Y_{it} - X_{it}'\tilde{\beta}$$

The variance of the residuals (reported as SIGMA**2 on the SHAZAM output) is computed as:

$$\hat{\sigma}^2 = \frac{1}{NT - K} \sum_{i=1}^{N} \sum_{t=1}^{T} \tilde{v}_{it}^2$$

When the **DN** option is used the divisor is NT instead of NT–K.

As a goodness-of-fit measure the SHAZAM output reports the Buse R^2 (see Buse [1973]) as described in the chapter *GENERALIZED LEAST SQUARES*. This is computed using the *estimated* PHI MATRIX. The result is that, unlike the usual R^2, the Buse R^2 is not guaranteed to be a nondecreasing function of the number of explanatory variables.

The Durbin-Watson statistic (reported with the **RSTAT** option) is calculated as:

$$\sum_{i=1}^{N} \sum_{t=2}^{T} (\tilde{v}_{it} - \tilde{v}_{i,t-1})^2 \Big/ \sum_{i=1}^{N} \sum_{t=1}^{T} \tilde{v}_{it}^2$$

Note that the Durbin-Watson statistic is appropriate as a test for autocorrelation only when the option **RHO=0** is used and when there are no lagged dependent variables as explanatory variables.

Other Pooling Methods

Other pooling methods may be appropriate to investigate. For example, Judge, Hill, Griffiths, Lütkepohl and Lee [1988, Chapter 11] compare two approaches for allowing different intercept effects for each cross-section. One approach is to introduce dummy variables and estimate the parameters by OLS. A second approach is to assume a random intercept to give an error components (or variance components) model that can be estimated by generalized least squares. Examples of SHAZAM commands for estimation of these models are given later in this chapter.

POOL *COMMAND OPTIONS*

The format of the **POOL** command is:

POOL *depvar indeps* / **NCROSS=** *options*

where *depvar* and *indeps* are the names of the dependent and independent variables. The **NCROSS=** option **must** specify the number of cross-sectional units in the data. SHAZAM will then figure out the number of time periods from the total number of observations. In some cases it is easier to specify the number of time periods with the **NTIME=** option. In this case SHAZAM will figure out the number of cross-sectional units.

The data should be arranged so that all observations of a particular cross-sectional unit are together. Therefore, SHAZAM will require a complete time-series for the first group followed by a time-series for the second group, etc. If the data is not set up in this fashion it must be sorted before estimation of the model. In some cases the SHAZAM **SORT** command will help to rearrange the data. With N cross-sectional units observed for T time periods the total number of observations will then be N x T. Each cross-sectional unit must have the same number of time-series observations.

Options as defined for the **OLS** command that are available are:

ANOVA, DLAG, DUMP, GF, LINLOG, LIST, LM, LOGLIN, LOGLOG, MAX, NOCONSTANT, PCOR, PCOV, RESTRICT, RSTAT, COV=, PREDICT=, RESID=, STDERR= and **TRATIO=**

Options as defined for the **GLS** command that are available are:

BLUP and **UT**

The following additional options are available on the **POOL** command:

CORCOEF   Estimates the autoregressive parameters ρ_i using the correlation coefficient form, the alternative method described by Kmenta [1986, Equation 12.26]. This method confines the estimate of ρ_i to the interval $[-1,+1]$.

DN   Uses a divisor of T instead of T–K when calculating the PHI matrix.

FULL   Estimates the **FULL** cross-sectionally correlated and time-wise autoregressive model (see Kmenta [1986, pp. 622-625]). If this option is not specified then the model assumptions are cross-sectional heteroskedasticity with cross-sectional independence. The **UT** or **BLUP** options are recommended as the transformed residuals in the **FULL** model are sensitive to order of the cross-sections and have no useful interpretation. The **FULL** option is not available when N > T (when there are a large number of cross-sections but the number of time series is few). When N > T the estimated error covariance matrix PHI is singular and SHAZAM will terminate with the message MATRIX IS NOT POSITIVE DEFINITE.

MULSIGSQ   The estimated covariance matrix of coefficients is calculated using Equation 12.39 in Kmenta [1986, p. 623]. However, some econometricians believe that this matrix should be multiplied by the overall estimate of $\hat{\sigma}^2$. The **MULSIGSQ** option does this multiplication. This option is the default, but could be turned off with the **NOMULSIGSQ** option.

PCOV   Prints the covariance matrix of coefficients. In addition it prints the PHI matrix if **NCROSS=** is greater than 8. If **NCROSS=** is less than 8 the PHI matrix is always printed.

SAME   Forces the ρ_i to be the same for each of the cross-sectional units.

COEF=   Saves the estimated coefficients, the RHO vector, and the square root of the diagonal elements of the PHI matrix in the variable specified.

CONV=   Specifies a convergence criterion to stop the iterative procedure when the **ITER=** option is used. The default is .001.

ITER=   Specifies the maximum number of iterations if an iterative procedure is desired. If this option is not specified then one iteration is done.

NCROSS=   Specifies the number of cross-sectional units in the data. This option is required unless the **NTIME=** option is used.

NTIME=   Specifies the number of time periods in the data. This option is required if the **NCROSS=** option is not used. If both **NCROSS=** and **NTIME=** are specified, **NCROSS=** is ignored.

RHO=   Specifies a fixed value of ρ to use. If this is not specified the autoregressive parameters are estimated. When this option is used the **SAME** option is automatically in effect. This option is commonly used with **RHO=0** to suppress the autocorrelation correction so that only the heteroskedastic correction is performed.

The available temporary variables on the **POOL** command are:

$ANF, $DF, $DW, $ERR, $K, $LLF, $N, $R2, $R2OP, $RAW, $RHO, $SIG2, $SSE, $SSR, $SST, $ZANF, $ZDF, $ZSSR and *$ZSST*.

For more information on temporary variables see the chapter *MISCELLANEOUS COMMANDS AND INFORMATION* and the chapter *ORDINARY LEAST SQUARES*.

EXAMPLES

Cross-Section Heteroskedasticity and Time-wise Autoregression

This example is adapted from Chapter 11 of the *Judge Handbook*. The data set contains 10 years of cost and production data for four industries. The SHAZAM commands set the data up in the form that is accepted by the **POOL** command. That is, the cost data is stacked in the variable *C* and the production data is stacked in the variable *Q*. The SHAZAM commands to read the data set and implement model estimation are as follows:

```
SAMPLE 1 10
READ C1 C2 C3 C4 Q1 Q2 Q3 Q4
   43.72   51.03   43.90   64.29   38.46   32.52   32.86   41.86
   45.86   27.75   23.77   42.16   35.32   18.71   18.52   28.33
    4.74   35.72   28.60   61.99    3.78   27.01   22.93   34.21
   40.58   35.85   27.71   34.26   35.34   18.66   25.02   15.69
   25.86   43.28   40.38   47.67   20.83   25.58   35.13   29.70
   36.05   48.52   36.43   45.14   36.72   39.19   27.29   23.03
   50.94   64.18   19.31   35.31   41.67   47.70   16.99   14.80
   42.48   38.34   16.55   35.43   30.71   27.01   12.56   21.53
   25.60   45.39   30.97   54.33   23.70   33.57   26.76   32.86
   49.81   43.69   46.60   59.23   39.53   27.32   41.42   42.25
* Stack the columns into a long vector
MATRIX C=(C1'|C2'|C3'|C4')'
MATRIX Q=(Q1'|Q2'|Q3'|Q4')'
```

```
* Pooling by OLS
SAMPLE 1 40
OLS C Q
* Pooling with the POOL command
POOL C Q / NCROSS=4 FULL
```

Note that the **FULL** option is used on the **POOL** command. The estimation results from the **POOL** command are shown below.

```
|_POOL C Q / NCROSS=4 FULL
POOLED CROSS-SECTION TIME-SERIES ESTIMATION
     4 CROSS-SECTIONS AND      10 TIME-PERIODS
     40 TOTAL OBSERVATIONS
DEPENDENT VARIABLE = C

MODEL ASSUMPTIONS:
    DIFFERENT ESTIMATED RHO FOR EACH CROSS-SECTION
    FULL PHI MATRIX - CROSS-SECTION CORRELATION

OLS COEFFICIENTS
   1.1316       7.3852

RHO VECTOR
   .53953      .45388E-02   .94290       .70678

SAME ESTIMATED RHO FOR ALL CROSS-SECTIONS =    .63342

VARIANCES (DIAGONAL OF PHI MATRIX)
   41.507       20.575       11.336       45.057

PHI MATRIX
   41.507
   1.4891       20.575
  -2.8462       -6.4657      11.336
  -31.859       -9.5802      .85767       45.057

BUSE [1973] R-SQUARE =  .9260     BUSE RAW-MOMENT R-SQUARE =  .9920
VARIANCE OF THE ESTIMATE-SIGMA**2 =   .83872
STANDARD ERROR OF THE ESTIMATE-SIGMA =   .91582
SUM OF SQUARED ERRORS-SSE=   31.871
MEAN OF DEPENDENT VARIABLE =   39.836
LOG OF THE LIKELIHOOD FUNCTION = -112.331
```

VARIABLE NAME	ESTIMATED COEFFICIENT	STANDARD ERROR	T-RATIO 38 DF	P-VALUE	PARTIAL CORR.	STANDARDIZED COEFFICIENT	ELASTICITY AT MEANS
Q	1.1658	.5346E-01	21.81	.000	.962	.8710	.8392
CONSTANT	7.4442	1.784	4.174	.000	.561	.0000	.1869

Pooling by OLS with Dummy Variables

This example uses the data set of the previous example. Cross-section dummy variables are generated and an OLS dummy variable regression is run. The example also shows how to construct a time index for each cross-section. The SHAZAM output follows.

```
|_* Generate cross-section dummy variables
|_DIM CS1 40 CS2 40 CS3 40 CS4 40
|_SAMPLE 1 10
|_GENR CS1=1
|_SAMPLE 11 20
|_GENR CS2=1
|_SAMPLE 21 30
|_GENR CS3=1
|_SAMPLE 31 40
|_GENR CS4=1
|_SAMPLE 1 40
|_* Generate an index to represent each cross-section
|_GENR CSINDEX=SUM(SEAS(10))
|_* Generate a repeating time index for the 10 observations
|_GENR TINDEX=TIME(0)-10*(CSINDEX-1)
|_* Print some data for the first 2 cross-sections
|_PRINT C CSINDEX TINDEX CS1 CS2 / BEG=1 END=20
        C           CSINDEX         TINDEX           CS1            CS2
     43.72000      1.000000       1.000000       1.000000       .0000000
     45.86000      1.000000       2.000000       1.000000       .0000000
     4.740000      1.000000       3.000000       1.000000       .0000000
     40.58000      1.000000       4.000000       1.000000       .0000000
     25.86000      1.000000       5.000000       1.000000       .0000000
     36.05000      1.000000       6.000000       1.000000       .0000000
     50.94000      1.000000       7.000000       1.000000       .0000000
     42.48000      1.000000       8.000000       1.000000       .0000000
     25.60000      1.000000       9.000000       1.000000       .0000000
     49.81000      1.000000       10.00000       1.000000       .0000000
     51.03000      2.000000       1.000000       .0000000       1.000000
     27.75000      2.000000       2.000000       .0000000       1.000000
     35.72000      2.000000       3.000000       .0000000       1.000000
     35.85000      2.000000       4.000000       .0000000       1.000000
     43.28000      2.000000       5.000000       .0000000       1.000000
     48.52000      2.000000       6.000000       .0000000       1.000000
     64.18000      2.000000       7.000000       .0000000       1.000000
     38.34000      2.000000       8.000000       .0000000       1.000000
     45.39000      2.000000       9.000000       .0000000       1.000000
     43.69000      2.000000       10.00000       .0000000       1.000000
|_SAMPLE 1 40
|_OLS C Q CS1 CS2 CS3 CS4 / NOCONSTANT
 OLS ESTIMATION
        40 OBSERVATIONS        DEPENDENT VARIABLE = C
...NOTE..SAMPLE RANGE SET TO:     1,    40

  R-SQUARE =    .9238     R-SQUARE ADJUSTED =    .9150
 VARIANCE OF THE ESTIMATE-SIGMA**2 =    14.042
 STANDARD ERROR OF THE ESTIMATE-SIGMA =   3.7473
 SUM OF SQUARED ERRORS-SSE=    491.48
 MEAN OF DEPENDENT VARIABLE =   39.836
 LOG OF THE LIKELIHOOD FUNCTION = -106.928
```

```
RAW MOMENT R-SQUARE =     .9930
```

VARIABLE NAME	ESTIMATED COEFFICIENT	STANDARD ERROR	T-RATIO 35 DF	P-VALUE	PARTIAL CORR.	STANDARDIZED COEFFICIENT	ELASTICITY AT MEANS
Q	1.1190	.6357E-01	17.60	.000	.948	.8360	.8056
CS1	2.3150	2.278	1.016	.317	.169	.0790	.0145
CS2	10.110	2.231	4.532	.000	.608	.3448	.0634
CS3	2.3854	2.031	1.174	.248	.195	.0814	.0150
CS4	16.171	2.161	7.484	.000	.784	.5516	.1015

Pooling with Error Components

This example shows the procedure for estimation of an error components model using the steps described in Judge, Hill, Griffiths, Lütkepohl and Lee [1988, Section 11.5.2]. The first step is to run an OLS with dummy variables regression as given in the previous example. The method proceeds by appropriately transforming the observations and then applying OLS to the transformed observations. The SHAZAM output follows.

```
|_* Use results from OLS with dummy variables to estimate variance components
|_SAMPLE 1 40
|_?OLS C Q CS1 CS2 CS3 CS4 / NOCONSTANT
|_?GEN1 SIG2E=$SIG2
|_SAMPLE 1 10
|_?STAT C1-C4 / MEAN=CBAR
|_?STAT Q1-Q4 / MEAN=QBAR
|_GEN1 T=10
|_SAMPLE 1 4
|_?OLS CBAR QBAR
|_?GEN1 SIG21=$SIG2*T
|_GEN1 SIG2U=(SIG21-SIG2E)/T
|_* Check that SIG2U is positive
|_PRINT SIG2U
   SIG2U
   65.17116
|_GEN1 ALPHA=1-SQRT(SIG2E)/SQRT(SIG21)
|_PRINT ALPHA
   ALPHA
   .8547682
|_* Now transform the observations
|_DIM CSTAR 40 QSTAR 40
|_SAMPLE 1 10
|_GENR CSTAR=C-ALPHA*CBAR:1
|_GENR QSTAR=Q-ALPHA*QBAR:1
|_SAMPLE 11 20
|_GENR CSTAR=C-ALPHA*CBAR:2
|_GENR QSTAR=Q-ALPHA*QBAR:2
|_SAMPLE 21 30
|_GENR CSTAR=C-ALPHA*CBAR:3
|_GENR QSTAR=Q-ALPHA*QBAR:3
|_SAMPLE 31 40
|_GENR CSTAR=C-ALPHA*CBAR:4
|_GENR QSTAR=Q-ALPHA*QBAR:4
|_SAMPLE 1 40
|_GENR INTERCEP=1-ALPHA
|_* Apply OLS to the transformed observations to get the GLS estimator
```

```
|_OLS CSTAR QSTAR INTERCEP / NOCONSTANT
 OLS ESTIMATION
        40 OBSERVATIONS       DEPENDENT VARIABLE = CSTAR
...NOTE..SAMPLE RANGE SET TO:     1,    40


 R-SQUARE =    .8934     R-SQUARE ADJUSTED =     .8906
VARIANCE OF THE ESTIMATE-SIGMA**2 =   13.682
STANDARD ERROR OF THE ESTIMATE-SIGMA =   3.6989
SUM OF SQUARED ERRORS-SSE=   519.91
MEAN OF DEPENDENT VARIABLE =   5.7854
LOG OF THE LIKELIHOOD FUNCTION = -108.053
RAW MOMENT R-SQUARE =    .9164
```

VARIABLE NAME	ESTIMATED COEFFICIENT	STANDARD ERROR	T-RATIO 38 DF	P-VALUE	PARTIAL CORR.	STANDARDIZED COEFFICIENT	ELASTICITY AT MEANS
QSTAR	1.1193	.6273E-01	17.84	.000	.945	.9452	.8058
INTERCEP	7.7375	4.410	1.754	.087	.274	.0000	.1942

24. PROBIT AND LOGIT REGRESSION

"The deliverance of the saints must take place some time before 1914."
Charles Taze Russell
American religious leader, 1910

"The deliverance of the saints must take place some time after 1914."
Charles Taze Russell
American religious leader, 1923

The probit and logit models can be used for the analysis of binary choice models where the dependent variable Y_t is a 0-1 dummy variable. Some references are Chow [1983, Chapter 8]; Greene [1993, Chapter 21]; Griffiths, Hill and Judge [1993, Chapter 23]; Hanushek and Jackson [1977, Chapter 7]; Judge, Griffiths, Hill, Lütkepohl and Lee [1985, Chapter 18]; Judge, Hill, Griffiths, Lütkepohl and Lee [1988, Chapter 19]; Maddala [1977, Chapter 9-7]; Maddala [1983, Chapter 2]; and Pindyck and Rubinfeld [1991, Chapter 10]. Examples of probit and logit estimation using SHAZAM can be found in, respectively, White [1975] and Cameron and White [1986].

The estimation algorithms implemented with the **PROBIT** and **LOGIT** commands use fast iterative methods which usually converge in 4 or 5 iterations. The maximum likelihood estimation routines are based on computer programs originally written by John Cragg. SHAZAM **TEST** commands can be used following estimation. **RESTRICT** commands are not permitted.

A "utility index" I is defined for individual t as $I_t = X'_t\beta$.

The choice probabilities must lie between zero and one. However, the index I is in the range $(-\infty, +\infty)$. This can be translated to a 0-1 range by the use of a cumulative distribution function so that $\mathrm{Prob}(Y_t = 1) = P_t = F(I_t) = F(X'_t\beta)$.

Two alternative choices for F are:

The probit model: $$F(X'_t\beta) = \int_{-\infty}^{I_t} \frac{1}{\sqrt{2\pi}} \exp(-t^2/2)\, dt$$

The logit model: $$F(X'_t\beta) = \frac{1}{1 + \exp(-X'_t\beta)}$$

Maximum Likelihood Estimation

With the assumption of independent observations the log-likelihood function for a sample of N observations is:

$$L(\beta) = \sum_{t=1}^{N} \left\{ Y_t \ln\left[F(X_t'\beta)\right] + (1 - Y_t)\ln\left[1 - F(X_t'\beta)\right] \right\}$$

The estimate of the asymptotic covariance matrix for the maximum likelihood estimates $\hat{\beta}$ is computed as the inverse of the negative of the matrix of second derivatives of the log-likelihood function.

A test of the null hypothesis that all the slope coefficients are zero can be carried out using a likelihood ratio test. If S is the number of successes ($Y_t=1$) observed in N observations, then for both the probit and logit models, the maximum value of the log likelihood function under the null hypothesis is:

$$L(0) = S \ln\left(\frac{S}{N}\right) + (N - S)\ln\left(\frac{N - S}{N}\right)$$

The above statistic is printed on the SHAZAM output as LOG-LIKELIHOOD FUNCTION WITH CONSTANT TERM ONLY or as LOG-LIKELIHOOD (0). If all coefficients except the intercept are zero the LIKELIHOOD RATIO TEST statistic $2[L(\hat{\beta}) - L(0)]$ has an asymptotic $\chi^2_{(k-1)}$ distribution.

Interpreting the Results

Predicted probabilities are computed as $\hat{Y}_t = \hat{P}_t = F(X_t'\hat{\beta})$.

The coefficients tell the effect of a change in the independent variable on the utility index. The impact of a unit increase in an explanatory variable on the choice probability is obtained by estimating the marginal effects as follows:

The probit model: $\qquad \dfrac{\partial \hat{P}_t}{\partial X_{kt}} = f(X_t'\hat{\beta})\,\hat{\beta}_k \quad$, f() is the normal density function

The logit model: $\qquad \dfrac{\partial \hat{P}_t}{\partial X_{kt}} = \dfrac{\hat{\beta}_k \exp(-X_t'\hat{\beta})}{[1 + \exp(-X_t'\hat{\beta})]^2}$

The elasticity gives the percentage change in the choice probability in response to a percentage change in the explanatory variable. For the kth coefficient this is estimated as:

$$E_{kt} = \left(\frac{\partial \hat{P}_t}{\partial X_{kt}}\right) \frac{X_{kt}}{F(X_t'\hat{\beta})}$$

Since the elasticity is different for every observation it is often reported at the mean values of X. On the SHAZAM output the ELASTICITY AT MEANS is computed as:

$$\overline{E}_k = \left(\frac{\partial \hat{P}}{\partial \overline{X}_k}\right) \frac{\overline{X}_k}{F(\overline{X}'\hat{\beta})}$$

Following Hensher and Johnson [1981, Eq. 3.44] the WEIGHTED AGGREGATE ELASTICITY is computed as:

$$\overline{E}_k^W = \sum_{t=1}^{N} \hat{P}_t E_{kt} \Bigg/ \sum_{t=1}^{N} \hat{P}_t$$

Measuring Goodness of Fit

Various researchers have proposed different ways of computing R^2 measures for the probit and logit models and the practitioner must decide which statistic is the most appealing. The SHAZAM output prints a variety of these statistics to choose from.

	Goodness-of-fit measure	Reference
MADDALA R-SQUARE	$1 - \exp\{2[L(0) - L(\hat{\beta})] / N\}$	Maddala [1983, Eq.2.44]
CRAGG-UHLER R-SQUARE	$\dfrac{1 - \exp\{2[L(0) - L(\hat{\beta})] / N\}}{1 - \exp\{2\,L(0) / N\}}$	Cragg &Uhler [1970, p. 400]
MCFADDEN R-SQUARE	$1 - L(\hat{\beta}) / L(0)$	McFadden [1974]
CHOW R-SQUARE	$1 - \dfrac{\sum_{t=1}^{N}(Y_t - \hat{Y}_t)^2}{\sum_{t=1}^{N}(Y_t - \overline{Y})^2}$	Chow [1983, p. 262, Eq. 47]

Denote R^2 as the McFadden goodness-of-fit measure. Hensher and Johnson [1981, p. 52] recommend adjusting this for degrees of freedom and on the SHAZAM output the statistic ADJUSTED FOR DEGREES OF FREEDOM is computed as:

$$1 - \frac{L(\hat{\beta})/(N-K)}{L(0)/(N-1)}$$

An alternative to the likelihood ratio test is proposed in Chow [1983, p. 263]. Under the null hypothesis that all the slope coefficients are zero the statistic:

$$\frac{R^2/(K-1)}{(1-R^2)/K}$$

is APPROXIMATELY F DISTRIBUTED with (K–1,K) degrees of freedom.

A summary of predictive ability is the 2 x 2 PREDICTION SUCCESS TABLE reported as:

		ACTUAL	
		0	1
	0	N_{11}	N_{12}
PREDICTED	1	N_{21}	N_{22}

The decision rule is to predict $Y_t = 0$ when $\hat{P}_t < .5$ (equivalent to $\hat{I}_t < 0$) and predict $Y_t = 1$ when $\hat{P}_t \geq .5$. The table tells the numeric counts of hits and misses using this decision rule. Other calculated statistics are:

EXPECTED OBSERVATIONS AT 0	$\sum_{t=1}^{N}(1-\hat{P}_t)$
EXPECTED OBSERVATIONS AT 1	$\sum_{t=1}^{N}\hat{P}_t$
SUM OF SQUARED RESIDUALS	$\sum_{t=1}^{N}(Y_t - \hat{Y}_t)^2$
WEIGHTED SUM OF SQUARED RESIDUALS	$\sum_{t=1}^{N}\frac{(Y_t - \hat{Y}_t)^2}{\hat{Y}_t(1-\hat{Y}_t)}$

A discussion on the interpretation of these statistics in the context of binary choice models is given in Amemiya [1981, pp. 1502-7].

Hensher and Johnson [1981, p.54] provide a more enhanced version of the prediction success table where the N_{ij} elements are defined somewhat differently as:

$$N_{11} = \sum_{t=1}^{N}(1-Y_t)(1-\hat{P}_t) \ ; N_{12} = \sum_{t=1}^{N}(1-Y_t)\hat{P}_t \ ; N_{21} = \sum_{t=1}^{N}Y_t(1-\hat{P}_t) \ \text{ and } \ N_{22} = \sum_{t=1}^{N}Y_t\hat{P}_t$$

The HENSHER-JOHNSON PREDICTION SUCCESS TABLE is then obtained as:

ACTUAL	PREDICTED 0	CHOICE 1	OBSERVED COUNT	OBSERVED SHARE
0	N_{11}	N_{12}	$N_{1.}$	$N_{1.}/N_{..}$
1	N_{21}	N_{22}	$N_{2.}$	$N_{2.}/N_{..}$
PREDICTED COUNT	$N_{.1}$	$N_{.2}$	$N_{..}$	1
PREDICTED SHARE	$N_{.1}/N_{..}$	$N_{.2}/N_{..}$	1	
PROP. SUCCESSFUL	$N_{11}/N_{.1}$	$N_{22}/N_{.2}$	$(N_{11}+N_{22})/N_{..}$	
SUCCESS INDEX	$\dfrac{N_{11}}{N_{.1}} - \dfrac{N_{.1}}{N_{..}}$	$\dfrac{N_{22}}{N_{.2}} - \dfrac{N_{.2}}{N_{..}}$	$\sum\limits_{i=1}^{2}\dfrac{N_{ii}}{N_{..}} - \left(\dfrac{N_{.i}}{N_{..}}\right)^2$	
PROPORTIONAL ERROR	$(N_{.1}-N_{1.})/N_{..}$	$(N_{.2}-N_{2.})/N_{..}$		

The NORMALIZED SUCCESS INDEX is the sum of the SUCCESS INDEXES weighted by the PROPORTIONAL ERROR.

PROBIT *AND LOGIT COMMAND OPTIONS*

In general, the formats of the **PROBIT** and **LOGIT** commands are:

PROBIT *depvar indeps / options*

LOGIT *depvar indeps / options*

where *depvar* is the dependent variable, *indeps* is a list of independent variables, and *options* is a list of desired options. Options as defined for the **OLS** command that are available are:

MAX, NOCONSTANT, NONORM, PCOR, BEG=, END= COEF=, COV=, STDERR=, TRATIO= and **WEIGHT=**

Additional options available on the **PROBIT** and **LOGIT** commands are:

DUMP	**DUMP**s the matrix of second derivatives and possibly some other output that the user normally does not want to see.
LIST	**LIST**s, for each observation, the value of the index I, the predicted and observed values of the dependent variable, and a plot of the predicted values. It will also print the residual statistics obtained with **RSTAT**. Note that the predicted values, rather than the residuals, are plotted with the **LIST** option in the probit and logit models since a plot of the residuals is less useful.
PCOV	Prints the estimated asymptotic **COV**ariance matrix of the coefficients. The matrix is the inverse of the negative of the matrix of second derivatives of the log-likelihood function.
RSTAT	Prints Residual **STAT**istics, but no listing of the observations. While a variety of statistics are printed (for example, Durbin-Watson), they should be used with care since they may not be valid for the probit and logit models.
CONV=	Sets the **CONV**ergence criterion for the log-likelihood function. Let $L^{(i)}$ be the value of the log-likelihood function at iteration i. The estimation converges when $(L^{(i)} - L^{(i-1)})/|L^{(i)}| < \delta$. The value for δ is set with **CONV=** and the default is .001.
IMR=	Saves the computed inverse Mill's ratio (or hazard rate) in the variable specified (only for use with **PROBIT**). This is estimated as $f(X'_t\hat{\beta})/F(X'_t\hat{\beta})$ if $Y_t=1$ where f( ) is the standard normal density function and F( ) is the standard normal cumulative distribution function. When $Y_t=0$ SHAZAM computes the negative of the hazard rate as $f(X'_t\hat{\beta})/[F(X'_t\hat{\beta})-1]$. The ratio is discussed in Heckman [1979, p.156] and applications can be found in Maddala [1983, Chapter 8-9] and Berndt [1991, Chapter 11]. An example of the use of the **IMR=** option is given for a two-stage estimation procedure at the end of this chapter. In the first stage a probit model is specified and estimated. In the second stage the inverse Mill's ratio is included as a regressor in an OLS estimation with a selected sample. This is intended as a correction for sample selection bias.
INDEX=	Saves the computed **INDEX** in the variable specified.

ITER=   Sets the maximum number of **ITER**ations allowed. The default is 25.

PITER=   Specifies the frequency with which the **ITER**ations will be Printed. The default is **PITER=1**. To prevent any information from being printed **PITER=0** must be specified.

PREDICT=   Saves the **PREDICT**ed probabilities in the variable specified.

If the **WEIGHT=** option is used, the method used follows that described for the **REPLICATE** option in **OLS**.

EXAMPLES

Logit Model Estimation

This example shows the estimation results from the logit procedure using the voting data set from Pindyck and Rubinfeld [1991, Table 10.8, p. 283]. The variable *YESVM* is equal to 1 if the individual voted yes and 0 if the individual voted no.

```
|_LOGIT YESVM PUB12 PUB34 PUB5 PRIV YEARS SCHOOL LOGINC PTCON / PITER=0
 LOGIT ANALYSIS       DEPENDENT VARIABLE =YESVM      CHOICES = 2
     95. TOTAL OBSERVATIONS
     59. OBSERVATIONS AT ONE
     36. OBSERVATIONS AT ZERO
  25 MAXIMUM ITERATIONS
CONVERGENCE TOLERANCE = .00100


LOG OF LIKELIHOOD WITH CONSTANT TERM ONLY =    -63.037
BINOMIAL  ESTIMATE = .6211
ITERATION  5       LOG OF LIKELIHOOD FUNCTION =   -53.303

ITERATION  5 ESTIMATES
   .58364      1.1261        .52606       -.34142       -.26127E-01  2.6250
  2.1872      -2.3945      -5.2014

                                    ASYMPTOTIC                        WEIGHTED
VARIABLE     ESTIMATED      STANDARD     T-RATIO    ELASTICITY     AGGREGATE
  NAME       COEFFICIENT     ERROR                  AT MEANS       ELASTICITY
PUB12          .58364        .68778       .84858     .93986E-01    .91051E-01
PUB34         1.1261         .76820      1.4659      .11827        .96460E-01
PUB5           .52606       1.2693        .41445     .73664E-02    .69375E-02
PRIV          -.34142        .78299      -.43605    -.11952E-01   -.12037E-01
YEARS         -.26127E-01    .26934E-01  -.97006    -.73996E-01   -.68592E-01
SCHOOL        2.6250        1.4101       1.8616      .10108        .28999E-01
LOGINC        2.1872         .78781      2.7763     7.2529        6.7561
PTCON        -2.3945        1.0813      -2.2145    -5.5262       -5.1745
CONSTANT     -5.2014        7.5503       -.68890    -1.7298       -1.6137

LOG-LIKELIHOOD FUNCTION =  -53.303
LOG-LIKELIHOOD(0)   =    -63.037
LIKELIHOOD RATIO TEST  =    19.4681    WITH      8 D.F.
```

```
MADDALA R-SQUARE              .1853
CRAGG-UHLER R-SQUARE         .25218
MCFADDEN R-SQUARE            .15442
    ADJUSTED FOR DEGREES OF FREEDOM            .75759E-01
    APPROXIMATELY F-DISTRIBUTED     .20544      WITH        8  AND      9  D.F.
CHOW R-SQUARE               .17197

              PREDICTION SUCCESS TABLE
                    ACTUAL
                0              1
        0      18.            7.
PREDICTED 1    18.           52.

NUMBER OF RIGHT PREDICTIONS =        70.0
PERCENTAGE OF RIGHT PREDICTIONS =     .73684

EXPECTED OBSERVATIONS AT 0  =        36.0    OBSERVED =      36.0
EXPECTED OBSERVATIONS AT 1  =        59.0    OBSERVED =      59.0
SUM OF SQUARED "RESIDUALS" =         18.513
WEIGHTED SUM OF SQUARED "RESIDUALS" =      86.839

HENSHER-JOHNSON PREDICTION SUCCESS TABLE
                                        OBSERVED     OBSERVED
                    PREDICTED  CHOICE      COUNT        SHARE
        ACTUAL          0         1
          0         17.591    18.409     36.000        .379
          1         18.409    40.591     59.000        .621

PREDICTED COUNT       36.000    59.000     95.000       1.000
PREDICTED SHARE         .379      .621      1.000
PROP. SUCCESSFUL        .489      .688       .612
SUCCESS INDEX           .110      .067       .083
PROPORTIONAL ERROR      .000      .000
NORMALIZED SUCCESS INDEX                     .177
```

Probit Model Estimation

The SHAZAM output given below uses data from T. Mroz included in Berndt [1991, Chapter 11]. The labor force participation for married women is given by the 0-1 dummy variable *LFP*. The explanatory variables measure various attributes of the woman and her family. The wage rate *WW* is observed only for the working women in the sample. To obtain a wage rate estimate for the entire sample a wage determination equation is first estimated and used for extrapolation purposes. The **PROBIT** command is then used to estimate a model of labor force participation that predicts the probability that an individual will join the labor force.

```
|_SAMPLE 1 753
|_READ (MROZ) LFP WHRS KL6 K618 WA WE WW RPWG HHRS HA HE HW FAMINC &
|            MTR WMED WFED UN CIT AX  / SKIPLINES=1
UNIT 88 IS NOW ASSIGNED TO: MROZ
   19 VARIABLES AND       753 OBSERVATIONS STARTING AT OBS        1
|_* Analyze wife's property income
|_GENR PRIN=(FAMINC-WW*WHRS)/1000
```

```
|_DIM LWW 753
|_GENR WA2=WA*WA
|_* Restrict the sample to those who work
|_SAMPLE 1 428
|_GENR LWW=LOG(WW)
|_* Estimate a wage determination equation
|_?OLS LWW WA WA2 WE CIT AX
|_* Estimate a predicted wage for non-workers
|_?FC / PREDICT=LWW BEG=429 END=753
|_* Probit Estimation
|_SAMPLE 1 753
|_PROBIT LFP LWW PRIN KL6 K618 WA WE UN CIT / PITER=0
PROBIT ANALYSIS      DEPENDENT VARIABLE =LFP      CHOICES = 2
     753. TOTAL OBSERVATIONS
     428. OBSERVATIONS AT ONE
     325. OBSERVATIONS AT ZERO
   25 MAXIMUM ITERATIONS
CONVERGENCE TOLERANCE = .00100


LOG OF LIKELIHOOD WITH CONSTANT TERM ONLY =     -514.87
BINOMIAL  ESTIMATE = .5684
ITERATION  3      LOG OF LIKELIHOOD FUNCTION =     -450.72


ITERATION  3 ESTIMATES
 .23998     -.21238E-01 -.87938     -.32061E-01 -.34542E-01  .13204
 -.10666E-01  .11466E-01  .53839
```

		ASYMPTOTIC			WEIGHTED
VARIABLE NAME	ESTIMATED COEFFICIENT	STANDARD ERROR	T-RATIO	ELASTICITY AT MEANS	AGGREGATE ELASTICITY
LWW	.23998	.93507E-01	2.5664	.18017	.15423
PRIN	-.21238E-01	.46991E-02	-4.5195	-.29063	-.25371
KL6	-.87938	.11450	-7.6799	-.14212	-.11515
K618	-.32061E-01	.40672E-01	-.78829	-.29497E-01	-.25672E-01
WA	-.34542E-01	.76642E-02	-4.5069	-.99895	-.88764
WE	.13204	.25962E-01	5.0861	1.1030	.95967
UN	-.10666E-01	.15955E-01	-.66851	-.62531E-01	-.54989E-01
CIT	.11466E-01	.10749	.10667	.50106E-02	.44439E-02
CONSTANT	.53839	.48129	1.1186	.36602	.32165

```
LOG-LIKELIHOOD FUNCTION =  -450.72
LOG-LIKELIHOOD(0)   =   -514.87
LIKELIHOOD RATIO TEST  =   128.306    WITH     8  D.F.


MADDALA R-SQUARE              .1567
CRAGG-UHLER R-SQUARE          .21022
MCFADDEN R-SQUARE             .12460
     ADJUSTED FOR DEGREES OF FREEDOM          .11519
     APPROXIMATELY F-DISTRIBUTED     .16013     WITH     8 AND     9 D.F.
CHOW R-SQUARE                 .15809

          PREDICTION SUCCESS TABLE
                ACTUAL
               0            1
       0    163.          79.
PREDICTED 1  162.         349.

NUMBER OF RIGHT PREDICTIONS =        512.
```

```
PERCENTAGE OF RIGHT PREDICTIONS =        .67995

EXPECTED OBSERVATIONS AT 0  =         323.5   OBSERVED =    325.0
EXPECTED OBSERVATIONS AT 1  =         429.5   OBSERVED =    428.0
SUM OF SQUARED "RESIDUALS" =          155.52
WEIGHTED SUM OF SQUARED "RESIDUALS" =    746.36

HENSHER-JOHNSON PREDICTION SUCCESS TABLE
                                            OBSERVED      OBSERVED
                   PREDICTED  CHOICE          COUNT         SHARE
       ACTUAL         0         1
         0         168.692   156.308        325.000         .432
         1         154.761   273.239        428.000         .568

PREDICTED COUNT      323.454   429.546      753.000        1.000
PREDICTED SHARE         .430      .570        1.000
PROP. SUCCESSFUL        .522      .636         .587
SUCCESS INDEX           .092      .066         .077
PROPORTIONAL ERROR     -.002      .002
NORMALIZED SUCCESS INDEX                       .157
```

Heckit Sample Selectivity Procedure

The following SHAZAM command file was written by David Jaeger of the University
of Michigan to do sample selection-corrected two-stage estimation by the method in
Heckman [1979]. The first stage uses probit estimation. The program includes
corrections for standard errors in the second step. The commands illustrate an
application with the Mroz data set that was used in the previous example. The
commands can be modified to read in any set of data.

```
SAMPLE 1 753
READ (MROZ) LFP WHRS KL6 K618 WA WE WW RPWG HHRS HA HE HW FAMINC &
            MTR WMED WFED UN CIT AX   / SKIPLINES=1
* Analyze wife's property income
GENR PRIN=(FAMINC-WW*WHRS)/1000
DIM LWW 753 LTWW 753
GENR WA2=WA*WA
* Restrict the sample to those who work
SAMPLE 1 428
GENR LWW=LOG(WW)
* Estimate a wage determination equation
OLS LWW WA WA2 WE CIT AX
* Estimate a predicted wage for non-workers
FC / PREDICT=LWW BEG=429 END=753
GENR LTAX=LOG(1-MTR)
* Calculate an after-tax wage rate variable
GENR LTWW=LTAX+LWW

*********************************************************************
* Sample Selection-Corrected Estimation ("Heckit")
*
* Programmmer:
*    David A. Jaeger
*    The University of Michigan
```

```
*
* Background:
*     Heckman (1979) discusses the bias that results from using
*     nonrandomly selected samples when estimating behavioral
*     relationships as "omitted variables" bias.  He proposes
*     a simple consistent method to estimate these models,
*     using a bivariate normal model for the selection equation,
*     and ordinary least squares to estimate the behavioral
*     equation with the selected sample.
*
*     Greene (1981) notes that the standard errors in the OLS
*     stage that are typically computed can either be smaller
*     or larger than the correct standard errors, not
*     just smaller as Heckman had asserted.  He then derives
*     a simple-to-compute formula for the correct variance-
*     covariance matrix of the OLS estimates.
*
* Description:
*     This program uses SHAZAM's PROBIT and OLS routines to
*     estimate the parameters of the Heckman model and SHAZAM's
*     MATRIX language to calculate the correct standard errors
*     for the second stage (OLS).
*
************************************************************************

* ================= DATA INPUT REQUIREMENTS ====================
*
* Modify this section as appropriate
SAMPLE 1 753
* List of independent variables for the 1st-stage probit estimation
X1: PRIN KL6 K618 WA WE UN CIT WA2 WFED WMED
* List of independent variables for the 2nd-stage OLS estimation
X2: PRIN KL6 K618 WA WE UN CIT WA2 WFED WMED
* Binary variable for probit estimation
RENAME LFP SEL
* Dependent variable for 2nd-stage OLS estimation
RENAME LTWW DEP
* ==================== END OF DATA INPUT =======================

***** First Stage:   Run Probit

PROBIT SEL [X1] / INDEX=ALPHAW COV=SIG IMR=LAMBDA PCOV

***** Second Stage:  Run OLS on the selected sample
SET NOWARNSKIP
SKIPIF (SEL.EQ.0)
   OLS DEP LAMBDA [X2] / RESID=ERR COEF=BETA STDERR=OLSSTD
   GEN1 N=$N
   GEN1 K=$K
   GEN1 THETA=BETA:1
   PRINT THETA
   GENR CONSTANT=1
   GENR DELTA=LAMBDA*(LAMBDA+ALPHAW)
   COPY ERR E
   COPY DELTA CAPDELTA
   COPY [X1] CONSTANT W
   COPY LAMBDA [X2] CONSTANT XSTAR
DELETE SKIP$
```

```
MATRIX CAPDELTA=DIAG(CAPDELTA)
MATRIX DELTABAR=TRACE(CAPDELTA)/N
MATRIX SIGSQE=E'E/N+THETA**2*DELTABAR
MATRIX SIGE=SQRT(SIGSQE)

***** Standard Error of 2nd Stage (OLS) corrected for selection
PRINT SIGE

GEN1 RHOSQ=THETA**2/SIGSQE
GEN1 RHO=(ABS(THETA)/THETA)*SQRT(RHOSQ)

***** Correlation Between error in regression and error in selection
PRINT RHO

MATRIX Q=RHOSQ*(XSTAR'CAPDELTA*W)*SIG*(W'*CAPDELTA*XSTAR)
MATRIX ASYVCOV=SIGSQE*INV(XSTAR'XSTAR)* &
       (XSTAR'(IDEN(N)-RHOSQ*CAPDELTA)*XSTAR + Q)*INV(XSTAR'*XSTAR)

***** Consistent Variance-Covariance Matrix of 2nd Stage (OLS)
PRINT ASYVCOV

MATRIX ASYSE=DIAG(ASYVCOV)
MATRIX ASYSE=SQRT(ASYSE)

***** Consistent Standard Errors for 2nd Stage (OLS)
SAMPLE 1 K
PRINT BETA OLSSTD ASYSE
STOP
```

25. ROBUST ESTIMATION

"39..This appears to be the first uninteresting number, which of course makes it an especially interesting number, because it is the smallest number to have the property of being uninteresting. It is therefore also the first number to be simultaneously interesting and uninteresting."

David Wells, 1986
The Penguin Dictionary of Curious and Interesting Numbers

SHAZAM can perform the robust estimation methods described in Judge, Hill, Griffiths, Lütkepohl and Lee [1988, Chapter 22]. As a prelude to this chapter, the **OLS** command can be used to obtain regression diagnostics such as tests for normal errors and tests for detecting influential observations (see the **OLS** command options **DFBETAS, GF, LM, INFLUENCE** and **RSTAT**). The **ROBUST** command provides a number of alternative robust estimation methods. These methods give coefficient estimators that do not necessarily follow a t-distribution, so hypothesis testing must be done carefully. Often the distribution is unknown.

ESTIMATION UNDER MULTIVARIATE t ERRORS

The multivariate-t regression model specifies an error distribution with fatter tails than the normal distribution. Two cases to consider are one where the residuals are independent and one where the residuals are uncorrelated but not independent. For the uncorrelated but not independent error case (specified with the **UNCOR** option on the **ROBUST** command) the coefficient estimates are identical to OLS estimates but the covariance matrix is estimated as:

$$\frac{v\tilde{\sigma}^2}{v-2}(X'X)^{-1} \quad \text{where} \quad \tilde{\sigma}^2 = \frac{e'e}{N}$$

and v is the degrees of freedom specified with the **MULTIT=** option and is only defined for v>2.

The independent error case is discussed in Kelejian and Prucha [1985] and Judge, Hill, Griffiths, Lütkepohl and Lee [1988, Chapter 22.3].

ESTIMATION USING REGRESSION QUANTILES

The method of regression quantiles is described in Koenker and Bassett [1978] and in Koenker and D'Orey [1987]. For a given a value of θ such that $0<\theta<1$ the θth sample regression quantile is found by minimizing the function:

$$\sum_{(t|Y_t \geq X_t'\beta)} \theta|Y_t - X_t'\beta| + \sum_{(t|Y_t < X_t'\beta)} (1-\theta)|Y_t - X_t'\beta|$$

The solution to the minimization problem is the estimator $\hat{\beta}^*(\theta)$. The value of the minimized function is printed on the SHAZAM output as OBJECTIVE FUNCTION. The output also includes a statistic labelled EMPIRICAL QUANTILE FUNCTION AT MEANS which is computed as the predicted value at the mean values of the independent variables.

Least Absolute Error Estimation

When $\theta=.5$ the objective is to find the set of coefficients that minimizes the sum of absolute errors:

$$\sum_{t=1}^{N} |Y_t - X_t'\beta|$$

The estimator $\hat{\beta}^*(0.5)$ is the least absolute errors (LAE) estimator, also known as minimum absolute deviations (MAD), least absolute values (LAV) or the L1 estimator. The covariance matrix of the LAE estimator is estimated as:

$$[2\hat{f}(0)]^{-2}(X'X)^{-1}$$

where f(0) is the value of the density at the median and an estimator is:

$$\hat{f}(0) = \frac{2d}{N(e_{(m+d)} - e_{(m-d)})}$$

where $e_{(t)}$ are ordered residuals and $m \approx N/2$. The value of d can be specified with the **DIFF=** option on the **ROBUST** command.

Linear Functions of Regression Quantiles

An estimator that is a linear function of regression quantiles is given by:

$$\hat{\beta}(\pi) = \sum_{i=1}^{M} \pi_i \hat{\beta}^*(\theta_i)$$

where $\pi = (\pi_1, \ldots, \pi_M)'$ is a symmetric weighting scheme. Alternative schemes described in Judge, Hill, Griffiths, Lütkepohl and Lee [1988, Chapter 22.4.2] and implemented with the **ROBUST** command are as follows:

Estimator	ROBUST option	θ	π
Five quantile	**FIVEQUAN**	(.1, .25, .5, .75, .9)	(.05, .25, .4, .25, .05)
Gastwirth	**GASTWIRT**	(.33, .5, .67)	(.3, .4, .3)
Tukey trimean	**TUKEY**	(.25, .5, .75)	(.25, .5, .25)

Another estimator is: $\quad \hat{\beta} = \dfrac{1}{M} \sum_{i=1}^{M} \hat{\beta}^*(\theta_i)$

where the θ_i values are equally spaced. This rule is used by specifying the **THETAB=**, **THETAE=** and **THETAI=** options on the **ROBUST** command.

Trimmed Least Squares

The trimmed least squares method constructs the estimators $\hat{\beta}^*(\alpha)$ and $\hat{\beta}^*(1-\alpha)$ where α is the desired trimming proportion ($0<\alpha<0.5$). The value for α is specified with the **TRIM=** option on the **ROBUST** command. The observations where $Y_t - X_t'\hat{\beta}^*(\alpha) \leq 0$ or $Y_t - X_t'\hat{\beta}^*(1-\alpha) \geq 0$ are discarded and OLS is then applied to the remaining observations to get the estimator $\tilde{\beta}_\alpha$. The covariance matrix is estimated as:

$$V(\tilde{\beta}_\alpha) = \hat{\sigma}^2(\alpha)(X'X)^{-1} \qquad \text{where}$$

$$\hat{\sigma}^2(\alpha) = \frac{1}{(1-2\alpha)^2}\left(\frac{e'e}{N-K} + \alpha(c_1^2 + c_2^2) - \alpha^2(c_1 + c_2)^2 \right) \ ,$$

$$c_1 = \overline{X}'[\hat{\beta}^*(\alpha) - \tilde{\beta}_\alpha] \qquad \text{and} \qquad c_2 = \overline{X}'[\hat{\beta}^*(1-\alpha) - \tilde{\beta}_\alpha]$$

ROBUST *COMMAND OPTIONS*

In general, the format of the **ROBUST** command is:

ROBUST *depvar indeps / options*

where *depvar* is the dependent variable, *indeps* is a list of independent variables, and *options* is a list of options.

Options as defined for the **OLS** command that are available are:

GNU, LINLOG, LIST, LOGLIN, LOGLOG, MAX, NOCONSTANT, PCOR, PCOV, RSTAT, BEG=, END=, COEF=, COV=, PREDICT=, RESID=, STDERR= and **TRATIO=**

The following additional options are available on the **ROBUST** command:

FIVEQUAN   Specifies the "five quantile estimator" as described above.

GASTWIRT   Specifies the Gastwirth weighting scheme for the regression quantile estimator as described above.

LAE   Specifies that least absolute error (**LAE**) estimation is desired. This is the default method. Also see the **DIFF=** option.

TUKEY   Specifies the Tukey trimean weighting scheme in computing regression quantiles as described above.

UNCOR   Used with the **MULTIT=** option described below to specify that the *uncorrelated* error model is requested. If this option is not used the *independent* error model is assumed.

CONV=   Used with the **MULTIT=** option described below to specify a convergence criterion δ to stop the iterative procedure used to obtain the estimates. For $S^{(i)}$ the sum of squared errors at iteration i the iterations will stop when:

$$\left| S^{(i)} - S^{(i-1)} \right| < \delta$$

The default is **CONV=.01**.

DIFF=   Specifies a value of d to use with the **LAE** and **THETA=** options and for methods that use linear functions of regression quantiles. The parameter d is the differential used when selecting ordered residuals to use in computing the covariance matrix (details are in Judge, Hill,

Griffiths, Lütkepohl and Lee [1988, Chapter 22.4]). The default value for d is $(N-K-1)/6$ (rounded down to the nearest integer). However, the maximum permitted value for d is $N \cdot \theta / 2$ (rounded down to the nearest integer). Judge et al. [1988, p. 903-4] note that the covariance estimator is unlikely to be satisfactory for large K/N.

If you specify **DIFF=-1** the method of Bofinger [1975] and Siddiqui [1960] is used which gives:

$$d = N^{(-1/5)} \left[\frac{4.5 \varphi(x)^4}{(2x^2+1)^2} \right]^{(1/5)} \qquad \text{where} \quad x = \Phi^{-1}(\theta)$$

φ and Φ^{-1} represent the standard normal density function, and inverse of the standard normal cumulative distribution function respectively. In the above equation θ is the quantile required so $\theta=.5$ in the case of the LAE model. If **DIFF=-2** SHAZAM will use the method suggested by Hall and Sheather [1988] and Siddiqui [1960]:

$$d = N^{(-1/3)} z_\alpha^{2/3} \left[\frac{1.5 \varphi(x)^2}{(2x^2+1)} \right]^{(1/3)} \qquad \text{where} \quad x = \Phi^{-1}(\theta)$$

and z_α is the $\alpha/2$ critical value from the normal distribution. SHAZAM uses $\alpha=.05$ and therefore $z_\alpha=1.96$.

ITER=   Used with the **MULTIT=** option described below to specify the maximum number of iterations allowed in the iterative procedure used to obtain the estimates. The default is **ITER=10**.

MULTIT=   Specifies the degrees of freedom parameter to be used for the multivariate-t error distribution. See also the **UNCOR, CONV=**, and **ITER=** options which can be used with the **MULTIT=** option.

THETA=   Specifies a single value of θ to use for the regression quantile method.

THETAB=,
THETAE=,
THETAI=   Specifies beginning (**THETAB=**), ending (**THETAE=**), and increments (**THETAI=**) to be used for θ. A sequence of regression quantile estimates is generated and coefficient estimates are obtained as the average (equal weights). If these options are specified the **THETA=** option is ignored.

TRIM=   Specifies the value of the **TRIM**ming proportion α to use for the trimmed least squares estimation method. The value specified for α should be between 0 and .5. A listing of the observation numbers for the deleted observations is printed unless the **SET NOWARN** command has been used.

Only one estimation method is permitted on any **ROBUST** command. The default is the **LAE** method. Note that calculations of R^2 are not well defined in these models. Users may prefer to use the R^2 measure that is reported with the **RSTAT** option.

EXAMPLES

Examples of the use of the **ROBUST** command are provided in Chapter 22 of the *Judge Handbook*. The following is an example of the **ROBUST** command to obtain the LAE estimates for the Theil textile data set.

```
|_ROBUST CONSUME INCOME PRICE / LAE RSTAT
LEAST ABSOLUTE ERRORS REGRESSION
OBJECTIVE FUNCTION  =   35.244
NUMBER OF SIMPLEX ITERATIONS =   5.0000
EMPIRICAL QUANTILE FUNCTION AT MEANS =   136.24
SUM OF ABSOLUTE ERRORS =   70.487
   USING DIFF=   2 FOR COVARIANCE CALCULATIONS

VARIANCE OF THE ESTIMATE-SIGMA**2 =   68.326
STANDARD ERROR OF THE ESTIMATE-SIGMA =   8.2659
SUM OF SQUARED ERRORS-SSE=   570.95
MEAN OF DEPENDENT VARIABLE =   134.51

VARIABLE    ESTIMATED   STANDARD   T-RATIO          PARTIAL STANDARDIZED ELASTICITY
  NAME      COEFFICIENT   ERROR      14 DF   P-VALUE CORR. COEFFICIENT   AT MEANS
INCOME       .69851       .3962      1.763    .100   .426    .1570        .5348
PRICE      -1.4421        .1245    -11.58     .000  -.952  -1.0316       -.8182
CONSTANT   174.36       40.26       4.331     .001   .757    .0000       1.2963

DURBIN-WATSON = 1.5333   VON NEUMANN RATIO = 1.6291   RHO =    .19972
RESIDUAL SUM = -29.563     RESIDUAL VARIANCE =   40.782
SUM OF ABSOLUTE ERRORS=   70.487
R-SQUARE BETWEEN OBSERVED AND PREDICTED =  .9435
RUNS TEST:    7 RUNS,   10 POSITIVE,    7 NEGATIVE, NORMAL STATISTIC = -1.1583
```

26. TIME-VARYING LINEAR REGRESSION

"If a man's wit be wandering, let him study the mathematics."
Francis Bacon, 1625

Consider a linear regression model with time-varying coefficients:

$$Y_t = X_t'\beta_t + \varepsilon_t \qquad \text{for } t=1,\ldots,N$$

The flexible least squares (FLS) method developed by Kalaba and Tesfatsion [1989] finds time paths of the coefficients which minimize the "incompatibility cost" function:

$$C(\beta;\delta,N) = \frac{1}{1-\delta}\left[\delta \sum_{t=1}^{N-1}(\beta_{t+1}-\beta_t)'(\beta_{t+1}-\beta_t) + (1-\delta)\sum_{t=1}^{N}(Y_t - X_t'\beta_t)^2\right]$$

$$= \frac{1}{1-\delta}\left[\delta\, r_D^2(\beta;N) + (1-\delta)\, r_M^2(\beta;N)\right]$$

where $\beta = (\beta_1,\beta_2,\ldots,\beta_N)$ is the time-path of coefficient vectors, r_D^2 is the sum of squared residual dynamic errors, r_M^2 is the sum of squared residual measurement errors and $\delta \in (0,1)$ is a smoothness weight. The OLS extreme point occurs at $\delta=1$ and equal weights apply when $\delta=.5$. The FLS solution is conditional on the choice of δ. The implementation of FLS with the **FLS** command is based on a program provided by Tesfatsion and Kalaba.

A strength of FLS is its ability to capture turning points and other systematic time variation in the coefficients. This is highlighted in the applied work of Tesfatsion and Veitch [1990] and Lütkepohl [1993]. FLS can be compared with other tests such as the Chow test and the CUSUM of recursive residuals tests (available with the **DIAGNOS** command). The Chow test requires the specification of a break-point and assumes coefficient constancy over a sub-period. Schneider [1991, p. 210] comments that the CUSUM test provides a global stability test and, in contrast to FLS, does not identify the sources of instability.

FLS offers an exploratory data analysis tool and requires no distributional assumptions on the error terms. However, Lütkepohl [1993, p. 733] discusses that, with some stochastic assumptions, a likelihood function can be formed from a random walk model for the regression coefficients and FLS may be interpreted as a special Kalman filter.

FLS COMMAND OPTIONS

In general, the format of the **FLS** command is:

FLS *depvar indeps* / *options*

where *depvar* is the dependent variable, *indeps* is a list of independent variables with coefficients which evolve over time and *options* is a list of desired options.

Options as defined for the **OLS** command that are available are:

BEG=, END=, PREDICT= and **RESID=**

Additional options available on the **FLS** command are:

GNU   Prepares **GNUPLOT** plots of the time paths of the coefficients as well as the residuals and predicted values. For more information on this option see the *GNUPLOT* section in the *PLOTS* chapter. With the **GNU** option the **APPEND, OUTPUT=, DEVICE=, PORT=** and **COMMFILE=** options are also available as described for the **PLOT** command.

MAX   Reports the first-order necessary conditions for the minimization of the cost function as described in Kalaba and Tesfatsion [1989, Appendix A]. The columns on the output give the evaluations of the partial derivatives of the cost function with respect to the variables. The results should be close to zero and therefore may be machine dependent. The **MAX** option also prints the coefficient estimates.

NOCONSTANT Do not include an intercept term. Otherwise, a time-varying intercept is included in the model.

PCOEF   Prints the coefficient estimates over the sample period.

COEF=   Saves the FLS estimates in a N x K matrix.

DELTA=   Specifies the smoothing weight δ in the range $0<\delta<1$. The default setting is **DELTA=.5**.

The temporary variables available after the **FLS** command are:

$ERR	Error code
$K	Number of coefficients
$LLF	Value of the incompatibility cost function
$N	Number of observations
$SSE	Sum of squared residual measurement errors
$SSR	Sum of squared residual dynamic errors
$R2	R-square

Note that some of these temporary variables may have different definitions than that used by other SHAZAM commands.

EXAMPLES

This example is inspired by simulation experiments reported in Kalaba and Tesfatsion [1989, Section 8]. The true coefficients $\beta_t = (\beta_{t1}, \beta_{t2})$ are generated so that they trace out an ellipse over time. The experiment illustrates the degree to which the FLS coefficient estimates are able to recover this time variation. The SHAZAM command file that generates the data and runs the FLS estimation is shown below.

```
SAMPLE 1 30
* Generate the time-varying coefficients
GENR AI=TIME(0)
GENR B1=.5*SIN(AI*2*$PI/30)
GENR B2=SIN( (AI*2*$PI/30) + $PI/2)
* Generate the data
GENR X1=1
GENR X2=1
SAMPLE 2 30
GENR X1=SIN(10+AI)+.01
* The next command uses the SIN function to generate COS(10 + AI)
GENR X2=SIN(10+AI + $PI/2)
SAMPLE 1 30
GENR Y=B1*X1+B2*X2
* Get the FLS estimates
FLS Y X1 X2 / NOCONSTANT PCOEF
STOP
```

The FLS estimation output follows.

```
|_FLS Y X1 X2 / NOCONSTANT PCOEF
     30 OBSERVATIONS      DEPENDENT VARIABLE = Y
...NOTE..SAMPLE RANGE SET TO:    1,   30

SMOOTHING WEIGHT : DELTA =   .500
```

```
FLEXIBLE LEAST SQUARES ESTIMATES
              X1              X2
        1    .26646          .81866
        2    .26947          .82167
        3    .33164          .72990
        4    .36991          .58770
        5    .39536          .44375
        6    .43262          .28622
        7    .46050          .96371E-01
        8    .45298         -.10372
        9    .42074         -.28179
       10    .39140         -.44191
       11    .34850         -.60802
       12    .26072         -.74510
       13    .17287         -.81824
       14    .10615         -.87791
       15    .31137E-02     -.92037
       16   -.10953         -.88498
       17   -.17895         -.81339
       18   -.25383         -.74014
       19   -.34417         -.61391
       20   -.39581         -.44338
       21   -.42039         -.27711
       22   -.44792         -.10402
       23   -.45966          .92531E-01
       24   -.43288          .28858
       25   -.38436          .45040
       26   -.34608          .59009
       27   -.29316          .73170
       28   -.20245          .82765
       29   -.13678          .84552
       30   -.13669          .84543


SUM OF SQUARED RESIDUAL MEASUREMENT ERRORS =    .65723E-01
SUM OF SQUARED RESIDUAL DYNAMIC ERRORS =        .62918
THE INCOMPATIBILITY COST =                      .69491


R-SQUARE =   .99328


  SUMMARY STATISTICS FOR THE FLS ESTIMATES
VARIABLE    MEAN         STDEV        STDEV        COEFFICIENT
  NAME                                OF MEAN      OF VARIATION
X1          .46592E-02   .33747       .61614E-01   72.431
X2         -.72609E-02   .64204       .11722      -88.425

OLS ESTIMATES CALCULATED FROM A MATRIX AVERAGE OF FLS ESTIMATES
   .38463E-01    .37439E-01
```

The first graph below compares the true sequence of coefficients for the variable *X1* with the FLS estimates. The second graph shows the elliptical shape traced out by the FLS estimates.

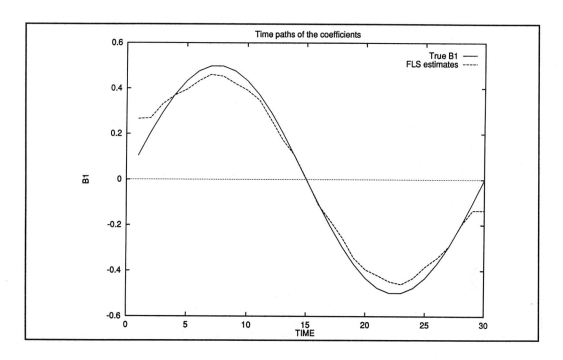

Time paths of the coefficients

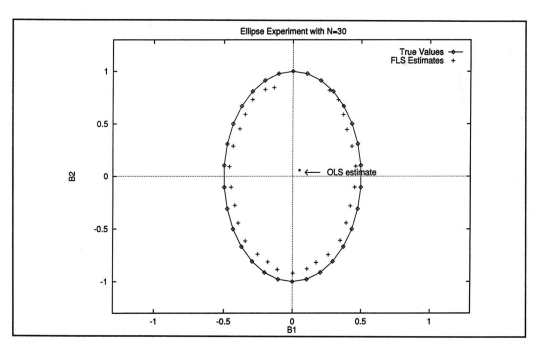

Ellipse Experiment with N=30

27. TOBIT REGRESSION

"That the automobile has reached the limit of its development is suggested by the fact that during the past year no improvements of a radical nature have been introduced."
Scientific American
January 2, 1909

The **TOBIT** command is available for regressions with limited dependent variables. The model is described in Tobin [1958, pp. 24-36]. Other references for tobit analysis (the name is coined from "Tobin's probit") are Goldberger [1964, pp. 248-255]; Maddala [1977, Chapter 9.7]; Greene [1993, Chapter 22]; Judge, Hill, Griffiths, Lütkepohl and Lee [1988, Chapter 19]; and Maddala [1983, Chapter 6]. An application of tobit analysis using SHAZAM can be found in Deegan and White [1976].

The tobit model estimation algorithm is based on a computer program originally written by John Cragg. SHAZAM **TEST** commands can be used following estimation. **RESTRICT** commands are not permitted.

The tobit model can be defined with the use of a latent variable as:

$$Y_t^* = X_t'\beta + \varepsilon_t$$
$$Y_t = 0 \qquad \text{if} \quad Y_t^* \le 0$$
$$Y_t = Y_t^* \qquad \text{if} \quad Y_t^* > 0$$

If a limit value other than 0 is required this can be specified with the **LIMIT=** option on the **TOBIT** command. For the latent variable,

$$E(Y_t^*) = \sigma I_t \qquad \text{where} \quad I_t = X_t'\alpha = X_t'(\beta / \sigma)$$

The conditional expectation is:

$$E(Y_t | I_t) = \sigma I_t \, F(I_t) + \sigma \, f(I_t)$$

where F() is the cumulative normal distribution function and f() is the normal density function. The conditional expectation given that Y>0 is:

$$E(Y_t | I_t, Y_t > 0) = \sigma I_t + \frac{\sigma f(I_t)}{F(I_t)}$$

The parameters of the tobit model are the vector α and a normalizing parameter σ. Users should note that other computer programs may use a different parameterization.

Maximum Likelihood Estimation

The log-likelihood function for the tobit model can be expressed as:

$$L = \sum_{Y_t > 0} -\frac{1}{2}\left[\ln(2\pi) + \ln(\sigma^2) + (\frac{1}{\sigma}Y_t - X_t'\alpha)^2\right] + \sum_{Y_t = 0} \ln[1 - F(X_t'\alpha)]$$

The maximum likelihood estimates of α and σ are denoted by $\hat{\alpha}$ and $\hat{\sigma}$. An estimate of the index variable is $\hat{I}_t = X_t'\hat{\alpha}$. The regression coefficients are estimated as $\hat{\beta} = \hat{\sigma}\hat{\alpha}$. On the SHAZAM output the column NORMALIZED COEFFICIENT reports $\hat{\alpha}$ and the column REGRESSION COEFFICIENT reports $\hat{\beta}$. The coefficient listed for the dependent variable is actually equal to $(1/\hat{\sigma})$ while the statistic labelled STANDARD ERROR OF ESTIMATE is $\hat{\sigma}$ and VARIANCE OF THE ESTIMATE is $\hat{\sigma}^2$.

Interpreting the Results

Analysis of the tobit results is complicated by the fact that all computations are performed on the *normalized* α vector, and the estimated standard errors of the coefficients are those of the α vector and not the β. However, it is quite easy to perform hypotheses on the regression coefficients β by working on the α vector in the manner described in the Tobin article. SHAZAM **TEST** commands can be used to test hypotheses about the β vector as shown in the example in this chapter.

The predicted value of the dependent variable can be computed as:

$$\hat{Y}_t = \hat{\sigma}\hat{I}_t \, F\left(\hat{I}_t\right) + \hat{\sigma} \, f\left(\hat{I}_t\right)$$

The conditional expectation of Y estimated at the mean values is given by:

$$Y^E = \hat{\sigma}(\overline{X}'\hat{\alpha}) \, F\left(\overline{X}'\hat{\alpha}\right) + \hat{\sigma} \, f\left(\overline{X}'\hat{\alpha}\right)$$

Alternative approaches to the interpretation of results from tobit analysis can be considered and this may depend on the specific goals of the study (see, for example, the discussion in Greene [1993, pp. 694-5]). Therefore, before proceeding with the reporting of estimation results, the user should carefully study applied work available in good journals and textbooks.

The ELASTICITY OF INDEX for the kth variable (the percentage change in the index I for a percentage change in X_k at the sample means) is estimated as:

$$\hat{\beta}_k \left(\frac{\overline{X}_k}{\overline{Y}\hat{\sigma}} \right)$$

Another response to consider is that for Y, given the censoring, the marginal effect is:

$$\frac{\partial E(Y_t|I_t)}{\partial X_t} = \beta F(I_t)$$

This result is then used to compute the ELASTICITY OF E(Y) for the kth variable as:

$$\hat{\beta}_k \frac{\overline{X}_k F(\overline{X}'\hat{\alpha})}{\hat{\sigma} Y^E}$$

With S the number of NON-LIMIT OBSERVATIONS the calculations for other statistics on the SHAZAM output are:

PREDICTED PROBABILITY OF Y > LIMIT GIVEN AVERAGE X(I) = $\quad F(\overline{X}'\hat{\alpha})$

THE OBSERVED FREQUENCY OF Y > LIMIT IS = $\quad S/N$

AT MEAN VALUES OF ALL X(I), E(Y) = $\quad Y^E$

MEAN SQUARE ERROR $\quad \dfrac{1}{N}\sum_{t=1}^{N}(Y_t - \hat{Y}_t)^2$

MEAN ABSOLUTE ERROR $\quad \dfrac{1}{N}\sum_{t=1}^{N}|Y_t - \hat{Y}_t|$

When the **LIST** or **MAX** options are used output will include, for each observation:

INDEX	$\hat{I}_t$	OBSERVED	Y_t
PROB(X)	$F(\hat{I}_t)$	EXPECTED	$\hat{Y}_t$
DENSITY(X)	$f(\hat{I}_t)$	CONDITIONAL	$\hat{Y}_t / F(\hat{I}_t)$ for $Y_t > 0$

TOBIT *COMMAND OPTIONS*

In general, the format of the **TOBIT** command is:

TOBIT *depvar indeps /options*

where *depvar* is the dependent variable, *indeps* is a list of independent variables, and *options* is a list of desired options. Options as defined for the **OLS** command that are available are:

MAX, NOCONSTANT, NONORM, BEG=, END=, COEF=, COV=, STDERR=, TRATIO= and **WEIGHT=**

The following additional options are available on the **TOBIT** command:

DUMP	**DUMP**s the matrix of second derivatives, the moment matrices of limit and non-limit observations, and some other output that is probably not useful to the average user.
LIST	**LIST**s, for each observation, the value of the index I, the density and cumulative probabilities corresponding to the index I, and the observed, expected and conditional values of the dependent variable. No plot is produced.
PCOR	Prints the **COR**relation matrix of the *normalized* coefficients.
PCOV	Prints the estimated asymptotic **COV**ariance matrix of the *normalized* coefficients. The matrix is the inverse of the negative of the matrix of second derivatives of the log-likelihood function. In a large sample the *normalized* coefficients will be normally distributed.
UPPER	Used if the limit is an **UPPER** limit rather than a lower limit.
CONV=	Sets the **CON**vergence criterion for the *normalized* coefficients. The default is .00000001 (that is, 1×10^{-8}). This is the same as using **CONV=1E-8**.
INDEX=	Saves the computed **INDEX** in the variable specified.
ITER=	Sets the maximum number of **ITER**ations allowed. The default is 25.
LIMIT=	Specifies the **LIMIT**ing value of the dependent variable. The default is **LIMIT=** 0.

PITER=   Specifies the frequency with which **ITER**ations are to be **P**rinted. The default is **PITER=1**. If **PITER=0** is specified, no iterations are printed.

PREDICT=   Saves the **PREDICT**ed expected values in the variable specified.

Note that the **PCOR, COEF=, COV=, STDERR=** and **TRATIO=** options all refer to the *normalized* coefficients. If the **WEIGHT=** option is used the method performed follows that described for the **REPLICATE** option in **OLS**.

The temporary variables available with the **TOBIT** command are:

$ERR, $K, $LLF, $N, $SIG2,* and *$SSE.

The variable *$K* is the number of estimated coefficients (the number of independent variables plus one for the estimate of σ).

EXAMPLES

The following is an example of tobit model estimation using data found in Judge, Hill, Griffiths, Lütkepohl and Lee [1988, Table 19.2, p. 800]. The SHAZAM commands include **TEST** commands to derive the standard error and associated asymptotic normal test statistics for the regression coefficients. This is easy to do since as explained earlier the coefficient on the dependent variable Y is simply $1/\sigma$. The command file is:

```
SAMPLE 1 20
READ (TABLE19.2) Y X
TOBIT Y X / LIST PITER=0
TEST X/Y
TEST CONSTANT/Y
STOP
```

The SHAZAM output is:

```
|_SAMPLE 1 20
|_READ (TABLE19.2) Y X
   2 VARIABLES AND        20 OBSERVATIONS STARTING AT OBS       1

|_TOBIT Y X / LIST PITER=0
TOBIT ANALYSIS, LIMIT=      .00        25 MAX ITERATIONS
        6 LIMIT OBSERVATIONS
       14 NON-LIMIT OBSERVATIONS

 FIRST DERIVATIVES OF LOG OF LIKELIHOOD FUNCTION EVALUATED AT MAXIMUM
      .19539925E-13     .88817842E-15    -.23236187E-13

NUMBER OF ITERATIONS =  3

 DEPENDENT VARIABLE = Y
```

```
VARIANCE OF THE ESTIMATE =   13.184
STANDARD ERROR OF THE ESTIMATE =   3.6310


                              ASYMPTOTIC
VARIABLE  NORMALIZED     STANDARD   T-RATIO    REGRESSION ELASTICITY ELASTICITY
          COEFFICIENT    ERROR                 COEFFICIENT OF INDEX   OF E(Y)
X           .24820       .58959E-01  4.2096       .90120     1.9458    1.9970
CONSTANT  -1.5786        .60413     -2.6130     -5.7319
Y           .27541       .53292E-01  5.1679

THE PREDICTED PROBABILITY OF Y > LIMIT GIVEN AVERAGE X (I) =   .8479
 THE OBSERVED FREQUENCY OF Y > LIMIT IS =   .7000
 AT MEAN VALUES OF ALL X(I), E(Y) =        4.0177

                                           DEPENDENT VARIABLE
 OB    INDEX       PROB(X)     DENSITY(X)  OBSERVED    EXPECTED   CONDITIONAL
  1   -1.3304     .91692E-01   .16465       .00000      .15491    ------
  2   -1.0822     .13958       .22212       .00000      .25805    ------
  3   -.83402     .20214       .28175       .00000      .41091    ------
  4   -.58582     .27900       .33604       .00000      .62670    ------
  5   -.33762     .36782       .37684      3.1348       .91739    2.4941
  6   -.89429E-01 .46437       .39735      3.5080      1.2920     2.7822
  7    .15877     .56307       .39395       .83120     1.7550     3.1169
  8    .40696     .65798       .36724      8.0064      2.3057     3.5042
  9    .65516     .74382       .32189       .00000     2.9382     ------
 10    .90335     .81683       .26528       .00000     3.6425     ------
 11   1.1515      .87525       .20557      2.9352      4.4061     5.0341
 12   1.3997      .91921       .14978      3.9048      5.2157     5.6741
 13   1.6479      .95032       .10261      6.5144      6.0590     6.3758
 14   1.8961      .97103       .66099E-01  5.9772      6.9254     7.1321
 15   2.1443      .98400       .40034E-01  3.7260      7.8069     7.9338
 16   2.3925      .99163       .22799E-01 10.412       8.6974     8.7708
 17   2.6407      .99586       .12208E-01 16.906       9.5932     9.6330
 18   2.8889      .99807       .61466E-02  9.2968     10.492     10.512
 19   3.1371      .99915       .29098E-02  7.8916     11.392     11.401
 20   3.3853      .99964       .12952E-02 14.216      12.292     12.297

LOG-LIKELIHOOD FUNCTION= -41.255240
MEAN-SQUARE ERROR=  8.0589568
MEAN ERROR= -.40295353E-02
MEAN ABSOLUTE ERROR=  2.1501402
SQUARED CORRELATION BETWEEN OBSERVED AND EXPECTED VALUES=   .66061
|_TEST X/Y
TEST VALUE =   .90120    STD. ERROR OF TEST VALUE   .17186
ASYMPTOTIC NORMAL STATISTIC =   5.2437210     P-VALUE=  .00000
WALD CHI-SQUARE STATISTIC =  27.496610    WITH    1 D.F.  P-VALUE=   .00000
UPPER BOUND ON P-VALUE BY CHEBYCHEV INEQUALITY =  .03637
|_TEST CONSTANT/Y
TEST VALUE =  -5.7319    STD. ERROR OF TEST VALUE   2.2383
ASYMPTOTIC NORMAL STATISTIC =  -2.5608774     P-VALUE=  .01044
WALD CHI-SQUARE STATISTIC =   6.5580928    WITH    1 D.F.  P-VALUE=   .01044
UPPER BOUND ON P-VALUE BY CHEBYCHEV INEQUALITY =  .15248
|_STOP
```

28. TWO-STAGE LEAST SQUARES AND SYSTEMS OF EQUATIONS

> *"You won't have Nixon to kick around anymore – because, gentlemen, this is my last press conference."*
>
> Richard M. Nixon
> November 7, 1962
> (after losing the California Governor Election)

A single linear equation can be estimated by Two Stage Least Squares (2SLS) with the **2SLS** command in SHAZAM. The **2SLS** command can be used for any instrumental variables estimation. The **INST** command can also be used, but the output is identical to **2SLS**. The **SYSTEM** command in SHAZAM provides features for joint estimation of a set of linear equations by either seemingly unrelated regression (SUR) estimation or by Three Stage Least Squares (3SLS). A reference for 2SLS and 3SLS is Judge, Hill, Griffiths, Lütkepohl and Lee [1988, Chapters 14-15], a reference for instrumental variables estimation is Judge et al. [1988, Chapter 13] and a reference for SUR is Judge et al. [1988, Chapter 11]. Other references are Theil [1971, Chapters 7,9 and 10], Judge, Griffiths, Hill, Lütkepohl and Lee [1985, Chapter 12] and Srivastava and Giles [1987].

Note that these estimation techniques are available for nonlinear models with the **NL** command described in the chapter *NONLINEAR REGRESSION.* An alternative to 2SLS is the Limited Information Maximum Likelihood (LIML) method described in the chapter *SHAZAM PROCEDURES.* The **SYSTEM** command does not estimate models with autoregressive errors. A set of seemingly unrelated regression equations with autoregressive errors can be estimated by using the **NL** command with the **AUTO** option.

2SLS *OR INSTRUMENTAL VARIABLE ESTIMATION*

Since 2SLS is a single equation technique for estimating equations in a simultaneous equation model, each equation is estimated separately and it is not necessary to estimate all equations in the model. However, it is necessary to know which variables are endogenous and which are exogenous. The statistical model for the ith equation in a system of equations may be written:

$$y_i = Z_i \delta_i + \varepsilon_i$$

where y_i is a (Nx1) vector of observations on the left-hand side dependent variable, Z_i is a (Nxp_i) matrix that includes observations on the exogenous variables as well as the jointly endogenous variables in the ith equation, ε_i is a (Nx1) vector of disturbances and the number of unknown parameters in the vector δ_i is p_i.

Consider X as the $(N \times K)$ matrix of observations on all exogenous and predetermined variables in the entire system. Premultiplying the above statistical model by X gives the transformed statistical model:

$$X'y_i = X'Z_i\delta_i + X'\varepsilon_i$$

The 2SLS estimator is:

$$\hat{\delta}_i = \left[Z_i' X(X'X)^{-1} X'Z_i \right]^{-1} Z_i' X(X'X)^{-1} X'y_i$$

and the estimated covariance matrix of coefficients is given by:

$$\hat{\sigma}^2 \left[Z_i' X(X'X)^{-1} X' Z_i \right]^{-1}$$

where the estimator for $\hat{\sigma}^2$ used by SHAZAM is:

$$\hat{\sigma}^2 = \frac{1}{N - p_i} \left[y_i - Z_i\hat{\delta}_i \right]' \left[y_i - Z_i\hat{\delta}_i \right]$$

Some econometricians would argue that the denominator should just be N, since the 2SLS estimator is only consistent when the small sample distribution is unknown. If it is preferable to the user that the estimates be done by dividing by N instead of $N-p_i$ the **DN** options should be used on the **2SLS** command. The estimated coefficients are not affected in either case, but all the variances and t-ratios will be. Users should note that R^2 in **2SLS**, and in many other models, is not well defined and could easily be negative. In fact, the lower bound is minus infinity. This usually indicates that the equation does not fit the data very well. Many econometricians would prefer to use the squared-correlation coefficient between the observed and predicted dependent variable instead for these models. This is obtained with the **RSTAT** option and is reported as R-SQUARE BETWEEN OBSERVED AND PREDICTED. It is also available in the temporary variable $R2OP$.

2SLS and INST Command Options

In general, the format of the **2SLS** command is:

2SLS *depvar rhsvars (exogs) / options*

where *depvar* is the dependent variable, *rhsvars* is a list of all the right-hand side variables in the equation, *exogs* is a list of all the exogenous variables in the system, and *options* is a list of desired options.

Note that the list of *exogs* must be enclosed in parentheses, and that SHAZAM automatically includes a constant in the list of exogenous variables unless the **NOCONEXOG** option is used. If the number of exogenous variables is less than the number of right-hand side variables, the equation will be underidentified. Equation estimation requires $N \geq K \geq p_i$.

While most of the **OLS** options are also available as *options* on **2SLS**, the user should be aware that hypothesis testing in **2SLS** is complicated by the unknown distributions, so the normal t and F tests are invalid. At best these can be interpreted as being asymptotically normal and chi-square. The F test from an Analysis of Variance table is invalid, and the printed R^2, which is defined as 1 minus the unexplained proportion of the total variance, may not coincide with that obtained by using other programs which do the calculation differently.

If the interest is instrumental variables estimation then the **INST** command can be used with the general format:

INST *depvar rhsvars (exogs) / options*

The output for the **INST** command is identical to **2SLS**.

The following **OLS** options may be used on the **2SLS** and **INST** commands:

DN, DUMP, GF, LIST, MAX, NOCONSTANT, PCOR, PCOV, RESTRICT, RSTAT, BEG=, END=, COEF=, COV=, PREDICT= and RESID=.

In addition, the following option is available:

NOCONEXOG   Specifies that a constant is not to be included in the list of exogenous variables. If this option is not specified then SHAZAM includes a column of 1's in the X matrix.

The temporary variables available on the **2SLS** command are:

$ADR2, $DF, $DW, $ERR, $K, $N, $R2, $R2OP, $RAW, $RHO, $SIG2 and *$SSE.*

For more information on temporary variables see the chapter *MISCELLANEOUS COMMANDS AND INFORMATION* and the chapter *ORDINARY LEAST SQUARES.*

Example

An example of a **2SLS** command and the resulting SHAZAM output using the first equation of the Klein model [Theil, 1971] is the following:

```
|_2SLS C PLAG P WGWP (WG T G TIME PLAG KLAG XLAG) /  DN RSTAT
 TWO STAGE LEAST SQUARES - DEPENDENT VARIABLE = C
  7 EXOGENOUS VARIABLES
  3 POSSIBLE ENDOGENOUS VARIABLES
       21 OBSERVATIONS
DN OPTION IN EFFECT - DIVISOR IS N

 R-SQUARE =    .9767     R-SQUARE ADJUSTED =     .9726
VARIANCE OF THE ESTIMATE-SIGMA**2 =   1.0441
STANDARD ERROR OF THE ESTIMATE-SIGMA =   1.0218
SUM OF SQUARED ERRORS-SSE=   21.925
MEAN OF DEPENDENT VARIABLE =   53.995

                          ASYMPTOTIC
VARIABLE   ESTIMATED  STANDARD   T-RATIO         PARTIAL STANDARDIZED ELASTICITY
  NAME     COEFFICIENT  ERROR   ***** DF   P-VALUE CORR. COEFFICIENT  AT MEANS
PLAG        .21623      .1073     2.016     .044  .439     .1270       .0656
P           .17302E-01  .1180     .1466     .883  .036     .0106       .0054
WGWP        .81018      .4025E-01 20.13     .000  .980     .8922       .6224
CONSTANT   16.555      1.321     12.53      .000  .950     .0000       .3066

DURBIN-WATSON = 1.4851    VON NEUMANN RATIO = 1.5593   RHO =    .20423
RESIDUAL SUM = -.15632E-12  RESIDUAL VARIANCE =   1.0441
SUM OF ABSOLUTE ERRORS=   17.866
R-SQUARE BETWEEN OBSERVED AND PREDICTED =  .9768
RUNS TEST:     9 RUNS,    9 POSITIVE,   12 NEGATIVE, NORMAL STATISTIC = -1.0460
```

SYSTEMS OF EQUATIONS

SHAZAM can estimate a system of linear equations. Linear restrictions can be imposed on the coefficients within or across equations. The seemingly unrelated regressions (SUR) case is also known as Zellner estimation, or multivariate regression. The simultaneous equation estimation technique is three-stage least squares (3SLS). As an option, SHAZAM will iterate until convergence.

A system of M equations may be written as:

$$y_1 = Z_1 \delta_1 + \varepsilon_1$$
$$y_2 = Z_2 \delta_2 + \varepsilon_2$$
$$\cdots$$
$$y_M = Z_M \delta_M + \varepsilon_M$$

or, more compactly, as:

$$y = Z\delta + \varepsilon \qquad \text{where}$$

$$y = \begin{bmatrix} y_1 \\ y_2 \\ . \\ . \\ y_M \end{bmatrix}$$ is a (MNx1) vector of observations on the left-hand side dependent variable.

$$Z = \begin{bmatrix} Z_1 & 0 & . & 0 \\ 0 & Z_2 & . & 0 \\ . & . & . & . \\ 0 & 0 & . & Z_M \end{bmatrix}$$ is a (MNxP) matrix of jointly endogenous and exogenous variables in the system and $P = p_1 + p_2 + \ldots + p_M$ where p_i is the number of right hand side variables in equation i.

$\delta = [\delta_1' \ \delta_2' \ldots \delta_M']'$ is a (Px1) vector of unknown parameters.

$\varepsilon = [\varepsilon_1' \ \varepsilon_2' \ldots \varepsilon_M']'$ is a (MNx1) vector of disturbances.

All exogenous variables of the system are in the matrix X. In the case of SUR Z=X since there are no jointly endogenous variables in a SUR system.

The variance-covariance matrix of disturbances is given by:

$$E[\varepsilon\varepsilon'] = \begin{bmatrix} \sigma_{11}I & \sigma_{12}I & . & \sigma_{1M}I \\ \sigma_{21}I & \sigma_{22}I & . & \sigma_{2M}I \\ . & . & . & . \\ \sigma_{M1}I & \sigma_{M2}I & . & \sigma_{MM}I \end{bmatrix} = \Sigma \otimes I_N$$

Seemingly Unrelated Regression

The first step in the SUR estimation procedure is to estimate the σ_{ij} from OLS residuals as:

$$\hat{\sigma}_{ij} = \frac{1}{\tau} \left(y_i - Z_i \hat{\delta}_{OLS,i} \right)' \left(y_j - Z_j \hat{\delta}_{OLS,j} \right)$$

where $\hat{\delta}_{OLS,i} = (Z_i'Z_i)^{-1}Z_i'y_i$ and τ can be calculated using:

$$\tau_1 = N \qquad \text{or} \qquad \tau_2 = \frac{MN - P}{M}$$

If the **DN** option is used SHAZAM will use $\tau = \tau_1$, otherwise $\tau = \tau_2$ is used.

With the matrix $\hat{\Sigma}$ containing individual elements $\hat{\sigma}_{ij}$ the SUR estimator is:

$$\hat{\delta}_{SUR} = [Z'(\hat{\Sigma}^{-1} \otimes I_N)Z]^{-1}Z'(\hat{\Sigma}^{-1} \otimes I_N)y$$

and the covariance matrix of the parameter estimates is estimated as:

$$[Z'(\hat{\Sigma}^{-1} \otimes I_N)Z]^{-1}$$

With the assumption of normality the log-likelihood function can be expressed as:

$$L = -\frac{MN}{2}\ln(2\pi) - \frac{N}{2}\ln|\Sigma| - \frac{1}{2}(y - Z\delta)'(\Sigma^{-1} \otimes I_N)(y - Z\delta)$$

Restricted Seemingly Unrelated Regression

A set of q linear restrictions may be written in the form $R\delta=r$ where R and r are known matrices of dimensions (q x P) and (q x 1) respectively. When the **RESTRICT** and **ITER=0** options are specified on the **SYSTEM** command the restricted estimator is obtained from:

$$\hat{\delta}_R = \hat{\delta}_{OLS} + (Z'Z)^{-1}R'(R(Z'Z)^{-1}R')^{-1}(r - R\hat{\delta}_{OLS})$$

Estimates of the error variances and covariances are obtained from the residuals from the restricted estimation as:

$$\hat{\sigma}_{ij} = \frac{1}{\tau}\left(y_i - Z_i\hat{\delta}_{R,i}\right)'\left(y_j - Z_j\hat{\delta}_{R,j}\right)$$

With the **DN** option $\tau=\tau_1$ otherwise $\tau=\tau_2$ where

$$\tau_1 = N \qquad \text{or} \qquad \tau_2 = \frac{MN - (P - q)}{M}$$

When the **RESTRICT** and **ITER=1** options are specified on the **SYSTEM** command the restricted seemingly unrelated regression estimator is obtained from:

$$\hat{\delta}_{RSUR} = \hat{\hat{\delta}} + \hat{C}R'(R\hat{C}R')^{-1}(r - R\hat{\hat{\delta}})$$

where

$$\hat{C} = [Z'(\hat{\Sigma}^{-1} \otimes I_N)Z]^{-1} \qquad \text{and} \qquad \hat{\delta} = \hat{C}Z'(\hat{\Sigma}^{-1} \otimes I_N)y$$

Three Stage Least Squares

The first step in the 3SLS estimation procedure is to estimate the σ_{ij} from 2SLS residuals as:

$$\hat{\sigma}_{ij} = \frac{1}{\tau}\left(y_i - Z_i\hat{\delta}_{2SLS,i}\right)'\left(y_j - Z_j\hat{\delta}_{2SLS,j}\right)$$

where τ is as described above. The 3SLS estimator is given by:

$$\hat{\delta} = \left\{Z'\left[\hat{\Sigma}^{-1} \otimes X(X'X)^{-1}X'\right]Z\right\}^{-1}Z'\left[\hat{\Sigma}^{-1} \otimes X(X'X)^{-1}X'\right]y$$

and the covariance matrix of coefficients is estimated by:

$$\left[Z'\left(\hat{\Sigma}^{-1} \otimes X(X'X)^{-1}X'\right)Z\right]^{-1}$$

Iterative Estimation

When estimating a system of equations by SUR or 3SLS, the estimation may be iterated by using the **ITER=** option. In this case, the initial estimation is done to estimate $\hat{\delta}$. A new set of residuals is generated and used to estimate a new variance-covariance matrix. This matrix is then used to compute a new set of parameter estimates. The iterations proceed until the parameters converge or until the maximum number of iterations specified on the **ITER=** option is reached.

Model Diagnostics

Unless the **NOCONSTANT** option is used, a system R^2 is reported. This is computed as:

$$\tilde{R}^2 = 1 - |E'E|/|Y_*'Y_*|$$

where Y_* is an (NxM) matrix with column i containing the observations on the left hand side variable for equation i measured as deviations from the sample mean and E is an (NxM) matrix with the estimated residuals for equation i in column i. This statistic is frequently very high and should be interpreted with caution (see Berndt [1991, p. 468]).

The SHAZAM output from systems estimation includes a test of the null hypothesis that the slope coefficients are jointly zero. This is equivalent to the F-statistic used to determine whether all the slope coefficients in a multiple regression model are zero. The CHI-SQUARE statistic is calculated as:

$$\chi^2 = -N \ln(1 - \tilde{R}^2)$$

The statistic can be compared with a chi-square distribution with degrees of freedom equal to the number of slope coefficients in the system.

The Breusch-Pagan [1980] Lagrange multiplier test gives a test for a diagonal covariance matrix. With the squared correlation coefficient of residuals given by:

$$r_{ij}^2 = \frac{\hat{\sigma}_{ij}^2}{\hat{\sigma}_{ii}\hat{\sigma}_{jj}}$$

the statistic reported on SHAZAM output as BREUSCH-PAGAN LM TEST FOR DIAGONAL COVARIANCE MATRIX is computed as:

$$\lambda = N \sum_{i=2}^{M} \sum_{j=1}^{i-1} r_{ij}^2$$

Under the null hypothesis of a diagonal covariance structure the statistic has an asymptotic $\chi^2_{(M(M-1)/2)}$ distribution.

With SUR estimation the SHAZAM output reports the LIKELIHOOD RATIO TEST OF DIAGONAL COVARIANCE MATRIX as an alternative to the Breusch-Pagan Lagrange multiplier test. This statistic is computed as:

$$N \left[\sum_{i=1}^{M} \ln(\hat{\sigma}_{ii}^2) - \ln|\hat{\Sigma}| \right] \qquad \text{with} \quad \tau = N$$

The statistic has an asymptotic $\chi^2_{(M(M-1)/2)}$ distribution. For discussion see, for example, Greene [1993, p. 492].

SYSTEMS MODEL SPECIFICATION

As the setup for equation systems is quite general SHAZAM will handle many types of linear models. To set up a set of seemingly unrelated regression equations for estimation, the following commands are used:

SYSTEM *neq / options*
OLS *depvar indeps*
. . .
OLS *depvar indeps*

where *neq* is the number of equations, and *options* is a list of desired options. After the **SYSTEM** command there should be an **OLS** command for each equation in the system. Do NOT use *options* on the **OLS** commands. They must only be used with the **SYSTEM** command.

To set up a restricted SUR estimation, the following commands are used:

SYSTEM *neq / **RESTRICT** options*
OLS *depvar indeps*
. . .
OLS *depvar indeps*
RESTRICT *restriction*
. . .
RESTRICT *restriction*
END

The **RESTRICT** option on the **SYSTEM** command specifies that linear restrictions are to be imposed on the parameters in the system. The restrictions must be linear and are entered in a set of **RESTRICT** commands followed by **END**. Note that when **RESTRICT** commands are used the **RESTRICT** option on the **SYSTEM** command must be specified.

To set up a simultaneous equations system for estimation by 3SLS, the following commands are used:

SYSTEM *neq exogs / options*
OLS *depvar indeps*
. . .
OLS *depvar indeps*

where *neq* is the number of equations, *exogs* is a list of the exogenous variables and *options* is a list of desired options. **The *exogs* must ONLY be included for Three Stage**

Least Squares and not for Zellner estimation. Linear restrictions on the parameters can be imposed by specifying the **RESTRICT** option on the **SYSTEM** command and including a set of **RESTRICT** commands terminated by an **END** command. Nonlinear restrictions cannot be imposed but may be tested using **TEST** commands.

Following model estimation linear or nonlinear hypotheses may be tested with **TEST** commands. For a discussion about linear and non-linear hypothesis testing, see the chapter *HYPOTHESIS TESTING*.

Estimation of systems of equations can be rather slow, especially if there are many equations or variables in the system. Options should be carefully specified so the system does not have to be re-estimated. Imposing restrictions on the coefficients will also slow the estimation. In large models, it is possible that SHAZAM will require additional memory. For information on how to proceed in this case, see the **PAR** command discussed in the chapter *HOW TO RUN SHAZAM* and the chapter *MISCELLANEOUS COMMANDS AND INFORMATION*.

SYSTEM *Command Options*

The available options on the **SYSTEM** command are:

DN   This is a useful option and its use is strongly recommended. With this option the fact that the estimation procedure has good asymptotic properties is recognized. The covariance matrix is computed using **N** as the **D**ivisor, rather than a measure which provides a dubious degrees of freedom adjustment. The use of the **DN** option is consistent with Theil's development. Without the **DN** option, the degrees of freedom correction for the covariances is as described above.

DUMP   DUMPs a lot of intermediate output after each iteration, including the system **X'X** matrix and its inverse, and the inverse of the residual covariance matrix (SIGMA). This option is primarily of interest to SHAZAM consultants.

FULL   Lists **FULL** equation output. This output is similar to that of regular **OLS** regressions. **FULL** is automatically in effect except in TALK mode. It can be turned off with the **NOFULL** option.

LIST
RSTAT
MAX
GF
Used as on **OLS** commands to control output. They should only be used when full output is required for each equation. Users should be aware when interpreting the equation-by-equation output that some statistics printed are not valid in system estimation. If systems analysis is properly understood the questionable statistics are easily identified. Since the analysis of variance F-test is invalid it is not printed; if it is desired, **TEST** commands should be used.

NOCONEXOG
If a list of exogenous variables is included for either Two or Three Stage Least Squares SHAZAM will automatically add a *CONSTANT* to the list. If you do not want SHAZAM to automatically include a constant in the list of exogenous variables, specify the **NOCONEXOG** option.

NOCONSTANT
Normally, SHAZAM will automatically put an intercept in each equation in the system. If there are some (or all) equations in which no intercept is desired the **NOCONSTANT** option should be specified. Then, an intercept should be created by generating a variable of ones (1) with a **GENR** command and this variable should be included in each equation in which an intercept is desired. Without the **NOCONSTANT** option the intercept will only be printed in the **FULL** equation-by-equation output, and the variances of the intercepts will only be approximate unless the model converges.

PCOR
PCOV
Prints the **COR**relation and **COV**ariance matrices of all coefficients in the system after convergence. If these options are specified the matrices will also be printed for each equation in the equation-by-equation output.

PINVEV
Prints the **INV**erse of the Exogenous Variables matrix $(X'X)^{-1}$ when 3SLS estimation is being used. This option is rarely needed.

PSIGMA
Prints the residual covariance matrix (**SIGMA**) after each iteration. If this option is not used the matrix will be printed for the first and final iterations. This option can add pages of output if there are many equations in the system and, thus, should not be specified unless this information is specifically needed.

RESTRICT
Forces linear restrictions as specified with **RESTRICT** commands. The **RESTRICT** commands follow the **OLS** commands. Only linear restrictions are permitted. Users should be aware that iterative estimates may not necessarily be maximum likelihood estimates if restrictions on the intercepts of the equation are imposed.

COEF=   Saves the values of the **COEF**ficients in the variable specified. The values for all equations will be in a single vector. No values for the equation intercepts will be saved so if these are required the directions above for the **NOCONSTANT** option should be followed.

COEFMAT=   Saves the values of the **COEF**ficients in the variable specified in **MAT**rix form with each column of the matrix representing one equation. Equation intercepts will also be saved. This is useful if the coefficients for a single equation need to be specified on the **F C** command.

CONV=   Specifies a **CONV**ergence criterion to stop the iterative procedure (subject to the maximum number of iterations specified with the **ITER=** option). The criterion is the maximum desired percentage change in each of the coefficients. The default is .001.

COV=   Saves the **COV**ariance matrix in the variable specified. No values for the variances and covariances of equation intercepts will be saved so if these are required the directions above for the **NOCONSTANT** option should be followed.

ITER=   Specifies the maximum number of **ITER**ations performed if an iterative procedure is desired. If this option is not specified, one iteration is done. If **ITER=0** is specified, the system is estimated without the Generalized Least Squares procedure which uses the covariance matrix of residuals. This would be equivalent to running separate **OLS** regressions (or **2SLS**), but more expensive. **ITER=0** would be appropriate only if there were restrictions across equations or hypothesis testing across equations.

OUT=_unit_   These options are used to **OUT**put a dump of useful information on
IN= _unit_   the unit specified at each iteration, so that the system can be restarted in another run at the same point by **IN**putting the dump. This can be very useful in expensive models to avoid re-estimation of already calculated data in the event that a time limit is reached. With the **OUT=** option, the information from the most recent iteration will be written on the specified unit. **OUT=** and **IN=** are usually assigned to the same unit so the latest information replaces existing information. Units 11-49 are available and may be assigned to a file with the SHAZAM **FILE** command or an operating system command.

NOTE: It is important to remember to create a system file to be attached to the appropriate unit before using the **OUT=** option. Without this file the information will be lost. The use of **OUT=** will add slightly to the cost, but will substantially lower the cost of restarting the model. It is also important to run the same system on subsequent runs with the **IN=** option. The **IN=** option should *never* be run before there is anything to input. See the example at the end of this chapter.

PITER=   Specifies the frequency with which **ITER**ations are to be Printed. The default is **PITER=1**. If **PITER=0** is specified, no iterations are printed.

PREDICT=   Saves the **PREDICT**ed values of the dependent variable in a N x M matrix, where N is the number of observations and M is the number of equations.

RESID=   Saves the values of the estimated **RESID**uals in a N x M matrix.

SIGMA=   Saves the residual covariance matrix $\hat{\Sigma}$ in the variable specified.

The temporary variables available are:

$ERR, $N and *$SIG2*

When more than one equation is estimated the value of the temporary variable *$SIG2* is the value $\ln|\hat{\Sigma}|$. If there is only one equation, *$SIG2* will be the same as that obtained from OLS estimation.

With SUR estimation the temporary variable *$LLF* is also available.

EXAMPLES

The next list of SHAZAM commands shows the use of the **SYSTEM** command for 3SLS estimation of Klein's model I described in Theil [1971, Chapter 9.2].

```
SYSTEM 3 WG T G TIME1 PLAG KLAG XLAG / DN
OLS C PLAG P WGWP
OLS I PLAG KLAG P
OLS WP TIME1 XLAG X
TEST P:1=P:2
```

There are 3 equations in the system and the variables *WG, T, G, TIME, PLAG, DLAG* and *XLAG* are the exogenous variables. SHAZAM automatically includes a constant in the list of exogenous variables. (All identities have already been substituted.) Three **OLS** commands are included to describe the three equations in the system. The **TEST** command will test the hypothesis that the coefficient on variable *P* in equation 1 is equal to the coefficient on variable *P* in equation 2.

The SHAZAM output from the 3SLS estimation follows.

```
|_SYSTEM 3 WG T G TIME1 PLAG KLAG XLAG / DN
|_OLS C PLAG P WGWP
|_OLS I PLAG KLAG P
|_OLS WP TIME1 XLAG X
THREE STAGE LEAST SQUARES--    3 EQUATIONS
   7 EXOGENOUS VARIABLES
   9 RIGHT-HAND SIDE VARIABLES IN SYSTEM
MAX ITERATIONS = 1         CONVERGENCE TOLERANCE =   0.01000
        21 OBSERVATIONS


DN OPTION IN EFFECT - DIVISOR IS N
ITERATION  0 COEFFICIENTS
   0.21623     0.17302E-01 0.81018     0.61594    -0.15779     0.15022
   0.13040     0.14667     0.43886


ITERATION    0 SIGMA
   1.0441
   0.43785       1.3832
  -0.38523       0.19261     0.47643


BREUSCH-PAGAN LM TEST FOR DIAGONAL COVARIANCE MATRIX
    CHI-SQUARE =    10.235    WITH     3 DEGREES OF FREEDOM
LOG OF DETERMINANT OF SIGMA= -1.2458


ITERATION    1 SIGMA INVERSE
   2.1615
  -0.98292       1.2131
   2.1451       -1.2852      4.3530


ITERATION    1 COEFFICIENTS
   0.16314     0.12489     0.79008     0.75572    -0.19485    -0.013079
   0.14967     0.18129     0.40049


ITERATION    1 SIGMA
   0.89176
   0.41132       2.0930
  -0.39361       0.40305     0.52003
LOG OF DETERMINANT OF SIGMA= -1.2623


SYSTEM R-SQUARE = 0.9995 ... CHI-SQUARE = 159.41  WITH 9 D.F.

VARIABLE       COEFFICIENT    ST.ERROR      T-RATIO
PLAG           0.16314        0.10044       1.6243
P              0.12489        0.10813       1.1550
WGWP           0.79008        0.37938E-01   20.826
PLAG           0.75572        0.15293       4.9415
KLAG          -0.19485        0.32531E-01   -5.9897
P             -0.13079E-01    0.16190       -0.80787E-01
TIME1          0.14967        0.27935E-01   5.3579
XLAG           0.18129        0.34159E-01   5.3073
X              0.40049        0.31813E-01   12.589


EQUATION  1 OF  3 EQUATIONS
DEPENDENT VARIABLE = C                 21 OBSERVATIONS
  R-SQUARE =    .9801
```

```
VARIANCE OF THE ESTIMATE-SIGMA**2 =   .89176
STANDARD ERROR OF THE ESTIMATE-SIGMA =   .94433
SUM OF SQUARED ERRORS-SSE=   18.727
MEAN OF DEPENDENT VARIABLE =   53.995
```

			ASYMPTOTIC			PARTIAL	STANDARDIZED	ELASTICITY
VARIABLE	ESTIMATED	STANDARD	T-RATIO			PARTIAL	STANDARDIZED	ELASTICITY
NAME	COEFFICIENT	ERROR	***** DF	P-VALUE	CORR.	COEFFICIENT	AT	MEANS
PLAG	.16314	.1004	1.624	.104	.367	.0958	.0495	
P	.12489	.1081	1.155	.248	.270	.0768	.0391	
WGWP	.79008	.3794E-01	20.83	.000	.981	.8701	.6070	
CONSTANT	16.441	1.302	12.63	.000	.951	.0000	.3045	

```
EQUATION  2 OF  3 EQUATIONS
DEPENDENT VARIABLE = I                 21 OBSERVATIONS
 R-SQUARE =   .8258
VARIANCE OF THE ESTIMATE-SIGMA**2 =   2.0930
STANDARD ERROR OF THE ESTIMATE-SIGMA =   1.4467
SUM OF SQUARED ERRORS-SSE=   43.954
MEAN OF DEPENDENT VARIABLE =   1.2667
```

			ASYMPTOTIC			PARTIAL	STANDARDIZED	ELASTICITY
VARIABLE	ESTIMATED	STANDARD	T-RATIO			PARTIAL	STANDARDIZED	ELASTICITY
NAME	COEFFICIENT	ERROR	***** DF	P-VALUE	CORR.	COEFFICIENT	AT MEANS	
PLAG	.75572	.1529	4.942	.000	.768	.8570	9.7704	
KLAG	-.19485	.3253E-01	-5.990	.000	-.824	-.5441	-30.8417	
P	-.13079E-01	.1619	-.8079E-01	.936	-.020	-.0155	-.1744	
CONSTANT	28.178	6.796	4.146	.000	.709	.0000	22.2457	

```
EQUATION  3 OF  3 EQUATIONS
DEPENDENT VARIABLE = WP                 21 OBSERVATIONS
 R-SQUARE =   .9863
VARIANCE OF THE ESTIMATE-SIGMA**2 =   .52003
STANDARD ERROR OF THE ESTIMATE-SIGMA =   .72113
SUM OF SQUARED ERRORS-SSE=   10.921
MEAN OF DEPENDENT VARIABLE =   36.362
```

			ASYMPTOTIC			PARTIAL	STANDARDIZED	ELASTICITY
VARIABLE	ESTIMATED	STANDARD	T-RATIO			PARTIAL	STANDARDIZED	ELASTICITY
NAME	COEFFICIENT	ERROR	***** DF	P-VALUE	CORR.	COEFFICIENT	AT MEANS	
TIME1	.14967	.2794E-01	5.358	.000	.793	.1473	.0453	
XLAG	.18129	.3416E-01	5.307	.000	.790	.2565	.2891	
X	.40049	.3181E-01	12.59	.000	.950	.6745	.6615	
CONSTANT	.15080	1.016	.1484	.882	.036	.0000	.0041	

```
|_TEST P:1=P:2
 TEST VALUE=  0.13797    STD. ERROR OF TEST VALUE = 0.16036
 ASYMPTOTIC NORMAL STATISTIC =  0.86037777
 WALD CHI-SQUARE STATISTIC =  0.74024991      WITH   1 D.F.
```

Restrictions in a Systems Estimation

In this example a set of Seemingly Unrelated Regression equations is estimated. The iteration option is not requested. The model is estimated subject to the restriction that the coefficient on variable *B* in equation 1 plus the coefficient on variable *E* in equation 2 sum to zero.

```
SYSTEM 2 / RESTRICT
OLS A B C
OLS D E F
RESTRICT B:1+E:2=0
END
```

Note that SHAZAM always puts a constant term in each equation unless the **NOCONSTANT** option is specified on the **SYSTEM** command. If restrictions are required on the constant terms, you should generate your own constant by creating a variable which is always equal to 1 and then suppress the usual SHAZAM constant term with the **NOCONSTANT** option. The next example illustrates a model where two constant terms must sum to one.

```
GENR CONST=1
SYSTEM 2 / RESTRICT NOCONSTANT
OLS A B C CONST
OLS D E F CONST
RESTRICT B:1+E:2=0
RESTRICT CONST:1+CONST:2=1
END
```

Example using a restart file

If you use the **OUT=** and **IN=** options in a **SYSTEM** (or **NL**) problem, the first run would assign a file to a unit between from 11-49. Note that a decimal point is included after the unit number on the **FILE** command because a **BINARY** file is required. The general form is as follows:

FILE 17. restartfile
SAMPLE *beg end*
. . .
SYSTEM 3 / DN ITER=10 OUT=17
OLS *depvar indeps*
OLS *depvar indeps*
OLS *depvar indeps*
. . .
STOP

In the next run, to restart where you left off, you should add the **IN=** option. The **SYSTEM** command might read as follows:

SYSTEM 3 / DN ITER=20 OUT=17 IN=17

In this case, the model will continue at the point it left off in the first run and update the file assigned to unit 17 until iteration 20 is reached. Do not attempt to use the **IN=** option before you have anything to **IN**put.

29. LINEAR PROGRAMMING

"Programming, both linear and nonlinear, is entirely a mathematical technique. Its economic content is therefore nil."
William J. Baumol
Professor of Economics, 1977

The **LP** command is available to compute the solution to a linear programming problem. For discussion of linear programming methods see, for example, Baumol [1977]. The purpose is to solve for the vector x and the shadow values of the constraints for the problem:

Maximize $c'x$

subject to: $Ax \leq b$

$x \geq 0$

where A is a M x N matrix, b is a M x 1 vector and c is a N x 1 vector of coefficients in the objective function. The solution algorithm is a contracted simplex algorithm based on a program written by David Ryan. Note that the second set of constraints ($x \geq 0$) is automatically imposed and does not need to be specified.

SHAZAM expects the first set of constraints ($Ax \leq b$) to be in the form of less than or equal to ($\leq$) inequalities. However, inequalities of the form $Ax \geq b$ can be used if the signs of the elements in the A matrix and b vector are all reversed as shown in the second example below. If an exact equality constraint is required it should be specified as two inequality constraints using both $\leq$ and $\geq$ notation. If the problem is set up as a minimization rather than a maximization problem, the **MIN** option should be specified.

LP COMMAND OPTIONS

In general, the format of the **LP** command is:

LP *c A b / options*

where *c*, *A* and *b* are the vectors and matrices defined above. The available options are:

DUMP   Prints information for SHAZAM consultants.

MIN   Indicates that the problem is a **MIN**imization problem.

DSLACK=   Saves the dual slack variables in the vector specified.

DUAL=   Saves the dual solution in the vector specified.

ITER=   Specifies the maximum number of iterations. The default is 15.

PRIMAL=   Saves the primal solution in the vector specified.

PSLACK=   Saves the primal slack variables in the vector specified.

EXAMPLES

Consider the following linear programming problem:

$$\text{Maximize} \quad x_1 + 3\,x_2$$

$$\text{subject to:} \quad x_1 \leq 300$$

$$x_2 \leq 100$$

$$.1\,x_1 + .2\,x_2 \leq 40$$

$$x_1, x_2 \geq 0$$

The SHAZAM commands to input the coefficients and solve the the maximization problem are:

```
READ C / ROWS=2 COLS=1
 1
 3
READ A / ROWS=3 COLS=2
 1   0
 0   1
.1  .2
READ B / ROWS=3 COLS=1
300
100
 40
LP  C  A  B
```

The output follows.

```
|_READ C / ROWS=2 COLS=1
    1 VARIABLES AND          2 OBSERVATIONS STARTING AT OBS        1
...SAMPLE RANGE IS NOW SET TO:          1        2
|_READ A / ROWS=3 COLS=2
    3 ROWS AND               2 COLUMNS, BEGINNING AT ROW          1
|_READ B / ROWS=3 COLS=1
    1 VARIABLES AND          3 OBSERVATIONS STARTING AT OBS        1

|_LP C A B
NUMBER OF VARIABLES=    2 NUMBER OF CONSTRAINTS=     3
COEFFICIENTS ON VARIABLES IN OBJECTIVE FUNCTION
    1.0000        3.0000
CONSTRAINT COEFFICIENTS AND CONSTRAINT VALUES
    1.0000       0.00000E+00    300.00
  0.00000E+00    1.0000         100.00
  0.10000        0.20000        40.000

MAXIMIZED VALUE OF OBJECTIVE FUNCTION IS      500.0
PRIMAL SOLUTION
  200.00        100.00
SLACK VARIABLES
  100.00        0.00000E+00   0.00000E+00
DUAL SOLUTION
  0.00000E+00    1.0000         10.000
DUAL SLACK VARIABLES
  0.00000E+00   0.00000E+00
```

The dual linear programming problem with variables $\lambda_1, \lambda_2, \ldots$, can be constructed from the primal problem. For example, the dual solution to the above problem can be obtained as the primal solution to the following minimization problem:

Minimize $300\,\lambda_1 + 100\,\lambda_2 + 40\,\lambda_3$

subject to: $\lambda_1 + .1\,\lambda_3 \geq 1$

$\lambda_2 + .2\,\lambda_3 \geq 3$

$\lambda_1, \lambda_2, \lambda_3 \geq 0$

Since the constraints are of the form $\geq$ rather than $\leq$ it is necessary to reverse the signs of the coefficients in the A matrix and b vector. The SHAZAM commands for solving this problem are:

```
READ C / ROWS=3 COLS=1
300
100
 40
READ A / ROWS=2 COLS=3
-1  0 -.1
 0 -1 -.2
```

```
READ B / ROWS=2 COLS=1
-1
-3
LP C A B / MIN
STOP
```

The output follows.

```
|_READ C / ROWS=3 COLS=1
    1 VARIABLES AND         3 OBSERVATIONS STARTING AT OBS        1
...SAMPLE RANGE IS NOW SET TO:           1         3
|_READ A / ROWS=2 COLS=3
    2 ROWS AND              3 COLUMNS, BEGINNING AT ROW           1
|_READ B / ROWS=2 COLS=1
    1 VARIABLES AND         2 OBSERVATIONS STARTING AT OBS        1

|_LP  C  A  B  / MIN
NUMBER OF VARIABLES=    3 NUMBER OF CONSTRAINTS=     2
COEFFICIENTS ON VARIABLES IN OBJECTIVE FUNCTION
  300.00      100.00      40.000
CONSTRAINT COEFFICIENTS AND CONSTRAINT VALUES
  -1.0000      0.00000E+00 -0.10000      -1.0000
  0.00000E+00  -1.0000     -0.20000      -3.0000
MINIMIZATION  PROBLEM

MINIMIZED VALUE OF OBJECTIVE FUNCTION IS      500.0
PRIMAL SOLUTION
 0.00000E+00   1.0000       10.000
SLACK VARIABLES
 0.00000E+00  0.00000E+00
DUAL SOLUTION
  200.00       100.00
DUAL SLACK VARIABLES
  100.00       0.00000E+00  0.00000E+00
|_STOP
```

30. MATRIX MANIPULATION

"I am tired of all this thing called science...We have spent millions in that
sort of thing for the last few years, and it is time it should be stopped."
Simon Cameron
U.S. Senator from Pennsylvania, 1861

The **MATRIX** and **COPY** commands can be used to create and manipulate matrices in
SHAZAM. The **MATRIX** command will do matrix operations and create and transform
matrices instead of vectors. It is similar to the **GENR** command except matrices are
used. In contrast to the **GENR** command the **MATRIX** command ignores the current
SAMPLE command. Also, **SKIPIF** commands have no effect on the **MATRIX**
command.

THE MATRIX COMMAND

In general, the format of the **MATRIX** command is:

MATRIX *mat = equation*

where *mat* is the name of the matrix to be generated from an *equation*.

The following operators are valid on the **MATRIX** command:

–	Negation
*	Matrix Multiplication
+	Addition
–	Subtraction
'	Transpose
/	Hadamard Division
@	Kronecker Multiplication
|	Concatenation

Regular matrix rules apply on the **MATRIX** command. So, when multiplying with *
the first matrix to be multiplied must have the same number of columns as the second
matrix has rows. Addition (+), and subtraction (–), of matrices are done element by
element, so only matrices with the same dimensions may be added to and subtracted
from one another. Concatenation puts two matrices together side by side so both must
have the same number of rows. Kronecker multiplication can be done with matrices of

any dimension. The following examples illustrate concatenation and stacking matrices. The final example shows that the Kronecker product of a 3 x 3 matrix B and a 2 x 2 matrix A results in a 6 x 6 matrix K.

```
|_READ A / ROWS=3 COLS=3 LIST
      3 ROWS AND            3 COLUMNS, BEGINNING AT ROW         1
   ...SAMPLE RANGE IS NOW SET TO:        1           3
      A
    3 BY      3 MATRIX
    1.000000        19.00000       -2.000000
    354.0000        0.0             28.00000
   -3.000000        15.00000        7.000000
|_READ B / ROWS=2 COLS=2 LIST
      2 ROWS AND            2 COLUMNS, BEGINNING AT ROW         1
     B
    2 BY      2 MATRIX
   78.00000         592.0000
   4.000000        -65.00000
|_READ C / ROWS=3 COLS=2 LIST
      3 ROWS AND            2 COLUMNS, BEGINNING AT ROW         1
     C
    3 BY      2 MATRIX
   16.00000         44.00000
   -3.000000        13.00000
   0.0              23.00000
|_* CONCATENATE A AND C SIDE BY SIDE
|_MATRIX AC=A|C
|_PRINT AC
     AC
    3 BY      5 MATRIX
    1.000000   19.00000    -2.000000    16.00000    44.00000
    354.0000   0.0          28.00000    -3.000000   13.00000
   -3.000000   15.00000     7.000000    0.0         23.00000
|_* STACK B AND C WITH B ON TOP
|_MATRIX BC=(B'|C')'
|_PRINT BC
     BC
    5 BY      2 MATRIX
   78.00000         592.0000
   4.000000        -65.00000
   16.00000         44.00000
   -3.000000        13.00000
   0.0              23.00000
|_* GET KRONECKER PRODUCT OF A AND B
|_MATRIX K=A@B
|_PRINT K
     K
    6 BY      6 MATRIX
   78.00000    592.0000    1482.000    11248.00    -156.0000    -1184.000
   4.000000   -65.00000    76.00000    -1235.000   -8.000000     130.0000
   27612.00    209568.0    0.0         0.0          2184.000     16576.00
   1416.000   -23010.00    0.0         0.0          112.0000     -1820.000
   -234.0000  -1776.000    1170.000    8880.000     546.0000      4144.000
   -12.00000   195.0000    60.00000    -975.0000    28.00000     -455.0000
```

Of course, any matrix can be multiplied by a constant.

The following functions are also available with the **MATRIX** command:

CHOL(*matrix*)   Cholesky's decomposition of *matrix* is performed. The *matrix* must be symmetric positive definite. For a symmetric positive definite matrix A, **CHOL(A)** returns a lower triangular matrix L such that $LL'=A$.

DET(*matrix*)   Determinant of *matrix*.

DIAG(*matrix*)   If *matrix* is N x N the DIAG function will create an N x 1 vector that consists of the diagonal elements of *matrix*. If *matrix* is an N x 1 vector the DIAG function will create an N x N matrix with zeros off the diagonal and the vector along the diagonal.

EIGVAL(*matrix*)   The eigenvalues of *matrix* are computed and sorted in descending order (that is, the largest eigenvalue is first).

EIGVEC(*matrix*)   The eigenvectors of *matrix* are computed.

EXP(*matrix*)   The exponential operator is applied to each element of *matrix*.

FACT(*matrix*)   If the *matrix* A is symmetric positive definite, then **FACT(A)** factors the inverse of the matrix and returns a lower triangular matrix P such that $P'P=A^{-1}$.

IDEN(*ndim*)   An identity matrix with *ndim* rows and columns is created.

IDEN(*ndim,ndiag*)   A matrix with *ndim* rows and columns is created with a diagonal of ones on the *ndiag* lower diagonal (*ndiag*=1 gives an identity matrix).

INT(*matrix*)   Integer truncation of each element of *matrix* is performed.

INV(*matrix*)   Inverse of *matrix*.

LAG(*matrix,n*)   Each column of *matrix* is lagged *n* times.

LOG(*matrix*)   The natural log of each element of *matrix* is taken.

NCDF(*matrix*)   Normal cumulative distribution function. The probability of each element of *matrix* is taken.

NOR(*nrow,ncol*)   Generates a matrix of random numbers from a standard normal distribution. The number of rows and columns is specified by *nrow,ncol*.

RANK(*matrix*)   The rank, or the number of independent rows, of *matrix* is calculated. Calculation of the rank of a matrix is often numerically difficult especially in the case of a near singular matrix, therefore the value returned by the RANK function should be used with caution.

SAMP(*matrix,nrows*)   A new matrix with *nrows* is created from the old *matrix* by random sampling with replacement.

SEAS(*nob,nseas*)	A series of seasonal dummy variables is created. The number of observations and the number of seasons are specified by *nob* and *nseas*.
SIN(*matrix*)	The sine of each element of *matrix* is computed.
SQRT(*matrix*)	The square root of each element of *matrix* is computed.
SVD(*matrix*)	The Singular Value Decomposition of *matrix* is performed. The singular values are returned.
SYM(*matrix*)	Creates a symmetric matrix using the lower triangle from a square full *matrix*.
TIME(*nob,x*)	A vector with *nob* observations is created with values equal to a time index plus *x*.
TRACE(*matrix*)	The trace, or the sum of the diagonal elements, of *matrix* is calculated.
TRI(*matrix*)	Creates a lower triangular matrix from a square full *matrix*.
UNI(*nrow,ncol*)	A matrix of random numbers between 0 and 1 is created. The number of rows and columns is specified by *nrow,ncol*.
VEC(*matrix*)	Stacks columns of *matrix* into a long vector.
VEC(*vector,nrows*)	Unstacks *vector* into a matrix with *nrows*.

Following a **MATRIX** command the dimension of the matrix is saved in the temporary variables *$ROWS* and *$COLS*.

Although it is not a common matrix operation, SHAZAM can do multiplication and division element-by-element. These are often called Hadamard product and division (see Rao [1973, p. 30]). For example, Hadamard division is done as follows:

```
MATRIX M=A/B
```

In the above example each element in the matrix *A* is divided by each element of the matrix *B* and the results of this operation are put in the matrix *M*. Of course, *A* and *B* must have the same dimensions unless either *A* or *B* is a constant.

It is also possible to perform Hadamard products or element-by-element multiplication. This is done in the following way:

```
MATRIX M=A/(1/B)
```

Again, *A* and *B* must have the same dimensions.

If multiplying an N x 1 vector by a matrix with N rows and any number of columns, SHAZAM will do element-by-element multiplication of the N x 1 vector times each column of the matrix so that the result will have the same number of columns as the original matrix.

The example below shows how to extract pieces of a matrix.

```
|_SAMPLE 1 5
|_READ X / ROWS=5 COLS=3 LIST
                    5 ROWS AND          3 COLUMNS, BEGINNING AT ROW       1
             X
         5 BY       3 MATRIX
      1.000000    3.000000    5.000000
      1.000000    1.000000    4.000000
      1.000000    5.000000    6.000000
      1.000000    2.000000    4.000000
      1.000000    4.000000    6.000000

|_* SHOW HOW TO PICK OUT ELEMENTS, AND ROWS, OR COLUMNS OF A MATRIX
|_* CHANGE ROW 3 COLUMN 2 TO A 7
|_MATRIX X(3,2)=7
|_* GET THE SECOND COLUMN OF X
|_MATRIX XTWO=X(0,2)
|_PRINT XTWO / NOBYVAR
                    XTWO
      3.000000
      1.000000
      7.000000
      2.000000
      4.000000
|_* GET THE FOURTH ROW OF X
|_MATRIX XFOUR=X(4,0)
|_PRINT XFOUR
            XFOUR
            1 BY       3 MATRIX
      1.000000    2.000000    4.000000
|_* GET ELEMENT (4,2) OF X
|_MATRIX X42=X(4,2)
|_PRINT X42
            X42
      2.000000
```

Note that when referring to an element of a matrix there must be no embedded blanks between the variable name and the left bracket. As well, for left-hand side variables there must be no embedded blanks between the brackets.

The next example shows how to extract the upper block of a symmetric matrix.

```
* Run OLS and save the estimated covariance matrix in the symmetric matrix BVAR.
OLS Y X1 X2 X3 X4 X5 / COV=BVAR
PRINT BVAR
* Extract the 3 x 3 upper block
MATRIX BUP=BVAR(1;3,1;3)
* Print the result
PRINT BUP
```

The next example shows the use of the **MATRIX** command to calculate the vector of OLS parameter estimates in one step. The example uses the same X matrix that was used above. The matrix calculation uses the ubiquitous formula $\hat{\beta} = (X'X)^{-1}X'Y$. When the transpose operator (') is used it is not necessary to use the multiplication operator (*) if multiplication between the transposed matrix and the following matrix is desired. However, without the transpose operator the multiplication operator is required. The example also shows the calculation of an F-test using matrices. This formula is given in the chapter *HYPOTHESIS TESTING AND CONFIDENCE INTERVALS*.

```
|_SAMPLE 1 5
|_READ Y / BYVAR LIST
   1 VARIABLES AND        5 OBSERVATIONS STARTING AT OBS       1
   Y
   3.000000        1.000000        8.000000        3.000000        5.000000
|_READ X / ROWS=5 COLS=3
      5 ROWS AND         3 COLUMNS, BEGINNING AT ROW      1
|_MATRIX B=INV(X'X)*X'Y
|_PRINT B
   B
   4.000000        2.500000       -1.500000
|_MATRIX EE=Y'Y-(B'(X'Y))
|_PRINT EE
   EE
   1.500000
|_READ R / ROWS=1 COLS=3 LIST
      1 ROWS AND         3 COLUMNS, BEGINNING AT ROW      1
   R
   1 BY      3 MATRIX
   .0000000        1.000000        1.000000
|_READ LR / ROWS=1 COLS=1 LIST
   1 VARIABLES AND        1 OBSERVATIONS STARTING AT OBS       1
      LR
   .0000000
|_MATRIX F=((R*B-LR)'(INV(R*(INV(X'X)*R')))*(R*B-LR))/(EE/2)
|_PRINT F
   F
   2.666667
```

It is apparent from the above SHAZAM output that many calculations can be done on one **MATRIX** command. See the chapter *PROGRAMMING IN SHAZAM* for more examples of the **MATRIX** command.

THE COPY COMMAND

The **COPY** command is used to copy vectors or matrices into other matrices. It is also possible to partition matrices, delete rows and columns, and create matrices from vectors by using the **COPY** command. The format of the **COPY** command is:

COPY *fromvar(s) tovar / options*

where *fromvar(s)* is either a list of vectors or a single matrix, *tovar* is the variable into which the *fromvar(s)* are to be copied and *options* is a list of desired options. The available options on the **COPY** command are:

FROW=*beg;end* Specifies the rows of the *fromvar(s)* that are to be copied into the *tovar*. If this option is not specified the current **SAMPLE** command will be used.

FCOL=*beg;end* Specifies the columns of the *fromvar* that are to be copied into the new variable. If the old variables are a list of vectors the **FCOL**= option need not be used as SHAZAM will automatically treat each vector as a column. Therefore, this option is only used if the old variable is a matrix.

TROW=*beg;end* Specifies the rows of the *tovar* into which the *fromvar(s)* are to be copied. If this option is not specified the current **SAMPLE** command will be used.

TCOL=*beg;end* Specifies the columns of the *tovar* into which the old variables are to be copied.

If no options are specified on the **COPY** command all the *fromvar(s)* will be copied into the *tovar*. It is impossible to copy from vectors and a matrix simultaneously. It is very important to specify consistent options on the **COPY** command, that is, the dimensions specified with the **COPY** options must be compatible with the dimensions of the *fromvar(s)* and *tovar*. It is also important to remember to use a semicolon (;) only to separate *beg* and *end* and no more than 8 characters are allowed.

If **SKIPIF** commands or the expanded form of the **SAMPLE** have been used the *tovar* matrix will be reduced in size. This is useful in deleting rows of a matrix to create a new matrix. For example, if A is a 15 by 5 matrix, the following commands will create a new matrix B which is 4 by 12 because rows 4, 10, 11 and column 3 of A have been deleted:

```
|_PRINT A
   A
   15 BY      5 MATRIX
   40.05292       1170.600      97.80000       2.528130      191.5000
   54.64859       2015.800     104.4000       24.91888      516.0000
   40.31206       2803.300     118.0000       29.34270      729.0000
   84.21099       2039.700     156.2000       27.61823      560.4000
   127.5724       2256.200     172.6000       60.35945      519.9000
   124.8797       2132.200     186.6000       50.61588      628.5000
   96.55514       1834.100     220.9000       30.70955      537.1000
   131.1601       1588.000     287.8000       60.69605      561.2000
   77.02764       1749.400     319.9000       30.00972      617.2000
   46.96689       1687.200     321.3000       42.50750      626.7000
   100.6597       2007.700     319.6000       58.61146      737.2000
   115.7467       2208.300     346.0000       46.96287      760.5000
```

```
   114.5826        1656.700        456.4000        57.87651        581.4000
   119.8762        1604.400        543.4000        43.22093        662.3000
   105.5699        1431.800        618.3000        22.87143        583.8000
|_SAMPLE 1 3 5 9 12 15
|_COPY A:1 A:2 A:4 A:5 B
...NOTE..SOME OBSERVATIONS MAY BE SKIPPED
|_PRINT B
   B
   12 BY     4 MATRIX
   40.05292        1170.600        2.528130        191.5000
   54.64859        2015.800        24.91888        516.0000
   40.31206        2803.300        29.34270        729.0000
   127.5724        2256.200        60.35945        519.9000
   124.8797        2132.200        50.61588        628.5000
   96.55514        1834.100        30.70955        537.1000
   131.1601        1588.000        60.69605        561.2000
   77.02764        1749.400        30.00972        617.2000
   115.7467        2208.300        46.96287        760.5000
   114.5826        1656.700        57.87651        581.4000
   119.8762        1604.400        43.22093        662.3000
   105.5699        1431.800        22.87143        583.8000
```

31. PRICE INDEXES

"When the U.S. government stops wasting our resources by trying to maintain the price of gold, its price will sink to...$6 an ounce rather than the current $35 an ounce."

Henry Reuss
U.S. Senator from Wisconsin, 1967

The **INDEX** command computes price indexes from a set of price and quantity data on a number of commodities. To calculate an index, it is necessary to have prices and quantities for at least two commodities. Let p_{it} and q_{it} be the price and quantity for variable i in period t for i=1,2,...,K and t=1,2,...,N. The period t price and quantity vectors that are to be aggregated into scalars are given by:

$$q_t' = (q_{1t}, q_{2t}, \ldots, q_{Kt}) \quad \text{and} \quad p_t' = (p_{1t}, p_{2t}, \ldots, p_{Kt})$$

Weighted Aggregate Price Indexes

Let p_{i0} and q_{i0} be the price and quantity for variable i in the base period. Alternative price index calculations are:

Laspeyres index	$L_t = (p_t' q_0) / (p_0' q_0)$
Paasche index	$P_t = (p_t' q_t) / (p_0' q_t)$
Fisher index	$F_t = \sqrt{L_t P_t}$

Chained Price Indexes

Chained price indexes are computed when the **CHAIN** option is specified on the **INDEX** command. The level of prices in period t relative to period t−1, for t=2,3,...,N, for the alternative price index formulas are:

Laspeyres index	$L_t = (p_t' q_{t-1}) / (p_{t-1}' q_{t-1})$
Paasche index	$P_t = (p_t' q_t) / (p_{t-1}' q_t)$
Fisher index	$F_t = \sqrt{L_t P_t}$

Discrete approx. to the
Divisia (Törnqvist or
Translog)

$$D_t = \exp\left[.5\sum_{i=1}^{K}(s_{it} + s_{i,t-1})\log(p_{it} / p_{i,t-1})\right]$$

where $s_{it} = (p_{it}q_{it}) / (p_t'q_t)$

These are chain links that are used in constructing the final price index series. For example, for a base period at observation 1, the Laspeyres price index series computed with the **CHAIN** option is:

$$1,\ L_2,\ L_2L_3,\ldots,\ \prod_{t=2}^{N}L_t.$$

For the Paasche, Fisher or Divisia price indexes, the L_t are replaced by P_t, F_t or D_t respectively. If this new price series is denoted by R, then the corresponding quantity series, Q, is computed as:

$$Q_t = (p_t'q_t) / R_t$$

These index number formulas are explained more fully in Diewert [1978].

INDEX *COMMAND OPTIONS*

In general, the format of the **INDEX** command is:

INDEX p_1 q_1 p_2 q_2 p_3 q_3 ... / *options*

where the *p* and *q* are names of the variables for the prices and quantities of the commodities.

As well as the **BEG=** and **END=** options as defined for **OLS**, the following options are available on the **INDEX** command:

CHAIN   CHAINs the Laspeyres, Paasche or Fisher indexes using the method described above. The Divisia index is always chained.

EXPEND   Indicates that the quantity variables measure **EXPEND**itures rather than quantities. SHAZAM will first divide each **EXPEND**iture variable by its respective price to get the quantities.

NOALTERN   Normally, variables are listed as described above, with p and q
                    alternating in the list. Sometimes, it is more convenient to list all the
                    prices followed by all the quantities. This would be the case if the
                    prices were in one matrix and the quantities in another matrix. In
                    this case, **NOALTERN** should be specified. The default is **ALTERN**.

NOLIST   With this option the price and quantity indexes are not printed.

BASE=   Specifies the observation number to be used as the **BASE** period for
                    the index. The value of the index in the base period will be 1.0. If the
                    BASE= option is not specified SHAZAM will use the first available
                    observation as the base period. Use of **SKIPIF** commands is not
                    recommended when computing Divisia indexes since the index
                    needs to be chained.

DIVISIA=   These options specify the variable where the index will be stored for
PAASCHE=   this SHAZAM run. Note that the options beginning with the letter
LASPEYRES=   **Q**, (**QDIVISIA=**, **QPAASCHE=**, etc.) tell SHAZAM to store the
FISHER=   *quantity* in the variable specified. Those options not preceded by **Q**
QDIVISIA=   tell SHAZAM to store the *price index* in the variable specified. The
QPAASCHE=   quantity is computed residually in this option, i.e. according to the
QLASPEYRES=   method described above. To compute quantity indexes and prices
QFISHER=   residually, interchange the role of prices and quantities in the **INDEX**
                    command.

EXAMPLES

An example of the **INDEX** command is:

```
INDEX PFOOD FOOD PCLOTHES CLOTHES PHOUSE HOUSE / EXPEND BASE=23
```

In this example the quantity data is in expenditure form and observation 23 is to be
used as the base year.

A problem arises if there is a zero price or quantity in any year. SHAZAM handles this
problem by ignoring any commodity whenever a zero price or quantity would have to
be used in a calculation. The remaining quantities are then assumed to exhaust the set
for that year. A good reference for treatment of zero price and quantities is Diewert
[1980].

Some users may wish to compute quantity indexes directly. To do this, reverse the p
and q variables on the **INDEX** command.

The following is an example of the SHAZAM output obtained from the **INDEX** command using data for price and quantity of cars for various corporations found in Newbold [1984, Chapter 16]:

```
|_INDEX P1 Q1 P2 Q2 P3 Q3 P4 Q4 / QDIVISIA=QD PAASCHE=PA

BASE PERIOD IS OBSERVATION       1
PAASCHE  WILL BE STORED AS VARIABLE: PA
QDIVISIA WILL BE STORED AS VARIABLE: QD
                      PRICE INDEX                    QUANTITY
   DIVISIA PAASCHE LASPEYRES FISHER  DIVISIA  PAASCHE  LASPEYRES  FISHER
 1  1.000   1.000   1.000   1.000    1509.    1509.    1509.     1509.
 2  0.994   0.998   0.989   0.994    816.0    812.8    819.8     816.3
 3  0.979   0.977   0.980   0.978    733.3    735.4    732.9     734.1
 4  0.999   0.997   0.999   0.998    747.9    749.4    748.1     748.7
 5  1.045   1.044   1.045   1.044    1133.    1135.    1134.     1134.
 6  1.048   1.044   1.043   1.044    930.6    933.4    934.3     933.9
 7  1.029   1.025   1.025   1.025    637.5    639.9    639.6     639.8
 8  1.075   1.077   1.069   1.073    1213.    1211.    1219.     1215.
 9  1.110   1.106   1.106   1.106    923.6    926.6    926.9     926.8
10  1.109   1.104   1.101   1.102    1210.    1215.    1218.     1217.
11  1.198   1.195   1.188   1.191    1540.    1544.    1553.     1548.
12  1.153   1.148   1.148   1.148    1178.    1184.    1184.     1184.
|_PRINT QD PA
       QD              PA
   1509.375        1.000000
   816.0446        0.9979699
   733.3490        0.9765596
   747.8928        0.9969307
   1133.374        1.043727
   930.5681        1.044271
   637.4855        1.024789
   1212.867        1.076632
   923.5981        1.106354
   1210.000        1.103586
   1540.261        1.194918
   1178.282        1.147695
```

As the above example shows, all the price indexes and quantities are computed and printed. Note that the Divisia price index is computed as a chained price index but the other price indexes are computed using the weighted aggregate price index method. The Divisia quantity and the Paasche price index are saved. The **BASE=** option is not specified, so the base period is the first period.

32. PRINCIPAL COMPONENTS AND FACTOR ANALYSIS

"That's an amazing invention, but who would ever want to use one of them?"

Rutherford B. Hayes
U.S. President, 1876
(after seeing the telephone)

The **PC** command is available to extract principal components from a set of data and, as an option, do a varimax rotation for factor analysis. A good reference on principal components is Jolliffe [1986]. Output may include the eigenvalues, eigenvectors, components, factor matrix, and rotated factor matrix. It is possible to specify conditions under which factors are retained. Multicollinearity diagnostics including condition numbers, condition indexes, and variance proportions may also be printed. These diagnostics are discussed in Belsley, Kuh and Welsch [1980]; Judge, Griffiths, Hill, Lütkepohl, and Lee [1985, Chapter 22.3] and Judge, Hill, Griffiths, Lütkepohl and Lee [1988, pp. 872-4].

Consider a data set in the (N x K) matrix X. The principal components analysis is based on a matrix C that can be set as one of the following:

PC option	C =
default	matrix of cross-products of deviations about the mean
COR	the correlation matrix
RAW	the cross-product matrix $(X'X)$
SCALE	the matrix $(S'S)$ where $S_{kt} = X_{kt} / \left[\sum_{t=1}^{N} X_{kt}^2 \right]^{1/2}$

The (N x 1) vectors of principal components are obtained as:

$$Z_k = X \cdot a_k \qquad \text{for } k=1, \dots, K$$

where a_k is a (K x 1) eigenvector of C. The corresponding eigenvalue is λ_k. The eigenvalues are arranged in descending order. The variance of the principal component Z_k is $\lambda_k / (N-1)$. The principal components can be normalized four different ways with the use of the **NC=** option on the **PC** command.

The value:
$$\lambda_1 / \sum_{i=1}^{K} \lambda_i$$

gives the proportionate contribution of the first principal component to the total variation in the X variables. The cumulative percentage of eigenvalues is:

$$\sum_{i=1}^{k} \lambda_i \Big/ \sum_{i=1}^{K} \lambda_i \qquad \text{for } k=1,\ldots,K$$

The variance reduction benchmark function (see Judge et al. [1985, p. 912]) is:

$$100 \sum_{i=k}^{K} \left(\frac{1}{\lambda_i}\right) \Big/ \sum_{i=1}^{K} \left(\frac{1}{\lambda_i}\right) \qquad \text{for } k=1,\ldots,K$$

An inspection of the eigenvectors and eigenvalues can aid in the detection of multicollinearity. The condition numbers are λ_1 / λ_k and the condition indexes are $\sqrt{\lambda_1 / \lambda_k}$. Belsley, Kuh and Welsch [1980] suggest that condition indexes around 5 or 10 reveal weak dependencies and condition indexes around 30 to 100 demonstrate strong linear dependencies. The finding of several large condition indexes indicates more than one near exact dependency. The **PCOLLIN** option reports a table of variance-decomposition proportions. The values in the table are computed as:

$$\phi_{kj} = \frac{a_{jk}^2 / \lambda_k}{\sum_{i=1}^{K} a_{ki}^2 / \lambda_i} \qquad \text{for } k,j=1,\ldots,K$$

The columns in the variance proportions table sum to one. Multicollinearity is indicated if a *row* that is associated with an eigenvalue that has a high condition index contains two or more values of ϕ_{kj} that are greater than the rule of thumb value of 0.50. This diagnostic procedure is discussed in Belsley et al. [1980, p. 112].

The model for factor analysis has the form:

$$X_k = \Lambda f_k + \varepsilon_k \qquad \text{for } k=1,\ldots,K$$

where Λ is an (N x M) factor loading matrix and the f_k are (M x 1) vectors of factors. The ε_k is a zero mean error vector. As an estimate, the columns of Λ are constructed from the first M principal components as $Z_j / \sqrt{\lambda_j}$ for j=1, . . . , M. The factors f_k are then computed from OLS estimation and are listed with the **PFM** option on the **PC** command.

PC COMMAND OPTIONS

In general, the format of the **PC** command is:

PC *vars / options*

where *vars* is a list of the variables desired in the analysis, and *options* is a list of desired options. The available options are:

COR   Specifies that the analysis is to be done on the **COR**relation matrix. If this option is not specified, the analysis is done on the deviations from the means cross-product matrix. Since the components are sensitive to transformations, it is important that the user be sure this option is needed. If all the variables are measured in the same units, it is probably better to use the cross-product matrix. This is often the case for economists. If the variables are all measured differently, it may be more appropriate to use the correlation matrix which, in effect, normalizes all variables. See also the **SCALE** option.

LIST   **LIST**s the matrix of principal components. If there are many observations the list of all the components will be very long.

MAX   Sets the **PEVEC, PFM,** and **PRM** options.

PCOLLIN   Prints the table of variance-decomposition proportions that can be used for the detection of multi**COLLIN**earity.

PEVEC   Prints all the Eigen**VEC**tors for the retained components. If there are many variables this option could yield a lot of costly output which may have little value.

PFM   Prints the Factor Matrix for the retained factors.

PRM   Computes and Prints the Rotated factor Matrix by a varimax rotation. The method is described in Kaiser [1959]. The varimax rotation is one of the most common types of rotation.

RAW   Specifies that the analysis is to be done on the **RAW** cross-product matrix. If this option is not specified, the analysis is done on the deviations from the means cross-product matrix. The same warnings specified for the **COR** option apply here.

SCALE   Specifies that the analysis is to be done on a scaled cross-product matrix. The scaled matrix transforms a **RAW** cross-product matrix into one where the data vectors all have unit length so that the diagonals of the cross-product matrix are all equal to 1. Note that this is *not* the same as the **COR** option. If the **SCALE** option is not specified, the analysis is done on the deviations from the means cross-product matrix. The same warnings specified for the **COR** option apply here.

BEG=, END= Specifies the **BEG**inning and **END**ing observations to be used in the analysis. This option overrides the **SAMPLE** command and defaults to the sample range in effect.

EVAL= Saves the Eigen**VAL**ues in the vector specified.

EVEC= Saves the Eigen**VEC**tors in the matrix specified.

MAXFACT= Specifies the **MAX**imum number of **FACT**ors to be retained. If no value of **MINEIG** is specified **MAXFACT** will be the actual number retained. If **MAXFACT** is not specified, all will be included.

MINEIG= Specifies the **MIN**imum **EIG**envalue allowed to be retained. If the **COR** option is specified, the eigenvalues will range from 0 to the number of variables in the analysis. Sometimes a convenient value is **MINEIG=1**. This rule of thumb does not work if the analysis is done on the cross-product matrix. The default is **MINEIG=0**.

NC= Specifies the Normalization Code. The default is **NC=1**. There does not appear to be much agreement in other computer programs on how the components should be normalized, so SHAZAM offers the options:

NC=	Method	Variance of principal component
1	No normalization	$\lambda_k / (N-1)$
2	Theil's method	$1 / (N-1)$
3	BMDP method	λ_k
4	standard normal	1

PCINFO= Saves a matrix of **INFO**rmation needed for regressions on Principal Components.

PCOMP= Saves the matrix of Principal **COMP**onents in the matrix specified.

PRINCIPAL COMPONENTS REGRESSION

A consequence of multicollinearity is that the OLS estimators may have large standard errors. A solution is to consider a restricted least squares estimator. One approach is to use principal components analysis to reduce the dimensionality of the data set. A set of principal components is generated and a sub-set is selected to include as regressors in an OLS regression. The estimators are then transformed to obtain estimators for the coefficients of the original model. The resulting estimator has an interpretation as a restricted least squares estimator and therefore has smaller sampling variance compared to the unrestricted OLS estimator. Discussion with further references is available in Judge, Griffiths, Hill, Lütkepohl, and Lee [1985, Chapter 22.5]; Mundlak [1981]; Jolliffe [1986, Chapter 8] and Maddala [1992, Chapter 7.6].

The general command format for principal components regression is:

PC *vars* / **PCOMP=***pc* **PCINFO=***info options*
OLS *depvar indeps* / **PCOMP=***pc* **PCINFO=***info options*

Note that the **PCOMP=** and the **PCINFO=** options are used in both the **PC** and the **OLS** commands. In the **PC** command, they are used to store the information for later use in the **OLS** command. On the **OLS** command *indeps* is a list of variables that must contain a sub-set of the principal components saved in the matrix *pc*.

The next example illustrates principal components regression using the data set described in Judge, Griffiths, Hill, Lütkepohl, and Lee [1985, p. 930]. First, the **PC** command is used to obtain principal components and some multicollinearity diagnostics. The output CUMULATIVE PERCENTAGE OF EIGENVALUES shows that the first two principal components account for 97.340% of the total variation in the variables. These two components are selected for the principal components regression that is implemented with the **OLS** command.

```
|_SAMPLE 1 20
|_READ (JUDGE22.DAT) X1 X2 X3 X4 X5 Y1

   6 VARIABLES AND      20 OBSERVATIONS STARTING AT OBS        1

|_PC X2 X3 X4 X5 / PCOMP=PC PCINFO=INFO PCOLLIN
  PRINCIPAL COMPONENTS ON   4 VARIABLES      MAXIMUM OF    4 FACTORS RETAINED

EIGENVALUES
   33.645        5.7812        .95354        .12366

SUM OF EIGENVALUES =    40.504

CUMULATIVE PERCENTAGE OF EIGENVALUES
   .83067        .97340        .99695       1.0000
```

```
VARIANCE REDUCTION BENCHMARK FUNCTION
  100.00        99.682        97.829        86.599

CONDITION NUMBERS
  1.0000        5.8197        35.285        272.08

CONDITION INDEXES
  1.0000        2.4124        5.9401        16.495

VARIANCE PROPORTIONS
       X2         X3         X4         X5
  1   .00149    .00059    .00250    .02602
  2   .00540    .11700    .00730    .05538
  3   .00349    .53393    .08059    .64291
  4   .98962    .34848    .90960    .27570


  4 COMPONENTS STORED IN MATRIX PC

|_OLS Y1 PC:1 PC:2 / PCINFO=INFO PCOMP=PC
 OLS ESTIMATION
        20 OBSERVATIONS     DEPENDENT VARIABLE = Y1
...NOTE..SAMPLE RANGE SET TO:    1,   20

 R-SQUARE =     .8913     R-SQUARE ADJUSTED =     .8786
VARIANCE OF THE ESTIMATE-SIGMA**2 =    .91550
STANDARD ERROR OF THE ESTIMATE-SIGMA =    .95682
SUM OF SQUARED ERRORS-SSE=    15.564
MEAN OF DEPENDENT VARIABLE =    20.107
LOG OF THE LIKELIHOOD FUNCTION = -25.8708
```

VARIABLE NAME	ESTIMATED COEFFICIENT	STANDARD ERROR	T-RATIO 17 DF	P-VALUE	PARTIAL CORR.	STANDARDIZED COEFFICIENT	ELASTICITY AT MEANS
PC	1.8892	.1650	11.45	.000	.941	.9156	.0000
PC	-1.1455	.3979	-2.878	.010	-.572	-.2301	.0000
CONSTANT	20.107	.2140	93.98	.000	.999	.0000	1.0000

```
ORIGINAL COEFFICIENTS TRANSFORMED BACK FROM COMPONENTS
```

VARIABLE NAME	ESTIMATED COEFFICIENT	STANDARD ERROR	T-RATIO 17 DF	P-VALUE	PARTIAL CORR.	STANDARDIZED COEFFICIENT	ELASTICITY AT MEANS
X2	.48574	.1745	2.783	.013	.559	.1226	.0375
X3	1.0811	.2936	3.682	.002	.666	.1820	.0680
X4	.55642	.1686	3.300	.004	.625	.1472	.0497
X5	1.7796	.2011	8.849	.000	.906	.6186	.2994
CONSTANT	10.968	.8434	13.00	.000	.953	.0000	.5455

33. PROBABILITY DISTRIBUTIONS

"A severe depression like that of 1920-21 is outside the range of probability."

Harvard Economic Society
November 16, 1929

The **DISTRIB** command provides functions of probability distributions. For a continuous random variable X the cumulative distribution function (CDF) is defined for a value x as:

$$F(x) = Pr(X \leq x)$$

and the probability density function (PDF) satisfies

$$f(x) = \frac{d\,F(x)}{dx} \geq 0 \qquad \text{and} \qquad \int_{-\infty}^{\infty} f(x)dx = 1$$

The **DISTRIB** command can provide critical values for use if adequate statistical tables are unavailable. Since approximation formulas are often used to compute probabilities users may find that the numbers printed may not exactly match those found in statistical tables which are usually computed with far greater precision. However, the approximation formulas are usually accurate to at least two significant digits. In some cases either the PDF or CDF is difficult to compute and so is not calculated. A handbook for statistical distributions is Evans, Hastings and Peacock [1993].

DISTRIB COMMAND OPTIONS

In general, the format of the **DISTRIB** command is:

DISTRIB *vars / options*

where *vars* is a list of variables and *options* is a list of the options that are required on the specified type of distribution. The available options are:

INVERSE   Computes the inverse survival function. The data in *vars* must contain probabilities. With a probability α the inverse survival function $Z(\alpha)$ is such that $Pr[X > Z(\alpha)] = \alpha$. The relation to the inverse cumulative distribution function is $Z(\alpha) = F^{-1}(1-\alpha)$. The **INVERSE** option is useful for obtaining critical values. For example, when the

TYPE=CHI option is also specified the values tabulated in chi-square tables will be obtained. The **INVERSE** option may not be used with **TYPE=BURRII, BURRIII, BURRXII, DAVIES, EDGE, IMHOF, BINOMIAL,** or **HYPERGEO**.

LLF Computes the Log of the Likelihood Function for the data and prints it and stores it in the temporary variable *$LLF*. This option may not be used with **TYPE=IMHOF**, non-central distributions, or the **INVERSE** option.

NOLIST Suppresses the listing of probability densities or critical values for each observation. It would normally be used only if these numbers were saved in temporary or permanent variables for later use and the listing was not required.

ACCURACY= Specifies the level of accuracy required for the **TYPE=DAVIES** option. The default is **ACCURACY=1E-6**. Computational time can be reduced by specifying a lower value, for example **ACCURACY=.001** (that is, 1E-3).

BEG=, END= Specifies the **BEG**inning and **END** observations to be used for the given **DISTRIB** command. If none are specified the current **SAMPLE** range is used.

BIGN= Specifies the population size (N) for the Hypergeometric distribution. It must be specified along with the **BIGX=** and **N=** options.

BIGX= Specifies the population number of successes (X) for the Hypergeometric distribution. It must be specified along with the **BIGN=** and **N=** options.

C= Specifies the non-Centrality parameter for a non-central F-distribution. It specifies the parameter C for the BURR distribution. This option is only used with **TYPE=F,BURRII,BURRIII,BURRXII**.

CDF= Saves the Cumulative Distribution Function values in the variable specified.

CRITICAL= Saves the **CRITICAL** values in the variable specified when the **INVERSE** option is being used.

DF= Specifies the Degrees of Freedom. This option is used only with **TYPE=T** and **TYPE=CHI**.

DFVEC=	Specifies a vector of N elements containing the **Degrees of Freedom** for the **TYPE=DAVIES** option.
DF1=, DF2=	Specifies the **Degrees of Freedom** for the numerator (**DF1**) and the denominator (**DF2**) respectively. This option is used only with **TYPE=F**.
EIGENVAL=	Specifies the vector of **EIGENVAL**ues to be used with the **TYPE=IMHOF** option.
H=	Specifies the Precision Parameter for the t-distribution. The default is **H=1** which corresponds to the most common use of the t-distribution. For examples of situations where $H \neq 1$ see Zellner [1971] or Chapters 4 and 7 of the *Judge Handbook*.
K=	Specifies the parameter **K** for **TYPE=BURRII,BURRIII,BURRXII** .
KURTOSIS=	Specifies the population excess **KURTOSIS** parameter for **TYPE=EDGE**. The coefficient of excess kurtosis is equal to 0 for a normal distribution.
LAMBDA=	Specifies the name of an N element λ vector to be used with **TYPE=DAVIES**.
LIMIT=	Specifies the maximum number of integration terms to be used with **TYPE=DAVIES**. The default is 10000.
MEAN=	Specifies the population **MEAN** value. This option is only used with **TYPE=NORMAL** , **TYPE=EDGE** or **TYPE=BETA**.
N=	Specifies the sample size (**N**) for use with **TYPE=BINOMIAL** or **TYPE=HYPERGEO**. With **TYPE=DAVIES** this option specifies the number of chi-square variables.
NEIGEN=	Specifies the Number of **EIGEN**values to be used with **TYPE=IMHOF** if the entire vector is not required.
NONCEN=	Specifies a vector of non-centrality parameters with the **TYPE=DAVIES** option. An example of the use of this option is given later in this chapter.
P=	Specifies a parameter value with **TYPE=BETA**, **TYPE=BINOMIAL** or **TYPE=GAMMA**. This is not needed with **TYPE=BETA** if **MEAN=** and **VAR=** are used.

PDF=   Saves the Probability Density Function for each observation in the
                     variable specified. It may not be used with **TYPE=IMHOF**.

Q=   Specifies a parameter value for **TYPE=BETA** or **TYPE=GAMMA**. This
                     is not needed with **TYPE=BETA** if **MEAN=** and **VAR=** are used.

S=   Specifies a parameter value for **TYPE=IG2**. For **TYPE=DAVIES**, the **S=**
                     option specifies the value of σ and the default value is zero.

SKEWNESS=   Specifies the population **SKEWNESS** coefficient for **TYPE=EDGE**. The
                     coefficient of skewness is equal to 0 for a normal distribution.

TYPE=   Specifies the **TYPE** of distribution. If the type is not specified
                     SHAZAM assumes **TYPE=NORMAL**. The other choices, described in
                     detail later in this chapter, are **BETA, BINOMIAL, BURRII, BURRIII,
                     BURRXII, CHI, DAVIES, EDGE, F, GAMMA, HYPERGEO, IG2,
                     IMHOF** and **T**.

V=   Specifies the degrees for freedom for **TYPE=IG2**.

VAR=   Specifies the population **VAR**iance. This option is only used with
                     TYPE=NORMAL, TYPE=EDGE or **TYPE=BETA**.

There are several temporary variables available from the last observation of the
previous **DISTRIB** command. These are *$CDF, $CRIT* and *$PDF*. For more information
on temporary variables see the chapter *MISCELLANEOUS COMMANDS AND
INFORMATION*.

TYPES OF DISTRIBUTIONS

The distributions available on the **TYPE=** option are:

BETA   *Beta Distribution*
                     Required options: **P=**p and **Q=**q (p>0; q>0) or **MEAN=** and **VAR=**. The
                     range is $0 \leq x \leq 1$.
                     The probability density function is:

$$f(x) = \frac{x^{p-1}(1-x)^{q-1}}{B(p,q)} \quad \text{where B is the beta function.}$$

BINOMIAL   *Binomial Distribution*
                     Required options: **N=**n and **P=**p $(0 \leq p \leq 1)$; x is an integer and the
                     range is $0 \leq x \leq n$.

The probability density function is:

$$f(x) = \binom{n}{x} p^x (1-p)^{n-x}$$

BURRII   *Burr Distribution*
BURRIII   The Burr family of distributions is quite general and contains many
BURRXII   other distributions. The type must be specified as **TYPE=BURRII**,
                    TYPE=BURRIII, or **TYPE=BURRXII** (see Burr [1968] and Johnson and
                    Kotz [1970, pp. 30-31]).
                    Required options: **C=c** and **K=k** (c and k are positive parameters).
                    The cumulative distribution functions are:

$$\text{(II)} \quad F(x) = (\exp(-x) + 1)^{-k}$$

$$\text{(III)} \quad F(x) = (x^{-c} + 1)^{-k} \qquad (0 < x)$$

$$\text{(XII)} \quad F(x) = 1 - (1 + x^c)^{-k} \qquad (0 < x)$$

CHI   *Chi-Squared Distribution*
                    Required options: **DF=v**. The range is $0 \leq x < \infty$.
                    The probability density function for v degrees of freedom is:

$$f(x) = \frac{x^{(v-2)/2} \exp(-x/2)}{2^{(v/2)} \Gamma(v/2)}$$

DAVIES   *Davies Method*
                    Davies [1980] describes an algorithm to compute the distribution of a
                    linear combination of chi-squared random variables. Consider:

$$Q = \sum_{j=1}^{N} \lambda_j Z_j + \sigma Z_0$$

where Z_j are independent random variables each having a chi-square
distribution with n_j degrees of freedom and non-centrality parameter
δj^2 and Z_0 has a standard normal distribution. The algorithm
computes the cumulative distribution function $F(x) = \Pr(Q \leq x)$. The
Davies algorithm can be used to compute a wide variety of
distributions including non-central chi-square, non-central F and the
distribution of the Durbin-Watson statistic (that is, the algorithm can
be used for obtaining the distribution function of quadratic forms as
computed with **TYPE=IMHOF**).
Required options: **N=N** (the number of variables), **LAMBDA=** (an
Nx1 λ vector), **DFVEC=** (an Nx1 vector of degrees of freedom) and
NONCEN= (an Nx1 vector of non-centrality parameters). Other

options are: $S=\sigma$ (the default value of σ is zero), **LIMIT=** and **ACCURACY=**.

The algorithm can be used to find the distribution of the ratio of two quadratic forms. To calculate the F distribution with the Davies method the ratio of two χ^2 distributions must be expressed as the sum of two χ^2 distributions. That is,

$$F_{v,w} = \frac{(\chi^2_v / v)}{(\chi^2_w / w)} \quad \text{is stated as} \quad 0 = \left(\frac{\chi^2_v}{v}\right) - F_{v,w}\left(\frac{\chi^2_w}{w}\right)$$

An example of how this works is given at the end of this chapter.

EDGE

Edgeworth Approximation
The Edgeworth expansion is a method for obtaining approximations to many distributions and is described in Bickel and Doksum [1977, p. 33].
Required options: **MEAN=μ, VAR=σ^2, SKEWNESS=γ_1,** and **KURTOSIS=γ_2**. The defaults with **TYPE=EDGE** are **MEAN=0, VAR=1, SKEWNESS=0** and **KURTOSIS=0**. γ_1 and γ_2 are the coefficient of skewness and excess kurtosis of the standardized variable.

The Edgeworth expansion for the cumulative distribution function of the standardized variable is given by:

$$F(x) = \Phi(x) - \phi(x)\left[\frac{1}{6}\gamma_1 H_2(x) + \frac{1}{24}\gamma_2 H_3(x) + \frac{1}{72}\gamma_1^2 H_5(x)\right]$$

where $\phi(x)$ and $\Phi(x)$ are the standard normal probability density and cumulative distribution functions respectively and H_2, H_3 and H_5 are Hermite polynomials defined by:

$$H_2(x) = x^2 - 1, \quad H_3(x) = x^3 - 3x, \quad H_5(x) = x^5 - 10x^3 + 15x$$

An example of the Edgeworth approximation to the χ^2 distribution is given in Bickel and Doksum [1977, p. 33].

F

F-Distribution
Required options: **DF1=v** and **DF2=w**. The range is $0 \leq x < \infty$. In addition, the **C=** option is required for the non-central F-distribution. The probability density function for the central F-distribution with v and w degrees of freedom is:

$$f(x) = \frac{\Gamma[(v+w)/2](v/w)^{(v/2)}x^{(v-2)/2}}{\Gamma(v/2)\Gamma(w/2)((1+v/w)x)^{((v+w)/2)}}$$

GAMMA

Gamma Distribution
Required options: **P**=p (the scale parameter p>0) and **Q**=q (the shape parameter q>0). The range is $0 \leq x < \infty$.
The probability density function is:

$$f(x) = \frac{(x/p)^{q-1}\exp(-x/p)}{p\Gamma(q)}$$

HYPERGEO

Hypergeometric Distribution
Required options: **BIGN**=N (number of elements in the population), **N**=n (the sample size) and **BIGX**=X (number of successes in the population). The range is $\max[0, n-N+X] \leq x \leq \min[X,n]$.
The probability of exactly x successes is:

$$f(x) = \binom{X}{x}\binom{N-X}{n-x} \Big/ \binom{N}{n}$$

IG2

Inverted Gamma Distribution - Type 2
Required options: **S**=$\hat{\sigma}$ (the estimate of σ) and **V**=v (the degrees of freedom).
The probability density function is:

$$f(\sigma) = \left(\frac{2}{\Gamma(v/2)}\right)\left(\frac{v\hat{\sigma}^2}{2}\right)^{v/2}\frac{1}{\sigma^{v+1}}\exp\left(-\frac{v\hat{\sigma}^2}{2\sigma^2}\right)$$

The inverted-gamma probability density function is shown in Judge, Griffiths, Hill, Lütkepohl and Lee [1985, Equation 4.2.5]. See Chapters 4 and 7 of the *Judge Handbook* for examples of the **TYPE=IG2** option.

IMHOF

Imhof Method
The **TYPE=IMHOF** option computes the cumulative distribution function for the quadratic form in normal variables: Q=X'AX. The method is described in Imhof [1961] and Koerts and Abrahamse [1968 and 1969].
Required options: **EIGENVAL**= . The **NEIGEN**= option may also be used.

The cumulative distribution function is obtained by using the result:

$$F(x) = Pr(Q \leq x) = Pr(R < 0) \qquad \text{where} \quad R = \sum_{j=1}^{n} (\lambda_j - x) Z_j^2$$

and λ_j are the nonzero eigenvalues of the matrix A and the Z_j are standard normal variables. The cumulative distribution function is:

$$F(x) = \frac{1}{2} - \frac{1}{\pi} \int_0^\infty \frac{\sin \varepsilon(u)}{u\gamma(u)} \, du \qquad \text{where}$$

$$\varepsilon(u) = \frac{1}{2} \sum_{j=1}^{n} \arctan\{(\lambda_j - x)u\} \quad ; \quad \gamma(u) = \prod_{j=1}^{n} \{1 + (\lambda_j - x)^2 u^2\}^{\frac{1}{4}}$$

The integral is computed by numerical integration.

An example of the use of **TYPE=IMHOF** for the computation of an exact p-value for the Durbin-Watson test statistic is given in the chapter *PROGRAMMING IN SHAZAM*. An alternative method is obtained with the **TYPE=DAVIES** option.

NORMAL

Normal Distribution
TYPE=NORMAL is the default distribution.
Required options: **MEAN**=μ and **VAR**=σ^2 (the default is **MEAN=0** and **VAR=1**). The range is $-\infty < x < \infty$.
The probability density function is:

$$f(x) = \frac{1}{\sqrt{2\pi\sigma^2}} \exp\left[-\frac{(x-\mu)^2}{2\sigma^2} \right]$$

T

Student's t-Distribution
Required options: **DF**=v (the degrees of freedom). The range is $-\infty < x < \infty$.
The probability density function is:

$$f(x) = \frac{\Gamma[(v+1)/2]}{\sqrt{v\pi}\ \Gamma(v/2)} \cdot \frac{1}{(1+x^2/v)^{(v+1)/2}}$$

EXAMPLES

The following example shows how the **DISTRIB** command can return p-values for test statistics (for a discussion of p-values see, for example, Griffiths, Hill and Judge [1993, p. 138]). The example uses the Theil textile data set and the t-statistics from an **OLS** regression are saved in the variable *TR*. The degrees of freedom for the **OLS** regression is available in the temporary variable *$DF*. The **DISTRIB** command is then used to get the p-values for the t-statistics.

```
|_OLS CONSUME INCOME PRICE / TRATIO=TR
 OLS ESTIMATION
        17 OBSERVATIONS      DEPENDENT VARIABLE = CONSUME
...NOTE..SAMPLE RANGE SET TO:      1,    17

 R-SQUARE  =     .9513     R-SQUARE ADJUSTED =      .9443
 VARIANCE OF THE ESTIMATE-SIGMA**2 =    30.951
 STANDARD ERROR OF THE ESTIMATE-SIGMA =    5.5634
 SUM OF SQUARED ERRORS-SSE=    433.31
 MEAN OF DEPENDENT VARIABLE =    134.51
 LOG OF THE LIKELIHOOD FUNCTION = -51.6471

 VARIABLE    ESTIMATED   STANDARD    T-RATIO        PARTIAL STANDARDIZED ELASTICITY
   NAME      COEFFICIENT   ERROR      14 DF   P-VALUE CORR. COEFFICIENT  AT MEANS
 INCOME       1.0617      .2667       3.981     .001  .729     .2387      .8129
 PRICE       -1.3830      .8381E-01  -16.50     .000 -.975    -.9893     -.7846
 CONSTANT    130.71      27.09        4.824     .000  .790     .0000      .9718
|_SAMPLE 1 3
|_GENR TR=ABS(TR)
|_DISTRIB TR / TYPE=T DF=$DF CDF=CDF
 T DISTRIBUTION DF=    14.000
 VARIANCE=   1.1667      H=    1.0000

                 DATA        PDF         CDF         1-CDF
   TR
 ROW      1      3.9813    .13395E-02  .99932     .68261E-03
 ROW      2      16.501    .57984E-10  1.0000     .71625E-10
 ROW      3      4.8241    .25335E-03  .99986     .13502E-03
|_* Now get the p-value for a 2-sided test.
|_GENR P_VAL=2*(1-CDF)
|_PRINT TR P_VAL
      TR              P_VAL
   3.981302        .1365218E-02
  16.50060         .1432510E-09
   4.824139        .2700419E-03
```

In the above example, a one-sided test of the hypothesis that the coefficient on *INCOME* is equal to zero would be rejected at the .00068261 level of confidence. The p-values for a 2-sided test are also computed and reported and these are identical to the values listed in the column labelled p-value on the OLS output.

The next example shows how to compute probability values for the chi-square distribution using the option **TYPE=CHI**. An alternative calculation is done using the Davies algorithm with **TYPE=DAVIES**.

```
|_* Program to compute the chi-square distribution function.
|_* Find the probability (CHI-SQUARE<3) with 1 degree of freedom
|_SAMPLE 1 1
|_GEN1 C=3
|_DISTRIB C / TYPE=CHI DF=1
CHI-SQUARE PARAMETERS- DF=    1.0000
MEAN=    1.0000    VARIANCE=   2.0000    MODE=    .00000


                   DATA        PDF         CDF         1-CDF
  C
  ROW      1     3.0000     .51393E-01  .91674      .83265E-01
|_*
|_* Now use the Davies algorithm
|_GEN1 DF=1
|_GEN1 LAMB=1
|_DISTRIB C / TYPE=DAVIES N=1 DFVEC=DF LAM=LAMB
DAVIES ALGORITHM N=   1 ACCURACY=   .1000000E-05 LIMIT= 10000 S=    .00000
DF
  1.0000
LAMB
  1.0000


                   DATA        CDF         1-CDF
  C
  ROW      1     3.0000     .91674      .83265E-01
```

The next example computes probability values for the non-central F distribution using the option **TYPE=F**. An alternative calculation is also done using the Davies algorithm with **TYPE=DAVIES**.

```
|_* PROGRAM FOR NON-CENTRAL F(1,4,5) DISTRIBUTION
|_SAMPLE 1 1
|_GEN1 CRIT=16
|_DISTRIB CRIT / TYPE=F DF1=1 DF2=4 C=5

                   DATA        CDF         1-CDF
  CRIT
  ROW      1     16.000     .81373      .18627
|_* Now use the Davies algorithm
|_* SINCE DAVIES WORKS ON CHI-SQUARE AND F IS THE RATIO OF
|_* TWO CHI-SQUARES, YOU MUST CONVERT THE STATISTIC TO THE
|_* SUM OF CHI-SQUARES BY MOVING THE DENOMINATOR TO THE LEFT
|_* SO F=(CHI1/DF1)/(CHI2/DF2) BECOMES 0=(1/DF1)CHI1-(F/DF2)CHI2
|_GEN1 DF1=1
|_GEN1 DF2=4
|_DIM LAMB 2 DF 2 NC 2
|_GENR DF=DF1
|_GENR LAMB=1/DF
|_GENR NC=5
|_SAMPLE 2 2
|_GENR DF=DF2
```

```
|_GENR LAMB=-CRIT/DF2
|_GENR NC=0
|_SAMPLE 1 1
|_GEN1 C=0
|_DISTRIB C / TYPE=DAVIES N=2 DFVEC=DF LAM=LAMB NONCEN=NC
DAVIES ALGORITHM N=    2 ACCURACY=    .1000000E-05 LIMIT= 10000 S=    .00000
DF
  1.0000        4.0000
LAMB
  1.0000       -4.0000
NC
  5.0000        .00000

                   DATA        CDF       1-CDF
  C
ROW      1       .00000      .81375      .18625
```

34. SORTING DATA

"Where a calculator on the ENIAC is equipped with 18,000 vacuum tubes and weighs 30 tons, computers in the future may have only 1,000 vacuum tubes and perhaps weigh only 1.5 tons."
Popular Mechanics
March 1949

The **SORT** command allows the user to sort data. A variable which will be used to sort the data must be specified. When completed, all observations of the specified variables will be rearranged in ascending order according to the ranking in the sort variable.

SORT *COMMAND OPTIONS*

In general, the format of the **SORT** command is:

SORT *sortvar vars / options*

where *sortvar* is the variable name of the sorting variable, *vars* is a list of the variables to be sorted and *options* is a list of desired options. Note that only the variables listed in *sortvars* and *vars* will be sorted, that only the observations for the currently defined **SAMPLE** will be sorted, and that **SKIPIF** commands are not in effect.

The available options on the **SORT** command are:

DESC   This option will cause the specified variables to be sorted in **DESC**ending, rather than ascending order.

LIST   This option will **LIST** all the sorted data. That is, it will print the sorted *vars* and the *sortvar*.

BEG=, END=   Specify the sample range for the given **SORT** command. If these are not specified, the current **SAMPLE** range is used.

EXAMPLES

The following is an example of the **SORT** command using Theil's [1971, p. 102] textile data. This example shows how a data file that has been typed in backward could be sorted using the **SORT** command.

```
|_SAMPLE 1 17
|_READ(11) YEAR CONSUME INCOME PRICE
   4 VARIABLES AND        17 OBSERVATIONS STARTING AT OBS 1
|_PRINT YEAR CONSUME INCOME PRICE
   YEAR              CONSUME           INCOME            PRICE
   1939.000          165.5000          103.8000          61.30000
   1938.000          149.0000          101.6000          59.50000
   1937.000          154.3000          102.4000          59.70000
   1936.000          168.0000          97.60000          52.60000
   1935.000          136.2000          96.40000          63.60000
   1934.000          140.6000          95.40000          62.50000
   1933.000          158.5000          101.7000          61.30000
   1932.000          153.6000          105.3000          65.40000
   1931.000          154.2000          109.3000          70.10000
   1930.000          136.0000          112.3000          82.80000
   1929.000          121.1000          110.8000          90.60000
   1928.000          117.6000          109.5000          89.70000
   1927.000          122.2000          104.9000          86.50000
   1926.000          111.6000          104.9000          90.60000
   1925.000          100.0000          100.0000          100.0000
   1924.000          99.00000          98.10000          100.1000
   1923.000          99.20000          96.70000          101.0000
|_SORT YEAR CONSUME INCOME PRICE
DATA HAS BEEN SORTED BY VARIABLE YEAR
|_PRINT YEAR CONSUME INCOME PRICE
   YEAR              CONSUME           INCOME            PRICE
   1923.000          99.20000          96.70000          101.0000
   1924.000          99.00000          98.10000          100.1000
   1925.000          100.0000          100.0000          100.0000
   1926.000          111.6000          104.9000          90.60000
   1927.000          122.2000          104.9000          86.50000
   1928.000          117.6000          109.5000          89.70000
   1929.000          121.1000          110.8000          90.60000
   1930.000          136.0000          112.3000          82.80000
   1931.000          154.2000          109.3000          70.10000
   1932.000          153.6000          105.3000          65.40000
   1933.000          158.5000          101.7000          61.30000
   1934.000          140.6000          95.40000          62.50000
   1935.000          136.2000          96.40000          63.60000
   1936.000          168.0000          97.60000          52.60000
   1937.000          154.3000          102.4000          59.70000
   1938.000          149.0000          101.6000          59.50000
   1939.000          165.5000          103.8000          61.30000
```

It is important to realize that once the data has been sorted it can only be unsorted back to its original state if, prior to the sort, there was a variable which was in either ascending or descending order. This type of variable may be created on a **GENR** command with the **TIME(0)** function.

35. SET AND DISPLAY

"Gone With The Wind is going to be the biggest flop in Hollywood history. I'm just glad it'll be Clark Gable who's falling flat on his face and not Gary Cooper."

Gary Cooper
Actor, 1938

This chapter describes the **SET** command and the **DISPLAY** command.

SET *COMMAND OPTIONS*

SET commands make it possible to turn certain options on or off. In general, the format of the **SET** command to turn options on is:

SET *option*

To turn options off, the format of the **SET** command is:

SET NO*option*

where *option* is the desired option. The available options on the **SET** command are:

BATCH	Used in **BATCH** mode or when more extensive output is desired or when the OUTPUT unit is assigned to a file. Most modern operating systems can detect a batch run, so this option is rarely used. If the operating system is not able to do this, **BATCH** is the default.
COLOR **NOCOLOR**	The **COLOR** option is used on MS-DOS and OS/2 computers with a Color EGA or VGA monitor to obtain a color background that changes depending on the command in use. If you do not want color, type **SET NOCOLOR**.
CPUTIME	The **DISPLAY CPUTIME** command will print the amount of computer time used in the current SHAZAM run. The **SET CPUTIME** command resets the timer to zero.

DELETE/
NODELETE

In distributed-lag models, before estimation, SHAZAM will automatically delete the number of observations equal to the longest lag. If you do not want SHAZAM to do this and prefer to adjust this yourself with the **SAMPLE** command, use **SET NODELETE**. The default is **SET DELETE**.

DOECHO

Commands are normally printed for each cycle through a SHAZAM **DO**-loop. To prevent these commands from being printed, **SET NODOECHO**.

DUMP

DUMPs a lot of output which is primarily of interest to SHAZAM consultants.

ECHO

Causes commands to be printed in the output. In interactive mode it may be necessary to use **NOECHO** to prevent the repetition of each command, however most modern operating systems can set this automatically. The default is **ECHO** in BATCH and TERMINAL modes and **NOECHO** in TALK mode.

FRENCH

Allows all command names to be typed in **FRENCH** or **ENGLISH**. Output will still appear in English. A list of French commands is shown in the chapter *FRENCH COMMAND NAMES*.

LASTCOM

Creates a variable called *C$* which will contain the previous command typed. This variable can then be printed at any time after the **LASTCOM** option is **SET** by typing **PRINT C$**. This option is only useful in TALK mode.

LCUC/
NOLCUC

When this option is specified, all lower case characters will be converted to upper case before processing by SHAZAM. This is the default on most computers. If you wish to distinguish upper and lower case variable names and file names in SHAZAM then use **SET NOLCUC**.

MAX

The **MAX** option can be **SET** to turn on the **MAX** option on each command. This eliminates the need to use the **MAX** option on every individual command if it is always desired.

NOCC

Used to turn off carriage control. When **SET CC** is in effect, some commands (like **OLS**) will still skip to a new page. The default is **SET CC**. For more information on carriage control in SHAZAM see the chapter *MISCELLANEOUS COMMANDS AND INFORMATION*.

OPTIONS   Displays the value of all command **OPTIONS** in subsequent commands. This option is primarily of interest to SHAZAM consultants.

OUTPUT/   These options are used to turn off or on the output for all following
NOOUTPUT   commands. **SET NOOUTPUT** is equivalent to putting a "?" in front of every command.

PAUSE   Causes a pause to occur after each command or screen of output. This is useful when the user is working on a machine which has no pause control on its keyboard and therefore much of the output is missed as it appears on the screen. The default is **SET NOPAUSE**. On some systems the user can simply press *RETURN* on the keyboard to resume execution. However, this may not be the case on all operating systems. This option has no effect in BATCH mode.

RANFIX   When **RANFIX** is **SET** the random number generator is not set by the system clock. Thus, the same set of random numbers will be obtained in repeated jobs.

SAMPLE/   These options allow the use of the omitted observations in the
NOSAMPLE   expanded form of the **SAMPLE** command to be turned on and off.

SCREEN/   Works on some (but not all computers) to turn on and off the display
NOSCREEN   of the SHAZAM output on the terminal screen when the output has been redirected to a file assigned with the **FILE SCREEN** command. Due to the peculiarities of various operating systems the option may or may not work. Try it and see.

SKIP/   These options allow **SKIPIF** commands to be turned on and off. For
NOSKIP   an example of these options, see the chapter *GENERATING VARIABLES*.

SKIPMISS   This option is used to turn on automatic deletion of missing observations in any data analysis or estimation command such as **OLS, NL, ROBUST, STAT, FC** etc. If any observation has a missing value code for any of the dependent or independent variables on that command, then the observation will be omitted for that particular command.

                       Missing values are checked by scanning whether a variable is equal to the missing value code. The missing value code has a default of −99999 but can be changed with the **SET MISSVALU=** option. The option can be turned off with **SET NOSKIPMISS**.

The **AUTO** command should also specify the **MISS** option when estimation with missing observations is considered. Estimation with missing observations in time series may not be appropriate with the **POOL**, **ARIMA**, or **COINT** commands or ARCH estimation with the **HET** command.

When the **SET SKIPMISS** command is in effect the **GENR** command will assign a missing value code to results that involve a computation with a missing observation.

This is less general than the **SKIPIF** command which will delete an observation for all subsequent commands since the observation will only be deleted if the variable is actually used.

STATUS
This option is used on the PC and Macintosh Microcomputers to display a status line for some SHAZAM operations. The status line differs among operating systems and can include the index of the current **DO** loop, or the name of the current command. If this status line is not desired it can be turned off with **SET NOSTATUS.**

TALK
TALK is **SET** at the beginning of an interactive session when typing commands in interactive mode. If all commands are in a file then the user is not "talking" and should use the **TERMINAL** option instead. Most modern operating systems can detect an interactive run, so it may not be necessary to **SET** this option.

TERMINAL
TERMINAL is used when the job is run at the terminal; the SHAZAM commands are typed into a separate file and the output is not placed in a file. Most modern operating systems can detect if this is the case, so it may not be necessary to **SET** this option.

TIMER
Times each command and the CPU time is printed out after execution of each command.

TRACE
This option is primarily of interest to SHAZAM consultants. It prints the name of each subroutine as it is executed.

WARN/
NOWARN
Warning messages are normally printed for illegal operations in **GENR, MATRIX, IF, SKIPIF** and **ENDIF** statements. These messages can be turned off with **SET NOWARN.**

WARNSKIP
A warning message is printed for every observation skipped by a **SKIPIF** command. There may be a large number of these warnings if the sample is large. These warnings can be turned off with **SET NOWARNSKIP.**

WIDE/
NOWIDE
The **WIDE** option is used to control the line length of printed output. **WIDE** will assume that up to 120 columns are available. **NOWIDE** will try to fit all output in 80 columns. This option mainly affects the **PRINT** and **PLOT** commands. The default is **WIDE** in Batch operation and **NOWIDE** in Talk mode at a terminal.

COMLEN=
The maximum number of characters in a command line is 255 on some computers but on others the maximum length is only 80. You can see the length for your computer with the command **DISPLAY COMLEN**. This option can be used to prevent SHAZAM from reading commands beyond a certain column. For example, for a file with sequence numbers in columns 73-80, **COMLEN=72** would be appropriate. **COMLEN=** should never be specified at a value of greater than 255 under any circumstance. Note that on all computers, commands can be continued onto additional lines if the continuation symbol (&) is used at the end of a line. The use of continuation lines allows a total command length on all computers of 4096 characters.

MAXCOL=
When using the colon (:) function to specify a row of a matrix or a number in a vector, the default maximum number is at least 1000 or twice the maximum number of variables specified on the **SIZE** command. If a larger number is required a **SET** command such as **SET MAXCOL=1500** should be used.

MISSVALU=
Used with the **SET SKIPMISS** option to specify a missing value code. The default is −99999.

OUTUNIT=
The **OUTUNIT=** option is **SET** when the SHAZAM output for the run is to be put into more than one file. In this case, the output files are assigned to appropriate units and addressed with the **OUTUNIT=** option. Of course, if one of the files is originally assigned to Unit 6, SHAZAM automatically outputs into this file and continues until another file is specified on a **SET OUTUNIT=** command. This option is rarely used.

RANSEED=
If you wish to initialize the random number generator with a particular integer number use the **SET RANSEED=xxx** option where xxx is a positive integer. This can be used to obtain the same set of random numbers in different runs. This option should be used before any random numbers are generated in the run. **SET RANSEED=0** is the same as **SET RANFIX**.

DISPLAY *COMMAND OPTIONS*

The **DISPLAY** command displays the current value of any option that has been specified with the **SET** command. The format of the **DISPLAY** command is:

DISPLAY *option*

where *option* is the option or a list of the options previously set on a **SET** command.

In addition to the **DISPLAY** command, the **DUMP** command described in the chapter *MISCELLANEOUS COMMANDS AND INFORMATION* is useful for SHAZAM consultants who wish to see technical debugging output.

36. MISCELLANEOUS COMMANDS AND INFORMATION

"If God had wanted a Panama Canal, he would have put one here."
King Philip II of Spain
1552

This is a very important chapter that all users should read. There are various SHAZAM commands available that do not require separate chapters, but are very useful.

Carriage Control

Users can manipulate printer carriage control in SHAZAM on some machines. For example, by inserting the number one (1) before a command the user can ensure that the output for that command will be printed on a new page. Similarily, a zero (0) inserted before a command tells the printer to skip a line before printing output. Consider, for example, the following commands:

```
SAMPLE 1 10
READ A B
1PRINT A B
```

The **SAMPLE** and the **READ** commands will appear on the first page of the output and the results of the **PRINT** command will appear on the following page. Some commands (like **OLS**) automatically start a new page.

NOTE: Carriage control can be turned on or off for commands that automatically start a new page by using the **SET CC** or **SET NOCC** commands. The default is **SET CC**. For more information on **SET CC** see the chapter *SET AND DISPLAY*.

The CHECKOUT Command

The **CHECKOUT** command prints information about the machine being used. This information is primarily of interest to SHAZAM consultants. The format of the **CHECKOUT** command is:

CHECKOUT

Comment Lines

Comment lines are permitted in SHAZAM. The first column of the line must have an asterisk (*), but the rest of the line may contain anything the user desires. Thus, a comment line might look like the following:

```
* ORDINARY LEAST SQUARES REGRESSION USING TEXTILE DATA
```

This comment line will appear in the output for the run and can be used to identify which regressions were run. Comment lines may not be placed inside data to be read.

The COMPRESS Command

The **COMPRESS** command is used to retrieve the space of deleted variables. The **DELETE** command for deleting variables does not automatically free previously occupied space. Since there is a limited amount of memory available in a SHAZAM run the **COMPRESS** command is useful after **DELETE** commands have been used. The format of the **COMPRESS** command is:

COMPRESS

The **COMPRESS** command is not allowed in **DO**-loops or procedures.

Continuation Lines

Continuation lines are permitted in SHAZAM. An ampersand (&) is used at the end of the line to be continued. For example, if a long and complicated equation were to be given on a **GENR** command, it could be continued onto the following line in this way:

```
GENR Y=LOG(X)+P**16*T/(X-2/P)*203 &
-6042
```

SHAZAM will remove the & from the equation and put the two pieces together. The continued line need not start in the first column. Any space typed before the ampersand will be retained in the equation. The maximum length of a command including continuation lines is 4096 characters. Also see the **SET COMLEN=** command described in the chapter *SET AND DISPLAY*.

The DELETE Command

The **DELETE** command is used to delete variables. The format of the **DELETE** command is:

DELETE *vars*

where *vars* is a list of variables to be deleted. All variables can be deleted with the command:

DELETE / ALL

The special **ALL_** option can be used to delete all variables with an underscore as a final character (see the chapter *SHAZAM PROCEDURES*). The command is:

DELETE / ALL_

Also see the **COMPRESS** command described above.

The **DEMO** *Command*

The **DEMO** command is used to teach beginners the basic commands in SHAZAM. To see a SHAZAM **DEMO**nstration type **DEMO** and follow the instructions displayed at the terminal. The **DEMO** can be restarted at any time with: **DEMO START**.

The **DIM** *Command*

The **DIM** command dimensions a vector or matrix before any data is defined. This is useful if the data for a given variable or matrix comes from several sources. In this case, **COPY** commands are useful for filling the previously dimensioned vector or matrix. The format of the **DIM** command is:

DIM *var size var size ...*

where *var* is the name of the vector or matrix to be dimensioned, and *size* is either one or two numbers separated by a space to indicate the size of the *var* to be dimensioned. The *size* parameter can also be a scalar variable name. If only one number is given, SHAZAM assumes the *var* is a vector. If two numbers are given, SHAZAM assumes that the *var* specified is a matrix and that the first number given specifies the rows of the matrix, and the second number specifies the columns. More than one vector or matrix can be dimensioned with a single **DIM** command, as shown above. In the example below, the vector *V* is dimensioned to 12 rows (or observations).

```
DIM V 12
```

Similarly, if a matrix *M* were to be dimensioned to 4 rows and 5 columns, the following **DIM** command would be appropriate (matrices may have a maximum of 2 dimensions):

```
DIM M 4 5
```

DO-*loops*

DO-loops perform repeat operations. For instructions on the use of DO-loops see the chapter *PROGRAMMING IN SHAZAM*.

The DUMP *Command*

The **DUMP** command prints out information that is primarily of interest to SHAZAM consultants. The format of the **DUMP** command is:

DUMP *options*

where *options* is a list of desired options.

There are many options available on the **DUMP** command, although most of these options are only useful for those who have a source listing of SHAZAM. **DUMP DATA** prints a chart of all the current variables, their addresses, increment, type, their number of observations and their second dimension. **DUMP VNAME** lists all the current variable names. **DUMP KADD** prints the first address of each variable. The following common block options are also available for SHAZAM consultants: **ADDCOM, DATCOM, FCOM, GENCOM, INPCOM, IOCOM, LODCOM, MACOM, NLCOM, OCOM, OLSCOM, OPTCOM, OSCOM, RANCOM, SCNCOM, SYSCOM, TEMCOM, VCOM, VLCOM, VPLCOM, VTCOM, VTECOM** and **VTICOM**. Finally, any range of data in the SHAZAM workspace can be dumped by typing the first and last word desired. For example, the command **DUMP 30 50** would print words 30 through 50 of SHAZAM memory. This would normally be used in conjunction with the information obtained from the **DUMP DATA** command.

The FILE *Command*

The **FILE** command is used to specify a particular action for a file, or assign a search path, or assign units to files. This command is described in the chapter *DATA INPUT AND OUTPUT*.

The HELP *Command*

Help on various SHAZAM commands and options is available on the **HELP** command. The format of the **HELP** command is:

HELP *command*

where *command* is any SHAZAM command name.

The MENU *Command*

The **MENU** command is useful when you are running SHAZAM interactively and you need a list of available commands. At any point in time some commands may not be valid. These are indicated by an * in the menu list.

The NAMES *Command*

The **NAMES** command will print out the **NAMES** of all the variables that have been read or generated in a particular SHAZAM run. It is mainly used in TALK mode to see which variables are currently defined. The format of the **NAMES** command is:

NAMES

or

NAMES *

which will print a table of names, the type of variable and the size of the variable.

The PAR *Command*

The **PAR** command sets the **PAR** value. The **PAR** value specifies the amount of memory (in batches of 1024 bytes) that is needed for the SHAZAM run. The format of the **PAR** command is:

PAR *number*

where *number* specifies the amount of memory that is needed. This command may have different machine implementations. Check the installation instructions for details on raising **PAR** for your version.

The PAUSE *Command*

The **PAUSE** command can be used anywhere in a SHAZAM run to cause a display on the screen to pause on some computers after the chosen commands. This command might be used, for example, on a machine that has no scroll key on the keyboard. Strategically placed **PAUSE** commands make it possible to view the output from commands as they are executed even when there is no scroll control. Users who wish to **PAUSE** after every command may use the **SET PAUSE** command. This command has no effect in BATCH mode.

The **RENAME** *Command*

The **RENAME** command is used to rename variables that already exist in the current run. The format of the **RENAME** command is:

RENAME *oldname   newname*

where *oldname* is the name of the variable whose name is to be changed, and *newname* is the new name to be given to that variable.

The **REWIND** *Command*

The **REWIND** command is used to rewind any unit, usually the **WRITE** unit. **REWIND** is also available as an option on the **WRITE** command. After a **REWIND** command, anything written to the specified unit will overlay what was already there. The format of the **REWIND** command is:

REWIND *unit*

where *unit* is the unit assigned to the **WRITE** file.

The **SIZE** *Command*

Normally, SHAZAM allows at least 300 variables. This can be changed with the **SIZE** command on most (but not all) systems. The format of the **SIZE** command is:

SIZE *maximum*

For example:

```
SIZE 500
```

The **SIZE** command should be placed at the beginning of the command file. This command may have different machine implementations. Check the installation instructions for your version.

The **STOP** *Command*

The **STOP** command is used to indicate that the SHAZAM run is finished. If no **STOP** command is included SHAZAM will read to the end of the command file.

Temporary Variables

Temporary variables are scalar variables that contain values from current computations. They are redefined each time a new estimation is performed. For example, temporary variables that are generally available are:

$N   The number of observations

$ERR   An error code

$PI   The value for π ($PI = 3.1415926535898).

Note that the value for $PI may be printed in a shortened form on the SHAZAM output even though the number printed above is used in the calculations.

The matrix dimensions from a **MATRIX** command are in:

$ROWS and $COLS.

The current values of each index from the **DO** command are in:

$DO and $DO2 -$DO8.

Temporary variables available following the **TEST** command are:

$CHI, $DF1, $DF2, $F, $STES, $T, $VAL, $VAL1, $VAL2, $CT11, $CT22, $CT12

Temporary variables available following the **DISTRIB** command are:

$CDF, $CRIT, $LLF and $PDF.

Some temporary variables available following the **AUTO, BOX, GLS, MLE, OLS, POOL** or **2SLS** regression commands are:

$ADR2, $ANF, $DF, $DW, $ERR, $K, $LLF, $N, $R2, $R2OP, $RAW, $RHO, $SIG2, $SSE, $SSR, $SST, $ZANF, $ZDF and $ZSSR.

Further description is in the chapter *ORDINARY LEAST SQUARES* and other chapters.

Temporary variables are useful for subsequent calculations. For example, suppose the adjusted R^2 (described in the chapter *A CHILD'S GUIDE TO RUNNING REGRESSIONS*) is needed. This variable could be calculated in the following way:

```
OLS CONSUME INCOME PRICE
GEN1 AR2=1-($N-1)/($N-$K)*(1-$R2)
```

where $N is the number of observations, $K is the number of parameters, and $R2 is the R-SQUARE statistic. However, the adjusted R^2 is also automatically available in the temporary variable $ADR2.

The TIME Command

The **TIME** command specifies the beginning year and frequency for a time series so that an alternate form of the **SAMPLE** command can be used. The format is:

TIME *beg freq var*

where *beg* is the beginning year, *freq* is the frequency of the data (for example, use 1 for annual data, 4 for quarterly data and 12 for monthly data), and *var* is an optional variable name to store dates. An example is:

```
TIME 1981 12
SAMPLE 1982.3 1984.10
```

When a dot "." is included, as in the example above, it is assumed to be a date according to the specification of the **TIME** command. This sets the **SAMPLE** from March of 1982 to October of 1984 for monthly data. The date can also be saved in a variable by specifying a variable name in *var* if a **SAMPLE** range for *var* has previously been defined. However, this variable should only be used for labelling output and not in calculations as it often has no useful numerical meaning.

If yearly data is used a decimal point must be included. For example, for Theil's [1971, p. 102] Textile data you could use:

```
SAMPLE 1 17
TIME 1923 1 YEAR
SAMPLE 1930.0 1939.0
```

A **SAMPLE** command without a decimal point is interpreted to be the observation number.

The TITLE Command

The **TITLE** command prints the specified title at the top of selected pages of output. The **TITLE** may be changed at any time, and as many times as desired. The format of the **TITLE** command is:

TITLE *title*

where *title* is any title the user requires.

Suppressing Output

To suppress the output from SHAZAM commands a question mark (?) may be placed in the first column of the line on which the command is typed. For example, to suppress the output from an **OLS** command, use:

```
?OLS  A  B  C  /  RSTAT
```

This is useful when a particular statistic is needed (say the Durbin-Watson statistic) for a subsequent test, but no other output is needed. In this case the Durbin-Watson statistic would have been stored in the temporary variable *$DW*, and can easily be retrieved when required.

The command **SET NOOUTPUT** (see the chapter *SET AND DISPLAY*) is equivalent to using the ? prefix on every command. This is recommended for Monte Carlo studies (an example of a Monte Carlo study is given in the chapter *PROGRAMMING IN SHAZAM*).

To suppress the printing of the command itself, but not the output an equal sign (=) may be placed in the first column of the line on which the command is typed. For example, to suppress the **OLS** command, type:

```
=OLS  A  B  C
```

To suppress both the command and the output from that command an equal sign and a question mark are placed in the first and second columns of the line on which the command is typed. To suppress both an **OLS** command and its output, use:

```
=?OLS  A  B  C
```

Error Codes

When an error occurs in executing a SHAZAM command an error code will often be set in the temporary variable *$ERR*. This variable can then be examined following each command to keep track of the type of error. If *$ERR* is a zero then an error code was not set. An example is:

```
HET CONSUME INCOME PRICE  / STDRESID=E
IF($ERR.EQ.0)
ARIMA E
```

A list of error codes is available with the command **HELP ERROR**. A list of the most common error codes is shown below.

```
ALL commands
     1010 ...INSUFFICIENT MEMORY-AT LEAST ??? MORE WORDS NEEDED
          THIS REQUIRES AT LEAST PAR=???  CURRENT PAR=???
     1011 ...ERROR..DATA ON VARIABLE ??? DOES NOT EXIST
     1012 ..INVALID OPTION
     1013 ..ERROR.. ??? EXCEEDS MAXCOL=??? USE SET MAXCOL=
     1014 ...ERROR..VARIABLE ??? DOES NOT EXIST
     1015 ..ERROR.. ??? EXCEEDS MAXCOL= ??? USE SET MAXCOL=
     1016 .SYNTAX ERROR IN LINE ABOVE NEAR $
     1017 ...ERROR ... COMMAND TOO LONG
OLS
     6010 ..ERROR..VARIABLE ??? IS ON BOTH SIDES OF EQUATION
     6011 ...ERROR..IN RIGHT HAND SIDE OF OPTION ???
     6012 ...ERROR..INCOMPATIBLE OPTIONS
     6013 ...INSUFFICIENT NUMBER OF VARIABLES SPECIFIED
     6014 .ERROR ??? OBSERVATIONS IS NOT ENOUGH FOR ESTIMATION
     6015 ..ERROR..RESTRICT AND RIDGE OPTIONS NOT ALLOWED
     6016 ..ERROR..VARIABLE ??? IS NOT VALID
     6017 .INSUFFICIENT MEMORY TO CORRECT COVARIANCE MATRIX
TEST, RESTRICT, LAMBDA
     15008 ...INSUFFICIENT MEMORY FOR THIS CALCULATION
     15009 ..SYNTAX ERROR IN LINE ABOVE
     15010
     15011 ...ERROR..??? DOES NOT EXIST
     15012 ...ERROR.. ??? IS NOT IN EQUATION
     15013 ...ERROR..MORE EQUATIONS THAN PARAMETERS
     15014 ..ERROR..THIS COMMAND MUST FOLLOW AN ESTIMATION COMMAND
     15015 ...TEST COULD NOT BE DONE
     15016 ...RESTRICTIONS COULD NOT BE DONE
     15017 .ABOVE COMMAND IS INVALID FOR THIS PROBLEM
     15018 ..ERROR.COMMAND IS NOT A RESTRICT, TEST, OR END COMMAND
PLOT, CONFID
     28010 ...ERROR IN RIGHT HAND SIDE OF OPTION ???
     28011 ...ERROR..INVALID COEFFICIENTS OR OPTIONS
     28012 ...AXIS ERROR: TRY NOPRETTY OPTION ??? ??? ??? ???
POOL
     29010 ...ERROR..MISSING RIGHT HAND SIDE OF OPTION ???
     29011 ...ERROR..INCOMPATIBLE OPTIONS
     29012 ...ERROR..NCROSS= OR NTIME= NOT SPECIFIED
     29013 ...ERROR..INVALID LIST OF EXOGENOUS VARIABLES
     29014 ...ERROR..TIME-PERIODS NOT OF EQUAL LENGTH
     29015 ..ESTIMATION FAILED DUE TO UNSTABLE RHO = ???
     29016 ..ERROR..FOUND IN ROW ???
     29017 ..MATRIX IS NOT POSITIVE DEFINITE
     29018    ITERATION LIMIT EXCEEDED
SYSTEM, 2SLS
     50010 ...ERROR..MISSING RIGHT HAND SIDE OF OPTION ???
     50011 ...ERROR..NO. OF EQUATIONS NOT GIVEN ON SYSTEM COMMAND
     50012 .ABOVE COMMAND IGNORED, IS NOT ALLOWED AT THIS TIME
     50013 ...ERROR..UNIT ??? IS RESERVED FOR INTERNAL USE
     50014 ...PROBLEM TOO LARGE.TOO MANY VARIABLES OR RESTRICTIONS
```

```
      50015 ...ERROR...EQUATION ??? IS UNDERIDENTIFIED
      50016 SIGMA.MATRIX IS NOT POSITIVE DEFINITE
      50017 .MATRIX IS NOT POSITIVE DEFINITE
      50018 ..ERROR..EXOG VAR ?? IS A CONSTANT..A CONSTANT IS
            AUTOMATICALLY INCLUDED
      50019 .MATRIX OF EXOGENOUS VARIABLES IS NOT POSITIVE DEFINITE
NL, MLE, HET
      52010 ...ERROR..SAME OPTION NEEDS PREVIOUS NL OR MLE COMMAND
      52011 ...ERROR.. START= VARIABLE DOES NOT EXIST
      52012 ..ERROR..LOGLOG, LOGLIN, LINLOG OPTIONS NOT AVAILABLE
      52013 ..ERROR..CONVERGENCE SET TO ZERO
      52014 ...ERROR..IN RIGHT HAND SIDE OF OPTION ??
      52015 ...ERROR.. YOU FORGOT TO SPECIFY NCOEF=
      52016 ...ERROR.. EXOGENOUS VARIABLES NOT ALLOWED
      52017 ...ERROR.. ARCH ERRORS NOT ALLOWED
      52018 ...ERROR.. INVALID MODEL= OPTION
      52019 ...ERROR.. TYPE= OPTION NOT ALLOWED
      52020 ...SYNTAX ERROR IN LINE ABOVE
      52021 ...ERROR..ATTEMPT TO USE ??? PARAMETERS FROM UNIT ??? FAILED
      52022 ...ERROR..SET SAMPLE COMMAND TO USE ONLY ONE OBSERVATION
      52023 *** FAILURE TO COMPLETE A LINE SEARCH IN 20 FUNCTION
            EVALUATIONS. THIS IS PROBABLY BECAUSE THE LIKELIHOOD
            FUNCTION HAS NO GLOBAL MAXIMUM
      52024 No Message: Too Many Parameters required, XXIT(10)
      52025 COVARIANCE MATRIX AND STD ERRORS ARE INCORRECT
      52026 .ERROR..DEP VAR IN OB. NO. ??? IS NOT POSITIVE
      52027 ...MAXIMUM NUMBER OF ITERATIONS
      52028 ...ERROR..GMM=??? IS INVALID OR WRONG DIMENSION
      52029 ...HESSIAN IS NOT POSITIVE DEFINITE
      52030 ...GRAD TRANSPOSE TIMES X GREATER THAN OR EQUAL ZERO
                CONV SET TOO SMALL?
PROBIT, LOGIT, TOBIT
      55010 ...ERROR IN RIGHT HAND SIDE OF OPTION ???
      55011 .ERROR ??? OBSERVATIONS IS NOT ENOUGH FOR ESTIMATION
      55012 .MAXIMUM ITERATIONS REACHED
      55013 ...MODEL HAS BLOWN UP WITH -XB= ???
      55014 ...ERROR..DEPENDENT VARIABLE IS A CONSTANT
      55015 OBSERVATION ??? HAS ILLEGAL DEP VAR ??
TOBIT
      57012 ...THERE ARE NO OBSERVATIONS AT THE LIMIT
      57013 ...ALL OBSERVATIONS ARE AT THE LIMIT
PC
      65010 ...MISSING RIGHT HAND SIDE OF OPTION ???
      65011 ...DISASTER..IN EIGENVALUE OF ROW ???
ARIMA
      72010 ...ERROR..MISSING RIGHT HAND SIDE OF OPTION ???
      72011 ...ERROR..INVALID TYPE= OPTION
      72012 ...ERROR..INVALID NLAG OR NLAGP
      72013 ...ERROR..SPAN OF SEASONAL CYCLE NOT SET
      72014 ...ERROR..THE FORECAST LIMIT IS 200
      72015 ...ERROR..REQUIRE FEND>FBEG
      72016 ...ERROR..FBEG IS OUTSIDE SAMPLE RANGE
      72017 ...ERROR..START= VARIABLE DOES NOT EXIST
      72018 ...ERROR..NO VARIABLE SPECIFIED FOR ANALYSIS
      72019 ...ERROR..PRE-SAMPLE VALUES EXCEEDS 104
      72020 ...ERROR..TOO FEW OBSERVATIONS
      72021 ...ERROR..TOO FEW COEFFICIENTS OR INVALID COEFFICIENTS
      72022 ...ERROR..ORIGIN DATE IS LESS THAN MAXIMUM AR LAG
```

```
      72023 ...ERROR..INVALID PARAMETER LIST
      72024 *** SPECIFICATION ERROR, PLEASE CHANGE ***
      72028 ...NO CONVERGENCE AFTER ??? ITERATIONS
            INITIAL SUM OF SQS= ???    FINAL SUM OF SQS =???
      72029 ...FAILED TO REDUCE SSE FURTHER AFTER ??? ITERATIONS
            INITIAL SSE = ???  FINAL SSE = ???
COINT
      72025 ...ERROR..COINTEGRATION TESTS NEED MORE VARIABLES
      72026 ...ERROR..NDIFF= OPTION NOT AVAILABLE
      72027 ...ERROR..TOO FEW OBSERVATIONS
ROBUST
      77010 ...ERROR..MISSING RIGHT HAND SIDE OF OPTION ???
      77011 ..ILLEGAL THETA VALUES ??? ??? ???
      77012 .SOLUTION NONUNIQUE
      77013 .PREMATURE END
      77014 .EXIT CODE=??? DEGREES OF FREEDOM PROBLEM
      77015 ...TRIM PROPORTION OF ??? TOO LOW OR TOO HIGH WITH ONLY ???
                  OBSERVATIONS
      77016 ...ESTIMATION FAILED WITH DIFF=???  USE DIFF= OPTION
      77017 ...MATRIX IS NOT POSITIVE DEFINITE
HET
      79001 THE STARTING VALUES GIVE NEGATIVE VARIANCE OR OVERFLOWS
NONPAR
      96010 ...ERROR... CONSTANT OPTION NOT ALLOWED
      96011 ...ERROR... SMOOTH= OPTION INVALID
      96012 ...ERROR... A REGRESSOR IS REQUIRED
      96013 ...ERROR... ONLY ONE REGRESSOR ALLOWED
      96014 ..ERROR.. xxxx VARIABLE NOT VALID
      96015 ...ERROR... SKIPPED OBSERVATIONS NOT ALLOWED
      96016 ..ERROR.. xxxx OPTION NOT VALID
      96017 ..ERROR.. INCOVAR= ARRAY HAS TOO FEW ELEMENTS
      96020 INVALID METHOD= OPTION
      96021 ... ERROR .. DIVIDE BY ZERO
```

37. PROGRAMMING IN SHAZAM

"Everything that can be invented has been invented."
Charles H. Duell
U.S. Patent Office, 1899

SHAZAM provides many features to aid users who wish to write their own algorithms or procedures. This chapter provides a few programming examples. More examples of programming in SHAZAM are in the *Judge Handbook* and the Coelli and Griffiths [1989] manual that accompanies Judge, Griffiths, Hill, Lütkepohl and Lee [1985] as well as the Chotikapanich and Griffiths [1993] *Learning SHAZAM Handbook*.

DO-LOOPS

DO-loops provide repeat operations. The general format of DO-loops is:

DO *dovar=start,stop,inc*
commands
. . .
ENDO

The statements between the **DO** and **ENDO** commands are repeatedly executed. The *dovar* variable is the loop variable and this must be set as a symbol such as #, %, ! or ?. Other symbols on the keyboard can also be used (provided it does not have another purpose). Warning: Some operating systems do not permit the use of the # symbol and another one must be used. For example, on CMS operating systems the # sometimes indicates the end of a line. The $ symbol must not be used as a loop variable when a **DELETE SKIP$** command is used in the do-loop commands.

The **DO**-loop facility provides a numeric character substitution for the *dovar* variable. The *dovar* is incremented by the value of *inc*. If *inc* is not specified then an increment of one is set.

The **ENDIF** command can be used inside the **DO**-loop to terminate the **DO**-loop and then continue execution with the command after the **ENDO**. This is described in the chapter *GENERATING VARIABLES* and an example is given in the example on iterative Cochrane-Orcutt estimation later in this chapter.

The **DO**-loop execution can generate a large amount of repetitive output and this can be suppressed by using the command **SET NODOECHO** before the **DO** command. For applications like Monte Carlo studies, the command **SET NOOUTPUT** may also be useful.

DO-loops can be nested up to 8 levels. Each level must use a different **DO**-loop symbol. The value of the **DO**-loop index is contained in the temporary variable $DO. The value of the second loop and following loops are contained in the temporary variables $DO2 - $DO8.

An example of the use of a **DO**-loop is as follows.

```
READ(11) VAR1-VAR10
DO # = 1,10
GENR LVAR# = LOG(VAR#)
PLOT LVAR# VAR#
ENDO
```

This example will create 10 new variables and 10 plots of the log of each variable against each original variable. (It is assumed that the variables *VAR1, VAR2,...VAR10* are in a file.) This example also shows how a series of variables with the same initial letters (in this case, *VAR*) can be easily specified.

The next example shows how a second level **DO**-loop can be used to run a total of 6 regressions. In this case the dependent variables *VAR1, VAR2,* and *VAR3,* are each run with *VAR4* and then run with *VAR5* as independent variables. Note that when a second level is used the first **ENDO** closes the **DO %=4,5** loop and the second **ENDO** closes the **DO #=1,3** loop.

```
SAMPLE 1 10
READ(11) VAR1-VAR5
DO #=1,3
DO %=4,5
OLS VAR# VAR%
ENDO
ENDO
```

The next example takes the variables *X1, X2* and *X3* and divides them by 2 to get *X21, X22, X23* and then by 3 to get *X31, X32, X33*.

```
DO # = 2,3
DO % = 1,3
GENR X#% = X%/#
ENDO
ENDO
```

It is also possible to increment the **DO**-loop by any integer. For example, **DO # = 1,9,2** would set # to the numbers: 1, 3, 5, 7, 9.

EXAMPLES

Splicing Index Number Series

Suppose you have 2 overlapping price indexes where the base year has changed from 1971=100 to 1976=100 and you want to create a new spliced index with 1976=100. You can use the overlapping year, 1976, to adjust the 1971 data as follows:

```
|_* Data set from: Newbold, Statistics for Business and Economics,
|_*     Fourth Edition, 1995, Table 17.8, p. 685.
|_* First READ the data for the 1971 and 1976 based indexes.
|_SAMPLE 1 10
|_READ YEAR  P71 P76 / LIST
   3 VARIABLES AND        10 OBSERVATIONS STARTING AT OBS       1
   1971.000        100.0000        0.0
   1972.000        92.20000        0.0
   1973.000        131.2000        0.0
   1974.000        212.0000        0.0
   1975.000        243.0000        0.0
   1976.000        198.5000        100.0000
   1977.000        0.0             94.00000
   1978.000        0.0             86.70000
   1979.000        0.0             94.90000
   1980.000        0.0             107.0000
|_SAMPLE 6 10
|_* Copy the last 5 years of P76 into the SPLICE index.
|_GENR SPLICE=P76
|_SAMPLE 1 5
|_* Compute the first 5 years of P71 using 1976 base.
|_GENR SPLICE=P71*P76:6/P71:6
|_SAMPLE 1 10
|_* Now PRINT all 10 years of the SPLICED INDEX.
|_PRINT YEAR SPLICE
     YEAR          SPLICE
   1971.000        50.37783
   1972.000        46.44836
   1973.000        66.09572
   1974.000        106.8010
   1975.000        122.4181
   1976.000        100.0000
   1977.000        94.00000
   1978.000        86.70000
   1979.000        94.90000
   1980.000        107.0000
```

Computing the Power of a Test

DO-loops can be useful in computing the power of tests. This example uses the Theil textile data set. The power function is computed for the **TEST** that the coefficient on *INCOME* is equal to 1 in an OLS regression. The power function is then plotted.

```
|_SAMPLE 1 17
|_* Convert data to base 10 logs since that is what Theil uses.
|_GENR CONSUME=LOG(CONSUME)/2.3026
|_GENR INCOME=LOG(INCOME)/2.3026
|_GENR PRICE=LOG(PRICE)/2.3026
|_* Run OLS save coefficients, assume these are true coefficients.
|_OLS CONSUME INCOME PRICE / COEF=BETA
  OLS ESTIMATION
     17 OBSERVATIONS     DEPENDENT VARIABLE = CONSUME
...NOTE..SAMPLE RANGE SET TO:    1,   17


 R-SQUARE =     .9744     R-SQUARE ADJUSTED =     .9707
VARIANCE OF THE ESTIMATE-SIGMA**2 =    .18340E-03
STANDARD ERROR OF THE ESTIMATE-SIGMA =    .13542E-01
SUM OF SQUARED ERRORS-SSE=    .25675E-02
MEAN OF DEPENDENT VARIABLE =    2.1221
LOG OF THE LIKELIHOOD FUNCTION =   50.6612
```

VARIABLE NAME	ESTIMATED COEFFICIENT	STANDARD ERROR	T-RATIO 14 DF	P-VALUE	PARTIAL CORR.	STANDARDIZED COEFFICIENT	ELASTICITY AT MEANS
INCOME	1.1432	.1560	7.328	.000	.891	.3216	1.0839
PRICE	-.82884	.3611E-01	-22.95	.000	-.987	-1.0074	-.7314
CONSTANT	1.3739	.3061	4.489	.001	.768	.0000	.6474

```
|_* Dimension room for 11 values of Power Function.
|_DIM  P 11 B 11
|_SAMPLE 1 1
|_* Assume true SIGMA**2 is the OLS SIGMA**2.
|_GEN1 SIG2=$SIG2
..NOTE..CURRENT VALUE OF $SIG2=  0.18340E-03
|_* Next find the alpha critical value (Type I error).
|_GEN1 ALPHA=.05
|_DISTRIB ALPHA/ TYPE=F DF1=1 DF2=14 INVERSE
            PROBABILITY    CRITICAL VALUE
  ALPHA
 ROW    1    0.50000E-01  4.6000
|_GEN1 CR=$CRIT
..NOTE..CURRENT VALUE OF $CRIT=   4.6000

|_* Turn off the DO-LOOP ECHOing of commands.
|_SET NODOECHO
|_DO #=1,11
|_* Let BETA:1(INCOME) vary between .5 and 1.5, other BETAS unchanged.
|_GEN1 BETA:1=.4+.1*#
|_* Store the hypothesized value of BETA:1(INCOME) in vector B.
|_GEN1 B:#=BETA:1
|_SAMPLE 1 17
|_* Now substitute in the "true" BETAS in OLS.
|_* The next OLS is simply to compute information with given BETA
|_* and SIG2 so the TEST command can be used. Since the OLS output
|_* itself is useless it is suppressed by using ? before the OLS.
|_?OLS CONSUME INCOME PRICE / INCOEF=BETA INSIG2=SIG2
|_* Compute the non-centrality parameter.
|_* It is the same as the chi-square statistic for TEST and is
|_* in $CHI.
|_* Suppress the TEST output with "?".
|_?TEST INCOME=1
|_SAMPLE 1 1
```

```
|_* Also, suppress the DISTRIB output with "?".
|_?DISTRIB CR / TYPE=F DF1=$DF1 DF2=$DF2 C=$CHI
|_* P is now the Power (the probability of rejecting the null if
|_* the alternative is true).
|_?GENR P:#=1-$CDF
|_ENDO
***** EXECUTION BEGINNING FOR DO LOOP
***** EXECUTION FINISHED FOR DO LOOP

|_SAMPLE 1 11
|_* Now print the Power for INCOME coefficient varying between .5 and 1.5
|_PRINT B P
        B                   P
   0.5000000          0.8459275
   0.6000000          0.6648547
   0.7000000          0.4330394
   0.8000000          0.2230297
   0.9000000          0.9189934E-01
   1.000000           0.5000252E-01
   1.100000           0.9189934E-01
   1.200000           0.2230297
   1.300000           0.4330394
   1.400000           0.6648547
   1.500000           0.8459275
|_PLOT P B
        11 OBSERVATIONS
                       *=P
                    M=MULTIPLE POINT
    0.84593     |*                                      *
    0.80404     |
    0.76215     |
    0.72026     |
    0.67836     |
    0.63647     |    *                          *
    0.59458     |
    0.55269     |
    0.51080     |
    0.46891     |
    0.42702     |       *                    *
    0.38513     |
    0.34324     |
    0.30135     |
    0.25946     |
    0.21757     |        *              *
    0.17567     |
    0.13378     |
    0.91893E-01 |            *       *
    0.50003E-01 |               *
                _____
                0.500    0.750     1.000     1.250     1.500

                                  B
```

Initially it is assumed that the coefficients from the first **OLS** regression are the true coefficients and the critical value is calculated on the basis of the "true" coefficient for *INCOME*. Next, a **DO**-loop is set up in which 11 hypothetical coefficients are generated and 11 power values (in the variable P) are generated in conjunction with the hypothetical coefficients. Notice that the variables for the hypothetical coefficients and the power values are **DIM**ensioned before the **DO** -loop to be vectors of 11 observations so that their values will be saved as they are calculated in the **DO**-loop. Several commands are used to generate P within the **DO**-loop. The **OLS** command is used in order to allow the subsequent **TEST** command since **TEST** commands must directly follow a regression command. The **TEST** command results in the calculation of the chi-square statistic which is stored in the temporary variable $\$CHI$ and used in the **DISTRIB** command which follows. The **DISTRIB** command calculates the CDF which is stored in the temporary variable $\$CDF$ (Cumulative Distribution Function) and is used in the final command of the **DO**-loop to compute the power value for the particular hypothetical coefficient. Finally, the power values are plotted against the coefficient values.

The values of the power in the variable P are the probabilities of rejecting the null hypothesis when the alternative is true. The hypothetical values of the $INCOME$ coefficient are the alternatives. Thus, we would hope that the probability of rejecting the null hypothesis (that the coefficient on $INCOME$ is 1) would increase as the alternative (B) moves away from 1. This turns out to be the case as can be seen from the plotted power function. Of course, the ideal power function is one in which the probability of rejecting the null hypothesis when it is true is extremely low and in which the probabilities increase rapidly as the alternatives (the true values) move away from the null value.

A good reference on the non-central F-distribution and power functions can be found in Graybill [1976, Chapter 4.3].

Ridge Regression

DO-loops can also be used to plot a ridge trace for ridge regressions (see, for example, the explanation in Watson and White [1976]). The following output computes a ridge trace for Theil's textile data.

```
|_READ(11) YEAR CONSUME INCOME PRICE
...SAMPLE RANGE IS NOW SET TO:              1        17
|_* Make room for 10 different sets of coefficients.
|_DIM BETA 3 10  K 10
|_* Let Ridge k go from .1 to .9, turn off warning messages.
|_SET NOWARN
|_DO #=1,9
|_GENR K:#=.#
|_* Suppress printing of OLS output by using "?".
|_?OLS CONSUME INCOME PRICE / RIDGE=.# COEF=BETA:#
|_ENDO
****** EXECUTION BEGINNING FOR DO LOOP
#_GENR K:1=.1
#_?OLS CONSUME INCOME PRICE / RIDGE=.1 COEF=BETA:1
#_ENDO
```

```
#_GENR K:2=.2
#_?OLS CONSUME INCOME PRICE / RIDGE=.2 COEF=BETA:2
#_ENDO
#_GENR K:3=.3
#_?OLS CONSUME INCOME PRICE / RIDGE=.3 COEF=BETA:3
#_ENDO
#_GENR K:4=.4
#_?OLS CONSUME INCOME PRICE / RIDGE=.4 COEF=BETA:4
#_ENDO
#_GENR K:5=.5
#_?OLS CONSUME INCOME PRICE / RIDGE=.5 COEF=BETA:5
#_ENDO
#_GENR K:6=.6
#_?OLS CONSUME INCOME PRICE / RIDGE=.6 COEF=BETA:6
#_ENDO
#_GENR K:7=.7
#_?OLS CONSUME INCOME PRICE / RIDGE=.7 COEF=BETA:7
#_ENDO
#_GENR K:8=.8
#_?OLS CONSUME INCOME PRICE / RIDGE=.8 COEF=BETA:8
#_ENDO
#_GENR K:9=.9
#_?OLS CONSUME INCOME PRICE / RIDGE=.9 COEF=BETA:9
#_ENDO
****** EXECUTION FINISHED FOR DO LOOP
|_* Now put OLS coefs in the 10th column, ridge k=0.
|_GENR K:10=0
|_?OLS CONSUME INCOME PRICE / COEF=BETA:10
|_* Now transpose the beta matrix to make it easier to plot.
|_MATRIX BETA=BETA'
|_PRINT K BETA
K
  0.10      0.20      0.30      0.40      0.50      0.60      0.70      0.80
  0.90      0.0

BETA
  10 BY      3 MATRIX
  0.8957645     -1.248780      137.5545
  0.7689530     -1.138775      142.2192
  0.6695782     -1.046880      145.4404
  0.5900597     -0.9689098     147.6794
  0.5252973     -0.9018889     149.2343
  0.4717498     -0.8436397     150.3036
  0.4268921     -0.7925306     151.0229
  0.3888814     -0.7473141     151.4868
  0.3563458     -0.7070192     151.7624
  1.061710      -1.382985      130.7066
```

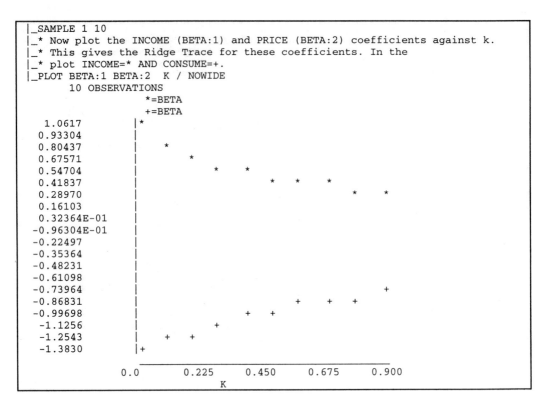

```
|_SAMPLE 1 10
|_* Now plot the INCOME (BETA:1) and PRICE (BETA:2) coefficients against k.
|_* This gives the Ridge Trace for these coefficients. In the
|_* plot INCOME=* AND CONSUME=+.
|_PLOT BETA:1 BETA:2  K / NOWIDE
        10 OBSERVATIONS
                          *=BETA
                          +=BETA
      1.0617           | *
      0.93304          |
      0.80437          |      *
      0.67571          |        *
      0.54704          |          *    *
      0.41837          |            *    *    *
      0.28970          |                       *    *
      0.16103          |
      0.32364E-01      |
     -0.96304E-01      |
     -0.22497          |
     -0.35364          |
     -0.48231          |
     -0.61098          |
     -0.73964          |                              +
     -0.86831          |           +    +    +
     -0.99698          |        +    +
     -1.1256           |     +
     -1.2543           |   +    +
     -1.3830           |+
                        _____
                 0.0        0.225      0.450      0.675      0.900
                                      K
```

In the above program, the Theil textile data is read in. Next, two variables, *BETA* and *K* are dimensioned to be a 3 x 10 matrix and a vector of 10 observations, respectively. *BETA* will be used in the subsequent **DO**-loop to store the values of the coefficients for each ridge regression. *K* will be used in the subsequent **DO**-loop to increment the value of k used in the ridge regressions. In this way, the ridge parameter k goes from .1 to .9 in increments of .1. Notice the **SET NOWARN** command turns off the printing of any warning message that may occur, thus minimizing the amount of output generated. Notice also the question mark (?) that is typed before the **OLS** commands to suppress the output. Since **OLS** is a special case of ridge regression where k=0, an additional **OLS** regression is run without the **RIDGE** option. In all, 10 regressions are run and the intercept and the coefficients on each of *INCOME* and *PRICE* for each of these regressions are saved in the variable *BETA*. *BETA* is then transposed to facilitate the plotting of the coefficients of each *INCOME* and *PRICE* against *K*. In the plot *INCOME* is * and *PRICE* is +. This plot is known as the ridge trace.

An Exact p-value for the Durbin-Watson Test

The following SHAZAM run computes (the hard way) an exact p-value value for the Durbin-Watson test. This is illustrated with the Theil textile data. The SHAZAM commands reproduce the method used by SHAZAM with the **DWPVALUE** option on the **OLS** command. A useful discussion is in Judge, Griffiths, Hill, Lütkepohl and Lee [1985, p. 323]. The Imhof technique applied in Koerts and Abrahamse [1968 and 1969] is used to obtain the distribution of the Durbin-Watson test statistic. Other methods are discussed in Durbin and Watson [1971] and Pan, Jei-jian [1968].

The Durbin-Watson test is based on the statistic:

$$d = \sum_{t=2}^{N}(e_t - e_{t-1})^2 \bigg/ \sum_{t=1}^{N} e_t^2$$

where the e_t are OLS residuals. In matrix notation this can be stated as:

$$d = e'MAMe/e'Me$$

where $M = I - X(X'X)^{-1}X'$ and A is a matrix with 2 on the main diagonal (except in the extreme corners where there is a 1), the upper and lower off diagonals have the value −1, and 0 is everywhere else.

The computations are shown in the following SHAZAM output.

```
|_READ(11) YEAR CONSUME INCOME PRICE
...SAMPLE RANGE IS NOW SET TO:            1        17
|_* Create X.
|_GENR ONE=1
|_COPY INCOME PRICE ONE X
|_* Compute M.
|_MATRIX M=IDEN(17)-X*INV(X'X)*X'
|_* Generate the "A" matrix.
|_* The Diagonal has 2 everywhere except 1 in the corners.
|_GENR D=1
|_SAMPLE 2 16
|_GENR D=2
|_SAMPLE 1 17
|_* Put 1 on the off-diagonals.
|_MATRIX A=IDEN(17,2)
|_* Turn off diagonal to -1 and add the diagonal.
|_MATRIX A=-(A+A')+DIAG(D)
|_* Compute the eigenvalues of "MA" (Eigenvalues are sorted so largest is first)
|_MATRIX MA=M*A
|_MATRIX E=EIGVAL(MA)
|_* Run OLS just to get the DW statistic from $DW when RSTAT is used.
|_OLS CONSUME INCOME PRICE / RSTAT
OLS ESTIMATION
      17 OBSERVATIONS       DEPENDENT VARIABLE = CONSUME
...NOTE..SAMPLE RANGE SET TO:     1,    17

 R-SQUARE =     .9513    R-SQUARE ADJUSTED =      .9443
VARIANCE OF THE ESTIMATE-SIGMA**2 =    30.951
STANDARD ERROR OF THE ESTIMATE-SIGMA =    5.5634
```

```
SUM OF SQUARED ERRORS-SSE=    433.31
MEAN OF DEPENDENT VARIABLE =    134.51
LOG OF THE LIKELIHOOD FUNCTION = -51.6471


VARIABLE    ESTIMATED  STANDARD   T-RATIO        PARTIAL STANDARDIZED ELASTICITY
  NAME      COEFFICIENT  ERROR      14 DF   P-VALUE CORR. COEFFICIENT  AT MEANS
INCOME       1.0617     .2667      3.981      .001  .729    .2387       .8129
PRICE       -1.3830     .8381E-01 -16.50      .000 -.975   -.9893      -.7846
CONSTANT    130.71     27.09       4.824      .000  .790    .0000       .9718


DURBIN-WATSON = 2.0185     VON NEUMAN RATIO = 2.1447     RHO = -0.18239
RESIDUAL SUM =  0.96212E-12  RESIDUAL VARIANCE =    30.951
SUM OF ABSOLUTE ERRORS=    72.787
R-SQUARE BETWEEN OBSERVED AND PREDICTED = 0.9513


|_* Use the DISTRIB command to compute the exact DW probability.
|_DISTRIB $DW / EIGENVAL=E TYPE=IMHOF NEIGEN=14
                     DATA         CDF       1-CDF
  $DW
ROW     1      2.0185     0.30127      0.69873
```

First, A and M are generated in matrix form and stored in the variables A and M. The generation of M is straightforward; the independent variables, *INCOME* and *PRICE*, and a column of ones for the intercept, are copied into a matrix, X, with a **COPY** command and M is then generated with a **MATRIX** command. The generation of A, however, takes several steps. First, to create the diagonal of twos with ones in the extreme corners, a vector of twos is generated with a **GENR** command and this vector is then modified to have ones in the first and last rows (which will later become the extreme corners of the A matrix) with the use of two **IF** commands. The A matrix is then generated as an identity matrix with the ones starting on the second row. The A matrix is then transformed again to its final form with another **MATRIX** command. This is done by adding A and A' and multiplying the result by –1 (thus creating the upper and lower off-diagonals of –1) and adding D to be the diagonal of the A matrix. Next, the N–K=14 eigenvalues of the product of M and A are computed.

The Durbin-Watson statistic from the **OLS** regression is saved in a temporary variable called $DW. This value is then used with the **DISTRIB** command to compute the exact Durbin-Watson p-value. The **TYPE=IMHOF, EIGENVAL=** and **NEIGEN=** options must be used for correct results.

In this example we find that d=2.0185. For a test of the null hypothesis of no autocorrelation in the residuals against positive autocorrelation the critical region is in the left hand tail of the distribution of d. The output of the **DISTRIB** command reports this probability in the cdf column. The p-value of 0.30127 suggests that we cannot reject the null hypothesis.

Iterative Cochrane-Orcutt Estimation

The easy way to implement iterative Cochrane-Orcutt estimation of the model with
first-order autoregressive errors is to use the **AUTO** command. However, the example
below shows how the method can also be programmed in SHAZAM. The final results
are compared to the SHAZAM **AUTO** command:

```
|_* Program to perform Iterative Cochrane-Orcutt estimation of AR(1) Model.
|_READ (11) CONSUME INCOME PRICE
...SAMPLE RANGE IS NOW SET TO:          1         17
|_* Initialize RHO to first estimate OLS.
|_GEN1 RHO=0
|_* Initialize LASTRHO to a high number.
|_GEN1 LASTRHO=999
|_* Turn off useless output in DO-loop.
|_SET NODOECHO NOWARN
|_* Try up to 20 iterations.
|_DO #=1,20
|_* Transform all but first observation including CONSTANT.
|_SAMPLE 2 17
|_GENR C=CONSUME-RHO*LAG(CONSUME)
|_GENR I=INCOME-RHO*LAG(INCOME)
|_GENR P=PRICE-RHO*LAG(PRICE)
|_GENR CONS=1-RHO
|_* Transform first observation.
|_SAMPLE 1 1
|_GENR C=SQRT(1-RHO**2)*CONSUME
|_GENR I=SQRT(1-RHO**2)*INCOME
|_GENR P=SQRT(1-RHO**2)*PRICE
|_GENR CONS=SQRT(1-RHO**2)
|_* Run OLS on transformed data, suppress OLS output with "?".
|_SAMPLE 1 17
|_* Check for convergence, if so jump out of loop.
|_ENDIF(ABS(RHO-LASTRHO).LT.0.01)
|_?OLS C I P CONS / NOCONSTANT  COEF=BETA
|_* Take OLS coefficients and get RHO using original data.
|_?FC CONSUME INCOME PRICE / COEF=BETA
|_* Save RHO to check for convergence next time.
|_GEN1 LASTRHO=RHO
|_PRINT $DO $SSE $RHO
|_* Put latest value of $RHO into RHO.
|_GEN1 RHO=$RHO
|_ENDO
****** EXECUTION BEGINNING FOR DO LOOP  # =  1
   $DO        1.000000
   $SSE       433.3130
   $RHO      -0.1823932
   $DO        2.000000
   $SSE       419.9997
   $RHO      -0.1947947
   $DO        3.000000
   $SSE       419.8044
   $RHO      -0.1953525
...ENDIF IS TRUE AT OBSERVATION          1
...DO LOOP ENDED AT   #=        4
|_* Print final results.
```

```
|_OLS C I P CONS / NOCONSTANT
  OLS ESTIMATION
      17 OBSERVATIONS      DEPENDENT VARIABLE = C
...NOTE..SAMPLE RANGE SET TO:    1,   17


 R-SQUARE =    .9709    R-SQUARE ADJUSTED =    .9668
VARIANCE OF THE ESTIMATE-SIGMA**2 =   29.986
STANDARD ERROR OF THE ESTIMATE-SIGMA =   5.4759
SUM OF SQUARED ERRORS-SSE=   419.80
MEAN OF DEPENDENT VARIABLE =   158.77
LOG OF THE LIKELIHOOD FUNCTION = -51.3777
RAW MOMENT R-SQUARE =    .9991


VARIABLE    ESTIMATED   STANDARD   T-RATIO             PARTIAL STANDARDIZED ELASTICITY
  NAME     COEFFICIENT   ERROR     14 DF    P-VALUE CORR. COEFFICIENT AT MEANS
I            1.0650      .2282      4.667     .000  .780    .3237      .8170
P           -1.3751     .7105E-01  -19.35     .000 -.982   -.8615     -.7830
CONST       129.62      23.05      5.624      .000  .833    .2247      .9656

|_* Compare to SHAZAM AUTO command.
|_AUTO CONSUME INCOME PRICE /  CONV=.01
DEPENDENT VARIABLE =   CONSUME
..NOTE..R-SQUARE,ANOVA,RESIDUALS DONE ON ORIGINAL VARS

LEAST SQUARES ESTIMATION               17 OBSERVATIONS
BY COCHRANE-ORCUTT TYPE PROCEDURE WITH CONVERGENCE = 0.01000


    ITERATION          RHO             LOG L.F.            SSE
        1             0.0            -51.6471            433.31
        2            -0.18239        -51.3987            420.00
        3            -0.19479        -51.3972            419.80
        4            -0.19535        -51.3972            419.80


 LOG L.F. =   -51.3972       AT RHO =    -0.19535

                   ASYMPTOTIC  ASYMPTOTIC  ASYMPTOTIC
             ESTIMATE  VARIANCE   ST.ERROR    T-RATIO
RHO         -0.19535   0.05658    0.23786   -0.82128


 R-SQUARE =    .9528    R-SQUARE ADJUSTED =    .9461
VARIANCE OF THE ESTIMATE-SIGMA**2 =   29.986
STANDARD ERROR OF THE ESTIMATE-SIGMA =   5.4759
SUM OF SQUARED ERRORS-SSE=   419.80
MEAN OF DEPENDENT VARIABLE =   134.51
LOG OF THE LIKELIHOOD FUNCTION = -51.3972


VARIABLE    ESTIMATED   STANDARD   T-RATIO             PARTIAL STANDARDIZED ELASTICITY
  NAME     COEFFICIENT   ERROR     14 DF    P-VALUE CORR. COEFFICIENT AT MEANS
INCOME       1.0650      .2282      4.667     .000  .780    .2394      .8154
PRICE       -1.3751     .7105E-01  -19.35     .000 -.982   -.9837     -.7802
CONSTANT    129.62      23.05      5.624      .000  .833    .0000      .9637
```

Note that the output from the programmed procedure matches that of the **AUTO** command except for certain statistics like R-SQUARE, LOG OF THE LIKELIHOOD FUNCTION, STANDARDIZED COEFFICIENT and ELASTICITY AT MEANS which are not properly computed with an OLS algorithm. The **AUTO** output has the correct values of these statistics.

Nonlinear Least Squares by the Rank One Correction Method

The next example illustrates how to write a SHAZAM program to do least squares by the rank one correction (ROC) method described in Judge, Griffiths, Hill, Lütkepohl and Lee [1985, p. 959]. This method merely minimizes the sum of squared residuals and thus produces the same results as the **OLS** run. The following commands assume use of the data from Table B.2 on page 956 of the above reference.

```
SAMPLE 1 20
READ (TABLEB.2) Y ONE X1 X2
GEN1 NOBS=20
COPY X1 X2 ONE X
MATRIX YY=Y'Y
MATRIX XX=X'X
MATRIX XY=X'Y
MATRIX H=2*XX
MATRIX HINV=INV(H)
MATRIX P=IDEN(3)
SAMPLE 1 3
READ B / BYVAR LIST
   1  1  1
MATRIX S=YY-2*B'XY+B'XX*B
MATRIX G=-2*XY+2*XX*B
* Print starting value info.
PRINT B S G YY XX XY H HINV
* Program to do least squares by rank one correction (ROC) method.
* Allow up to 10 iterations.
DO #=1,10
* First compute the gradient.
MATRIX GLAST=G
* Now get next round betas.
MATRIX BLAST=B
MATRIX B=B-P*G
MATRIX G=-2*XY+2*XX*B
* Now compute S.
MATRIX S=YY-2*B'XY+B'XX*B
MATRIX ETA=(B-BLAST)-P*(G-GLAST)
MATRIX M=(ETA*ETA')/(ETA'(G-GLAST))
MATRIX P=P+M
PRINT B S G P M
MATRIX GG=G'G
* Now check for convergence.
ENDIF(GG.LT.0.0000001)
ENDO
* End of loop
MATRIX VB=2*(S/NOBS)*P
MATRIX SE=SQRT(DIAG(VB))
MATRIX T=B/SE
PRINT B SE T
PRINT VB
* Now compare to regular OLS.
SAMPLE 1 NOBS
OLS Y X1 X2 / DN PCOV
STOP
```

As can be seen in the above example, the ROC method involves computing the gradient at each iteration to see if it is close to zero and thus minimized. To do this, first S is computed, which is the objective function to be minimized. G, the gradient, is then computed from S. Next, a **DO**-loop is initiated to perform the necessary computations until convergence, i.e. until $G'G$ is close to zero. The starting value for B (beta) is one, but this value is transformed on each iteration, thus transforming the values for G and P. P is the inverse of the Hessian and is transformed on each iteration by M, a correction matrix. When convergence occurs, or when the **DO**-loop is performed 10 times, the current values of S and P are used to compute the variance of beta and ultimately to compute a t-ratio. In the commands above, a **PRINT** command is used to print out the final values of beta, the standard error and the t-ratio. These results can then be compared to the **OLS** results which will be generated by the final **OLS** command. The results should be the same.

Monte Carlo Experiments

This example is from an exercise in Judge, Hill, Griffiths, Lütkepohl and Lee [1988, Section 9.6.2, pp. 411-412]. A Monte Carlo experiment is designed to compare the parameter estimates obtained with OLS, GLS, and feasible GLS estimation of a model with AR(1) errors. A feature of the SHAZAM program to note is the use of the **GENR** command to generate the AR(1) errors by recursive calculations. The **SET RANFIX** command is used to ensure that the same set of random numbers will be used in repeated runs of the program so that the results can be replicated.

```
* Design Matrix
SAMPLE 1 20
READ X1 X2 / LIST
14.53   16.74
15.30   16.81
15.92   19.50
17.41   22.12
18.37   22.34
18.83   17.47
18.84   20.24
19.71   20.37
20.01   12.71
20.26   22.98
20.77   19.33
21.17   17.04
21.34   16.74
22.91   19.81
22.96   31.92
23.69   26.31
24.82   25.93
25.54   21.96
25.63   24.05
28.73   25.66
* Generate 1000 samples with true model:  Y = 10 + X1 + X2 + e
* where e is an AR(1) process with:       e = 0.8*e(-1) + v
* and v is independent normally distributed with 0 mean and var.=6.4.
GEN1 SE=SQRT(6.4)
```

```
* Allocate arrays to hold the estimates
DIM BOLS 4 1000 STDOLS 4 1000 BGLS 4 1000 STDGLS 4 1000
DIM BEGLS 4 1000 STDEG 4 1000
* Request the same set of random numbers in repeated runs
SET RANFIX
* Suppress useless output
SET NODOECHO
DO #=1,1000
SAMPLE 1 20
* Generate v
GENR V=NOR(SE)
* Set an initial condition for e
GENR E=0
* Generate e - recursive calculations
SAMPLE 2 20
GENR E=0.8*LAG(E)+V
SAMPLE 1 20
* Generate Y given X and e.
GENR Y=10+X1+X2+E
* OLS estimation, suppress the output with ?
?OLS Y X1 X2 / COEF=BOLS:# STDERR=STDOLS:#
* GLS estimation (RHO is known)
?AUTO Y X1 X2 / RHO=0.8 COEF=BGLS:# STDERR=STDGLS:#
* Estimated GLS (RHO is estimated - iterated Cochrane-Orcutt)
?AUTO Y X1 X2 / COEF=BEGLS:# STDERR=STDEG:#
ENDO
* Transpose the arrays so that the STAT command can be used
MATRIX BOLS=BOLS'
MATRIX STDOLS=STDOLS'
MATRIX BGLS=BGLS'
MATRIX STDGLS=STDGLS'
MATRIX BEGLS=BEGLS'
MATRIX STDEG=STDEG'
SAMPLE 1 1000
STAT BOLS    BGLS    BEGLS / MEAN=B STDEV=ASE
STAT STDOLS STDGLS STDEG / MEAN=ESE STDEV=STDSE
SAMPLE 1 12
FORMAT(4F12.4)
PRINT B ASE ESE STDSE / FORMAT
STOP
```

Annotated results obtained from the above program follow. *B* is the average parameter estimate, *ASE* is the standard deviation of the parameter estimate, *ESE* is the average standard error and *STDSE* is the standard deviation of the standard errors.

B	ASE	ESE	STDSE
OLS ESTIMATION			
.9957	.4091	.2092	.0540
.9986	.2093	.1768	.0456
10.1006	8.8212	3.8956	1.0047
.0000	.0000	.0000	.0000
GLS estimation (with RHO=0.8)			
.9889	.3080	.3802	.0649
1.0032	.1345	.1291	.0220
10.1398	5.7728	8.3551	1.4261
.8000	.0000	.0000	.0000

```
EGLS estimation (by iterative Cochrane-Orcutt)
        .9905         .3424        .2700         .0907
       1.0051         .1433        .1348         .0242
      10.0649        6.5016       5.6791        2.1816
        .5031         .2589        .0000         .0000
```

The results show that the parameter estimates from the three estimation methods are unbiased with the exception of the parameter estimate for the autocorrelation parameter RHO that is obtained by iterative Cochrane-Orcutt estimation. The average parameter estimate for RHO is 0.5031 which is less than the true parameter value of 0.8. The standard deviations of the parameter estimates are smaller for EGLS (Estimated GLS or feasible GLS) estimation compared to OLS estimation to demonstrate that EGLS is efficient.

Bootstrapping Regression Coefficients

This example shows how to approximate the distribution of an estimator by using the Efron [1979] bootstrapping method that is discussed in Freedman and Peters [1984]. This is illustrated with an OLS regression using the Theil textile data set. A more automatic way of getting the results produced in the SHAZAM program below is with the commands:

```
SET RANFIX
OLS CONSUME INCOME PRICE
DIAGNOS / BOOTSAMP=1000
```

Note that the bootstrap method is a computationally slow and inaccurate way of getting OLS standard errors, but might be useful on other kinds of models. A valuable way to view the results is with a graphical presentation. The commands show two methods of obtaining a graphical display. First, a histogram is produced with the **PLOT** command. Second, the **NONPAR** command is used to construct a nonparametric kernel density estimate. The **GNU** option specifies that the plots are produced with the GNUPLOT interface.

```
* Read the Theil textile data set
READ(THEIL.DAT) YEAR CONSUME INCOME PRICE
* Program to get OLS standard errors by Bootstrapping.
* Warning: This is a computationally expensive run.
* Run the original regression, save residuals and predicted values.
OLS CONSUME INCOME PRICE / RESID=E PREDICT=YHAT
GEN1 N=$N
GEN1 K=$K
GEN1 NREP=1000
* Create space to hold vectors of bootstrapped coefficients.
DIM BETA K NREP
* Turn off DO-loop printing or you will get lots of output.
SET NODOECHO
SET NOOUTPUT
SET RANFIX
```

```
DO #=1,NREP
* Draw a random sample of errors with replacement.
GENR NEWE=SAMP(E)*SQRT(N/(N-K))
* Generate new dependent variable by using NEWE.
GENR Y=YHAT+NEWE
OLS Y INCOME PRICE / COEF=BETA:#
ENDO
* Transpose the BETA matrix for use in STAT and PLOT commands.
* This is needed to get the numbers in column order.
MATRIX BETA=BETA'
SET OUTPUT
* Set the sample size to number of replications.
SAMPLE 1 NREP
* Get the statistics on the replications.
STAT BETA
*
* Look at the frequency distribution for the INCOME coefficient.
GENR B1=BETA:1
* Plot a histogram
PLOT B1 / HISTO GNU GROUPS=30
* Now get a nonparametric density estimate
NONPAR B1 / DENSITY GNU
STOP
```

The histogram presentation of the distribution for the coefficient on *INCOME* is as follows:

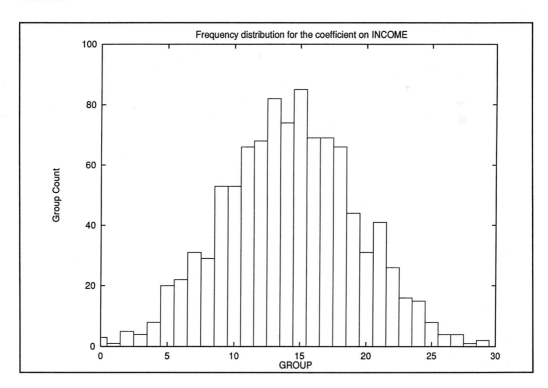

The above histogram can be compared with the nonparametric density estimate that is generated with the **NONPAR** command. The GNUPLOT graph of this estimate is as follows:

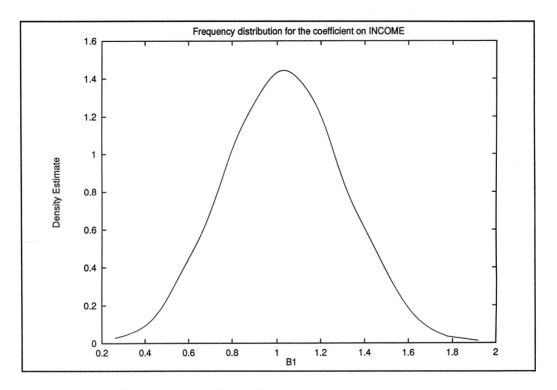

Heteroskedastic Consistent Covariance Matrices

The easy way to get White's [1980] heteroskedastic consistent covariance matrix is to use the **HETCOV** option on **OLS**. However, this example shows how to program it and some variations discussed in MacKinnon and White [1985]. The example also shows how to use the estimator proposed by Cragg [1983].

```
|_READ(11) YEAR CONSUME INCOME PRICE
...SAMPLE RANGE IS NOW SET TO:        1        17
|_* First run OLS, save residuals
|_OLS CONSUME INCOME PRICE / RESID=U STDERR=OSE
 OLS ESTIMATION
      17 OBSERVATIONS     DEPENDENT VARIABLE = CONSUME
...NOTE..SAMPLE RANGE SET TO:    1,   17

 R-SQUARE =    .9513    R-SQUARE ADJUSTED =     .9443
 VARIANCE OF THE ESTIMATE-SIGMA**2 =   30.951
 STANDARD ERROR OF THE ESTIMATE-SIGMA =   5.5634
 SUM OF SQUARED ERRORS-SSE=    433.31
```

```
MEAN OF DEPENDENT VARIABLE =    134.51
LOG OF THE LIKELIHOOD FUNCTION = -51.6471


VARIABLE   ESTIMATED  STANDARD   T-RATIO       PARTIAL STANDARDIZED ELASTICITY
  NAME     COEFFICIENT  ERROR      14 DF   P-VALUE CORR. COEFFICIENT AT MEANS
INCOME      1.0617      .2667      3.981     .001   .729     .2387      .8129
PRICE      -1.3830      .8381E-01 -16.50     .000  -.975    -.9893     -.7846
CONSTANT   130.71      27.09       4.824     .000   .790     .0000      .9718
```

```
|_* Next square the residuals and copy the independent variables
|_* into the X matrix.
|_GENR U2=U**2
|_GENR ONE=1
|_COPY INCOME PRICE ONE X
|_* Now HC is White's(1980) covariance matrix for heteroskedasticity.
|_MATRIX HC=INV(X'X)*X'DIAG(U2)*X*INV(X'X)
|_* Now get the corrected standard errors and print them out.
|_MATRIX HSE=SQRT(DIAG(HC))
|_PRINT OSE
OSE
  0.2666740      0.8381426E-01   27.09429
|_PRINT HSE
HSE
  0.2172196      0.7422455E-01   23.66507
|_* Note that the corrected standard errors are smaller.
|_* Now get HC1, the Hinkley method of estimation.
|_MATRIX HC1=($N/$DF)*HC
..NOTE..CURRENT VALUE OF $N   =   17.000
..NOTE..CURRENT VALUE OF $DF  =   14.000
|_MATRIX KTT=DIAG(X*INV(X'X)*X')
|_MATRIX SIG2=U2/(1-KTT)
|_* HC2 is the Horn and Duncan estimate.
|_MATRIX HC2=INV(X'X)*X'DIAG(SIG2)*X*INV(X'X)
|_MATRIX USTAR=U/(1-KTT)
|_MATRIX OM=DIAG(USTAR**2)
|_* HC3 is the MacKinnon and White(1985) Jackknife estimate.
|_MATRIX HC3=(($N-1)/$N)*INV(X'X)*(X'OM*X-(1/$N)*(X'USTAR*USTAR'X))*INV(X'X)
|_* Now print out the 4 different covariance matrix estimates.
|_PRINT HC HC1 HC2 HC3
HC
    3 BY     3 MATRIX
  0.4718433E-01  0.2076371E-03  -4.957136
  0.2076371E-03  0.5509284E-02  -0.4802344
  -4.957136     -0.4802344      560.0357
HC1
    3 BY     3 MATRIX
  0.5729526E-01  0.2521307E-03  -6.019380
  0.2521307E-03  0.6689845E-02  -0.5831418
  -6.019380     -0.5831418      680.0433
HC2
    3 BY     3 MATRIX
  0.6044015E-01 -0.5570915E-03  -6.295172
 -0.5570915E-03  0.6942529E-02  -0.5138845
  -6.295172     -0.5138845      704.1588
HC3
    3 BY     3 MATRIX
  0.7333148E-01 -0.1782186E-02  -7.563165
 -0.1782186E-02  0.8325627E-02  -0.4927166
```

```
   -7.563165      -0.4927166        836.8303
|_* Now do the Cragg (1983) estimator using X**2 as auxiliary variables.
|_GENR INCOME2=INCOME**2
|_GENR PRICE2=PRICE**2
|_COPY INCOME PRICE ONE INCOME2 PRICE2 Q
|_* The coefficient vector BA is Cragg's equation (13), p. 753.
|_MATRIX BA=INV(X'Q*INV(Q'DIAG(U2)*Q)*Q'X)*X'Q*INV(Q'DIAG(U2)*Q)*Q'CONSUME
|_* The covariance matrix VBA is Cragg's equation (14), p. 754.
|_MATRIX VBA=INV(X'Q*INV(Q'DIAG(U2)*Q)*Q'X)
|_* Note that BA and VBA have many similar terms. It would have
|_* been cheaper to compute them separately first.
|_PRINT BA VBA
BA
   0.9725258       -1.367748        138.8088
VBA
     3 BY     3 MATRIX
  0.3068722E-01  0.1126381E-02  -3.324788
  0.1126381E-02  0.5418412E-02  -0.5683495
  -3.324788      -0.5683495        398.3224
```

Hausman Specification Test

This example shows how to use Hausman's [1978] specification test in an errors in variables model. The model is a regression of consumption on income where it is suspected that income is measured with error. The investment variable is used as an instrumental variable.

```
|_* Hausman specification test of error in variables
|_* EXAMPLE:   The data set on investment (I), consumption (C) and
|_* income (Y) is from Griffiths, Hill and Judge (1993, Table 14.2, p. 464).
|_SAMPLE 1 20
|_READ I C Y
   3 VARIABLES AND       20 OBSERVATIONS STARTING AT OBS        1

|_* Estimation using the consistent estimator (IV) under both
|_* the null and the alternative hypotheses;
|_* in SHAZAM, the 2SLS command is used for instrumental variable estimation
|_2SLS C Y (I) / DN COEF=B1 PCOV COV=V1
 TWO STAGE LEAST SQUARES - DEPENDENT VARIABLE = C
   1 EXOGENOUS VARIABLES
   2 POSSIBLE ENDOGENOUS VARIABLES
       20 OBSERVATIONS
DN OPTION IN EFFECT - DIVISOR IS N


 R-SQUARE =    .9893    R-SQUARE ADJUSTED =    .9887
VARIANCE OF THE ESTIMATE-SIGMA**2 =   .67175E-01
STANDARD ERROR OF THE ESTIMATE-SIGMA =   .25918
SUM OF SQUARED ERRORS-SSE=   1.3435
MEAN OF DEPENDENT VARIABLE =   21.747

                             ASYMPTOTIC
VARIABLE   ESTIMATED   STANDARD   T-RATIO          PARTIAL STANDARDIZED ELASTICITY
  NAME    COEFFICIENT   ERROR    --------   P-VALUE CORR. COEFFICIENT  AT MEANS
Y           .79036    .2074E-01   38.12      .000   .994     .9560      .8955
CONSTANT   2.2734      .5142       4.421     .000   .722     .0000      .1045
```

```
VARIANCE-COVARIANCE MATRIX OF COEFFICIENTS
Y           .42995E-03
CONSTANT  -.10594E-01    .26437
             Y                CONSTANT


|_GEN1 SIGIV=$SIG2
..NOTE..CURRENT VALUE OF $SIG2=   .67175E-01

|_* Estimation using the efficient estimator (OLS) under the null
|_OLS C Y / DN COEF=B0 COV=V0 NOMULSIGSQ
 OLS ESTIMATION
      20 OBSERVATIONS     DEPENDENT VARIABLE = C
...NOTE..SAMPLE RANGE SET TO:    1,   20

 R-SQUARE =    .9908     R-SQUARE ADJUSTED =     .9903
VARIANCE OF THE ESTIMATE-SIGMA**2 =   .57482E-01
STANDARD ERROR OF THE ESTIMATE-SIGMA =   .23975
SUM OF SQUARED ERRORS-SSE=   1.1496
MEAN OF DEPENDENT VARIABLE =    21.747
LOG OF THE LIKELIHOOD FUNCTION =  .184015


                          ASYMPTOTIC
VARIABLE   ESTIMATED   STANDARD   T-RATIO        PARTIAL STANDARDIZED ELASTICITY
  NAME     COEFFICIENT   ERROR    --------  P-VALUE CORR. COEFFICIENT AT MEANS
Y           .82289     .7389E-01   11.14     .000   .934     .9954     .9323
CONSTANT   1.4718      1.834        .8024    .422   .186     .0000     .0677

|_* Use the error variance estimate obtained from IV estimation.
|_MATRIX V0=SIGIV*V0
|_PRINT V0
   V0
   2 BY    2 MATRIX
   .3667221E-03  -.9035666E-02
  -.9035666E-02   .2259885

|_* Compute the Hausman specification test statistic using the method
|_* illustrated in Griffiths, Hill and Judge (1993, p. 465)
|_SAMPLE 1 2
|_GENR Q=B1-B0
|_MATRIX VQ=V1-V0
|_MATRIX M=(Q(1)**2) / VQ(1,1)
|_* The statistic M is distributed chi-square with 1 degree of freedom
|_* under the null hypothesis. The 5% critical value is 3.84.
|_PRINT M
   M
   16.73798
```

A general version of the Hausman specification test is described in Griffiths, Hill and Judge [1993, Appendix 14A.4, pp. 475-6].

Non-Nested Model Testing

This example shows how to apply the nonnested Cox test and the Davidson-MacKinnon [1981] J-test described in Judge, Griffiths, Hill, Lütkepohl and Lee [1985, pp. 883-884]. Theil's textile data is used to test the two linear regressions *CONSUME* on *INCOME* and *CONSUME* on *PRICE*. The test procedure first tests H1 (*INCOME* is the correct variable) and then H2 (*PRICE* is the correct variable). It should be noted that we have strong theoretical reasons to believe that both *INCOME* and *PRICE* belong in the regression in this example.

In the output below the Cox test statistics indicate that the *INCOME* model is rejected, but the *PRICE* model is not rejected. However, the J-test statistics reject both models.

```
|_SAMPLE 1 17
|_READ(11) YEAR CONSUME INCOME PRICE
    4 VARIABLES AND       17 OBSERVATIONS STARTING AT OBS       1
|_* Non-nested Cox Test, H1: Consume on income, H2: Consume on price.
|_*  See BIG JUDGE pp. 883-884.
|_OLS CONSUME INCOME / COEF=B1 DN PREDICT=Y1HAT
 OLS ESTIMATION
       17 OBSERVATIONS     DEPENDENT VARIABLE = CONSUME
...NOTE..SAMPLE RANGE SET TO:    1,   17

 R-SQUARE =    .0038   R-SQUARE ADJUSTED =    -.0626
VARIANCE OF THE ESTIMATE-SIGMA**2 =   521.19
STANDARD ERROR OF THE ESTIMATE-SIGMA =   22.830
SUM OF SQUARED ERRORS-SSE=   8860.3
MEAN OF DEPENDENT VARIABLE =   134.51
LOG OF THE LIKELIHOOD FUNCTION = -77.2990

                              ASYMPTOTIC
VARIABLE    ESTIMATED  STANDARD    T-RATIO          PARTIAL STANDARDIZED ELASTICITY
  NAME      COEFFICIENT  ERROR    **** DF    P-VALUE CORR. COEFFICIENT  AT MEANS
INCOME      .27473      1.077      .2552      .799  .066     .0618       .2103
CONSTANT    106.21      111.0      .9567      .339  .240     .0000       .7897
|_GEN1 S1=$SIG2
..NOTE..CURRENT VALUE OF $SIG2=   521.19
|_OLS CONSUME PRICE / COEF=B2 DN PREDICT=Y2HAT
 OLS ESTIMATION
       17 OBSERVATIONS     DEPENDENT VARIABLE = CONSUME
...NOTE..SAMPLE RANGE SET TO:    1,   17

 R-SQUARE =    .8961   R-SQUARE ADJUSTED =    .8892
VARIANCE OF THE ESTIMATE-SIGMA**2 =    54.348
STANDARD ERROR OF THE ESTIMATE-SIGMA =    7.3721
SUM OF SQUARED ERRORS-SSE=   923.91
MEAN OF DEPENDENT VARIABLE =   134.51
LOG OF THE LIKELIHOOD FUNCTION = -58.0829

                              ASYMPTOTIC
VARIABLE    ESTIMATED  STANDARD    T-RATIO          PARTIAL STANDARDIZED ELASTICITY
  NAME      COEFFICIENT  ERROR    **** DF    P-VALUE CORR. COEFFICIENT  AT MEANS
PRICE       -1.3233     .1093     -12.11      .000 -.952    -.9466      -.7508
CONSTANT    235.49      8.528      27.61      .000  .990     .0000      1.7508
```

```
|_GEN1 S2=$SIG2
..NOTE..CURRENT VALUE OF $SIG2=   54.348
|_* Create the X and Z matrices, X for H1, Z for H2.
|_GENR ONE=1
|_COPY INCOME ONE X
|_COPY PRICE ONE Z
|_* Create the M matrices, M1 for H1, M2 for H2.
|_MATRIX M2=IDEN(17)-Z*INV(Z'Z)*Z'
|_MATRIX M1=IDEN(17)-X*INV(X'X)*X'
|_* Test H1: The hypothesis that income is the true model.
|_* The test statistic H1 is asymptotically normally distributed.
|_MATRIX S21=S1+1/$N*(B1'X'M2*X*B1)
..NOTE..CURRENT VALUE OF $N   =   17.000
|_MATRIX C12=$N/2*LOG(S2/S21)
..NOTE..CURRENT VALUE OF $N   =   17.000
|_MATRIX VC12=(S1/S21**2)*(B1'X'M2*M1*M2*X*B1)
|_MATRIX H1=C12/SQRT(VC12)
|_PRINT C12 VC12 H1
    C12
  -19.24761
    VC12
  0.2001174E-02
    H1
  -430.2633
|_* Now test H2: The hypothesis that price is the true model.
|_* The test statistic H2 is asymptotically normally distributed.
|_MATRIX S12=S2+1/$N*(B2'Z'M1*Z*B2)
..NOTE..CURRENT VALUE OF $N   =   17.000
|_MATRIX C21=$N/2*LOG(S1/S12)
..NOTE..CURRENT VALUE OF $N   =   17.000
|_MATRIX VC21=(S2/S12**2)*(B2'Z'M1*M2*M1*Z*B2)
|_MATRIX H2=C21/SQRT(VC21)
|_PRINT C21 VC21 H2
    C21
  0.2147064
    VC21
  0.5193263E-01
    H2
  0.9421603
|_* Now try the Davidson-MacKinnon J Test.
|_* To test H1, see if coef on Y2HAT is zero.
|_OLS CONSUME INCOME Y2HAT
 OLS ESTIMATION
      17 OBSERVATIONS     DEPENDENT VARIABLE = CONSUME
...NOTE..SAMPLE RANGE SET TO:    1,   17


 R-SQUARE =    .9513    R-SQUARE ADJUSTED =    .9443
VARIANCE OF THE ESTIMATE-SIGMA**2 =   30.951
STANDARD ERROR OF THE ESTIMATE-SIGMA =   5.5634
SUM OF SQUARED ERRORS-SSE=   433.31
MEAN OF DEPENDENT VARIABLE =   134.51
LOG OF THE LIKELIHOOD FUNCTION = -51.6471
```

VARIABLE NAME	ESTIMATED COEFFICIENT	STANDARD ERROR	T-RATIO 14 DF	P-VALUE	PARTIAL CORR.	STANDARDIZED COEFFICIENT	ELASTICITY AT MEANS
INCOME	1.0617	.2667	3.981	.001	.729	.2387	.8129
Y2HAT	1.0451	.6334E-01	16.50	.000	.975	.9893	1.0451
CONSTANT	-115.40	30.20	-3.821	.002	-.714	.0000	-.8580

```
|_* To test H2, see if coef on Y1HAT is zero.
|_OLS CONSUME PRICE Y1HAT
 OLS ESTIMATION
      17 OBSERVATIONS       DEPENDENT VARIABLE = CONSUME
...NOTE..SAMPLE RANGE SET TO:     1,    17


 R-SQUARE =    .9513    R-SQUARE ADJUSTED =     .9443
 VARIANCE OF THE ESTIMATE-SIGMA**2 =    30.951
 STANDARD ERROR OF THE ESTIMATE-SIGMA =    5.5634
 SUM OF SQUARED ERRORS-SSE=    433.31
 MEAN OF DEPENDENT VARIABLE =     134.51
 LOG OF THE LIKELIHOOD FUNCTION = -51.6471


 VARIABLE    ESTIMATED   STANDARD   T-RATIO        PARTIAL STANDARDIZED ELASTICITY
   NAME     COEFFICIENT   ERROR     14 DF     P-VALUE CORR. COEFFICIENT  AT MEANS
 PRICE       -1.3830    .8381E-01   -16.50      .000 -.975    -.9893       -.7846
 Y1HAT        3.8645     .9707       3.981      .001  .729     .2387       3.8645
 CONSTANT   -279.75     129.6       -2.159      .049 -.500     .0000      -2.0799
```

Solving Nonlinear Sets of Equations

Consider the task of finding a solution X to the equation $f(X)=0$ (where X may be a vector). For example, in the single variable case,

$$X^2 - 4X = -4$$

This can be expressed in implicit function form as:

$$X^2 - 4X + 4 = 0$$

A solution can be obtained by a numerical iterative method with the use of the **SOLVE** option on the **NL** command. The **SAMPLE** command must be set to one observation. The implicit function form of the equation (excluding the = sign) is specified on the **EQ** command. This is shown in the SHAZAM output below.

```
|_SAMPLE 1 1
|_NL 1 / NCOEF=1 SOLVE PITER=50
...NOTE..SAMPLE RANGE SET TO:     1,     1
|_EQ (X*X)-4*X+4
|_COEF X 5
     0 VARIABLES IN  1 EQUATIONS WITH   1 COEFFICIENTS
         1 OBSERVATIONS


COEFFICIENT STARTING VALUES
X          5.0000
      100 MAXIMUM ITERATIONS, CONVERGENCE =  .000010


INITIAL STATISTICS :
TIME =         .250 SEC.   ITER. NO.     0   FUNCT. EVALUATIONS     1
FUNCTION VALUE=   81.00000     FUNCTION VALUE/N =    81.00000
```

```
COEFFICIENTS
   5.000000
GRADIENT
   108.0000

FINAL STATISTICS :
TIME =        .340 SEC.   ITER. NO.    34   FUNCT. EVALUATIONS    35
FUNCTION VALUE=    .8261134E-15 FUNCTION VALUE/N =    .8261134E-15
COEFFICIENTS
   2.000128
GRADIENT
   .1949125E-10
        COEFFICIENT
X         2.0001
|_END
```

The solution of the equation is near X=2. The FUNCTION VALUE (in this case the value reported is $f^2(X)$) and the GRADIENT should be very close to zero if a solution has been found.

This technique can be generalized to solve a set of equations simultaneously. For example, consider two equations with variables X1 and X2. The implicit function form in SHAZAM notation is:

X1**2 + 3*X1*X2 – 22

X2**2 + 2*X1*X2 – 21

The following output shows the solution.

```
|_SAMPLE 1 1
|_NL 2 / NCOEF=2 SOLVE
...NOTE..SAMPLE RANGE SET TO:     1,      1
|_EQ X1**2 + 3*X1*X2 - 22
|_EQ X2**2 + 2*X1*X2 - 21
|_COEF X1 1 X2 1
     0 VARIABLES IN  2 EQUATIONS WITH   2 COEFFICIENTS
          1 OBSERVATIONS

COEFFICIENT STARTING VALUES
X1        1.0000      X2        1.0000
     100 MAXIMUM ITERATIONS, CONVERGENCE =   .000010

INITIAL STATISTICS :
TIME =        .040 SEC.   ITER. NO.    0    FUNCT. EVALUATIONS    1
FUNCTION VALUE=    972.0000    FUNCTION VALUE/N =    972.0000
COEFFICIENTS
   1.000000      1.000000
GRADIENT
  -252.0000     -252.0000

FINAL STATISTICS :
```

```
TIME =          .070 SEC.    ITER. NO.     10    FUNCT. EVALUATIONS      19
FUNCTION VALUE=       .9305198E-11 FUNCTION VALUE/N =    .9305198E-11
COEFFICIENTS
    2.000000         3.000000
GRADIENT
    .7605076E-04    .4753829E-04
        COEFFICIENT
X1          2.0000
X2          3.0000
|_END
```

The solution to the equations is near X1=2 and X2=3. Remember that there may be multiple answers, so you may need to experiment with different starting values.

Full Information Maximum Likelihood

This example was proposed by Professor Ray Byron of Bond University in Australia. This supplements the example on LIML given in the chapter *SHAZAM PROCEDURES*. Although this method may not be the fastest (or most appealing) way to compute FIML estimates it does illustrate very advanced SHAZAM programming.

The example shows FIML estimation of Klein's model I. The starting values for the iterative estimation are obtained from 3SLS estimation (see the example in the chapter *TWO-STAGE LEAST SQUARES AND SYSTEMS OF EQUATIONS*). The parameter estimates from the FIML estimation are saved in the variable *BFIML*.

```
SAMPLE 1 21
READ (KLEIN.DAT) WG T GE TIME1 PLAG KLAG XLAG C I WP PR WGWP PP
* ===== KLEIN'S MODEL I - 3SLS =====
SYSTEM 3 WG T GE TIME1 PLAG KLAG XLAG / DN COEF=B3SLS
OLS C PLAG PR WGWP
OLS I PLAG KLAG PR
OLS WP XLAG TIME1 PP
* ===== KLEIN'S MODEL I - FIML =====
* Programmed by Ray Byron, Bond University, Queensland, Australia
* Note - this can be improved upon with two sided derivatives and
* better programming.
*
* The model is  YB + XG = E
DIM B 7 7 G 7 7
* Exogenous variables
COPY PLAG KLAG XLAG TIME1 WG T GE   X
* Endogenous variables
GENR YY=C+I+GE-T
COPY C I WP YY PR WGWP PP   Y
* Number of observations
GEN1 NOB=21
* Number of stochastic equations
GEN1 NEQ=3
* Number of parameters
GEN1 NCOEF=9
GEN1 NM=NOB*NEQ
SET NODOECHO
```

```
* Specify the identities
*   (4) YY=C+I+GE-T
*   (5) PR=YY-WGWP
*   (6) WGWP=WP+WG
*   (7) PP=YY-WG+T
MATRIX B=-IDEN(7)
MATRIX G(6,4)=-1
MATRIX G(7,4)=1
MATRIX G(5,6)=1
MATRIX G(5,7)=-1
MATRIX G(6,7)=1
MATRIX B(1,4)=1
MATRIX B(2,4)=1
MATRIX B(4,5)=1
MATRIX B(6,5)=-1
MATRIX B(3,6)=1
MATRIX B(4,7)=1
* Express data in deviations about the mean
GENR ONE=1
MATRIX XM=ONE'X/NOB
MATRIX YM=ONE'Y/NOB
MATRIX X=X-ONE*XM
MATRIX Y=Y-ONE*YM
* Starting values
MATRIX BB=B3SLS
DIM F 3 1  DV NM NCOEF  E0 NM 1  E NM 1  V1 NOB NEQ
*
PROC ML_CALC
* Specify the stochastic equations
* (1) C = f(PLAG, PR, WGWP)      Consumption
* (2) I = f(PLAG, KLAG, PR)      Investment
* (3) WP= f(XLAG, TIME1, PP)     Private Wages
   MATRIX B(5,1)=BB(2)
   MATRIX B(6,1)=BB(3)
   MATRIX B(5,2)=BB(6)
   MATRIX B(7,3)=BB(9)
   MATRIX G(1,1)=BB(1)
   MATRIX G(1,2)=BB(4)
   MATRIX G(2,2)=BB(5)
   MATRIX G(3,3)=BB(7)
   MATRIX G(4,3)=BB(8)
   MATRIX P=-G*INV(B)
   MATRIX V=Y-X*P
   COPY V V1 / FROW=1;NOB TROW=1;NOB FCOL=1;NEQ TCOL=1;NEQ
   MATRIX VV=V1'V1/NOB
* DT is the value of the likelihood function
   MATRIX DT=DET(VV)
PROCEND
*
EXEC ML_CALC
*
MATRIX FX1=DT
MATRIX BFIML=BB
MATRIX F(2)=DT
* set up matrix for solving quadratics later on
READ AA / ROWS=3 COLS=3
.01 -.1 1
 0   0  1
```

```
.01 .1  1
* loop for optimum searching
DO %=1,20
* routine to evaluate derivatives and get search direction
* vectorise v1
MATRIX E=VEC(V1)
MATRIX E0=E
MATRIX SIG=INV(VV)
* get dv/db numerically
DO #=1,NCOEF
* evaluate residuals in response to increments in coefficients
    MATRIX C=BFIML(#)*.01
    MATRIX BB(#)=BFIML(#)+C
    EXEC ML_CALC
    MATRIX E=VEC(V1)
    MATRIX DIF=(E-E0)/C
    COPY DIF DV / FROW=1;NM TROW=1;NM FCOL=1;1 TCOL=#;#
    MATRIX BB(#)=BFIML(#)
ENDO
* get weighting matrix and first derivatives for Gauss method
MATRIX DD=DV'(SIG@IDEN(NOB))*DV
MATRIX D1=DV'(SIG@IDEN(NOB))*E
* get direction
MATRIX DIR=INV(DD)*D1
* test both sides of previous position
MATRIX BB=BFIML-.1*DIR
EXEC ML_CALC
MATRIX F(1)=DT
MATRIX BB=BFIML+.1*DIR
EXEC ML_CALC
MATRIX F(3)=DT
* solve quadratic
MATRIX ABC=INV(AA)*F
MATRIX LEN=-ABC(2)/(2*ABC(1))
MATRIX BB=BFIML+LEN*DIR
EXEC ML_CALC
GEN1 TEST=ABS((F(2)-DT)/F(2))
GEN1 F(2)=DT
MATRIX BFIML=BB
GEN1 DT1=1.0/DT
PRINT LEN DT1 BFIML
* Stopping criterion
ENDIF(TEST.LT..001)
ENDO
* Compare 3SLS and FIML
SAMPLE 1 NCOEF
PRINT B3SLS BFIML
STOP
```

Multinomial Logit Models

An introduction to multinomial choice models is available in Judge, Griffiths, Hill, Lütkepohl and Lee [1985, Chapter 18.3]. Suppose that J+1 alternatives are available. For the multinomial logit model consider that the probability that individual (or firm) t will select alternative j for j=0,...,J is:

$$P_{t0} = 1 / [1 + \sum_{j=1}^{J} \exp(X_t' \beta_j)] \quad \text{and} \quad P_{tj} = \exp(X_t' \beta_j) / [1 + \sum_{j=1}^{J} \exp(X_t' \beta_j)] \quad \text{for } j=1,...,J$$

where X_t is a vector of variables and the β_j are vectors of unknown parameters. For individual t let Y_{tj} be a binary variable that is 1 if alternative j is chosen and 0 otherwise. The log-density for observation t can be stated as:

$$L_t = \sum_{j=1}^{J} Y_{tj} (X_t' \beta_j) - \log[1 + \sum_{j=1}^{J} \exp(X_t' \beta_j)]$$

With the assumption of independence the log-likelihood function is obtained by summing the individual log-densities. Maximum likelihood estimation of this model can be implemented with the **LOGDEN** option on the **NL** command. The **EQ** statement is used to give the formula for the log-density of a single observation.

To interpret the results it is useful to evaluate how the choice probabilities change in response to changes in the independent variables. For predicted choice probabilities $\hat{P}_{tj}$ the elasticities are calculated as:

$$(X_{tk} / \hat{P}_{tj}) (\partial \hat{P}_{tj} / \partial X_{tk})$$

The **DERIV** command can be used to compute the required derivatives and then the estimated elasticities can be obtained. Elasticities can be computed as weighted aggregated elasticities as described in the chapter *PROBIT AND LOGIT REGRESSION* and given in Hensher and Johnson [1981, Equation 3.44].

The SHAZAM program that follows shows the steps involved in the estimation and analysis of a multinomial logit model. It is assumed that three alternatives are available and a data file **FIRMS.DAT** contains binary variables *Y1* and *Y2* that indicate choices for alternatives 1 and 2. The variable calculated as *1−Y1−Y2* is then 1 if the third alternative is chosen and 0 otherwise. The data file also contains independent variables *X1, X2* and *X3*.

The first task is to determine sensible starting values for the multinomial logit estimation. The approach illustrated here is to estimate a "null model" with constant terms only. The estimates are used to initialize starting values in the variable *BETA*. The value of the log-likelihood function for the null model is computed in the variable *LL0*. The multinomial logit model is then specified and estimated with the **N L** command. Note that the value of the log-likelihood function at the first iteration should be identical to the value of *LL0*.

A number of goodness-of-fit measures can be considered (see, for example, Maddala [1983, Chapter 3]). A measure that is easily computed is a likelihood ratio test statistic. The value of the log-likelihood function at the final iteration of the **NL** procedure is available in the temporary variable *$LLF*. The commands below show the calculation of the likelihood ratio test statistic in the variable *LR*. Predicted choice probabilities are then computed. For each observation, the alternative with the highest probability can be determined and a prediction success table can be formed. This is left to the user as an exercise. Finally, derivatives and elasticities are calculated.

The commands demonstrated here can be modified to estimate nested logit models as described in Amemiya [1985, Chapter 9]. That is, the main requirement for maximum likelihood estimation of these models in SHAZAM is to write an expression for the log-density of a single observation.

```
READ (FIRMS.DAT) Y1 Y2 X1 X2 X3
GENR Y0=1-Y1-Y2
?STAT Y1 Y2 Y0 / SUMS=STOT
GEN1 NTOT=STOT:1+STOT:2+STOT:3
GEN1 A1=LOG(STOT:1/STOT:3)
GEN1 A2=LOG(STOT:2/STOT:3)
* Value of log-likelihood function for "null" model
GEN1 LL0=STOT:1*A1+STOT:2*A2-NTOT*LOG(1+EXP(A1)+EXP(A2))
PRINT STOT NTOT A1 A2 LL0
* Set starting values
DIM BETA 8
GEN1 BETA:1=A1
GEN1 BETA:5=A2
* Specify the parameterization of the model.
EQ1: (B10+B11*X1+B12*X2+B13*X3)
EQ2: (B20+B21*X1+B22*X2+B23*X3)
* Multinomial logit estimation by maximum likelihood
NL 1 / LOGDEN NCOEF=8 START=BETA PITER=100 GENRVAR
EQ  Y1*[EQ1] + Y2*[EQ2] -LOG(1+EXP([EQ1])+EXP([EQ2]))
END
* A goodness-of-fit measure is the likelihood ratio test.
* The test can be compared with a Chi-square distribution with 6 d.f.
GEN1 LR=2*($LLF-LL0)
PRINT LR
* Calculate the predicted choice probabilities
GENR P1=EXP([EQ1]) / (1+EXP([EQ1])+EXP([EQ2]))
GENR P2=EXP([EQ2]) / (1+EXP([EQ1])+EXP([EQ2]))
* Calculate derivatives and elasticities
SET NODOECHO
DO #=1,3
DERIV X# VP1=EXP([EQ1]) / (1+EXP([EQ1])+EXP([EQ2]))
DERIV X# VP2=EXP([EQ2]) / (1+EXP([EQ1])+EXP([EQ2]))
DO %=1,2
GENR VE=VP%*X#
?STAT VE P% / SUMS=TOT
GEN1 VE#%=TOT:1/TOT:2
ENDO
ENDO
* Weighted Aggregate Elasticities
PRINT VE11 VE21 VE31  VE12 VE22 VE32
```

38. SHAZAM PROCEDURES

"It will take six months or more for the colonial secretary to deal with the matter and months more before we learn of his decision. But you will not be interested in what he decides for you are to be hanged on Monday morning"

Matthew B. Begbie
Canadian Judge, 19th Century

SHAZAM provides many features to aid users who wish to write their own programs. SHAZAM PROCS require the knowledge of three commands: **PROC, PROCEND,** and **EXEC** as well as the concept of SHAZAM character strings.

SHAZAM *CHARACTER STRINGS*

A character string is actually a SHAZAM variable which contains a set of characters rather than numeric data. Character strings can be used at any time and are not restricted for use in SHAZAM procedures. They can simplify the use of repeated character sequences in a SHAZAM program. For example, if you always use the list of variable names: CONSUME INCOME PRICE in many parts of your SHAZAM program, you can define a character variable which contains these characters. Note that the character string contains only the characters and not the actual data. To define a character string, simply chose a variable name that is not used in your SHAZAM program and place a colon ":" after the name and follow it with the desired character string, as in:

MYLIST:CONSUME INCOME PRICE

In this case the SHAZAM variable *MYLIST* is created and it contains only the characters "CONSUME INCOME PRICE". If any spaces are included immediately following the ":" they will be included in the character string.

Next, you could use the contents of the variable *MYLIST* in any SHAZAM command by enclosing the character variable in left and right brackets as in:

OLS [MYLIST] / RSTAT

SHAZAM would then interpret the above command as:

OLS CONSUME INCOME PRICE / RSTAT

If you wish to see the actual characters in the variable *MYLIST,* just print it with:

```
PRINT MYLIST
```

The output from the above SHAZAM commands would look like:

```
|_MYLIST:CONSUME INCOME PRICE
|_OLS CONSUME INCOME PRICE / RSTAT
 OLS ESTIMATION
       17 OBSERVATIONS      DEPENDENT VARIABLE = CONSUME
 ...NOTE..SAMPLE RANGE SET TO:     1,    17

  R-SQUARE =    .9513    R-SQUARE ADJUSTED =     .9443
 VARIANCE OF THE ESTIMATE-SIGMA**2 =    30.951
 STANDARD ERROR OF THE ESTIMATE-SIGMA =   5.5634
 SUM OF SQUARED ERRORS-SSE=    433.31
 MEAN OF DEPENDENT VARIABLE =    134.51
 LOG OF THE LIKELIHOOD FUNCTION = -51.6471

 VARIABLE    ESTIMATED  STANDARD   T-RATIO          PARTIAL STANDARDIZED ELASTICITY
   NAME     COEFFICIENT   ERROR    14 DF   P-VALUE  CORR. COEFFICIENT  AT MEANS
 INCOME       1.0617     .2667     3.981    .001  .729     .2387        .8129
 PRICE       -1.3830   0.8381E-01 -16.50    .000 -.975    -.9893       -.7846
 CONSTANT    130.71     27.09      4.824    .000  .790     .0000        .9718

 DURBIN-WATSON = 2.0185   VON NEUMANN RATIO = 2.1447    RHO =  -.18239
 RESIDUAL SUM =  0.53291E-14  RESIDUAL VARIANCE =    30.951
 SUM OF ABSOLUTE ERRORS=    72.787
 R-SQUARE BETWEEN OBSERVED AND PREDICTED =  .9513
 RUNS TEST:    7 RUNS,    9 POSITIVE,    8 NEGATIVE, NORMAL STATISTIC = -1.2423
|_PRINT MYLIST
  CONSUME INCOME PRICE
```

Character strings are used heavily in SHAZAM procedures to define lists of variables at execution time rather than in the procedure itself. Examples will be detailed below.

While character strings are frequently used to contain a list of variable names, they could also be used to contain any set of characters including an entire equation. For example suppose you wanted to square a set of variables, you could first define the character variable:

```
MYMATH:**2
GENR Y=X[MYMATH]
GENR Z=W[MYMATH]
```

This would be equivalent to:

```
GENR Y=X**2
GENR Z=W**2
```

If you later decide to divide by 3 instead of squaring the variable it would only be necessary to change one line of the program and use:

```
MYMATH:/3
```

and this would be equivalent to:

```
GENR Y=X/3
GENR X=W/3
```

WRITING A SHAZAM PROCEDURE

A SHAZAM procedure requires the use of the **PROC, PROCEND** and often the **FILE PROCPATH** commands. A SHAZAM procedure is simply a set of SHAZAM commands contained within **PROC** and **PROCEND** commands. The SHAZAM commands are executed with the SHAZAM **EXEC** command. Every SHAZAM procedure must have a name which has not been used as a previous SHAZAM variable. The procedure name is specified on the **PROC** command and also on the **EXEC** command. A simple SHAZAM procedure is:

```
PROC OLSYX
SAMPLE 1 20
GENR Y=NOR(1)
GENR X=NOR(1)
OLS Y X
PROCEND
```

The above commands will simply define two random variables using the normal random number generator and then run an OLS regression. The procedure is executed with the **EXEC** command. Suppose you want to run the procedure three times and hence obtain three different OLS regressions since different random numbers would be generated each time. The command file would look like:

```
PROC OLSYX
SAMPLE 1 20
GENR Y=NOR(1)
GENR X=NOR(1)
OLS Y X
PROCEND
EXEC OLSYX
EXEC OLSYX
EXEC OLSYX
STOP
```

You might decide that you like your *OLSYX* procedure so much that you want to keep it in your library of procedures. In that case you would simply create a file with a filename identical to the PROC name. Use a file with the name **OLSYX** and put the commands from **PROC** to **PROCEND** in the file. After the file has been saved, your SHAZAM command file only requires the commands:

```
EXEC OLSYX
EXEC OLSYX
EXEC OLSYX
STOP
```

SHAZAM will search your current default directory for a file with the name **OLSYX** and load the procedure and then execute it three times.

It is also possible to use SHAZAM **DO**-loops to avoid repetitive commands as in:

```
DO #=1,3
EXEC OLSYX
ENDO
STOP
```

Most users like to keep their SHAZAM procedures in a separate directory. For example: in the DOS and OS/2 operating systems, if all procedures are in the directory **C:\SHAZAM\SHAZPROCS** then you would include the **FILE PROCPATH** command in your SHAZAM command file so that the proper directory is searched as in:

```
FILE PROCPATH C:\SHAZAM\SHAZPROCS\
EXEC OLSYX
EXEC OLSYX
EXEC OLSYX
STOP
```

Alternatively, you can use the **FILE PROC** command to load the PROC from any directory as in:

```
FILE PROC C:\PROCS\OLSYX
EXEC OLSYX
EXEC OLSYX
EXEC OLSYX
STOP
```

If a Macintosh is used the directory might appear something like:

```
FILE PROCPATH HARDDISK:SHAZAM:SHAZPROCS:
```

Note that blank characters are not allowed in the disk and folder names on the Macintosh. Other systems should have a **FILE PROCPATH** corresponding to filename conventions for that system.

While the *OLSYX* procedure will certainly prove valuable in your research you might find that it is too restrictive because sometimes you would like to add additional variables to the regression. This is where character variables are used. However, first the *OLSYX* proc will be modified to reduce potential confusion in a SHAZAM program. It will be convenient to use an underscore "_" in variable names inside a procedure so they would not get confused with variable names outside the procedure. For example you might already have a variable with the name Y and it could be unexpectedly redefined if the *OLSYX* procedure were used in its current form. Hence, the procedure will use the variables Y_ and X_ instead of Y and X. The **ALL_** option on the **DELETE** command can be used to delete all variables with an underscore at the end. The second modification to the procedure will allow you to include additional variables and change them each time the procedure is executed. This feature will require a character string which will be given the name *MOREVARS* in the revised procedure below. In addition, a character string with the name *OPTS* will be used to pass options for the **OLS** command down to the revised *OLSYX* procedure.

```
PROC OLSYX
SAMPLE 1 20
GENR Y_=NOR(1)
GENR X_=NOR(1)
OLS Y X [MOREVARS] / [OPTS]
PROCEND
```

Now consider the following SHAZAM command file:

```
SAMPLE 1 20
GENR Z=UNI(1)
GENR W=UNI(1)
MOREVARS:Z W
OPTS:ANOVA
EXEC OLSYX
MOREVARS:Z
OPTS:
EXEC OLSYX
MOREVARS:
OPTS:MAX
EXEC OLSYX
STOP
```

It should be easy to figure out that the above program would be equivalent to the following three OLS commands:

```
OLS Y X Z W / ANOVA
OLS Y X Z
OLS Y X / MAX
```

In summary, the general format for using SHAZAM procedures is:

FILE PROCPATH *pathname*   or   **FILE PROC** *filename*
charname: string
EXEC *proc_name*

The general format for the PROC is:

PROC *proc_name*

. . .

(SHAZAM commands)

. . .

PROCEND

CONTROLLING PROCEDURE OUTPUT

SHAZAM procedures can often become quite long and you will not want to see the commands printed when the procedure is loaded or when it is executed. It is easy to stop the procedure from printing when loaded by placing the commands **SET NOECHO** before the procedure and then include **SET ECHO** after the procedure to allow commands to appear again. In addition it is sometimes useful to begin certain commands with an "=" which suppresses the printing of that particular command. Commands that begin with "?" will suppress the output of the command. Furthermore, the **SET NODOECHO** command will suppress the echoing of commands within a **DO**-loop and the **SET NOOUTPUT** command will turn off most (but not all) output). These features are used in the example below. You will want to experiment with these features to obtain desired results. Comments that begin with a single * will not be printed in the output but comments that begin with a double ** will be printed.

EXAMPLES

Square Root of a Matrix

For a given matrix A it is sometimes necessary to find the square root of A. The **SQRT( )** function on the **MATRIX** command simply takes the square root of each element of the matrix but it may be necessary to find the matrix X such that XX=A. The **SQRT()** function does not do this. Various algorithms have been proposed from time to time and they usually involve matrix decompositions. For example: if A is a real, symmetric matrix then an eigenvalue-eigenvector decomposition can be used such that new matrices are defined where V'V=I, AV=VD, D is a diagonal matrix, A–VQV'VQV', QQ=D, and XX=A, where X=VQV'. A procedure named *SQRTA* to compute X is:

```
PROC SQRTA
*  [AMATRIX]=INPUT MATRIX
*  [XMATRIX]=OUTPUT MATRIX
* GET SQRT OF A MATRIX
MATRIX A_=[AMATRIX]
MATRIX V_=EIGVEC(A_)
MATRIX D_=EIGVAL(A_)
MATRIX Q_=SQRT(D_)
MATRIX X_=V_*DIAG(Q_)*V_'
MATRIX [XMATRIX]=X_
DELETE A_ X_ V_ D_ Q_
PROCEND
```

However, another method is an iterative procedure described in Golub and Van Loan [1983, p.395]. This method says to simply iterate on the formula:

$$X_{k+1} = \frac{1}{2}(X_k + AX_k^{-1})$$

where the initial matrix X_0 is an identity matrix. A SHAZAM procedure to do this for up to 20 iterations and check for convergence is:

```
SET NOECHO
=PROC SQRTM
=SET NODOECHO NOOUTPUT
* [AMATRIX]=INPUT MATRIX
* [XMATRIX]=OUTPUT MATRIX
* GET SQRT OF A MATRIX
MATRIX A_=[AMATRIX]
?GEN1 N_=$ROWS
MATRIX X_=IDEN(N_)
* ALLOW UP TO 20 ITERATIONS BUT WE PROBABLY DONT NEED THAT MANY
DO #=1,20
MATRIX X_=.5*(X_+A_*INV(X_))
* SEE HOW CLOSE WE ARE BY FIRST TURNING THE WHOLE MATRIX INTO A VECTOR
MATRIX C_=VEC(X_*X_)-VEC(A_)
* FIND OUT THE SUM OF SQUARED DISCREPANCIES
MATRIX CC_=C_'C_
* IF WE HAVE CONVERGED GET OUT
?ENDIF(C_.LT.1E-15)
?ENDO
MATRIX [XMATRIX]=X_
DELETE A_ N_ X_ C_ CC_
SET DOECHO
PROCEND
=SET ECHO
```

The input to this procedure is the matrix $A\_$ and the solution will be in the matrix $X\_$. An example is to find the square root of the matrix:

$$\begin{bmatrix} 10 & 5 & 3 \\ 5 & 12 & 2 \\ 3 & 2 & 11 \end{bmatrix}$$

Assume that the *SQRTM* procedure is contained in the file **SQRTM**. SHAZAM will automatically search for the *SQRTM* procedure if it has not been previously defined in the command file. SHAZAM will search the directory specified by the **FILE PROCPATH** statement or look in the default directory if there is no defined PROCPATH. For example, if the file **SQRTM** were in an alternate directory such as **C:\SHAZAM\PROCS\SQRTM** then the PROCPATH should be defined as:

```
FILE PROCPATH C:\SHAZAM\PROCS\
```

Then the SHAZAM command file will be:

```
SAMPLE 1 3
READ  A / ROWS=3 COLS=3
10 5 3
5 12 2
3 2 11
AMATRIX:A
XMATRIX:X
EXEC SQRTM
PRINT A X
* Check the result
MATRIX XX=X*X
PRINT XX
STOP
```

The output from this exercise will be:

```
|_SAMPLE 1 3
|_READ A / ROWS=3 COLS=3 LIST
      3 ROWS AND          3 COLUMNS, BEGINNING AT ROW          1
|_AMATRIX:A
|_XMATRIX:X
|_EXEC SQRTM
...DO LOOP ENDED AT  #=        7
#_          PROCEND
|_PRINT A
   10.00000       5.000000        3.000000
   5.000000       12.00000        2.000000
   3.000000       2.000000        11.00000
|_PRINT X
   3.036379       .7631512        .4449762
   .7631512       3.369748        .2498038
   .4449762       .2498038        3.277132
|_* Check the result
|_MATRIX XX=X*X
|_PRINT XX
   10.00000       5.000000        3.000000
   5.000000       12.00000        2.000000
   3.000000       2.000000        11.00000
|_STOP
```

Black-Scholes Option Pricing Model

The Black-Scholes [1973] equation gives a formula for pricing call options. The formula gives the value of the call option at time t (C_t) as a function of the current price of the stock (S_t), the exercise price of the option (K), the time to expiration (τ), the risk free interest rate (r) and the standard deviation of the stock's log return (σ) as follows:

$$C_t = S_t F(d_1) - K e^{-r\tau} F(d_2) \qquad \text{where}$$

$$d_1 = \frac{\ln(S_t / K) + (r + \sigma^2 / 2)\tau}{\sigma\sqrt{\tau}} \quad \text{and} \quad d_2 = d_1 - \sigma\sqrt{\tau}$$

F() represents the cumulative normal distribution function. The put price (P_t) can also be computed by substituting negative values of S_t, d_1, and d_2 so that:

$$P_t = -S_t F(-d_1) + Ke^{-r\tau}F(-d_2)$$

A procedure to compute the option price given other known inputs follows:

```
PROC BS
* INPUTS: [K] EXERCISE PRICE
*         [S] STOCK PRICE
*         [SIG] STANDARD DEVIATION
*         [TAU] TIME TO EXPIRATION
*         [R] RISK FREE INTEREST RATE
* OUTPUTS: [C] CALL PRICE
*          [P] PUT PRICE
GENR D1_=(LOG([S]/[K])+([R]+([SIG]**2)/2)*[TAU])/([SIG]*SQRT([TAU]))
GENR D2_=D1_-[SIG]*SQRT([TAU])
GENR [C]=[S]*NCDF(D1_)-[K]*EXP(-[R]*[TAU])*NCDF(D2_)
GENR [P]=-[S]*NCDF(-D1_)+[K]*EXP(-[R]*[TAU])*NCDF(-D2_)
PRINT [S] [K] [C] [P]
PROCEND
```

To run the *BS* PROC, one needs only to set the inputs as illustrated in the following SHAZAM commands.

```
SAMPLE 1 1
READ EXPRICE SPRICE
50 50
SIG:.35
R:.08
TAU:.25
K:EXPRICE
S:SPRICE
C:CALL
P:PUT
EXEC BS
PRINT [C] [P]
STOP
```

This produces the following output. Note that a listing of the PROC and all commands occur because no options were used to suppress this output.

```
|_PROC BS
|_* INPUTS: [K] EXERCISE PRICE
|_*         [S] STOCK PRICE
|_*         [SIG] STANDARD DEVIATION
|_*         [TAU] TIME TO EXPIRATION
|_*         [R] RISK FREE INTEREST RATE
```

```
|_* OUTPUTS: [C] CALL PRICE
|_*         [P] PUT PRICE
|_GENR D1_=(LOG([S]/[K])+([R]+([SIG]**2)/2)*[TAU])/([SIG]*SQRT([TAU]))
|_GENR D2_=D1_-[SIG]*SQRT([TAU])
|_GENR [C]=[S]*NCDF(D1_)-[K]*EXP(-[R]*[TAU])*NCDF(D2_)
|_GENR [P]=-[S]*NCDF(-D1_)+[K]*EXP(-[R]*[TAU])*NCDF(-D2_)
|_PRINT [S] [K] [C] [P]
|_PROCEND
|_SAMPLE 1 1
|_READ EXPRICE SPRICE
    2 VARIABLES AND         1 OBSERVATIONS STARTING AT OBS        1

|_SIG:.35
|_R:.08
|_TAU:.25
|_K:EXPRICE
|_S:SPRICE
|_C:CALL
|_P:PUT
|_EXEC BS
 _PROC BS
  _        GENR D1_=(LOG(SPRICE/EXPRICE)+(.08+(.35**2)/2)*.25)/(.35*SQRT(.25))
  _        GENR D2_=D1_-.35*SQRT(.25)
  _        GENR CALL=SPRICE*NCDF(D1_)-EXPRICE*EXP(-.08*.25)*NCDF(D2_)
  _        GENR PUT=-SPRICE*NCDF(-D1_)+EXPRICE*EXP(-.08*.25)*NCDF(-D2_)
  _        PRINT SPRICE EXPRICE CALL PUT
   50.00000        50.00000        3.969272        2.979205
  _        PROCEND
|_PRINT CALL PUT
   3.969272        2.979205
```

From the output one can see that the Black-Scholes model predicts a call option price of $3.96 and a put option price of $2.97.

It is also possible to write a procedure to compute the Black-Scholes implied volatility (σ) given the current stock price (S_t), strike price (K), interest rate (r), time to maturity (τ) and call price (C). This requires an iterative algorithm based on the Newton-Raphson method for solving a nonlinear equation as described in Benninga [1989, pp. 139-154]. The algorithm uses a starting value for σ based on the formula:

$$\sigma^2 = \left| \ln(S_t / K) + r\tau \right| \frac{2}{\tau}$$

then uses a series of iterations to solve for σ in the formula:

$$\sigma(i+1) = \sigma(i) - \frac{f(\sigma(i)) - C}{f'(\sigma)} \qquad \text{where}$$

$$f'(\sigma) = \frac{\partial f(\sigma)}{\partial \sigma} = S_t \sqrt{\tau} F'(d_1) \qquad \text{and} \qquad F'(x) = \frac{1}{\sqrt{2\pi}} \exp(-x^2 / 2)$$

The SHAZAM PROC is:

```
PROC IMPVOL
SET NODOECHO
* PROGRAM TO COMPUTE BLACK-SCHOLES IMPLIED VOLATILITY
* INPUTS: [S] STOCK PRICE
*         [K] STRIKE PRICE
*         [R] INTEREST RATE, EXAMPLE .12
*         [TAU] TIME TO MATURITY IN YEARS, EXAMPLE .25
*         [C]  CALL PRICE
GENR STARTS_=ABS(LOG([S]/[K])+[R]*[TAU])*(2/[TAU]))
GENR SIG_=SQRT(STARTS_)
?DO #=1,20
GENR D1_=(LOG([S]/[K])+([R]+SIG_*SIG_/2)*[TAU])/(SIG_*SQRT([TAU]))
GENR FN_=EXP(-D1_*D1_/2)/SQRT(2*3.14159)
GENR FPRIME_=[S]*SQRT([TAU])*FN_
GENR D2_=D1_-SIG_*SQRT([TAU])
GENR C_=[S]*NCDF(D1_)-[K]*EXP(-[R]*[TAU])*NCDF(D2_)
GENR SIG_=SIG_-(C_-[C])/FPRIME_
?ENDIF(ABS(C_-[C]).LT.0.00001)
ENDO
PRINT SIG_ C_
PROCEND
```

To run the PROC use the SHAZAM commands:

```
* AN Example
SAMPLE 1 1
READ STOCK STRIKE CALL / LIST
     100    125      2
S:STOCK
K:STRIKE
C:CALL
R:.12
TAU:.25
EXEC IMPVOL
* Another Example
READ STOCK STRIKE CALL / LIST
     122    125      3
S:STOCK
K:STRIKE
C:CALL
R:.1
TAU:.25
EXEC IMPVOL
STOP
```

The output is:

```
|_* AN Example
|_SAMPLE 1 1
|_READ STOCK STRIKE CALL / LIST
   3 VARIABLES AND         1 OBSERVATIONS STARTING AT OBS         1

      STOCK           STRIKE           CALL
```

```
    100.0000        125.0000        2.000000
|_S:STOCK
|_K:STRIKE
|_C:CALL
|_R:.12
|_TAU:.25
|_EXEC IMPVOL
 _PROC IMPVOL
  _          SET NODOECHO
       SIG_            C_
   0.4034792        2.000000
|_* Another Example
|_READ STOCK STRIKE CALL / LIST
    3 VARIABLES AND          1 OBSERVATIONS STARTING AT OBS          1

       STOCK           STRIKE          CALL
   122.0000        125.0000        3.000000
|_S:STOCK
|_K:STRIKE
|_C:CALL
|_R:.1
|_TAU:.25
|_EXEC IMPVOL
       SIG_            C_
   0.1215579        3.000000
|_STOP
```

Reproducing the OLS Command

This example shows how a procedure could be written to actually reproduce almost all
the calculations of the SHAZAM **OLS** command. While this procedure is not necessary
since the **OLS** command is easier and faster, the method does illustrate and verify the
precise calculations used in the **OLS** command. The *OLS* PROC which is placed in the
file **OLS** is:

```
SET NOECHO
PROC OLS
* THIS PROC WILL PRODUCE THE SAME OUTPUT AS THE SHAZAM OLS COMMAND
SET NODOECHO
COPY [DEPVAR] Y_
* DEFINE THE VECTOR OF ONES AS BELOW TO GET THE DIMENSIONS RIGHT
MATRIX ONE_=Y_-Y_+1
GEN1 N_=$ROWS
COPY [INDEPS] ONE_ X_
SAMPLE 1 N_
MATRIX B_=INV(X_'X_)*X_'Y_
GEN1 K_=$ROWS
MATRIX YHAT_=X_*B_
MATRIX E_=Y_-YHAT_
MATRIX SSE_=E_'E_
GEN1 DF_=N_-K_
MATRIX SIG2_=SSE_/DF_
* COMPUTE Y'Y IN DEVIATIONS FROM MEAN, THIS REQUIRES THE A MATRIX, THEIL 4.2
MATRIX A_=IDEN(N_)-(1/N_)*(ONE_*ONE_')
* DO ANOVA STUFF FROM MEAN
```

```
MATRIX SST_=Y_'A_*Y_
MATRIX SSR_=SST_-SSE_
MATRIX R2_=1-SSE_/SST_
MATRIX KM1_=K_-1
MATRIX NM1_=N_-1
MATRIX R2ADJ_=1-(NM1_/DF_)*(1-R2_)
MAT SIGMA_=SQRT(SIG2_)
MAT YMEAN_=Y_'ONE_/N_
MATRIX MST_=SST_/NM1_
MAT SIGML_=SSE_/N_
MAT LLF_=-(N_/2)*LOG(2*3.14159*SIGML_)-(N_/2)
PRINT N_ R2_ R2ADJ_ SIG2_ SIGMA_ SSE_ YMEAN_ LLF_
* DO THE MODEL SELECTION TESTS
GEN1 FPE_=SIG2_*(1+K_/N_)
GEN1 LOGAIC_=LOG(SIGML_)+2*K_/N_
GEN1 LOGSC_=LOG(SIGML_)+K_*LOG(N_)/N_
GEN1 GCV_=SIGML_*(1-K_/N_)**(-2)
GEN1 HQ_=SIGML_*LOG(N_)**(2*K_/N_)
GEN1 RICE_=SIGML_/(1-2*K_/N_)
GEN1 SHIBATA_=SIGML_*(N_+2*K_)/N_
GEN1 SC_=SIGML_*N_**(K_/N_)
GEN1 AIC_=SIGML_*EXP(2*K_/N_)
PRINT FPE_ LOGAIC_ LOGSC_ GCV_ HQ_ RICE_ SHIBATA_ SC_ AIC_
MATRIX MSR_=SSR_/KM1_
MATRIX F_=MSR_/SIG2_
*PRINT SSR_ SSE_ SST_ KM1_ DF_ NM1_ MSR_ SIG2_ MST_ F_
* MAKE AN ANOVA TABLE
DIM ANOVA_ 3 4
MATRIX ANOVA_(1,1)=SSR_
MATRIX ANOVA_(2,1)=SSE_
MATRIX ANOVA_(3,1)=SST_
MAT ANOVA_(1,2)=KM1_
MAT ANOVA_(2,2)=DF_
MAT ANOVA_(3,2)=NM1_
MAT ANOVA_(1,3)=MSR_
MAT ANOVA_(2,3)=SIG2_
MAT ANOVA_(3,3)=MST_
MAT ANOVA_(1,4)=F_
PRINT ANOVA_
* DO ANOVA STUFF FROM ZERO
MATRIX ZSST_=Y_'Y_
MATRIX ZSSR_=ZSST_-SSE_
MATRIX ZMSR_=ZSSR_/K_
MATRIX ZMST_=ZSST_/N_
MATRIX ZF_=ZMSR_/SIG2_
* MAKE A ZANOVA TABLE
DIM ZANOVA_ 3 4
MATRIX ZANOVA_(1,1)=ZSSR_
MATRIX ZANOVA_(2,1)=SSE_
MATRIX ZANOVA_(3,1)=ZSST_
MAT ZANOVA_(1,2)=K_
MAT ZANOVA_(2,2)=DF_
MAT ZANOVA_(3,2)=N_
MAT ZANOVA_(1,3)=ZMSR_
MAT ZANOVA_(2,3)=SIG2_
MAT ZANOVA_(3,3)=ZMST_
MAT ZANOVA_(1,4)=ZF_
*PRINT ZSSR_ SSE_ ZSST_ K_ DF_ N_ ZMSR_ SIG2_ ZMST_ ZF_
```

```
PRINT ZANOVA_
* PRINT COEFFICENT TABLE
MATRIX VB_=SIG2_*INV(X_'X_)
MATRIX SE_=SQRT(DIAG(VB_))
MATRIX T_=B_/SE_
MATRIX PARTIAL_=T_/SQRT(T_**2+DF_)
?STAT X_ / MEAN=XBAR_ STDEV=SD_
MATRIX STANDB_=B_*SD_/SQRT(MST_)
MATRIX ELAS_=B_*XBAR_/YMEAN_
PRINT B_ SE_ T_ PARTIAL_ STANDB_ ELAS_ VB_
* RESIDUALS
*PRINT Y_ YHAT_ E_
* DURBIN-WATSON
* NEED TO GENERATE THE DW A MATRIX AS SHOW IN THE SHAZAM MANUAL
* PROGRAMMING EXAMPLE FOR THE EXACT DW TEST
GENR D_=2
SAMPLE 1 1
GENR D_=1
SAMPLE N_ N_
GENR D_=1
SAMPLE 1 N_
MATRIX A_=IDEN(N_,2)
MATRIX A_=-(A_+A_')+DIAG(D_)
MATRIX DW_=(E_'A_*E_)/SSE_
MATRIX VN_=DW_*(N_/NM1_)
* NOW WE NEED AN A MATRIX THAT WILL GENERATE RHO
?DELETE A_
MAT A_=IDEN(N_,2)
MAT RHO_=(E_'A_*E_)/(SSE_ - ((E_(N_))**2) )
MAT ESUM_=E_'ONE_
MAT EABS_=ABS(E_)'ONE_
* NEED THE DEVIATION A MATRIX AGAIN FOR Y AND YHAT
MATRIX A_=IDEN(N_)-(1/N_)*(ONE_*ONE_')
MAT R2OP_=(YHAT_'A_*Y_)**2/((YHAT_'A_*Y_)*(Y_'A_*Y_))
PRINT DW_ VN_ RHO_ ESUM_ SIG2_ EABS_ R2OP_
* NOW FOR THE RUNS TEST
MAT DUME_=DUM(E_)
MAT N1_=DUME_'ONE_
MAT N2_=DUM(-E_)'ONE_
MAT EN_=(2*N1_*N2_)/(N1_+N2_) +1
*PRINT EN_
MAT SN_=SQRT((2*N1_*N2_*(2*N1_*N2_-N1_-N2_))/((N1_+N2_)**2*(N1_+N2_-1)))
*PRINT SN_
* GET THE NUMBER OF RUNS
SAMPLE 2 N_
GENR DIFF_=DUME_.NE.LAG(DUME_)
SAMPLE 1 N_
MATRIX NRUNS_=DIFF_'ONE_ +1
MAT NORMSTA_=(NRUNS_-EN_)/SN_
PRINT NRUNS_ N1_ N2_ NORMSTA_
* NOW FOR THE SKEWNESS AND KURTOSIS
MATRIX S1_=E_'ONE_/N_
MATRIX S2_=(E_**2)'ONE_/N_
MATRIX S3_=(E_**3)'ONE_/N_
MATRIX S4_=(E_**4)'ONE_/N_
GEN1 M2_=S2_-S1_**2
GEN1 M3_=S3_-3*S1_*S2_+2*S1_**3
GEN1 M4_=S4_-4*S1_*S3_+6*S1_**2*S2_-3*S1_**4
```

```
GEN1 K2_=N_*M2_/(N_-1)
GEN1 K3_=N_**2*M3_/((N_-1)*(N_-2))
GEN1 K4_=N_**2*((N_+1)*M4_-3*(N_-1)*M2_**2)/((N_-1)*(N_-2)*(N_-3))
GEN1 G1_=K3_/(K2_**1.5)
GEN1 G2_=K4_/(K2_**2)
GEN1 SG1_=SQRT(6*N_*(N_-1)/((N_-2)*(N_+1)*(N_+3)))
GEN1 SG2_=SQRT(24*N_*(N_-1)**2/((N_-3)*(N_-2)*(N_+3)*(N_+5)))
PRINT G1_ SG1_ G2_ SG2_
* THE ONLY THING MISSING IS THE CHI-SQUARE GOODNESS OF FIT TEST
* NOT DONE HERE BECAUSE IT IS DIFFICULT TO GET RESIDUALS IN GROUPS
DELETE / ALL_
SET DOECHO
PROCEND
SET ECHO
```

To execute the *OLS* PROC on the Theil textile data which is built into the **DEMO** command simply use:

```
?DEMO
DEPVAR:CONSUME
INDEPS:INCOME PRICE
FILE PROC OLS
EXEC OLS
STOP
```

The output from the *OLS* PROC would be:

```
|_?DEMO
|_DEPVAR:CONSUME
|_INDEPS:INCOME PRICE
|_FILE PROC OLS.SHA
|_SET NOECHO
|_EXEC OLS
 _PROC OLS
    _          SET NODOECHO
..NOTE..CURRENT VALUE OF $ROWS=    17.000
..NOTE..CURRENT VALUE OF $ROWS=    3.0000
    N_
  17.00000
    R2_
  0.9512817
    R2ADJ_
  0.9443220
    SIG2_
  30.95090
    SIGMA_
  5.563353
    SSE_
  433.3126
    YMEAN_
  134.5059
    LLF_
 -51.64704
    FPE_
  36.41282
```

```
 LOGAIC_
 3.591187
 LOGSC_
 3.738225
 GCV_
 37.58323
 HQ_
 36.81123
 RICE_
 39.39205
 SHIBATA_
 34.48508
 SC_
 42.02332
 AIC_
 36.27712
 ANOVA_
 3 BY     4 MATRIX
 8460.937      2.000000      4230.468       136.6832
 433.3126      14.00000      30.95090      0.0000000E+00
 8894.249      16.00000      555.8906      0.0000000E+00
 ZANOVA_
 3 BY     4 MATRIX
 316022.1      3.000000      105340.7       3403.478
 433.3126      14.00000      30.95090      0.0000000E+00
 316455.4      17.00000      18615.02      0.0000000E+00
 B_
 1.061710      -1.382985      130.7066
 SE_
 0.2666738      0.8381422E-01      27.09427
 T_
 3.981306      -16.50061      4.824140
 PARTIAL_
 0.7286980      -0.9752411      0.7901811
 STANDB_
 0.2387079      -0.9893298      0.0000000E+00
 ELAS_
 0.8128818      -0.7846353      0.9717535
 VB_
 3 BY     3 MATRIX
 0.7111490E-01 -0.3997410E-02  -7.018530
-0.3997410E-02  0.7024823E-02 -0.1244140
 -7.018530      -0.1244140      734.0997
 DW_
 2.018550
 VN_
 2.144710
 RHO_
-0.1823939
 ESUM_
-0.8701306E-10
 SIG2_
 30.95090
 EABS_
 72.78664
 R2OP_
 0.9512817
 NRUNS_
```

```
     7.000000
     N1_
     9.000000
     N2_
     8.000000
     NORMSTA_
    -1.242299
     G1_
   -0.3426591E-01
     SG1_
    0.5497474
     G2_
   -0.8700860
     SG2_
    1.063198
    _          PROCEND
|_STOP
```

Limited Information Maximum Likelihood

This example was proposed by Professor Ray Byron of Bond University in Australia. SHAZAM easily computes Two-Stage Least Squares estimation of a single equation in a simultaneous equation model with the **2SLS** command as described in the chapter *TWO-STAGE LEAST SQUARES AND SYSTEMS OF EQUATIONS*. An alternative estimation method is Limited Information Maximum Likelihood (LIML) which can be computed with a set of **MATRIX** commands as shown below for the Consumption equation of Klein's Model I. The method shown can be also be used to compute k-Class estimates by selecting a desired value of k. The results from the LIML estimation can be compared to the 2SLS results. See Amemiya [1985, Section 7.3.2] for further information on the LIML model and the notation used in this example. The SHAZAM procedure LIML below can be used to compute the estimates.

```
set noecho
* Turn off printing the proc while reading it in with FILE PROC
* THE PROC STARTS HERE
PROC LIML
* If you do not want the PROC commands to print during the EXEC phase
* then SET NODOECHO here, only do this after the PROC is working properly.
set nodoecho
****************************************************************
* INPUTS REQUIRED: EXOG, RHSEXOG RHSENDOG ENDOG
****************************************************************
* FIRST DELETE ALL VARIABLES CREATED BY PROC
* To keep Proc variables distinct from others append the _ symbol
* This is not required but it eliminates confusion
?DELETE X_ X1_ Y1_ Y2_ Y_ Z_ M_ W_ W1_ LAMBDA_ K_ ALPHA_ E_ SIG2_ V_ SE_
* A shortcut is to delete all variables containing _ in the name with:
DELETE / ALL_
****************************************************************
* PUT THE INPUT DATA IN THE RIGHT PLACE
* Define X as all exogenous variables in system
COPY [EXOG] X_
* Define X1 as right-hand-side exogenous variables
COPY [RHSEXOG] X1_
```

```
* Define Y1 as all right-hand-side endogenous variables
COPY [RHSENDOG] Y1_
* Define Y as all endogenous variables in equation
COPY [ENDOG]  Y_
* Define the Left hand side endogenous variable
COPY [LHS] Y2_
****************************************************************
* Define Z as all right-hand-side variables, exogenous first
MATRIX Z_= X1_ | Y1_
* Compute the M matrices for X and X1
GEN1 ROWS_=$ROWS
GEN1 COLS_=$COLS
MATRIX M_=IDEN(ROWS_)-X_*INV(X_'X_)*X_'
MATRIX M1_=IDEN(ROWS_)-X1_*INV(X1_'X1_)*X1_'
* Compute W and W1
MATRIX W_=Y_'M_*Y_
MATRIX W1_=Y_'M1_*Y_
* Get the eigenvalues from the W1 and INV(W) matrix computations
MATRIX LAMBDA_=EIGVAL(W1_*INV(W_))
PRINT LAMBDA_
* Get the minimum eigenvalue and use it for k
STAT LAMBDA_ / MIN=K_
PRINT K_
* Note that k-class estimation can be done by choosing
* a different value of k
MATRIX ALPHA_=INV(Z_'(IDEN(ROWS_)-K_*M_)*Z_) * Z_'(IDEN(ROWS_)-K_*M_)*Y2_
* Now print the LIML coefficients
* The order is: CONSTANT PLAG P WGWP
ATITLE_: The estimated coefficient vector is
=PRINT ATITLE_ / NONAME
=PRINT ALPHA_ / NONAME
* Get the residuals and variance
MATRIX E_=Y2_-Z_*ALPHA_
* Print SIGMA**2 using  Degrees of freedom
MATRIX SIG2_=E_'E_/(ROWS_-COLS_)
PRINT SIG2_
* Get the Covariance matrix
MATRIX V_=SIG2_*INV(Z_'(IDEN(ROWS_)-K_*M_)*Z_)
PRINT V_
* Get the standard errors
MATRIX SE_=SQRT(DIAG(V_))
PRINT SE_
* Now delete all the PROC variables
DELETE / ALL_
set doecho
PROCEND
* THE PROC is over, turn echo back on again
set echo
```

Next, the LIML procedure can be run with:

```
SAMPLE 1 21
READ(KLEIN.DAT) WG T G TIME1 PLAG KLAG XLAG C I WP P WGWP PP
* ONE CONSTANT
* PLAG PROFITS LAGGED ONE PERIOD
* KLAG STOCK OF CAPITAL AT END OF PREVIOUS PERIOD
* XLAG PRIVATE PRODUCT LAGGED ONE PERIOD
```

```
* TIME1 TIME TREND
* W2 GOVERNMENT WAGE BILL
* T INDIRECT TAXES
* G GOVERNMENT EXPENDITURES
* C CONSUMPTION
* I INVESTMENT
* WP PRIVATE WAGE BILL
* P PROFITS
* WGWP WAGES
* PP PRIVATE PRODUCT
GENR ONE=1
* Define all exogenous variables in system
EXOG:ONE PLAG KLAG XLAG TIME1 WG T G
* Define all endogenous variables in equation
ENDOG:C P WGWP
* Define right-hand-side exogenous variables
RHSEXOG:ONE PLAG
* Define all right-hand-side endogenous variables
RHSENDOG:P WGWP
* Define the Left-hand-side endogenous variable
LHS:C
* First equation of Klein Model is C= f( ONE, PLAG, P, WGWP)
* Now run the PROC
EXEC LIML
STOP
```

The output will appear as:

```
|_SAMPLE 1 21
|_READ(KLEIN.DAT) WG T G TIME1 PLAG KLAG XLAG C I WP P WGWP PP
  13 VARIABLES AND        21 OBSERVATIONS STARTING AT OBS        1

|_* ONE CONSTANT
|_* PLAG PROFITS LAGGED ONE PERIOD
|_* KLAG STOCK OF CAPITAL AT END OF PREVIOUS PERIOD
|_* XLAG PRIVATE PRODUCT LAGGED ONE PERIOD
|_* TIME1 TIME TREND
|_* W2 GOVERNMENT WAGE BILL
|_* T INDIRECT TAXES
|_* G GOVERNMENT EXPENDITURES
|_* C CONSUMPTION
|_* I INVESTMENT
|_* WP PRIVATE WAGE BILL
|_* P PROFITS
|_* WGWP WAGES
|_* PP PRIVATE PRODUCT
|_GENR ONE=1
|_* Define all exogenous variables in system
|_EXOG:ONE PLAG KLAG XLAG TIME1 WG T G
|_* Define all endogenous variables in equation
|_ENDOG:C P WGWP
|_* Define right-hand-side exogenous variables
|_RHSEXOG:ONE PLAG
|_* Define all right-hand-side endogenous variables
|_RHSENDOG:P WGWP
|_* Define the Left-hand-side endogenous variable
|_LHS:C
```

```
|_* First equation of Klein Model is C= f( ONE, PLAG, P, WGWP)
|_* Now run the PROC
|_EXEC LIML
UNIT 82 IS NOW ASSIGNED TO: LIML
|_set noecho
 _PROC LIML
 _         set nodoecho
|_         ******************************************************
..NOTE..CURRENT VALUE OF $ROWS=   21.000
..NOTE..CURRENT VALUE OF $COLS=    4.0000
     LAMBDA_
    186.1614          7.617559         1.498746
 NAME        N     MEAN       ST. DEV      VARIANCE      MINIMUM      MAXIMUM
COEF.OF.VARIATION CONSTANT-DIGITS
   LAMBDA_    3    65.093       104.89       11003.       1.4987       186.16
1.6114        0.00000E+00
     K_
    1.498746
 The estimated coefficient vector is
    17.14765        0.3960273       -0.2225131        0.8225587
     SIG2_
    2.404952
     V_
     4 BY     4 MATRIX
    4.183554        0.2948809E-01 -0.8698058E-01 -0.7431826E-01
    0.2948809E-01   0.3722705E-01 -0.3598255E-01 -0.7560770E-03
   -0.8698058E-01  -0.3598255E-01  0.5027916E-01 -0.4170617E-02
   -0.7431826E-01  -0.7560770E-03 -0.4170617E-02  0.3788332E-02
     SE_
    2.045374        0.1929431       0.2242301       0.6154943E-01
 _         PROCEND
|_STOP
```

Generating Multivariate Random Numbers

This example shows how to generate random numbers from a bivariate normal distribution for a given covariance matrix. The method is explained in Judge et al. [1988, Chapter 11A] and the corresponding chapter in the *Judge Handbook*. The *MULTI* PROC is included directly in the command file in this example.

```
SET NOECHO
PROC MULTI
* INPUTS: [SIGMA] DESIRED COVARIANCE MATRIX
*         [N] SAMPLE SIZE
* OUTPUT: [MRAN] MATRIX OF RANDOM NUMBERS
* Do a Cholesky factorization of the Sigma Matrix
MATRIX P_=CHOL([SIGMA])
?GEN1 K_=$ROWS
PRINT P_
* Check it out
MATRIX CHECK_=P_*IDEN(K_)*P_'
PRINT CHECK_
* Now use the P_ matrix to generate MRAN
SAMPLE 1 [N]
MATRIX E_=NOR([N],K_)
```

```
MATRIX [MRAN]=E_*P_'
* Check the sample covariance of the orignal independent random numbers
STAT E_ / PCOV
* Now check the sample of correlated random numbers
STAT [MRAN] / PCOV
DELETE / ALL_
PROCEND
SET ECHO
* End of Proc
* Beginning of Calling Program
SET RANFIX
* READ IN A SIGMA MATRIX AND GENERATE 100 RANDOM VECTORS
READ S / ROWS=2 COLS=2 LIST
5 2
2 8
* Specify the Inputs to the MULTI PROC
SIGMA:S
N:100
MRAN:U
EXEC MULTI
* Print the matrix
PRINT U
STOP
```

The output is:

```
|_SET NOECHO
|_* End of Proc
|_* Beginning of Calling Program
|_* READ IN A SIGMA MATRIX AND GENERATE 100 RANDOM VECTORS
|_READ S / ROWS=2 COLS=2 LIST
     2 ROWS AND              2 COLUMNS, BEGINNING AT ROW         1

...SAMPLE RANGE IS NOW SET TO:            1         2
   S
   2 BY     2 MATRIX
  5.000000        2.000000
  2.000000        8.000000
|_* Specify the Inputs to the MULTI PROC
|_SIGMA:S
|_N:100
|_MRAN:U
|_EXEC MULTI
 _PROC MULTI
 _        MATRIX P_=CHOL(S)
 _        ?GEN1 K_=$ROWS
 _        PRINT P_
   P_
  2.236068
 0.8944272        2.683282
 _        MATRIX CHECK_=P_*IDEN(K_)*P_'
 _        PRINT CHECK_
   CHECK_
   2 BY     2 MATRIX
  5.000000        2.000000
  2.000000        8.000000
 _        SAMPLE 1 100
```

```
    _          MATRIX E_=NOR(100,K_)
    _          MATRIX U=E_*P_'
    _          STAT E_ / PCOV
NAME      N     MEAN       ST. DEV      VARIANCE     MINIMUM      MAXIMUM
...NOTE...TREATING COLUMNS OF E_    AS VECTORS
E_       100   0.94483E-01  0.96477      0.93078     -2.9865      2.4730
E_       100   0.11050      0.99368      0.98740     -2.0836      2.6220

   COVARIANCE MATRIX OF VARIABLES -        100 OBSERVATIONS
E_         0.93078
E_        -0.75042E-01  0.98740
            E_            E_
    _          STAT U / PCOV
NAME      N     MEAN       ST. DEV      VARIANCE     MINIMUM      MAXIMUM
...NOTE...TREATING COLUMNS OF U     AS VECTORS
U        100   0.21127      2.1573       4.6539      -6.6781      5.5299
U        100   0.38100      2.7375       7.4937      -6.3243      6.4619

   COVARIANCE MATRIX OF VARIABLES -        100 OBSERVATIONS
U          4.6539
U          1.4113        7.4937
            U             U
    _          DELETE / ALL_
    _          PROCEND


|_* Print the matrix
|_PRINT U
    U
  100 BY      2 MATRIX
 -0.6990535       2.138877
  -2.902652       0.6931440
 -0.6460146       3.504951
  0.4849795      -1.069619
   2.435809       5.103048
   etc.
```

39. FRENCH COMMAND NAMES

"I tell you Wellington is a bad general, the English are bad soldiers; we will settle the matter by lunch time."

Napolean Bonaparte
Waterloo, June 18, 1815

The following are French equivalents to English SHAZAM commands. To use French commands the **SET FRENCH** command must be used. This will allow either English or French commands. To return to English only, type: **OUVRE NOFRANCAIS**.

ARIMA	ARIMA	GME	GME
AUTO	AUTO	HELP	AIDE
BAYES	BAYES	HET	HET
BOX	BOX	IF	SI
CHECKOUT	VERIFIE	INDEX	INDEX
COEF	COEF	INST	INST
COINT	COINT	INTEG	INTEG
COMPRESS	COMPRIME	LAG	RETARD
CONFID	INTCONF	LOGIT	LOGLA
COPY	COPIE	LP	PLI
DELETE	SUPPRIME	MATRIX	MATRICE
DEMO	DEMO	MLE	EMV
DERIV	DERIV	NAMES	NOMS
DIAGNOS	DIAGNOS	NLIN	NLIN
DIM	DIM	NONPAR	NONPAR
DISPLAY	VISUEL	OLS	MCO
DISTRIB	DISTRIB	PAR	PAR
DO	FAIS	PAUSE	PAUSE
DUMP	DEVERSE	PCOMP	COMPR
END	FIN	PROBIT	PROBLA
ENDIF	FINSI	PC	CP
ENDO	FFIN	PLOT	TRACE
EXEC	EXEC	POOL	MELE
EQ	EQ	PRINT	IMPRIME
FCAST	PREVOIS	PROC	PROC
FILE	FICHIER	PROCEND	PROCFIN
FLS	FLS	READ	LIS
FORMAT	FORMAT	RENAME	RENOMME
GENR	GENR	RESTORE	RETABLIS
GEN1	GEN1	RESTRICT	RESTR
GLS	MCG	REWIND	REBOBINE

ROBUST	ROBUSTE
SAMPLE	PRENDS
SAVE	GARDE
SET	OUVRE
SIZE	NOMBRE
SKIPIF	SAUTESI
SORT	CLASSE
STAT	STAT
STOP	ARRETE
SYSTEM	SYSTEME
TEST	TESTE
TIME	CHRONO
TITLE	TITRE
TOBIT	TOBLA
WRITE	ECRIS
2SLS	2MC

40. SUMMARY OF COMMANDS

"The Sun never sets on the SHAZAM empire."
Kenneth J. White
1980

The following is a list of all the available SHAZAM commands and their available options. The underlined letters of each command and option are the acceptable abbreviations.

ARIMA *var*

ALL, DN, GNU, IAC, LOG, NOCONSTANT, NOWIDE, PITER, PLOTAC, PLOTDATA, PLOTFORC, PLOTPAC, PLOTRES, RESTRICT, START, STOCHAST, WIDE, ACF=, BEG=, END=, COEF=, COV=, FBEG=, FCSE=, FEND=, ITER=, NAR=, NDIFF=, NLAG=, NLAGP=, NMA=, NSAR=, NSDIFF=, NSMA=, NSPAN=, PACF=, PREDICT=, RESID=, SIGMA=, START=, STDERR=, STEPSIZE=, TESTSTAT=, TRATIO=

AUTO *depvar indeps*

ANOVA, DLAG, DN, DROP, DUMP, GF, GS, LINLOG, LIST, LOGLIN, LOGLOG, MAX, MISS, ML, NOCONSTANT, NOPITER, NOWIDE, PAGAN, PCOR, PCOV, RESTRICT, RSTAT, WIDE, BEG=, END=, COEF=, CONV=, COV=, GAP=, ITER=, NMISS=, NUMARMA=, ORDER=, PREDICT=, RESID=, RHO=, SRHO=, STDERR=, TRATIO=.

BAYES *options*

NOANTITHET, NORMAL, , PSIGMA, DF=, NSAMP=, OUTUNIT=.

BOX *depvar indeps*

ACCUR, ALL, ANOVA, AUTO, DN, DUMP, FULL, GF, LIST, MAX, NOCONSTANT, PCOR, PCOV, RESTRICT, RSTAT, TIDWELL, UT, BEG=, END=, COEF=, COV=, LAMBDA=, LAME=, LAMI=, LAMS=, PREDICT=, RESID=, RHO=.

CHECKOUT

No options.

COEF *names values*

No options.

COINT *vars*

DN, DUMP, LOG, MAX, BEG=, END=, NDIFF=, NLAG=, RESID=, SIGLEVEL=, TESTSTAT=, TYPE=

COMPRESS	No options.
CONFID *coef1 coef2*	EGA, GNU, GOAWAY, GRAPHICS, HERCULES, HOLD, NOBLANK, NOFPLOT, NOMID, NORMAL, NOTPLOT, NOWIDE, PAUSE, PRINT, SYMBOL, VGA, WIDE, COEF1=, COEF2=, COVAR12=, DF=, FCRIT=, POINTS=, TCRIT=, VAR1=, VAR2=, XMAX=, XMIN=, YMAX=, YMIN=.
COPY *fromvar(s) tovar*	FCOL=, FROW=, TCOL=, TROW=.
DELETE *vars*	ALL.
DEMO	START.
DERIV *var res=equation*	No options.
DIAGNOS *options*	ACF, BACKWARD, BOOTLIST, CHOWTEST, CTEST, GNU, HET, JACKKNIFE, LIST, MAX, NORECEST, NORECRESID, NOWIDE, RECEST, RECRESID, RECUR, RESET, WIDE, BOOTSAMP=, BOOTUNIT=, CHOWONE=, GQOBS=, MHET=, RECUNIT=, SIGLEVEL=.
DIM *var size*	No options.
DISPLAY *option*	Options same as for the SET command.
DISTRIB *vars*	INVERSE, LLF, NOLIST, ACCURACY=, BEG=, END=, BIGN=, BIGX=, C=, CDF=, CRITICAL=, DF=, DFVEC=, DF1=, DF2=, EIGENVAL=, H=, K=, KURTOSIS=, LAMBDA=, LIMIT=, MEAN=, N=, NEIGEN=, NONCEN=, P=, PDF=, Q=, S=, SKEWNESS=, TYPE=, V=, VAR=.
DO *dovar=beg,end,inc*	No options.
DUMP *option*	ADDCOM, DATA, DATCOM, FCOM, GENCOM, INPCOM, IOCOM, KADD, LODCOM, MACOM, NLCOM, OCOM, OLSCOM, OPTCOM, OSCOM, RANCOM, SCNCOM, SYSCOM, TEMCOM, VCOM, VLCOM, VNAME, VPLCOM, VTCOM, VTECOM, VTICOM.

<u>END</u>	No options.
<u>ENDIF</u> *(equation)*	No options.
<u>ENDO</u>	No options.
<u>EQ</u> *equation*	No options.
<u>EXEC</u> *proc_name*	No options.
<u>FC</u> *depvar indeps*	<u>AFCSE</u>, <u>BLUP</u>, <u>IBLUP</u>, <u>DY</u>NAMIC, <u>GF</u>, LIST, <u>MAX</u>, <u>NOCONS</u>TANT, <u>PERCENT</u>, <u>UPPER</u>, <u>BEG</u>=, <u>END</u>=, <u>COEF</u>=, <u>CSNUM</u>=, <u>ESTEND</u>=, <u>FCSE</u>=, <u>LIMIT</u>=, <u>MOD</u>EL=, <u>NC</u>=, <u>ORDER</u>=, <u>POOLSE</u>=, <u>PRE</u>DICT=, <u>RESID</u>=, <u>RHO</u>=, <u>SRHO</u>=.
<u>FILE</u> *option filename*	*Option* can be unit from 11-49 or the keywords: CLOSE, DELETE, HELPDEMO, INPUT, KEYBOARD, LIST, OUTPUT, PATH, PLOTPATH, PRINT, PROCPATH, SCREEN or TEMP.
<u>FLS</u> *depvar indeps*	<u>GNU</u>, <u>MAX</u>, <u>NOCONS</u>TANT, <u>PCOEF</u>, <u>BEG</u>=, <u>END</u>=, <u>COEF</u>=, <u>DELTA</u>=, <u>PRE</u>DICT=, <u>RESID</u>=.
<u>FORMAT</u> *statement*	No options.
<u>GENR</u> *newvar=equation*	No options.
<u>GEN1</u> *equation*	No options.
<u>GLS</u> *depvar indeps*	ANOVA, <u>BLUP</u>, <u>DLAG</u>, <u>DN</u>, <u>DUMP</u>, <u>FULLMAT</u>, <u>GF</u>, LIST, <u>MAX</u>, <u>NOCONS</u>TANT, <u>NOMULSIGSQ</u>, <u>PCOR</u>, <u>PCOV</u>, RSTAT, <u>UT</u>, <u>BEG</u>=, <u>END</u>=, <u>COEF</u>=, <u>COV</u>=, <u>OMEGA</u>=, <u>OMINV</u>=, <u>PMATRIX</u>=, <u>PRE</u>DICT=, <u>RESID</u>=, <u>STDERR</u>=, <u>T</u>RATIO=.
<u>GME</u> *depvar indeps*	DEVIATION, <u>LINLOG</u>, LIST, <u>LOGLIN</u>, <u>LOGLOG</u>, <u>NOCON</u>STANT, <u>PCOV</u>, <u>RS</u>TAT, <u>BEG</u>=, <u>END</u>=, <u>COEF</u>=, <u>CONV</u>=, <u>COV</u>=, <u>ITER</u>=, <u>LOGEPS</u>=, <u>PITER</u>=, <u>PRE</u>DICT=, <u>QPRIOR</u>=, <u>RESID</u>=, <u>START</u>=, <u>STDERR</u>=, <u>T</u>RATIO=, <u>UPRIOR</u>=, <u>V</u>ENTROPY=, <u>Z</u>ENTROPY=.

HELP *command*	ARIMA, AUTO, BAYES, BOX, CHECKOUT, COEF, COINT, COMPRESS, CONFID, COPY, DELETE, DEMO, DERIV, DIAGNOS, DIM, DISPLAY, DISTRIB, DO, DUMP, END, ENDIF, ENDO, EQ, ERROR, FC, FILE, FLS, FORMAT, GENR, GEN1, GLS, GME, HELP, HET, IF, IF1, INDEX, INST, INTEG, LAMBDA, LOGIT, LP, MATRIX, MENU, MLE, NAMES, NL, NONPAR, OLS, PAR, PAUSE, PC, PLOT, POOL, PRINT, PROBIT, READ, RENAME, RESTORE, RESTRICT, REWIND, ROBUST, SAMPLE, SET, SIZE, SKIPIF, SORT, STAT, STOP, SYSTEM, TEST, TIME, TITLE, TOBIT, WRITE, 2SLS.
HET *depvar indeps (exogs)*	DUMP, LIST, MAX, NOCONSTANT, NOWIDE, NUMERIC, OPGCOV, PCOR, PCOV , PRESAMP, RSTAT, WIDE, ARCH=, ARCHM=, BEG=, END=, COEF=, CONV=, COV=, GARCH=, GMATRIX=, ITER=, MACH=, METHOD=, MODEL=, PITER=, PREDICT=, RESID=, START=, STDERR=, STDRESID=, STEPSIZE=, TRATIO=.
IF *(expression)*	No options.
IF1 *(expression)*	No options.
INDEX *p1 q1...pn qn*	ALTERN, CHAIN, EXPEND, NOALTERN, NOLIST, BASE=, BEG=, END=, DIVISIA=, FISHER=, LASPEYRES=, PAASCHE=, QDIVISIA=, QFISHER=, QLASPEYRES=, QPAASCHE=.
INST *dep ind (inst)*	DUMP, GF, LIST, MAX, NOCONSTANT, PCOR, PCOV, RESTRICT, RSTAT, BEG=, END=, COEF=, COV=, PREDICT=, RESID=.
INTEG *var lo up res=equ*	No options.
LAMBDA *var=value*	No options.
LOGIT *depvar indeps*	DUMP, LIST, MAX, NOCONSTANT, NONORM, PCOR, PCOV, RSTAT, BEG=, END=, COEF=, CONV=, COV=, INDEX=, ITER=, PITER=, PREDICT=, STDERR=, TRATIO=, WEIGHT=.

LP *c A b*

DUMP, MIN, DSLACK=, DUAL=, ITER=, PRIMAL=, PSLACK=.

MATRIX *newmat=equation*

No options.

MENU

No options.

MLE *depvar indeps*

ANOVA, DUMP, GF, LINLOG, LIST, LM, LOGLIN, LOGLOG, MAX, NOCONSTANT, NONORM, PCOR, PCOV, RSTAT, BEG=, END=, COEF=, CONV=, COV=, IN=, OUT=, ITER=, METHOD=, PREDICT=, PITER=, RESID=, STDERR=, TRATIO=, TYPE=, WEIGHT=.

NAMES *options*

LIST

NL *neq (exogs)*

ACROSS, AUTO, DRHO, DUMP, EVAL, GENRVAR, LIST, LOGDEN, MINFUNC, MAXFUNC, NOCONEXOG, NOPSIGMA, NUMCOV, NUMERIC, OPGCOV, PCOV, RSTAT, SAME, SOLVE, AUTCOV= BEG=, END=, COEF=, CONV=, COV=, GMM= IN=, OUT=, ITER=, METHOD=, NCOEF=, ORDER=, PITER=, PREDICT=, RESID=, SIGMA=, START=, STDERR=, STEPSIZE=, TRATIO=, ZMATRIX=.

NONPAR *depvar indeps*

DENSITY, GNU, LIST, PCOEF, BEG=, END=, BRHO=, COEF=, DELTA=, FCSE=, HATDIAG=, INCOVAR=, ITER=, METHOD=, PREDICT=, RESID=, RWEIGHTS=, SIGMA=, SMATRIX=, SMOOTH=.

OLS *depvar indeps*

ANOVA, AUXRSQR, DFBETAS, DLAG, DN, DUMP, DWPVALUE, GF, GNU, HETCOV, INFLUENCE, LINLOG, LIST, LM, LOGLIN, LOGLOG, MAX, NOCONSTANT, NOMULSIGSQ, NONORM, PCOR, PCOV, PLUSH, REPLICATE, RESTRICT, RSTAT, UT, AUTCOV=, BEG=, END=, COEF=, COV=, FE=, FX=, HATDIAG=, IDVAR=, INCOEF=, INCOVAR=, INDW=, INSIG2=, METHOD=, PCINFO=, PCOMP =, PE=, PX=, PREDICT=, RESID=, RIDGE=, STDERR=, TRATIO=, WEIGHT=.

PAR *number*

No options.

PAUSE

No options.

PC *vars*

COR, LIST, MAX, PCOLLIN, PEVEC, PFM, PRM, RAW, SCALE, BEG=, END=, EVAL=, EVEC=, MAXFACT=, MINEIG=, NC=, PCINFO=, PCOMP=.

PLOT *depvars indep*

ALTERNATE, APPEND, AXIS, DASH, EGA, GNU, GOAWAY, GRAPHICS, HERCULES, HISTO, HOLD, KEY, LINE, LINEONLY, NOBLANK, NOPRETTY, NOSAME, NOWIDE, PAUSE, PRINT, RANGE, SAME, TIME, VGA, WIDE, BEG=, END=, CHARSIZE=, COMMFILE=, DATAFILE=, DEVICE=, GROUPS=, OUTPUT=, PORT=, SYMBOL=, XMAX=, XMIN=, YMAX=, YMIN=.

POOL *depvar indeps*

ANOVA, CORCOEF, DLAG, DN, DUMP, FULL, GF, LIST, MAX, MULSIGSQ, NOCONSTANT, PCOR, PCOV, RESTRICT, RSTAT, SAME, UT, BEG=, END=, COEF=, CONV=, COV=, ITER=, NC=, NCROSS=, NTIME=, PREDICT=, RESID=, RHO=, STDERR=, TRATIO=.

PRINT *vars*

BYVAR, FORMAT, NEWLINE, NEWPAGE, NEWSHEET, NONAMES, NOWIDE, WIDE, BEG=, END=.

PROBIT *depv indeps*

DUMP, LIST, MAX, NOCONSTANT, NONORM, PCOR, PCOV, RSTAT, BEG=, END=, COEF=, CONV=, COV=, IMR=, INDEX=, ITER=, PITER=, PREDICT=, STDERR=, TRATIO=, WEIGHT=.

PROC *proc_name*

No options.

PROCEND

No options.

READ *(unit) vars*

BINARY, BYVAR, CLOSE, DIF, EOF, FORMAT, LIST, REWIND, TSP, BEG=, END=, COLS=, ROWS=, SKIPLINES=.

RENAME *old new*

No options.

RESTORE *vars*

CITIBASE, CITINEW, UNIT=.

RESTRICT *equation*

No options.

REWIND *unit*

No options.

ROBUST *depvar indeps*

FIVEQUAN, GASTWIRT, GNU, LAE, LINLOG, LIST, LOGLIN, LOGLOG, MAX, NOCONSTANT, PCOR, PCOV, RSTAT, TUKEY, UNCOR, BEG=, END=, COEF=, CONV, COV=, DIFF=, ITER=, MULTIT=, PREDICT=, RESID=, STDERR=, THETA=, THETAB=, THETAE=, THETAI=, TRATIO=, TRIM=.

SAMPLE *beg end beg end*

No options.

SET *option*

BATCH, CPUTIME, COLOR, DELETE, DOECHO, DUMP, ECHO, FRENCH, LASTCOM, LCUC, MAX, NOCC, NOCOLOR, NODELETE, NOLCUC, NOSKIP, NOOUTPUT, NOSAMPLE, NOSCREEN, NOSTATUS, NOWARN, NOWARNSKIP, NOWIDE, OPTIONS, OUTPUT, PAUSE, RANFIX, SAMPLE, SCREEN, SKIP, SKIPMISS STATUS, TALK, TERMINAL, TIMER, TRACE, WARN, WARNSKIP, WIDE, COMLEN=, MAXCOL=, MISSVALU=, OUTUNIT=, RANSEED=.

SIZE *maximum*

No options.

SKIPIF*(expression)*

No options.

SORT *sortvar vars*

DESC, LIST, BEG=, END=.

STAT *vars*

ALL, ANOVA, BARTLETT, DN, MATRIX, MAX, PCOR, PCOV, PCP, PCPDEV, PFREQ, PMEDIAN, PRANKCOR, REPLICATE, WIDE, BEG=, END=, COR=, COV=, CP=, CPDEV=, MAXIM=, MEAN=, MEDIANS=, MINIM=, MODES=, RANKCOR=, STDEV=, SUMS=, VAR=, WEIGHT=.

STOP

No options.

SYSTEM *neq exogs*

DN, DUMP, FULL, GF, LIST, MAX, NOCONSTANT, NOCONEXOG PCOR, PCOV, PINVEV, PSIGMA, RESTRICT, RSTAT, COEF=, COEFMAT=, CONV=, COV=, IN=, OUT=, ITER=, PITER=, PREDICT=, RESID=, SIGMA=.

TEST *equation*

No options.

<u>TI</u>ME *beg freq var*   No options.

<u>TI</u>TLE *title*   No options.

<u>TO</u>BIT *depvar indeps*   <u>DU</u>MP, <u>LIST</u>, <u>MAX</u>, <u>NOCON</u>STANT, <u>NONORM</u>, <u>PCOR</u>, <u>PCOV</u>, <u>UPPER</u>, <u>BEG</u>=, <u>END</u>=, <u>COEF</u>=, <u>CONV</u>=, <u>COV</u>=, <u>INDEX</u>=, <u>ITER</u>=, <u>LIMIT</u>=, <u>PITER</u>=, <u>PR</u>EDICT=, <u>STDERR</u>=, <u>TR</u>ATIO=, <u>W</u>EIGHT=.

<u>W</u>RITE(*unit*) *vars*   <u>BINARY</u>, <u>BY</u>VAR, <u>CLOSE</u>, <u>DIF</u>, <u>F</u>ORMAT, <u>NA</u>MES, <u>NONA</u>MES, <u>REWIND</u>, <u>WIDE</u>, <u>BEG</u>=, <u>END</u>=.

<u>2</u>SLS *depvar rhsvars (exogs)* <u>D</u>UMP, <u>GF</u>, <u>LIST</u>, <u>MAX</u>, <u>NOCONS</u>TANT, <u>NOCONEX</u>OG, <u>PCOR</u>, <u>PCOV</u>, <u>RESTRICT</u>, <u>RS</u>TAT, <u>BEG</u>=, <u>END</u>=, <u>COEF</u>=, <u>COV</u>=, <u>PR</u>EDICT=, <u>RESID</u>=.

41. NEW FEATURES IN SHAZAM

"I've changed a lot in the past year."
Margaret Trudeau
1979

There are many differences between SHAZAM Versions. This appendix itemizes a few of these differences. SHAZAM is a continuously expanding program with many new capabilities in econometrics. Always use the latest version available, older versions may not contain the new features.

VERSION 5.0

Before Version 5.0 was released in 1985, SHAZAM was completely rewritten to make it a modern and flexible package. Users of Versions 1.0-4.6 found that they had entered a new world of econometric computing. A matrix programming language had been added and all procedures had been rewritten to provide the flexibility that researchers require. Versions prior to Version 5.0 are called *OLD-OLD* **SHAZAM** and should no longer be used by anyone except Econometric Historians.

VERSION 5.1

The following are some of the major changes and additions to Version 5.1 of SHAZAM:

COMMAND	*NEW AVAILABLE OPTIONS*
DISTRIB	LLF, S= and V=
GENR	MOD(X,Y)
MLE	LM
OLS	DFBETAS, INFLUENCE, REPLICATE, HATDIAG= and UT=
PROBIT /LOGIT	NONORM
SET	NOWIDE, WIDE and RANSEED=
STAT	WEIGHT=
TOBIT	NONORM

VERSION 6.0

A large number of changes were made to SHAZAM between Versions 5.1 and 6.0. Version 6.0 SHAZAM is capable of computing Box-Jenkins Models (ARIMA) Time-Series models, Bayesian Inequality Restrictions, Confidence Intervals and Ellipses, and Robust Regressions. It can also perform a variety of Regression Diagnostic Tests including many Heteroskedasticity Tests, Recursive Residuals, CUSUM tests and Specification Error Tests as well as Jackknife and Bootstrap estimates. Furthermore, many new options were developed for existing commands. The following are some of the major new commands and options found in Version 6.0 of SHAZAM:

COMMAND	_NEW AVAILABLE OPTIONS_
ARIMA	New Command:
	Identification Phase: **ALL , NOWIDE, PLOTAC, PLOTDATA, PLOTPAC, WIDE, BEG= END=, NDIFF=, NLAG=, NLAGP=, NSDIFF= and NSPAN=**
	Estimation Phase: **DN, NOCONSTANT, PITER, PLOTRES, START, BEG= END=, COEF=, ITER= , NAR=, NDIFF=, NMA=, NSAR=, NSDIFF=, NSMA= , NSPAN= and PREDICT=**
	Forecasting Phase: **LOG, NOCONSTANT, PLOTFORC, COEF=, FBEG= FEND=, NAR=, NDIFF=, NMA=, NSAR=, NSDIFF=, NSMA=, NSPAN=, PREDICT= and RESID=**
AUTO	**NOWIDE, PAGAN and WIDE**
BAYES	New Command: **NOANTHITHET, NORMAL, NSAMP= and OUTUNIT=**
CONFID	New Command: **EGA, GRAPHICS, HERCULES, HOLD, NOBLANK, NOWIDE, SYMBOL, TOSHIBA and WIDE**
DIAGNOS	New Command: **ACF, BACKWARD, CHOWTEST, HET, JACKKNIFE, LIST, MAX, NOWIDE, RECEST, RECRESID, RECUR, RESET, WIDE, GQOBS=, RECUNIT= and SIGLEVEL=**
DISTRIB	**LLF, H=, P= N=, S= V= and TYPE=BINOMIAL**
FC	**FCSE=**
MATRIX	**Concatenation (│), SYM(_matrix_), TRI(_matrix_), VEC(_matrix_) and VEC(_matrix,nrows_)**
MENU	Gives the list of available commands in SHAZAM while in interactive mode.

NL	**LOGDEN, NUMCOV, START=, STDERR=, STEPSIZE=** and **TRATIO=**
OLS	**GF** and **INCOVAR=**
PLOT	**ALTERNATE , EGA, GRAPHICS, HERCULES** and **TOSHIBA**
POOL	**MULSIGSQ, CORCOEF=** and **RHO=**
PC	**PCOLLIN, RAW** and **SCALE**
PROBIT / LOGIT	**IMR=** and **WEIGHT=**
ROBUST	New command: **FIVEQUAN, GASTWIRT, LAE, LINLOG, LIST, LOGLIN, LOGLOG, MAX, PCOR, PCOV, RSTAT, TUKEY , UNCOR, BEG= END=, COEF=, CONV=, COV=, DIFF= , ITER=, MULTIT=, RESID=, STDERR=, THETA=, THETAB=, THETAE=, THETAI=, TRATIO=** and **TRIM=**
SAMPLE	Formerly called **SMPL**
SYSTEM	**COEF=, COEFMAT=, COV=, PITER=** and **SIGMA=**
TOBIT	**NONORM**
2SLS	**COV=**

VERSION 6.1

Further additions were made after Version 6.0 to make SHAZAM Version 6.1 a more powerful program than ever before. The Macintosh version of SHAZAM now supports the Macintosh interface and graphics, and many other substantial changes have been made. Some of the major new options are:

COMMAND	*NEW AVAILABLE OPTIONS*
AUTO	**DLAG**
CONFID	**GOAWAY, PAUSE, PRINT** and Macintosh **GRAPHICS**
DIAGNOS	**BOOTLIST, NORECEST, NORECRESID, BOOTSAMP=** and **MHET=**
DISPLAY	**CPUTIME, SCREEN** and **WARNSKIP**
DLAG	Command is no longer needed. Distributed lags are now specified on **AUTO, BOX, GLS, OLS** and **POOL** commands directly. The command is redesigned to make Almon Lag estimation even easier.
FC	**AFCSE, CSNUM=, ESTEND=, LIMIT=** and **POOLSE=**
FILE	Available for many machines: **CLOSE, INPUT, LIST, OUTPUT** and **SCREEN**

	Available for the Macintosh only: **PRINT**
GLS	**DLAG**
MATRIX	More flexible definition of matrix multiplication added.
NL	**GENRVAR** and **OPGCOV**
OLS	**DLAG**
PLOT	**GOAWAY, PAUSE, PRINT** and Macintosh **GRAPHICS**
POOL	**DLAG, MULSIGSQ** and **PCOV**
READ	**CLOSE** and **SKIPLINES=**
SET	**NOSCREEN, NOWARNSKIP** and **WARNSKIP**
STAT	**SUMS=**
WRITE	**CLOSE**

VERSION 6.2

Version 6.2 includes several new options on existing commands and a new command to estimate Heteroskedastic and ARCH models as well as new commands to compute derivatives and integrals. A new Macintosh interface has been developed. The OS/2 Version has been released and includes Presentation Manager Scrollable Windows and Graphics. The OS/2 Version allows massive amounts of virtual memory not available in the DOS version and allows multitasking and many other features. Some of the new options are:

COMMAND	*NEW AVAILABLE OPTIONS*
AUTO	**NUMARMA=**
CONFID	**VGA**
DERIV	New command: *var resultvar = equation*
DISTRIB	**BIGN=, BIGX=** and **TYPE=HYPERGEO**
FILE	**KEYBOARD** and **PATH**
HELP	**HET, DERIV** and **INTEG**
HET	New command: **DUMP, LIST, MAX, NOCONSTANT, NOWIDE, NUMERIC, OPGCOV, PCOR, PCOV, PRESAMP, RSTAT, WIDE, ARCH=, ARCHM=, BEG= END=, COEF=, CONV=, COV= , GARCH=, ITER=, MACH=, METHOD=, MODEL=, PITER=, PREDICT=, RESID=, START=, STDERR=, STDRESID= , STEPSIZE=** and **TRATIO=**

INTEG	New command:
	var lower upper resultvar = equation
MATRIX	**FACT**(*matrix*)
NL	**MINFUNC, MAXFUNC , SOLVE** and **ZMATRIX=**
OLS	**AUXRSQR** and **AUTCOV=**
PLOT	**VGA**
READ	**DIF** and **TSP**
SET	**COLOR, CPUTIME, DELETE, LCUC, NOCOLOR, NODELETE, NOLCUC, NOOUTPUT , OUTPUT** and **PAUSE**
WRITE	**DIF**

VERSION 7.0

Version 7.0 offers a variety of new econometric techniques including a new command for Unit Roots and Cointegration testing and new options for model estimation by Nonlinear Two Stage Least Squares and Nonlinear Three Stage Least Squares and Generalized Method of Moments. $ERR is a new Temporary Variable to give Error Codes. An important new feature is the capability to program SHAZAM procedures. An interface to the GNUPLOT package provides high quality graphics. In addition, system commands can be entered from a SHAZAM command prompt on some versions. A large number of minor improvements have also been made.

SHAZAM is maintained as a machine portable system and versions are now available for the following operating systems: DOS Extended Memory Version for 80386 and 80486 PC Computers, the NeXT computer, WINDOWS, OS/2 Version 2.0 and the SUN SPARCstation (in addition to operating systems supported by previous SHAZAM versions).

Some of the new options are :

COMMAND	*NEW AVAILABLE OPTIONS*
ARIMA	*Identification phase :*
	GNU, IAC, ACF=, PACF= and **TESTSTAT=**
	Estimation phase:
	GNU, RESTRICT, ACF=, COV=, START=, STDERR=, STEPSIZE=, TESTSTAT= and **TRATIO=**
	Forecasting phase:
	GNU, STOCHAST, FCSE= and **SIGMA=**
	An interface to the GNUPLOT package is available to provide high quality graphics. The options are:

GNU, COMMFILE=, DEVICE=, OUTPUT= and PORT=

Program revisions were made including changes to some calculations to give consistency with other SHAZAM commands. Also, the estimation algorithm was improved to provide greater accuracy. As a result, output from the **ARIMA** command may give slightly different answers than previous SHAZAM versions.

AUTO	**NOPITER**
	Tests for autocorrelation after correcting for autocorrelation.
COINT	New command for Cointegration and Unit Roots: **DN, DUMP, LOG, MAX, BEG=, END=, NDIFF=, NLAG=, TESTSTAT= and TYPE=.**
COMPRESS	Improved algorithm.
CONFID	**GNU**
DELETE	**ALL_**
DISTRIB	**TYPE=(BURRII, BURRIII, BURRXII, DAVIES), DFVEC=, K=, LAMBDA=, LIMIT=**
DO	Up to 8 levels are now allowed.
EXEC	A new command to execute SHAZAM procedures.
FILE	**PROCPATH, HELPDEMO, PROC**
GEN1	Calculator Mode
HET	**GMATRIX=**
	Exogenous variables may be included in the ARCH variance equation. Some changes were made to the estimation algorithm so that results may be different from previous versions.
IF1	IF command for the first observation only.
LP	New command for Linear Programming: **DUMP, MIN, PRIMAL=, DUAL=, PSLACK=, DSLACK=, ITER=**
MAP	This command has been removed.
MATRIX	Temporary variables are *$ROWS* and *$COLS*.
NL	**NOCONEXOG, AUTCOV=, GMM=, PREDICT=, RESID=**
	Nonlinear Two Stage Least Squares, Nonlinear Three Least Squares and Generalized Method of Moments are available.
OLS	**AUTCOV=** gives the Newey-West Autocorrelation Consistent Covariance Matrix.
PLOT	An interface to the GNUPLOT package is available to provide high quality graphics. The options are: **GNU, KEY/NOKEY, COMMFILE=, DEVICE=, OUTPUT= and PORT=.**

PROC	Beginning of SHAZAM procedures.
PROCEND	End of SHAZAM Procedure.
SET	**SKIPMISS, MISSVAL=** options for missing values.
SYSTEM	**NOCONEXOG**
2SLS	**NOCONEXOG**

VERSION 8.0

A SHAZAM World Wide Web page has been developed to offer a variety of useful information and services related to SHAZAM.

Version 8.0 introduces the following new commands: **FLS** for the estimation of equations with time-varying coefficients; **NONPAR** for nonparametric density estimation and regression smoothing methods; and **GME** for equation estimation by generalized entropy methods.

Program improvements include the following. New temporary variables are PI that contains the value of π and $PVAL$ that contains the p-value from some tests. On the **OLS** command new temporary variables to save model selection test statistics reported with the **ANOVA** option are: FPE, $LAIC$, LSC, GCV, HQ, $RICE$, $SHIB$, SC, and AIC; the **DLAG** option returns $DURH$, and the **LM** option returns JB. Some of the new options are:

COMMAND	*NEW AVAILABLE OPTIONS*
COINT	**RESID=, SIGLEVEL=**
DIAGNOS	**CTEST** **GNU** can be used with the **RECUR** option to get a plot of the CUSUM and CUSUMSQ of the recursive residuals.
FILE	**DELETE , PLOTPATH, TEMP**
FLS	New command: **GNU, MAX, NOCONSTANT, PCOEF, BEG=, END=, COEF=, DELTA=, PREDICT=** and **RESID=**
GME	New command: **DEVIATION, LINLOG, LIST, LOGLIN, LOGLOG, NOCONSTANT, PCOV, RSTAT, BEG=, END=, COEF=, CONV=, COV=, ITER=, LOGEPS=, PITER=, PREDICT=, QPRIOR=, RESID=, START=, STDERR=, TRATIO=, UPRIOR=, VENTROPY=** and **ZENTROPY=**
HELP	**ERROR, FLS, GME, NONPAR**
NL	**NOPSIGMA, SIGMA=**

NONPAR	New command: **DENSITY, GNU, LIST, PCOEF, BEG=, END=, BRHO=, COEF=, DELTA=, FCSE=, HATDIAG=, INCOVAR=, ITER=, METHOD=, PREDICT=, RESID=, RWEIGHTS=, SIGMA=, SMATRIX=** and **SMOOTH=**
OLS	**GNU, INDW=** The **EXACTDW** option has been renamed to **DWPVALUE** and the 200 observation limit has been removed.
PLOT	**GNU** can be used with the **HISTO** option. **APPEND** is available with the **GNU** option.
ROBUST	**GNU**
SET SKIPMISS	Improved implementation. **GENR** commands set missing value codes when computations involve a missing observation.
STAT	**REPLICATE, MEDIANS=** and **MODES=**

FEATURES UNDER DEVELOPMENT

The ongoing design and testing of new features ensures that SHAZAM offers a comprehensive range of econometric and statistical techniques. To obtain details of new features that may be available on a pre-release basis on some computers use the command:

HELP   NEW

42. HOW TO RUN SHAZAM ON MSDOS AND WINDOWS

"The computer has no commercial future."
IBM
1948

There are several different SHAZAM systems that are designed for specific hardware requirements. Each of these SHAZAM systems supports identical SHAZAM commands and features. Detailed information on the installation and running of SHAZAM is contained in the **README** documentation files supplied with the program disks. All the files from the SHAZAM program disks should be installed on the hard disk in a directory called **SHAZAM**.

This chapter describes SHAZAME for use in a MSDOS session and SHAZAMW for use as a Microsoft Windows application.

Creating Files with an Editor

Command and data files are typically created and modified with an editor. The Microsoft operating system provides a built-in editor called **edit**. Alternatively, there are many commercial and public-domain shareware editors that can be used. The PC MAGAZINE program **ted** is recommended for small files. A word processing program can be used as an editor but the file must be saved as an ASCII (plain text) file before using the file as an input file to SHAZAM.

MSDOS Editor

To use the MSDOS editor **edit** to create the SHAZAM command file **COMMAND.SHA** at the MSDOS command prompt type:

```
edit command.sha
```

The **edit** program will load and a file called **COMMAND.SHA** will be created. A blank screen with a menu at the top will appear. The following is an example of SHAZAM commands that can be typed:

```
SAMPLE 1 17
READ(TEXTILE.DAT) YEAR CONSUME INCOME PRICE
PRINT YEAR CONSUME INCOME PRICE
STAT CONSUME INCOME PRICE
STOP
```

After typing in the **STOP** command press the return/enter key to advance the cursor to the next line to signal to the SHAZAM program no additional commands are to follow. Press the Alt-F keys to highlight the features under the File command. To save the file and exit out of the editor **edit** press the X key. The editor will prompt you with the statement:

```
Loaded file is not saved.   Save it now?

< Yes >   <  No  >   <Cancel>   < Help >
```

Press the Y key to state yes to save the file.

To create the data file at the MSDOS prompt type:

```
edit textile.dat
```

The **edit** program will load and a file called **TEXTILE.DAT** will be created. A blank screen with a menu at the top will appear. Begin typing in the following data set:

1923	96.7	99.2	101.0
1924	98.1	99.0	100.1
1925	100.0	100.0	100.0
1926	104.9	111.6	90.6
1927	104.9	122.2	86.5
1928	109.5	117.6	89.7
1929	110.8	121.1	90.6
1930	112.3	136.0	82.8
1931	109.3	154.2	70.1
1932	105.3	153.6	65.4
1933	101.7	158.5	61.3
1934	95.4	140.6	62.5
1935	96.4	136.2	63.6
1936	97.6	168.0	52.6
1937	102.4	154.3	59.7
1938	101.6	149.0	59.5
1939	103.8	165.5	61.3

After typing in the last row and column of data press the return/enter key to advance the cursor to the next line to signal to SHAZAM that no additional data is to follow. Press the Alt-F keys to highlight the features under the File command and then save the file and exit out of the editor as described above.

TED Editor

For the above example, if the editor **ted** is used then at the MSDOS prompt type:

```
ted command.sha
```

to create the command file. A blank screen will appear with function keys listed at the bottom of the screen. Type in the SHAZAM commands as in the above example. Remember to press the enter/return key after the **STOP** command has been typed in to ensure the cursor is advanced to the next line to signal to the SHAZAM program no additional commands are to follow. To save and exit **ted** press the F7 key and then the return/enter key to execute the command.

SHAZAME

The SHAZAME system runs in a MSDOS session and requires a 80386DX / 80486DX or Pentium processor as well as a minimum of 4 MB of memory. SHAZAME can be run in a MSDOS session under OS/2 and Microsoft Windows.

In the following examples commands typed in lower case indicate commands typed at the MSDOS command prompt. Commands typed in upper case indicate SHAZAM commands, although in actual practice you may type your commands in either upper or lower case.

Most applications will have the SHAZAM commands (and sometimes the data) in a file. Note: The control-S and control-Q keys are useful for "freezing" and "unfreezing" output to the screen. The control-PrintSc key is useful for turning the printer on or off during an interactive session.

To run SHAZAM interactively when your data is not in a separate file at the MSDOS prompt type:

```
shazame
```

This will load SHAZAM and a banner with copyright information will be displayed. At the SHAZAM **TYPE COMMAND** prompt any SHAZAM command can be entered. An example of a list of commands is:

```
SAMPLE beg end
READ vars / options
(data goes here)
(other commands)
STOP
```

The output from each command should appear on the screen immediately following the command.

If you want the output to go into a file instead of appearing on screen you should assign an output file. If the output is placed in a file then you will have a permanent record of the results. For example, if the SHAZAM commands are prepared in the file **COMMAND.SHA** then an output file can be assigned with the command:

```
shazame command.sha output.out
```

In this example the output file called **OUTPUT.OUT** will be created by SHAZAM if it does not exist in the current directory. All the output from this run will be dumped into this file rather than appearing on the screen. If the file, **OUTPUT.OUT** currently exists the new output may overwrite the existing file.

The output file can be viewed by using the MSDOS command:

```
type output.out | more
```

The display will pause after each screen. Press the Enter key to continue the display. Alternatively, the SHAZAM output file can be viewed with an editor or preferably the shareware program **LIST**. The output file can also be sent to a printer.

Running out of Memory

Use the **par=** parameter to increase memory, for example, to 1000K at the MSDOS prompt type:

```
shazame command.sha output.out par=1000
```

SHAZAME allows disk space to be used as virtual memory. Before running SHAZAME, to turn off the virtual memory feature to make SHAZAME run faster at the MSDOS command prompt type:

```
novm
```

To turn back on the virutal memory feature type:

```
vm
```

The **size=** parameter can increase the number of variables allowed from the default of 1000 to a higher value. An example of the use of this option is:

```
shazame command.sha output.out size=1500
```

To use both the **par=** and **size=** parameters at the MSDOS command prompt type:

```
shazame command.sha output.out size=1500 par=2000
```

Note: You might be able to obtain additional memory by removing any space allocated to a RAM-DISK or RAM-CACHE or memory resident programs such as BACKSCRL, Network, etc.

To raise the memory under the Windows 95 operating system you should go to the MSDOS box Properties and try setting the DPMI=65535. This is not one of the options in the pull down list, but it will take this value. Alternatively, you can raise the PAR to a much higher level if you reboot the computer in MSDOS mode only.

SHAZAMW

To run SHAZAMW under Windows 3.1 at the MSDOS command prompt type:

```
win shazamw
```

To run the SHAZAMW under Windows 95 or Windows NT at the MSDOS command prompt type:

```
shazamw
```

Once the system has finished loading at the SHAZAM **TYPE COMMAND** prompt type:

```
FILE INPUT COMMAND.SHA
```

or in Windows you can make a shortcut icon to link to the **SHAZAMW.EXE** file. Read your Windows manual for instructions on making a shortcut icon.

Running out of Memory

Memory can be increased with the **PAR** command. At the SHAZAM **TYPE COMMAND** prompt type:

```
PAR number
```

where *number* specifies the amount of memory required (in batches of 1024 bytes). For example, to raise the **PAR** to 600K at the SHAZAM **TYPE COMMAND** prompt type:

```
PAR 600
```

You will be able to increase the **PAR** to use all of the computer's real memory.

Using the Absoft Command Shell

When running SHAZAMW it will be easier if you load the Absoft Command Shell. This will also make it easier to enter other MSDOS commands. The main feature of the Absoft Command Shell is that it will allow you to scroll the output back and forth on your screen.

Under Windows 3.1 the Absoft Command Shell may be required before SHAZAMW will run. Check the **README** file before using the Absoft Command Shell.

SHAZAME and SHAZAMW

Executing MSDOS Programs Within **SHAZAM**

SHAZAME will permit you to execute other MSDOS programs if sufficient memory is available while SHAZAM is loaded by preceding the MSDOS program name with a "$". For example, if you wanted to edit the data file **TEXTILE.DAT** with the MSDOS editor **edit** at the SHAZAM **TYPE COMMAND** prompt type:

```
$EDIT TEXTILE.DAT
```

Once you have completed your editing of the data file **TEXTILE.DAT** the system will return to SHAZAM.

Another example, would be to list the current directory during a SHAZAM session. At the SHAZAM **TYPE COMMAND** prompt type:

```
$DIR
```

Graphics

SHAZAM provides an interface to the GNUPLOT graphics program. Further details are in the chapter *PLOTS*.

SHAZAM will write a file of GNUPLOT commands called **COMM.GNU** and data files with the extension **.GNU** that can be run with the GNUPLOT program. To use this, specify the **GNU** option on the SHAZAM **PLOT, ARIMA, CONFID, DIAGNOS, FLS, NONPAR, OLS,** or **ROBUST** command. For example,

```
PLOT CONSUME INCOME PRICE YEAR / GNU LINE
```

If for some reason GNUPLOT does not run within SHAZAME it probably means you have exhausted all of your computer's memory. GNUPLOT can then be executed from the MSDOS command prompt after you have exited SHAZAM by typing:

```
gnuplot comm.gnu
```

Obtaining a Hard Copy of the **SHAZAM** *Output*

To obtain a hard copy of the SHAZAM output you may use the MSDOS **print** command. For example, if you wanted to print out a hard copy of the SHAZAM output file in your current working directory called **SHAZ.OUT** then at the MSDOS command prompt type:

```
print shaz.out
```

The above **print** command assumes that your computer is connected to the printer. Alternatively, if your output file, **SHAZ.OUT**, is in the directory called **work** on your hard drive **c:** then at the MSDOS command prompt type:

```
print c:\work\shaz.out
```

If the above MSDOS **print** command does not work then try the MSDOS **copy** command. For example, if you wanted to print out a hard copy of the SHAZAM output file in your current working directory called **SHAZ.OUT** then at the MSDOS command prompt type:

```
copy shaz.out lpt1
```

The above **copy** command assumes that your computer is connected to the printer port lpt1. If your printer is connected to lpt2 then replace lpt1 with lpt2 in the above **copy** command. Alternatively, if your output file, **SHAZ.OUT**, is in the directory called **work** on your hard drive **c:** then at the MSDOS command prompt type:

```
copy c:\work\shaz.out lpt1
```

43. HOW TO RUN SHAZAM ON MACINTOSH

"Every regression matters."
Angela Redish
1986

SHAZAM requires at least 4 Meg of Memory and a Hard Disk. The Macintosh SHAZAM installation disks include a **README** file and other instruction files which contain additional instructions not provided in this manual. After installation the SHAZAM program should be in a folder on the hard disk with the name **SHAZAM**.

All your SHAZAM data files and SHAZAM command files should also be inside the **SHAZAM** folder. If not, they can be accessed with the SHAZAM **FILE** command and the complete **diskname:***foldername:filename* as discussed below. To run SHAZAM, open the **SHAZAM** folder then double click the SHAZAM icon (it looks like the World) and follow the examples in this chapter.

When SHAZAM begins a standard Macintosh Menu Bar will appear on the screen. Check the **README** file for a description of the menu items. This file also explains how to increase memory.

The **File** menu contains INPUT and OUTPUT options to select the files to be assigned to your SHAZAM run. If you wish to assign input and output files you may find it more convenient to use the SHAZAM commands:

FILE OUTPUT*diskname:foldername:outputfile*

and

FILE INPUT *diskname:foldername:inputfile*

In the examples below, when reference is made to a file, it is *always* assumed that this file was created by a text editor such as SimpleText or was saved with the SAVE AS... option in the **File** menu with the TEXT ONLY option (if MacWrite is used). Using files that are not text only will result in error messages.

Files on other disks that have already been loaded can be accessed by using the diskname with a colon (:) on the SHAZAM **FILE** command. For example:

FILE 11 diskname:*diskfile*

or

FILE 11 diskname:*foldername:diskfile*

The SHAZAM **FILE PATH** command is useful for specifying a default path.

It would be a good idea to type **DEMO** to learn how to use SHAZAM.

EXAMPLE 1

To run SHAZAM when your data is not in a separate file open SHAZAM and type:

SAMPLE *beg end*
READ *vars / options*
(data goes here)
(other commands)
STOP

EXAMPLE 2

A SHAZAM command file that has been prepared with an editor can be specified with the **FILE INPUT** command. Open SHAZAM and type:

FILE INPUT *commandfilename*

(the output will appear on the terminal screen here)

After all output has finished, to leave SHAZAM type:

STOP

EXAMPLE 3

Suppose you want your output to go into a file rather than the screen:

FILE OUTPUT *outputfilename*
FILE INPUT *commandfilename*
STOP

EXAMPLE 4

Suppose you want your output to come to the screen and go to a file:

FILE SCREEN *outputfilename*
FILE INPUT *commandfilename*
STOP

You can print your output file (or any other file) by typing the command:

FILE PRINT *outputfilename*

This can also be done with the PRINT option on the **File** menu. Be sure to turn on
your printer before executing this command. You could also print it as you would print
any document by selecting its icon and choosing the PRINT option from the **File**
menu.

To display a file from one of the loaded disks on screen use the LIST option on the
File menu or type:

FILE LIST *filename*

Sometimes SHAZAM will not allow you access to a file that has previously been
assigned. In this case you must close the file first with:

FILE CLOSE *filename*

How to Pause or Break Out of a **SHAZAM** Run

If you wish to stop execution before the run finishes you should try pressing the
Command key and the "." key simultaneously. *Command-.* will usually cause
SHAZAM to stop and you will be able to return to the Finder with a carriage return. If
this does not work then you can always simply turn off your machine. If the Mac says
"CR TO EXIT" it wants you to press *Command-.* a second time. You might also be able
to stop execution by pressing down the mouse in the menu bar. This occassionally
works, but it depends on what SHAZAM is doing at the time.

SHAZAM Scratch Files

Occasionally SHAZAM will need to create temporary scratch files during a run.
SHAZAM will attempt to trash these files when it is finished with them, but they often
will remain around on your disk. These files have names like: **-SHAZ#8**   o r
00000001. You can trash them yourself if you see them on your disk.

System Bombs

SHAZAM often attempts to use every bit of memory it can find. Occasionally you may find that SHAZAM runs fine, but when SHAZAM attempts to return to the Finder, a System Bomb will occur. This happens when there is simply no memory left for the Finder to take control. In this case you may have to restart the machine.

Sometimes SHAZAM cannot return directly to the Finder and it will say:

ERROR 35 - CR to exit

This is harmless, simply press the *Command-.* key to get back to the Finder.

When SHAZAM abnormally terminates for some reason, it is possible that a dialog box will pop up the next time you run SHAZAM which says something like: **SHAZAM HAS UNEXPECTEDLY QUIT.** If this occurs you will probably have to restart your Macintosh before SHAZAM will work again.

Some Macintosh Error Codes

34 Disk full
43 File not found
49 File already assigned (restart system)
35 No such volume name
54 File assigned to another task
64 Insufficient Memory
65 Numeric Overflow
66 Divide by zero
67 Insufficient Memory
75 Subprogram not found
76 FORMAT syntax error

Macintosh System Alert Error Codes (Bombs)

2 Address error (Usually Means Out of Memory)
3 Illegal Instruction (Usually Means Out of Memory)
10 Possibly running MacII/SE30 version on MacPlus, SE, or Portable
25 Out of Memory
28 Out of Memory
35 Make Block Free Error (Usually Means Out of Memory)

44. HOW TO RUN SHAZAM ON UNIX COMPUTERS

"There is no reason for any individual to have a computer in their home"
Ken Olson
President, DEC Corp, 1977

This chapter explains how to run SHAZAM with UNIX operating systems. These instructions should be used for the SUN Sparcstation, Linux and NeXT computers as well as all other UNIX workstations. SHAZAM command lines may be up to 80 characters. Continuation lines allow a SHAZAM command to be as long as 4096 characters. SHAZAM automatically converts lower case commands to upper case. However, if you wish to distinguish lower and upper case filenames and variables you should use the **SET NOLCUC** command.

The instructions in this chapter may differ for each installation. For more details refer to the SHAZAM installation instructions, or to the system administrator or to the SHAZAM manual page that may be available by typing: **man shazam**.

You could have all your SHAZAM commands and data together in one file: *infile.* To run SHAZAM use:

% **shazam** *<infile*

Note that % is the system prompt and this may vary from user to user.

If you wish to place the output in a file, use:

% **shazam** *<infile >outfile*

To print this file, use:

% **lpr** *outfile*

To print this file with the carriage control in effect, use:

% **lpr -f** *outfile*

or

%**fpr** *<outfile* l **lpr**

To obtain this output directly in a batch run, create a file, say **zap,** which contains the line:

shazam *<infile*

Next, type:

chmod a+rx zap

to make the file executable. To run the commands in the *infile*, type:

% batch zap

The output will be posted as a mail message. To view the output type: **mail** and read the results. If the **batch** command is not available then the **at** command can be used. For example type:

% at now +1 min zap

RUNNING OUT OF MEMORY

When SHAZAM is unable to run a problem because of insufficient memory you will usually get a message telling you how to set the **PAR** value. The **PAR** value specifies the amount of memory (in batches of 1024 bytes) that is needed. If you need to specify the **PAR** value, it should be done with the **PAR** command. For example, if you run SHAZAM and get the message:

RUN AGAIN WITH PAR=96

you should then use:

% shazam

PAR 96

(continue with the rest of the SHAZAM commands)

If used, the **PAR** command should be the first command in the SHAZAM run.

45. HOW TO RUN SHAZAM ON VAX AND ALPHA COMPUTERS

"If it works, it's obsolete"
Marshal McLuhan
1971

This chapter explains how to run SHAZAM on a VAX with VMS or ALPHA with VMS operating systems. In the examples below operating system commands are typed in lower case to distinguish them from SHAZAM commands. SHAZAM commands may be up to 80 columns. WARNING: The instructions in this section may differ for each installation.

You could have all your SHAZAM commands and data together in one file which should be read as follows:

$ shazam inputfile

You could have the output also go into a file with:

$ shazam inputfile outputfile

When SHAZAM is unable to run a problem because of insufficient memory, you will usually get a message telling you how to set the **PAR** value. The **PAR** value specifies the amount of memory (in batches of 1024 bytes) that is needed. If you need to specify the **PAR** value, it should be done with the **PAR** command. For example, if you run SHAZAM and get the message:

```
RUN AGAIN WITH PAR=96
```

you should then use:

$ shazam
PAR 96

(continue with the rest of SHAZAM commands)

If used, the **PAR** command must be the first command in the SHAZAM run.

Using **SHAZAM** *Interactively at a Terminal*

With a little care, you can easily run SHAZAM interactively at a terminal. The procedure is exactly the same as in batch, except some of the usual output will be deleted unless specifically requested. At a terminal, it is almost always useful to have your data in a file. This is not necessary if you want to input your data directly. However, direct data input is not recommended since an error would require that you start over. To exit SHAZAM at any time simply type **STOP**. It is possible to execute a VMS command within SHAZAM by preceding it with a $. For example:

$dir

would list your files.

46. HOW TO RUN SHAZAM FROM THE INTERNET

> *"Thank you for your email. I appreciate you taking the time to write to me. As you can probably imagine, I receive hundreds of messages from outside of Microsoft each day. While I love to read people's views and share ideas about technology, unfortunately, I am not able to answer each and every inquiry.*
>
> *...Thank you for your continued support of Microsoft and our products and best of luck with all your endeavours."*
>
> Bill Gates
> (computer generated reply to email asking for help with Windows 95)

Running SHAZAM via Email

SHAZAM programs can be submitted via email to a UNIX machine. The SHAZAM command file (all data must be inserted after a **READ** command) can be submitted as an email message to:

> runshazam@shazam.econ.ubc.ca

Alternatively, the SHAZAM command file can be posted to any UNIX machine that has the SHAZAM email software installed. For example, type the following SHAZAM commands and data as the text of your email message:

```
SAMPLE 1 3
READ A B C
1 10 1000
2 20 2000
3 30 3000
STAT A B C / NOWIDE
STOP
```

Now send the email message to the above address. When the SHAZAM run is finished the SHAZAM output will be posted back to you as an email message. For example, the output from the above commands should look like:

```
Hello/Bonjour/Aloha/Howdy/G Day/Kia Ora/Konnichiwa/Buenos Dias/Nee Hau
Welcome to SHAZAM - Version 8.0  -  DEC 1996 SYSTEM=SUNSPARC PAR=    234
|_SAMPLE 1 3
|_READ A B C
    3 VARIABLES AND       3 OBSERVATIONS STARTING AT OBS       1

|_STAT A B C / NOWIDE
NAME         N    MEAN       ST. DEV      VARIANCE     MINIMUM      MAXIMUM
A            3    2.0000     1.0000       1.0000       1.0000       3.0000
B            3    20.000     10.000       100.00       10.000       30.000
```

| C | | 3 | 2000.0 | 1000.0 | 0.10000E+07 | 1000.0 | 3000.0 |
| _STOP | | | | | | | |

Running **SHAZAM** *from the World Wide Web Browser*

SHAZAM programs can be run from the Internet with a recent version of a World Wide Web browser such as Netscape. The web site address (known as a URL or Uniform Resource Locator) for this service is `http://shazam.econ.ubc.ca/runshazam/`. Alternatively, you can use the URL of any UNIX machine running SHAZAM with the World Wide Web interface. The SHAZAM web page will be split into two frames as follows:

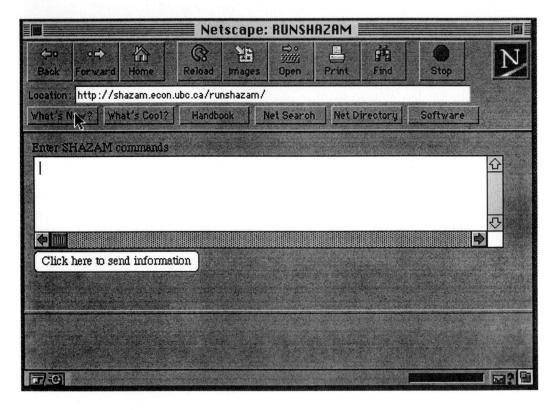

The SHAZAM commands are entered in the box contained in the upper frame while the lower frame displays the output. Using the mouse, the proportion of the page dedicated to each frame can be altered. SHAZAM cannot be run interactively through the Internet so BATCH mode must be used (see the *INTRODUCTION* chapter). When the commands are ready to be run, click on the box labeled *Click here to send information* located just below the command box. A warning regarding possible third party viewing of the information being sent may appear. Click on *Don't Show Again* to turn off the warning in future applications. At this point, the input frame might appear as follows:

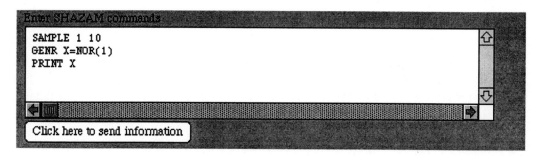

and the output frame will be:

```
Hello/Bonjour/Aloha/Howdy/G Day/Kia Ora/Konnichiwa/Buenos Dias/Nee Hau
Welcome to SHAZAM - Version 8.0  -  DEC 1996 SYSTEM=SUNSPARC PAR=    234
|_SAMPLE 1 10
|_GENR X=NOR(1)
|_PRINT X
    X
   1.133890     -2.231024    -0.9088095    -0.6669198    -1.291996    0.8289343
   0.6196108E-01   1.073122    0.6959795    0.5624666
|_STOP
```

It should be noted that some versions place constraints on the operations available with SHAZAM. There may be a character limit to the number of command lines written and the user should only attempt to run small SHAZAM command files. If SHAZAM appears to be ignoring the latter part of a program more than one hundred lines long, the character limit has likely been reached.

When writing the command file, most SHAZAM commands are available. If the user has access to files on the UNIX system that is running SHAZAM then it is possible to reference these files by using the full pathname. For example, a data file can be read as follows:

```
READ(/home/sam/data1) A B C
```

However, in general, **FILE INPUT**, **FILE OUTPUT**, and **WRITE** commands cannot be used. The user must import and export text by using copy and paste method to the SHAZAM input window.

Data can be typed directly into the input window following a **READ** command (see the chapter *A CHILD'S GUIDE TO RUNNING REGRESSIONS*). Alternatively, it is often the case that the user has a data file that he would like to use. Open the data file in an editor and copy and paste it to place the data in the input frame after a **READ** command. The example below shows the result after a data file has been copied and pasted from a data file.

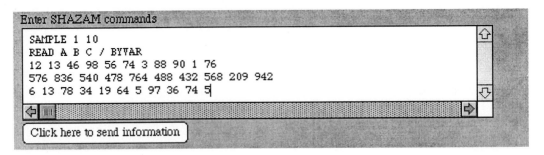

```
Enter SHAZAM commands
SAMPLE 1 10
READ A B C / BYVAR
12 13 46 98 56 74 3 88 90 1 76
576 836 540 478 764 488 432 568 209 942
6 13 78 34 19 64 5 97 36 74 5
```

Click here to send information

To save SHAZAM generated data use the **PRINT** command to list the required variables in the output frame (see the chapter *DATA INPUT AND OUTPUT*). Then use the copy option under the Edit menu to copy and paste the data from the output screen to another program.

The World Wide Web Browser Save Frame option allows the text found in the output frame itself to be saved into a file on your computer.

New features on the SHAZAM World Wide Web interface will be described at the SHAZAM WWW site. For information on an enhanced World Wide Web interface to SHAZAM see Nakano and White [1996].

Updates of this chapter *HOW TO RUN SHAZAM FROM THE INTERNET* are available at http://shazam.econ.ubc.ca/.

47. REFERENCES

Akaike, H., "Fitting Autoregressive Models for Prediction", *Annals of the Institute of Statistical Mathematics*, Vol. 21, 1969, pp. 243-247.

Akaike, H., "Information Theory and an Extension of the Maximum Likelihood Principle", in B.N. Petrov and F. Csáki, eds. *2nd International Symposium on Information Theory*, Akadémiai Kiadó, Budapest, 1973, pp. 267-281.

Akaike, H., "A New Look at Statistical Model Identification", *IEEE Transactions on Automatic Control*, Vol. 19, 1974, pp. 716-723.

Almon, S., "The Distributed Lag Between Capital Appropriations and Expenditures", *Econometrica*, Vol. 33, 1965, pp.178-196.

Amemiya, T., "Qualitative Response Models: A Survey", *Journal of Economic Literature*, Vol. XIX, 1981, pp. 1483-1536.

Amemiya, T., "Nonlinear Regression Models", Chapter 6 in Z. Griliches and M.D. Intriligator, eds., *Handbook of Econometrics*, Vol. 1, North-Holland, 1983.

Amemiya, T., *Advanced Econometrics*, Harvard University Press, 1985.

Andrews, D., "Heteroskedasticity and Autocorrelation Consistent Covariance Matrix Estimation", *Econometrica*, Vol. 59, 1991, pp. 817-858.

Baillie, R., "The Asymptotic Mean Squared Error of Multistep Prediction from the Regression Model with Autoregressive Errors", *Journal of the American Statistical Association*, Vol. 74, 1979, pp. 179-184.

Baumol, W.J., *Economic Theory and Operations Analysis,* 4th Edition, Prentice-Hall, 1977.

Beach, C., and MacKinnon, J., "A Maximum Likelihood Procedure for Regression with Autocorrelated Errors", *Econometrica*, Vol. 46, 1978, pp. 51-58.

Belsley, D., "On the Computation of the Nonlinear Full-Information Maximum-Likelihood Estimation", *Journal of Econometrics*, Vol. 14, 1980, pp. 203-278.

Belsley, D., Kuh, E., and Welsch, R., *Regression Diagnostics*, Wiley, 1980.

Benninga, S., *Numerical Techniques in Finance,* MIT Press, 1989

Berndt, E.R., *The Practice Of Econometrics*, Addison-Wesley, 1991.

Beveridge, S., and Nelson, C.R., "A New Approach to Decomposition of Economic Time Series into Permanent and Transitory Components with Particular Attention to Measurement of the Business Cycle", *Journal of Monetary Economics*, Vol. 7, 1981, pp. 151-174.

Bickel, P., and Doksum, K., *Mathematical Statistics: Basic Ideas and Selected Topics*, Holden-Day, 1977.

Black, F., and Scholes, M., "The Pricing of Options and Corporate Liabilities", *Journal of Political Economy*, Vol. 81, 1973, pp. 637-659.

Bollerslev, T., "Generalized Autoregressive Conditional Heteroskedasticity", *Journal of Econometrics*, Vol. 31, 1986, pp. 307-327.

Box, G.E.P., and Cox, D.R., "An Analysis of Transformations", *Journal of the Royal Statistical Society*, Series B, Vol. 26, 1964, pp. 211-243.

Box, G.E.P., and Jenkins, G.M., *Time Series Analysis: Forecasting and Control*, Holden-Day, 1976.

Box, G.E.P., and Pierce, D.A., "Distribution of Residual Autocorrelations in Autoregressive Integrated Moving Average Time Series Models", *Journal of the American Statistical Association*, Vol. 65, 1970, pp. 1509-1526.

Box, G.E.P., and Tidwell, P., "Transformation of the Independent Variables", *Technometrics*, Vol. 4, 1962, pp. 531-550.

Bofinger, E., "Estimation of a Density Function using Order Statistics", *Australian Journal of Statistics*, Vol. 17, 1975, pp. 1-7.

Brent, R.P., "Algorithm 488: A Gaussian Pseudo-Random Number Generator", *Communications of the ACM*, Vol. 17, 1974, pp. 704-706.

Breusch, T.S., and Pagan, A.R., "A Simple Test For Heteroscedasticity And Random Coefficient Variation", *Econometrica*, Vol. 47, 1979, pp. 1287-1294.

Breusch, T.S., and Pagan, A.R., "The Lagrange Multiplier Test and its Applications to Model Specification in Econometrics", *Review of Economic Studies*, Vol. 47, 1980, pp. 239-254.

Brown, R.L., Durbin, J., and Evans, J.M., "Techniques for Testing the Constancy of Regression Relationships over Time", *Journal of the Royal Statistical Society*, B, Vol. 37, 1975, pp. 149-163.

Buja, A., Hastie, T., and Tibshirani, R., "Linear Smoothers and Additive Models", *The Annals of Statistics*, Vol. 17, 1989, pp. 453-555.

Burr, I.W., "On a General System of Distributions III", *Journal of the American Statistical Association*, Vol. 63, 1968, pp. 636-643.

Buse, A., "Goodness of Fit in Generalized Least Squares Estimation", *American Statistician*, Vol. 27, 1973, pp. 106-108.

Buse, A., "Goodness of Fit in the Seemingly Unrelated Regressions Model", *Journal of Econometrics*, Vol. 10, 1979, pp. 109-113.

Businger, P., and Golub, G.H., "Linear Least Squares Solutions by Householder Transformations", *Numerische Mathematik*, Vol. 7, 1965, pp. 269-276.

Cameron, T.A., and White, K.J., "Generalized Gamma Family Regression Models for Long-distance Telephone Call Durations" in A. de Fontenay, M. Shugard, and D. Sibley (eds.) *Telecommunications Demand Modelling*, Amsterdam: North Holland, 1990.

Cameron, T.A., and White, K.J., "The Demand for Computer Services: A Disaggregate Decision Model", *Managerial and Decision Economics*, Vol. 7, 1986, pp. 37-41.

Cassing, S.A., and White, K.J., "An Analysis of the Eigenvector Condition in the Durbin-Watson Test", *Australian Journal of Statistics*, Vol. 25, 1983, pp. 17-22.

Cerf, C., and Navasky, V. *The Experts Speak: The Definitive Compendium of Authoritative Misinformation*, Pantheon Books, 1984.

Chalfant J., and White, K.J., "Estimation of Demand Systems with Concavity and Monotonicity Constraints", University of British Columbia Discussion Paper, 1988.

Chalfant, J, Gray, R., and White, K., "Evaluating Prior Beliefs in a Demand System: The Case of Meats Demand in Canada", *American Journal of Agricultural Economics*, Vol. 73, 1991, pp. 476-490.

Chotikapanich, D., and Griffiths, W.E., *Learning SHAZAM™: A Computer Handbook for Econometrics*, Wiley, 1993.

Chow, G., "Tests for Equality Between Sets of Coefficients in Two Linear Regressions", *Econometrica*, Vol. 28, 1960, pp. 591-605.

Chow, G., *Econometrics*, McGraw-Hill, 1983.

Cleveland, W.S., "The Inverse Autocorrelations of a Time Series and Their Applications", *Technometrics*, Vol. 14, 1972, pp. 277-293.

Cleveland, W. S., "Robust Locally Weighted Regression and Smoothing Scatterplots", *Journal of the American Statistical Association*, Vol. 74, 1979, pp. 829-836.

Cleveland, W. S., and Devlin S. J., "Locally Weighted Regression: An Approach to Regression Analysis by Local Fitting", *Journal of the American Statistical Association*, Vol. 83, 1988, pp. 596-610.

Cleveland, W. S., Devlin S. J., and Grosse, E., "Regression by Local Fitting: Methods, Properties and Computational Algorithms", *Journal of Econometrics*, Vol. 37, 1988, pp. 87-114.

Cochrane, D., and Orcutt, G.H., "Application of Least Squares Regressions to Relationships Containing Autocorrelated Error Terms", *Journal of the American Statistical Association*, Vol. 44, 1949, pp. 32-61.

Coelli, T.J., and Griffiths, W., *Computer and Exercise Solutions Manual*, Wiley, 1989: To accompany Judge, G., Griffiths, W., Hill, R., Lütkepohl, H., and Lee, T., *The Theory and Practice of Econometrics, Second Edition*.

Cragg, J.G., "More Efficient Estimation in the Presence of Heteroscedasticity of Unknown Form", *Econometrica*, Vol. 51, 1983, pp. 751-763.

Cragg, J.G., and Uhler, R.S., "The Demand for Automobiles", *Canadian Journal of Economics*, Vol. 3, 1970, pp. 386-406.

Craven, P., and Wahba, G., "Smoothing Noisy Data with Spline Functions: Estimating the Correct Degree of Smoothing by the Method of Generalized Cross-Validation", *Numerishce Mathematik*, Vol. 31, 1979, pp. 377-403.

Davidson, R., and MacKinnon, J.G., "Several Tests for Model Specification in the Presence of Alternative Hypotheses", *Econometrica*, Vol. 49, 1981, pp. 781-793.

Davidson, R., and MacKinnon, J.G., *Estimation and Inference in Econometrics*, Oxford University Press, 1993.

Davies, R.B., "The Distribution of a Linear Combination of χ^2 Random Variables, Algorithm AS 155", *Applied Statistics*, Vol. 29, 1980, pp. 323-333.

Deegan, J., and White, K., "An Analysis of Nonpartisan Election Media Expenditure Decisions Using Limited Dependent Variable Methods", *Social Science Research*, Vol. 5, 1976, pp. 127-135.

Dhrymes, P., *Econometrics*, Harper and Row, 1970.

Dhrymes, P., *Distributed Lags: Problems of Estimation and Formulation*, Holden-Day, 1971.

Dickey, D.A., and Fuller, W.A., "Likelihood Ratio Statistics for Autoregressive Time Series with a Unit Root", *Econometrica*, Vol. 49, 1981, pp. 1057-1072.

Diewert, W.E., "Superlative Index Numbers and Consistency in Aggregation", *Econometrica*, Vol. 46, 1978, pp. 883-900.

Diewert, W.E., "Aggregation Problems in the Measurement of Capital", in D. Usher, ed., *The Measurement of Capital*, NBER, University of Chicago Press, 1980, pp. 433-528.

Diewert, W.E., and Wales, T.J., "Linear and Quadratic Spline Models for Consumer Demand Functions", *Canadian Journal of Economics*, Vol. 26, 1993, pp. 77-106.

Durbin, J., "Testing for Serial Correlation in Systems of Simultaneous Regression Equations", *Biometrika*, Vol. 44, 1957, pp. 370-377.

Durbin, J., "Testing for Serial Correlation in Regression Analysis based on the Periodogram of Least-Squares Residuals", *Biometrika*, Vol. 56, 1969, pp. 1-15.

Durbin, J., "Testing for Serial Correlation in Least-Squares Regression When Some of the Regressors are Lagged Dependent Variables", *Econometrica*, Vol. 38, 1970, pp. 410-421.

Durbin, J., and Watson, G.S., "Testing for Serial Correlation in Least Squares Regression I", *Biometrika*, Vol. 37, 1950, pp. 409-428.

Durbin, J., and Watson, G.S., "Testing for Serial Correlation in Least Squares Regression II", *Biometrika*, Vol. 38, 1951, pp. 159-178.

Durbin, J., and Watson, G.S., "Testing for Serial Correlation in Least Squares Regression III", *Biometrika*, Vol. 58, 1971, pp. 1-19.

Dyer, D.D., and Keating, J.P., "On the Determination of Critical Values for Bartlett's Test", *Journal of the American Statistical Association*, Vol. 75, 1980, pp. 313-319.

Efron, B., "Bootstrap Methods: Another Look at the Jackknife", *Annals of Statistics*, Vol. 7, 1979, pp. 1-26.

Engle, R.F., "Autoregressive Conditional Heteroscedastity with Estimates of the Variance of United Kingdom Inflation", *Econometrica*, Vol. 50, 1982, pp. 987-1007.

Engle, R.F., and Granger, C.W., "Cointegration and Error Correction: Representation, Estimation and Testing", *Econometrica*, Vol. 55, 1987, pp. 251-276.

Engle, R.F., Lilien, D.M., and Robins, R.P., "Estimating Time Varying Risk Premia in the Term Structure: The ARCH-M Model", *Econometrica*, Vol. 55, 1987, pp. 391-407.

Eubank, R. L., *Spline Smoothing and Nonparametric Regression*, Marcel Dekker, 1988.

Evans, M., Hastings, N., and Peacock, J., *Statistical Distributions, Second Edition*, Wiley, 1993.

Fan, J., and Marron, J. S., "Fast Implementations of Nonparametric Curve Estimators", *Journal of Computational and Graphical Statistics*, Vol. 3, 1994, pp. 35-56.

Farebrother, R.W., "Gram-Schmidt Regression", *Applied Statistics*, Vol. 23, 1974, pp. 470-476.

Fomby, T., Hill, R., and Johnson, S., *Advanced Econometric Methods*, Springer-Verlag, 1984.

Freedman, D.A., and Peters, S.C., "Bootstrapping a Regression Equation: Some Empirical Results", *Journal of the American Statistical Association*, Vol. 79, 1984, pp. 97-106.

Fuller, W.A., *Introduction to Statistical Time Series*, Wiley, 1976.

Gallant, A.R., *Nonlinear Statistical Models* , Wiley, 1987.

Geweke, J., "Exact Inference in the Inequality Constrained Normal Linear Regression Model", *Journal of Applied Econometrics*, Vol. 1, 1986, pp. 127-141.

Geweke, J., "Antithetic Acceleration of Monte Carlo Integration In Bayesian Inference", *Journal of Econometrics*, Vol. 38, 1988, pp. 72-89.

Glejser, H., "A New Test for Heteroscedasticity", *Journal of the American Statistical Association*, Vol. 64, 1969, pp. 316-323.

Godfrey, L.G., "Testing for Multiplicative Heteroskedasticity", *Journal of Econometrics*, Vol. 8, 1978, pp. 227-236.

Godfrey, L.G., "Discriminating Between Autocorrelation and Misspecification in Regression Analysis: An Alternative Test Strategy", *Review of Economics and Statistics* , Vol. 69, 1987, pp. 128-134.

Godfrey, L.G., McAleer, M., and McKenzie, C.R., "Variable Addition and Lagrange Multipler Tests for Linear and Logarithmic Regression Models", *Review of Economics and Statistics*, Vol. 70, 1988, pp. 492-503.

Golan, A., Judge, G., and Miller, D., *Maximum Entropy Econometrics: Robust Estimation with Limited Data*, Wiley, 1996.

Goldberger, A.S., "Best Linear Unbiased Prediction in the Linear Regression Model", *Journal of the American Statistical Association*, Vol. 57, 1962, pp. 369-375.

Goldberger, A.S., *Econometric Theory*, Wiley, 1964.

Goldfeld, S., and Quandt, R., "Some Tests for Homoscedasticity", *Journal of the American Statistical Association*, Vol. 60, 1965, pp. 539-547.

Goldfeld, S., and Quandt, R., *Nonlinear Methods in Econometrics*, North-Holland, 1972.

Golub, G.H., and Styan, G.P.H., "Numerical Computations for Univariate Linear Models", *Journal of Statistical Computation and Simulation*, Vol. 2, 1973, pp. 253-274.

Golub, G.H., and Van Loan, C.F., *Matrix Computations*, Johns Hopkins University Press, Baltimore, 1983.

Graybill, F., *Theory and Application of the Linear Model*, Duxbury Press, 1976.

Greene, W., "Sample Selection Bias as a Specification Error: Comment", *Econometrica*, Vol. 49, No. 3, 1981, pp. 795-798.

Greene, W.H., *Econometric Analysis, Second Edition*, Macmillan, 1993.

Gregory, A., and Veall, M., "On Formulating Wald Tests of Nonlinear Restrictions", *Econometrica*, Vol. 53, 1985, pp. 1465-1468.

Griffiths, W.E., Hill, R.C., and Judge, G.G., *Learning and Practicing Econometrics*, John Wiley & Sons, 1993.

Griliches, Z., and Intriligator, M., *Handbook of Econometrics*, North-Holland, 1983.

Guilkey, D.K., and Schmidt, P., "Estimation of Seemingly Unrelated Regressions with Vector Autoregressive Errors", *Journal of the American Statistical Association*, Vol. 68, 1973, pp.642-647.

Guilkey, D.K., and Schmidt, P., "Extended Tabulations for Dickey-Fuller Tests", *Economic Letters*, Vol. 31, 1989, pp. 355-57.

Gujarati, D., *Basic Econometrics*, Third Edition, McGraw-Hill, 1995; (Second Edition, 1988).

Hall, P., and Marron, J. S., "On Variance Estimation in Nonparametric Regression", *Biometrika*, Vol. 77, 1990, pp. 415-419.

Hall, P., and Sheather, S.J., "On the Distribution of a Studentised Quantile", *Journal of the Royal Statistical Society*, Series B, Vol. 50, 1988, pp. 381-391.

Hall, P., and Wehrly, T. E., "A Geometrical Method for Removing Edge Effects from Kernel-type Nonparametric Regression Estimators", *Journal of the American Statistical Association*, Vol. 86, 1991, pp. 665-672.

Hannan, E.J., and Quinn, B., "The Determination of the Order of an Autoregression", *Journal of the Royal Statistical Society*, Series B, Vol. 41, 1979, pp. 190-195.

Hansen, L., and Singleton, K. "Generalized Instrumental Variables Estimation of Nonlinear Rational Expectations Models", *Econometrica*, Vol. 50, 1982, pp. 1269-1286.

Hanushek, E., and Jackson, J., *Statistical Methods for Social Scientists*, Academic Press, 1977.

Härdle, W., "Resistant Smoothing Using the Fast Fourier Transform", *Applied Statistics*, Vol. 36, 1987, pp. 104-111.

Härdle, W., *Applied Nonparametric Regression*, Cambridge University Press, 1990.

Harvey, A.C., "Estimating Regression Models with Multiplicative Heteroscedasticity", *Econometrica*, Vol. 44, 1976, pp. 461-465.

Harvey, A.C., *Time Series Models*, Philip Allan, 1981.

Harvey, A.C., *The Econometric Analysis of Time Series, Second Edition*, MIT Press, 1990.

Harvey, A.C., and Collier, P., "Testing for Functional Misspecification in Regression Analysis", *Journal of Econometrics*, Vol. 6, 1977, pp. 103-119.

Harvey, A.C., and Phillips, G.D.A., "A Comparison of the Power of some Tests for Heteroskedasticity in the General Linear Model", *Journal of Econometrics*, Vol. 2, 1974, pp. 307-316.

Hausman, J.A., "Specification Tests in Econometrics", *Econometrica*, Vol. 46, 1978, pp. 1251-1271.

Heckman, J., "Sample Bias as a Specification Error", *Econometrica*, Vol. 47, 1979, pp. 153-161.

Hensher, D.A., and Johnson, L.W., *Applied Discrete Choice Modeling*, Wiley, 1981.

Hildreth, C., and Lu, J.Y., "Demand Relations with Autocorrelated Disturbances", *Technical Bulletin 276*, Michigan State University Agricultural Experiment Station, May 1960.

Hylleberg, S., Engle, R.F., Granger, C.W.J., and Yoo, B.S.,"Seasonal Integration and Cointegration", *Journal of Econometrics*, Vol. 44, 1990, pp. 215-238.

Imhof, J.P., "Computing the Distribution of Quadratic Forms in Normal Variables", *Biometrika*, Vol. 48, 1961, pp. 419-426.

Intriligator, M., *Econometric Models, Techniques and Applications*, Prentice-Hall, 1978.

Jarque, C.M., and Bera, A.K., "Efficient Tests for Normality, Homoscedasticity and Serial Independence of Regression Residuals", *Economics Letters*, Vol. 6, 1980, pp. 255-259.

Jarque, C.M., and Bera, A.K., "A Test for Normality of Observations and Regression Residuals", *International Statistical Review*, Vol. 55, 1987, pp. 163-172.

Johansen, S., and Juselius, K., "Maximum Likelihood Estimation and Inference on Cointegration - with Applications to the Demand for Money", *Oxford Bulletin of Economics and Statistics*, Vol. 52, 1990, pp. 169-210.

Johnson, N.L., and Kotz, S., *Continuous Univariate Distributions-1*, John Wiley, New York, 1970.

Johnston, J., *Econometric Methods*, McGraw-Hill, 1984.

Jolliffe, I.T., *Principal Component Analysis*, Springer-Verlag, 1986.

Judge, G., Hill, R., Griffiths, W., Lütkepohl, H., and Lee, T., *Introduction to the Theory and Practice of Econometrics , Second Edition*, Wiley, 1988.

Judge, G., Griffiths, W., Hill, R., Lütkepohl, H., and Lee, T., *The Theory and Practice of Econometrics, Second Edition*, Wiley, 1985.

Kalaba, R., and Tesfatsion, L., "Time-Varying Linear Regression via Flexible Least Squares", *Computers and Mathematics with Applications*, Vol. 17, 1989, pp. 1215-1245.

Kaiser, H.F., "Computer Program for Varimax Rotation in Factor Analysis", *Educational and Psychological Measurement*, Vol. XIX, 1959, pp. 413-420.

Kelejian, H., and Purcha, I., "Independent or Uncorrelated Disturbances in Linear Regression: An Illustration of the Difference", *Economics Letters*, Vol. 19, 1985, pp. 35-38.

Kennedy, P., *A Guide to Econometrics*, MIT Press, 1985.

Kiefer, N.M., "Economic Duration Data and Hazard Functions", *Journal of Economic Literature*, Vol. XXVI, 1988, pp. 646-679.

Klein, L., *Textbook of Econometrics*, Prentice-Hall, 1974.

Kmenta, J., *Elements of Econometrics*, Second Edition, Macmillan, 1986.

Koenker, R., and Bassett, G., "Regression Quantiles", *Econometrica*, Vol. 46, 1978, pp. 33-50.

Koenker, R., and D'Orey, V., "Computing Regression Quantiles", *Applied Statistics*, Vol. 36, 1987, pp. 383-393.

Koerts, J., and Abrahamse, A.P.J., "On the Power of the BLUS Procedure", *Journal of the American Statistical Association*, Vol. 63, 1968, pp. 1227-1236.

Koerts, J., and Abrahamse, A.P.J., *On the Theory and Application of the General Linear Model*, Rotterdam University Press, 1969.

Kvalseth, T. O., "Cautionary Note About R^2", *American Statistician*, Vol. 39, 1985, pp. 279-285.

Lafontaine, F., and White, K.J., "Obtaining Any Wald Statistic You Want", *Economics Letters*, Vol. 21, 1986, pp. 35-40.

Lee, H.S., and Siklos, P.L., "Unit Roots and Seasonal Unit Roots in Macroeconomic Time Series", *Economics Letters*, Vol. 35, 1991, pp. 273-277.

Ljung, G.M., and Box, G.E.P., "On a Measure of Lack of Fit in Time Series Models", *Biometrika*, Vol. 66, 1978, pp. 297-303.

Lütkepohl, H., "The Sources of the U.S. Money Demand Instability", *Empirical Economics*, Vol. 18, 1993, pp. 729-743.

McDonald, J.B., "Some Generalized Functions for the Size Distribution of Income", *Econometrica*, Vol. 52, 1984, pp. 647-663.

McKelvey, R.D., and Zavoina, W., "A Statistical Model for the Analysis of Ordinal Level Dependent Variables", *Journal of Mathematical Sociology*, Vol. 4, 1975, pp. 103-120.

MacKinnon, J.G., and White, H., "Some Heteroskedasticity Consistent Covariance Matrix Estimators with Improved Finite Sample Properties", *Journal of Econometrics*, Vol. 29, 1985, pp. 305-325.

MacKinnon, J.G., "Critical Values for Cointegration Tests", Chapter 13 in R.F. Engle and C.W.J. Granger, eds., *Long-Run Economic Relationships: Readings in Cointegration*, Oxford University Press, 1991.

Maddala, G.S., *Econometrics*, McGraw-Hill, 1977.

Maddala, G.S., *Introduction to Econometrics, Second Edition*, Macmillan, 1992.

Maddala, G.S., *Limited Dependent and Qualitative Variables in Econometrics*, Cambridge University Press, 1983.

Marquardt, D.W.,"An Algorithm for Least-Squares Estimation of Nonlinear Parameters", *Journal of the Society for Industrial and Applied Mathematics*, Vol. 2, 1963, pp. 431-441.

Magee, L., "The Behaviour of a Modified Box-Cox Regression Model When Some Values of the Dependent Variable are Close to Zero", *Review of Economics and Statistics*, Vol. 70, 1988, pp. 362-366.

Mood, A.M., Graybill, F.A., and Boes, D.C., *Introduction to the Theory of Statistics*, McGraw Hill, 1974.

Mundlak, Y., "On the Concept of Non-Significant Functions and its Implications for Regression Analysis", *Journal of Econometrics*, Vol. 16, 1981, pp. 139-150.

Murphy, J., *Introductory Econometrics*, Irwin, 1973.

Nakano, J., and White, K.J., "Using WWW abilities from SHAZAM Statistical Program", *Proceedings of the Institute of Statistical Mathematics*, Vol. 44, No. 2, 1996 (in Japanese). http://shazam.econ.ubc.ca/ (in English).

Nelson, C., *Applied Time Series Analysis*, Holden-Day, 1973.

Newbold, P., *Statistics for Business and Economics*, Prentice-Hall, 1984.

Newbold, P., *Statistics for Business and Economics, Fourth Edition*, Prentice-Hall, 1995.

Newey, W., and West, K., "A Simple, Positive Semi-definite, Heteroskedasticity and Autocorrelation Consistent Covariance Matrix", *Econometrica*, Vol. 55, 1987, pp. 703-708.

Newey, W., and West K., "Automatic Lag Selection in Covariance Matrix Estimation", Unpublished University of Wisconsin Paper, 1991.

Nguyen, T.T., *Statistics with SHAZAM*, Narada Press, 1993. ISBN 1-895938-00-7.

Otto, G., and Wirjanto, T., "Seasonal Unit Root Tests on Canadian Macroeconomic Time Series", *Economics Letters*, Vol. 34, 1990, pp. 117-120.

Ouliaris, S., Park, J.Y., and Phillips, P.C.B., "Testing for a Unit Root in the Presence of a Maintained Trend", Chapter 1 in B. Raj ed., *Advances in Econometrics and Modelling*, Kluwer Academic Publishers, 1989.

Pagan, A.R., "A Generalized Approach to the Treatment of Autocorrelation", *Australian Economic Papers*, Vol. 13, 1974, pp. 267-280.

Pagan, A.R., and Hall, A.D., "Diagnostic Tests As Residual Analysis", *Econometric Reviews*, Vol. 2, 1983, pp. 159-218.

Pagan, A.R., and Nichols, D.F., "Estimating Predictions, Prediction Errors and their Standard Deviations Using Constructed Variables", *Journal of Econometrics*, Vol. 24, 1984, pp. 293-310.

Pan, Jie-Jian, "Distribution of Noncircular Serial Correlation Coefficients", *Selected Translations in Mathematical Statistics and Probability*, (Printed for the Institute of Mathematical Statistics by the American Mathematical Society), Vol. 7, 1968, pp. 281-291.

Parks, R.W., "Efficient Estimation of a System of Regression Equations when Disturbances are Both Serially and Contemporaneously Correlated", *Journal of the American Statistical Association*, Vol. 62, 1967, pp. 500-509.

Perron, P., "The Great Crash, the Oil Price Shock and the Unit Root Hypothesis", *Econometrica*, Vol. 57, 1989, pp. 1361-1402.

Perron, P., "Trends and Random Walks in Macroeconomic Time Series", *Journal of Economic Dynamics and Control*, Vol. 12, 1988, pp. 297-332.

Phillips, P.C.B., "Time Series Regression with a Unit Root", *Econometrica*, Vol. 55, 1987, pp. 277-301.

Phillips, P.C.B., and Ouliaris, S., "Asymptotic Properties of Residual Based Tests for Cointegration", *Econometrica*, Vol. 58, 1990, pp. 165-193.

Pindyck, R., and Rubinfeld, D., *Econometric Models & Economic Forecasts, Third Edition*, McGraw-Hill, 1991.

Pinkse, J., "A Consistent Nonparametric Characteristic Function Based Test for Serial Independence", *Journal of Econometrics*, 1996, forthcoming.

Poirier, D.J., "The Effect of the First Observation in Regression Models with First-order Autoregressive Disturbances", *Applied Statistics*, Vol. 27, 1978, pp. 67-68.

Poirier, D.J., and Melino A., "A Note on the Interpretation of Regression Coefficients within a Class of Truncated Distributions", *Econometrica*, Vol. 46, 1978, pp. 1207-1209.

Prais, S.J., and Houthakker, H.S., *The Analysis of Family Budgets*, Cambridge University Press, 1955.

Prais, S.J., and Winsten, C.B., "Trend Estimators and Serial Correlation", Cowles Commission Discussion Paper No. 383, Chicago, 1954.

Ramanathan, R., *Introductory Econometrics with Applications, Third Edition*, The Dryden Press - Harcourt Brace College Publishers, 1995; (*Second Edition*, Harcourt Brace Jovanovich, 1992.)

Ramsey, J.B., "Tests for Specification Errors in Classical Linear Least Squares Regression Analysis", *Journal of the Royal Statistical Society*, Series B, Vol. 31, 1969, pp. 350-371.

Rao, C.R., *Linear Statistical Inference and its Applications*, Wiley, 1973.

Rice, J. "Bandwidth Choice for Nonparametric Kernel Regression", *Annals of Statistics*, Vol. 12, 1984, pp. 1215-1230.

Rice, J., "Boundary Modification for Kernel Regression", *Communications in Statistics, Series A*, Vol. 13, 1984, pp. 893-900.

Richardson, S.M., and White, K., "The Power of Tests for Autocorrelation with Missing Observations", *Econometrica*, Vol. 47, 1979, pp. 785-788.

Rust, R. T., "Flexible Regression", *Journal of Marketing Research*, Vol. 25, 1988, pp. 10-24.

Salkever, S., "The Use of Dummy Variables to Compute Predictions, Prediction Errors, and Confidence Intervals", *Journal of Econometrics*, Vol. 4, 1976, pp. 393-397.

Savin, N.E., "Conflict Among Testing Procedures in a Linear Regression Model With Autoregressive Disturbances", *Econometrica*, Vol. 44, 1976, pp. 1303-1315.

Savin, N.E., "Friedman-Meiselman Revisited: A Study in Autocorrelation", *Economic Inquiry*, Vol. 16, 1978, pp. 37-52.

Savin, N.E., and White, K.J., "Estimation and Testing for Functional Form and Autocorrelation: A Simultaneous Approach", *Journal of Econometrics*, Vol. 8, 1978, pp. 1-12.

Savin, N.E., and White, K.J., "The Durbin-Watson Test for Autocorrelation with Extreme Sample Sizes or Many Regressors", *Econometrica*, Vol. 45, 1977, pp. 1989-1996.

Savin, N.E., and White, K.J., "Testing for Autocorrelation With Missing Observations", *Econometrica*, Vol. 46, 1978, pp. 59-68.

Schmidt, P., "Estimation of a Distributed Lag Model With Second Order Autoregressive Disturbances: A Monte Carlo Experiment", *International Economic Review*, Vol. 12, 1971, pp. 372-380.

Schneider, W., "Stability Analysis using Kalman Filtering, Scoring, EM and an Adaptive EM Method", Chapter 14 in Hackl, P. and Westlund, A., ed., *Economic Structural Change*, 1991, Springer-Verlag.

Schwarz, G., "Estimating the Dimension of a Model", *The Annals of Statistics*, Vol. 8, 1978, pp. 461-464.

Shibata, R. "An Optimal Selection of Regression Variables", *Biometrika*, Vol. 68, 1981, pp. 45-54.

Siddiqui, M. "Distribution of Quantiles in Samples from a Bivariate Population", *Journal of Research National Bureau of Standards* Sect B. 64, 1960, pp. 145-150.

Silk, J., "Systems Estimation: A Comparison of SAS, SHAZAM and TSP", *Journal of Applied Econometrics*, Vol. 11, 1996, pp. 437-450.

Silverman, B. W., *Density Estimation*, Chapman and Hall, 1986.

Simon, S., and Lesage, J., "Assessing the Accuracy of ANOVA Calculations in Statistical Software", *Computational Statistics and Data Analysis*, Vol. 8, 1989, pp. 325-332.

Smillie, K.R., *An Introduction to Regression and Correlation*, Ryerson Press, 1966.

Srivastava, V.K., and Giles, D.E.A., *Seemingly Unrelated Regression Equations Models*, Dekker, 1987.

Tesfatsion, L., and Veitch, J., "U.S. Money Demand Instability", *Journal of Economic Dynamics and Control*, Vol. 14, 1990, pp. 151-173.

Theil, H., *Economic Forecasts and Policy*, North-Holland, 1961.

Theil, H., *Applied Economic Forecasting*, North-Holland, 1966.

Theil, H., *Principles of Econometrics*, Wiley, 1971.

Tobin, J., "Estimation of Relationships for Limited Dependent Variables", *Econometrica*, Vol. 26, 1958, pp. 24-36.

Vinod, H., "Generalization of the Durbin-Watson Statistic for Higher Order Autoregressive Processes", *Communications In Statistics*, Vol. 2, 1973, pp. 115-144.

Wallace, T., and Silver, J., *Econometrics: An Introduction*, Addison-Wesley, 1988.

Watson, D.E., and White, K.J., "Forecasting the Demand for Money Under Changing Term Structure of Interest Rates: An Application of Ridge Regression", *Southern Economic Journal*, Vol. 43, 1976, pp. 1096-1105.

Weiss, A.A., "ARMA Models with ARCH Errors", *Journal of Time Series Analysis*, Vol. 5, 1984, pp. 129-143.

Weiss, A.A., "Asymptotic Theory for ARCH Models: Estimation and Testing", *Econometric Theory*, Vol. 2, 1986, pp. 107-131.

Wells, D., *The Penguin Dictionary of Curious and Interesting Numbers*, Penguin Books, 1986.

Whistler, D., "An Introductory Guide To SHAZAM", http://shazam.econ.ubc.ca/intro.

White, H., "A Heteroskedasticity-Consistent Covariance Matrix Estimator and a Direct Test for Heteroskedasticity", *Econometrica*, Vol. 48, 1980, pp. 817-838.

White, H., "Using Least Squares to Approximate Unknown Regression Functions", *International Economic Review*, Vol. 21, 1980, pp. 149-170.

White, H., "Maximum Likelihood Estimation of Misspecified Models", *Econometrica*, Vol. 50, 1982, pp. 1-25.

White, H., *Asymptotic Theory for Econometricians*, Academic Press, 1984.

White, H., and Domowitz, I., "Nonlinear Regression with Dependent Observations", *Econometrica*, Vol. 52, 1984, pp. 143-162.

White, K.J., "Estimation of the Liquidity Trap With a Generalized Functional Form", *Econometrica*, Vol. 40, 1972, pp. 193-199.

White, K.J., "Consumer Choice and Use of Bank Credit Cards: A Model and Cross-Section Results", *Journal of Consumer Research*, Vol. 2, 1975, pp. 10-18.

White, K.J., "A General Computer Program for Econometric Methods - SHAZAM", *Econometrica*, Vol. 46, 1978, pp. 239-240.

White, K.J., "Applications in Econometrics: Problems, Programs, and Procedures", *Proceedings of the Third Annual Conference of the SAS Users Group International*, January 1978.

White, K.J., "SHAZAM: A General Computer Program for Econometric Methods (Version 5)", *American Statistician*, Vol. 41, 1987, p. 80.

White, K.J., "SHAZAM: A Comprehensive Computer Program For Regression Models (Version 6)", *Computational Statistics & Data Analysis*, Vol. 7, 1988, pp. 102-104.

White, K.J., "The Durbin-Watson Test for Autocorrelation in Nonlinear Models", *Review of Economics and Statistics*, Vol. 74, 1992, pp. 370-373.

White, K.J., Boyd, J.A.J., Wong, S.D., and Whistler, D. *SHAZY: The SHAZAM Student Version*, McGraw-Hill, 1993. ISBN 0-07-833562-0.

White, K.J., and Bui, L.T.M., *Basic Econometrics: A Computer Handbook Using SHAZAM*, McGraw-Hill, 1988. ISBN 0-07-834463-8, *Gujarati (2nd Edition) Handbook*.

White, K.J., and Bui, L.T.M., *The Practice of Econometrics: A Computer Handbook Using SHAZAM*, Addison-Wesley, 1991. ISBN 0-201-50048-5, *Berndt Handbook*.

White, K.J., Haun, S.A., and Gow, D.J., *Introduction to the Theory and Practice of Econometrics: A Computer Handbook Using SHAZAM and SAS*, John Wiley and Sons, 1988. ISBN 0-471-85946-X, *Judge Handbook*.

White, K.J., and Theobald, S.A., *Basic Econometrics: A Computer Handbook Using SHAZAM*, McGraw-Hill, 1995. ISBN 0-07-069864-3, *Gujarati (3rd Edition) Handbook*.

White, K.J., Wong, S.D., Whistler, D., Grafton, R.Q., and Scantlen, M., *Econometric Models & Economic Forecasts: A Computer Handbook Using SHAZAM*, McGraw-Hill, 1991. ISBN 0-07-050101-7, *Pindyck-Rubinfeld Handbook*.

Yule, G., and M.G. Kendall, *An Introduction to the Theory of Statistics*, Charles Griffen and Company, Ltd. London, 1953.

Zarembka, P., *Frontiers of Econometrics*, Academic Press, 1974.

Zellner, A., "An Efficient Method of Estimating Seemingly Unrelated Regressions and Tests for Aggregation Bias", *Journal of the American Statistical Association*, Vol. 57, 1962, pp. 348-368.

Zellner, A., *An Introduction to Bayesian Inference in Econometrics*, John Wiley and Sons, 1971.

Zellner, A., and Theil, H., "Three-stage Least Squares: Simultaneous Estimation of Simultaneous Equations", *Econometrica*, Vol. 30, 1962, pp. 54-78.

INDEX

INTRODUCING

THE SHAZAM FREQUENT REGRESSORS CLUB

SHAZAM is now the first Econometrics Computer Program to give bonus awards for Frequent Regressors.

Save all your old regressions for valuable awards. The more regressions you run the more awards you can receive. Members receive 1 point for each regression run.

AWARD SCHEDULE

10,000 pts.: Regression upgrade. Run **OLS**; get output for Two Stage Least Squares.
20,000 pts.: One free Computer Handbook for Econometrics.
30,000 pts.: One free **SHAZAM** manual.
40,000 pts.: One free **SHAZAM** t-shirt.
50,000 pts.: 10% off on the purchase of your next version of **SHAZAM**.

Now for a limited time only you will start off with 3,000 points just for joining the Frequent Regressors Club.

Now, you can accumulate regressions even faster with SHAZAM bonus awards:

1. *Obtain double points for all regressions run in Version 8.0 (up to 100 bonus points allowed).*
2. *500 bonus points for regressions run while flying on United Airlines or Air Canada (up to 1000 bonus points allowed).*
3. *Systems of equations yield multiple points. For example, a 3 equation system will yield 3 points.*
4. *1000 bonus points for running **SHAZAM** regressions at over 100 different **SHAZAM** installations.*
5. *Receive 1 bonus point for every R^2 over .99 (up to 100 bonus points allowed).*

Now, SHAZAM is the only program with penalty points:

1. *Subtract 1 point for every negative R^2.*
2. *Subtract 2 points for every stepwise regression.*
3. *Subtract 3 points for every non-linear model that does not converge.*

How do I enroll?

It's easy! Simply fill out the application form on the reverse and mail it in. You may start running regressions as soon as your form is postmarked.

How do I claim my awards?

It's simple! When you have run enough regressions to qualify simply mail copies of the regressions to the **SHAZAM** *processing center. Your award will be mailed as soon as your output is verified. To receive your 10,000 point award regression upgrade you should also send your data.*

What does it cost to join?

This is the best part! Enrollment is free.

How do I keep track of my points?

It's simple! Just count them.

Do all regressions count?

No. Only regressions run with **SHAZAM** *are eligible. Each regression must be different; duplicate results are not allowed. Regressions run in* **DO-loops** *are also not eligible. All other regressions are eligible, even simple regressions.*

How much time do I have to accumulate regressions?

At present, there is no time limit. However, **SHAZAM** *reserves the right to modify the rules and awards and introduce new award levels.*

ENROLL NOW! Don't let any of your regressions go to waste.

Date: _____

Name: _____

Address: _____

_____

_____

Telephone/FAX: _____

Send this form to:

SHAZAM
997 - 1873 East Mall
Vancouver, British Columbia
V6T 1Z1
Canada

300